John Foley, S.J.

Creativity
and the Roots
of Liturgy

The Pastoral Press

Washington, DC

ISBN: 1-56929-015-6

The Pastoral Press
225 Sheridan Street, NW
Washington, DC 20011

The Pastoral Press is the publications division of the National Association of Pastoral Musicians, a membership organization of musicians and clergy dedicated to fostering the art of musical liturgy.

Printed in the United States of America.

TABLE OF CONTENTS

Part Two

Appendices

ABBREVIATIONS

AP	*Art and poetry,* Maritain
AS	*Art and scholasticism,* Maritain
BP	*Bergsonian philosophy,* Maritain
CA	The principles of creation in art, Langer
CI	*Creative intuition,* Maritain
CL I	*Christian liturgy.* Vol. I. Theology, Kilmartin
CP	*Christ proclaimed: christology as rhetoric,* van Beeck
DK	*The degrees of knowledge,* Maritain
EE	*Existence and the existent ,* Maritain
FF	*Feeling and form,* Langer
FP	*Frontiers of poetry,* Maritain
GE I	*God encountered,* Vol. 1, van Beeck
GE II	*God encountered,* Vol. 2, van Beeck
GFU	*God for us,* LaCugna
GGHS	*Grace, the gift of the Holy Spirit*
MIND I	*Mind: an essay on human feeling,* Vol. 1, Langer
PA	*Problems of Art,* Langer
PI	The primary illusions and the great orders of art, Langer
PM	*A preface to metaphysics,* Maritain
PNK	*Philosophy in a new key,* Langer
PP	*The practice of philosophy,* Langer
PS	*Philosophical sketches,* Langer
RR	*The range of reason,* Maritain
RT	*Ransoming the time,* Maritain
SP	*The situation of poetry,* Jacques & Raissa Maritain

FOREWORD

Creativity has become a kind of "buzz-word" for anyone involved in liturgical ministry in the contemporary Church. For many it has come to mean "what can I do to make the liturgy a more interesting experience for the people?" Unfortunately this approach often ends up being "what meaning can I—or we as a group—impose upon the liturgy?"

John Foley, the noted Jesuit liturgical composer and musician and now director of the *Center for Liturgy at Saint Louis University*, takes a fresh approach to the topic of liturgical creativity in this book. Taking as his key analogy the human process of conception, gestation and birth, he plumbs the depths of the philosophy of art in the works of Susanne Langer and Jacques Maritain, two widely divergent twentieth century thinkers.

Even more significant is Foley's insistence that liturgical creativity cannot be understood outside of the context of a true theology—for Christians the theology of the Triune God. Employing the best of contemporary trinitarian theology in David Coffey, Catherine LaCugna, F. J. van Beeck and Edward Kilmartin, he shows how at its very depths liturgy shares in the trinitarian project of divinizing human life.

The pay-off in this book comes in chapter five where Foley applies his sophisticated analysis to the liturgy itself and shows that the liturgy is not so much a combination of the various arts as an art in itself, its own "commanding form," to use the terminology he adopts from Langer. Best of all, Foley gives profound theological grounding to the involvement of the artist with the assembly in the assembly's response to the promptings of the Triune God—a response so intimately connected to the liturgy's primary purpose.

I am confident that this work will place John Foley prominently among American liturgical theologians. In addition to providing a useful guide to modern aesthetic philosophy and contemporary trinitarian theology, *Creativity and the Roots of Liturgy* deserves to be read by anyone reflecting upon Christian worship today. With its applicability as well to Roman Catholic and other Christian forms of liturgy this work should also be read by those responsible for worship. It will help them to understand the depth of creativity as God's work comes to birth in the assembly of the Church.

John F. Baldovin, S. J.
Jesuit School of Theology
Berkeley, California

PREFACE

The congenial task of this preface is simple but far-reaching: to give thanks to those who have helped this book into existence. I will wait until chapter one to introduce the order and content of presentation.

It was Kathleen Kanavy from the University of Scranton who brought the inciting question of this book. She asked me to respond to a paper of hers on the Mass as an aesthetic event. After my formal reply, conversations with her, with Tom Stahel, and especially with John Haughey lodged the problem fiercely and frankly in me, pushing me toward further elaboration. I wrote a larger paper, therefore, upon which James Empereur, Kevin Waters, and Louis Weil were kind enough to comment.

When it came to writing the present book, my friendly ally and firm critic was John Baldovin. He read and reacted to the entire opus as it developed, and I am grateful for his careful attention. Thomas Anderson of Marquette University pointed me toward Edwin Block of the Marquette English department, who not only engaged me at length on my ideas, but also helped me with style, flow, and meaning. I value his friendship. And I had the formal opportunity at the North American Academy of Liturgy to converse at length with Don Saliers, Gerard Sloyan, Mark Garrett, and Fred Anderson. Their reactions and minute attention to my text have enriched this book greatly. I have also been blessed by discussions with Gordon Lathrop and Virgil Funk.

Several special helps need mention. Richard Liddy not only aided me in the aesthetic portion of the text, but he also gave me access to Bernard Lonergan's unpublished manuscript on Susanne Langer (Lonergan 1959). This let me introduce Langer succinctly. Frans Jozef van Beeck gave me helpful reactions and also was so kind as to send me a pre-publication copy of his *God Encountered*, part II. Roselyn Schmitt of the College of St. Benedict offered not only her professional philosopher's reaction to the relevant portions of this book, but gave her time and sharp eye for proofreading the various versions of it. I am very grateful. Finally, Thomas Kavanaugh of Triune Communications in St. Louis was a real friend in need when it came to tailoring the diagrams in this book, and to working out an initial design for the cover.

Without such aid to the beleaguered, the present book would have had a much greater struggle toward life. Of course I hold these people free and harmless from any and all deficiencies in my theory and text, since I myself am responsible for the final product.

I am excited about *Creativity and the Roots of Liturgy*. I permit myself the hope that it will lead to serious conversation and even a sharpened practice in that most essential and pregnant area of the Church's life: its liturgical celebration.

John B. Foley, S. J.
The Center for Liturgy
at Saint Louis University
St. Louis, Missouri

CHAPTER ONE

THE CREATIVE QUESTION

The question that will occupy this book can be simply stated. Is liturgy creative at its core in the same way that the various genres of art are creative? Liturgy may resemble art not only in many details, but also at its very root. If that is so, then the subsidiary arts should find in liturgy a creative home. A unified vision of the liturgy might be at hand: an aesthetical one.[1]

But let us not go too fast. Is there a reason why the eucharistic liturgy might qualify as an aesthetical event? The answer will require a whole book, but a moment's reflection will help establish the question. In every art form there is a "material" (e.g., sounds, paints on canvas, bodies in motion). The art-work is not the same thing as this material. The painting is not the paint. If we took a magnifying glass to the Mona Lisa, we would see some very old, scruffy paint, and some brush strokes. The Louvre would never let us touch the paint, but if it did, or if we were to sneak in, Pink-Panther style, we would only feel roughness, not anything Mona-Lisa-like. Our hearts and minds would not be moved by the gritty, coarse surface our fingers moved along. Might we not be correct if we played the scientist and declared that the world-famous, universally admired painting called the Mona Lisa stands before us . . . as a fraud? It is only a square of dried, rough, calcified stuff called paint.

Not according to admirers of art. The long lines who daily gaze at Leonardo's masterpiece do not look for the substance called paint at all. They look at something that was somehow persuaded into the pigments by the mighty genius of Leonardo. By his use of brush and hue, the master has instilled there not only the likeness of an enigmatic woman, but lines and spaces and colors that agree heartily with something profound inside the human soul. He has projected an artistic vision. Just as the symphony is not just buzzing instruments, the painting is not just the paint. Every work of art transcends its mere materials and projects by means of them the presence of something that is not literally there, but is present in a far more important way.

The eucharist too projects a reality that is not present in a literal, physical way. When the gospel reading tells a story about Jesus' life, Jesus does not appear in person to act it out, as if he had arrived in a time machine. His presence is projected by the working of words. The eucharistic prayer does not provide flashbacks, as movies do, so that we can observe the historical Jesus at the Last Supper. Its words and actions tell us what happened at that supper, thus rendering present Jesus' body and blood.[2] And the body and blood of Jesus are (at least) symbolized in the action of communion, not presented literally as a piece of flesh and a cup of blood. Jesus is present throughout the eucharistic liturgy because his presence is projected, by means of the actions and elements of that liturgy. This it has in common with the arts.

Immediately the Roman Catholic question of "real presence" arises. If Jesus is *merely* projected by the liturgy, in the same way that Leonardo projected Mona Lisa, then Jesus is not "there" except in the way a friend is in a snapshot. This question will demand treatment as the book proceeds, and it will receive that treatment. But I believe one of the best advantages of the theory I am going to present will be that it gives a new theological underpinning for the real presence, one that is different from "transubstantiation," and one that is much more satisfactory than any theory of mere symbolic representation.

Another connection to art is suggested by the word "feeling." Feeling, in its spiritual sense, has never been absent from liturgy.[3] Since Vatican II, felt experience has become an explicit ingredient in liturgy. Parishioners sing music that stirs them or comforts them. The Easter Vigil, with its hand-held candles and its multiple readings, has become an event to feel and remember.

One can grieve and rejoice at a funeral. Liturgical space is recognized as providing—or not—"atmosphere" and "aura."[4] The word "celebration" was re-chosen by the liturgical renewers as a name for the liturgical event, suggesting precisely a feeling state. None of this is really new: the Latin Mass was far from a dry, emotionless event. The faithful knew they could expect in it a certain majesty, mystery, peace, holiness, and power. Even if presiders and congregations were not explicitly aware of this fact, it happened anyway; the "feel" had settled into the rite itself.[5] Feeling edges into the realm of aesthetics, one of the prime concerns of which is artistic emotion.

The main motivation for seeking an aesthetic basis for liturgy flows from an urgent problem: the integration of liturgy and its arts. Granted, music, dance, homiletics, and the other arts are touted for the wonderful addition they make to liturgical celebration. Music is said to be normative for the liturgy.[6] This contribution is certainly to be praised, but it must not obscure the ever-present competition between liturgy and its arts. Each art has its own engine, its own inspiration, which is fostered, nurtured, and guarded by the artist. What is to keep a piece of music or a dance from overshadowing the very liturgy it is meant to serve? Through history, as we will see, music for the Mass has seemed to escape control. The Council of Trent, for example, and popes before it, saw the florid polyphony of Mass music gradually separating from ritual intent, becoming music for music's own sake. Palestrina invented a whole new style of music to remedy this problem, but just sixteen years after his death Monteverdi and others replaced that style with one aimed at pure dramatic interpretation of the text, to the detriment of ritual action.[7]

If we hold the liturgy to be in no way artistic, to belong to a different category altogether, then it will be it difficult to find a reason for the *intrinsic* joining of it to its arts. Liturgical music would develop according to its own aesthetic principles, and the Mass would work according to its own laws. In time two events would be taking place at the same time: one aesthetic, the other religious. Coordination of the two would depend entirely upon external mandate.

Liturgists have not yet faced this problem of restraining liturgy's arts. The renewal is too new to need such deliberations yet. The questions, however, are very real. Can a Mozart Mass be

used at the eucharist without overshadowing and even depart-
ing from the ritual? If not, then what place is there for professional composers in the liturgy? And what about folk or pop
music for liturgy? Can it serve liturgy's purpose, or does it
compete? What about rock music? Or jazz, polka, and "easy
listening" music? True, there are guidelines, documents such as
Music in Catholic Worship (Simcoe 1985, 217–240), but what guides
the guidelines? In other words, we have to understand liturgy
itself in order to see how music and the other arts operate *within*
the liturgy, *for the purposes* of it, rather than outside it for other
purposes. Otherwise we will finally be stumped when the awful
question surfaces at last: "Why have the arts in liturgy at all?"

If there are reasons for a theory of liturgy as aesthetical or
creative, there are dangers as well. For instance, the danger of
misinterpreting the congregation. An assembly cannot be an
audience, as it might be at an aesthetical event such as a play or
a movie. Vatican II says that liturgy requires full, conscious, and
active participation by the people. What gives them this right to
participation? They used to just "go to" or "hear" Mass. Does the
assembly in fact have some kind of constitutive, originating role
in liturgical ritual—is that the source of their "right" of participation?[8] I believe the answer lies in the realm of creativity properly understood—the same creativity that brings forth works of
art in all the genres. If such creativity lies at the heart of both art
and liturgy, if each is therefore intrinsically aesthetical, the congregation will be included as an active agent. The reasons why
await, in the pages to follow.[9]

And there is the dangerous question of God. What role could
God play in an aesthetical event? The great artist? The subject
matter? Or could God be thought of as an audience for liturgical
prayer? After all, worship and prayer are directed primarily to
God, not to creatures. Whatever the answer, no theory of liturgy
can ignore God's role.

Another danger is that already too much artistic skill is being
asked of the ministers. Aesthetic liturgy may well require more
talent than we can supply. The ability to project felt meaning—
as opposed to simply experiencing it—is a special aptitude, an
aesthetical one. If a presider is supposed to lead and interact
with the congregation in this way, his (and in other traditions,
her) ability to do so becomes paramount. There is less shelter
now. Pianists say the hardest music to play is the (seemingly)

simple music of Haydn because each line is exposed and the audience can hear everything. The priest's role can be like that today. If a presider lacks style or conviction, this lack will be felt. Personal manner now enters into the substance of the liturgical experience. Of course such skill is needed not only in the presider but in the musicians, the composers, the greeters, the readers, the ministers of communion, and for that matter the assembly as a whole.

Whether such a ministerial requirement can be met is another question. Where would such a vast pool of ability come from? For Roman Catholic parishes there would typically be four or five Masses every weekend for at least fifty-two weeks a year, not counting Christmas, Holy Week, and Easter. Multiply these Masses by the number of parishes per diocese, times the number of dioceses in the United States alone, and the yield is a very high number of Masses to be planned and carried out by ordinary ministers and presiders as an aesthetic accomplishment. Is this possible? Or is the lack of such abundant talent one reason people say they find Mass "boring"? The thesis I am proposing about liturgy does not assume that the high talent requirement will remain in its present form as decades roll by. It seeks a foundation theory for aesthetical creativity in liturgy, however this may be required.

Let me be clear. I am saying that I seek a foundation theory. Instead of talking mainly about the liturgical arts, I want to pursue a systematic vision of the liturgy itself in its relation to aesthetics. Such is the purpose of the present book. After working toward that vision I will look for the way liturgical arts support liturgy and integrate within it. A less ambitious approach would finally leave the aesthetical nature of the liturgy unsupported, and therefore unconvincing in the long run.

One drawback to my procedure is that I must talk about what is an essentially pastoral event in a way that is not primarily pastoral. I have to speak of liturgy in a philosophical and theological way. The reader should note this from the outset, that the present book is an academic one, an attempt to undergird the pastoral.[10]

By the word academic, I do not mean impenetrable. I try to assume that the reader and I are asking new questions together, that we do not have insiders' knowledge of this or that philosophy or theology. I avoid terms and concepts that would be known only to a professional aesthetician or theologian. Where this is impossible I attempt to explain clearly what I mean when I use such terms. I examine several philosophers of art, and of course this requires an understanding of at least some portions of their philosophy. I try to explain what I understand of these. Obviously a book like this does not propose any one system of philosophy or theology over others; yet certain insights from a system used by a Susanne Langer, for example, can help disclose the aesthetical theory in question. I also try to guide readers who seek the main line of argument of the book but not the minutiae. I say what sections the overviewer can safely skip. This will assist, for instance, a first reading, and prepare the way for more details at a later time.

In sum, the present book is not mainly an investigation of the liturgical arts, but of liturgy itself. Only by originating a new theory of liturgy can a theologian show that the subsidiary arts *share intrinsically* in the activity known as liturgy. While appropriate hesitation is in order in mounting such a task, still it must be said that such is the goal of the present book: to move toward a new theology of the liturgy.

I. The Beginning

In 1989 I was asked to respond at an academic conference to the following proposition: *liturgy represents the highest form of aesthetic experience.* I had been involved in liturgical music for more than two decades, and surely this hypothesis should have appealed to me strongly. But what is an aesthetical event? And in whose opinion? Aesthetic critics and theoreticians differ widely in their approach to art. Would we hold Andy Warhol as the aesthetic ideal—and therefore propose liturgy as pop-art? Or is Rembrandt the exemplar? Clearly one would have to understand both art and liturgy to make a conjunction.

So I began to formulate an initial proposition about art, stemming from my interest in creativity. If art is an act of creation, (1) what is creativity? Finding a basis for creativity in human affairs might (2) open up the aesthetic realm and (3) provide a breakthrough to liturgy as well.

I started with the most ubiquitous example of creativity there is, one of which all human beings have first-hand experience: birth. We have each been born. And no one who has seen the birth of a baby can fail to have been touched by the miracle of it: new life from old; a tiny, beautiful, needy, perfect human child. Look first to how this new creation came to be and then see if the same ebb and flow can be glimpsed in other kinds of creativity, and finally in liturgy itself. I proposed to myself a kind of journey: begin from an understanding of creativity in human conception, gestation, and birth; go next to creativity as found in the making of art works; end with the liturgy, asking the question "is a liturgical event creative in any of the senses already uncovered, and is it therefore aesthetic?"

Very soon I arrived at a core insight that would guide the entire journey. I will state it here without further ceremony:

every significant union is fruitful.

This guiding insight provided the path for the further study implied. Creativity cannot exist as an individualistic, solo event. Man and woman cannot conceive without one another. Even the painter ensconced in a garret cannot proceed without "inspiration" from outside him/herself. And liturgy itself is a union. In some traditions this means a union of believers celebrating in memory of Jesus. In the Roman Catholic tradition there is a strong tradition of sacramental "presence," the union of God with the individual and with the assembly. Since I know the Roman tradition best, I will search sacramental liturgy for the union whose fruit is the liturgical event.

The beginning point of this quest may already have surprised the reader. Section III of this chapter involves a somewhat detailed description of the world of birthing—tracing the conception, the gestation, and finally the birth of any human child. "Creative principles" derived there will then apply in what follows. Part One (chapters two and three) will let us see what two aestheticians say about creative art, especially in the context of my hypothesis. Part Two (chapters four and five) is a look at liturgy itself, first developing a theory about what it is, and then again applying the principles now derived both from procreation and from aesthetics.

The present writer does not claim to be an original philosopher of aesthetics. Many theorists in many schools have approached the question of art,[11] but I believe the present investigation will be served best by intension rather than extension. That is to say, I want to delve rather deeply into the work of two aesthetical philosophers, not pretending that they are the last and only word on the subject, but deriving from them a somewhat detailed understanding of the artist and the art. Of course, I have chosen the two writers because of their hospitality to the union/birth metaphor. A second reason is that their insights about art can be taken over into the liturgical discussion.

As for liturgy, I will come to it through God as Trinity. This may seem a surprising detour to something as practical as liturgy. But if God really does exist as a Trinity, then no relating with God can happen unless it is a relation to the trinitarian persons. This holds for liturgy as well, which is at the very least a relating with God. If I succeed, then the kinds of liturgical problems we have raised so far can be revisited with more hope of a unified answer. It is a longish effort, I know, but I already know the harvest to be great, and I invite the reader to join in.

Is art like birth? And is liturgy like art—both in its creativity and in its quality of craft? The answer to these questions may help till the earth so that liturgy can flourish. Not only the Roman Catholic but all the liturgical churches have begun a new era of ritual. Eucharistic prayers in the Roman Catholic, Lutheran, Anglican, and Methodist traditions are now nearly identical. The calendar of readings is largely the same. The western church at large needs some signposts about the future paths all its liturgies will take.

II. The Plot and Two Devices

Here is a somewhat more defined shape for the hypothesis I am proposing. In human conception, one fact is even more remarkable than the wondrous emergence of a new child. It is this: conception of that child represents a *merging to oneness of two coequal partners*. We do not ordinarily think of this radical oneness. Though the realities of a man and woman are made one at many levels (ideally), we want to concentrate on the moment of conception. The mother's reality and the father's reality, as concentrated and symbolized within the sperm and ovum which were made for each other, come together so that there are *no longer two but one*. From a biological viewpoint, we call this union the *zygote* (from the Gk *zygotos*, meaning yoked). It is not that the man and woman have *caused* a child to be conceived; it is that the union of their selves *itself becomes the new being*. The two identities that belonged to each alone now unite to become a new one identity, and that one differentiates itself from them to become eventually a free-standing third party. Tucked within that microscopic entity (initially of four to eight cells) we could find all the potential for hands, feet, organs, brilliant or ordinary mind, flashing or quiet personality, love, talent, and all the rest. These dormancies begin to develop immediately, to unfold from the germ of a life that contains them. We call it "gestation."

Conception was a work of equal partners;[12] now the woman becomes procreation's privileged place, its mothering womb. When articulation is complete enough, all the drama of labor and birth come about. The child—who is nothing but the developed and differentiated union of father and mother—emerges into a less sheltering world, to be seen and cared for and learned from by admiring (and frustrated) adults.

Creative art does the same thing; artistic creation mimes human procreation. This is a big statement and we will have opportunity to test it, but here are some broad strokes. Instead of a poem being simply and only the "self-expression" of an individual artist, it represents a yoked reality just as does the zygote. An artist of any kind—painter, poet, musician, dancer, architect—comes into union with the world in all its vagaries. At a special moment conception occurs, a union called "inspiration" that happens deep within the artistic soul. Like a physical mother, the artist may not even know it has happened. He or she may think that a commission from a performing group gave the "reason" for the work of gestation that now begins. But in fact the new life came from and must differentiate from the mothering artist and the fathering world. Instead of being an exercise in self-expression, creative art is an expression of the artist's soul as filled with some beloved aspect of the inrushing world around him or her. Its beginning was as a new conception. The zygote then began to stir, to articulate itself until, after nine months (or years or minutes) the work is complete. It enters the world before admiring beholders (or arch-critics) and makes its way through time. An artist-mother has childed the world.

Artists often refer to their "children," meaning their creations. Their "labor" is clearly difficult and wearing. After a work is finished many will speak of *post partum* depression. The artist feels empty. His or her constant companion and drudge no longer resides within; maternal empathy for the newborn work cannot mask the fact that it now lives "out there," not needing any more intrinsic efforts. Some artists leap immediately to a new project to shake this feeling. A being that was part of myself—not identical to me but marked by its origins in me—has come to significant separation.

There are both male and female artisans, but artists are always mother of the art work, not father. Theirs is the mothering womb without which gestation could not ensue. Birth is a relatively stable externalization that continues the trend toward separation from and union with this sheltering, mothering environment. A baby cannot exist without great care from its mother: food, drink, touch, changing, presence all are surely required. Neglect will result in incalculable harm. The work of art, once finished, needs a different kind of care; it is more stable than a baby. But the present writer has found that an infinite number of birthing details have to be attended to before a piece of music can be played. It has to be copied legibly; checking has to be done—to add or subtract a note or accidental; copies have to be made and distributed. These are birth-room details. Paintings must be displayed and sold. Poems need readers. Stories wait for publication. Music remains a series of dots on the page until someone plays them. Only when beheld do works of art have full life. The artist-mother swaddles the art-work till it can stand without support. Others share in the maternal role.

At this point a clarification is needed. The work of art does not exist in order to be seen; it is not simply communication. Like the baby, it exists because it exists, because it was born, not because individual consumers need some pleasure. On the other hand, the work's very substance does call out for beholders. Like everything else significant in the world, its nature is relational. It calls out for beholders who will enter its world, not to wrench it into gratification, but to love it for what it is. We could say that the work of art is *centripetal* in its effect: it draws its observers into its world for the time span during which it is beheld. This does not deny its accompanying *centrifugal* action, the way it enters the beholder and changes him or her. Both actions take place, as in any human relation, but the latter is an effect of the former. Like a baby, the work of art requires those who love it to bend toward it.[13]

If such comparisons hold good, we have an approach to art. Can we apply it also to liturgy? The task will not be easy. A "mother" and "father" for liturgy will have to be sought. Their union will itself become the liturgy as conceived. Could the work of preparation and enactment of ritual activities then serve as gestation, and liturgy itself the babe? The advantage of such an approach, if it can be made, is to discover liturgy at least as creativity and perhaps as art as well. Roles of presiding and ministering could then safely evidence an artistic flow. Music, dance and movement, proclaiming, etc., so crucial to liturgy, could find a firm basis in the overall creative event and yet still remain creativities in themselves. We would have to establish the role of the assembly: could it claim a significant place, and as per Vatican II, an active participation? What about God's place in the scheme? If such questions could find an answer in the theory of this book, liturgy would find itself not remodeled but re-focused.

The conclusion can be previewed here. Instead of forcing the planner or the presider to parent the liturgy, to be its creative artist, I will name a different father and an analogous mother. *The Church-assembled serves as mother of the liturgical event.* The people unify with God's Spirit and they conceive. This union with God gestates within the assembly, with the help of specific assembly members, the ministers of liturgy; finally it comes to birth as the liturgy. Like the baby and the art-work, liturgy has an integrity of its own: it does not exist to communicate. Yet, communicate it does to those who love both it and the Christ it contains.

This is the general shape of the present book's thesis. We are about to begin. One further task calls to us first: to discover the mechanics involved in using a comparison. I am comparing procreation to artistic creativity to the liturgical event. Does my thesis serve mainly to amuse or to foster cute remarks like "the liturgy is our baby"? Or does it locate something deeply present within art and within liturgy? To answer we must look briefly to the matter of metaphor and analogy: both are comparisons, but with a difference.

In metaphor a quality of one object is transferred to another where it does not ordinarily belong.[14] Upon hearing a (verbal) metaphor, one works fast to understand the comparison between the two objects (on the basis of that quality) and then harvests the new insights. If I am told of "the rosy fingered dawn," for instance, I do not conclude that the morning sky has real human fingers which are colored light red. Somehow I comprehend almost instantly that dawn and rosy fingers, so very unlike each other, nevertheless have something in common. I call up memories of cloud patterns streaked with colors from dawn's early light, or maybe I recall just the colorful rays of the sun. I see the light "reaching out." Fingers. Dawn discloses the day, as fingers do packages. A comparison has been made.

But the real heft of metaphor does not lie in literal correspondences like these. Much comes to the hearer that defies explicit statement. Perhaps I remember the airy and placid feel of sunrise and of a caress from caring hands, fingers careful to console. Perhaps both have comforted me beyond words. The adjective "rosy" grants a loveliness to these fingers of the sun that can only be suggested, not explicated. Metaphor creates a conscious and subconscious *tension energy* within us,[15] a need to resolve an utterance that at first seems at war with itself. Dawn does not have fingers—what is he talking about? We resolve this discrepancy, this tension, by putting into play our own felt, sensed, intuited, remembered encounters. I know more than an explicit definition of the rose, of the dawn, of the nimble human hand. Swimming in my subconscious pool are images of the beauty, newness, sweetness, and comfort I have taken from them—and much more besides. From these I understand without thinking why dawn has rosy fingers. Thus, metaphor is not a direct statement; it is a verbal *device* that invokes the hearer's own experience by use of just a few words. The meaning comes from the hearer as much as from the words.[16]

"Analogy" is another kind of comparison of two unlike objects on the basis of some similarity. But as we will use it here, analogy performs a different function from metaphor. It is a businesslike *statement* of the similarity-in-diversity between two things, not an *evocation* of that similarity from within the hearer. Instead of trading on the multiple suggestive meanings of words, analogy attempts to hold them to only an intended meaning or two. It aims to make a clear statement. If I say that the old man's face has something in common with an old, worn out piece of paper, for instance, in that both have creases, I have expressed an analogy. But if instead I say with Shakespeare, "Thus is his cheek the map of days outworn" (Sonnet 68), I have used complicated metaphor. His cheek is not a map, and one cannot make a map of days. Yet the meaning is immediately and piercingly felt.

Let us try both analogy and metaphor on the present subject. A poet resembles a mother. We will make it a male poet, to increase the contrast. He loves the poem he has just written and re-written, but like a mother with her child, he knows that it is still fragile and uncertain. Is it too intimate to be seen? He senses he must shield his still private poem for the time being from people who might reject it or take it too literally. We have stated an analogy between the poet and the mother. They both protect what they have brought forth.

If I tried (shakily) to speak poetically (clumsily) I might say that "the poet wraps his newborn verse against the light of day." Light and day represent the cool, objective world, as contrasted with the warm, pleasantly dark interior of the poet. They are cool because, unlike the artist's own realm of associations in which the forming poem was fully supported, they represent an atmosphere of (possible) readers who may not share the meanings at all. We picture this poet folding up his sheet of paper and stashing it away, "wrapping it up" for safety. A mother might swathe her child in the same way. Of course, I am trying to make explicit what is only implicit in the words. If a metaphor succeeds, we will find that it *evokes* telling associations within its hearer instead of spelling them out. "The poet wraps his newborn verse. . . ." Enough said.

This is the sense in which I will use the words "metaphor" and "analogy" throughout the present book. Sometimes I will spell out the comparison, making an analogy; sometimes merely invoke it by talking of art or liturgy using words from parenting, thus making metaphor. Associations may well be stirred within the reader.

Notice that in both instances we will be referencing an *intrinsic* quality in the members of the comparison, not just something superadded. Let us speak of that for a moment. The scholastics noticed how the term "existence" in its many forms is said of very different items.[17] An ape and a boulder both can be pronounced to exist. Both could be painted with red paint which could then be shellacked off without affecting the boulder very deeply—though the ape might become testy. But we cannot imagine taking existence away and having anything left. Existence is intrinsic to both the ape and the rock, but in a very different way. One is alive, dynamically processing, yelling, and beating its chest. The other lies inert, passive. Their existences have quite different identities. When we say that each exists, we are applying an analogy. Something intrinsic to each is named, which nevertheless is the same only with important differences.

There is no space here, of course, to trace further how this could be so. We have to leave off explaining analogy and metaphor by saying that we will find analogous and metaphorical meanings of creativity in our three instances—birthing, art, and liturgy. In a loose way, we have already sketched a metaphor of reproduction and art. If the reader assented to any degree, then perhaps he or she will find energy to pursue with me the interesting analogy that underlies it.

Analogy forms the bedrock for this book; metaphor does not. Several paragraphs here might show why this is so. The analogy we will carry through all three models, procreation, art, and liturgy, is the principle we have seen: *every significant union is a generative union.* The generativity happens one way in human conception, gestation, and birth, another in the union between an artist and reality, and still another in the case of God's involvement with humanity. The differences we will note as we go. The similarity consists in the strong presence of significant, engendering union. All the details, all the theoretical discourses of this book exist to establish this similarity-in-difference, or in other words, this analogy of significant union in the three areas.

Then why bother with metaphor? The reason has to do with the process of discovery. Using an ancient distinction, philosophy talks of *via inventionis* and of *via judicii.* The Way of Discovery (*via inventionis*) means the order in which one discovers facts. An Agatha Christi detective, for instance, might detect first a broken door, then muddy footsteps inside, then a dangling door to the safe in the living-room wall, and finally the fact that jewelry is missing. The detective might justly conclude that someone had broken into the house, walked to the safe, blown it open, and stolen the jewelry. But study might finally lead to the conclusion that a family member, already in the house, had rigged the safe to look as if it had been broken into, walked backwards to the door with muddy feet, gone out, closed the door, and finally smashed it down to simulate a break-in. In this manner, the Way of Judgment (*via judicii*) has provided a different ordering of events and importance than did the Way of Discovery. The smashing of the door happened last, not first; the perpetrator started inside the house, not outside. Both "Ways" are important. One must "discover" the facts one at a time, in the order in which they present themselves. But one must also determine the true relationship between them, not assuming them to be ordered in the same way in which they were discovered.

In this book metaphor is a *via inventionis*, a manner of discovering: it presents the muddy footsteps. We use procreation as a metaphor for the rest because it is the easiest to see, the fact most open to first understanding. We use it in order to proceed from the more well known to the less well known and finally to the least well known. Metaphor, therefore, aids in the Way of Discovery. Use of it, as we noted above, provokes thought, creates a tension in the hearer that urges him or her to ferret out the similarity between the first example and the other realities. If we were to begin, for example, with the Holy Trinity, and then use it as a metaphor for art and finally for procreation, we would have begun with the least well known and gone on to the most. The Way of Discovery does not work well in this manner.

Analogy, on the other hand, belongs to the Way of Judgment. Our conclusion will not be that, since we use procreation as a first metaphor, art and liturgy must be erotic, just as conception is. Rather, we will judge that all three are analogous realizations of the same principle: that *all significant unions are engendering unions*. Thus, the prime analogate is fruitful union, not erotic union. Procreation helps us discover the similarity, which we state as a fact we judge to be true. In a moment we will delineate seven characteristics of such unions whenever they involve human beings. Since both art and liturgy pertain (at least) to human activities, these seven features will be found analogously realized in each of the analogates, even though we will discover them first in procreation.

III. Human Conception, Gestation, and Birth

Now we must speak of conception, gestation, and birth. Some notes are needed about why we concentrate on the biological level.

(1) The "biological" events of reproduction will serve as icons for the relation of mother and father *in toto*. In other words, we do not intend to chart mere free-standing biological events and then twist them into a theory of art and liturgy. A human relationship coordinates all its levels, including biological, and

therefore even the least of these levels will show forth principles true of the human realities that surround them.[18]

Let us talk briefly about the other levels of a personal relationship, in order to illustrate. At its best, human procreation involves profound union of two people, a union of love. Such love is the grounding for *any* relationship between people and most certainly the desired foundation for sexual union. This is not to deny that sexual union happens frequently without the presence or even desire for integration with the rest of life. The four letter word so preferred in 1990s culture says that it does. And advertising, driven by the need to coerce sales, has co-opted human sexuality as a mechanism to move product. We could multiply such examples. The reality to which we will refer, though, is not sex as a style or an amusement, but as the integrated center of a complex human process, fruitful at every level.[19]

(2) Today society has a bit more clarity as to the role of the two genders within relationship. We are no longer strapped with a culture-wide presupposition that women are inferior to men, that they mainly carry out functions of producing and caring for children and household. These are marvelous tasks, but no longer simply stereotypical. American society is growing toward an understanding that marriage is a relation of equal parties, each of which brings a highly valuable but different set of strengths (and weaknesses) to bear. On the decline is the opinion, current only decades ago, that woman endures sex not for her own pleasure or support but to supply the man his needs. Such a characterization speaks of private satisfaction and martyrdom rather than true relationship. It is not individualistic pleasures I am referencing, but pleasure as a by-product of something much more important: true exchange between loving parties.[20] I see persons as open-to and unhappy-without exchange at every level of their lives. Procreation of children therefore mirrors the still more encompassing reality of such a relationship. In this it is iconic.

In the case of procreation, the partners are equal, and therefore able to come to significant union.[21] Soon I will begin to use the term "connaturality" instead of equality. Connaturality is a kind of *congeniality* that exists between two beings. Two partners to a significant union do not have to be equal in every respect in order to have the equivalency implied by connaturality. They must simply have—or be given—a certain correspondence that is open to union. When we come to apply the analogy (of significant generative union) to the union of God and creatures, for instance, there will be no way to iron out the differences between God and persons in order to assert equality. God and human persons can never be equals. But if God is ever to come to creatures in a union of love, there will have to come into being a connaturality, given by God, that allows union. In conception there is connaturality plus equality; in art and in the God/human relationship there is only a bestowed connaturality, not equality. We will see more of this in due time, but noting this difference now will prevent misunderstanding.

(3) We might be thought to imply that sexual union exists only to beget a child. This is a pinched view. Sexual union exists for the purpose of exchange or relation, which is always generative of a new reality and often of a baby. Whenever significant union takes place, that union is by its essence generative. When I love and am loved, I am different from what I was before, and so is my beloved. This difference pools out into our whole life together and apart. I can ward off the beloved, of course, in which case I am untouched. But if I open up and make space, he or she can make a home with and within me, a union called friendship. It is said that marriages are most deeply of all friendships, whatever may happen to the transitory quality known as "being in love." The union of friendship generates vitality, new patterns of behavior, self-discovery, comfort, self-donation, being together, etc. Friendship does not deny sexuality, which is somehow involved in every human relationship. In certain unions this sexual aspect mirrors all the other aspects: comfort, self-discovery, play, etc. It produces, at least on occasion, the new life of a child. Again, sexual oneing[22] is in this way an iconic surface of a relation that exists or is striven for on many different levels.[23]

(4) Talk of relationship might suggest engulfment to the reader. It might sound as if one no longer has possession of oneself, as if individualism had swung to the opposite pole and become sticky togetherness. This difficulty presupposes two extremes: either I am me, by myself, or else I am fused with someone else. Under such polarized togetherness I could no longer possess my own life: I would have to do what he or she wants me to, who is my harness, my dominator. The answer to such a dilemma does not so much lie between the two polarities

of isolation versus engulfment as outside their continuum. Healthy relationship presupposes *differentiation*. I am not identical to someone else, I am different from them. But my own differentiated realm, which I have striven for and have still to complete, includes as a constituent part of itself openness to the other person. Through a series of intricate, alternatively successful and always growthful moves, the two learn to retain their own lives but at the same time to open them to the other so that a union is achieved that does not compromise the individual's selfhood. Marriage unions of friendship depend on this kind of differentiation. How often is it achieved? Probably more often than we imagine, but not easily or automatically. If in our descriptions we assume the completion of this goal, it is for the purpose of illustration.

I am saying, then, that the biological operation of conception, gestation, and birth resides within a higher level of human affairs. It is iconic of them. Like an icon it presents what is truly there.[24] Because what we call the "biological" level of marriage exists as unified with and conjoined with every other level—psychological, personal, interpersonal, connubial—our consideration of the wonders we find at the "biological" level will reveal all the other levels with which it is unified. It acts as a symbol—or icon, in this applied sense. We will have the opportunity in chapter four to examine Karl Rahner's philosophical statement of this symbolic nature of such reality.

So let us speak of the biology of such a union, with some comments on its surroundings, but always assuming the context in which all of it is imbedded. Our subheadings will highlight the principles we wish to draw forth.

IV. Physical Conception, Gestation, and Birth

In describing human reproduction, I want to enumerate seven essential characteristics of the process. These will serve as markers for *each* discussion of creativity in this book: analogies for any human creativity.

1. Connaturality. This is a term I am borrowing from later chapters of our discussion. As I have noted already, it means simply that two realities are "made for each other": they are so configured that they fit together well. The sperm of a father naturally unites with the egg of the mother: the chromosomes of each combine readily in a complex process.

And so we begin the way of discovery, the way of metaphor.

Chromosomes are strands of rods containing the "instructions" for the human being in whom they reside. Chromosomes reflect that which they contain, the reality of the whole person. That reality is relational. The DNA information within a chromosome not only determines the structures of the person; it is also intrinsically prepared to be united with another chromosome in a pair. In every other cell of the body there are twenty-three chromosomes paired off with twenty-three others for a total of forty-six. But sperm and egg each have *half that number*, only twenty-three unpaired chromosomes, so that they will be able to combine with twenty-three from another human being. When the sperm cell fuses with an egg cell, each chromosome unites with its opposite number, creating a new cell with the full number of chromosomes. Thus reproductive cells are naturally disposed to each other, and we give that disposition here the name connaturality.

So we have already nuanced the beginning description of creativity we gave above. In order for there to be significant union, *partners must be inclined connaturally to each other.* Dogs and zebras cannot produce offspring if they mate. The predilection of human reproductive cells for each other is not only marvelous but is also connatural. Two vitalities carrying all the traits of their human person are built to unite. Again, we will see that connaturality is not always a given in art and in theology; that is, it must be achieved by an elevation of the lower party by the higher.

2. Fertility. A second trait must be recognized. Though common language reserves the word "fertilization" for the mother's cell when it has been penetrated by the father's, we would do well to widen the meaning of the word "fertile." It is based on the Latin word *ferre,* meaning "to bear," with a connotation of "the power to reproduce in kind or to assist in reproduction and growth." Both man and woman are fertile in this sense *before* the act of conception: they bear life to each other. This is the fertility we will now review.

The mother's fertile potential is astonishing in its breadth. A baby girl's ovaries at her own birth contain almost five hundred thousand potential single-cell eggs.[25] They are the largest single cells in the human body. Only a number of these will ripen into a tiny egg when the time comes. The ones that will not ripen serve as nourishment for the ones that do. There could be as many as four thousand ripe eggs for a woman during her life. One hundred to 150 will begin to ripen each month during her child-bearing years. One usually reaches full maturity each month, therefore becoming capable of impregnation. This is a superabundance of potential, so that of all the initial candidates at least one egg per month will be ready for a possible union. Nature seems to be taking no chances.

Sperm are the other fertile vitality. They are tinier than the egg: they are the smallest cells in the human body. Thirty thousand sperm placed side by side on a nickel would only just stretch across it. The appearance of a sperm is more or less well known through educational television: it is like a tadpole, with a long, lashing tail which gives mobility and drive for its journey. Fertility abounds. In a male orgasm there are literally hundreds of millions of sperm. Several thousand of these make the trip up the vagina to the fallopian tubes where a ripened egg awaits.

The fallopian tube's long canal is about the thickness of a ballpoint pen refill. A follicle holds the egg in place during the time it waits. If impregnation does not happen within a few days, this follicle dries up and decomposes, and the cycle begins again. Notice that the egg itself is a minute speck, barely visible to the naked eye, even though it is the largest cell in the body. It is more than a mere target; it is the fertile potential of the woman, open to and ripe for union.

So fertility, applying not just to the woman but to both man and woman, consists of an abundant supply of what within the two partners is made for union. Two vitalities with an innate capacity to become one. Let us add this to our description of creative unions. The significant union is prepared by abundance upon abundance, a sort of creational "fail-safe."

3. *Conception.* The sperm's round head holds its important, gene-carrying nucleus. Only a few sperm arrive at the egg. They compete, each trying to penetrate the egg cell-wall, which puts up resistance. One sperm rams its way through. The cell-wall's toughness seems to be a way to avoid multiple conceptions. When one sperm gets in, the egg immediately puts up a chemical

barrier to keep all other sperm out. The head of the sperm separates from the tail and goes toward the nucleus of the egg. When these two nuclei unite, the two sets of chromosomes become one.

Even though the journey and implantation of a sperm is dramatic and interesting, it is not the most significant fact about conception. The union is. The energetic sperm journey and the patient waiting of the resistant egg provide only a *means* by which the cells can come together. Everything leads to the union. When chromosomes combine, they are not doer and receiver—the popular stereotype of man and woman—but complete equals. Each has a full half of what is needed. In combination they now become a whole.

As I said above, we will have to nuance this connaturality when we come to art and to theology of liturgy, since there the parties are not equal, and have to be *made* connatural. But, to stay with the present discussion, and to say it another way: when sperm and egg unite

> *two different and differentiated beings*
> *unite as one*
>
> *to become three.*

Each part of this curious dictum has consequence. The man and the woman are two complete human entities. They have emerged from their own childhoods and have assumed responsibility for their lives. They unite, and portions of themselves, burrowing inside that union, iconic of it, seek each other for a oneing of cells that happens relatively seldom, considering the amount of fertility that each lavishes upon the other.

But when it does, instead of the resulting number being one, as it seemingly should be ("two become one"), the new count is three. Two parents and one child-to-be. The new little being is not the man or the woman, but something new. This onehood achieved in conception is so much a life force, such a combination of vitalities that it cannot be held tightly in orbit by its former owners. The yoking of the two becomes *zygote*. Two parents-to-be hold each other to themselves, and the result is a *conception* (whose Latin forbear is a word meaning "to take to oneself and hold"). Now they must let go and let the yoked reality enjoy its own new vitality.

4. The Union Is the Offspring. That which has been conceived *differentiates* from the very two whose union it is, and is from then on a third being. This statement is exact, even though all the questions of viability of the fetus have to be considered. It cannot survive by itself, but it is nevertheless a unique being. The immediate combination of chromosomes begins as soon as fertilization takes place. These are no longer activities of the man's or woman's body but a new purposive endeavor of independent (or better, interdependent) human life bent on development. No longer two people, no longer two made one, but now three. The mother now must begin learning how to eat both for herself and the new party within her.

Thus we come again to a key characteristic of this significant, pregnant union. In spite of all that comes before it, conception is not *caused* by the union of a man and woman, like pressing a button; at its very centermost core,

the union of man and woman itself IS the new being.

Even though it happens every day, we are not prepared to take in the significance of this fact. The union, with all its iconic reality, *is* the zygote. This is the manner in which a significant union is fruitful. The "onement," as we have called it, has such importance and vitality that, instead of "causing" the new being, it *is* the new being. In each case of creativity, then, we will have to look for this amazing fact. We will find that the very uniting of diverse, fertile, connatural beings itself takes on a differentiated reality of its own. This is the fourth characteristic of creativity.

5 Gestation. The united reality burgeons, a being still in shadow, but growing into itself. Its potentials start unfolding at once. Gestation's intricate beauty deserves some attention here, especially because we will spend time on it in each of the analogates. Of course we can only select certain striking features of this great progress, and we must say them in summary form.

By three days the zygote is a sixteen to thirty-two cell, raspberry-shaped ball. At eighteen days the nervous system begins to develop. At twenty-eight days the embryo (from the Greek *en* + *bryein*, to swell) is a quarter of an inch long. Tiny buds appear which will grow into arms that are, by forty-two days, still too short to meet. Rudiments of fingers and toes have appeared. By seven weeks it becomes a fetus (from the Latin *fetus*, newly delivered, fruitful). In three months, at an inch and a half long all the organs and features of the fetus are completed. In four months the heart of the now six inch fetus has become fully developed and the eyes are sensitive to light. By five months it could survive outside the womb if it had to, and the hearing apparatus is complete. It is half as long as it will be when delivered and weighs seven ounces. By thirty-two weeks it has grown to fourteen inches and the right and left hemispheres of the brain begin working together. Finally it descends, at thirty-six weeks, into the pelvis "with its head firmly fixed like an egg in an eggcup" (Kitzinger 1989, 69).[26]

Surely parents are correct in saying that this is the most amazing process they ever hope to witness. What was microscopic in size has emerged as a full baby, ready for birth. Everything that burgeoned outwards was contained in potential within the few celled being, the differentiated union between father and mother.

6. *Labor*. Now the work begins in earnest. The mother has been host to many possible afflictions before now. The beloved other within her had sapped her strength, bloated her figure, increased her weight, given her a sore back, made her throat and chest burn, and generally changed her life.[27] The mother has been at pains to enlarge herself gradually to give it room. Now there may be false labor (though "prelabor" might be a better name), which consists of contractions too far apart to produce results. When this early labor begins there are mild contractions about every five minutes, with mild to moderate cramping in the lower abdomen, thighs, and lower back. If early labor is prolonged, the mother can become exhausted. Women say that the contraction feels like a strong menstrual cramp. In the early stage there is excitement that the baby is about to be born. The mother can laugh and chat.

Then active labor. The pain is real and intense. Advisors tell the woman to "work-with" the contractions, to "let-go" to their power, and to *push*. One writer says the mother should talk to her cervix: "let the baby out, let the cervix open, open up inside . . . let the baby come down" (McCartney and van der Meer 1991, 139). Back pain is common, but pushing makes it go away. Relaxation is important and possible between contractions, which are not continuous, but last for a minute to a minute and a half, with one about every three to four minutes. In the interim, ice applied to the lower back is in order, or a hot-water bottle on the lower abdomen, and massages. The goal is important, the baby is at hand. The strain and pain have purpose.

The first stage of active labor lasts typically three to four hours. There is a one to two hour "transition" with strong contractions every two to three minutes. The cervix is dilated to ten centimeters. The woman may feel panicked and trapped. The second stage follows, with contractions farther apart again, and the automatic urge to push. The mother is happier now and communicating. This stage lasts one to two hours and ends with the birth of the baby.

The experience reported by mothers varies widely, of course. One woman may say that the back pain was "as though someone was bashing my lower back with a baseball bat" (McCartney and van der Meer 1991, 139). Another might say it was calm and quick, and still another that a Jacuzzi made her hardly feel it. The length of labors also varies greatly. Some take thirty minutes, others forty-eight hours.[28]

More and more fathers are taking part in the labor process. Instead of barring men from the birthing room, as happened universally in the colonial United States, or making the male doctor—not the father—the ordinary deliverer,[29] women now train for labor with their husbands, and receive assistance, support, and actual participation from their mates. Some of these fathers had already been talking to their child-to-be when it was in the womb, and after it is born it recognizes their voice. This cooperation in birthing mirrors the fact that, even though women are the privileged place for gestation and labor, the child is literally the union of *both*, grown to (relative) stability.

The important observation for our purposes here is that labor is an inevitable accompaniment to childbirth. A new human being is being pushed out from the middle of another human being. The woman's body may be built for it, but extraordinary strains are placed on that body. All human creativity requires labor, which is the sixth mark of that creativity. Maybe in art too it is the conjunction of creativity with human, material bodies that enjoins labor and explains it. We will see the same thing in the birth of a liturgy.

7. *Birth—Emergence into the World.* At last the two who became one are *seen* to be three. Birthing is the stage at which the new being can shed its protection and continue differentiating,

now physically outside the mother, but still emphatically within the mothering environment, at gradually increasing distances from her. Her shelter let the new person's "intense fragility," to use e. e. cummings' phrase, receive protection and nourishment during the comfort of first its night, then its early light, and finally now the full light of day.

What happens in birth? It includes "an active, very physical drive that compels a woman to push the baby forcefully out of her body" (McCartney and van der Meer 1991, 146). There are different possible positions for delivery, and various pushing strategies. Not all women like to push. The urge is there, but several hours of this may not even seem possible. It can seem that the baby will never fit through, or if it does that the woman will burst. She may be exhausted by this point. Midwives sometimes urge her to take a fifteen minute break, and maybe to vocalize her fears—of tearing, or feeling out of control. Continuing praise for her efforts helps a lot. Of course not all births are difficult. Some mothers simply push from instinct and the baby is there.

The head comes first (normally), and this must not be rushed. The midwife might place a hand lightly on it to make sure it doesn't slide out too fast. When the birthing is nearly complete the mother can even reach down and help the baby out, and then cuddle it in her arms.[30] Other children from the family can give assistance throughout the birth and even cut the umbilical cord![31] The baby cries, to expand its lungs and get them working. Its bluish color changes to pink. It is wet from amniotic fluid and another protective substance called *vernix caseosa*. Its head may be molded into an elongated shape, which allowed it to fit through the mother's pelvis. All this is fine and normal. The last necessary effort, which may even have been forgotten by the mother, consists of two or three more pushes to deliver the placenta.

It seems obvious that the baby belongs with its parents after being born, but until recently this was not a common practice. After newborn babies are dried and warmed (they have gone from a womb of ninety plus degrees to a delivery location of around seventy degrees), they have to be given lots of skin-to-skin contact, which benefits both the baby and the mother. The baby looks at the mother in response to her voice. Its eyes can see about twelve inches, about the distance to the mother's face when she holds it in her arms. Human bonding now begins, a future of love and battle and growth, the life of a thoroughly relational being ready for care and lots of it. This is the miracle of birth. The union of man and woman—striven for in their whole life together, but in particular within the wonder of conception—now puts its face toward the world.

We can now summarize the whole difficult and wondrous process from its beginning. We have placed markers at various points above to highlight analogous principles for other creative events. First, we saw that the partners must be *connatural*, that is, fitted to each other. This became obvious in the case of human parents, but will need attention in the case of art or liturgy. Second, we remarked the abundant *fertility* of the partners and their possibility of union. Nature's generosity seemed endless. Third, we saw the wonder of union at the very core of these human beings, a *conception* in which chromosomes automatically united, once they had found one another. This onement is iconic of the hoped for union at many levels of the human partners. Fourth, we observed the curious and singular fact of creative union: the *union itself becomes the third party*. Conception does not consist of "a man causing a woman to be pregnant"; it is the joining of two connatural realities into a union that itself comes to life. We will see this characteristic throughout created and uncreated reality.

Fifth, we found an intricate and beautiful *gestation*, in which the tiny zygote unfolded its potentials outwards to articulation. Analogous applications already come to mind: the semi-conscious shaping of the art work, and the planning and preparation of a liturgical event. Sixth, we saw the generous *labor* required by human birth, required not because the event is unnatural but because human structures are still human, not angelic. Finally, we have just seen the difficult, triumphant, othering summit of all that went before, birth of the child and the toil this requires. The helpless newborn at last parts company with its physical home and begins life in a new mother-infant unit, this time outside the womb. The parents, especially the mother, now bond with the newborn life that began as the man and woman's union with each other and now takes shelter within it.

Many artists I know could find themselves within this recounting of the reproductive process, especially labor and birthing. I certainly do find my own experiences of composing present metaphorically in these pages. But we must go a greater distance if we are to apply the analogy in earnest. We must now investigate formally the creative process of artists. We turn to aesthetical theory.

NOTES

1. It has often been thought since 1963 or so that creativity is the key to liturgy. The elements of rite are to be, or we are free to make them be, fresh and artistic. This will keep the liturgy alive. I do not hold this thesis. There is another way, one which I will explicate in this book, in which liturgy is deeply creative and artistic, a way that yields far more important results in understanding and carrying out ritual ceremony. It is true to the surest principles of liturgy throughout the centuries, and is faithful to the very essence of the rite.

2. The eucharistic prayer of course does more than just tell the story of the Last Supper. It gives thanks, renders certain prayers as well, and invokes the Holy Spirit, who establishes the presence of God.

3. We will see why "brute emotion" is not aesthetical or liturgical, but that events-as-felt are.

4. Cf. Baldovin 1991, 204-205.

5. Throughout this book I will use the word rite in its non-technical sense, to indicate simply the enacted liturgy.

6. "Music is integral to full and active participation in the liturgy. Music is not decorative and it is not a dispensable addition. A genuine act of communal, public prayer is musical by definition" (Keifer 1980, 100).

7. "In the preface to his masses, 1567, Palestrina himself made mention of a *novum genus musicum*. It meant assembling all the stylistic tendencies of his age and recasting them into the unity of an ideal style which could produce the text-music compromise sought by the Council of Trent . . . . [His] techniques demonstrate the dominant position of the text in this style of Palestrina, in contrast to the violence frequently done the words by the early Netherlanders in their contrapuntal settings or by the isorhythmic devices of an earlier period" (Fellerer 1961, 95). Monteverdi's new style involved long melismas (many notes for each syllable) to achieve expressiveness, and was called *stile concitato*.

8. John Baldovin says that the eucharist "has often been perceived as the action of a special class of persons endowed with supernatural powers and controlling an activity over which the nonordained members of the assembly have no power. Such a cultic understanding of sacramental activity runs counter to the prophetic critique of worship

engaged in by Jesus himself" (Baldovin 1991, 104) Cf. Keifer 1980, 100: "The ministers celebrated the liturgy, and the liturgy functioned simply as the occasion for the prayer of the people."

9. A second question has to do, again, with music. How can the worshiping churches arrive at a truly beautiful and appropriate musical repertory, while still remembering the taste and preferences of the participators?

10. A distinction has to be made between "academic" and "scientific," at least as the latter word has tended to be defined. I do not approach any subject in this book as if I had withdrawn myself from it and had achieved an "objective" viewpoint. Jonathan Lear calls the desire to thus abstract oneself an "obsessional strategy" which is held unconsciously by western culture. The hidden assumption is that "the world is itself devoid of value, purpose or meaning. For if the world were purpose-full, there could be no objection in principle to a science that embodied the very purpose it investigated in nature. It is because the world is assumed to be neutral that science must somehow reflect that neutrality" (Lear 1990, 218). I believe that the subjects of the present book are value laden, and can be approached only by recognition of that fact.

11. At least one major theologian, Hans Urs von Balthasar, has an aesthetical basis for his theology (cf., for example, von Balthasar 1973, 83).

12. We will see in detail how, in each of the other analogates to conception and birth, the partners are not equal at all, but are made "connatural" to each other (to use a word that will assume great importance in the following discussions).

13. Centrifugal and centripetal as expressive of love relationships are terms I encountered first in Coffey (1979) and in LaCugna (1991).

14. To say it another way, *"The essence of metaphor is understanding and experiencing one kind of thing in terms of another"* (Lakoff and Johnson 1980, 5).

15. A term promoted by Wheelwright 1982, chapter 6.

16. Metaphors are common in English words. The verb "to abstract," so pale in today's light, originally came from the Latin *ab* + *traho*, meaning to draw or pull away from. It started as a metaphorically vivid image.

17. Even this word has a metaphorical basis. Philip Wheelwright mentions Müller's evidence of an Indo-European root for both the word "be" and the Sanskrit *bhu*, meaning "to grow, or make grow," as well as a Sanskrit base (*amsi*) meaning "to breathe" for "am" and "is." "The irregular conjugation of the English verb 'to be' can thus be regarded as an abbreviated record of a time when men had no independent word for 'existence' and could reach toward the idea only by

choosing whether to say that something 'grows' or that it 'breathes'" (Wheelwright 1982, 121). Lakoff and Johnson claim on the basis of linguistic evidence that "most of our ordinary conceptual system is metaphorical in nature" (Lakoff and Johnson 1980, 4).

18. Jonathan Lear interprets Freud as saying that "human sexuality is an incarnation of love, a force for unification present wherever there is life" (Lear 1990, 147).

19. We are not by this trying to present an argument for natural law, but merely an observation that sexual union, on a large scale, and unless thwarted, tends to be creative at all levels. For philosophers who work from the idea of relationship as constitutive of the human person, see Lear 1990, 157, n 2.

20. The word "exchange" to characterize such realities comes originally from Rosemary Haughton (1981). Her work establishes universal prominence for exchange, and thus comports quite well to the large hypothesis of the present book. We will have opportunity in chapter four to view Haughton's theory in greater detail.

21. Freud: ". . . the libidinal, sexual or life instincts . . . are best comprised under the name *love*; their purpose would be to form living substance into ever greater unities, so that life may be prolonged and brought to higher development." Quoted in Lear 1990, 150.

22. If I speak of *oneing, onehood,* or *onement,* I ask the reader to listen for echoes of an ancient usage rather than the more trendy speech of today. In the sixteenth century a verb *to one* was utilized, though it later became obsolete, replaced by the word *atone,* which emerged around 1550. The combined form, to *at-one,* or *attone* or finally *atone,* meant "to set or make at one." It can be found in Shakespeare, meaning not *to expiate* but *to unite:* "Since we cannot attone you, you shall see justice designe the Victors Chiualre." Richard II, 1.i.202. In the course of time atone took on an applied meaning, *expiation,* and thus does not mean *to unite* anymore. In this book I am bringing the original sixteenth-century verb, *to one,* back into use in its original meaning, as well as its other forms from that era: *onement,* which originally meant physical union but later came to signify union of mind and feeling; and the word *onehood,* which was common from about the thirteenth century onwards (in 1575 it was written that "where onehood reinz, ther quiet bears rule, and discord fliez a pase").

23. Separation of people who love each other presents an interesting test case of this theory, which unfortunately we can only touch upon here. The best way to say it in a few words is this stanza from John Donne, quoted by Wheelwright (1982, 106):

> Our two souls therefore, which are one,
> > Though I must go, endure not yet
> A breach, but an expansion,
> > Like gold to airy thinness beat.

24. An icon is not just a picture, but a window into the sacred realm of God, which now is not separate and distant from the material world but present therein. By the icon's "centripetal" force, the contemplator is drawn into the mystery of God's presence (in the sacraments). The eastern church holds that Jesus' incarnation let the divine be present in matter, and that therefore God's image was restored in every human being. Ouspensky quotes St. John of Damascus to this effect: "God, who has neither body nor form, was never represented in days of old. But now that He has come in the flesh and has lived among men, *I* represent the visible appearance of God" (Ouspensky 1978, 55, italic mine). Through the human being, the material world is converted and can once again mediate divine beauty. For more on icon, see Ouspensky 1978, Mitchell 1982, 376-77.

25. These descriptions drawn from Kitzinger 1989, 56-63.

26. The description of gestation is taken mostly from Verny and Weintraub 1991, 26–27, 48–49, 74–75. 100–101, 116–117, 134–135, 162–163, 179, 187.

27. Possible problems include heartburn, hemorrhoids, varicose veins, Braxton-Hicks contractions, breast soreness, swelling of hands and ankles, exhaustion, fainting, feeling hot, inverted nipples, leg cramps, nasal congestion and nosebleeds, nausea, aching pelvis bones, sciatic nerve pain, difficulty in sleeping, and stretch marks. (Taken from McCartney and van der Meer 1991, chapter 5.)

28. Descriptions of labor are based on McCartney and van der Meer 1991, 129–145.

29. See Wertz and Wertz 1989 for a history of such practices of childbirth in the United States.

30. "The mother was giving birth for the first time, but the minute the baby was halfway out and crying, she instinctively reached down and picked the baby up from my hands. The rest of his body slid out and she lifted the child to her chest and began rocking, cuddling, and talking to the crying baby. This mother was doing something that came naturally to her, and it was working beautifully. This is the way birth has gone on for centuries. . . . " (McCartney and van der Meer 1991, 191).

31. An eleven-year-old girl said "It was really neat to help with the birth of my new sister. I ran lots of errands for everybody and . . . I got to cut the umbilical cord after she was born. That makes me feel even more special and close to her. She's so tiny and cute and cuddly. I knew she'd be small but not as small as she actually is. She feels soft and comfortable in my arms" (McCartney and van der Meer 1991, 158).

PART ONE

CHAPTER TWO

THE INSIDE OF
ARTISTIC KNOWING

The fine delight that fathers thought; the strong
Spur, live and lancing like the blowpipe flame,
Breathes once and, quenchèd faster than it came,
Leaves yet the mind a mother of immortal song.
Nine months she then, nay years, nine years she long
Within her wears, bears, cares and combs the same:
The widow of an insight lost she lives, with aim
Now known and hand at work now never wrong.
Sweet fire the sire of muse, my soul needs this;
I want the one rapture of an inspiration.
O then if in my lagging lines you miss
The roll, the rise, the carol, the creation,
My winter world, that scarcely breathes that bliss
Now, yields you, with some sighs, our explanation.

Gerard Manley Hopkins, "To R. B."

I. Introduction

I have dared the hypothesis that every significant union is a generative union. We can say it the other way around: every human act of creativity is a *co*-creation. I will expand that hypothesis now as we apply it to our second test case: the making of works of art. If this process meets with success we will be able to carry two metaphoric bundles, human reproduction and artistic creation, to the third case, liturgy. This is the way of discovery. We will see whether the analogy undergirding all creativity bears the weight of these applications.

Convenience dictates that language be consistent in a study such as the present one, and so a brief moment on vocabulary is needed here. Since it is difficult to find terms in English to designate "creative works" without ambiguity I will continue to use "art" or "works of art" to mean the creative product. I will refer to the one who creates such a work as "artist." These words will carry these meanings only, and will never refer to a painting or a painter, even though common usage allows them to. When I do speak of the "plastic art" called painting I will consistently call it just that, painting.

We have already noted that, if the analogy holds, it will undercut an opinion about art held even by artists: that art is primarily a matter of "self-expression." To put it another way, the artist has a right to say who he or she is, and to do so by means of an art work. There is something right about this statement, and something wrong as well. As our investigations go by we will see the part that is right. Here we note the problem: this vision tends to use an exclusively masculine prototype. It emphasizes doing, causing, making—not relating, receiving, growing. The artist extends himself outward into the world, thrusting part of himself into it, demanding freedom to do this without sanction. e.e. cummings parodies a view of something like this in a poem:

> "Let's start a magazine
>
> to hell with literature
> we want something
> redblooded
>
> lousy with pure
> reeking with stark
> and fearlessly obscene
>
> but really clean
> get what I mean
> let's not spoil it
> let's make it serious
>
> something authentic and delirious
> you know something genuine
> like a mark
> in a toilet

> graced with guts and
> gutted
> with grace"
>
> squeeze your nuts and
> open your face[1]

By the irreverent mention of male anatomy, cummings seems to be letting us know with a wink about this kind of gender analogy to creativity. The poem is sarcastic throughout—the resulting product is compared to something found in a toilet because half of the partnership is left out. This is an ad-man's idea of how to create, and pressure on the anatomy will make it happen. But procreation is not an event for one person; it is mutual causation by two equal partners. So is poetry.

No act of human artistic creation can be anything but co-creation because artistic conception cannot take place without the vitality of inrushing inspiration. The artist is conjoined to the world about him or her, is made fertile by it, is ravished by it. Reality of the world of experience becomes simultaneously the reality of the poetic soul, in a confluence that can truly be called "conception." The poem is fathered by those privileged moments when a particular scene captivates, as when Hopkins "caught this morning morning's minion," or grieved "Felix Randal the farrier," or "lay wrestling with (my God!) my God." These happenings so penetrate the inner soul of the poet that the soul conceives.[2]

We already heard Hopkins put it this way:

> The fine delight that fathers thought; the strong
> Spur, live and lancing like the blowpipe flame,
> Breathes once and, quenched faster than it came,
> Leaves yet the mind a mother of immortal song.[3]

The "mind" in these lines begins in emptiness; it is not initially full and poised to create. A poet is only half of what is needed, the womanly half. The "mind" is fertile and mature; eggs are ripe and have descended in readiness. Fathering comes from elsewhere, unspecified by Hopkins, but strong and alive, like the sperm activity we saw above. A strong spur is needed to get the poet with poem, which is to say that *another* is needed, the other of the *two that come together as one*. Impregnation, true to what we saw above, is quick and then gone. Perhaps the poet's egg-soul even sends out chemicals to stop other conceptions from spoiling the first. The quenched moment leaves behind new being, the *third*.

Later in his poem Hopkins intimates that he is not currently able to write many poems. "I want the one rapture of an inspiration," he says. Poets, artists, do not do the fathering. Inspiration, the blowpipe flame, sires the poem. Without it, nothing happens. The poet is mother, the place where the newly formed third will take up residence as it gains viability and growth. Both are needed.

We could summarize as follows:

> *creativity,*
> *like physical conception*
> *is always CO-creative*

> *and*

> *the artist is not*
> *the father/begetter of the artwork*
> *but the mother*

The artist is mothering womb. After conception, she is the privileged place where the speck of a poem or painting resides, growing, pushing outwards to its realization as an art work.

Music and colors and tastes of everyday life make love to the artist. Real events come colliding in, overwhelming him or her, giving rapture to the artistic soul. It cannot resist them. Keats said he was born without skin. The things of life are somehow transfigured and become lancing flame, making onement. They leave "yet the mind a mother of immortal song." This is a co-creative project because there is a terrible influx, sometimes a piercing wind, sometimes a still small voice, but always an inpouring that activates. The high fertility of the artistic soul lets the fertile real come into it, and at unforeseen times one gesture, one word, one burning glimpse of life below its surface rushes in and strikes to the core. Unless this happens the poet must wander in a sterile "winter world."

What is it about the world that the artist takes in? One might be skeptical here. Certainly we understand the poet to be necessarily describing events as brooded upon. These come from the world of experience. What external world of experience consorts with architects? And what about abstract art, or dance? Does it not seem a bit far fetched to say that an external event fathers a moment of inspiration for music? This is a difficult question for any theory of art and certainly for the metaphoric analogy we are pursuing. Langer will be of particular help in this realm, possibly giving her greatest contribution by deliberately parsing the arts and their contents in order to find this very thing. The work of this chapter will prepare us for her answer. For now we can say that there has to be a profound *connaturality* of the artist for *whatever it is* in the world that gives (or is) the seed. An artistic soul cannot be weatherproofed against events—their in-rush must not bead and run off. Soul and world are magnets with polar attraction for each other, and in the vast profusion of inseminating data, something grabs hold. This is conception.

After conception, much more takes place within the poet, painter, composer, etc., to make the work of art ready for birth: gestation. The old popular image of a composer leaping from bed to piano at midnight to capture an inspiration seems to imply that there is very little time if any between fancy and fact. Nothing could be further from the truth.

> Nine months she then, nay years, nine years she long
> Within her wears, bears, cares and combs the same:
> the widow of an insight lost she lives, with aim
> Now known and hand at work now never wrong.

No longer conceiving, having come into union, the artist quickly makes a home for the embryo. Inside her/his body, within sub-jective depths, the artist is one with and shelters that which is even so not him/her. "I am so astonished to think that there is another life in there," says a mother in early pregnancy. Her body knows without knowing the exact procedures for nurtur-ing this new being, as does the artist soul know how to haven the speck-sized inspiration.

Jacques Maritain has three stages to this nine month/year/infinite process, which we will see. The tiny, poetic zygote wiggles out of the dark and stilly womb of night (to borrow a phrase from T.H. White), into the early morning light where it gradu-ally unfolds and articulates itself toward day.

Gestation of an art work requires talent. Who can be a poet, composer, or painter? Who is equipped? Langer makes a helpful distinction between talent and genius.

> Talent is essentially the native ability to handle such ideas as one has, to achieve desired effects. It seems to be closely linked

with body-feeling, sensitivity, muscular control, verbal or tonal memory, as well as the one great mental requirement, aesthetic responsiveness.

Genius is... not a degree of talent at all. Talent is special ability to express what you can conceive; but genius is the power of conception (FF 407).

Or, in Maritain's words, ". . . genius has essentially to do with the fact of poetic intuition taking shape in the inaccessible recesses of the soul at an exceptional degree of depth" (CI 370). Genius means openness in one's subjective depths: the amount of creative room there is in those depths. It has to do with conception. Everyone has the capacity to be open to the subjective depths, though many prefer to stay away from them.[4] Genius has an extraordinary ability to be open. Anyone—genius or not—who has an openness to the world can conceive, can be creative. The highly specialized talents of an artist provide the manner and skill of gestation and birth.

Maslow said he had to make a distinction along these lines:

I found it necessary to distinguish "special talent creativeness" from "self-actualizing creativeness" which sprang much more directly from the personality, and which showed itself widely in the ordinary affairs of life, for instance, in a certain kind of humor. It looked like a tendency to do *anything* creatively: e.g., housekeeping, teaching, etc. (Maslow 1962, 129).

Talents differ, but are a necessity across the board. They have to do with gestation. Maslow's two types of creativity help us here to see that in the traditional categories of art very special dispositions are put into play once the inspiration has been had. There must be talent of the requisite kind if the work is not to be stillborn. Langer notes that

great artists have not always had extraordinary technical ability; they have often struggled for expression, but the urgency of their ideas caused them to develop every vestige of talent until it rose to their demands (FF 408).[5]

The stages of procreation are not as neatly ordered in artistic production as they are in making babies. In the arts, gestation and even conception can take place *concurrently* with the "external" activity that could be called birthing. As we know from his unfinished works, Hopkins "hand that is never wrong" is crossing out various lines and holding them up to other versions to see which displays better the original conception as it grows. This *external* gestation process actually takes place simultaneously with the "earlier" stages of *internal* development. In this matter the analogy must be allowed some room. We will have a good idea why by the end of two chapters.

We will trace the work of art from fertile potential through conception, gestation, and finally to a description of the newly birthed baby. Artistic conception is, like physical conception, an act of momentous oneing, a coming together of inciting flame with illuminated emotion. Then the artist is concerned only with gestation of the zygote-like work-to-be, unfolding the "commanding form" given at conception. Finally birth, when the new child goes on display before adoring beholders. Thus art acts like reproduction in a way that is more than fanciful. The same dynamic gestalt is seen in both because creativity acts according to profound dynamics at work in any creative act.

We can complete this overview by summarizing the seven dynamic characteristics derived from human conception in Chapter One. This will help us scout for such evidence in the discussions to follow. (1) In art we will find a powerful *connaturality* obtaining between the partners who will come to one, a sympathetic likeness that allows them to come together. (2) Fertility will abound, numerical potential for significant union. Eventual onement cannot be stopped unless the two are held apart. (3) Then onement of the artist and the world: two separated entities merge. This oneing becomes a new reality, numerically different from the two that preceded it. (4) The "offspring" is not simply a result or effect of the union, it *is* the union. The zygote is the combined reality of the man and woman, and the poem is the oneing of poet with the world. (5) Gestation involves movement of the poem or painting from the less stable but nurturing darkness toward the articulate light. (6) There is labor in both pregnancy/birth and artistic conception/creation, not because connaturality is lacking, but because human structures strain under so great a burden. (7) Then birth: the finished work takes up life amid generations to come.

It is time now to have a longer look at the world of painting, sculpture, architecture, music, dance, poetry, novel, drama, and motion pictures. Who would dare such a task except in the company of astute and ardent observers? I have chosen two, both remarkable in themselves. Each was knowledgeably engaged in the art world, not as a deduction from philosophy or theory, but because of art itself. Susanne Langer's is a breathtaking intimacy with each art genre, the knowledge of a true lover and student of them each. Jacques Maritain could say, "One day, after a walk in the wintertime, Rouault told me he had just discovered, by looking at snow-clad fields in the sunshine, how to paint the white trees of spring" (CI 224–25). Maritain lived alongside both the art and the artist. His love for and knowledge of each are evident.[6]

A second benefit is that both writers hover about the same realities of art and artistry. Sometimes they have a similar insight regarding the same materials, though using different names for it. Yet each tends, without design of course, to cover areas the other does not. Much of Langer's work is concerned with the work of art after it has been born. Much of Maritain's interest is the interior of the artist and how the work makes its way outward. In both there is authentic witness to the physical, touchable stuff of song, poem, paint, dance, stage, and movement.[7]

By coincidence Maritain's and Langer's major books on aesthetical theory were published in the same year, 1953, yet it appears that never in their long lives did either read the other. Each is a philosopher as well as an aesthetician, but their schools of thought could hardly be more opposed. Langer began her work from a Kantian/empiricist starting place, Maritain from a vigorous and life-long pursuit of Thomism. Yet in so unique and unmapped a reality as art, philosophy serves only as a foundation. When hers does not extend far enough, Langer gets another one, while Maritain pulls his into larger shapes.[8] Maritain even apologizes humorously at one point for a "brief and rather chill irruption of Scholastic lecturing" (CI 98).[9] His is a discerning and idiomatic interest in the subject, not that of an apologist. Let us move on to the theories, to see if our analogical metaphor can find a home there.

II. Jacques Maritain

On his way to Europe a young man carried with him and read, on commuters, on buses, on the plane, in hostels and in lobbies of concert halls, a book by an author known to him only by the title page. The young man was already, and wanted to be, a composer: the book, *Creative Intuition in Art and Poetry* by Jacques Maritain, held out a complicated ideal.

I cannot say how much light broke into my young mind from those wise pages. Many years thence, in new company, I take it up again, this great and now generally overlooked tome. Can it engage the nuanced theories of Susanne Langer that we will pursue? Will it support and even enhance the theory of creativity I am proposing?

I will organize my exposition according to three sections of our operating metaphor: union of artist and world (conception), emergence of poetic knowledge from interior dark to the light of day (gestation), and the shape and structure of the work of art (birth and life outside the womb). It is at once easier and more possible to divide Maritain's work this way than Langer's. Maritain himself has so sectioned his thoughts, though sporadically and certainly without use of my metaphor. Langer's exposition will help us more when we examine conception—making us able to say which thing or things of the world come together with an artist in order to conceive, say, a symphony, or a dance—and of the art work's subsequent life in the world.

There is a deeper reason for the form these pages will take. If my thesis is near the mark, the work of all artists ("poets," Maritain would say) and art forms proceeds in at least the manner this metaphor suggests. Art begins within the artist, works its way out from soul-depth, and issues forth. Maritain's is a careful and long look into the person and process of art and the artist. Instead of an imposition, I believe that the form of our discussion will elicit most clearly what Maritain meant.

Another word about terminology is needed, since we are beginning an academic discussion of his work. The words in Maritain's title, *Creative Intuition in Art and Poetry*, seem straightforward enough, but they are not. What is "art," for Maritain? What is "poetry," and, at least in an initial understanding, what is "intuition"? We will find out the meaning of "creativity" in the course of the chapter.

Regarding the two words "art" and "poetry," the obvious meanings do apply, at least often. As regards painting, *Creative Intuition* in its original edition contains sixty-eight full color plates of paintings throughout history, from ancient India to Marc Chagall. These are "art" in the sense of "painting." Maritain does not ordinarily use "art" in any sense but this. As

I have said, however, for continuity throughout the present book I will restrict the word "art" so that it refers to all the creative genres, allowing the word "painting" to mean the specific painterly art.

The "Texts Without Comment" that follow various chapters in the same book contain a total of fifty-one poems, or texts regarding poetry. There, "poetry" is used in the ordinary sense of the word: a particular type of artifact containing written words. There is another, more characteristic way Maritain employs the word poetry. In an early book called *The Frontiers of Poetry* (1927) he says that the "divination of the spiritual in the things of sense, and which expresses itself in the things of sense, is precisely what we call poetry" (FP 128). Here, poetry means the *knowing* that lies at the base of the act of making any work of art. Again, as he says in *Creative Intuition,*

> the essential need of the poet is to create, but he [or she] cannot do so without passing through the door of the knowing, as obscure as it may be, of his [or her] own subjectivity. For *poetry means first of all an intellective act which by its essence is creative* (CI 114, italics mine).[10]

Here again Maritain uses the term poetry to designate not the poem but the knowledge that is behind it.[11] We will be aware of this wider meaning of "poetry." It is often conjoined to words like intuition, knowledge, or experience. In this sense, poetic knowledge is a central act of knowledge, lying at the root of all the art forms (poem-writing included). Therefore we feel free to call it also creative knowledge, or artistic knowledge.[12]

As for intuition, in *Bergsonian Philosophy* Maritain gives the word a general meaning: "to divine, to know without reasoning, to form a just idea or correct judgment without any discursive preparation" (BP 162). But this word too, in Maritain's treatment of the arts, has a wandering import. There are times when it seems to designate the act of artistic *knowing* we have just called creative or poetic knowledge. The epigraph for section A below contains such a usage. But more often intuition seems to be the *power of the artist's human spirit* that enacts such knowing, not the knowledge as such. Perhaps its meaning in this sense could be "the free creativity of the spirit" (CI 238). When he uses "creative intuition" in this sense, he seems to *contrast* it with "poetic knowledge" or "poetic experience."[13]

My concern here is to adopt somewhat consistent terminology without having to assume in advance the entire chapter's work in order to do so. Therefore let us try to speak of the artist's "knowledge" or "experience" whenever referring to the root act of knowing behind artistic production, and to let Maritain's two verging meanings of "intuition" stand whenever he speaks. Here too we must gracefully allow him "poetic" as a designation of this type of knowledge and activity, understanding by it the act of knowing foundational to all the arts, rather than the specific one of writing a poem.

A. Conception—the Primordial Translucid Night

The content of poetic intuition is both the reality of the things of the world and the subjectivity of the poet, both obscurely conveyed through an intentional or spiritualized emotion. The soul is known in the experience of the world and the world is known in the experience of the soul, through a knowledge which does not know itself. For such knowledge knows, not in order to know, but in order to produce. It is toward creation that it tends (CI 124).[14]

In this statement we could find an outline of Maritain's whole aesthetics. We must begin at the beginning, however, with the act of knowing that grounds artistic activity. This section, then, is about artistic knowing. We will begin with a first overview (including the topics of spiritual unconscious, connaturality, the union of world and artist within poetic knowledge, and creative intuition's need to make a work of art), move on to a sketch of a theory of knowledge, and end with a second, closer view of creative knowledge, with an eye more toward details.

1. Level One—Overview. In his mature vision, Maritain found it compelling to posit an "unconscious" or, as he corrects himself, a "preconscious," that stands behind human knowing. He distinguishes it sharply from the Freudian notion of unconscious, which he says comprises "the unconscious of blood and flesh, instincts, tendencies, complexes, repressed images and desires, traumatic memories, as constituting a closed or autonomous dynamic whole." This is an automatic or *deaf* unconscious— "deaf to the intellect, and structured into a world of its own apart from the intellect" (CI 91–92). In intimate connection and in unceasing communication with this "Freudian unconscious" is *spiritual unconscious or preconscious,* which is the activity of the spirit "in its living springs."[15]

For an example of spiritual preconscious, Maritain turns first to the functions of everyday intelligence. The new discoveries we make, "the new ideas that come to us; every genuine intellectual grasping, or every new discovery," have their start in this place. So do free decisions, especially about one's entire life.[16]

The primary powers in this unconscious realm are the intellect and will—though we will see that all other human knowing capacities are involved as well (CI 93–94).

> Far beneath the sunlit surface thronged with explicit concepts and judgments, words and expressed resolutions or movements of the will, are the sources of knowledge and creativity, of love and supra-sensuous desires, hidden in the primordial translucid night of the intimate vitality of the soul (CI 94).

Maritain says that this spiritual unconscious was recognized by Plato and other ancient writers, but in modern times has been disregarded in favor of Freudian unconscious. Nevertheless, the existence of a spiritual unconscious, hidden within each human being, is Maritain's "first preliminary thesis," and upon it depend all his further insights.[17]

So daily knowledge makes its roots in spiritual unconscious, and its flowering is in explicit discoveries, insights, decisions. The same is true of the speculative knowledge practiced by philosophers and scientists, originating in preconscious but emerging as specific and fully "objective" theory, description, etc. This topic requires an extensive philosophy of human knowledge, as Maritain notes (CI 91), to which he attends in other books.

"Poetic" or creative knowing is another operation that roots in the unconscious. Describing it, Maritain says

> we would have only a very incomplete picture of human knowledge if we did not take into account another type of knowledge, entirely different, which is not acquired through concepts and reasoning, but through *inclination,* as St. Thomas says,[18] or through sympathy, congeniality or connaturality (RR 16).

Here Maritain begins to use the term he will carry with him throughout his writings, and which we borrowed liberally in chapter one: connaturality. This is a knowledge by *inclination* to its objects, by a kind of *sympathy* with them, by a *congeniality* that exists between them and the knower. Poetic experience is this kind of knowing. The artist knows the things of the world by connatural knowledge. We should spend a few pages on this important idea for Maritain.

Maritain supplies identical exemplars of connatural knowing in at least five places.[19] We can look at them briefly, though the reader may wish to skip over their details (in the next three paragraphs) and go to the question of what is expressed in a work of art.

First, there is connaturality in a moral virtue such as prudence. Ask a good person what the right thing to do might be in, for example, a school bussing problem, and after some consideration the correct answer will out. Moral science or rational knowledge did not prompt the reply—the person just consulted inner bents or propensities of his or her own being and gave the good answer. This is an affective connatural knowledge directed toward the ends of human action, a knowledge of that which is already within oneself naturally.

A second example is mysticism. Though Maritain speaks of a *natural* mysticism (an emptying out of one's consciousness, as in Hinduism[20]), he is more intent on the supernatural kind, in spite of its more properly theological, not philosophical, nature. Here a "transcendent reality inexpressible in itself" (SP 66) becomes one with the mystic in a union of love that is not a natural love but an infused one. This is a knowledge in darkness, since no human concept or created word is capable of containing it. God's love enters the human being and itself becomes the way that the person knows God, like the way a concept is the way one knows in everyday knowledge.[21]

The third example is our topic: poetic knowledge represents an affective connatural union with reality. It too is non-conceptualizable. Things of the world become intimate to the unconscious of the artist, and since they are then one with the artistic soul, connatural to it, they are known inexplicitly.

> Is it possible to show that poetry and the intellect are of the same race and blood, and call to one another; and that poetry not only requires artistic or technical reason with regard to the particular ways of making, but, much more profoundly, depends on intuitive reason with regard to poetry's own essence and to the very touch of madness it involves (CI 90–91)?

Poetry and the soul of the artist are connatural to each other, and so is the stuff of the world, as we shall see. They are *like* each other, sharing something of the same nature.

We will see in the next chapter how different a work of art is from a concept or a word. The latter are general, which is to say that they apply to many instances, but the poem or the play is completely singular, incapable of being applied to anything but itself. Maritain's notion of poetic "knowledge" is helpful here. Creative knowing never reaches beyond particularity. It terminates not in a concept but in the work of art. If ordinary knowledge is always completed somewhere within the knower (e.g., the concept), poetic knowing is not consummated within the knower at all, but only in the exterior world. It is called *creative* for this reason. It exists in order to complete itself in the art product.

Maritain says, as will Langer, that art is fully a representation of the inner life of the artist. In this sense it can be called "self-expression." But he adds that subjective life cannot be known or expressed unless it is filled with the things of the external world. To put it otherwise, all knowledge has to be *of something* or that knowledge does not exist;

> it is only by receiving and suffering things, by awakening to the world, that our substance awakens to itself. The poet's own substance can only be expressed in a work if things resound within, and if at the same awakening, they and the artistic soul emerge together from sleep. All that the artist discerns and divines in things is thus inseparable from the artist and his or her emotion, and it is actually as a part of oneself that the artist discerns and divines it, and in order to grasp obscurely his or her own being through a knowledge the end of which is to create (Cf. RR 18).[22]

Poetic knowledge does not know anything conceptually, but it knows the world by receiving into its very passion "the realities, correspondences, ciphered writings that are at the core of actual existence" (CI 115). Artists "discern and divine" the secrets of the things of the world not as if they were outside and other than the artist, but as inseparable from the artist's soul and emotion. Things become identified with the unconscious. A germ is created that contains a "humble revelation . . . *both of the Self of the poet and of some particular flash of reality in the God-made universe* . . . in its unforgettable individuality" (CI 115). This is poetic experience (in Maritain's sense of the word poetic), a knowledge of the world that is connatural knowing because at the unconscious level poet and world are one. It is almost too little to say they are therefore congenial to each other, inclined toward one another, connatural one to the other.

We see at work the governing metaphor of this book. In our language, a kind of deep knowledge takes place in which the fathering world becomes one with the artistic soul's mothering unconscious. The artist-mother receives things of the world as a part of him or herself. But this knowledge is not for its own sake. It is not complete until the fertile bud of union has grown and been born into the world as a child whose name is work-of-art.

I have said that the metaphor of this book depends for its life on this significant union at the root of artistic knowing. We are compelled therefore to look through Maritain's glasses not only at artistic expression, but at the act of knowing itself, since only a coherent theory of knowledge will ground artistic experience as described above. We need to see why poetic experience is based on not just the union but the *identity* of knower with what is known.

2. Excursus: A Story of Knowing. This section may well contain terms and ideas comprising what some see as a system no longer current or even relevant. Whatever one thinks about a philosophical system, however, intellectual courtesy urges us to hear out any writer, especially one who will stretch the boundaries of the system he or she inherited in order to explain aesthetical creation.

Let us spend a section, then, understanding generally Maritain's theory of knowing. Because I believe in the intelligibility of metaphor, I have adopted a basic metaphorical structure for this discussion. I speak of things "outside" consciousness, of "entering the realm of knowing," of "being elevated." These are my way of achieving an initial understanding of Maritain—they do not represent his expressions. Call this a poetic account.

In *The Degrees of Knowledge* (112–118) Maritain gives a summary of his (Thomistic) theory of knowing.[23] Toward the beginning he makes a foundational statement:

> *"a being is a knowing being*
> *to the extent that it is immaterial"* (DK 112).

Material things do not know; beings which are to some degree immaterial do.

I will not be able to give extensive treatment to the notions of material and immaterial realities in this discussion. Perhaps here we can arrive merely at Maritain's notion of immateriality as related to knowledge. He points to a peculiar fact about consciousness,[24] as follows: whenever one knows, there is nothing in one's awareness except the object being known. When, as the present writer, I look at the desk I am using, for instance, or at least at the crowd of papers and books strewn upon it, I definitely am unaware of any of my mechanisms of knowing, either physical (photons, refraction, nerve impulses, stimulations, interpretation, figure/ground, etc.) or mental (for Maritain: sense images, concepts, judgments). More than that, I am not even aware of *myself* in the knowing process. To become aware in that way, I have to take a kind of indirect backward glance at the "me" behind the knowing. Knowledge of the self is a most obscure knowledge, as counselors can affirm.[25]

The wonderful thing about consciousness, therefore, is its ability to suppress its own identity and *become* the object. We will hear Lonergan quote Aristotle to that effect in Appendix Four: *the sense in act is the sensed thing in act.* The one becomes the other and there is no trace of duality in that coming-to-one. Maritain says this "becoming" is very different from what happens in the strictly material world (which we can also name the "entitative world"—from Latin *ens,* meaning "thing"). There each thing is strictly its own self and nothing else. No item on my cluttered desk can be in the same space as any other thing (to my disadvantage), unless the other thing is first removed. Matter seems to bring with it a heaviness, a torpor in which an item cannot release its identity, its place, its characteristics, on pain of ceasing to be what it is, in the place where it is. It is stuck to itself. My consciousness can become anything else; a pencil cannot. This gives rise to what is termed the principle of identity or of non-contradiction. *A thing cannot both be and not be at the same time.* It cannot be brown and not brown in the same regard at the same time. Or cluttered and non-cluttered. Or desk and not desk. For Maritain, this principle of identity is the first rule of material reality.[26]

Consciousness is immaterial because it has a different rule. If the knowing powers can lose themselves and *become* the desk reality (or whatever else), then the principle of identity does not apply within the conscious realm. Here is an entity that *can* be both itself and something else at the same time and in the same respect. Consciousness can remain consciousness and at the same moment manage to be the piled-high desk (as an object within consciousness). The more a being lets go of its materiality the more it can be a knowing being. Consciousness is not stuck to itself.

Unfortunately, the freedom that belongs to consciousness is not enough. As long as the material thing still clings to itself it cannot be known. It has to let go of its own stickiness *to some degree* in order to enter into consciousness. *Both* it and consciousness have to be unstuck from themselves. We have seen that the material thing cannot release itself as long as it remains only in the entitative order of existence—if it could, the clutter could fall through my desk. Childhood dreams sometimes involve relief from the entitative world's material rules so that we have x-ray vision, can fly, can stretch our arms and legs as if they were rubber, or be in more than one location at the same time. Since this is impossible in the "real world," and since dreams are exceptions to prove that rule, then where can the material thing go to free itself from its stuckness? The answer: it has to go to a new order of existence, the conscious one.[27]

The desk must take up residence in the conscious or intentional realm. This may seem redundant: of course it has to enter into knowledge if it is to be known. To clarify, we must make an acute distinction:

Union of consciousness with a known thing is an act by which consciousness receives the thing.

But helping the thing to become unstuck from its materiality requires activity on the part of the knower.

Therefore two steps are needed, one receptive, the other active.

Active consciousness helps the desk to be a *desk in the order of conscious existence*, and then, since both partners have at that point become free from the heavy principle of identity, receptive consciousness *receives* the desk as one with itself. To say it another way, the thing has to enter the conscious realm through the enlightening *power* of consciousness, and only then be received into oneness with consciousness. There is always first an elevation, then a union.[28] This is an important principle that we will see repeated in the traditional trinitarian theology of Part Two of this book. (I give the stages of this elevation and union in Appendix Two).

Let us now retrace our steps. We have wandered into the realm of consciousness, where laws of materiality do not fully apply, and found our way back to the world beyond our object knowledge, the "trans-objective world" of the material realm. We started with the homely reality of my desk, fully subject to material laws (especially the law of identity or non-contradiction) in the material world. We learned that the desk could escape those laws and be known beyond the mere physical self that it is. If it can be paired with the knowing power of my consciousness it can escape its "either/or" status and enter as a potential partner within a new "both/and" conscious sphere where my knowing and it can be one. Maritain called this realm "intentional existence." The thing enters this realm by means of the active power of consciousness, which frees it in various ways to unite with consciousness. Then the receptive power of consciousness receives the object, even as an ovum receives the sperm, and oneness is achieved.

We are now able to continue with *creative* knowing, which is our main topic. A small matter must be taken care of first. Several disclaimers have to be registered or repeated regarding the manner we have just spoken about knowledge. First, stories love places, and therefore the conscious realms we have discussed may well have sounded like locations that are walkable and measurable. But these words are solely metaphorical when applied to the intentional order of existence. Second, time does not apply either. Because of the semi-narrative shape of the preceding paragraphs, our account of knowledge theory had to take a temporal form: *first* the thing enters the intentional sense realm, *then* consciousness receives it and becomes one with it (at various levels: please see Appendix Two). But the "steps" do not really happen before and after each other. They are simultaneous, not progressive. The only ordering is that one depends on the other.[29]

Third, it is important to remark the degree to which this process is *not explicit within* consciousness. For Maritain, some of the above features of knowledge cannot even be known directly; they are just deductions about what has to be there.[30] They are that *by which* the object is known, not *that which* is known. The processes resemble the tape and CD and their respective playback units in modern stereo systems: we hear the sound, but the equipment and discs *by which* it is given to us are not "known" in the music. All the equipment of knowledge is "invisible," to use a sight metaphor. Perception's content is "the other," with no awareness of the regions of consciousness; it knows the object with complete self abandon so that its regard is completely filled with the thing as other than itself.

Obviously, Maritain's theory of knowledge carries the marks of significant union specific to our metaphor, a union-to-identity of two connatural beings, which union is the act of knowing ("the act of simple intelligence" SP 80). This union has an analogy to physical conception as found in human procreation, with only one discord: in ordinary knowledge, once the union has taken place, birth does not follow gestation. The act of knowledge has knowing as its purpose, not making. To find gestation and birth we will have to turn to Maritain's aesthetic theory. We advance to poetic knowledge, the conception that precedes gestation, this time with a more nuanced view, and with the tools to probe it deeper.[31]

3. *Level Two—Creative Knowledge at Closer Range.* We said above that, for Maritain, *creative knowledge* bypasses conceptual knowledge and finds its completion only in the artifact it creates. Let us now examine that creative knowledge in greater detail. As we saw, Maritain anchors both everyday knowledge and creative knowing in his special form of "the unconscious."

> If there is in the spiritual unconscious a nonconceptual or preconceptual activity of the intellect even with regard to the birth of concepts, we can with greater reason assume that such a non-conceptual activity of the intellect, such a nonrational activity of reason, in the spiritual unconscious, plays an essential part in the genesis of poetry and poetic inspiration (CI 99–100).

What kind of essential part does it play? We must find out more about what happens in the stilly night of unconsciousness, and how poetic knowing differs from ordinary knowing. To do that, we have to look briefly to the *powers* that bring about knowing, insofar as they are present in the unconscious. It is their configuration that holds the clue.

Here we can share Maritain's love for diagrams, which he includes "for those readers (if there are any) who are fond of this innocent hobby" (CI 107, 318). There are, for Maritain, at least three areas where ordinary knowing took place. We could represent them by circles:

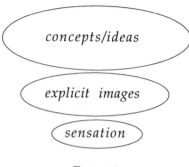

FIGURE 1

In the bottom circle the sense organs act as avenues through which a thing travels in order to take up residence in the conscious realm. In the middle circle the senses perform a union with the object as regards its sensed attributes. Since a name for this union is "image," the power of the soul that is involved here is the "imagination." When the intellect becomes one with these intelligibilities, consciousness has "become" the object (or oned with it). If we put a name on what results at this last stage, as separated from the preceding process of knowing, the name is "concepts" or "ideas."

Powers produce these results. Maritain appeals to Thomas Aquinas to say that the "powers" of the soul flow from the essence of the soul.[32] This could mean, of course, that they proceed in parallel fashion, something like this:

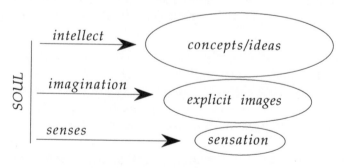

FIGURE 2

But in Maritain's view, Thomas also holds an *ordering* among the powers of the soul.[33] One power comes forth (a material metaphor) almost *through* the other, for the purpose of the other. External sensation emerges from the center point of the soul all the way toward material reality, *in order to begin the metamorphosis* to intellectual knowledge. The intellectual power stretches out to the material world by means of the senses, in order to bring the seed of intelligibility home. *The lower powers proceed through the higher ones.*

To illustrate this, Maritain attaches cones to the circles. Cones represent the powers of the knower and the way these powers operate. Instead of a mechanistic collection of concepts, images, and sense data, instead we now see an operational model:[34]

Maritain explains:

> Our three cones are not empty; each one should be imagined as filled with the life and activity of the power it symbolizes. The life and activity of the Intellect or Reason are not to be viewed only in the circle of the conceptualized externals of Reason. They are an immense dynamism emanating from the very center of the Soul and terminating in this circle of externals (CI 109).

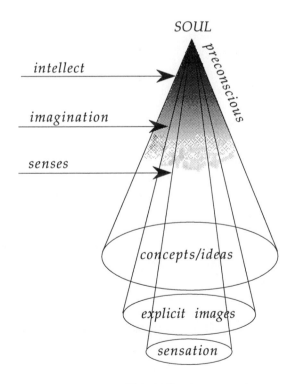

SOUL

intellect

imagination

senses

preconscious

concepts/ideas

explicit images

sensation

FIGURE 3

The same goes for the imagination (or imag-ination). There is an "immense dynamism" going upwards and downwards between the depths of the Soul and the external circles. This diagram is able to illustrate how the powers of consciousness come through each other and for the purpose of each other. Their goal, of course, is to grasp the entirety of the object, to become one with it in its most important aspects.

The lines grow ever closer as they near their soul source. At a certain stage we see them enveloped within the darker area of our drawing, which represents the knowing preconscious of the spirit. In this region the powers are not yet fully differentiated. Within the spiritual unconscious they are engaged in a root activity in common.

> The powers of the soul envelop one another, the universe of sense perception is in the universe of imagination, which is in the universe of intelligence. And they are all, within the intellect, stirred and activated by the light of the illuminating intellect (CI 110).

So we have an interpenetration of the knowing powers in their nascent or preconscious stage. They share each other's reality in a kind of mud bath of the unconscious.[35]

Preconsciousness is precisely *non-explicit* knowledge. It is an awareness that is prior to and undergirding explicit consciousness. But here a question occurs. If creative unconscious does not use concepts, how is the thing grasped at all by the unconscious? Traditional scholastic philosophy holds that the concept is the means, the carrier of knowledge. What carries pre-conceptional knowledge? The answer lies in a soul power not yet included in the diagram: emotion. Maritain and Langer each quote numerous artists and critics who place emotion at the center of the artistic act. Of course this is not the personal or (as Maritain calls it) crude emotion of the artist. "I do not mean," he says, "the inexhaustible flux of superficial feelings in which the sentimental reader recognizes his [or her] own cheap longings, and with which the songs to the Darling and Faithless One of generations of poets have desperately fed us" (CI 113).[36] Both Langer and Maritain are after the emotion "which *causes to express,* emotion as formative, emotion as intentional vehicle of reality known through inclination and as proper medium of poetic intuition" (CI 120–121, n 16). In other words, emotion is one of the powers involved in the preconscious interplay, is one of the main players in complex poetic knowledge. It is not "how I feel today"—or at some important time—but *how my feelings are a mode of oneing with reality.*

> I would say that in poetic [artistic] knowledge emotion carries the reality which the soul suffers—a world in a grain of sand— into the depth of subjectivity, and of the spiritual unconscious of the intellect. . . (CI 122).

Poetic emotion, before it emanates outward to become your or my emotional state, holds a privileged place in the artist's oneing with the world. It permeates the sense images which bring first union with the object. It is filled with the "diffuse light of the Illuminating Intellect." In that state emotion can *know* with the full power of the soul, "before" the conscious process yields an *explicit* image or concept or feeling. And the intelligibilities present within emotion are thus made able to be known.[37] Emotion therefore "takes the place of the concept in becoming for the intellect a determining means or instrumental vehicle through which reality is grasped" (CI 121).[38] In technical language, from which the reader may chose to abstain,

> while remaining emotion it is made—with respect to the aspects in things which are connatural to, or *like*, the soul it imbues—into an instrument of intelligence judging through connaturality, and plays, in the process of this knowledge through *likeness* between reality and subjectivity, the part of a nonconceptual intrinsic determination of intelligence in its preconscious activity. By this very fact it is . . . spiritualized, it becomes intentional, that is to say, conveying, in a state of immateriality, things other than itself (CI 123).

This is perhaps the most important comment for our own thesis, and for the philosophy of art that Maritain is setting up. Emotion is no longer to be considered an accompaniment to knowing. It is now illuminated by the intellect so that it has the capacity to convey things into deep consciousness, to become them. In order to make no mistake about the import of this doctrine, let us look at a short text from *The Situation of Poetry.*

> The real and the subjectivity, the world and the whole of the soul coexist actively and inseparably in the emotion at that moment. At that moment sense and sensation are gathered back into the heart, the blood into the spirit, the passion into the intuition. And by the virtual actuation of the intellect all the faculties are also actuated at their very root (SP 82).

If we transport this specifically Maritainian understanding into the language of our own metaphor, there is here significant oneing, described in the most urgent terms. The parenting elements in poetic knowledge now "coexist actively and inseparably," and the locale of this union is "in the emotion." Through this emotion the intellect itself is activated *virtually*, which is to say not in explicit concepts, but in the other-carrying-emotion. By means of this activation *"all the faculties"* of the poet are activated *at their very root*, since the nascent powers of the soul interpenetrate each other in the preconscious. This is a transfixing union, involving every power of the artist because something of the world has become one with his or her soul at the deepest preconscious level. In this act the first and most important characteristic of our governing metaphor is fulfilled. Within intellectualized emotion the artist can become "pregnant."[39]

Now we must ask in more detail exactly what creative knowledge knows. We have heard Maritain talk about "things" and about "the world." But what are the dimensions of these? When we have seen the answer, we will be in a position to discern whether the union achieved in poetic knowledge is truly a pregnancy leading to birth, or if that generative aspect is just something superadded. How does Maritain describe the things that poetic experience knows?

It knows the individual thing.

> Poetic intuition is directed toward concrete existence as connatural to the soul pierced by a given emotion: that is to say, each time toward *some singular existent*, toward some complex of concrete and individual reality, seized in the violence of its sudden self-assertion and in the total unicity of its passage in time. This transient motion of a beloved hand—it exists in an instant, and will disappear forever, and only in the memory of angels will it be preserved, above time. Poetic intuition catches it in passing, in a faint attempt to immortalize it in time (CI 126, italics mine).

This passage is itself a poetic description of what the artistic soul grasps of reality. The beloved hand has become one with the artist's preconscious knowledge and in that realm the merger is not just according to the two powers we saw above, sense and intellectual oneness, but is a merger (in the preconscious) of the known and knower in the emotional reality of the object. Such emotion includes all the memories, images, connections, desires, urges, longings, that the entire artistic soul possesses.

So the focus of creative knowledge is "some singular existent," in its whole range of relationships with my life—Maritain understood these as part of its reality. The beloved hand is precisely *the beloved* hand, known to the poet as a locus of dear and specific relationships to the self. In this way, spiritualized emotion lets the artist know it in a fuller way than everyday knowledge does.[40]

There is a seeming contradiction, one which tells directly on the question of art as "self-expression." Both Maritain and Langer say that the art work is an expression of the artist's subjectivity. Does this mean that art is simply self-revelation and nothing more? We answered briefly in the first section of this chapter, and now must go further.

We saw that in ordinary knowing the whole of consciousness is taken up with the *content* of knowledge, that is, with the things known. I am conscious of desk, not of concept-of-desk, or of me-knowing-desk. If there is to be knowledge of one's own inner self, it will never be direct in the way that knowledge of things is, never objective. A knower can cast a sidelong glance back as he or she is knowing things and can then have what is called "reflexive" awareness of the self who is knowing. We saw that this is so because consciousness of itself is empty. It exists to receive the other and has no content until that happens.

Creative knowledge involves more of the "flesh and blood" of consciousness: the images, associations, memories, feelings, proclivities, desires that take part so vigorously in any act of creative knowing.[41] Poetic knowledge is, for Maritain, a rich and varied, obscure *becoming* of the other at one significant moment. Here again, it is only by this becoming that the artist can arrive at knowledge of him- or herself. One's own knowing is obscure to oneself; it can awaken to itself only by awakening to the world, whose contents resound within. In creative knowledge

> such a grasp of the substance of the subject can only take place in a non-conceptual or non-logical mode, hence in an essentially obscure manner, at the very instant when some reality from the universe outside is grasped by mode of affective connaturality, in an intuitive emotion in which the universe and the subject are revealed together to the subject, as if by a beam of darkness. For it is in awakening to the world, it is in obscurely grasping some substantial secret in things, that the soul of a [human being] obscurely grasps itself (SP 73).[42]

Subjectivity in the artist consists of artistic consciousness filled with the object. This moment of union, Hopkins says, is live and lancing like a blowpipe flame. Maritain quotes a scholastic saying:

- "the content most immediately grasped is the world,

- the content *most principally* (and most secretly) grasped is the subjectivity" (SP 73–74).

We are clearly talking about a fecundation: an impregnating, conception-like union. But it is only fair to call it such if the act of union develops and is born into the world. Thus we must take time now to see whether gestation and birth are an integral part of poetic experience, something that *could not fail* to happen once "conception" has taken place, or whether the art work is merely fortuitous. We will look now at that inevitability and then move on to gestation.

Maritain seems never to tire of saying that the "poetic" knowledge is *creative*. It does not exist for the purpose of knowing but of making. It is

> a knowledge which is at the minimum of knowledge but at the maximum of germinative virtuality, a knowledge which is objectified completely only in the work, in an object made (SP 73).

As we saw, for Maritain, ordinary knowledge has stages, one event growing out of another event, moving from the unconscious into the conscious. Ordinary knowledge is just that, knowledge, not making.[43] In artistic knowing as such, we have seen that nothing gets beyond the preconscious. In fact, if it were able to proceed to conceptual knowledge it would no longer be artistic or "poetic" knowing.

Thus the completion of artistic knowledge takes place in the work of art. To put it another way, the procession toward an explicit or objective state does not take place within the knower's conscious field at all; it takes place always and only in the production of a work of art outside of the knower. Therefore artistic knowledge is intrinsically germinative and creative. Being denied the concept, which anyway could not hold the fullness of its union with the world, creative knowledge therefore needs to find another way to come adequately to the surface. The art work is that way.

Thus self-knowledge for the artist can come, in an obscure and intuitive manner, from beholding the completed work of art. Its being was born out of the artist's own subconscious. Like a new-born baby, it carries reflections of its parents. If we translate all of this into our own language, we can say that a very important oneing has taken place. Such onement always needs to grow and differentiate until it can take up life apart from its mothering environment. This is part of its nature, and does not happen for another prior reason. Therefore it is not simply "knowledge," in the sense of everyday knowing, nor is it a communication.[44]

> The poetic intuition demands to be objectized and expressed in a work. It is enough that the work exists, that this kind of a world is created. The fact that it makes the poet communicate with other human beings, even the fact that it is seen, or listened to, is itself an effect of superabundance (CI 307).[45]

The intuitive union, planted deep in the unconscious, is what will become the poem, song, painting, dance. The artist is pregnant and uncomfortable until the birth—at which point the suffering is all forgotten. Maritain quotes this line from Keats and then makes a comment:

> "I was taught in Paradise
> To ease my breast of melodies."

> Precisely so. The overcharged breast can find no ease but in suckling the
> baby-song (CI 306–07).

We can conclude then that poetic knowing, like the physical zygote, contains within itself the urge to grow and to be born. We are justified at this point in finding our governing metaphor and analogy confirmed in Maritain's aesthetics. This would hold even if there were no description of gestation in his doctrine. It happens, however, that one of his keener instincts is to trace what takes place after the conceiving union and before the birth. Let us summarize what we have said so far before moving on to gestation.

We took a look at Maritain's theory of ordinary knowledge and found it already a tale of union: consciousness and the thing becoming one, through achieved connaturality. Then we began to peruse the powers of consciousness that made all this union possible. With Maritain we traced the origin of these powers to the centering point of soul. While within the pre-conscious, the powers were not completely differentiated from one another; they intermingled and shared illumination from the nascent intellectual power.

Then we made room for another power that considerably enriched union with the object: emotion. Within the preconscious, emotion had the same status as the other powers: undifferentiated from the others and inexplicit. It partook of the light of the illuminating intellect just like all the others. As a result, emotion, instead of being a reaction subsequent to an already complete act of knowing, could itself become a vehicle to carry the object into the soul. It could do this while still mixed and interpenetrating with sense images, memory, and the rest.

The one thing that could jinx this knowing role of the emotions was if it ended in clear, conceptual knowledge. In ordinary knowing, explicit and distinct concepts characterize consciousness' ultimate union with the object (before existence). Poetic knowledge must not do that. It can never abandon the sense aspects of a thing in order to derive a mere concept. Luckily, in the preconscious—where everything is mixed with everything— the fences are down so that emotion and images have license to carry the intellectual import of these sense details without letting go of the details themselves. This kind of emotional (+ sensed + remembered + intellectual + etc.) union is the place of poetic or artistic knowledge.

Such experience, so far just in the preconscious, still needs completion. It is pregnant from its union with reality (within intellectualized emotion). It pushes toward expression. Since that expression cannot be a matter of explicit consciousness it has to push outwards toward the material world, where it is born as a new object, the work of art. Of course it cannot pass directly to such a state. Brooding and sitting are in store while its implicit parts firm toward explicitness, while it becomes viable for its life in the material world. We initially have called this brooding process "gestation," by analogy with the physical journey of a zygote toward birth. With that we said that the initial step of our governing metaphor/analogy was complete: there is a union of considerable import, a pregnant union.

> In poetic intuition objective reality and subjectivity, the world and the whole of the soul, coexist inseparably. At that moment sense and sensation are brought back to the heart, blood to the spirit, passion to intuition (CI 124).

Now it is time to trace, in Maritain's philosophy, the progress of this oned reality toward viability.

B. Gestation—Early Morning Vision

... Explicit images awaken, more distinct emotions resound in the fundamental emotion. Then there is in the soul of the poet an enlarged musical stir, a music no longer almost imperceptible, but more and more cogent, in which the soundless rhythmic and harmonic relations... together with their soundless melody, emerge into consciousness (CI 303).

So far we have seen Maritain's vision of conception. In explicitly terms he says that some particular thing ("the beloved hand") has come to onehood with the intimate, preconscious emotion of the artist. We have seen that it cannot stay there, that it must work its way outwards to an objective state, outside the artist. In gestation, it passes first into a new and partially objectivized state, beginning to become the work as mentally articulated, the work in the making. Intellect and concepts do get involved here, but not as a part of intuition itself. The passage must be outwards, toward the finalized artwork, through but not usurped by concepts. Now another union takes place, that of the artist with the medium of his or her art genre. The writer of poems must know and love words intimately. They are the body that the intuitive union will assume.[46] Surprises are in store here, because flesh has its own intractability, as does the material of the art form.

At three main places in *Creative Intuition* Maritain discusses the unfolding of poetic knowledge into a work of art.[47] The first (CI 238–243) has mainly to do with the common term "inspiration," which does not forward the line of thought we are pursuing. In his second discussion of the movement from knowledge to art work (CI 301–310) Maritain has to introduce a new idea and new terminology about poetic knowledge. The term, which he says was not easy to coin, is *intuitive pulsion*. He allows us also to name it "dynamic charge." Pulsions are partial units within the intuitive subjective union. Maritain is now speaking of the creative knowledge as if it were itself an entity, a union of the artist with the world which has taken on its own reality, as did the fetus in the first stage of physical gestation. It already has beginning parts or buds: pulsions. Each is "a complex of virtual images and emotion, stirred in the fluid and moving world of the creativity of the spirit, and essentially tendential, dynamic, and transient" (CI 302).[48] These are awakened by creative experience under the illumination of the intellect, and are parts, not complete expressions, of the oned poetic experience. They depend on its indivisible unity. They are on the edge of consciousness and all but imperceptible.

> Between them there is movement and continuity. And this moving continuity between partial units (which originates in the indivisible unity of poetic intuition, and through which poetic intuition passes) is nothing but a *meaning* set free in *a motion:* that is to say, a kind of melody—in the state of a source, a primeval melody—this word being taken in a merely analogical sense, having in no way to do with sounds, but only with inaudible psychic charges of images and emotion (CI 302).[49]

"Meaning set free in a motion" (as in amniotic fluid?) surely does reinforce our metaphor of gestation. But Maritain reaches for another metaphor. The freedom and flow of these pulsions is also like what we experience in a great melody. Maritain is not talking about actual music, but something *like* music. Each pulsion is a kind of "mental wave or vibration, charged with dynamic unity." Together the pulsions represent a *"musical stir immediately produced by poetic experience and poetic intuition"* (CI 302, n 3). They are the first commotion of the newly conceived child in its most embryonic state. Even though they are within the preconscious, they begin to protrude into consciousness. They are the very earliest tendency to gestate.[50]

This pulsive stir represents the first stage of gestation. At the second stage pulsions become more shaped. They emerge into what Maritain calls the morning light. Now practical intelligence (that is, intelligence which produces) comes into play, but as a secondary force, always subservient to poetic intuition, and to the "music" of the intuitive pulsions. Such intelligence listens carefully, putting into play only that which is from the artistic source. The penalty for inattention at this time is bad art.

But if the intellect remains true to intuitive pulsions, they begin to emerge.

> The expansion of the poetic intuition in its vital milieu develops, and at the same time the intuitive pulsions also expand and become more and more distinct; explicit images awaken,

more distinct emotions resound in the fundamental emotion. Then there is in the soul of the poet an enlarged musical stir, a music no longer almost imperceptible, but more and more cogent, in which the soundless rhythmic and harmonic relations between intuitive pulsions, together with their soundless melody, emerge into consciousness (CI 303).

Instead of being only peripherally aware of the pulsions, the artistic organism now becomes explicitly conscious of them, is able to promote what is good for the poem and eliminate what is not. On the part of a human mother gestation is autonomic and instinctive. Her physical, conscious skills are not greatly involved during gestation, except as sidelights. In the artist, this stage requires, not the rigors of forced development, but conscious and semi-conscious attention to what is gestating within. Now is the time for skills of mindfulness and making.

Here "secondary rules" of making become important. These involve what Maritain calls "working reason" (the "practical intellect") producing according to honed abilities. In a poem judgments must be made as to whether intuitive pulsions are to be put behind a single word or line, or else into the whole poem. Again, loyalty to the intuitive source of the work in process must guide all choices of materials and methods. The artist becomes accustomed to working in this way, and so it becomes almost habitual.[51]

Our governing metaphor tells us that these descriptions concern the ability of the artist to provide a mothering environment for the now developing zygote—the burgeoning union of artist and reality as it makes its way toward the world outside. The reason our metaphor conveys so much even on first hearing is that it presents a first model startlingly similar to poetic gestation, at least as observed by Maritain.

We are seeing the root analogy in its details: that significant union is always generative, or, as we rephrased it, creativity is always co-creativity. We have seen the first two stages of creative gestation: initial stirring of the pulsions in the pre-dawn of unconsciousness; the early morning light in which practical intelligence begins to work with the soundless music of pulsions. Maritain describes the third stage of gestation in what is actually a meditation on classical versus modern poetry (CI 310–324).

We will be able to view artistic gestation more clearly by spending a few moments on this meditation. Classical poetry, he says, is required to be *clear*. Its language is meant to *communicate notions*, and to do so in a logically *bound* form (CI 311). Thus, poetic imagination is required to submit itself to the regime of the rational, conceptual mind, and this is the third stage of gestation.

At this point Maritain suggests three "regions" of creative subjectivity, which correspond to the three stages we have been following, admitting however that this scheme oversimplifies. First the "captured" flash of reality becomes one with the diffuse poetic soul. Second it enters the area of the imagination, where a "first expression" comes about, not yet conscious, but not hidden in darkness either. In this second region, the intuitive pulsions, both imaginal and emotional, are at play.

The third step is what we are seeking. Now,

> the creative impulse enters the sphere of authority of conceptual reason, and conceptual reason claims its rights to sovereignty. The intuitive content which puts pressure on the poet must be translated into concepts, and this translation into concepts must comply with the absolute primacy of the rational connections and the logical objectivity to be expressed through the signs of this social instrument which is language (CI 310–311).

The classical poem will be constructed from conceptual units. It will be a logically bound form; it will be necessarily clear; it will be explicit. In other words to various degrees the rule of the rational realm will prevail. The inner music of the pulsions is often killed at this stage, Maritain says, or at least is superseded by the reign of the rational (CI 311).

But in good classical poems it prevails. It can do this because of what Maritain calls the "music of the words." This is not the same thing as the soundless melody of the pulsions, which was a metaphorical use of the word music—it is something else. But there is difficulty finding out just what "music of the words" is, and Maritain does not explain. He does say in parentheses that music of the words includes the music of "the proffered notions and images" (CI 312). He also furnishes an example, Blake's "The Sick Rose" (CI 313).

> O Rose, thou art sick!
> The invisible worm,
> That flies in the night
> In the howling storm,

Has found out thy bed
Of crimson joy:
And his dark secret love
Does thy life destroy.

It is up to the reader to intuit or "feel" the music in this most effective poem. But we are still left without exact meaning for "music of the words." Perhaps we can deduce its meaning from its activity. It has to be

> strong enough to overcome the obstacle created by the intermediary signification, the definite set of things, and to put the eyes of our logical reason to sleep, and to lead us, captive, to a participation in the poetic intuition which was born in the spiritual night of the preconceptual activity of the poet (CI 312).

Thus we might say that "music" is used metaphorically in this case too. It includes images and suggestions of images, the sequence of ideas, perhaps even the actual sound of the words—and maybe all the devices of writing that Langer will be so good at isolating. Whatever its technical apparatus, it creates an appeal to the deeper senses of the reader (or better, listener) and draws his or her soul beyond the mere ideas. If it can do this, the prior "music" of the pulsions will survive its packaging into concepts.

So the oned moment of poetic conception stirs, then passes through the imagination with its "full grown and definitely formed images," then through the conceptual realm with its forming and formed concepts. Maritain says that explicit concepts are then pulled forth, and images are sought and picked up to illustrate the pulsions. Notice that this description gets rid of a quasi-mechanical view of creativity, one in which the whole art-work would be contained, pre-packaged, within the initial conception, and then merely unfolded outwards, like unfolding a tent. Such a view ignores the qualitative difference between the first, yoked reality, and that same reality as cloaked with, as one with the materials of its art (in this case, concepts and images). The emergence of the intuitive union into consciousness is an enfleshment. The manner and kind of flesh can vary widely, as long as it is guided by and made perfectly one with the oned, intuitive reality. In a poem the reader meets first the flesh, the definite objects (logical meanings), and then catches what Maritain calls the "transreality" behind them, a pulsed intuitive meaning (CI 319).

On the other hand, in modern poetry, reason is dethroned. The necessity of fixed forms, rhyme, versification, and clarity of ideas has been thrown aside. At first Maritain says that the music of words is no longer necessary. The internal music of pulsions, no longer obliged to fight with logical meanings, can itself provide the law of making. "The music of intuitive pulsions appears in the foreground, it is revealed in full, it has become the royal instrument of poetic expression" (CI 316). Later he corrects two impressions that this statement might convey: that music of words is absent in modern poetry, and that concepts too are missing. He says that word music is certainly there, now "a tougher, not pleasurable, broken music, but still music." It cannot be lacking, for this kind of "music" is the way that the "music of the pulsions" gets expressed in any work of words. This music of words is a direct and necessary response to the inaudible internal music of poetic intuition.

And of course, since words are conceptual vehicles, concepts must be present even in modern poetry. But now they are

> in a nascent state, and virtual, as it were, carried along by the images; or implicit, unapparent concepts, serving only as supports for the expression of images; or concepts which are explicit and used with their full intellectual meaning (CI 323).[52]

Nevertheless, in modern poetry, music of intuitive pulsions is master of the work, assuming its throne in the absence of rational articulation and logical objectivity.

Maritain cites an excerpt from Hopkins and one from Eliot to illustrate the "prevalence of the music of intuitive pulsions."

> I am gall, I am heartburn./
> > God's most deep decree
> Bitter would have me taste./
> > My taste was me./
>
> We have lingered in the chambers of the sea
> > By sea-girls wreathed with seaweed red and brown/
> Till human voices wake us/
> > And we drown./[53]

We feel here the relaxation of logic. Hopkins wrote in "sprung" rhythm, only one step from rhythmicized prose. And certainly clarity was not a major goal for Hopkins. The present author has witnessed heated debates among scholars on the possible syntax of lines from this very poem.

Maritain's discussions of intuition's gestation outwards toward the world have yielded an interesting, if simplified, picture of this process. The pulsions or dynamic charges, given in the original "conception," are emotion laden images (emotion always considered as soaked in the light of the illuminating intellect). They take a first development away from strict preconscious, push through the region of imagination's fully articulate images, and through the realm of concepts—either being ruled by reason's laws or not—and nestle comfortably into the words on paper (or the sounds of literal music, or the colors of a painting). This last is their birth, complete only when the finishing caress has been applied to a work by the mothering hand.

What of the temporal nature of this procession? In poetic creation the events do seem to have a temporal succession. However the *ordering* of that time may not always be strict, like it is in physical conception, gestation, and birth. In fact, the first emergence of intuitive pulsions may, Maritain says, even be simultaneous with the writing or molding or painting. A poet may be going through *all* the stages at the same moment he or she is toying with words on paper. Nor is there a rigid temporal order for the composer, who may—as did Stravinsky—sound out the musical ideas on the piano as the work is generating.[54] Maritain takes this reality into account. Again he says he is trying to establish a priority *in nature* rather than in time.

> My contention is that these two stages in poetic expression are distinct in nature, and that the transient expression through those *natural* signs which are the imaginal and emotional pulsions comes first, and precedes in nature the expression through those *social* signs which are the words of the language (CI 304).

"In nature" is the operative phrase. One thing is first in the sense that it is the foundation of the other, not because it necessarily happened first.

Here then is a difference from our guiding metaphor. Conception and gestation in human biology necessarily follow a certain time sequence. Violation of it spells disaster. But at the higher level of human consciousness (operating within a material being but freed from material laws), it is less important that the order be segmented in time. To be explicit, Maritain is not saying that, *first*, fertilization of the subject's preconscious takes place, and *then*, only after that is over, the pulsions begin to emerge into the imagination, and when they have completed that task they can *subsequently* make their way into the intellective region and finally, when all other process are over, into the work. Because of the immateriality of consciousness—freedom from the principle of identity—this rigid temporal order yields to much interplay between and telescoping of the processes. A "later" sequence may be happening at the same moment as an "earlier" one. But even if all the stages were strictly concurrent with each other in time, the stirring of pulsive images could not take place except on the foundation of the intuitive reception of the world. They are given in it, or if not, a consonant work of art is impossible. And so on for all the stages.[55]

We said at the beginning that our ruling metaphor served as a means of discovering important facts about artistic creativity. Metaphor, we said, is a strategy by which content is activated in the hearer (or viewer) by the means of skillful comparison without explicit enumeration. Analogy is not a verbal strategy. It is the simple, direct statement of a sameness between two or more beings that are also different from each other in various important ways. Physical conception, gestation, and birth are very different from poetic knowledge as it leads to the art work; this softening of the temporal ordering is one of those differences. But the similarities are remarkably strong, based on the principle that all reality is inter-penetrative, and that any significant union is fecund, producing an other. A significant oneing itself gestates, achieving the explicitation of its parts until it is fully formed and ready to exist by itself in the world, outside its mothering environment. Human reproduction and art present analogous realities, similar within differences. Through our interesting journey with Maritain thus far we have been able to map the analogy.

Maritain's treatment of classical and modern poetry prompts an additional, final remark. Surely liturgical music and its words have to be "classical," in Maritain's sense, appealing to the assembly first by their logic and coherence, and only then delivering intuitive pulsions besides. On the other hand modern symphonic music since the early nineteen hundreds has taken a turn away from logic and coherence, to the dismay of many audiences. One reason given is that the harmonic, melodic, and formal language of serious music, which developed and innovated ceaselessly throughout history in the west, had finally run its course. New music had to be made of different stuff. Contemporary composers labor under the onus of creating not only a new work but an entirely new style and language as well. The twentieth century up through the 1960s saw new styles that, in their attempt to start over, often eliminated harmony and melody completely. Innovation seemed to become the rule. Music of the twentieth century came to be judged in part by whether it was "new" or at least not old.

Perhaps a much better reading of contemporary "classical" music could be gleaned from Maritain's analysis of poetry. Perhaps the decline of specific and logical melody (and harmony) is somehow parallel to the dethroning of logic and reason in poetry. It could be that twentieth-century music needs to be evaluated not on the basis of its novelty but of whether it takes advantage of the opening left by traditional harmony and melody in order to give sway to another (metaphorical) kind of music: that of internal pulsions. Composers of the 1990s say that their primary duty is to "make music," not to innovate. Does the reign of creative pulsions have full sway in their pieces, even though the language is free and non-classical? When it does, contemporary classical music has a chance to claim a place beside that of the Bachs and Mozarts—though some audiences may not agree.

It remains to say a bit more about the birth, and about what has been born: the work of art with its form and its beauty.

C. Birth—The Full Light of Day

Any poetic work is a revealer. A good work delights the sense and the intellect, but the radiance, in its beauty, is first of all the radiance of the ontologic mystery grasped by the intuition of the poet; then, when the work strikes the eyes of another, it causes a communication of intuition, a passage from creative intuition to receptive intuition (CI 307).

Of interest in this section is the art work once it has been finished. Two topics only make up this section: the issue of symbol/sign (something interesting also to Langer) and an interconnected problem, beauty in the arts.

Where there is obvious structure and ordering in a work, the "definite set of things," the pitcher or bowl or vase in a painting, is not what the work is meant to signify. The set of things is "only a means, and an intermediary, even an obstructive intermediary" (CI 311). A work of art signifies the "flash of reality" that has awakened poetic insight, and which has been "captured obscurely in the mystery of the world." The final task of creative intelligence is a choice between the words (or shapes, or movements of soul) spontaneously offered (CI 305), weighing and testing everything.

The reader's task consists of allowing the work to be "an engine to make us pass *through* or *beyond* things" (CI 318).

> Since the work is the final objectivization of poetic intuition, what the work tends finally to convey to the soul of others is the same poetic intuition which was in the soul of the poet: not precisely as creative, but as cognitive, both of the subjectivity of the poet and of a flash of reality echoing the world (CI 307).

The work, when it is beheld, causes, not a communication of ideas, but a display of the intuition.

In speaking of the beholder, Maritain says there is a passing from creative intuition to receptive intuition. The same kind of receptivity that brought about the work now is pressed into action by the observer, but with a simpler aim of receiving the already objectified intuition. This statement would seem to involve Maritain in some difficulties, such as how a power which is always intrinsically bent toward creation can now become receptive only, with no urge toward making. He does not seem to address this problem, so it remains an unresolved question. At any rate, much is lost upon the beholder's intuition, "lost or wasted in the process," because the work now exists in the world, among men and women, through time. A great work gains and changes significance through generations. The poetic intuition conveyed in it is vast, and within it is an enormous content delivered by the flash. If a beholder perceives at least something of that intuition, the experience is valid.

The last passage quoted contains an excellent pointer as to why "baby" or "offspring" is so fitting as a metaphor for the art work. Like a baby, the art work does not function to convey or communicate something to us about the world. Nor is it in essence a confession of the author, or a record of the emotional state of its writer. The parenting elements come together in a significant union that gestates to become *a new being*, with elements of both progenitors in its makeup. A child should not be defined as a coded message about either parent. A work of art is an end in itself. Its own life came forth from the vitalities of things insofar as they fecundated the creative consciousness of its mother, the artist. Art expresses not just the subjectivity of the poet, but that subjectivity as filled with the mysterious reality of some part of the world that has ravished it. The "same intuition" that fills the work and that filled the artist is precisely the union itself that has now gestated into the world, has taken on the flesh typical to the particular art form involved. As the birthed art object passes through time it will be understood this way and that way, but fortunate ones who meet it will catch something of its inner reality. The same is true of the baby as it becomes child and adult.

Now we need to address a technical issue, one that the critics will bring against Langer to her near peril: signification or sign value. The more casual reader will wish to skip ahead to Langer, even though the theory of sign is a significant feature of each aesthetician's theory. Langer will begin from the insight that the finished work of art is a symbol representing the inner organic life of its maker. Her critics will say a symbol (1) must have general meaning(s) so that it might speak to those who observe it, and that (2) a symbol is not significant in itself, but only insofar as it refers the observer away from itself and toward that which it signifies. But to accept either or both these conditions would violate the idea of a work of art, which has to be singular and important for itself. Thus if the work is a symbol of the inner life of the artist it can no longer be considered art.[56]

Maritain has a sophisticated theory of symbol or sign, inherited from and enlarged by the school of philosophy that is his background. We can get at it by looking first at how subjectivity is represented in a work of art and then seeing how that gives us a key to the theory of sign. We will then conclude by a consideration of beauty in art.

I will state first the principle, derived from an aspect of knowledge we have already seen. Maritain, we know, makes a parallel between ordinary knowing and artistic knowing in the respective role of each *as an apprehension of the self*. In ordinary knowledge, as we noticed, human beings cannot know themselves with a direct, objective knowledge. The self is known in its operations, and otherwise not, since consciousness is empty unless it is filled with object. Self knowledge, we remember, is a reflexive process, a shadowy glance back at ourselves in the act of knowing, feeling, remembering. The self is *within* the knowing operation, but invisibly.

In the same way the subjectivity of the artist can be discerned in the work, *but only by contemplating the work in its operations,* not as something referring elsewhere and therefore unimportant in itself.

> For the substance of [a human being] is obscurely grasped—by a knowledge which will have its word in the work of art—only at the same time as the reality of things is, so to speak, pierced by connaturality and emotion. Every work of art is an avowal, but it is by uncovering the secrets of being (divined by force of suffering the things of this world) that the work of art confesses the secret of the poet (RT 254).

For Maritain, the "secrets of being" in things are entirely singular, even though they "echo" the mysterious interrelationships they have with everything else. Works of art are not general meanings and they do not have to refer away from themselves because the substance of the work *consists of the very merged reality of the artist and things of the world itself.* To look away toward something else would be averting one's glance from that which one wants to know. Any sign which only refers to something else is based on the either/or of the material realm. But signs which convey meaning by being known *as* themselves are founded on the both/and of the realm of consciousness ("intentional existence"). Subjectivity is comprehended insofar as it is *both* present in the art work, *and* oned with the things portrayed.

This is the key to Maritain's theory of sign, found mainly in chapter nine of *Ransoming the Time.* He admits there are some signs that are known in themselves and only thereafter make another thing known. A ribbon of smoke in the air is known as itself, but as a sign it refers our mind to something else, the fire we cannot see. This he names an *instrumental sign,* since it is an instrument by which another thing is known (he also calls it a "sign thing"). All signs are of this type *except one.*

We are prepared to understand that "one" because of our work on Maritain's theory of knowledge. He calls it a *formal sign.*[57] We recall that concepts are that *by which* we know the object, not that which is known. Thus they are formal signs (he also calls them "pure signs") because they are the form of the object that is known. Consciousness is empty and unknowable until that form is present. Formal or pure signs can only exist in the realm of consciousness, not in the material realm.[58]

Here is a summary:

Instrumental sign	• known beforehand
	• passes attention along to that which is represented
Formal sign	• not known in itself at all
	• is simply a presence of the signified within consciousness

Strangely, the work of art is neither kind, or else it is both. Maritain says it is both: the work of art has characteristics of each of these types. We certainly know the art object itself, in the manner of an instrumental sign: it is not a transparency through which we know. On the other hand, we are knowing "directly" only the materiality of the art work. The real content, however, is "simply the presence of the signified" somehow within the art object. The painting is a *sign* of a fictive woman (Mona Lisa together with the subjectivity which gave the painting birth), and thus acts like a formal sign: we know the presence of something else which is in the patterns of the thing, which patterns exist to "make present for consciousness something other than" themselves.

Maritain confirms in a footnote to *Ransoming the Time* that a statue has characteristics of an intentional or formal sign, but one which is known beforehand like an instrumental sign.

> In the statue of Socrates . . . Socrates is present in a mode of *intentional* existence, but in another fashion: the statue is something itself known beforehand (according to a priority in nature, not in time), before it makes Socrates known. It is an "instrumental" sign, and the intentionality therein is merely virtual (RT 310, n 8).

The statue is an instrumental sign because it is a thing known, like the curl of smoke, not something unknown like the concept. But even so, it has a special place in the intentional or conscious realm. There is a *virtual* presence within the statue itself, waiting for consciousness to activate (or "elevate") it. Maritain seems to be saying that there is something within the statue that is intentional because it already *tends toward Socrates* so that consciousness can know "him" in the statue.

Thus there is a third kind of sign:

Art sign   • The object is known in itself

• but also contains virtually the presence of the signified (on the intentional level)

By calling its presence "virtual," Maritain means the sign is slumbering within the art object and must be awakened by powers that belong properly to the conscious realm (virtual, from *virtus*, strength: something there in effect but not in fact).[59] A dog would not respond to the Mona Lisa as if it were a person, would not feel an aesthetical reaction, since the doggy consciousness could not actuate her virtual presence.

> It is the act of vision which, immaterial as such although intrinsically subject to material conditions, awakens this intentionality in the statue—in so far as the latter is perceived or made one with the sense power in act (RT 310, n 8).

There is in the statue or art work *a pattern of intelligibility already virtually intentional* that consciousness unites with. This added pattern makes present to consciousness something that is not the block of marble. Intentional sign patterns make *Socrates* present to consciousness. Thus Socrates is in the statue *in alio esse*, in another mode of existence—the mode we have been calling intentional existence. [60]

The discussion of sign ushers us into the last important area of Maritain's theory that is relevant for our purpose: beauty. We must give quick heed to it, leaving aside Maritain's treatment of subservient arts versus fine arts, the relativity of taste, and even the difference between transcendental and aesthetic beauty. We want to find out, quite simply, the way in which an art work can be called beautiful. This discussion will help us in Part Two of the present book when we come to speak of beauty and the liturgical arts.

One conclusion from our quick look at knowledge-according-to-Maritain was this: ordinary knowledge is a knowing of the beings of the world, or simply, of *being*. Now we must say a bit more about being, since for Maritain beauty has an intimate connection with it.

First, for the Thomistic tradition, there are various "levels" of being. Humans have it to a certain degree, dogs to a less extent, rocks still less. At the other end of the spectrum is The Being, who is the highest realization of what it means to exist. Any statement about "being," then, is made primarily about The Being, God, and only in an applied manner to those who exist in a lower way. Second, being transcends all categories: anything which exists in any category can be called a being. This is not as obvious as it may seem. A speck of dust is a being, God is a Being. Some philosophers might say to the contrary that there is nothing in common between them. Maritain, following medieval thinkers, says that they have the act of existing in common, exercised in very different, analogous manners.

Third, there are various *aspects* of being that transcend categories just as it does. Scholastics hold, for instance, that *unity* is "being" when it is considered as undivided. *Truth* is being when it confronts the power of knowledge. *Goodness* is being as confronting the power of desire. Of course each of these words can be used in other, less exalted ways, but if they are used in the present way they are called *transcendentals*, since they refer to something that transcends all categories.

> The essential characteristic of transcendentals is the fact that they cannot be enclosed in any class; they transcend or go beyond any genus or category, because they permeate or imbue everything, and are present in any thing whatsoever. Thus, just as everything *is* in its own way, and is *good* in its own way, so everything is beautiful in its own way (CI 163).

Beauty is one of the ways of considering transcendental being. Beauty is being when it is "considered as delighting, by the mere intuition of it, an intellectual nature" (AS 30). Everything is good in its own way, and therefore everything is beautiful too.

At this point the question arises as to why a work of art should be any better than a dandelion or a sunset. Indeed, sometimes it is not better! But in a fine work of art, a simple answer would be that it exists at a higher level of being. This is not the complete answer, but let us pursue it for a moment. Maritain is careful to say that a work of art is *engendered in* beauty, rather than that the artist *creates* beauty. Like being, beauty just is. If it were created by a human being, it would be within a category, like a "product," and it would no longer transcend categories. Therefore it would not be beauty. [61]

The work therefore is engendered in beauty, ripe for the beholder. "Intentional" beauty has been added to the admirable piece of marble, and now the marble is *still more beautiful than it was, and than the sunset.*[62] The work possesses on the intentional level that rich beauty conceived at the center of the human artist's creative soul. The observer is able to come to this beauty because of his or her own poetic intuition, which recognizes it immediately, even as a mother has special knowledge of a baby, no matter whose it is.[63]

We have come a long way with Maritain. In this last section, after a brief look at the nature of the beholder of a work of art, we have studied his theory of sign. Maritain's "answer" to critics is precisely that there is another kind of sign besides the semanticist's. In a world where the principle of identity reigns, a sign has to be either the object of attention itself and therefore can refer to nothing, or else refer away from itself to something else, in which case it is irrelevant except as a pointer. But in the conscious realm, a sign can be both itself and at the same time contain within itself the reality of the other. Both/and. Its own meaning does not have to be evacuated in order to give room for the referent. Concept and image are signs of this type.

The work of art is an important variation on this kind of sign, we said. By means of the projection of the artist, the work partakes in intentionality, even though it remains a thing that can be known in itself. Insofar as it is known it is called an instrumental sign. Yet, instead of pointing away from itself, the art-sign asks that attention stay with the work itself, with the layer of intentional meaning that the artist has formed into it. This layer is *virtually* present, since it requires, like the tree falling in the forest, a beholder who will bring the intentional powers of knowing to it and make it actively present.

Finally, we saw that *beauty*, an important notion for Maritain, takes place through intentionality. Since beauty is an aspect of being, which evades all categories, beauty belongs to the art work insofar as it has being. It seemed reasonable to Maritain to say that since the intentional form resulted from a profound, subconscious, multi-faceted union of the artist with being, the "amount" of being in an art work (to speak figuratively) would be greater because of it. The art piece would be an imperfect reaching out toward perfect being, which alone would fulfill the complete meaning of the word beauty. Thus the artist must be said to "engender in beauty" rather than to create beauty.

In Maritain we have a Thomist-based theory of the artist and his or her motherly union with the world. As we have just seen, Maritain also gives a description of certain aspects of the work of art. It is time now to turn to an entirely different basis for a theory of art, one that will furnish a much more detailed view of both the art work and the genres of art. If we have examined the mother of the work of art, we now will be able to discern more about what we call the father of the work. What is it in the world of daily experience that brings forth music, painting, dance, poetry, story, and architecture? We turn to the writings of Susanne Langer.

NOTES

1. Cummings 1963, 99.

2. Hopkins references from Hopkins 1988: #13 "The Windhover," p 30; #30 "Felix Randal," p 47; #41 "Carrion Comfort," p 60. See Foley 1989, 87–88 for application of this theory to ordained priesthood.

3. Of course, the words Hopkins employs, "thought" and "mind," raise a question for this chapter and the next, whether it is the *emotion* which receives artistic knowledge, or the mind. Without attempting an exegesis of Hopkins, it is possible here to remark merely that Hopkins was not referring to the work of the mind *as opposed to* that of the whole spirit, including emotion.

4. Maritain says much the same thing. "In one sense it ['spiritualized emotion'] . . . a privilege of those souls in which the margin of dreaming activity and introverted natural spirituality, unemployed for the business of human life, is particularly large. In another sense, because it emanates from a most natural capacity of the human mind, we must say that every human being is potentially capable of it: among those who do not know it, many, in point of fact, have repressed it or murdered it within themselves" (CI 123).

5. "Calvocoressi reports that Musorgsky 'created laboriously, clumsily, imperfectly. It was truly owing to the power of his genius that he produced immortal pages: he always did this, when his inspiration was sufficiently powerful to record itself in its own way. . . .'" M.D. Calvocoressi, *Musorgsky, the Russian Musical Nationalist,* quoted by Langer (FF 408).

6. One commentator says "Maritain is uniquely qualified to explore and assess the revolution which we call modern poetry. He lived the life of art in the time and place, Paris in the twenties, when an unparalleled galaxy of poets, painters and musicians was exploiting the 'new

self-awareness of poetry' in countless ways. Maritain knew intimately not only the art but many of the artists themselves, and what he says of poetry comes out of that rich and diverse life which he shared" (Fergusson 1963, 129).

7. In both I find direct access to the movements I myself have experienced as a creative artist.

8. At least two authors have taken pains to deny that Maritain's aesthetics is contained in Thomas Aquinas. Umberto Eco's *The Aesthetics of Thomas Aquinas* (1988) traces Aquinas' position through its historical forebears and tries to show that certain underpinnings of Maritain's theory have no origin there. Unfortunately he understands Maritain to implicitly deny sensible intuition (i.e., the direct knowledge through the senses of things in ·the world) (Eco 63). This is explicitly false, since Maritain holds for not only sensible intuition but, surprisingly, for direct intellectual intuition of being as well. And Thomas Rover's purpose in *Imitation and Transcendence in the Poetics of Maritain* (1965) is to develop an aesthetics of Thomas and of Maritain in order to deflate what he calls a widespread opinion that Maritain is simply elaborating Thomas on the subject of aesthetics. But he also seems to mistake Maritain. He takes him to say that the form of an art work is simply a *material* form (or in Maritain's language, a form taken at the level of natural existence rather than conscious or intentional existence). This too is explicitly a mis-reading of Maritain, as we shall find. See Hanke 1973, 49-50, for a critique of Rover in this regard.

Maritain's position seems to me mainly inductive, rather than deductive. That is, he observes artists at great length and tries to account for what he finds, rather than starts from a philosophical position in order to conclude that there must be poetic intuition. His theory of knowing helps him to observe, rather than control. It is fair to say that Maritain has stretched the philosophical framework he inherited and interpreted, in order to provide an adequate scaffolding for what he discovers inductively in artistic knowing and creating. For this reason I speak in this book of "Maritain's" theories and refer them back to "the ancients," the "schoolmen," Thomas Aquinas, or John of St. Thomas only when he specifically does so.

9. All references to *Creative Intuition* (CI) are to the original, hardback edition. Page numbers are different in later editions.

10. Maritain's writings in English and the translations of his writing from French were made at a time when "man" and "he" were commonly used to indicate human beings without regard to gender. But today such usage can create an unnecessary bias toward the masculine *instead of* feminine, implying that artistic activity and masculinity are co-extensive. Maritain's deep regard for Raïssa Maritain's poetry and for her insight regarding it establish beyond question that he believed

no such thing. Therefore I have taken the liberty to insert inclusive language in brackets when I quote him in this chapter, because I think it is what he would have said if he had written in the 1990s.

11. "Poetry in this sense is clearly not the privilege of poets. It forces every lock, lies in wait for you where you least expect it. You can receive the little shock by which it makes its presence known, which makes the distance still recede and unrolls the horizon of the heart, as much when looking at any common thing, a pasteboard model, 'silly pictures, door mantels, stage decorations, back-cloths in the booths of a fair, sign-boards,' as when contemplating a masterpiece" (AP 11). Appendix One of the present book regards the ramifications for other art forms of Maritain's designation of "poetry" as creative knowledge.

12. It should be noted here that Maritain's frequent designation of "creative intuition" by the name "poetic" intuition, knowledge, or experience automatically prejudices the state of all the arts, since an art is free and true to itself insofar as it is controlled by "poetic knowledge." "Creative intuition is the only supreme gift that a poet, in any art whatsoever, ought to seek," he says (CI 405). Maritain treats painting and its history with vast erudition (CI 9–34, 71–90, 209–222, 333), and music less often (e.g., CI 402-405); but his major interest is not to differentiate them and the other arts from each other, but to trace how expressive they are of this kind of knowledge, which is "poetic."

13. Maritain makes explicit such a contrast in chapter seven of *Creative Intuition,* defining "poetic experience" as "a certain state of the soul in which self-communion makes the ordinary traffic of our thinking stop for a while, and which is linked with particularly intense poetic intuition" (CI 238-239).

The word "intuition," for Maritain, also has another constellation of meaning, a specific philosophical one, that of immediate perception. Thus "sense intuition" refers to the direct experience of the thing in its sense qualities. There is a second type of intuition in this sense, direct knowledge of the self, which can be known reflexively only in its operations. Maritain also holds for a third type, intellectual intuition of reality outside the self. He argues for this against philosophers of the Thomistic persuasion who might see the intellect only as abstracting away from the sense phantasm, which phantasm alone would be the result of intuition. See BP 149–162.

14. "[The Artist's] intuition, the creative intuition or emotion, is an obscure grasping of himself [or herself] and things together in a knowledge by union of connaturality, which only takes shape, bears fruit and finds expression in the work, and which, in all its vital weight, seeks to create and produce. This is a very different knowledge from what is generally called knowledge; a knowledge which cannot be expressed in notions and judgments, but which is experience rather than knowl-

edge, and creative experience, because it wants to be expressed, and it can only be expressed in a work. This knowledge is not previous or presupposed to creative activity, but integrated in it, consubstantial with the movement toward the work, and this is precisely what I call poetic knowledge" (RR 18).

15. "I have suggested calling it, also, musical unconscious, for, being one with the root activity of reason, it contains from the start a germ of melody" (CI 99).

16. Jonathan Lear notes that Freud had the same notion, that everyday intelligence (secondary-process thinking) develops out of (Maritain's) unconscious (primary-process activity): "Secondary-process thinking, Freud thought, developed out of the archaic, primary-process mental functioning. Primary-process mental activity tends to be expressed in concrete images, rather than in concepts, and it tends to proceed by loose associations" (Lear 1990, 76).

17. How can such a thesis be proved? As one commentator remarks with wisdom (in the midst of an otherwise tendentious review of AS): "M. Maritain betrays a tendency to explain his meaning rather than to prove it, to show that the truth *could* be so rather than that it could not be otherwise" (Little 1930, 471). Of course, "it could not be otherwise" if the rest of Maritain's extensive theory is to survive. But in a more profound sense, aesthetical theories must of necessity be merely suggested and not proved, since the unconscious cannot be traced very far on a conceptual level. For evidence both Maritain and Langer rely on their own extensive acquaintance with works of art, and Maritain acknowledges at the beginning of CI that "a philosopher would not dare to speak of poetry if he could not rely on the direct experience of a poet," in this case his own wife, Raïssa Maritain (CI xxx).

18. In RR (23), and CI (117). Thomas does use the word connaturality in *Summa Theologica*, II-II, 45, 2: "Rectitudo autem judicii potest contingere dupliciter: uno modo secundum perfectum usum rationis; alio modo propter connaturalitatem quamdam id ea de quibus jam est judicandum: sicut de his quae ad castitatem pertinent, per rationis inquisitionem recte judicat ille qui didicit scientiam moralem; sed per quamdam connaturalitatem ad ipsam recte judicat de eis ille qui habet habitum castitatis" (Aquinas 1846, Vol 3, 422).

19. In *The Situation of Poetry* (65–67), *Ransoming the Time* (255–266), in *The Range of Reason* (16–17, 22–29), the text of which is reprinted in *Creative Intuition* (117–118), and in *Existence and the Existent* (78).

20. See especially RT 264-289 for this, which is a fourth category of connatural knowledge. See also EE 76, and Chapter Three of *Quatre essais sur l'Esprit dans se condition charnelle*. For mystical contemplation esp. as in St. John of the Cross, see DK 338–351. There is a fifth example of *intellectual* connatural knowledge given in RT, by which "the intelli-

gence of the mathematician or of the metaphysician . . . is thus connaturalized with the things of mathematics or metaphysics." Maritain thinks that the metaphysician can even arrive at a *natural* contemplation of divine things, even though this is not a mystical experience (RT 257-262).

21. This mystical knowledge can take place because of the connaturality "that the love of charity, which is a participation in God's very love, produces between" human beings and God (RR 24). "In mystical experience this love grows into an *objective means* of knowing, *transit in conditionem objecti* [it goes out into the condition of the object], and replaces the concept as intentional instrument obscurely uniting the intellect with the thing known, in such a way that [the person] not only experiences [God's] love, but, through [God's] love that precisely which is still hidden in faith, the *still more* to be loved, which is the hidden substance of faith" (RR 24).

This is "knowledge," through love, of God who paradoxically remains unknown; it is a contemplation of the non-conceptualizable (SP 66). Love is like emotion, which as a means of knowing will interest us very much in the next section. Here, the meaning of "connatural" emerges a bit further: it is a "coming to one," a participation in God's very love, and a "oneing," to adopt the language of our hypothesis.

22. I have retranslated this passage because otherwise there would be too many bracketed intrusions such as "[and her]." Here is the passage in the original:

". . . c'est en recevant et souffrant les choses, c'est en s'éveillant au monde qu'elle s'éveille à elle-même. Le poète ne peut exprimer sa propre substance dans une œuvre qu'à condition que les choses résonnent en lui, et qu'en lui, d'un même éveil, elles et lui sortent ensemble du sommeil. Tout ce qu'il discerne et devine dans les choses, c'est ainsi comme inséparable de lui et de son émotion, et à vrai dire comme lui-même, qu'il le discerne et le devine, et pour saisir obscurément son être à lui, d'une connaissance qui n'aboutira qu'en étant créatrice" (Maritain 1946, 37).

23. "Permit us, *brevitatis studio*, to set forth at this juncture a very concise résumé in seven points of the Thomistic doctrine on the nature of knowledge. The advantage of condensations of this kind is to force one to a synthesis in which only what is essential is stated" (DK 112). See also DK 96–99 for existential judgment, EE 20-28 for a summary of simple apprehension and judgment, and DK especially chapter three, part three, and his appendix one for a much more extensive treatment.

By referring to the epistemology herein as "Maritain's," I have no intention of implying that it is his *exclusive* of Aristotle or Thomas or John of St. Thomas, or Gilson, etc.; merely that it is *at least* Maritain's, regardless of where he or others got it and how much he added to or subtracted from it.

24. Throughout this account I will use the term "consciousness" to refer to "the order of intentional existence" in human knowledge. I utilize it instead of the multiple technical terms found in Maritain and his predecessors, in order to gain clarity and simplicity. I do not mean to imply that it is a technical term for Maritain.

25. Cf. EE 75–79 for one of Maritain's vivid accounts of self knowledge. See also Lear 1990, 4: "For, as Freud realized, the deeper meanings which shape a person's soul and structure his outlook are not immediately available to his awareness. A person is, by his nature, out of touch with his own subjectivity. Thus one cannot find out what it is like for a person to be just by asking. Even if he is sincere, he won't know the answer." Lear believes that the only way such subjectivity to emerge is through psychoanalytic therapy.

26. Cf. PM 91–96, among other places, for the principle of identity.

27. Maritain calls this realm "the intentional order," from *tendere,* to go toward. This word does not carry the meaning "done on purpose or design," but rather "having external reference"; consciousness "tends" toward the other, toward the relationship of knower and known.

28. Once the thing has entered consciousness under the power of the senses, the entire act of knowing takes place within the knowing subject. For this reason, in Maritain's received doctrine, knowledge is an *immanent* activity (*in* + *manere:* to remain in). It is not what is called technically a transient activity (*trans* + *ire:* to go across), in which one being affects another. This position would seem at first glance to end all possibility for significant union with anything outside the knower. We will see why it does not.

29. For an exceptionally detailed treatment of the temporal complexities of what I am calling "ordinary know-ledge"—simple apprehension—see EE 32–40, especially n 13.

30. "For the philosophers, the notion of *species* is not, any more than the notion of *esse intentionale,* an explanatory factor already known and already clarified by some other means. Species are, as it were, the abutments upon which an analysis of the given leans for support, the reality of which the mind, by that very analysis, is compelled to recognize—with certainty, if the analysis itself has proceeded correctly and under the constant pressure of intelligible necessities" (DK 116).

31. "In God himself we must—according to our mode of conceiving—distinguish between knowledge "of simple intelligence" and the creative knowledge or the knowledge "of vision." In [human beings] this is a real distinction which, beginning at the very root, separates poetic knowledge from speculative knowledge" (SP 80).

32. *Summa Theologica,* I, 77, 6. "Unde manifestum est, quod omnes potentiae animae, sive subjectum earum sit anima sola, sive compositum, fluunt ab essentia animae, sicut a principio: quia iam

dictum est in isto art. quod accidens causatur a subjecto, secundum quod est actu; et recipitur in eo, inquantum est in potentia" (Aquinas 1846, Vol 1, 422).

It is not possible in these pages to delineate what Maritain means by "soul." It is enough for us to say that it is the center of activity or act, which seeks and coordinates the seeking, which is the great receiving part of a person, the ability to achieve union with another. It becomes active in order, through its powers, to affect the union. It can, through this activity, enable otherwise inert things also to enter into the union called knowledge. In the next chapter we will be interested in Langer's descriptions of organic activity, organized for a particular function, all functions working together toward their goal. We might say that Maritain has transferred this notion to the purposive reality of a human being, which purpose is to become one with the other.

33. *ST* I, 77, 4. ". . . potentiae intellectivae sunt priores potentiis sensitivis: unde dirigunt eas, et imperant eis; et similiter potentiae sensitivae hoc ordine sunt priores potentiis animae nutritivae" (Aquinas 1846, Vol 1, 420).

34. This diagram is an adaptation of Maritain's drawing from CI 108. The preceding ones are also extracted from it.

35. Consisting of "all the universe of fluid images, recollections, associations, feelings, and desires latent, under pressure, in the subjectivity, and now stirred" (CI 122).

36. T. S. Eliot: "It is not his [or her] personal emotions, the emotions provoked by particular events in his [or her] life, that for the poet is in any way remarkable or interesting. His [or her] particular emotions may be simple, or crude, or flat. The emotion in his [or her] poetry will be a very complex thing, but not with the complexity of the emotions of people who have very complex or unusual emotions in life. . . . The business of the poet is not to find new emotions, but to use the ordinary ones and, in working them up into poetry, to express feelings which are not in actual fact emotions at all" (CI 120, n 16; from Eliot 1920).

37. Maritain says that artistic knowing resembles the freedom of the child at play (CI 111), presumably because children have not yet learned to distinguish feeling out from knowing and especially purposive knowing. There is a deep adult state in which emotion still carries out a primitive (or exalted) function of being a vehicle of knowledge, knowledge as a union with the world. Langer will say that the artist must see and feel as a child (MIND I 178)—because, unlike the ordinary adult mode, thought comes from emotion for a child, rather than vice versa.

38. For Freud, according to Jonathan Lear, emotions "are, by their nature, attempts at rational orientation toward the world. Even an

archaic expression of emotion is an archaic attempt at rationality. It is the germ from which a rational orientation may grow" (Lear 1990, 51. See also p. 131).

39. "It is then, at the very moment that it falls into the living waters, that the emotion becomes intentional and intuitive, and passes to the condition of a grasp of the real: not that it serves to objectify some term which specifies a knowledge, but because it is itself taken into the indeterminate vitality and productivity of the spirit, to which it brings a determination by mode of term" (SP 82).

40. There is more to be known in individual things even than their emotionally significant aspects. Maritain's almost mystical interest in the *being* of things and of the artist causes him to say that the act of poetic knowing extends outward *toward the infinite*. Its lack of a conceptualized object allows it to know a reality about the singular being that far exceeds that being. Maritain holds that traces of infinite reality are found in every existing thing: "secret properties of being involved in its identity." Through these properties it has existential relations with other things in the world, not necessarily just through physical causality, but through a mysterious communication in being, that which makes all things real. The union of this existing thing with the subjectivity of the artist is fully existential, and therefore all these reverberations are conveyed into the soul of the artist. "Poetic intuition does not stop at this given existent; it goes beyond, and infinitely beyond. Precisely because it has no conceptualized object, it tends and extends to the infinite, it tends toward all the reality, the infinite reality which is engaged in any singular existing thing, either the secret properties of being involved in its identity and in its existential relations with other things, or the other realities, all the other aspects of fructifications of being, scattered in the entire world, which have in themselves the wherewithal to ground some ideal relation with this singular existing thing, and which it conveys to the mind, by the very fact that it is grasped through its union with, and resonance in, subjectivity spiritually awakened" (CI 126).

This knowledge can be traced both to the side of the knower and to the known. The artistic soul is *able* to allow all these relationships in, and the existent *has* the relationships. In *The Situation of Poetry* Maritain says of beings that "they communicate in existence, under an infinity of modes and by an infinity of actions and contacts, of correspondences, of sympathies and malices, of breakings and reformings, and—insofar as they possess immateriality—of forms of interiorization of being and forms of giving" (SP 79).

In *Creative Intuition,* fifteen years later, he repeats the same paragraph from which the above text is taken, but he drops the phrase "insofar as they possess immateriality" and adds "because they are permeated by the activating influx of the Prime Cause" (CI 127). There is for Maritain a communion of things with each other as well as with the artist in certain "passages of the spirit" (SP 80), tracing all the way back to the first cause, the one who is unlimited being. This knowledge of the singular existent, resounding in the subjectivity of the artist "together with all the other realities which echo in this existent," is the fullness of that which is grasped in the world by creative knowledge (CI 126).

If the reader finds this answer somewhat vague and cloaked in mystery, so does the present writer. Maritain's poetic description of it perhaps can be grasped only by poetic intuition itself. We will find a less poetic clarity in Langer's answer to the question "what does creative knowledge know in each of the arts?"—this will be the "fathering" agent in our metaphor.

41. In a sensory deprivation chamber anyone could bathe in the currents of memory without any new contact with the world. In a way memories would become quasi objects and fill consciousness. But this would be an exception that proves the rule.

42. "For an unconscious thought is not a fully conceptualized judgment, needing to be pulled through the looking glass by its conscious image. At least one of the reasons an unconscious thought is unconscious is that conscious mind does not easily recognize this form of mental activity" (Lear 1990, 8).

43. Though explicit knowledge can be "put to work" subsequently, repatterned to serve the ends of making. A carpenter "uses" his or her objective knowledge (and daily intuitions) to create a cabinet. Such work also involves what Maritain calls a "habitus" (Cf. AS, Chapter Three).

44. "From the very start poetic intuition is turned toward operation. As soon as it exists, the instant it awakens the substance of the poet to itself and to an echoing secret of the reality, it is, in the depth of the nonconceptual life of the intellect, an incitation to create" (CI 134).

45. An early critic (Little 1930) attempted to urge the opposite against Maritain, i.e., that the work of art is first, essentially, and perhaps only a communication of concepts to others. A passage from CI gives Maritain's answer: "It is enough that the work exists, that this kind of a world is created. The fact that it makes the poet communicate with other human beings, even the fact that it is seen, or listened to, is in itself an effect of superabundance, terribly important for the poet, for [the poet] is a man [or woman], but additional with respect to the prime essential requirement of poetry" (CI 307).

46. "The artist has to love, he has to love *what he is making*, so that his virtue may truly be, in Saint Augustine's words, *ordo amoris,* so that beauty may become connatural to him and inviscerate itself in him through affection, and so that his work may come forth from his heart and his bowels as well as from his lucid spirit" (AS 47). (In this

sentence we have to merely assume Maritain's meaning as "he *or she*" in today's language, since so many bracketed incursions would make reading arduous.)

47. Maritain distinguishes two phases in true inspiration: one systolic, the other diastolic. Systolic (from Gk. *systellein,* to contract) refers in ordinary usage to that contraction of the heart by which blood is forced onward to keep up circulation. Maritain borrows this word to describe the expelling of previous contents to quiet the preconscious powers. "In the first phase, then, in the phase of systole and unifying repose, all the forces of the soul, gathered together in quietude, were in a state of virtuality and dormant energy. And poetic intuition, still preconscious, was the only act formed within the preconscious life of the intellect, and was the secret reason for this silent concentration" (CI 242). The distractions of the world and of ordinary perception lose their grip. The soul takes on "a dreamlike condition, as it were, but integrated, with intelligence neither bound nor disconnected." It is a state of inner balance.

Diastolic action follows. Diastolic operation of the heart (from the Greek *diastole,* to expand) actually is the enlargement of the heart in order to fill with blood. Maritain is describing the moment when creative intuition enlarges beyond itself and presses outward to expression. "It is not surprising that at a given moment . . . poetic intuition, acting no longer in the manner of an hypnotic but rather of a catalytic agent, should make the virtual energies concentrated around it pass also to the act. Then, from the single actuation of all the forces of the soul withdrawn into their root vitality, a single transient motion will result, which manifests itself either negatively, by a breaking of barriers, or positively, by the entrance of poetic intuition into the field of consciousness" (CI 242–243). It is like a wind arising from the center of the soul, sometimes a strong wind, after "a silent gathering."

These descriptions of "inspiration" might seem to cancel our suggestion that gestation is necessary at all. It speaks of "sometimes a gale bursting all of a sudden, through which everything is given in violence and rapture; sometimes the gift of the beginning of a song; sometimes an outburst of unstoppable words" (CI 243). This sounds like an immediate passage from conception to birth. But Maritain is here aiming at a description of the report of artists that certain privileged times afford an eruption instead of a brooding. This is an experience, not an analysis. In fact later on he explicitly *denies* that poetic knowledge flows directly into the poem without intermediate process.

Also, Maritain admits that simultaneity of stages is possible. He says that the first stage, the coming to life of poetic intuition "is transient and tendential, it tends to verbal expression, and as a matter of fact *it may now and then take place at the same time as the outpouring of words and their 'arrangement on the paper'* (or the arrangement of colored spots on the canvas, or the arrangement of sounds on the score), which is the second and final stage. Yet my contention is that these two stages in poetic expression are distinct in nature, and that the transient expression through those *natural* signs which are the imaginal and emotional pulsions comes first, and precedes in nature the expression through those *social* signs which are the words of the language" (CI 304, lengthy italics mine). He notes that bad Romanticism "made of 'inspiration' an excuse for facility, or simple release of brute emotions and passions, or uncontrolled flux of shallow words and sentimentalism" (ibid.), and such an event is not what he is referring to. In this section Maritain is attempting simply to provide a basic description of authentic inspiration, taken from the reported accounts by poets (Raïssa Maritain, Carlyle, Hölderlin, T. S. Eliot).

48. Maritain says that there are three possible states or existential conditions in which images can exist. First is in the "externals of the imagination," where the senses explicitly become the object in its sensible qualities. Second, they can be in the "automatic or deaf unconscious" as a part of "instincts, repressed memories and tendencies, dreams, and libido [which] lead a life of their own." And third, they can be, as in the present case, within the preconscious under the illumination of the Illuminating Intellect. These are "virtual" because they are not (yet) part of explicit consciousness but still exist (CI 325–326).

49. Later in the book Maritain makes an attempt to indicate by division marks and brackets where and in what groupings the pulsions are finally *expressed* in the last stage of the process, the art product. Such an analysis belongs to birth, not gestation's first stage, but it might help us grasp the meaning of "pulsion." Here is Maritain's proviso regarding the lines: "I have put division marks in these lines, not to stress the scansion, but to indicate the dynamic charges or intuitive pulsions with which they are laden, and to beg the reader . . . to listen *within him- [or her-] self*, each time, to the awakening of these soundless, purely mental units of image and emotion" (CI 316-317). Here are the lines:

Speech after long silence; //
　　　　　　it is right,
All other lovers being estranged or dead,/
　　Unfriendly lamplight hid under its shade,/
　　The curtains drawn upon unfriendly night/
That we descant and yet again descant
　　Upon the supreme theme of Art and Song;//

Bodily decrepitude is wisdom://
　　　　　　young
We loved each other and were ignorant.//

50. At this point Maritain enters something of a methodological disclaimer. "I am confronted with a special difficulty, because I am dealing with something which I must look for *behind* the words, *as if* I were in the presence of the emotional movements within the imagination of the poet, *before* the production of words: well, no philosophical analysis is possible in this domain without such an effort as introspective reconstruction" (CI 304).

51. *Habitus* is a word (both singular and plural) Maritain spent time on in *Art and Scholasticism* (AS 10–14). It has no English equivalent, he says, and especially is not the same as a "habit" ("mere mechanical bent and routine"). The ancients, he says, knew *habitus* as "qualities which are essentially stable dispositions perfecting in the line of its own nature the subject in which they exist" (AS 10). Health and beauty are *habitus* of the body. Art is a *habitus* of the practical intellect. A *Habitus* of art directs what happens, in correspondence with what "ought" to take place in the thing to be made. It "is a *virtue*, that is to say, a quality which, triumphing over the original indetermination of the intellectual faculty, at once sharpening and tempering the point of its activity, draws it, with reference to a definite object, *to a certain maximum of perfection and thus of operative efficiency*" (AS 12).

Thus *habitus* are enrichments of the faculties. They render the difficult task easy and enjoyable. They are able to be acquired, but only by someone who is fully alive—"that is to say, intellectual beings, who alone are perfectly alive" (ibid.). "The craftsman's creative idea which is part of the virtue of art, improves from the very fact that this virtue itself improves, both by exercise and by discipline. The action of the *habitus* is not to be equated with manual skill. An artist with deficient skill can produce a bad work of art and still be fully endowed with *habitus*. Nor is it to be equated with 'opinion.'"

52. They are also present in the artist's storehouse of memory.

53. (CI 317). Here again the slash marks indicate externalized pulsions, not scansions. The Hopkins lines are from his "terrible sonnet" that begins "I wake and feel the fell of dark, not day. . . ." In the original edition of *Creative Intuition* a typist rendered the third line of Maritain's pulsion scansion as "Bitter would have *my* taste," instead of *me*. This error found its way into the Meridian paperback edition, and was compounded by replacing the word "was" by "*with*"! Thus,

"... God's most deep decree
Bitter would have *my* taste: my taste *with* me."

While this may seem to illustrate Maritain's point about the dethronement of logical expression, the correct words surely would do the same thing. Cf. *Creative Intuition*, Meridian Books edition (1955), p 217.

54. Stravinsky did not want his experiments to be heard. His mother said "he composes at a small upright piano that has been muted and

dampened with felt. Nevertheless, and though the room is sound-proofed and the door tightly closed, little noises as though from mice on the keyboard penetrate to the next room" (White 1979, 39–40). One of the greatest orchestrators in modern history, Stravinsky still produced a complete piano version of his orchestral works before beginning to orchestrate. After finishing, he then wrote a piano "reduction" (for practice purposes in vocal/orchestral works) from the fully orchestrated version, not from the original piano work.

55. More often than a converging of the processes is a long ripening period. The work of art has been "kneaded and prepared, formed, brooded over, ripened in a mind before passing into matter" (AS 9). Again, from CI: "Here all the patience and accuracy, all the virtues of craftsmanship are involved, and intelligence works and works again, takes up the task anew, uses all that it knows, displays the most active sagaciousness to be true to its own superior passivity, to the indivisible inspiring actuation received—poetic intuition and wordless meaning or melody—to which it does not cease listening. And this effort of supreme loyalty can be resumed even after years" (CI 305–306).

56. So at least one critic urged against Maritain also: ". . . if the work of art is a symbol in the semanticist's sense of 'symbol,' then the work of art must be thought of as transparent and thus trivial in relation to what it symbolizes. For the function of a symbol is to lead the mind beyond it to its object. But this runs contrary to a crucial characteristic of art: that it arrests attention so that the mind focuses on the object in aesthetic apprehension. The work of art, unlike the semanticist's symbol, is significant in its own right, for its own sake" (Hausman 1960, 219).

57. Maritain says that such signs "make present for knowledge something which is other than itself" (RT 218). He refers this definition to the "scholastics": "Signum est id quod repraesentat aliud a se potentiae cognoscenti" (RT 218).

58. Cf. also DK 119–128.

59. He also says that there is an intentional presence of the painting *in the paint brush.* The activity of the painter puts it there: ". . . c'est selon l'*être intentionnel* que les choses existent dans les signes ou similitudes qui les rendent présentes à la pensée: de même que dans l'ordre de la causalité efficiente, la vertu de l'agent principal passe intentionellement dans l'instrument en mouvement, à titre de tendance fluente *(intentio fluens)* qui a pour terme l'effet à produire, de même, dans l'ordre de la causalité formelle, telle que la comporte l'immaterialité du connaître, l'object de connaissance existe *intentionnellement* dans l'âme, à titre de tendance immobile *(intentio quiescens)* qui a pour terme ce même objet effectivement connu" (Maritain 1924, 61–62).

60. See RT 220. This theory seems to present an exact parallel to Langer's theory of "illusion" that we will see. She and Maritain even

use the same term for it, "virtual." The virtual organic life that has been molded into the art work, the illusion created, can be called, following Maritain, "a different order of existence": the intentional or conscious one. Distinguishing intentional from entitative might well remove the ambiguity Langer will find in the word "illusion." Considered as a part of the "entitative" order, there is no Mona Lisa present (just "materials" in Langer's meaning of the word). In that sense what is presented on the entitative order is an illusion. But considered within the intentional realm, there is a sign conveying the subjectivity of the artist in its oneness with some secret of the world's being. This sign signifies by being known in itself, not by referring away from itself. The reality being signified is within it. Maritain gives a formal name, reverse sign, to that which denotes the very subject who makes use of the sign: "secrets which he [or she] does not even admit to him- [or her-] self— the subject then taken as object by some observer." A direct sign indicates an object, a reverse sign makes the subject manifest. Cf. RT 253–254.

61. ". . . The work is a product; but its beauty is not a product that impregnates it as with a perfume or invests it as with a garb or an armor; the beauty of the work, which inherently results from its very production, is in its very being a particular mirroring of a transcendental or an infinite, and a *gift* from the spiritual source—poetry—in which the production of the work originates. Let us say, then, that art engenders in beauty, or produces in beauty, not that it produces beauty" (CI 173, n 22).

62. Maritain quotes the famous Thomistic dictum that beauty is "that which being seen pleases," because "it is essentially a certain excellence or perfection in the *proportion of things to the intellect*" (AS 24, italics mine). "Pulchrim autem respicit vim cognitivam, pulchra enim dicuntur quae visa placent. Unde pulchrum in debita proportione consistit, quia sensus delectatur in rebus debite proportionatis sicut in sibi similibus. . . ." ST 5.4. ad 1 (Aquinas 1846, Vol 1, 28). The observer does not seek some kind of pleasure as disconnected from the beholding of the work. But pleasure is there, from the proportion of the work to the beholder's own creative receptivity. There are three characteristics which describe this coherence of the work with the intellect. *Integrity* means that everything is there which should be; there is a fullness of being. *Proportion* means that there is order and unity, or an intelligent ordering: there is due order. Most importantly, *clarity* or *radiance* means that there is splendor as when the ontological secret of the thing, that by which it exists and acts, shines forth to the intelligence. All these are intrinsic to being, and thus more so to the work of the artist. The art work is a being that has had molded into itself an intentional sign. This sign makes the work a proper offspring of the

confluence of (1) being—with all its radiance—and (2) the immaterial soul of the artist. This is why it is more beautiful than a star.

63. "But beauty is a necessary correlative for poetry. It is like its native climate and the air it naturally breathes in, nay more, it is as life and existence are for a runner running toward the goal—an end beyond the end. For poetry there is no goal, no specifying end. But there is an *end beyond*. Beauty is the necessary *correlative* and *end beyond any end* of poetry" (CI 170).

CHAPTER THREE

ARTISTS AND THEIR OFFSPRING

Art does not always take well to systematic, discursive formulation of itself. It dwells in the un-conscious (or pre-conscious or sub-conscious or semi-conscious) where clarity need not apply. This is one reason why Susanne K. Langer's writing comes across to some as sprawling and unsystematic when in fact it is based on some highly systematic thinking. She is working a topic whose resistance is legendary.

Another important reason is a conviction that Langer states in the 1951 preface to *Philosophy in a New Key*.

> The process of philosophical thought moves typically from a first, inadequate, but ardent apprehension of some novel idea, figuratively expressed, to more and more precise comprehension, until language catches up to logical insight, the figure is dispensed with, and literal expression takes it place. Really new concepts, having no names in current language, always make their earliest appearance in metaphorical statements (PNK x–xi).

The "really new concept" in Langer's aesthetical writings has to do with music as a symbol: music symbolizes felt interior life, just as language symbolizes an idea. We will see what this insight is about in a moment. Here we can say that her writings on aesthetics exemplify how "language catches up to logical insight." As one critic put it, "we are forced to watch Mrs.

Langer's mind at work" (Margolis 1955, 292). Langer announces, unreels, applies her insight, now in this direction, now in that, always assuming that the reader shares at some depth the all-encompassing new idea.

Readers can be cut adrift by this procedure. Indeed, more than one critic has complained about her methods. Here are some samples: "*Philosophy in a New Key* gives the reader the impression that it is written in one breath" (Jeunhomme 1985, 159-160); Langer's writing is "difficult" (Carrit 1955, 75); her conclusions "tend to be a little curt," and there is an "oddly rebellious air" about *Feeling and Form* (Margolis 1955, 295, 296). But, if the reader will "break in with an old-fashioned pick-lock," a "pretty spacious structure might be found there" (Carrit, 75).

Because of the difficulty of her writing, I have tried to supply anchor points for the reader, in the form of three main topics. Section I mainly treats artistic experience or knowing. Here if anywhere in Langer we will find something of our analogy to physical conception. Section II goes on to the art work itself. Section III gives more detail about form and symbol—which necessarily includes a criticism of Langer's aesthetical theory and its underpinnings.[1] This way of dividing gains in clarity, though it may sacrifice "ardor." I think the basic reader can move on to Section B of the following without harm, though I warn that Section A contains the preconditions for her theory.

We will not "pinch and poke" Langer's theories to make them yield our own doctrine. We turn to her in order to get explicit about art and art works. Langer's brilliant theory will help us greatly when we come to liturgy.

I. Susanne Langer's Theory of Art

I will draw mainly from the aesthetical portion of Langer's writings, written chiefly in the middle period of her life, from the publication of *Philosophy in a New Key* in 1942 to *Philosophical Sketches* in 1962. Her thought before that, and afterwards until her death in 1985, will enter as needed.

A. What is to be Expressed

Art consists of "illusions achieved by abstracting semblances from the actual world, and then composing

these sheer appearances into new forms that mirror
the logic of feeling" (FF 228).[2]

This epigraph is a nearly complete description of Langer's theory of art. But we meet terms that need understanding: illusion, abstraction, semblance, actual world, sheer appearance, forms, the logic of feeling. We will befriend each word in due course, but I find that a simpler way to start is by marshaling still another technical sentence, one which, by Lonergan's claim, displays the complete essence of Langer. "Art is the objectification of a purely experiential pattern" (Lonergan 1959, 284 ff).[3]

1. Purely Experiential Patterns. For a moment we will let Lonergan speak for Langer, since he had a love for her writings. An "experiential pattern," he says, is a set of internal relations between a set of colors, tones, volumes, movements, etc. A simple example is the rhyming of verses, which makes them easier to remember (Lonergan 1959, 284). But in a deeper sense we are referring to any patterning of sense data. Such patterning is essential to consciousness.

To attend to an experiential pattern is liberating: the pattern's relationships within itself are spontaneous, and they comport with one's simple ability to know them. One does not have to do anything about the smell of the rose, just enjoy it. Langer notes that human beings instead often utilize their experience pragmatically. Rather than beholding the beauty of the room, they look for a place to sit down.

> If you come into a room in normal indoor daylight, you may see that it contains, say, a red-covered sofa, but you do not notice the gradations of red or even the appearance of other colors caused by the way the light strikes that sofa at the moment (PA 31).

Our vision becomes "highly specialized," seeing only what is needful for our purpose (PA 31). In a neat phrase, Lonergan calls this pragmatic overlay an "alien pattern" that "instrumentalizes experience."[4] Spontaneous organization is now reorganized from outside of itself. His examples are telling: to stop the car at a red light or to make it go at a green is to make one's experiential patterns into a mechanism to receive and transmit signals. Or they can become an instrument for doing science, or be harnessed by some theory about how human beings think, or be put to use by one's motives (e.g., "what I can get out of it"). All use is opposed to simply receiving the seen as seen, the heard as heard, the felt as felt (Lonergan 1959, 287–289).

Abraham Maslow, writing just nine years after *Feeling and Form*, but without reference to it, says something of the same thing:

> . . . To the extent that we can prevent ourselves from only abstracting, naming, placing, comparing, relating, to that extent will we be able to see more and more aspects of the many-sidedness of the person or of the painting (Maslow 1962, 85).[5]

Langer believes that art can help people break away from pragmatic perception, because it presents a "lure" away from the practical world. An art work "detaches itself from the rest of the world" so that the perceiver simply "sees it as it is presented to" him or her (FF 45). How does it do this?

Her main answer seems to be (in Lonergan's formulation) that the pattern of the art work is *"pure"*: the painting shows forth, without overlay, a patterning of color and lines. It no longer is required to be the actual looks of some here and now person. It doesn't have to present part of the real world to me. Now it can simply be a spontaneous pattern of colors and sounds, organized according to, e.g., the Mona Lisa countenance. It thus has freedom in three ways. (1) It has "otherness and self sufficiency" because it is estranged from "actuality." (2) It is rendered plastic, that is, able to undergo "deliberate torsion" and modification for the sake of expressiveness; and finally, (3) it is made transparent, which means it is able to express freely more than just the practical appearance of a daily object (CA 522–523, FF 59–60).[6]

This is the preparatory phase of Langer's main theory, and we can proceed to that theory after one additional observation about her use of the word "abstraction." Of itself, this word means simply "to draw something away from something else *(ab + trahere)*." But its customary philosophical employment has been more restricted: it has usually meant "to consider a *general* aspect apart from application to a *particular* instance." For example, I could juggle three oranges, and I would enjoy it. But I could also consider just their number, three, apart from their shaped, juicy, orange colored, throwable reality. "Three" does not care what it numbers: in this sense it is general, and this is the rudimentary sense of philosophy's usual kind of abstraction.[7]

On the contrary, in Langer's use of the word abstraction, the "particular instance" remains. A patterning of colors and lines *can only be* considered with both pattern and patterned intact. The lines and colors cannot be left behind while the pattern is considered; the pattern disappears when they do. It is unlike number, which does not mind being removed from that which it numbers. Then why speak of abstraction? Because, as we have seen, the combination of pattern + sense data (= the pure experiential pattern) *can* be considered, not as split apart inside itself, but as abstracted from that which it would usually represent— real people whose names are George Washington or Mona Lisa. To say it another way, in a painting, the experiential pattern

> presents itself *purely to our vision,* i.e., as a sheer visual form instead of a locally and practically related object. If we receive it as a completely visual thing, we abstract its appearance from its material existence. What we see in this way becomes *simply a thing of vision*—a form, an image. It detaches itself from its actual setting and acquires a different context (FF 47, italics mine).[8]

We can discern here the type of abstraction we have been treating, and another kind as well: not only consideration of the patterned experience apart from its reference to real things, but also *consideration of one plane or type of experience apart from other planes or types.* In this case it is the visual aspects. In each of the various arts one particular kind of patterning becomes central: the relation of colors to each other, in a painting, for example; or the patterning of sounds in their gradations and presence-from-afar (e.g., from orchestral instruments on stage), etc. There is a "selective character" about each art form and about artistic talent, which is the ability to work with a certain—abstracted— type of sense data (cf. PI 219).[9]

2. Feeling. To this point we have been speaking as if the experiential pattern were only an arrangement or forming of sheer sense data. But much more is involved, according to Langer's vision. In a little remarked passage she says that the artist brings a specialized viewpoint, a different ability to perceive. It is not just the high affinity for color or sound that we have noted in a specialized artist: the artist retains as well a proclivity to perceive in a way that is vital, sensory, emotive; to take in the world as a child does. The artist involuntarily perceives (and projects) feeling—vital, sensory and emotive—as the most obvious quality of a perceived gestalt. To take up this sort of emotive import is a natural propensity of percepts in childhood experience. It tends, also, to persist in some people's mature mentality; and there it becomes the source of artistic vision, the quality to be abstracted by the creation of forms so articulated as to emphasize their import and suppress any practical appeal they would normally make. This is the just ground for the frequent assertion that an artist must see and feel as a child; and it is, I think the only ground for that widely misused statement. For he must not "feel as a child," and project childish feeling, but only translate feeling into perceivable quality . . . (MIND I, 178).

This is a knowledge that derives from feeling, not vice versa. Or perhaps knowledge laced with feeling; knowledge that is sharper because of it, rather than duller. It is possible for anyone, but artists have been flooded with it willy nilly. We will see more about this as the discussion continues.

Tagore, in one of his poems, reminisces about childhood in a way that may illustrate the felt cognitions we are dealing with:

I REMEMBER my childhood when the sunrise, like my playfellow, would burst in to my bedside with its daily surprise of morning; when the faith in the marvelous bloomed like fresh flowers in my heart every day, looking into the face of the world in simple gladness; when insects, birds and beasts, the common weeds, grass and the clouds had their fullest value of wonder; when the patter of rain at night brought dreams from the fairyland, and mother's voice in the evening gave meaning to the stars.

And then I think of death, and the rise of the curtain and the new morning and my life awakened in its fresh surprise of love.

(Tagore 1939, 1972, 281)

Here we find a felt awareness of the world, a feeling that comes first and only secondarily gives rise to knowledge.

So we add the mark of *feeling* to our description of experiential patterns. In general we can say that feeling has two roles in Langer's philosophy of art: first, what we have just seen, feeling as part of the content of an experiential pattern as it is received; second, as the artist's inner life of feeling that is portrayed in or projected into the work of art. To this inner life we must now turn.

For Langer, feeling is not synonymous with emotion, especially emotion considered (sentimentally) as an entity unto itself. It is important not to confuse these two. Instead of emotion, Langer's word "feeling" refers to the entire range of all subjective experiences, all of which are known or "felt" according to an inner awareness. Felt awareness is

> the way feelings, emotions, and all other subjective experiences come and go—their rise and growth, their intricate synthesis that gives our inner life unity and personal identity. What we call a person's "inner life" is the inside story of his [or her] own history; the way living in the world feels.... This kind of experience is usually but vaguely known (PA 7).

In this sense, feeling is the subject's awareness of inner life, "what we sometimes call the *subjective aspect* of experience, the direct feeling of it" (PA 22).[10] Knowing one's inner life means knowing

> what it is like to be waking and moving, to be drowsy, slowing down, or to be sociable, or to feel self-sufficient but alone; what it feels like to pursue an elusive thought or to have a big idea (PA 22).[11]

Even philosophical and historical thought—the contents of non-fiction in general—can be felt. There is a

> feeling that naturally inheres in studious thinking, the growing intensity of a problem as it becomes more and more complex, and at the same time more definite and "thinkable," until the demand for the answer is urgent, touched with impatience; the holding back of assent as the explanation is prepared; the cadential feeling of solution, and the expansion of consciousness in new knowledge (FF 302).

When she says art expresses human feeling, far from meaning that art simply expresses emotion, Langer is saying that felt experience *of any movement whatsoever within us* is what art deals with. The feeling involved in studious thinking is one such movement. The felt range is broad, then.

How does the subjective, felt pattern get there? Langer's descriptions tend to shy away from interaction with the world, in order to concentrate on the felt life itself. Of course, to "be sociable" or "feel self-sufficient" in her list above could not take place without relation to the world and to others. The table at the end of Section B will show that the world is very much involved in such patterns. The artist must know—depending on the genre of the art—visible, colored shapes, or activities of a human culture, or human gestures with all they signify, or the qualities of felt events, in order to produce a work of art.

In fact, Langer does say that the subject is "influenced" from outside. She discusses this influence in *Feeling and Form* (370–371). When awake, sentient beings react to the world around them. They change their total condition constantly. Obviously they change the positions of their eyes or ears in order to see or hear better. But more, they change "hundreds of fibers in the body" in response. There is another "sequence of vital changes" underneath all this, the system of vital functions (involuntary muscles, heart, skin, glands, etc.). "Whether that system reflects the functions of outward awareness all the time, or only when the latter rise above some particular degree of disturbance, I do not know," says Langer. But certainly "major excitements" from the outside do throw the whole system into unusual activity. So can "ideation," or at least the continual process of it, since "intellectual and imaginative functions have a controlling share of influence on waking activity." We will have an opportunity to look back at these statements toward the end of this chapter. For now, this much is clear: whatever experiential pattern is involved, it will be so only insofar as it is *inwardly* felt.

To see how art, for Langer, is the means of conveying what feeling is about, it will help to examine two other interesting traits of feeling: its *organic* contour and its basis in *rhythm*.

Organic contour: in the functioning of any organism, it is clear that an entire range of operations through time prevails over a single incident. "It is the whole life of feeling—call it 'felt life,' 'subjectivity,' 'direct experience,' or what you will—which finds its articulate expression in art" (FF 366). No organism is constituted by one or two momentary states; its entire life over time is required.

With that proviso in mind, we can present a summary of organic life and its features:

- An organism is not a "thing" but a *process*.
- Organisms are *dynamic:* they exist only while they keep going.
- Their permanent structures present many distinct *activities* that coincide with each other "in a miracle of timing";

- there is an inevitable process of *growth and decay*, with either a balance between the two or else an increase or decrease in the system;
- they exhibit *inviolability* (i.e., if an organism is significantly violated it ceases to be) and *fragility*;
- finally, organic processes are *rhythmic* (PA 47–50).

The last quality needs explanation, which we will come to in a moment. First we will note that the form a particular organic life takes always reflects the *function* of the organism.

> Organisms, performing characteristic functions, *must* have certain general forms, or perish. For them there is a norm of organic structure according to which, inevitably, they build themselves up; . . . and their parts are built to carry on this process as it becomes more complex, so the parts have shapes necessary to their respective functions (FF 88–89).

When this functionality is in place, the performance of an organism can be described as "rhythmic."[12]

Rhythm has to do with tensions, which are the hallmark of inner life.[13] Rhythm is a relation between tensions. A new tension is set up by the very resolution of the old one, exactly in the way that one wave prepares for the next. Langer spends a moment on this example. When the momentum of one wave is spent, the slanted shore causes it to run back out to sea.

> But the piling of the second, incoming wave is also sucking back the spent water, and making its return a downward rush, that stops the bottom part of the new wave and causes it to break over itself (PA 51).

The closing action of the old prepares and causes the new. Put another way, everything that prepares a future creates rhythm; and everything that fulfills the promised future likewise creates rhythm. A pendulum models this. So do the human, organic processes of breathing and heartbeat.[14] In this sense, rhythm is the most characteristic principle of vital organic activity (FF 126–28).

So far we have said that feeling is a private awareness accompanying all the inner, ongoing processes of a human being. The artist feelingly takes in his or her experience (experiential pattern), which is organic in its contours (as are the processes), and in its most notable feature, rhythm. The rhythm of a feeling organism is altered by "things outside the creature's skin" (FF 371).

We have spoken of the quality of inner experience, but we have more to say about the pattern itself. What has all this to do with the second term in Langer's key aesthetical work, *Feeling and Form*?

3. *Form*. We need only a moment to explain this important term. Form is that which structures the elements of the art experience. One thing troubles us from the outset: form, in the way it is usually understood, does not seem dynamic in the way that organic life has to be. Let us examine this problem. The word "form" arose in Greek philosophy; it came from the metaphor of a statue, in which one could distinguish between the shape itself and the material which was shaped. Neither could exist on its own, by itself; form and matter needed each other as integral aspects of the unified statue. Philosophers used these words metaphorically to mean any distinction in which the observed realities are truly different from each other, cannot exist on their own, and yet take their meaning from one another. So, for instance, the patterning of our sense experience is its "form," and the sense data is the "matter" being formed.

Form is general—there could be fifty look-alike statues of Socrates, each with a form we perceive to be the same as the others. Langer says that form in this sense relates one thing to another in our understanding. Two lampshades of different shape and color are still known to us to be lampshades. She notes with astonishment that the shapes of my two palms are exact opposites of each other. In this sense they are not alike at all. But the "form" we perceive tells us that they are the same, since each is the palm of a hand. We do reverse readings of them, using a rule of correspondence of opposite parts (PA 16–17).[15]

But even in this meaning form seems mainly static—it represents that which is permanent and unchanging in the object. If I tear the lampshade to pieces, I have taken away the form and replaced it perhaps with multiple forms of torn paper. One static form is replaced by others. How does Langer solve this problem? How can form describe changing, rhythmic, organic activity? Langer introduces what she calls *dynamic forms* (PA 18–19). Gases, mist, water, streams, the waterfall, do not have fixed shapes with parts in fairly stable relation to each other, just the opposite. Yet they have dynamic unity. Their forms, rather than being forms of *things*—the statue metaphor—are forms of *motion*.

A quiet river, too, has dynamic form; if it stopped flowing it would either go dry or become a lake. Some twenty-five hundred years ago, Heracleitos was struck by the fact that you cannot step twice into the same river at the same place—at least, if the river means the water, not its dynamic form, the flow (PA 18).

Flow is the dynamic form of a river. Organic activity thus can have a form too, a dynamic one. When Langer lists the attributes of dynamic forms, we see that they have attributes similar to those of organisms, noted above: 1) their permanence is a pattern of changes, 2) they have interrelated, interdependent centers of activity (organs), 3) the whole system coheres by means of rhythmic activity (whether periodic or not), 4) major violation or cessation of the main rhythms for very long kills the organism, and 5) their dialectic is one of growth and decay (PA 52–53).

Dynamic forms are quite important, since Langer will say that felt life and the work of art both answer to the description of living organisms, and that in fact these share the same dynamic form. To see what this means we will have to move onwards to the second main part of our exploration. First let us gather into a summary our descriptions of experiential patterns, feeling, and form.

At a *first level of consideration* we saw experiential patterns separated/abstracted from

- practicality (colored shapes as defining a place to sit down),
- actual things (Mona Lisa as a real person's appearance),
- other "types" or planes of experience (e.g., colors, as opposed to sounds).

Those freed, plastic, and transparent patterns were joined at our *second level* of observation to vital, sensory, and emotive feeling. The artist and the child perceive in this way.

At a *third level*, the content of felt life was seen to be a dynamic relation of tensions. Felt life's form is similar to other observed organisms, and is in fact itself organic. Now it is time to see how these three levels get involved in the work of art.

B. Composing the Sheer Appearances into New Forms

We will begin with the work of art "in general" and then turn to the particulars of the various art forms. We have already looked at the experiential pattern found within an artist. What does the inner life of an artist have to do with the work of art? In brief, the experiential patterns can be *restructured* and fashioned into new, objective, dynamic patterns within the work of art. In the work the dynamic forms are now *like* (or "the same as") the feelingly experienced inner life of the artist. Two statements can be made, which we will explain in a moment. The work's dynamic forms are not representations of the artist's own inner emotions, nor are they "expressions" of another felt experience. Rather they represent the artist's *understanding* of the felt life and its contours. Such understanding enables him or her to fashion a work whose inner relationships have the *same dynamic form(s)* that the subjective life of feeling has.

This statement, together with texts by Langer such as our epigraph for this chapter, seem straightforward enough. Let us see if they are.

1. Symbol and Form in the Work of Art (FF 370–374). Langer says that all art "exhibits an interplay of what artists in every realm call 'tensions.'" The artist makes choices which create patterned tensions and are controlled by them. These comprise an organic image that is to be called forth. "The depth of color, the technique—smooth or bold, delicately suggestive like Japanese drawings, full and luminous like stained glass, chiaroscuro, or what not—" all these are patterned, or better *re-patterned* by the new dynamic form that the artist is creating. Interacting elements in their dynamic flow make up this art work.[16]

In other words, the work of art uses the various elements of its craft in order to show forth organic life (FF 270). But the work of art is not a real organism. The lines of the painting only appear to interact; in reality the canvas and its dried paint are quite inert. The painting *resembles* the life of an organism, but it is not itself an organism. It is a *simulation*.

We have come a distance from our former understanding of simulation. Earlier in this chapter we saw that the pattern of a painting was an illusion (semblance, simulation) because it was not, e.g., a real face, whose appearance we are beholding, but simply the appearance of one, without the reality "behind" it. At this point we are able to understand that Langer is talking about more than the representational qualities of a work. To say it briefly,

*what is being simulated is not primarily people and things
but organic, felt subjective life.*

This is a major tenet of Langer's theory. Art is never, in any of its
types, first or primarily representation of objects. To say otherwise would take us back to a pragmatic overlay, as Lonergan
had pointed out. Even the painting of recognizable portraits can
be an imposition of an alien pattern upon that of the artist's
intuition. Only when the artist is able to merge the two, the felt
experience and the desired representative qualities, can there be
uninhibited and free artistic expression.[17]

So, organic, felt subjective life is what art simulates, but this
can co-exist, for Langer, with literal elements. Elements used in
writing can be both literally true and also, at a different level, a
simulation. We have seen above that in non-fiction, for example,
an excellent writer might present his or her philosophy *as if* it
were just being unfolded, with the felt dynamism of philosophical discovery. Readers generally would know that the writer did
not make the discoveries at the moment of writing them in a
book, but would not mind granting "suspension of disbelief."
The philosophical propositions themselves are not illusions, only
the manner of presenting them with the semblance of breakthrough. Thus, statements can be illusions or semblances even
while being attempts at literal truth in another regard.

Let us look into Langer's major premise that art simulates
organic, felt life. Two dangers arise straightaway. A simulation
of "felt subjective life" could easily be a simple "duplication of
psychophysical events," an imitative structure which expresses
the artist's own feelings. Or it could be a string of events which
parallel the passage of emotive life in the artist; by tracking the
progress of the art work, we would be able to find out how the
artist felt in the discernible time when the work was being created (or some other time remembered) (FF 372).

This is forbidden territory. A work of art cannot be a recreation of any specific feeling at all. "It is neither a confessional
nor a frozen tantrum," Langer says vividly (PA 26). Art is its
own event, its own pattern of tensions, existing in its own right,
not as a way to refer to something else.[18] Instead of presenting
feeling itself, it presents a concept of feeling. Again, the word
"simulation" means only that it recreates the way such patterns
occur organically. The forms are true to inner life's forms, but

the content (that which is shaped) is different. The new form belongs intrinsically to the art work.

Langer wants to make sure that the emotion expressed in a work of art is not what Maritain called "crude" emotion, the simple emotional responses of the artist. Intelligence somehow observes the flow of feeling—noting its patterns, its dynamic form, all of which will be the form of the work. Intelligence knows organic, felt life from within. It also knows the artistic elements intricately and is able to create from them a (simulated) organic reality by merging them with that form. We see an intimacy here, of outside world with inner, of inner life felt and understood, and of artistic material known and loved. Langer does not say much about how the artist knows the materials (and elements) of his or her art, something that would have helped to round her theory.

Another danger lurks. If art expresses a "concept of feeling," then why not say it gives precisely a *general understanding* about felt life, a kind of illustration of the concept an artist has about it? Of course art would be ruined by this, so we must now distinguish between general and particular knowledge to see how Langer escapes this trap.[19]

Discursive language, for its part, takes an understood "pattern of intellectual activity" and renders it into a generalized pattern of language and grammar (cf. PNK, ch IV, and FF 377 ff). In other words, the forming element (e.g., number) is abstracted away from that which it forms (e.g., dogs), so that the now general pattern can be named: two and two make four. Two of what? Four of what? It makes no difference, because the number is being abstracted away from the dogs or candlesticks that have number; the form is what interests—not the material, sensible things. And since the form is not burdened with the specific, numbered, material things, it is general. Discursive language deals with general concepts.

We have seen that the work of art for Langer is by contrast a *non*-discursive symbol. It presents the dynamic form (organic tensions and resolutions) always and only as concretized in sensual matter.[20] We behold the dynamic form of felt life *precisely in its act of forming the sensual qualities*, not as removed from those qualities. The work of art is, in Langer's oft-used term, a "presentational symbol." In general it is called presentational because it *presents* the individually formed object instead of just the form (PNK 96).[21]

Our task is to understand presentational symbol, and thereby the work of art. To do that we must look at Langer's theory of symbol, and our understanding of form will help us. Here, we can use Berel Lang's analysis to glimpse the main elements of symbol for Langer.[22]

First, in her early book, *Practice of Philosophy*, Langer defines symbol—not presentational—very simply. It is *a correspondence in the form of two different objects (i.e., the terms of the logical relation)*.[23] If we analyze one entity, such as a map, we are able to know another entity, Siberia. The two are "put together" somehow in the same way. They share a form. The country Siberia could be taken as a symbol which refers back to my map, but we ordinarily would find the other way around more helpful.

Later, in *Philosophy in a New Key*, she begins to see symbol-making as an activity peculiar to human beings.[24] Instead of just a "signal," human beings are capable of "symbol." What do these words mean?

Signal is rather straightforward, having three terms:[25]

$$Subject \rightarrow\rightarrow\rightarrow Signal \rightarrow\rightarrow\rightarrow object$$
$$(me) \qquad (pointing\ finger) \qquad (bus\ coming)$$

All the signal does is to focus my attention. Symbol, however, has a fourth term.

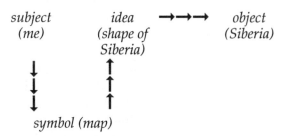

While signals *announce* their objects, symbols *lead us to conceive them;* symbolization is a human activity, since human beings can not only point to things, but represent them (PNK 30). Once I have seen the cave dweller's drawing on the cave wall, I have not a moment's pause before saying that it is an animal running. But in fact it lacks almost everything found in a real animal: no hair, no weight, no tangible properties, and what is worst, no power of movement. It consists merely of a few lines. However, those lines share the *form* of the animal in question. They point, Langer says, to the form as understood in my concept of bison. Because my concept and the bison have the same form, they can act as symbols one for the other. Langer says that the art object is a symbol also, because it has the same dynamic form that feeling has (PA 26).

Language is a form of symbolism. It is able to name things and actions because it can assign specific meanings to words, which refer in general to anything that corresponds to that meaning. Language is "discursive," in the sense we saw above. Presentational symbols are very different. They refer in a *non*-discursive manner to realities that are *not* able to be named (since names generalize). In a presentational reality such as music, no specific meanings are attached to particular elements. *Philosophy in a New Key* (PNK 240) has Langer calling music an "unconsummated symbol," since it does not refer to some specific reality. It is not completed or consummated. Finally, as we have seen, Langer holds that the "meaning" communicated by a presentational symbol is the *life of feeling* that we have examined above, emotional rhythms in organic existence.[26]

Not only does the presentational form remain with the "matter" it patterns, it *cannot* be removed and still retain its intelligibility. Presentational symbols therefore have to be known in their particularity. Let us try an example. The dynamic form of tension and release in a symphony can be known either generally or in particular, but with very different results. (1) I can *outline* the Sonata Allegro form of Beethoven's Fifth Symphony, first movement. The result will be a general pattern that can be applied to any musical composition that happens to use that format. This gives me real, referential knowledge. But if I stay with such general information alone, I will no longer be knowing that particular Beethoven movement, I will be knowing, *in abstracto*, a form for any Sonata Allegro movement—even though I got it in the beginning by outlining Beethoven. (2) I could instead apprehend the movement as it is played, with the kind of concrete apprehension appropriate for a work of art. Now I am knowing a form of tension and release that cannot be removed from the musical sounds exhibiting these tensions and releases. This aesthetic form is *particularized*, but still knowable. Example

(1) shows a discursive symbol. Example (2) illustrates a presentational symbol.

Two other loosely related aspects of form will complete this section about the work of art in general. First, form in the work of art is not simply a collection of smaller forms. It is centralized, so to speak, functionalized around a central node, giving it organic unity. What is this node, and where does it proceed from? Though Langer is never clear about it, she does offer one startling insight that contributes to our own argument. She says that the basic rhythm of an art work is contained in the *commanding form* of that work.

Commanding form is the original *conception* (note the use of that word both in art and in physical procreation), the general gestalt that is given in the artist's intercourse with reality. It is the fundamental organic form containing the basic movement or rhythm (FF 121–122) *even before the work is made*. It is the matrix in which lie all the motives for a specific piece. In music this would include the need for dissonance/consonance, for novelty/reiteration, length of phrase, timing of cadences, and so on (FF 123). The *performance* of a piece of music must be entirely unfolded from the commanding form contained within the work, in which case the performance is as creative as the composing (FF 137–141). Likewise, the art of listening to music, beholding the plastic art piece, or of reading the literary art, is entirely a matter of reaching through to the commanding form and therefore beholding the work in its intrinsic gestalt. Critics must grasp it too, or else their evaluation will be partial and peripheral (FF 147, 168). Since commanding form is the central element in the work, the subsidiary forms are elaborated from it. It is not a summation of the rhythms, cadences, movements within the work, but rather the source from which they flow. We remarked in passing its similarity to the embryo; it is a tiny bud from which parts will articulate outwards.

Finally, there is the *principle of assimilation*. It is not possible, according to Langer, to have more than one plane of commanding form in a work of art. When two types of art intersect in a work, as for instance music and poetry in the case of (classical) song, only one can win: music. The illusion created by the lyric or poem is subsumed under the musical gestalt. A good poem has an "expressive core" that provides the key to the poem and to which the music will give utterance, almost as if the poetic commanding form can be transmogrified and become music's. The music should sound as the poem feels, should have the very gist of the poem incorporated into it (FF 156–164). In Langer's words, "the poem should lie like a bride in the minstrel's arm, free, happy, and entire" (FF 154). This principle of assimilation will have relevance when we consider liturgy.

In brief summary, we have been looking at form in the work of art, the way the work is patterned. We saw Langer point to a type of form that is not static and unchanging but dynamic: a form that structures motion. Felt, interior life and the work of art both have the same dynamic forms; in fact the work is an illusion or semblance of organic, felt, subjective life—not primarily of people and things, or of specific emotion. Moreover, it is not itself a feeling but a "concept" of felt life. This concept is different than most because it does not represent a general understanding, but a specific and concrete realization of the dynamic form found in inner life. As such the work of art serves as a "presentational symbol," whose form cannot be abstracted away from that which it forms.

If we have an initial understanding of its form, then what is the matter of art? What *receives* the forms of tension and resolution? In subjective life one's inner experience receives the organic form. In the art work it is something else, something that undergoes the dynamic form given by the artist. He or she *composes* the work—and causes it therefore to share the same kind of organic forms that felt inner life has. But what is "it"?

"It" varies widely. Each art is concerned with the special elements that its own particular experiential pattern offers. It refashions these elements, re-forms them in the manner of felt life. A genre of art such as painting takes elements possible to and appropriate for its type and creates from them (an illusion of) the felt rhythm of inner life. Not every kind of illusion is possible in an order of art, only those aspects of organic inner life that are able to be projected into the medium. Since the different arts have different media, this one's *basic illusion* (of organic life) will be different from that one's. So, to ask about the medium of an art genre is to ask also about the *basic semblance* it creates.

2. *Art and the Arts*. Let us begin with music. Music is temporal or "occurrent." It happens over time. It therefore must create the tensions and resolutions of organic life by using materials

that can express its temporality. Painting's material is spatial, not temporal. It will have to simulate organic life—even its temporal aspect—with materials that are spatial.

Music's illusion, then, will have to capture the temporal aspect of organic life with elements that are themselves temporal. Let us ask first about the nature of temporality. Music does not express units of time, as does a clock. Langer makes a distinction important for her theory between types of time: time as felt and time as measured (PI 221–222). Clock time is really comparison of time to space, the distance that, e.g., the minute hand travels. The spatial distance from the numeral one to the numeral two represents the temporal five minutes, the "amount" of "time" that has elapsed. Since the motion of clock hands is entirely uniform, it can signify only a truly abstract portion of what goes on in the real world: the amount of uniformly progressing duration (represented as spatial but understood as temporal). No matter how meager or momentous, how many or few the events during that time, the minute hand still moves just its distance, and the "time" it counts out is only five durational units.

Langer contrasts this clock time with what she calls experiential or subjective time. Subjective time is filled with physical, emotional, or intellectual *tensions and resolutions.*

> Life is always a dense fabric of concurrent tensions, and as each of them is a measure of time, the measurements themselves do not coincide. This causes our time-experience to fall apart into incommensurate elements which cannot all be perceived together as clear forms. If one is taken as parameter others become "irrational," out of focus, ineffable. Some tensions, therefore, always sink into the background; some drive and some drag, but for perception they give *quality* rather than form to the passage of time, which unfolds in the pattern of the dominant and distinct strain whereby we are measuring it (PI 222)

We can measure duration not only by comparing it to the clock's spatial movement, but to anything that has motion. Interior subjective events move according to their tension ratio, so to speak, and any of them can serve as measurements of "time." I might refer my subjective experience of eating dinner to the hollow tension of a speech I am to give within the hour. If I did not "organize" events somehow, the "dense fabric of concurrent tensions" would be felt as a "confused experience of physical and mental strains—of waiting, expectation, fulfillment, sur-prises" (PI 223).[27]

What does this have to do with music? Music creates "the illusion of organic life in the subjective time dimension." In subjective life a subject organizes internal events by choosing a tension event to measure the others by. Music organizes its own organic tensions by means of a main illusion it is creating.

A work of art thus presents not a welter of illusions but what Langer names the *"primary illusion,"* a key term. Every element of the composition works together with the others to create one primary type of semblance: one of felt, subjective time (cf. FF 122). Thus it is not enough to say that music presents an illusion of temporality; one needs to know about the organization within that illusion. As with all the arts, then, we must discover the primary illusion for music.

In her 1950 article "The Primary Illusions and the Great Orders of Art," Langer begins to name one primary illusion for each art genre. Let us continue to deal mainly with music, to get the idea, and then apply that idea to one or two others. Music's semblance of subjective time (PA 39) is an illusion of the organic movement of tensions and release, or "the sonorous image of passage" (FF 113). This is its primary illusion.

> The creation of a self-contained temporal order, continuous, all-inclusive, and entirely given in direct experience, is the business of music. The elements of music therefore are sensu-ous images of the tensions and resolutions which constitute *passage* for us; and those sensuous images, creating the sem-blance of passage, are tonal forms in virtual motion. By these the illusion of time is achieved and its experiential character set forth—its complexity, density, and volume, its interwoven elements and indivisible flow (PI 223).

Langer compacts subjective time with all its moments into the word "passage." This word will indicate the particular aspect of felt inner life that is to be simulated in the art object. Music will display its elements, tonal forms in virtual motion, in a dynamic form that is found also in subjective life: passage.

Two very helpful technical terms appear in the above text. First, "element" is a word Langer employs with consistency throughout her writing. She means by it anything that enters into a primary illusion to "create, support, and organize" it. Various elements—tonal "images of passage"—work together to create the overall illusion in music of subjective time. What kind of tonal images?

> Movement and rest, swift movement or slow, stop, attack, direction, parallel and contrary motion, melody rising or soaring or sinking, harmonies crowding or resolving or clashing; moving forms in continuous flux (PI 220).

Each is an "element" of the whole. Each is already a semblance, that is, it contributes to the *appearance* of passage (not actual passage). When we speak of an element, then, we are not referring to middle C, for instance, but to the illusion it helps to establish. The composer uses elements because they already have the same forms of tension and release that internal subjective life has. That commonality is the reason the work of art is for Langer a symbol of subjective life.

Second, Langer uses the word "materials" in a specialized way, in conjunction with "element." Materials are the actual "stuff" out of which an art work is constructed. Paints in a tube or on the palette; words telling of deeds; bodily energy in dance; pitches in music. We are ordinarily unaware of materials, except when a work fails to marshal our attention.

> Music is the most enthralling, i.e., illusionistic, phenomenon in the world. What we hear [i.e., attend to] in listening to sounds "musically" is not their specific pitch and loudness, duration and timbre. Often we are not even specifically aware of melody, harmony, or rhythmic figure, yet the music is perfectly meaningful. What we hear is what Hanslick has properly described as *"tönend bewegte Formen"*—"sounding forms in motion" (PI 220).

In contrast to elements, then, materials are *not* illusions within the art work: they are real-life properties, the mechanical underpinning of the art, so to speak. As such they are not perceived as interacting with each other; they "lie side by side" in what Langer calls (with tongue in cheek) "their actual, undialectical materialism" (FF 84–85). In the art of painting, paints are *materials* that simply exist as themselves. But colorful shapes are illusionistic *elements* that interact with each other to create an illusion.

A single example will illustrate the difference. Langer contrasts the simulation of motion in music with actual physical motion. In this passage,

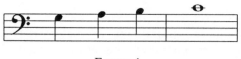

FIGURE 4

the *rest point* is middle C, and the other notes seem to be in motion toward it. But this motion is an illusion. Since sound consists of physical vibrations, the note we call "middle C" has more real, physical vibrations than any of the notes immediately below it; physical vibrations that cause sound get faster as the scale goes "up." The C, which *seems* to be at rest, actually is moving faster than the notes which *seem* to be in motion. *Felt* motion toward the resting middle C is therefore a semblance of motion, while the *actual* vibrations are just the "materials" by which it is accomplished (PI 220–221).

For dance, the motion of bodies is material; the human gestures which the motion simulates are elements (PI 225–226). In poetic composition grammar, accent, dialect, strong and weak stresses are materials; the sweep of an emotion or the intense experience of a mood is an element (PI 228, FF 259). And so on.

Musical works project tension/resolution patterns over a (simulated) span of (subjective) time. We said that painting cannot manage this in the same way, since its material is spatial, not temporal. A question arises. If the temporal span of organic life is as important as Langer claims,[28] how can any art genre fail to present that temporality and still be an art? A motionless art form is not like life at all.

To answer, Langer begins with the tendency of painters and critics to speak of "motion" in a painting or design. She quotes what she calls a "naive, normative statement" from a textbook of decorative drawing: "Borders must move forward and grow as they move" (FF 63).[29] In other words, lines have an ability to simulate motion. This motion "is not really movement in the scientific sense, change of place; it is the semblance of rhythm" (FF 63). What can this mean? In a particularly adept formulation, she says that "the path of a physical motion is an ideal line;" and, "in a line that 'has movement,' there is ideal motion" (FF 65–66). A well executed line contains the path of motion. And motion itself is likewise the tracing of a possible line. Langer calls the line and the motion "symbols" of each other:

> The running mouse seems to cover a path lying on the floor, and the still, painted line seems to run. The reason is that both exemplify the abstract principle of *direction*, by virtue of which they are logically congruent enough to be symbols for one another (CA 525; cf. 524–527).

Motion in art, then, is not necessarily actual change of place, but such a change made perceivable. What is really symbolized here is growth, organic growth.

We have said that an art genre can only use the elements that are possible to it. But the artist does not press into action every possible, or even every appropriate element of his or her art form in order to make a work of art. Of course (nearly) all the arts of poesis utilize words, but the actual, physical sound is of crucial importance in lyric poetry. Langer's explanation is very interesting. She says that the artist's first duty "is always to establish the primary illusion, i.e., to close the total form and set it apart from actuality" (PI 230). Those available elements are enlisted that will assure "psychical distance" for the work (i.e., mark it as an artful illusion, not reality). Sometimes a lot are needed. A true sonnet idea, she says, "calls for every device of fabrication, from word music to interlacing rhymes, to keep the thought in the realm of imagination" (PI 230). But if some other element performs the same function, the other virtual elements are not necessary. For instance, if there is great imagery and "a certain unrealism of subject matter," the poetry can dispense with other elements (PI 230). Narrative has such organizing force because of the unfolding of a story line. In narrative, all

> other devices have to adjust themselves: the choice of imagery is no longer free, as in the pure lyric, but is determined by the need of heightening some events and perhaps preparing others, and of slowing or hurrying the course of action (PI 232).

The Romance uses a different technique, a detailed account of *how* things are done, rather than just the fact *that* they are done. And so on.

Langer treats the primary illusions in groups. Music is one of what Langer calls the "occurrent arts," another of which is dance. These arts present, in general, the illusion of virtual time.

The "plastic arts" (painting, sculpture, architecture) fashion the illusion of virtual space. The primary illusion of painting, for Langer, is *virtual scene*: a space opposite the eye and related directly to the eye. That space is filled with shapes, visibly colored volumes, each of which contributes to the primary illusion. This, of course, does not eliminate but makes possible such divergent types as abstract art and portraits. These establish virtual scene—in Langer's sense of the term (not in the sense of a landscape) (FF 86).

Sculpture, contrary to what we might have said on first thought, does not just do the same thing as painting but in three dimensions. Sculpture provides as its primary illusion *organic volume*. It displays the vital structure, organic in its relation of tensions, that is (virtually) behind the surface (FF 86-90). This is the semblance the sculptor accomplishes, sculptural volume. The statue is a felt structure because the artist experiences his or her own organic volume in a way no eyes can comprehend: from within.

I have attempted to pull from Langer's writings of the period something like the nub of each art genre. If there were time and space in this chapter to consider each order of art in detail, Langer's greatest contribution would be set forth; but we must condense. She never made a chart like mine of the arts, perhaps to avoid a seeming compromise of their idiographic natures. Nevertheless, Table One is just such a chart, listing four things, three of which we have just described: the *materials*, the *elements*, and the *primary illusion*. I have included also an oft used category of Langer's, the "primary abstraction," or as I have rendered it for clarity, "the *primary element that is abstracted*." The primary element differs from elements only because of the word "primary." It is the main kind of elemental semblance that the art form deals with.

I have attempted to stay close to Langer's own words for descriptions in the chart. Obviously a table can only snapshot her attentive treatment of each art type. She is at her best here, in tangible, hands-on descriptions of each art. The reader will gain immeasurably by seeking out fuller descriptions in her writings.

TABLE ONE
Theory of the Various Art Forms
As Found in the Writings of Susanne Langer

Plastic arts: the illusion of virtual space

Painting:
  material: canvas, paints, the actual light on the picture
  elements: background, foreground, highlights, empty air,
    motion, accent, intensity of color, depth of darkness,
    objects in relation to each other (PA 39). Lines, colors
    (FF 31)
  the primary element that is abstracted: shapes, visible
    colored volumes
  primary illusion: virtual scene: a space opposite the eye
    and related directly and essentially to the eye (FF 86)

Sculpture:
  material: three dimensional structures: stone, wood,
    plaster, metal, etc.
  elements: sculptural volume, organic structure, the bulk of
    the figure, parts having shapes necessary for organic
    functions; (FF 88) tactual space (FF 90)
  the primary element that is abstracted: semblances of
    organism, (FF 88), especially shapes that reveal
    organic functioning (FF 88)
  primary illusion: organic, kinetic volume: the vital structure
    that has to be behind the surface. This includes the
    empty space around the figure (FF 86–89)

Architecture:
  material: wood, stone, clay, cement, metal, fabrics, even
    paper, grass and snow (FF 97)
  elements: dynamic, organic relations, intersecting spaces,
    interval tensions of space (FF 94)
  the primary element that is abstracted: activities of a human
    culture: the system of interlocking and intersecting
    actions; continuous functional patterns (FF 96);
    cultural patterns made visible (FF 98)
  primary illusion: "ethnic domain": a cultural place; a
    functional realm made visible (FF 95); a physically

present human environment that expresses the
characteristic rhythmic functional patterns which
constitute a culture (FF 96)

Occurrent arts: the illusion of virtual time

<u>Music:</u>
   material: sounds of a certain pitch & loudness, silences:
      composed into rhythmic, melodic, and harmonic
      patterns, enhanced by variations of loudness and
      timbre (PI 223)
   elements: sonorous moving forms (PA 39); images of the
      tensions and resolutions in simulated motion (PI 223);
      motions, tensions, resolutions, resting tones,
      emptiness, beginnings, ends (PA 39)
   the primary element that is abstracted: the forms that fill time:
      human tensions of any kind, physical, emotional, or
      intellectual (PI 222); sounding forms in motion; kinetic
      tonal forms (PI 220–21)
   primary illusion: the sonorous image of passage (FF 113):
      the motion of organic forms (FF 107–109);[30] subjective
      time in its passage (PA 39)

<u>Dance:</u>
   material: bodily energies limited by gravity and friction,
      muscular strength and control: i.e., the actual forces
      that move dancers (PI 194, 226). The floor, cloth that
      drapes the bodies, ambient space, light, musical tone
      (PA 4); actual motion (PI 223)
   elements: lures and excitements, prescribed paths, engulfing
      rhythms, personal wills: all as seen in gestures (PI 226)
   the primary element that is abstracted: virtual spontaneous
      gestures, that function as signals or symptoms of our
      desires, intentions, expectations, demands, feelings.
      Symbols of the will of a being who is a center of vital
      force. (FF 174, 187) Virtual powers that evoke virtual
      activities (PI 226)
   primary illusion: a virtual realm of power. Dance *driving*
      this way, *drawn* that way, *gathering* here, *spreading*
      there (PI 226–7); appearances of influence and agency,
      created by virtual gesture (FF 175) [31]

Arts of poesis:[32]*virtual events* (FF 217); *illusion of life*
    (virtual history) (FF 213)

<u>Lyric poetry</u>:
  material: word music, imagery, word pathos, "criticism of
      life," "dynamic" fantasy, sound and sense, implication
      and suggestion, derivations and metaphorical mean-
      ings, grammar, accent, dialect, strong and weak work-
      forms (PI 228)
  elements: thoughts with their emotional value and contour,
      as contrasted with the facts they may express; lived
      pieces of experience (PI 229); or the sweep of an
      emotion, the intense experience of a mood (FF 259)
  the primary element that is abstracted: the virtual history of a
      thought, emotion, mood, etc. (FF 259)
  primary illusion: illusion of impersonal subjectivity, in the
      natural tense of contemplation: the timeless present
      (PI 229–30)

<u>Narrative poetry</u>:
  material: telling of deeds; storytelling devices; colloquial
      language and (e.g.,) regular meter; slowing or hur-
      rying the course of action; descriptions (PI 231)
  elements: virtual events (remembered as separate instances)
      (FF 263)
  the primary element that is abstracted: significant virtual
      events in a mode of completed and unified qualitative
      experience (Liddy 1970, 80)
  primary illusion: virtual past: illusion of life in the mode of
      a virtual past. In the normal tenses for telling a story:
      perfect and pluperfect (FF 266–267, PI 231) or, to
      heighten vividness, the historical or "wandering"
      present (FF 269)

<u>Romance</u>:
  material: telling how things are done (PI 233); the narration
      often held back in service of description (FF 285 ff)
  elements: human types, like figures in a tapestry (PI 232)
  the primary element that is abstracted: events dwelt upon by
      imagination (PI 232)

    primary illusion: virtual life in history, in "three dimen-
    sions" like a tapestry (instead of a thread) (PI 232;
    FF 283-286)

Novel:
    material: discursive language as used in conversation: to
    inform, comment, inquire, confess; in short, to talk to
    people (FF 288). Character study, psychological in-
    sight
    elements: These are its most important creation: characters,
    individual human agents Also elements such as the
    inn, the garden, the days & nights, bearing the stamp
    of vivid memory (PI 232)
    the primary element that is abstracted: personalities with all
    their hazards, in interaction (FF 87–89)
    primary illusion: The contemporary scene: a virtual experi-
    ence on a large scale (FF 286–287)

Non-fiction:[33]
    material: opinions, attitudes, analysis, ascertainable facts of
    an actual past in their causal unity, personal history,
    exposition (FF 301)
    elements: ideas as experienced and felt (not as opposed to
    the same ideas as understood, but complementary to
    them) (FF 302)
    the primary element that is abstracted: the feeling that inheres
    in studious thinking (growing intensity as problem
    becomes more complicated and more thinkable,
    definite, more urgent and impatient) (FF 302)
    primary illusion: A semblance of organic unity of thought as
    it grows (FF 303)

Drama:
    material: Actors, stage, makeup, lights, audience, and, the
    quintessence of action: speech (FF 314–315)
    elements: actions[34] belonging to life, with motives that
    motivate other acts (FF 312)
    the primary element that is abstracted: actions within a situa-
    tion (FF 312)
    primary illusion: a virtual history in the mode of *destiny:* a
    present in which every action is oriented toward the
    future (FF 307). Indivisible virtual history is implicit in
    it, realized only as action is completed (FF 310–311)

Motion Pictures:
   material: cinema taken by a moving camera (cf. FF 411)
   elements: situations, objects, persons speaking and acting,
      with the dreamer equidistant from all (FF 413)
   the primary element that is abstracted: direct apparition
      (FF 414); immediacy of experience: "givenness"
      (FF 413)
   primary illusion: virtual history, in the dream mode. A
      virtual present in an order of direct apparition, with
      the dreamer always at the center (FF 412–413)

C. Assessment and Needed Additions

The word symbol, so central to Langer, imposes a question that some think dismantles Langer's theory by removing the cornerstone. We have reached the point in this discussion for critical remarks, more of which have been leveled at Langer than were at Maritain. This discussion will lead in the direction of our own grand picture. The leading question will be "what is symbol for Langer?" From the discussion thus far we are ready to fix on this topic in more detail, and to see if "presentational symbol" can withstand critique. The less detailed reader could well jump ahead to Part II of this chapter, conclusions, at this point.

Of course diverse objections have clustered about Langer's theories. A number of critics are displeased by the descriptions she gives of the various art types. Weitz (1954, 472–479) believes that she has stuffed the art genres into conceptual categories, to the detriment of each. This reductionism, he thinks, is accompanied by an outmoded theory of language-as-mirror. He also asks what happens if the non-theoretical audience member does not agree with or even know her theory: what if, being advised, the audience continues to "wallow in its emotions": what then (480)? Rader, whom Langer had read and whose influence she received, points out that the "art-genders" are usually distinguished from one another in aesthetic theory only on the basis of tools and materials, and that—as we have pointed out—Langer tends to slight the medium in order to emphasize the "illusion" (Rader 1954, 399). Margolis (1955) agrees with this. Carrit (1955, 75) believes that the common end of expressiveness is far more important than a theory of primary illusions.

Pursuit of these interesting criticisms would take us too far afield. The delineation of art types by their primary illusions (etc.) seems to the present writer a most valuable contribution to art appreciation, even if one or the other precise description could be seen as wide of its target. Each is at least near the target, and this nearness issues from astonishing insight into the nature of each art form.

The more serious criticism concerns the theory of form and symbolism itself. Certain critics of Langer think that her system simply fails at the level of symbol.[35] It is possible to get at this objection by talking again of "form." We said in part two of this chapter that a form, the design of a statue for instance, can be abstracted from that which it forms. The form of Socrates could be applied to many pieces of stone. It is general. Communication of general forms is easy. "Two," "chair," "cause and effect," "reaction formation," all these are able to be understood by me in the fullness with which you present them because they have been cut loose from their enfleshment as "two books," "I am sitting in your chair," "by lighting this match I cause this fire," "Sadie is smiling when she is really angry, which we psychologists call a 'reaction formation.'" We heard Langer talk about a certain form that cannot be abstracted from that which it informs. This "presentational form" is dependent on particular matter for its intelligibility. It cannot be thought of apart from its sensuous, singular content of feeling (i.e., the elements of an art work).

For Nagel, Weitz, and Lang, if a form cannot be known in general, apart from that which it forms, then it cannot *refer* to anything else. It is trapped by the matter which it informs and cannot have "meaning," since meaning is generalized (and its referents are specified). Thus it cannot be a symbol, since symbols count on the universality of the form for their ability to refer to something else. We saw the same critique of Maritain.

The experience of the present writer somehow counters this objection. I seemed to know the Taiko drum performance I went to last month with a type of knowledge that is very like the way I know my own inner felt life: I participated in it; I let myself take part; I grasped the performance "intuitively" in its fullness without passing on to a mode of "thinking." In that way I was aware that the flamboyant, screaming, gesticulating Taiko drummer was pressing out rhythmic passages exactly expressive of my own rudimentary and subconscious felt life.[36] The Taiko troupe was presenting vital, organic life in a way surely more profound than even the performers knew, especially if the word "know" has an intellectual cast.

For Langer, in order to grasp the intelligibility of that performance I must perceive the form in union with what it is forming at that moment. If I did that, I must have the ability to do so. *There must be a way to perceive concretely the generality of a form.*

> The "idea," as Flaubert called it, is not only perceived by one initial intuition, but also without being separated from its symbol; it is *universalium in re* (PA 69).

This "initial intuition" has to be a different way of perception, different from the one of knowing in general terms. It is a holistic manner of perceiving. It apprehends both form and matter in the concrete, without making an intellectual abstraction, without taking form away from content. Such an ability to know is necessary if "presentational form" is ever to be valid. I would propose, therefore, that an art object can act as a symbol as long as there is this kind of knowledge.

Langer seems to call this way of knowing "intuition." Unfortunately, she does not give intuition enough attention to make it prominent. As Lang notes, it is one of the most interesting though generally neglected aspects of her thought (1962, 359). In an otherwise tortured passage, she calls intuition "direct awareness of concrete reality" (PA 64); she also refers to it as "a recognition of non-discursive symbolization" (FF 377). She speaks of

> the exhilaration of a direct aesthetic experience [which] indicates the depth of human mentality to which that experience goes. . . . What it does to us is to formulate our conceptions of feeling and our conceptions of visual, factual, and audible reality together. It gives us *forms of imagination* and *forms of feeling* inseparably (FF 397).

In this passage a much more prominent place is given to the conjunction of external world and interior felt life than Langer usually does. Even so, she usually seems to assign other characteristics to intuition that appeal more to her than the strict epistemological necessity we want to urge.[37] For that reason, instead of pursuing her term I want to make the assumption that throughout her aesthetical writing she is reaching for a definition of a perception that takes in "forms" as they are enfleshed in the concrete, individual thing. In order to differentiate this from Maritain's solution, which we have seen, let us give such a perception a provisional name, "concrete apprehension." A working definition would speak of it as a perception in the singular of that which is not limited, of itself, to that particular instance (i.e., form).[38]

When I went to the Taiko performance I experienced forms that seemed to my intuition to be those of primordial human experience. The realization was instant and not cogitated. These "forms in the concrete," taken in by holistic "concrete apprehension," I must in some way be able to *compare* with the forms of my feeling life. My concrete perception at that Taiko festival was not an "objective" knowing, so I cannot place two empirical objects, Taiko and felt experience, beside each other and analyze their correspondences. But the form of each is still general (universal) even if it has to be apprehended only in conjunction with its matter. Form is entirely particular in the material thing, but it still has its general quality. Consciousness does not have to carry out an abstraction in order to "know" the form. I would propose that consciousness can perform a subconscious comparison of the concretized form of inner life and the concretized form of, e.g., the Taiko performance.

How does this apply to presentational symbol? We saw that Langer's specialized version of symbol does not refer me onward to another meaning. I attend to the dance for itself only. But as I perceive the work of art in its fullness, I can let its reality show me the life of feeling whose dynamic form I find realized *in it*. Of itself the form has meaning that is not exhausted by a particular Taiko incarnation—and therefore it can serve as incarnated form for my life of feeling. It is shared without being abstracted.

> A work of art is an expressive form, and therefore a symbol, but not a symbol which points beyond itself so that one's thought passes on to the concept symbolized. The idea remains bound up in the form that makes it conceivable. That is why I do not call the conveyed, or rather presented, idea the *meaning* of the sensuous form, but use the philosophically less committal word "import" to denote what sensuous form, the work of art, expresses (PA 67).

In concrete apprehension, we find roots for symbol in Langer's definition, since it fulfills all (Langer's) conditions for a symbol: (1) there is a correspondence or analogy between the art object and the felt, vital life which formed it and by which I know it; if

I could analyze the two I would understand that they are "put together in the same way." (2) Concrete apprehension is able to refer to ideas or concepts, as Langer would have a symbol do, though these are not intellectual ideas or concepts: they are the combined knowing powers working in tandem to grasp "the sensible form," so to speak. (3) And a common structure is known between the art object and the life of feeling. A common form: again, not an abstract form, but one whose universality is recognized but not abstracted, and here grasped along with its sensible content.

It is not necessary to endorse Maritain's philosophy to ratify a "subconscious" which does not enact the explicit, abstractive knowledge found in conscious thought. One of Maslow's "qualities of the peak experience and their subjects" suggests itself: people who have peak experiences have simultaneously the ability to abstract without giving up concreteness and the ability to be concrete without giving up abstractness. At these higher levels of human maturation, many dichotomies, polarities, and conflicts are fused, transcended or resolved (Maslow 1962, 83–86).

Berel Lang was right when he, following Nagel, warned that Langer's is not the "accepted usage of the terms" symbol and meaning (Lang 1962, 325; Nagel 1943, 326–328). If the type of perception I am suggesting does exist, Langer's different usage of the terms form and symbol becomes clear. Even so, it is not always obvious that Langer herself remained faithful to the distinction between these types of knowing, crucial as it is to her entire system. Lang thinks she capitulated in *Problems of Art* to Nagel and Rader in their insistence that "significance" and "symbol" are not commonly used by others in the fashion she did, and therefore should not be so used by her.

In fact, the passages that might seem to establish her capitulation really represent her attempt to nuance the theory in exactly the direction I am proposing. She says in *The Problems of Art* that

> the 'significance' of a work, by virtue of which some early twentieth-century writers called it 'significant form', is what is expressed. Since, however, *signification* [i.e., referring to something else by means of generality] is not its semantic function— it is quite particularly *not* a signal—I prefer Professor Melvin Rader's phrase, which he proposed in a review of *Feeling and Form*: 'expressive form'. This, he said, would be a better term than 'the art symbol.' I have used it ever since. Similarly,

> Professor Ernest Nagel objected to calling that which it expresses its 'meaning', since it is not 'meaning' in any of the precise senses known to semanticists; since then I have spoken of the *import* of an expressive form. This is the more convenient as the work may have *meanings* besides (PA 127).

Langer seems in this passage to withdraw the term "symbol." But she is only trying to nuance the normal impression conveyed by the word symbol in order to lose the generalized referring function. Its referential quality should instead be in the specialized, concrete manner that I have suggested. This is Langer's meaning of presentational symbol.[39]

My contention in this book is that one must somehow discover a foundation for the intimate relation that artists seem to have with the world. Without a true, unambiguous channel for commerce between these two, the importance of the art object seems to be severely degraded. Art is significant because it is an outcome of the closest possible relation between a human being and the perceived world. That world's rhythms are the human's rhythms. If this were not so, then a natural event such as a rainbow would be as important as—or more important than—any work of art, as we have remarked. We do not have to revert to Maritain's or Lonergan's philosophical stances to say that art is born out of a union of consciousness with the perceived forms of the world. Born, because no other metaphor carries as well the notion we have been urging: that when an artist observes life around—the motions, the passages, the figures and shapes of the experienced world—that artist is made one with them and therefore brings forth the work of art. These beloved and seductive forms of the humanly perceived world become the very motions of a life of feeling inside the artist. Every artist knows the materials and elements of his or her art form with an intimacy that cannot be described adequately as biological impact (see Appendix Four). In the words of the poet, "the world and my life have grown one."[40] The art product is conceived, and its birth has an importance like that of a new baby. It is not there to afford us verifiable knowledge of felt life, though perhaps it can do so on the side. Like a baby, the first reason for its being is that it is there. Like a poem, all art forms should not (primarily) mean but be.

With remarkable insight Langer describes the shapes and structure of the different art genres. Her theory of primary illusion gives cogency to the sentence "art is an experience of the inner, organic life of the artist." We could say metaphorically that the baby is very like its mother. And we can now see ways in which a fathering world plays its part. Subjective time, for instance, depends on an interaction with the world, events which impinge deeply at whatever level.

It is time for evaluation and conclusion to this whole part of the present book. We must pull together, not so much everything that Maritain and Langer have said, but the underlying unities that are relevant to our quest.

II. Conclusions

I have been careful thus far to avoid imposing my own hypothesis on the texts of the authors, but to note applications, where they exist, in passing. Now it is time to bring their theories into my structure. We will shape the discussion according to the list of characteristics of creativity. Though I derived this list primarily from physical conception, gestation, and birth, and though we have already sought traces of it while looking at Maritain and Langer, now the time has arrived to become explicit about the sphere of art. We seek metaphors to the procreation process, obviously not a literal repeat. Does it make sense to say that, *mutatis mutandis*, the creative process in the arts is truly *like* that in human reproduction? If enough of the marks of creativity do apply, the answer will be yes. At that point we will be justified in judging that an analogy exists between the two areas in that each realizes the principle, "Every significant union is a generative union," or put another way, "all creativity is co-creativity." They are also analogous in that they each exhibit in their own way the seven characteristics of human creativity.

We have discovered that Maritain's thought comports itself easily to our comparison, so much so that we could organize it according to conception, gestation, and birth. In general Langer is more resistant, but helps us in three ways. The first is by implication. The force of her argument can be bolstered if we posit beneath artistic production an act of knowing that is sensually and intellectually intimate (from L. *interus:* inward): what I have called "concrete apprehension." If the work is not an expression of this union, it is difficult to understand how, for instance, a painting is *able* to be expressive of the artist's subjectivity. But with this understanding the work of art is free to be an expressive form or "symbol," in her sense of the word. Table One testified to this necessity. Secondly, Langer has shown us what exactly can be expected to come together with the artistic soul in order to produce music or dance or any other art form. Third, she is of great help in speaking rationally about all the art genres in detail, and liturgy, when we come to it. But let us find these things out by walking, by commingling insights from both our authors.

A. The Marks of Creativity

1. Connaturality between partners. Man and woman are connatural to each other in a vast range of ways. Our discussion of connaturality in the arts shows us that the same is true of the artist and the world. Maritain's ordinary act of knowing displayed the aptitude that consciousness and being have for each other.[41] In artistic knowledge this connaturality is taken for granted and moved higher. Intimate union can happen because artistic knowledge happens close to the very center of the subjectivity of the knower. Now many connatural aspects can enter in: the felt relationship of "the beloved hand" to the poet, the interconnection of the ancient vase to other beings through history and through the world—a web of interrelationships, Maritain calls it. Artistic knowledge can open to such secrets of being because the beings of the world and artistic consciousness are made for one another, for the connatural union that is their goal.[42]

2. Abundant fertility. Langer's informative description of organic life numbered among its aspects that of organic activity's rhythm and timing, tuned in such a way as to ensure results. This description could be applied to the way in which human nature, normally parsimonious, abundantly supplies sperm and ova for possible conception. It is as if, in this important generative regard, chance should not be allowed power to defeat conception. If even one in a million achieve onement, the larger organic purpose is accomplished.

The same is true of art. A sculptor is inundated by bulks and structures all about. These cannot be avoided; they become natural environment to the sculptural wits that were born for them. When Michaelangelo at last looks on just the right marble block— after how many hundreds or thousands?—he conceives; conceives the *pieta* that just has to be rescued from its blockish surrounds. Or in music—the hardest of them all to describe because most abstract—the composer is, like everyone else, immersed in subjective time. That is to say, the composer has an especially acute receptiveness to the *passages* of daily life. The frantic rush, the cackling joke, the interminable wait, the clean winter's day. These the composer drinks in, noting at some level of consciousness their dynamic scope. But that is not all. The "sonorous moving forms" of music itself also invade the composer's sensitive soul. The cadence, the "tactile" nature of leading tone to tonic, the buzzing warmth of strings, the stabbing drums, and so on. These are connatural to the composer, they have to be, and they are passages *like* those of "subjective time" because they are taken into the subjectivity of the artist; they are one with it. Abundances encircle the writer of music. One day, when the time is right, or when the commission has arrived, one idea out of these many, one nuance, will lash its way to center and consort with the soul to conceive a tune, a toccata, or a symphonic strain. Startling abundances rush daily into every artistic soul, making artistic conception impossible to avoid, at least occasionally. The *organic* purpose of the overall act is thus ensured.

   3. Onement. We describe oneing as an important union of two distinct entities. Maritain's entire aesthetics is based on this possibility, from ordinary knowledge where "becoming" is the rule, all the way to artistic emotion where "objective reality and subjectivity, the world and the whole of the soul, coexist inseparably" (CI 124). For Maritain artistic subjectivity is never something on its own, quarantined from being(s) of the world. To think otherwise is to invite brutish "self-expression," which is, as we saw in Maritain, a betrayal of artistic knowledge.

   In his own way, Maritain put our case for onement quite clearly: poetic knowledge contains "both the reality of the things of the world and the subjectivity of the poet, both obscurely conveyed through an intentional or spiritualized emotion" (CI 124). Emotion,

> received in the preconscious life of the intellect, becomes intentional and intuitive, and causes the intellect obscurely to grasp some existential reality as *one* with the Self it has moved, and by the same stroke all that which this reality, emotionally grasped, calls forth in the manner of a sign: so as to have the self known in the experience of the world and the world known in

the experience of the self, through an intuition which essentially tends toward utterance and creation (RR 26).

The "existential reality as one with the Self it has moved" we call
here an analogy to physical conception in that each is an example of co-creativity and important oneing. The resulting germ
of creative knowledge is intrinsically oriented toward objective
utterance which is the offspring called the work of art.

Langer is never far from this.[43] The most convincing evidence
can be found in her statements about the elements and illusions
of the art genres. A glance back to Table One will make this
insight clear. The primary illusion of painting is virtual scene, a
space opposite the eye and related to it. But how can the painter
imbibe space and spaces and shapes without allowing the sight
of them into the soul? The architectural principle of "ethnic
domain" suggests an architect with deep-rooted sympathy for a
people and their "interlocking and intersecting" culture. The
contemplation of a "timeless present" found in lyric poetry does
not represent a shallow glance at love, which is the "wandering
bark"; or at "morning's minion" the Windhover. Drama's interest in destiny, with every action oriented toward the future,
means a dramatist acutely aware of lives and events on a touching, dramatic level. And so on, through all the genres. Because
artistic subjectivity is organic, as Langer insists, the knowledge
of these realities and aspects does not simply knock and then
remain outside the door of consciousness. These realities enter
and become working *parts* of the organic inner life that will be
expressed in the piece of art. They cause it to conceive.

Langer also makes statements about "intuition" that bend in
this direction. We heard her say that aesthetic exhilaration "indicates the depth of human mentality to which that experience
goes." She continues, "what it does is to formulate our conceptions of feeling and our conceptions of visual, factual, and audible reality together" (FF 397). Isolated statements such as these,
together with the otherwise inexplicable identity of form between the work and inner life give our assumption a home in her
aesthetical writings. There is a conceiving onement between the
artist and aspects of the world, which union is a direct analogy to
the conceiving of a human child: both are co-creativity.

4. *The union as viable.* The "zygote" is not just a *result* of the
union; it *is* the union, now initially differentiated from its sources.
We got one view of this process in Maritain's writings. "The

singular existent which resounds in the subjectivity of the poet, together with all the other realities which echo in this existent" becomes a yoked reality that will be expressed (CI 126). Intuitive pulsions or emotionalized charges are given within it. Deep but inaudible "music" is now lodged in the preconscious of the poet. The artist now has to be someone who "within her wears, bears, cares and combs the same" (Hopkins).

> . . . The totality of the work to be engendered was already present in advance, whether this totality is now virtually given in the first line of a poem, as a gift from the preconscious life of the soul, or virtually concentrated in the spiritual germ of a novel or a drama (CI 134).

This seed planted in the preconscious, this union of artistic subjectivity, will turn into the work.

Langer has a notion very like this. If we follow out the implications of *commanding form,* we will find a description of this zygote and its birth. In *Feeling and Form* she says it explicitly, using perhaps accidentally the metaphors of conception.

> The first stage is the process of conception, that takes place entirely within the composer's mind (no matter what outside stimuli may start or support it), and issues in a more or less sudden recognition of the total form to be achieved (FF 121).

She says this "conception" can happen in many different ways, from loose fantasy to hearing everything at once. But when it has happened, it forms a *gestalt,* and after it has firmed, the composer "is no longer free to wander irresponsibly from theme to theme, key to key, and mood to mood." There has been conceived something like an embryo, which she names as such.

> Once the essential musical form is found, a piece of music exists in embryo; it is implicit there, although its final, completely articulate character is not determined yet, because there are many possible ways of developing the composition. Yet in the whole process of subsequent invention and elaboration, the general *Gestalt* serves as a measure of right and wrong, too much and too little, strong and weak (FF 121-122).

This is the "commanding form," containing the total "idea" of the piece to be composed. I do not take the explicit metaphors from human reproduction as anything but that, metaphors. But perhaps they hint lightly that Langer at least at times knew the commanding form as that which is conceived and remains to be gestated. As she says, "the commanding form is not essentially restrictive, but fecund" (FF 123).[44]

5. *Gestation—a movement from the less stable but nurturing darkness toward articulate light.* We spent enough time above on Maritain's innovative notions of gestation to make summary statements sufficient. The intuitive pulsions edge over the brim of consciousness. Awareness is dim, but awareness there is. The skills of making come into play. The semi-conscious, instinctual actions in the artist are *like* the impulses of the mother's body, "with aim /Now known and hand at work now never wrong" (Hopkins). The embryo works through a region of emotion-charged images and into the conceptual realm. Here it either passes through concepts, or else gives itself over to them, depending on whether the work is to be classical or modern. Pulsions are like newly forming members of a fetus: they are in stir, like parts of a great melody, charged with dynamic unity. As they reach a state of open intelligence the pulsions receive shape, in what Maritain calls the morning light. All this is within the mothering womb of the artist, who is emphatically not the metaphorical *father* of the work, but mother, the place of all this gestation.

Of course, fertility means that not every conception will gestate and come forth. Many chances are given, few are taken. Maritain:

> This incitation can remain virtual. The poet, because poetic intuition is his [or her] ordinary frame of mind, is constantly open to such hidden incitations, . . . and not all of them can pass to the act. Nay more, a poetic intuition can be kept in the soul a long time, latent (though never forgotten), till some day it will come out of sleep, and compel to create. But at that moment there is no need of any additional element, it is only a question of application to actual exercise. Everything was already there, contained in poetic intuition, everything was given, all the vitality, all the insight, all the strength of creativity which is now in act. . . (CI 134).

However long it lies dormant, that which is contained in the embryo or commanding form is entirely sufficient to be the work of art, as long as it gets a chance to gestate, to become explicitly that which it is in seed.

6. *Labor.* There is hard work in both pregnancy/birth and in artistic gestation/creation, not because connaturality is lacking, but because human structures creak under so great a weight. Langer speaks of difficulty and sacrifice in the artist in a straightforward manner. She sees that there is a "relentless strain on a musician's faculties" because of the wealth of possibilities given in any commanding form once conceived. Not all can be realized and therefore every choice is a relinquishment for the good of the whole. All other developments that could have come out of a particular articulation now are taken out of viability. This labor is unconscious, but it is still labor, and painful (FF 122).

Maritain speaks often about the rigors demanded of an artist. In *Art and Scholasticism* he calls for asceticism in the artist's life. Artists must be on guard against the "banal attraction" of easy success; they must "pass through spiritual nights," purifying themselves without cease; they must work toward "humility and magnanimity, prudence, integrity, fortitude, temperance, simplicity, ingenuousness" in relation to the art-work-to-be (AS 78). They must remain true to the intuitive vision in its wildness, even while using reason and calculation to handle the fire.

> Consequently, they are aware in themselves of a torturing division, a rending of their own human substance, which they are condemned to bring to unity—enigmatic, unstable, never satisfying unity—not in themselves, but in their work. Hence their connatural torment. They are obliged to be at the same time at two different levels of the soul, out of their senses and rational, passively moved by inspiration and actively conscious, intent on an unknown more powerful than they are which a sagacious operative knowledge must serve and manifest in fear and trembling. No wonder that they live in inner solitude and insecurity (CI 249–250).

Surely Maritain had observed this torturing division in the poets, painters, and musicians he knew so well. His empathy let him see some reasons for their great madness of labor.

7. *Birth.* We have called physical birth a relatively stable externalization that continues the trend toward separation-in-union regarding the sheltering environment. In other words, now the work is delivered. Beholders now can find within the work the same poetic intuition that the artist had labored to bring forth (Maritain). They can participate in the work by grasp-

ing the commanding form that is its source of unity (Langer). There is beauty here, and it gives pleasure to the observer. Contemplation of the art work is the goal, not a kind of pleasure for its own sake. The work is not a pleasure machine and neither is a baby, obviously, even though it gives plenty of joy (amidst the pains). Technically the work is a sign or presentational symbol, which makes subjectivity present within its own being, and therefore does not send the observer elsewhere. The "other" that is being symbolized is the union of artistic soul and world, grown to viable life in that same world.

B. Codetta

Maritain is erudite, lyrical and—dare we say it—obscure in dealing with the art products of the various genres. He is most at home with poetry, as we have noted, but painting and music are included also. We would turn to Langer if we wanted to revel in the full panoply of the arts, to understand just how they combine subjectivity and the movements of the world. Semblances and illusions seem to me to be articulations of just what happens on Maritain's level of virtual intentionality in the art object. Without concrete apprehension Langer is left seeming like a trickster, perhaps even shading off from illusion into delusion. For his part, Maritain can seem too much at the mercy of a quasi-mystical vision of vast, interconnected being. Langer makes more practical, Maritain more profound our visit to the newly born work of art, where we notice dear features of the new child, and comment how it resembles both father and mother.

So we have now charted the analogy between procreation and art that we began with. Creativity is co-creativity. We have found the analogy strengthened not weakened at the hands of these two aestheticians. The likeness at every level between having a baby and making a work of art now seem unavoidable, even though they dwell amidst dissimilarities. Because there is a true analogy between the two, we see at last why the metaphor works so well. It does not need all the "drama of crossing" that these two chapters have supplied (since metaphor is a strategy of human speech) but our tracing of details shows us the profundity of both the analogy and the metaphor. The journey has also made us ready to set foot in the dangerous land of liturgical theory. We will see whether the analogy of creativity can survive this new excursion.

NOTES

1. See FF, chapter 2 for Langer's survey of theories of art that oppose her own. Also cf. FF 104–108, 176–179, 251–259, 303, 316–322, 394–395.

2. Liddy lists a number of statements—from among many—in Langer's writings giving a definition of art (Liddy 1970, 31–32). Examples are FF 40, 60; PA 53, 109, 111; and in MIND I 38.

3. Lonergan's unpublished paper, a chapter of a larger unpublished book, is 35 pages long, yet Lonergan ultimately seems to have condensed it, all of it, into about 4 pages in *Method in Theology* (Lonergan 1971, 61-64).

4. Lonergan: "Any type of subordination, of putting one's spontaneous consciousness at the disposal of intellect or at the disposal of a mechanical society, is an instrumentalization of experience. I do not say that there is anything wrong with such instrumentalization. But I think that is not what we want to talk about or think about when we think about art" (1959, 288).

5. Maslow refers to pragmatic perception as "deficiency-cognition" and contrasts it with "being-cognition" (1962, chap. 6). The former, he says, includes most human cognition experience. D-cognition categorizes or "rubricizes" what is perceived insofar as it is "relevant to human concerns" (72), and only as it is a member of a class of objects (e.g., "ashtray," "can") (70). B-cognition on the contrary attends to the percept fully and completely, on its own terms, with care, in an ego-transcending, self-forgetful manner (74). It is less active and more receptive and passive than d-cognition (81), and results in a sense of wonder, awe, reverence, humility, and surrender (82–3). See Appendix Three for a listing of the "Qualities of Peak-Experiences and Their Subjects."

6. Bufford took offense at Langer's calling a pure pattern an illusion. If it is simply "itself," a pattern, then it is *exactly what it seems to be*, not an illusion. He therefore resolves, intractably, to understand "illusion," in Langer's lexicon, as something which is exactly what it appears to be. In other words, he takes (with apparent sarcasm) the diametric opposite of the accepted meaning of the word (Bufford 1972). This is a polemic interpretation. Considered as material for the artist to work with, the pattern is innocent of connections to the daily world, and even of its customary job of being the appearance of someone or something. In that regard it is not an illusion. But considered as retaining its representative qualities (e.g., the appearance of George Washington) it is an illusion (since George is not there, only paint and canvas is).

7. Langer calls this type "generalizing abstraction" (MIND I, 153–56). In her discussion of abstraction (CA 518–523, FF 48–52 [a literal

reprinting of the pages from CA] and MIND I, chap. 6) Langer says that artistic or "presentational abstraction" is different in principle from other types, since the sensual qualities remain (cf. FF 51–52).

8. Her use here of all terms like material existence, form, and abstraction, is different from the traditional meanings.

9. It is selective also because the primary illusion differs in the different art types, as we shall see.

10. The dichotomy between "subjective" and "objective," and the terrible difficulty facing any philosopher who wishes to start with such a dichotomy and attempt to overcome it, will be an achilles' heel for Langer in her later writings. In *Feeling and Form* and the books that surround it, Langer sees the *lack* of such distinctions within the context of artistic creativity. As Maslow put it, in b-cognition the world is seen as a unity, and *in the same process*, the person is known concurrently, through the same act comes closer to his or her own inner being (1961, 89). Perhaps this clinical observation by Maslow should warn aestheticians away from a type of knowing in which subject/object dichotomies are prominent.

11. She continues, "All such directly felt experiences usually have no names—they are named, if at all, for the outward conditions that normally accompany their occurrence. Only the most striking ones have names like 'anger,' 'hate,' 'love,' 'fear,' and are collectively called 'emotion.' But we feel many things that never develop into any designatable emotion. The ways we are moved are as various as the lights in a forest; and they may intersect, sometimes without canceling each other, take shape and dissolve, conflict, explode into passion, or be transfigured. All these inseparable elements of subjective reality compose what we call the 'inward life' of human beings" (PA 22).

12. Rhythm "is, I think, something related to *function* rather than to time" (PA 50).

13. Langer says that knowledge, emotion, feeling tone, and even the very sense of identity, exhibit the interplay of nervous and muscular tensions within the subject. Even at this stage of her writing it is possible to wonder whether Langer means that feeling, mood, emotion, *and even the sense of identity!* are (1) accompanied by tensions, (2) can be described (also) by tension language, or (3) are *nothing more than* the interplay of tensions. In her later writing, something very like (3) will be her surprising choice.

14. "A rhythmic pattern arises wherever the completion of one event appears as the beginning of another" (PA 51). Or: rhythm is the "building up of a new dynamic *Gestalt* in the very process of a former one's passing away" (FF 128). "All life is rhythmic; under different circumstances, its rhythms may become very complex, but when they are really lost life cannot endure" (FF 126).

15. "Their respective shapes fit the same description, provided that the description is modified by a principle of application whereby the measures are read one way for the one hand and the other way for the other—like a timetable in which the list of stations is marked: 'Eastbound, read down; Westbound, read up'" (PA 17).

16. And as regards music, "the forms that fill time are *tensions*—physical, emotional, or intellectual" (PI 222). Time, a stream of tensions and resolutions (FF 372), is expressed in music.

17. "The form is that pattern of internal relations that will be immanent in the colours, in the tones, in the spaces. The expression, the work, the what is done, is isomorphic with the idealized pattern of experience. It may also be isomorphic with something else, and in that case your art is representative" (Lonergan 1959, 295).

18. "The function of music is not stimulation of feeling, but expression of it; and furthermore, not the symptomatic expression of feelings that beset the composer but a symbolic expression of the forms of sentience as he understands them. It bespeaks his imagination of feelings rather than his own emotional state, and expresses what he *knows about* the so-called 'inner life'; and this may exceed his personal case, because music is a symbolic form to him through which he may learn as well as utter ideas of human sensibility" (FF 28). Cf. PA 67.

19. Nagel finds this difficulty in the opinion Langer holds (PNK 238 ff) that, as he quotes her, "music actually reflects only 'the morphology of feeling'—so that it is plausible to hold that 'some sad and some happy conditions may have a very similar morphology.' But this is a more serious admission than Mrs. Langer seems to think, for it leads rather directly to the view, as she herself notes, that music conveys *general forms of feeling*—although earlier she maintained that general reference is reserved for discoursive [*sic*] symbols alone" (Nagel 1943, 327).

20. In normal symbolizing, then, a mapmaker abstracts a form, a shape, and re-presents it. But we have minimal interest in the sensual medium: it could be the back of an envelope or a marble wall. In music, however, the composer senses the formed matter of felt inner life, and presents that form in a new enfleshment.

21. "Form and content are one" in this kind of symbol, she says, relying on an analysis of the two by Morris Weitz (FF 51).

22. In a critique imaginatively entitled "Langer's Arabesque and the Collapse of the Symbol" (Lang 1962, 350–355), Lang purports to trace the collapse of her theory, though there are flaws in his analysis too as we will see in section three.

23. Lang says that already at this stage she saw also that there are meanings that do not admit of verbal formulation, that are incommunicable.

24. In FF 35 she complains that pragmatic philosophy reduces everything to *animal* needs instead of human.

25. She calls this reality "sign" in PNK (e.g., chap. 3), but decides later to re-title it "signal" (FF 26, n1).

26. Lang cites PA 58 and 91 for this insight, but of course it was present in PNK 228, and as early as 1950 in CA 527ff.

27. We might say that subjective awareness of time has not only "length," like clock time, but "volume." Common parlance has not only "a long time," but also "a big time." Much experience of tension/release is packed into it (PI 222).

28. For example, "'Living form' directly exhibits what is the essence of life—*incessant change, or process,* articulating a permanent form" (FF 65, italics mine).

29. Quoting Adolfo Best-Maugard 1937, 10.

30. Secondary illusion in music: virtual space: tonal space, deriving from harmony; a genuine semblance of distance and scope, musical elements as holding places in an ideal range (FF 127).

31. Especially the illusion of a conquest of gravity (e.g., leaps, dancing on toes), of the actual forces that are normally known and felt to control the dancer's body (FF 194). The play of virtual powers manifests itself particularly in the motions of illusory personages, whose passionate gestures fill the world they create—where forces seem to become visible (FF 195). Cf. Weitz 1954, p 476 for the opinion that modern dance "should *accept* and *exploit* the gravitational forces between the body and earth."

32. "'Poesis' is a wider term than literature, because there are other modes of poetic imagination than the presentation of life through language alone. Drama and its variants (pantomime, marionettes) and moving picture are essentially poetic arts in other modes; . . .they employ words in special ways, and sometimes even dispense with them altogether." (FF 267).

33. Includes: critical essay, philosophy, history, biography, reports, and all kinds of exposition. "Such writing is in essence not poetry (all poetry is fictive; 'non-fiction' is 'non-poetic'). Yet whenever it is well done, it meets a standard which is essentially literary, i.e., an artistic standard." It is "applied art" (FF 301).

34. I use the word "action" in place of Langer's "act," to avoid the confusion she acknowledges with "acts of a play." In this case she defines act as "any sort of human response, physical or mental. . . . The total structure of acts is a *virtual history in the mode of dramatic action*" (FF 307).

35. Cf. Nagel 1943, 324–325; Lang 1962, 349–365.

36. "The work of art . . . presents a form which is subtly but entirely congruent with forms of mentality and vital experience, which we recognize intuitively as something very much like feeling" (MIND I, 67).

37. For instance, later, in *Mind I*, she would refer to intuition as "direct logical or semantic perception; the perception of (1) relations, (2) forms, (3) instances, or exemplifications of forms, and (4) meaning." She calls this the strict sense that Locke gave the word (MIND I, 130).

38. Indeed, when Langer suggests later that the art work is a most helpful way to study psychological data about felt life, she is very careful to differentiate on the one hand an objective study that would use the art piece as a *model*, and on the other a "direct perception of artistic import," which is "not systematic and cannot be manipulated according to any rule. It is intuitive, immediate, and its deliverances are ineffable. That is why no amount of artistic perceptiveness ever leads to scientific knowledge of the reality expressed, which is the life of feeling" (MIND I, 65).

This "direct perception of artistic import" is what I am dubbing "concrete apprehension." If it is allowed its place in the discussion, many difficulties of Langer's theory dissolve.

39. In an odd passage from FF, Langer again appears to move in the direction Lang calls capitulation. She retracts the term "unconsummated symbol," which had meant the absence of an assigned connotation (PNK 240), and says that "every work of art . . . should express a particular feeling unambiguously; instead of being the 'unconsummated symbol' postulated in *Philosophy in a New Key*, it might have, indeed, a single reference. I suspect that this is the case. . . " (FF 373–374). This statement does not bear the weight assigned it by Lang, but instead is an incidental observation. In her last work, *Mind*, where her interest would be greatly served by tacking down the referential names for musical moods, she says that music "does much more than convey some nameable mood or emotion; it may even be given different names, but best none at all, for no name such as 'sorrow' or 'joy' fits any actual feeling throughout its course. . . . What makes a work important is not the category of its expressed feeling, which may be obvious or, on the contrary, impossible to name, but the articulation of the experiential form" (MIND I, 66–67). This also answers Nagel, who thought her remark about happy and sad moods in music having the same "morphology" was a dangerous move toward music having a generalized meaning (Nagel 1943, 327).

40. Tagore (1939, 1972, 203):

> I HAVE kissed this world with my eyes and my limbs; I have wrapt it within my heart in numberless folds; I have flooded its days and nights with thoughts till the world and my life have grown one,—and I love my life because I love the light of the sky so enwoven with me.

Also,

> WHEN I go from hence let this be my parting word, that what I have seen is unsurpassable (44).

41. Thomists hold that being is intelligible, or in other words that knowing and being were made for each other. The knowing powers boost things into the intentional realm and thereby make them equal partners in the becoming that is knowledge. The intellect's illumination brings out qualities that are already within the thing and need only light to be seen. This is connaturality.

42. "And it suffices for emotion disposing or inclining, as I have said, the entire soul in a certain determinate manner to be thus received in the undetermined vitality and productivity of the spirit, where it is permeated by the light of the Illuminating Intellect: then, while remaining emotion, it is made—with respect to the aspects in things which are connatural to, or *like,* the soul it imbues—into an instrument of intelligence judging through connaturality, and plays, in the process of this knowledge through *likeness* between reality and subjectivity, the part of a nonconceptual intrinsic determination of intelligence in its preconscious activity. By this very fact it is transferred into the state of objective intentionality; it is spiritualized, it becomes intentional, that is to say, conveying, in a state of immateriality, things other than itself" (CI 123). We are not interested here in whether there is a power called agent or "illuminating" intellect, but only in the connaturality such a theory can point to.

43. Maritain: "Since poetic imagination is born in these recesses [of subjectivity], where the intellect, the imagination, all the powers of the soul suffer in unity some reality of existence brought to them by intentional emotion, it involves first of all a certain alert receptivity. As the mystic suffers divine things, the poet is here to suffer the things of this world, and to suffer them so much that he [or she] is enabled to speak them and him- [or her-] self out. . . . The degree of creative strength of poetic intuition is proportional to the degree of depth of such attentive passivity" (CI 139–140).

44. But it is also restrictive. The composer, Wendy Carlos, put it this way: "When music feels like it's coming right, it definitely has the subjective feel that you're taking dictation, as it were. It doesn't feel like you're doing it. I mean, any creative process, I guess, really falls into this thing. You feel like you're sort of filtering this information through and being more an editor where you can say 'Oop, oop, I shouldn't go off in that direction,' and you halt yourself and you get the mechanism all up and rolling again in a different direction." From National Public Radio's Weekend Edition, Sunday, August 9, 1992.

PART TWO

INTRODUCTION

"Liturgical action does not simply use art," Don Saliers declares in the New Dictionary of Sacramental Worship, "it IS art—dialogue with God in symbolic form" (Saliers 1990, 33). Let us now approach this statement as a question, the one with which we began: can liturgy be considered an art form? If so, (1) who is the main artist in a liturgical event? (2) Who is the audience? (3) Where does God fit into the event—as one of the spectators, as a distant goal, as a co-partner in creative intuition? (4) In what way can individual liturgical art forms such as music find integration within what might itself already be an art form? (5) And how can ritual repetition be accounted for?

(1) In contemporary celebrations the planner or planners would seem most likely to merit the title "artist." Today more than ever they are the ones whose alert receptivity conceives the liturgy, especially as regards its tone, nuance, particular content, and shape. In Lawrence Hoffman's words,

> above all, liturgical planners must see the liturgy as a drama, and therefore, they must conceptualize it as a whole. It is not just the music, or the space, or the lives we lead, or the lesson for the morning, or the sermon of the day, or any other single thing. It is only the *totality* of the liturgical event that will present a coherent image of an alternate world (Hoffman 1988, 189).[1]

We saw in detail how the totality of artistic elements in a work of art must merge in dynamic unity around the "commanding form." Nothing short of a living conception was called for, since the oneness found in an artwork echoes a far more profound union at its source. If the liturgy is unified (at least potentially) in all its own elements, then surely a conceiving "artist" is called for.

Dangers lurk here. A primary "artist" of the liturgy has to act in the way all artists do: creative intelligence must come into significant union with some striking and beloved portion of the real world, which union itself gestates and becomes the art work. The work then represents the artist's soul insofar as it has mingled with the world. What model does this produce for liturgy? No matter how beautiful and holy that work of artistic production, it would have to be stamped with the person and personality of the particular creator. Does this ring true for liturgy? A single planner/artist calls to mind an older more common attitude in which the priest provided the Mass and the people attended. A sufficient aesthetic of the liturgy will have to discover how to name a principal artist while at the same time maintaining the important participation of people.[2]

(2) The nettlesome question of audience also lurks. Congregations become obvious candidates for this designation, but with terrible consequences of passivity. As we know, the Roman Catholic Constitution on Liturgy mandated "full, conscious, and active participation by the congregation," something that it called "their right and duty by reason of their baptism" ("Constitution on the Liturgy," #14: Abbott 1966, 144). Liturgical advances of this century all stand directly against the passivity and observer status implied in the word audience. Perhaps the present author's Taiko experience did represent some kind of "participation" in a performance, but at a distance, always an *observation* of the work of art already fully formed and in a sense complete without my attendance. Peter Fink says that the medievals understood liturgy as "sacred drama," observed by the assembly as if by an audience (Fink 1991, 9). Can this be true of contemporary Christian liturgy? What is the status of the assembly, then, if liturgy is an art form, but if they are to participate fully, consciously, actively?[3]

(3) And where is God's place in liturgy-as-art-form? If a planner serves as primary artist, does that artist go off to a quiet place with God-the-progenitor and conceive a liturgical event?

Piety might comfortably say yes, but then we are left watching the offspring of someone's soulful union with God. The assembly would resemble a spiritual director or confessor to this intimate event. Nor is it enough to say simply that God is simply within the liturgy "garbed in human attire" (Collins 1983, 79). This would render God a mysterious presence with no real role. Nor can we designate God merely as the projected result of a mainly human effort; liturgy surely does enact an image of God, importantly so, but if that is all it does, then again God is not described as an active participant in the event.[4] At the deepest level God has been amply revealed as three-personed and deeply at work in the world. Clearly, any theory of liturgy as art must grapple with the important, specific, difficult role of God in the ritual.

(4) Integration of creative arts into liturgy must also be taken into account. Any art form will tend to take center stage, so to speak, unless it is profoundly integrated into the larger form it would otherwise displace.[5] Throughout history music grew from its integrated role of *setting* liturgical words and action to a significantly non-integrated disposition, represented, say, by a Mozart Mass. One of the major benefits of calling liturgy itself an art form is to prevent such disintegration of the liturgy as a whole by bringing into play, for example, Langer's principle of assimilation. But to achieve this benefit, the problems we have charted above must be solved.

(5) Finally, a peculiar characteristic of liturgy and ritual has to be dealt with: repetition. With all the newness of each liturgical event, there is still a necessary and reassuring regularity of text, action, and intent. Congregations do not assemble to witness something new but rather something old. No ritual event could exist without the repetition of time-worn, traditional texts and actions. Such reiteration might fit well within the birth imagery we have used—the new infant is not a new invention but a fresh realization of the age-old human form—but it presents difficulties for liturgy-as-art. Even with the stylistic similarities in an era of painting such as the renaissance, for instance, no painter allowed him or herself to present the nearly identical material and form each time. Liturgy typically does do this.

Thus, at least five questions must be addressed in any theory of liturgy as art form: who is the artist, who is the audience, what part does God play, how are the subsidiary arts integrated not accidentally but in principle into the liturgy, and what do we make of literal repetition?

We saw that, because art is at root creative, the problem of liturgy as a form of art must be approached first from the prior question of *whether liturgy can be said to be creative* at least in its essence. If so, then the remaining task will be to describe how this creativity works. We will approach the question, therefore, from the basis of co-creativity. Can we find a significant union, a conception which gestates and then is born as the liturgical act?

In general, creativity can be predicated of liturgy in at least four ways, which we should distinguish from the outset. First there is the initial phase of *composing* the texts and actions. Through the long formative centuries of the rites, liturgical shapes became more and more fixed, some parts soon, some later, until finally the work of composition was done.[6] Creativity of this kind is rendered unnecessary in the Roman rite, except for subsidiary prayers and, say, the prayers of the faithful. Second there is creativity in the *manner of performing* the liturgy. Here "the climate is one of awe, mystery, wonder, reverence, thanksgiving and praise" (Environment and Art in Catholic Worship §34; Simcoe 1985). Suitably artful enactment of the rites represents an "opening of the mystery of the realities signified, proclaimed, and ritually participated in" (Saliers 1990, 37). Third is the creativity present within *liturgy's constituent arts*, as mentioned above: music, dance, homiletics, lighting, dramatic pace, etc. Fourth is the creativity which can be *intrinsically* predicated of liturgical celebration itself, not in the particular manner of this or that liturgical event, but in its dynamic essence. In other words, can liturgy be said to be *creative at its core*? The task of the next chapter will be to approach this last type of creativity.

An urgent clarification of this creativity may ward off misunderstandings. Words such as "essence" and "core" in no way refer to some kind of immobile substance of liturgy. If we do in fact establish liturgy as at least analogous to art, we will say that it is a performative or occurrent art, whose materials and elements are always actions, not simply a stationary nature on display. Liturgy is present only when it is being enacted or performed. The distinction I am drawing is not between the action and the essence, but between the particular action of a liturgy, and the commanding form that underlies, dynamically, all the actions of that ceremony. We will note in Chapter Five that this commanding form at times is being conceived even as the liturgy takes place.

Since all human creation at its inmost depth is always the union of two connatural partners whose union becomes the offspring, we will be seeking to identify such partners. We have already pointed toward God and the assembly as radically important to any Christian liturgical act, so we will begin our investigations by asking whether God and human beings are *"connatural"* to each other; whether, in other words, an important union could possibly take place between them. If we answer affirmatively we will then proceed to trace the union of the three-personed-God with the world, including the liturgical portion of that world. In chapter six we will begin to specify in what way such creativity applies to liturgy and whether it qualifies liturgy as an art form, with all the questions raised by Part One of this book then to the fore.

Before beginning we must first derive an initial overview of liturgy within the life of the Church. Such a survey proceeds from the very human necessity of locating a topic within its larger context before beginning to examine it. Those readers already well versed in liturgy may wish to skip directly to chapter four.

Liturgy in its Broadest Context

Franz Jozef van Beeck is one of a number of contemporary theologians who see liturgy as a starting place for theology instead of a stepchild. Both van Beeck and Edward Kilmartin cite the expression *lex orandi lex credendi* (the law of prayer is the law of belief) (GE I 224-231) to shape their teaching. This would mean that theologians could find liturgy a source of theology instead of an offspring of it.[7] Van Beeck positions this saying within a much larger dialectic that truly encompasses everything we refer to as faith and church. For this reason his large work now in progress, *God Encountered*, receives the subtitle "A Contemporary Catholic Systematic Theology": it is an integrated view of belief in every aspect.

Now that we have used the word "dialectic," we must give it brief attention here, though the philosophical notion in its fullness would require volumes. Hegel originated the usage van Beeck makes of it. We might say in brief that the word derives from three moments in a thought process: first a concept, then an opposing concept that fights against it, and finally a reconciliation of the two. A decorator, for instance, might approach a room with ideas of outfitting it in a highly ornamented, Baroque style. In consultation with the owners, she might find that they want instead a simple decor, with unadorned lines. Instead of merely capitulating, she might then come up with a way to suggest Baroque decor by means of very simple but decorous shapes. If this were possible, she would have effected a *synthesis* of the two, previously antithetical ideas. Hegel applied this kind of logic to all human knowing, including philosophy and even religion—an endeavor far beyond our present needs. Instead of "ideas," the "dialectic" applies to whole systems of thought, and to the material world itself. Marx applied it to human political activity. Therefore a new word is needed instead of "idea"; "*moment*" seems fill that role, since the process occurs in time. One "moment" interacts with a second which is quite different from it, and the two then issue in a third "moment." The liberal politics of the Democrats in the USA is replaced by a new moment of conservative control, which becomes a new entity having qualities of both.[8]

Van Beeck's first organizing principle is that the church acts in a dialectic manner, in this sense of the word. Its life consists of the threefold division "worship, conduct, and teaching."

> Together these form the threefold Tradition. This Tradition is the comprehensive, dynamic structure of the Church we live in, which *"in its teaching, life, and worship,* perpetuates and hands on to all generations all that it is itself, all that it believes"* (GE I 208).[9]

"Handing on through tradition" places doctrine in dialogue with Christian action and worship itself. The three—worship, conduct, and teaching—form dialectical centers of Christian life itself. Here the three remain in continuous tension and balance, without replacing one other. Early in volume one of *God Encountered* he says that there is nevertheless a hierarchy. "Teaching is informed by conduct and worship, and conduct by worship" (GE I 92). A diagram would yield the following:[10]

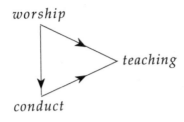

worship

teaching

conduct

FIGURE 5

The connections are of course highly nuanced and interconnected, as we will see.[11]

Van Beeck's second great organizing principle is historicity. Faith in each of its moments has to unfold over time, even as the events of Jesus' life did. We acknowledge Christ's presence to the world, but that acknowledgment itself *came to be*, and therefore it is intrinsically temporal. Faith with its moments unfolding through history is therefore a process.

The most important event in this process, the *resurrection motif*, lies at the center of Christian faith.[12] We find in Acts of the Apostles evidence of changes in understanding brought by knowledge of the resurrection (with the sending of the Spirit). The resurrection thus causes a *retrospect:* a reinterpretation of events that took place before it. Jesus' life and words now have a compelling new pattern, divinely warranted. Something like an insight, in Lonergan's language, has taken place. If an insight could be called a thread discerned between data formerly known only as unconnected or discordant, we see here an insight enfleshed. It interprets not only the deeds of Christ's life and death, but also those of all the world and all humanity. Everything is rearranged according to a new understanding given in the resurrection. The historical inbreaking of the resurrection emphasizes the point that access to God is available only as a process.[13]

Let us begin to look at the first moment of the historical dialectic, *worship*, keeping in mind the temporal nature of the faith. Then we can move on to conduct, and finally to teaching.

(1) Through history Christians wish to tell about this great presence of Christ in their midst by recounting the historical events by which it came about. Thus *narrative* is born.

> No wonder, then, that the Church, wherever and whenever it worships God in Jesus' name, should consciously and emphatically proclaim that it is relying on, and incorporating into its worship, historical, particular events of divine origin, which first prompted the mystery of its worship and continue to prompt it. *The worship that is the central focus of the Christian community takes the shape of divinely authorized realistic narrative* (GE I 182).

Van Beeck takes the telling of this narrative as the "concrete shape of the Church's act of worship" (GE I 466). It is authorized because it is guided by the Holy Spirit and has as its inciting moment the divinely caused resurrection. It is "realistic" not because it tries to ape newspaper reporting or modern historical writing, but because it is *based* on "historical events that took place in real, historical time" (GE I 196).

It could seem that the process stands complete once the resurrection has taken place. Instead, Christ can be compared to the firstfruits of the eschatological harvest, "God's own guarantee that all of the world and humanity are to share in the divine nature" (GE I 178). While Christ's resurrection did fulfill humankind's cry for union with God, still the

> *fulfillment remains only inchoative: the new heaven and the new earth, the general resurrection, the fullness of the love, which comes from God and embraces all, are still outstanding.* At the heart of its worship, therefore, the Church is living off a world yet invisible, off a liberation that is incomplete, off a future that remains to be seen, off a love that for the time being is desire rather than embrace (GE I 218).

This "eschatological" nature of worship—Christ's completed presence to the world which is not yet complete—means that it must be urged toward completion by Christians through their life and teaching. True encounter with others is called forth, a communication with them which displays "testimonial autobiography." In addition to "the facts," the Christian narrative has always included within itself the meaning of the people who tell it and who hear it. Their lives help shape it and are shaped by it. Narrative remains incomplete if it is simply a set of words.

In this way the Christian narrative acts in the way that *"myth"* acts. The community's sense of identity and destiny is renewed in the presence of the divine, replenished in each retelling of the mythic narrative. Myth thus shapes the *present* of the community and its purpose for the *future* by rehearsing the significant *past* (GE I 196–198). Now Jesus' story, realistic and mythic at the same time, can be told on the authority of God, and thus serve as a witness to the world.[14]

Van Beeck's notion of "rhetoric," developed at length in *Christ Proclaimed*, will help us expand this notion. *Rhetoric*, he says, is "language as activity in a situation" (CP 101) or "the expression, in language, of the Christian *act* of faith-surrender" (CP 145). The use of language is taken together with the life of belief that stands behind it, and with the effect it has on its hearers—who themselves already participate in the belief system. Christian narrative as rhetoric, for instance, cannot be separated from surrender of the self to God.

> Far from being a bare commemoration, the story is eucharistic *anamnesis*—the sacrifice of praise and thanksgiving in which the Church also identifies herself under invocation of the Name of Jesus. The story carries commitment, and thus it is the primary Christian self-expression, or witness, to the world (CP 466).

This is the *"performative function"* of the narrative. The commitment "behind it" is a direct act of worshipful surrender to God the Father in the Spirit. The story is thus given force and boldness by the Spirit whose utterance it is. Van Beeck uses the Greek name *parrhesia* to refer to this confidence.[15]

> Hence, though the risen One is re-presented in the act of speaking of the *witnesses*, it is nonetheless *he*, in his presence in the Spirit, who stands behind the witness as the reality that accounts for the urgency and the *parrhesia* with which he speaks, quite apart from what he says (CP 251).

The story of Jesus is told in the Spirit, and the telling "is the ultimate glorification of the Father—worship wholly and totally adequate to God" (CP 350). Boldness and confidence characterize a story that simply has to be told, that is a response to the fresh and surprising revelation of God-with-us. It is both a worship (a) unto the glory of the Father and at the same time (b) a "witnessing self-expression of the Church" (CP 397). This witnessing brings us back to the other two moments of the church.

Worship is the source of witness (cf. GE I 196–205) and witness has two parts: conduct and teaching.

(2) So, let us proceed to the second moment, *conduct*. Since we have already spoken about it in the midst of the above, we can simply recapitulate. Narrative brings forth conduct because when it is told over a period of time it draws out from the tellers the kind of commitment it expresses. In a sense it cannot really be told except under the aegis of surrender, since removal of its performative reality would render it hollow. Thus, the narrative of the *past* demands to become an expressive vehicle of Christian commitment in the *present*, an imitation of Christ who waits for the church in the *future* (GE I 198–202).

When the narrative with its *parrhesia* shapes worship, it demands testing and verification by conduct. Van Beeck adds that within communal and private prayer it must show its moral integrity by its "confession of unworthiness and failure," an awe that its boldness comes not from itself but from God. This is simultaneously an admission that its conduct does not live up to the praise that it utters. Petition and intercession result from this admission. In relation to the world, the verification is a striving toward observable holiness of conduct (GE I 221–224).

Thus conduct has its finality and motive in worship. Virtuous living is the result of the Holy Spirit, who is sent out by the resurrection, and who is the bold source of worship's shape. Virtuous living depends on grace, which is a participation in divine life as found in worship (GE I 234–244).

(3) The great narrative also forms the core of the church's tradition of *teaching*, the third moment of the great dialectic.

> This story is significant narrative, and thus it is only natural that the question should arise: What does the story mean? The Church is called to account for her faith. When this happens, it is not enough to point out that God is being praised by the story, or that people are being called to believe; worship may be the original performative function of the story of Jesus, and those who believe may be unable to resist the urge to testify to their faith; the question about the meaning of the story *as such* remains, and it requires an answer (CP 359).

Both authoritative and non-authoritative theological statements result from this question. Faith could be called the *actus directus* of Christian understanding, while reflection on that understanding is the *actus reflexus*, at only one remove from the former. "Teaching" is the expression of this reflexive understanding of Christianity. It addresses the community's need for coherence and fidelity. "Teaching serves, not simply to keep the truth intact, but to guide the community on its way, as it travels through the vicissitudes of history to its fulfillment" (GE I 252).

At the immediate level, *creeds* throughout the centuries impress van Beeck as a central way in which the faith has been taught. He sees their early textual stability within predominantly oral cultures as an indication of their obligatory, normative character. They fill the community's need to get down to essentials, to state that which is not to be forgotten. Creeds never lost touch with worship, according to van Beeck. Their original home was in the baptismal rites, but they migrated to eucharist.[16] Because they are outcroppings of worship to begin with ("the original performative function of the story of Jesus"), van Beeck does not see them as foreign to it, but rather as proper and integral. He believes that the teaching of Christian faith must retrieve its connection with community worship (GE I 260–267). *Kerygma* (CP 347-348) too serves as a recital of the great things God has done. It is spoken in praise of God, through Jesus, on the strength of the Spirit (GE I 260-261).[17]

Theoretical theology has a bit more complicated connection with worship. Let us look briefly at christology (summarized in *Christ Proclaimed*—CP 466-467) for an example. In order to develop any theology, that is, any proper understanding of the narrative, one must *subtract* from the story its performative elements: the eschatological expectation, the humble surrender, the tone of worship and witness. This subtraction does not negate or undervalue these elements, it just enables the theologian to focus on the narrative alone.

In christology, subtraction yields a portrait of Jesus as interpersonal. His relationships to all persons and to the world form an important or essential portion of his individualized personality.

> The human person Jesus Christ is decisively determined by his total surrender to his Father. This surrender is not limited to an identifiable core of his person; rather, it is a mode of being related to God as his Father, which includes his entire person. It accounts not only for the actual, effective relationships which he engages in, but also, and far more profoundly, for the active

stance of relatedness with which Jesus presents himself to all. This *modus* of being-related to the Father, moreover, is actual and gracious (CP 430).

Even though the realistic narrative has universal Godly implications, it is still the story of Jesus' compassionate welcome of individuals, a life of total surrender out of love, even unto death. This focus clarifies the tradition and makes confident narrative possible.

We have seen, then, more detail how conduct and teaching emerge from worship. In van Beeck's writing there is a difficulty with the word worship. He uses this same word to mean on the one hand worshipful attitudes and on the other the liturgical act of worship. For instance, in the passage cited just previous to the last one, we cannot be clear as to the meaning of the word "worship." Does it mean liturgical worship, in which case the liturgical act achieves an indispensable importance, or does it refer to Christians' attitude of faith, confidence, and awe, wherever this might take place? Let us attempt to detect van Beeck's stance in this regard.

Van Beeck seems to imply the thesis we will be working toward, that the root of Christian life *in toto* can be nothing other than union with God, in Christ, through the Holy Spirit. Each stage of growth in this reality can be understood in this context. Beginning Christians are learning to approach God in this way by learning the elements of the great Tradition. Proficient Christians have taken the root meaning into their motivations, which flow into action. Mystic Christians have grown to the state of direct experience in prayer of their (and all Christians') unity with God. For each stage the root is present in its own way, and we could call that presence a kind of worship. The first response of all Christians to this wonderful gift is to tell about it, a reaction we call narrative. The event exists to be shared in story, not to be hoarded. The communitarian aspect implied in that statement means that liturgy is therefore the prime mode of experiencing and celebrating Jesus alive within us. If worship is the name of the Christian attitude in response to union with God, then liturgy is necessarily implied in it, indeed cannot be dispensed with.[18] We might diagram this schema as follows:

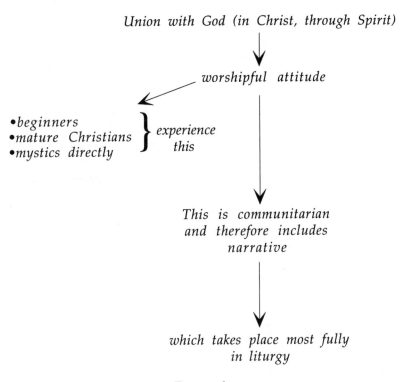

FIGURE 6

Thus van Beeck can say that "Christian worship and all Christian prayer is ultimately a matter of participating in an all-penetrating and all-encompassing *love*." Both liturgy and prayer are implied in the word "worship." Our arrows above do not indicate a succession of events, but different aspects of the same event.

We can summarize now our overview, which of course contains only glimpses of so expansive a theory as van Beeck's. We have seen that Christians respond to Jesus' life, death, and resurrection by means of narrative. This narrative forms the heart of worship. Christian conduct and teaching also are not only implied but always present in the true telling. That is to say, the story mandates an attitude of humble surrender before it, a "living it out." Otherwise the story cannot be told well. And it requires explanation and verification, which are "teaching." We saw also an eschatological orientation, which is the expectation of living up to the story by grace sometime in the future. Thus there is a rhetoric shaped by hope; Christians trust in the guidance of the Holy Spirit to bring it about.

We have done enough to situate liturgy in the life of the church. Clearly, with such an integral and important place for liturgy and worship, no concept of liturgy as *merely* a peak experience or an artful performance will satisfy. Because liturgy is the "wellspring" from which Christian life emerges; it represents the first dialectical moment of such life. Therefore its artistic quality will have to flow from its nature and not *vice versa*. To establish that nature in more detail we will leave the overview mode and concentrate in chapter five on the questions that concern us. How does the Holy Spirit guarantee the realistic narrative? Where did Jesus' relationality come from? What is the core, the underbedding of his surrender to the Father?

These questions will lead us in the direction of our own analysis. We will have to establish, for instance, the "connaturality" of God and human beings. In chapter one we saw that, in reproduction, men and women have a natural capacity to one with each other at their biological core. Chromosomes "know" what to do. Then we nuanced the term in detail when we came to the arts and Maritain's view of the artist. We realized that, for Maritain, the things of the world with which human beings have daily intercourse, do not *of themselves* possess a complete "connaturality" with the artist. If they are to enter significant union with the artist they have to be elevated by the consciousness of the creative artist. Now we have to face the question of God and human persons. Is it possible to say that God and persons are connatural to each other—God who is the highest and most rarified being of all, and ordinary folks, whose relationships with each other are at best checkered? Scripture and the church tell us that commerce does indeed come about between the two, and therefore they must have some kind of connaturality. What kind? Do persons merely receive the *influence* of grace, in the way that a nail receives blows from a hammer, or is there a much more intimate union? Do Christians in fact receive the very *self-communication* of God's being, as some theologians claim? If we can find a harbor for this viewpoint, we will have launched the liturgy, or to change images, will have found its conceiving moment.

A brief sample of this kind of thought would be the following: Jesus' unrestricted openness to the Father results in his very identity. His oneness with his *abba* is so complete that everything he is comes from that Source. There is such a creative oneing that Jesus himself is engendered by it. This making of Jesus is heralded in the great narrative: the Holy Spirit overshadows Mary and a child is conceived. From there the conception/gestation/birth model becomes literal. But also given to Jesus in his conception is the same unrestricted openness that the Father has. Thus a new project enters our description, Jesus' opening to all people and to the world that surrounds them. His openness to others results finally in a surrender all the way to death—closing no portal of his life to the entrance of good *and of evil* coming from people and the world. His love, since it is utter and Godly, cannot be annihilated, and so the resurrection results. The resurrection indicates that he remains alive even after his death, in the Spirit of relatedness that he pours out upon all people. Thus the resurrection enters history, and it makes its way down the river of time. This Spirit is the new sperm that ones with the fertile soul of people of the church. Like Mary they ponder in silence and then bring to birth the great narrative, with its performative elements of worship and witness (= conduct and teaching) through time.

The central thesis of this book is that *every significant union is generative.* Though we first experienced this principle in human conception, gestation, and birth, and we have used this reality as a metaphor throughout Part One, analogy of generative union is what we have been after, not just the metaphor of eros. In chapter four, after some reflections on the fact of God's oneing with the world (and therefore the prior connaturality that must have been given), we will attend to the series of consequential unions that God undertook and undertakes with the persons of the earth. We will begin with the most momentous oneings of all, those in the Trinity itself, and then with the union most significant to the peoples of the world, the incarnation. From there we will move on to Jesus' life, death, and resurrection; the sending of the Spirit as an offer of bestowal upon (union with) all persons, and the resulting birth of the liturgy itself.

But let us not get ahead of ourselves. If the Spirit and the people become our candidates for parents of the liturgy, we must ask first of all about connaturality.

NOTES

1. Hoffman's statement was made in a different context than the present discussion, so of course he is not implying that a planner should be the main artist or creator of the liturgy.

2. One way out of this dilemma would be to minimize an originating artist's part in the liturgy. This would involve humility, a movement away from egoism, "self"-expression, and so on. But even in the most anonymous work of art, as we have seen, the artist's soul, as opposed to his or her ego or personality, acts as one of the two principal agents in the (co-) creation of the work. As long as there is a primary artist in liturgy, this will apply. If it does not, then the artist in question is not at the creative center of the purported aesthetic event called liturgy, but plays an extrinsic role. Then either we conceive the liturgy as having nothing but an accidental coordination, or else the question reasserts itself: who is the primary artist of the liturgy?

3. "Those who lead worship must create conditions of possibility for those in the assembly which are similar to that created by actors *for their audience*. Each creates a virtual image *for the perceivers* to enter, a world-out-of-time for the sake of a real world in the future. One difference, of course, is that in ritual there is a 'performing' audience" (Collins 1983, 113, italics mine). Collins surely had in mind the influential book by Bernard Huibers called *The Performing Audience.* Huibers, however, is trying to establish ways in which the assembly can sing, not to designate them as observers. Cf. Huibers 1969.

Scott suggests also that the congregation members become primary actors, performing before "the true audience, namely, God" (Scott 1980, 104). One goal of the present book is to establish that God does indeed listen to the assembly's prayers, but it seems far-fetched to designate God therefore as "audience."

4. The job of liturgy, Lawrence Hoffman says, is to help establish the image of God. He sketches the master images of various eras: "what God enthroned in glorious light was to worshipers of the second century; what God transcendent was to nineteenth- and early twentieth-century Europe; that God *we find in intimate community*" (Hoffman 1988, 174, italics mine; cf. also 166–178).

5. One author, Thomas Day, urges *mediocre music* as a way to keep music in its place; we presume that, for him, music with only middling worth would not endanger liturgy's integrity because it would not be artistic in the first place (Day 1990). While Day draws attention to numerous problems about liturgy today, his solutions are often at the level of this suggestion. We might recall that Zwingli, alone among the reformers, banned music entirely and had the great organs destroyed, presumably because he knew the claim of excellent music upon the

attention. He was also a musician, which may account for his aware-ness of this danger.

6. Robert Taft speaks of "soft points" within the developing liturgy: spots within a ritual that were not yet canonically hardened (see for instance Taft 1984, 161, 168). Thus the *Sanctus* could be inserted into (a soft point in) the Anaphora late in the latter's development. E. C. Ratcliff produced an elaborate argument that the early third century *Apostolic Tradition*, which lacks a *Sanctus*, originally *ended* with one (Ratcliff 1950, 29–36, 125–134). See Jasper and Cumings 1987, 33, for a brief evaluation of this opinion.

I think there were "soft *layers*" also. In the east, for instance, by the middle ages when the liturgy had become fixed, there came to be extensive *interpretations* of it. In other words, instead of adding new material to the texts and actions, creativity added a new layer of interpretation (e. g., raising of the bread as the raising of Jesus on the cross; the transfer of gifts to the table of preparation as the ascension). This "representational thinking" became integrated with the liturgy without adding anything to the "horizontal" layer, and was therefore a "vertical" addition or layer (see for instance Schulz 1980, 100-131). When interpretation had run its course—by the 14th century with Nicolas Cabasilas—there came a third layer: depiction of the liturgy *as including* the second vertical layer. For instance, Christ and Bishop were painted together carrying out the liturgy. The same could be shown for music, which began as the unaccompanied, single line called chant. When the great system of chants became canonically hardened (and after *tropes* had been inserted into soft places), the layer of *polyphony* came into play. This is literally a vertical layer of melody added to the original chant without any horizontal change in the chant (cf., for example, Crocker 1966, 60–68).

7. Van Beeck is very careful to delimit the sense of the phrase. "The maxim *lex orandi lex credendi* is not a general norm that can be indis-criminately invoked to draw doctrine from each and every text used in liturgical settings. It is a general norm only in the sense that it points to Christ, present in the Spirit, as the ultimate authorization of all of the Church's worship" (GE I 226). He alludes to three norms, derived from the A.D. 440 document called the *Indiculus* of Prosper of Aquitaine. The usage must be in the area of *episcopal* (or presidential) prerogative at public liturgical functions; it must have *apostolic tradition* behind it; it must be in *universal* use" (ibid.). Kilmartin is more general on this point, saying that the liturgy is the most important place in which the Christian community expresses its nature: it is the symbolic expression of the community's self-understanding. Thus the two expressions "the law of prayer is the law of belief" and "the law of belief is the law of prayer" are interdependent (CL I 94–97).

8. According to van Beeck, a "moment" is for Hegel one of the partial pursuits that make up philosophy as a whole. Each actually *comprises* the whole (in the unique way of the part) and it enters into dynamic relationship with the other moments. One cannot exist without the other. Parts of a whole help one another come forth, and they refer back to each other. This organic inter-relationship of moments is what we are calling dialectic (GE I 209–210).

9. Quotation is from *Dei Verbum*: The Dogmatic Constitution on Divine Revelation (Vatican II), p. 8. According to van Beeck, the "great Tradition comprises, first of all, Scripture: Scripture read, by way of *lectio divina*, as the living Word of God, within the community of faith, and understood in the context of that community's present experience of the Holy Spirit; Scripture read, too, in its organic entirety, and reverenced as the first and original fruit of the community's Tradition of worship, conduct, and teaching, as well as the abiding canon by which the authority of all subsequent Tradition must be measured. . . . Furthermore, the great Tradition is the Tradition of worship, life, and teaching of the undivided Church. This implies that this book regards the record of the Christian Tradition before the Schism that divided West from East in the eleventh century as especially authoritative. But even after the Schism, East and West continued to cultivate what was in fact the great Tradition" (GE I 6–7).

10. The diagram makes clear what the sentence does not, that the structure quite interestingly mimics the procession model of the Trinity in the West, in which the Word proceeds from the Father, and the Holy Spirit spirates from both Father and Word.

11. Van Beeck structures chapters nine and ten of *God Encountered I* to reflect the dialectic. He speaks of Christian worship (first as it is related to conduct, and then to teaching), then of conduct (first as related to worship, then to teaching), and finally of teaching (as it is related to conduct, then to worship). He thus enfleshes his hypothesis in what we can well call a performative method: one finds it in the manner as well as in the telling.

12. Van Beeck traces the idea of resurrection to Israel's faith in God's absolute mastery of life and death. As such it conveys an integrated vision of God's design for humanity and the world across space and time (GE I 186-187).

13. Van Beeck says that the Resurrection is a metaphor (GE I 186), which is to say its full meaning depends on the realization of its bond with human concerns (CP 141). Though he does not seem to reject outright the possibility of physical resurrection, he clearly holds that the full meaning of the resurrection event must not be identified with a mere physical event. "Historical" records end at Jesus' execution and burial. The next event that can be established is statements by wit-

nesses: "He is not here. He is risen" (CP 255–256). But in a more profound sense, to assign the resurrection a mere place in the sequence of events would impoverish its real meaning, which is "the presence, in the Spirit, of the living Lord to the Church" (CP 322). This presence is connected with *eschatology*; that is, it is aims toward the future rather than just reciting past events. Van Beeck calls Pannenberg's consistently eschatological christology "an important event in the history of christology" (CP 323). It would seem, therefore, that rather than denying a historical bodily resurrection of Jesus, van Beeck is instead denying its importance. The resurrection is a metaphor for Jesus alive and with us, in the Spirit, today and always. Historical importance belongs to the witnessing "rhetoric" (in van Beeck's sense of the word), since, as we will see, it is the birth of the narrative which will found worship, conduct, and teaching.

14. Myth, of course, is enjoying a deep-rooted renewal of interest at the present time. For an exhaustive survey of the approach to it by various disciplines, see Doty 1986.

15. Van Beeck refers to Ian Ramsey on religious language, and Donald Evans' analysis of performative language. In general, statements perform a function besides merely denoting specific meanings. Religious language is expressive of a committed and full interpretation of reality which may not be present in the literal meanings. It performs the function of carrying the hearer beyond the literal meaning. Thus for van Beeck christological terminology is not meant just to present a "pictorially adequate representation of the truth," but to "help evoke the religious disclosure" (CP 77). Also, there is a self-involvement of the speaker, who is more than a conveyer of facts. This is true of God: "God does not (or does not merely) provide supernatural information concerning Himself, expressed in flat statements of fact; He 'addresses' man in an 'event' or 'deed' which commits Him to man and which expresses His inner Self" (Evans 1963, 14). For one treatment of the above, see (CP 73–79). For a summary of opinions on religious language, cf. Worgul 1985, chapter 5.

16. "The creed was one of the elements used *in worship* to impart to the baptizands their full *deputatio ad cultum*, that is to say, their *entitlement to participate in worship*—principally the Eucharist, which would follow immediately upon the rite of baptism. And the central action of that Eucharist, the presidential prayer, would include the solemn rehearsal of the christological narrative inserted, in summary form, into the baptismal creed" (GE I 262). In volume two, he speaks of the creed as a performative language act, like a "testimonial autobiography" (GE II §75,4), and as "traveling equipment" of the Christian on the way, a "wayfarer's charter," and a symbol of the Christian longing for God (GE II §77, 3).

Since volume two was not yet published at the time of writing the present book, my privilege of using portions of that volume came through the courtesy of Fr. van Beeck. The pagination of this pre-publication copy will not remain the same in the published version, of course, so I will cite portions of that volume by means of the excellent and consistent outline numbering system van Beeck has applied to the text.

17. Van Beeck credits C. H. Dodd's study of apostolic preaching with the origin of the term *kerygma*, which means "message." The kerygma, however, is more than just the apostolic preaching; it is the Christian *homologia*, that is, the essence of the great narrative we have been discussing.

18. cf. van Beeck 1985, 61-67.

CHAPTER FOUR

THE GREAT PLAN

I ask not only on behalf of these, but also on behalf of
those who will believe in me through their word, that
they may all be one. As you, Father, are in me and I am
in you, may they also be in us, so that the world may
believe that you have sent me (John 17:20-21).

In the act of physical conception we saw clearly that only
beings having physical connaturality with each other can "come
together as two to make three." Human sperm and ova lean out
to each other. Their most minute designs mirror each other,
provide the opening and the push toward union. Our question
here turns around the connaturality of the human being for that
which is in no way physical. Can the nature of a human being
exhibit openness to the eternal God such that a oneing can take
place?

Our first impulse would be to say no. The differences are too
great, no matter what people claim they experience. Are we
right? In order to understand whether both God and congregation have place at the very center of liturgical creation, we must
begin to ask whether God and human beings can come together
at all. A God who is transcendent and wholly other may live
somewhere far beyond, unreachable by any created agent. In
short, we must look at what is called the problem of nature and
grace.[1] We will not undertake technical considerations, but rather
put forward indicators and suggestive examples.

163

I. Connaturality

Rosemary Haughton has done major work in charting unity and separations in the universe. Her quasi-poetic viewpoint has great force, and in a way, it serves as another overview of Christ-life. Only a sketch of her thought is possible in these pages, but the reader will find its influence throughout the remaining discussion, even though here we will draw mainly the conclusion that not only is connaturality possible, it is the very stuff of all reality.

In *The Passionate God* Haughton uses the metaphor of "spheres." These characterize the basic nature of reality and are in part porous, part closed. Both halves of the equation are important in the breakthrough that she calls *exchange* between spheres. Beings of every stripe must let go of what they are and what they possess, in order to pass it on to others. And they must open themselves appropriately, so that they can receive from the other. This is exchange. When exchange fails, the pressure of growth within a sphere seeks a weak point in the increasingly non-porous sphere. When a boundary yields to the pressure, there is a *breakthrough* to exchange.[2] This thesis allows many capital insights, some of which now follow.

Human growth: Human beings can exist in a state of undifferentiated oneness with a beloved or with God. The spheres are not able to define themselves in such a state, and therefore the oneness has to be sundered so that the parties can "differentiate"—since love is a union of *differentiated* beings, not oneness to the point of identity. In the best circumstances, growing differentiation from one's mother, for instance, does not represent a choice between good and evil but a choice between the known good and an unknown one. The infant's undifferentiated oneness with the mother is well known and comfortable, but continued too long it wreaks havoc. Differentiation is a step into the unknown, and so is risky. If forced it will feel like a separation and a deprivation, in which case it is not an example of exchange. Exchange in this case means becoming one's own self and by that process being able to open to the other. Refusal of exchange makes life into something which exists for itself instead of in exchange.

Sin: There are two key aspects to exchange: to receive, and to let go of what one receives. If I grasp and take instead of receiving, then I am hardening the boundaries of my life. If, instead of letting what I receive rest lightly in my hand, I clutch it and hoard it, I have refused exchange in order to swell the proportions of my life, to exceed my creaturely condition and ultimately compete with God. In the western world the characterization of Satan has always had this face: one who intends ultimately to displace God by becoming bigger and better. Sin is, at root, the refusal of exchange. In it, love appears as conquest instead of opening. *Original sin* means our desire to stay with the known good. In this state, exchange seems evil, something that causes deprivation. The opening of one sphere to another then results in fear, since everything is *mine* and can be lost, leaving me alone.

> Sin is "in" human beings, in their total being, and it is, in every form it takes, basically a refusal, a deflecting back into the particular being of the energy of life whose nature is to be poured out. The very energy of sin, its power and malevolence, is in its origin the power whose nature is Love, the Spirit (Haughton 1981, 112–113).

Thus we find not two powers in competition—sin and love—but one: the power of creative love which the creature either accepts or refuses. Acceptance leads one inexorably to "the roots of life where the deeper exchanges take place, where human passion embraces and is embraced by God in the joy of differentiated love" (Haughton 1981, 124). Refusal diverts the same power inward.

Jesus: Haughton has a most compelling interpretation of the temptations in the Gospel of Luke.

> "Reading" through human minds, Satan recognized power in Jesus, on a scale he had not hitherto encountered. The idea that it could be the power of love was ruled out because love does not exist for him [Satan]; therefore it must be the kind of power he recognizes and understands very well: the power to dominate and manipulate—to "manage" the entire system. Satan does not, of course, "manage" it as totally as he thinks, because there is this other element in the situation which he is incapable of seeing—the element of love (Haughton 1981, 118).

If Jesus is one of the greatest "receivers" on earth, Satan must prevent the great exchange from happening in him. Jesus must refuse exchange and be co-opted into the great scheme of aggrandizement and competition with God. Then he can be plundered at will. The temptations in the desert are Satan's first attempt to do this, but Jesus refuses them. Satan presumes that Jesus is not as powerful as he seems, and leaves him "to return at the appointed time."[3]

The appointed time comes in the form of trial, torture, and execution. Diametrically opposed ways of life have to come into ultimate conflict. Satan must stop the breaching of spheres and Jesus must accomplish it. Satan had to reinterpret Jesus' life without the premise of love. For his part, Jesus understood intimately the power of evil because he lived more closely with it than others do: his "self" was *the same substance* in intensity as "the perverted energy one of whose names is Satan" (Haughton 1981, 148).

> The impulse of his whole being is a love poured out in detailed, personal care as it was poured out in the gift of his body to destruction. He did not merely surrender to death; he gave himself away, body and mind and human heart, all one gift (Haughton 1981, 148).

Jesus not only acts as the "great receiver," accepting from the Father all that he is, he also acts as the great giver. He pours out his whole being. He "lets go." In order to do this he opens himself in another way. He takes down the barriers not only to God but to all human persons. By this stroke, Jesus opens himself to the evil introduced throughout the whole universe by refusal. Fully human and in solidarity with all humanity, he finds that humanity has blocked the total self-giving of God-the-Source into human life, and therefore also the return of this love to God. To open the way for return, to allow the breakthrough, he has to accept everything it means to be human, including death, discouragement, unlove, betrayal, sin. Because the stability of exchange is real (throughout history), Jesus' breakthrough will be a breakthrough for the whole human race. Instead of clinging to the precious possessions of his own life against the great winds of sin, he throws open the doors and lets go.

Haughton suggests a simple image for the crucifixion/resurrection, which we can put in our own words. Everything that is not love could be said to have "handles" on it. Reputation, possessions, career, appearances—even marriage, devotion to children, noble ideals—all can be grasped and reinterpreted to mean self interest and refusal. "I'm getting what I want out of it," we might say. Satan—and Jesus—knew about the handles. These could be found even on Jesus' preaching, which could be a way to show off; on his "career" of itinerant preaching, which could mean power over the people; on his exultation by the crowds, which could prove the power and assuage the ego. Love is the one reality that has no handles because it is at root an opening of the spheres, a complete receiving and a complete giving. It cannot be "managed." Satan has interpreted everything about Jesus as "handleable," and now, with great passion and angst, Jesus surrenders. Grasp and take anything you can, he says.

> And into all the channels laid open by love the power of destruction thrust itself, to seize the very citadel of that power. It found nothing there. All was destroyed except love, and love is "nothing" to the intelligence and grasp of evil (Haughton 1981, 151).

Satan comes to the tabernacle, the inner sanctum of Jesus' life and discovers these doors open too. He lustfully enters but finds nothing at all inside. Only if love were itself power and grasping would it have handles. Satan therefore cannot grasp it, cannot see it at all. In this last great struggle love, therefore, evades the grip of evil.

> The Christian assertion, repeated liturgically again and again, is that by dying he "destroyed death." This is literally true, because the power of death is sin, and sin is that "defendedness" of human nature which keeps love confined. Where there is no sin, death finds nothing to "grip." Love is exchange of life, and sin, which blocks that exchange, is the place where death can hold on. In dying, Jesus, as it were, released the grip of death's power *to be evil* (Haughton 1981, 151-152).

The resurrection begins here and makes its way through time. Jesus is alive because the most inward secret of his identity, received freely and fully from God, is love. Human breakthrough, breaching the walls of sin and self aggrandizement, has been accomplished and now "rides time like riding a river," in Hopkins' words. The whole human race could join in the resurrection, but this "depends on the free response of human beings for its accomplishment" (Haughton 1981, 167).

Obviously, Haughton's vision far outstrips the purpose for which we are using it here, the pursuit of connaturality. Her poetic vision will inform this whole chapter. But if we narrow the question temporarily, we might ask Haughton whether nature and grace are made for each other. She would surely say that they are, but are held separate by compounded refusal. In a sense, Jesus was the one person in whom nature and grace truly cohered, truly broke through the walls that separate them. In the language we have been using, nature and grace are *connatural* for the rest of us, ripe for union, but only when the breakthrough can occur. We will have to ask after other authors to find the manner in which such breakthrough is possible. Haughton's difficult writing is itself passionate and stirring. Perhaps it "performs" the title under which it was written.

Let us, then, take a second approach. If exchange between human beings and God is so central to life, what allows it? First let us establish the fact and then the manner. Van Beeck clearly reports catholic tradition as insisting on the interaction between nature and grace (GE II §78, 1). In a word, "God most high is also God most nigh" (GE II §79, 2). Human beings have a *capacity* for actual sharing in God's being by grace (GE II §77, 1), and this means a *fundamental harmony* and concordance between the created order and divine life (GE II §78, 3). We can go a step further with van Beeck to understand. He notes that the Manichaeans of Augustine's time interpreted the universe as torn, victim of a "continuous standoff between God and Satan, light and darkness, spirit and matter" (GE II §79, 3a). This position sharpened Augustine's wits to reflect on the relation of God to all that is not God. He says that nothing can be the opposite of God. You can have cold as the opposite of hot, slow as the contrary of quick, white as opposed to black, and so on. But since God is the one who *is* without qualification, then the only opposition to God would be what *is not*. Since "what is not" does not exist, nothing is the opposite of God.[4] We might conclude with Maritain that whatever "is," at whatever level, has a connaturality with whatever else "is," even if that connaturality has to be elevated.

In another approach, van Beeck says that

> human nature is indeed marked by a native, dynamic luminosity that betrays an affinity with God. An inner light equips every human person for an understanding of (in principle) all things; single experiences of understanding can be so real that, whenever they occur, they can feel so delightfully genuine and authentic that they seem innate (GE II §87, 2a).

Human nature is defined not by fullness but by the quest for it; in fact, we could characterize Christian life as one holy desire.

It is grace that enables us to freely move by means of this desire toward God in total faith and abandon (GE II §87-88).[5] Here van Beeck seems to be echoing Karl Rahner, who founds his anthropology on the desiring openness to the supreme being.

We will have space later for a slightly more adequate treatment of Rahner's doctrine. Here let us note that he shares Maritain's (Thomistic) presupposition that the intellect can know whatever exists, but he transmutes it into what we might call question theory, or the theology of quest. I quest after whatever is because I already have a preconscious grasp of being (since my own consciousness itself exists), and I seek whatever will actualize this "pre-grasp." Thus I have a natural desire not only for *things* that exist, but for the most perfect realization of being, God. This is my nature. But if I could find God by use of my natural capacity, I would in a sense be equal to God. I could initiate a meeting without need for a prior move on God's part. Since this seems to compromise God, Roman Catholic theology holds that my nature must be *elevated* by grace in order to actually seek the real God, as opposed to seeking some possible fulfillment of my natural longing. Thus nature is perfected by grace, which elevates the human being's natural openness to all that is. Rahner changed the course of Catholic theology by his position that grace is the communication of God's own self to the individual's preconscious, resulting not in a knowledge or concept of God, but in an elevation *of the seeking* that is natural to that person.[6] Thus van Beeck's "luminosity that betrays an affinity to God" echoes Rahner, and testifies to a connaturality between God and human beings that is not completely "natural" because it is an elevation of nature's innate potential by grace. Haughton's expansive theory seems to assume but not deal directly with this need to be elevated.

For a third consideration of the possibility of union between God and the world we turn to an expert witness. If we find any first-hand witness to the merging of divine and human realities anywhere, then all argument about nature versus grace would be nulled. It is possible because it is (*ab esse ad posse*). In an old joke someone asks the Kansas farmer whether he believes in baptism. "Believe it?" he replies, "I've *seen* it!" This illustrates the problem, of course, with witnesses. While they "see" the event, the question is how they understand what they observe. Are they interpreting clearly what they think they see? The farmer bypasses the meaning of the event called "baptism" and thereby misses the point of the question.[7]

Can we trust our witness? The union of God and person takes place below the level of objective representation and therefore cannot be proved. But it can be observed and calibrated respectively by one who is deeply involved in it. In art it is the artist speaking through the artwork. In matters of union between God and humans, it is the mystic speaking in figures and parables.

Our trust of the mystic therefore revolves around our insertion into the whole life of the church. We then see the *place* of the mystic in the scheme of things.

> There is, in the great Tradition of the undivided Church, embodied especially in the tradition of ascetical and mystical theology, a consistent tendency, identifiable from the late second century on, to consider the Christian life, not as a reality in which all Christians participate in one identical, undifferentiated fashion, but as dynamic *process* by which Christians are *led* to God (GE I 268).

This process of insertion does not imply that some Christians are more in possession of the faith than others, since a person's "innate potential for human and religious growth" is actualized first by his or her thoroughgoing initial conversion. On this basis van Beeck says that the whole of the faith is actualized *mutatis mutandis* in each developmental stage.

After listing various three-stage schemas from the past, van Beeck tries to correlate growth stages with the threefold aspects of the church we have already looked at: worship, life, and teaching. To receive *teaching* one would be to some extent less knowledgeable. Therefore learning is most appropriate at the beginning stage. Christian *life* means a people on the way to the eschatological kingdom. The church is not yet identical to this kingdom and therefore the middle stage is implied, in which proficient Christians carry forward the great Tradition through action, shaping the history of salvation in the present moment, operating more from inner motivation than ecclesiastical authority.

And Christian *worship* conveys the reality that

> God is the central focus as well as the all-encompassing reality of the Christian faith: God approached with awe as well as confidence and praised, thanked, and implored in the Spirit, under invocation of Jesus Christ and in union with him.

> Without worship, Christianity ceases to be faith in God, that is
> to say, it ceases to be religious faith, except in the most theoreti-
> cal of senses (GE I 280).

As we saw above, mystics show forth this relation to God to best
advantage. Of course they need the requirements of conduct and
teaching as well. Experienced Christians discover that the road
of virtue is endless and wearying, and so they want more: God
approached in worship. And learners, like their counterparts,
are called to live the commandments, and to worship in Spirit
and truth (GE I 285–286). In this way the mystical union is not an
"exclusive prerogative" of the small number of mystics. It is
open to all in the eucharistic activity called thanksgiving. This is
the "Christ-mysticism" of the church at large (GE II §90, 6).[8]

What, then, does a privileged witness say about union with
God? Van Beeck translates the writing of the Dutch mystic Jan
van Ruusbroec. Ruusbroec writes of

> the nobility which we have, by nature, in the essential unity of
> our spirit, where it is naturally united with God. This makes us
> neither holy nor blessed, for all persons, good and evil, have
> this within themselves. It is, however, the first cause of all
> holiness and of all bliss. And this is the meeting and the union
> between God and our spirit in (our) bare nature (GE II §90, 3,
> toward the end).[9]

Van Beeck's translation brings out the place nature plays in this
union with God. As van Beeck puts it, the union with Christ "is
in its turn undergirded at the level of human nature itself: Christian prayer and Christian service are deeply natural" (GE II §90,
3). As we have seen, human nature consists of openness to God,
a kind of attunement, a *natural* desire for what God must be.
According to Ruusbroec, mystics discover God "in the very act
of establishing them in the divine image and likeness that defines their created being as such—their 'bare essence'" (GE II
§90, 4, toward the beginning).[10]

Ruusbroec, through van Beeck, seems to presage Rahner's
anthropology, as noted above, but perhaps to go a step beyond,
at least in presentation.

> We are naturally prepared to meet Christ as he comes to meet
> us. This means that the spiritual *eros* with which all human
> persons seek God, in virtue of the divine likeness that is theirs,
> is not a faceless homing instinct automatically impelling them
> to reunite with an impersonal divine Prototype. Quite the

> contrary: it is radically personalized. ... For human persons to
> be created in the image and likeness of God means: to be
> naturally stamped with the visage of Christ, the divine *Logos*
> (GE II §5, toward the beginning).

Creation itself, especially creation of human beings, is *personal*, because in it the Logos acts in the manner of relationship. We could have no better statement of the connaturality of human persons and God.

II. Theology of the Trinity

Perhaps now we are ready to summarize the wide and interconnected insights of our presentation so far, in preparation for our treatment of the Trinity. Haughton, we saw, does not deal with the question of connaturality directly, but her theology proclaims it anyway. No matter by what means, the "spheres" of all reality do stand open to one another—at times, and under the influence of breakthrough. In human terms, exchange between the spheres must take place, on pain of thwarting the great plan of love. Sin, or more specifically refusal, rejects exchange and closes the creature upon itself. In Luke's Gospel this closure, which results in competition with God, forms Satan's basic plan. Jesus takes not only the goodness of humanity to himself, but also and importantly the evil, and through it provides the breakthrough for all peoples. Haughton's most basic assumption, that of exchange, thus fulfills completely the need of our theory to find real reception of the Godly reality by Jesus (and therefore by human beings).

We discovered Augustine saying that God has no opposite, and therefore cannot constitute an antithesis to human beings. Then we traced briefly one root for van Beeck's position, that of Karl Rahner. The human person is intrinsically open to being, no matter how high or low the level of that being. This would seem to indicate that therefore a person is able to receive God. Rahner agrees with the tradition of the church, however, that no encounter with God can take place in the manner of a scientist discovering an inert substance. Encounter is personal, and for that reason must be *initiated* by God. Further, even as the material object has to be "elevated" to the conscious realm in order to become one with consciousness—though it already has a passive potential to be known—so the person must be "elevated" into the divine realm in order to activate his or her capacity to be one with God. This is a long way of saying that Sammy or Suzy must be elevated by grace in order to encounter God. In other words, connaturality does exist, once God has graciously raised a person to the divine realm.

When we sought the witness of an expert, a mystic, we saw that Christians from each of van Beeck's "moments," each in his or her own way, experience the worshipful attitude that results from their union with God in Christ. Mystics experience it most directly, but their stance in life cannot be separated from the learning and the conduct of the other moments. Mystics' response to union with God lies at the heart of the narrative outcry that worship compels: liturgy. When we listened briefly to Ruusbroec's testimony, we found him speaking of a "meeting" and "union between God and our spirit in (our) bare nature." Perhaps this takes us further than this section needed to go, but in any case, the union of God and mystic gives high testimony to the *possibility* of such union. In other words, connaturality cannot be denied.

The time has arrived, then, to describe the *manner* of union between God and people. We will best be served by a theology that concentrates most fully on union: the theology of the Trinity. This accounting will require the remainder of the present chapter, and we will have to see first why traditional theories of the Trinity might seem the very last place to look.

A. Trinity as Irrelevant

A revolution in trinitarian thinking has quietly burst in upon the church. Its form derives in part from early Church thinking, in which trinitarian being correlates closely with the life of people on earth. This new and old thinking should provide the most fruitful approach to liturgy today, especially in view of the hypothesis we are pursuing.

It is only fair, however, to begin with evidence to the contrary. If union of the trinitarian God with people is so rich a topic, then why has trinitarian doctrine seemed so obscure and far-removed? Why did it become an erudite doctrine interesting mainly to intellectuals? The present author was taught in his youth that to *begin* understanding the Trinity he would have to spend the same amount of time it would take a sparrow to wear down Mt. Everest by dragging its claws across the peak once every century. Trinity has seemed unrelated not only to liturgy but to life in general. To some it has seemed a doctrine in "defeat" for more than a millennium. We have said that human nature stands ready to receive God, but can the trinitarian God mingle with creatures? Has theology allowed enough room for God the transcendent to be present in people, no matter how much elevation they receive?

Catherine LaCugna details her theory of trinitarian defeat in the book *God For Us* (GFU).[11] We must spend some time with her in order to see the universal import of the otherwise trendy image of "defeat." The first half of her book gives the history of trinitarian doctrine in this regard. She begins with its early buildup, especially a certain ambiguity regarding the term "Father."[12] In the Bible, she says, this word applied to God as such, not to the first person of the still to be articulated triad. But no other existent could be conceived as the equal of God without ruining the idea of God. When "God" came to mean the first person, then, it was the Father who could have no equal. How then could the second person be equal to the Father? In the early fourth century the theologian Arius took scandal at such a possibility, and held the Son—and of course Jesus of Nazareth—to be *subordinate* to the originating Father. Here is one of the few extant texts from Arius:

> God being the cause of all is without beginning, most alone; but the Son, begotten by the Father, created and founded before the ages, *was not before he was begotten.* Rather, the Son begotten timelessly before everything, alone was caused to subsist by the Father. For he is not everlasting or co-everlasting or unbegotten with the Father. Nor does he have being with the Father (GFU 31).[13]

Councils, bishops, and theologians recoiled from a Christ who was not divine, who therefore could not save us. They moved to counter Arius, a move which was brilliant but which began to distance the Trinity from earth. The Council of Nicaea taught in 325 that Christ is of one essence or being (*ousia*) with the Father. This left unanswered the question about Jesus' humanity, which could not be equal to the Father. Athanasius and the "Cappadocians" (Basil, Gregory of Nyssa, Gregory of Nazianzus) responded that Christ of the Trinity and Christ of this world are to be considered differently. The trinitarian Christ is of one essence with the Father, but on earth Jesus was a union of divine and human natures. Thus the second person was in no way subordinate, while Jesus the human being could be at once subordinate to and equal to the Father.

By this stroke there began an abiding interest in the Trinity *as it is in itself*, in distinction from the Trinity as it comes into oneness with the world. In time, words for each view of the Trinity gained currency. "Immanent Trinity" meant the Trinity in its "inner" dimensions; "economic Trinity" (from the Greek *oikonomia*, originally meaning the administration and management of a household by plan or design, but used to mean the plan of salvation: how God administers the divine plan) referred to the Trinity as present in the world. The immanent Trinity could now be studied separately from and without necessary reference to the economic one.[14]

As regards the immanent Trinity, the Cappadocians introduced a (neo-Platonic) idea that the persons *emanate* from each other. The schema of the immanent Trinity was seen in a linear fashion:[15]

God the Father $\longrightarrow$ *Son* $\longrightarrow$ *Holy Spirit* $\longrightarrow$ *World*

FIGURE 7

In the early fifth century Augustine continued speculation on the immanent Trinity. Two main ideas are important to us here: relationality and psychological similarity. (1) Augustine, trying to fathom how three persons could exist within one God, introduced the analogy of relations. Father, Son, and Holy Spirit receive their differentiation solely by their relation to each other, and otherwise are the same essence.[16] (2) The "psychological analogy" arose through Augustine's own mystical introspection. Prayer, considered as contemplation or a "journey of the soul inward," discovers that one's soul is created in the image of the Trinity. Knowledge and love are then apt analogies for the inner constitution of the immanent Trinity. A person is of one unified substance, but still has self-knowledge, knowledge of the other, and love of the other. These do not disturb the essential oneness of that person. For Augustine "there is no other way to 'know' the unknowable One except through mystical union" (GFU 92). Would the soul have been able to know God if there had never been an incarnation in Jesus? LaCugna says that Augustine admitted this possibility in his early works (GFU 101)![17] We might state the case as follows: in order to preserve unity in God yet still retain God's intimate connection to creatures, Augustine seemed to de-emphasize the active roles of the trinitarian persons in Jesus and Church, and gave them a more passive presence in the inner shape of the soul.

De-emphasis meant that the Trinity-in-general originated many of God's actions. One could *"appropriate"* these activities, however, to one or the other person.

> It would be correct according to Augustine's theology to say that the Trinity creates, the Trinity redeems, the Trinity divinizes. It would also be correct to *appropriate* creation to the Father, redemption to the Son, and divinization to the Spirit (GFU 100; italics mine).

But in the Bible, God the Father is father of Christ, rather than "a non-specific God-person who, by being personal, reveals the divine essence as such" (ibid.).[18] LaCugna urges this statement, and holds that the missions of the Son and Spirit in Scripture are each an identifying characteristic of a unique person (a *proprium*), and cannot be appropriated.

Historically, then, according to LaCugna, the immanent Trinity grew in importance, but its relation to the world began to pale. The immanent Trinity could now receive this familiar diagram:

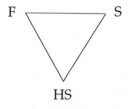

FIGURE 8

Whatever its advantages, such a model of the Trinity obviously carries with it an enclosed quality, an implication of the Trinity-*for-itself*, rather than -with-us. None of the thinkers took the economy of salvation to be unimportant, but their magnificent work *resulted in* thinking about the immanent Trinity separately from the world.[19]

Thomas Aquinas' *Summa Theologica* brought this kind of speculation to a high point. That work is too massive and detailed to admit summary here. LaCugna gives six objections to Thomas that have been urged as indicating separation of immanent and economic Trinity. We will list them without comment, except to note that a number of them have to do with the ordering of his great work.

1. Thomas places the topic of Trinity at the beginning of dogmatic theology. This inverts the order found in revelation and in experience.
2. He holds for the priority of essence over Trinity. This defeats biblical, liturgical, and credal ways of speaking (about God the Father who comes to us in Christ and the Spirit).
3. Separating the treatises *On the One God* and *On the Triune God* gives the impression that the Trinity is a secondary feature of the Christian faith.[20]
4. Therefore the Trinity and the incarnation are insufficiently related.
5. Like Augustine, Thomas develops a metaphysics of spirit which bypasses the historical economy of redemption.
6. The theology of creation as an act of the divine essence defunctionalizes the Trinity of divine persons (GFU 145).

For our part, we can delineate two historical trends throughout trinitarian thinking, trends that LaCugna thinks have inadvertently spelled defeat for the doctrine itself:

• *intensified interest in the Trinity considered in and by itself;*
• *intensified interest in the essence that undergirds that Trinity.*

The first—concentration (historically necessary) on the Trinity in its immanent existence—gives rise to a terrible problematic: that of reconnecting two realities which seem separate, the immanent and the economic Trinity. What if no satisfactory bridge can be established? Or if it can be, at least in theology, what if the gap is not thereby closed for worship and conduct in the church at large? If this were the case then van Beeck's "teaching moment" in Christianity would have unintentionally obstructed the other two (indispensable) moments, conduct and worship.

The second intensified interest—in God's essence to the possible detriment of the persons—further compromises the importance of the Trinity for the world. As Rahner comments, "despite their orthodox confession of the Trinity, Christians are, in their practical life, almost mere 'monotheists'" (Rahner 1967, 1970, 10). The *status questionis* of LaCugna, careful about the relevant details of every question, points to *a diminishment of the perceived relation that God has to human beings*. Such lessening mandates the task of thinking again about the Trinity, this time with the *relation* it has to the world kept first and foremost.[21]

Our premise about liturgy stands or falls on whether God can come to significant oneness with creatures, whether God can be said to grant in some way connaturality to us. We need to remark briefly on *God's* side of the connaturality question. We will draw a single thread from chapter two of this book and weave from it an insight that both clarifies the difficulties of the past and makes way for the new.

B. Trinity as Both/And Instead of Either/Or

LaCugna phrases the *desideratum* of new trinitarian study as follows: "Is there a way to preserve a distinction of reason between economic and immanent Trinity without allowing it to devolve into an ontological distinction?" (GFU 217) In other words, can we avoid making the distinction too complete. As regards the language we use in speaking of God, she says that

> the language of "in" God creates the impression first of all that God has an "inner life," second that we have access to this inner life, and third that speculative theology is mainly concerned with God's inner state or interior life. The immanent Trinity is then construed to be God's interior state, God *in se*, and the economic Trinity to be how God is in the world, God *pro nobis* or *quoad nos* (GFU 224).

The problematic consists not in overcoming God *in se* in order to strengthen God *pro nobis* or *quoad nos*, but in rooting the latter in a much more fundamental understanding of *God with us*. To put it another way, how can we begin to conceive God in a manner that brings together the different faces of God without thereby denying the distinctions.

It seems to this writer that a basic difficulty has plagued trinitarian thought. Because human beings are most at home in the world of matter, where—as we have noted—the principle of non contradiction applies with full force, it has been difficult to remember that such rules *do not and cannot apply to God*. If the principle of identity could be stated as "either/or" (either it is a desk or it is not), perhaps we could paraphrase the ground rule for God talk as "both/and." God is *both* one *and* Trinity. God is *both* God's own self *and* in the world to its depths. Jesus is *both* human being *and* God. Some theological thinking may have been afraid, for instance, that if Jesus is fully God, then God's complete divinity would be compromised. Therefore "subordinationism," the doctrine that the other persons in the Trinity are not equal to God-the-Source, and the resultant counter-measures. Or, if God is truly three persons then Christians stand in danger of affirming three Gods. Or, if God is truly with us (has *pitched his tent among us*, to paraphrase Scripture) then God is prohibited from being fully God—the God who exists before all ages without compromise. Because of the last difficulty there came forth theories of God relating to the world by means of *energies*, which are not the same as the essence of God—but exist from eternity with God (see, for example, GFU 39 and 188ff), and the theory that creatures have a real relation to God but that this relationship is *not real* from the side of God (Aquinas; cf. GFU 160ff).

We can think about such relations more integrally by bringing into play the metaphor of union that is the point of this book. In significant unions we do not find an obliteration of either party, but a fruitful union of two. The doctrine of the Trinity maintains *both* the distinction between persons *and* the unity of the three to the point of oneness. This is not an exception to the rule of oneing parties as we have seen it, but a higher level in which the persons are merged *almost* to the point of identity.

How to think in such terms? If the reader can be enticed momentarily back to section A. 2. of Chapter Two, we can discover there some tools necessary for clarity. In brief, and at the risk of repetitiveness, we found two different realms of existence: that of material things, and that of what we called "consciousness." We said that material things display a certain characteristic that we called, for short, "stickiness." Material things are what they are, and until a thing surrenders one identity it cannot have another one. Consciousness is less encumbered by this rule of "non-contradiction." In a manner of speaking my consciousness cannot be itself at all unless it is filled with the identity of something else, which it "knows." Thus, in order to remain fully itself, consciousness "becomes" something else. This would be contradictory at the material level. To phrase the argument in terms of the present discussion, my knowing is *both* consciousness *and* the desk. This traditional (Thomist based) analysis gives us an example of a both/and reality that is found implanted within the material world.

Consciousness has a "being" status for philosophers of this tradition. Langer's later thesis that knowing is merely a phase of the biological process (see Appendix Four) would find no home here. Consciousness is a "way of being," usually called "intentional being." Unless we hold that God is material, we would have to say that God's existence is more in the direction of intentional being than material. Thus there is an "analogy of being";[22] *things* exist but they are "stuck to themselves"; *human persons* exist, in part like material things do (my body is subject to the material laws) but in part also in a "higher manner." They are able to open to others, able to "become" the other in consciousness. Since God is (infinitely) higher than the human person, which is to say that God exists in a more perfect way, then we would be justified in saying that "both/and" language applies in a preeminent manner to God. Opening-to-the-other is not just a capacity of God, it belongs to the "essence" of what God is.[23] To put it another way, God is able to "one" with the other in a way that approaches the point of identity but stops just short of it. It stops not because of an imperfection but because the most deep definition of being is that it can become one with the other while remaining itself and while allowing the other to remain itself also. Neither is compromised, and neither is the union compromised. Being exists because it is in union. Therefore there must always remain an openness to plurality of some kind in all being, including God's. Otherwise we could not say that God "exists." The task of thinking about God then places the requirement on us that we hold under grave suspicion any conclusion whatsoever that smacks of either/or. Such basic opposition is appropriate to material beings, but decreases as the levels go higher, and disappears in God.

If such an argument holds, we should then be able to sort through the trinitarian controversies and stop them short of positing either/or. For instance, the initial concern of the early writers had to do with the nature of "God-as-such" in distinction to "God-with-us," to use LaCugna's terms. For reasons we saw above, these two "presences" of God had to be distinguished, so that certain things could be predicated of God-with-us that did not have to be held as regards God-as-such. Jesus' humanity could be subordinate to the Father, but the second person of the Trinity could be equal or co-extensive to the Father. Such distinctions started the ball rolling toward a separation of the two in practice, until finally the divine being would seem, in the words of Du Roy, "one unique God, thinking himself and loving himself, as a great egoist or a great celibate" (GFU 102).[24] While such a statement misunderstands the celibate state, it serves for emphasis. Likewise, the Roman preface for weekdays IV says to God that "you have no need of our praise, yet our desire to thank you is itself your gift." What kind of relation would it be in which we give something to a person who does not need it, and who in fact remains untouched by it, and makes our gratitude into something trapped within us, not reaching to the other? In that case our act of thanking is unmasked as medicinal, good for us but not for God. The God of Scriptures, questing after the people, hurt and angered by their intransigence, suddenly becomes a children's story, not true but "teaching us" some deeper truth, which unfortunately is that God does not need us at all.[25]

Such a separation does not come about if we think of God as the one who is most capable (essentially capable) of relating. God does not become identical with creatures unless we substitute "becoming-the-same-as" for "relation-with." God's presence to the world in Jesus is a supreme example of fertile union in which the one does not *become* the other, but becomes *one with the other* in an important and intrinsic union. In this union God is really present with and merged with human reality, but in a way that preserves otherness for each.[26] In this sense there can be no "God-as-such" if this means God existing alone, without relation to everything else that is. It is the nature and prime ability of God to "be-with," not to be alone. God-as-such *is* God-with-us. [27]

The great controversies about God's essence versus the Trinity of persons also find salve in this viewpoint. We saw Augustine concentrating on the divine essence as a way of preserving God's unity. He was then forced to escape modalism (the persons as modes of God, not really distinct persons) by the doctrine of appropriation, which we have seen. But if the persons are necessary pluralities within God they do not have to be modes of the essence; they are discrete persons whose union is so complete that it gives oneness: one God. Union and diversity in God have come to be co-equal with each other.[28]

Subordinationism was a way of preserving the underived character of the Father by saying that the other two persons are engendered not as equals but "lower grades," so to speak, of Godliness. The horns of this dilemma turn around the need to (1) avoid blurring the divine persons and (2) avoid positing three Gods. These alternatives are inescapable and dangerous only insofar as we think in quasi-material categories. *Either* God is one *or* God is three; to posit both would repel our thinking. If on the other hand we begin to think of God as the supreme instance of what we saw present (deficiently) in the intentional mode of existence (human consciousness) we see that God's ability to become one with the other is ultimate, so much so that for the Godhead to have multiplicity within it not only is possible but is the only way ultimate being could exist. The persons retain their individual identities even while simultaneously partaking of a union so complete that it must be called oneness.[29]

The same reasoning discloses the personal nature of God's relations to the world. God enters the world not through general godly action which is then appropriated to one or the other person of God. God-with-us is the individuated activity of the three persons, each in its own appropriate manner. Rahner's tradition-altering statement that "the immanent Trinity is the economic Trinity and *vice versa*" depends on this statement.[30] We will spend the next section on these oneing relationships of God's persons, so we need not preview them here. We will only say that God relates to the world in the way that God is. If there is a primordial unity of persons in God, then those persons must enact God's primordial unity with the world. The fear of positing this truth centers around a fear of compromising God's oneness by allowing that one person does one thing and another the second. If the relation-unto-unity within God is not subject to question, since God could not be otherwise, then this fear is allayed.

Traditionally theologians have spoken of *"perichoresis"* to depict the mutual permeation of one another that the persons carry on. Metaphors have been offered to help "feel" this reality: the way in which light from one lamp pervades the light from another. Or the metaphor of perfume: when it is sprayed into the air one cannot say where the scent begins and ends. Or the example of the three dimensions of a physical object; width implies (and supplies) length, and these two presuppose depth. And there is the image of "the dance."

> The dancers (and the observers) experience one fluid motion of encircling, encompassing, permeating, enveloping, outstretching. There are neither leaders nor followers in the divine dance,

only an eternal movement of reciprocal giving and receiving, giving again and receiving again (GFU 272).

LaCugna uses the metaphor of "begetting" to illustrate the divine dance. "God is eternally begetting and being begotten, spirating and being spirated" (ibid.). This is the image to which we would gravitate, given the nature of our central thesis. The persons of the Trinity interpenetrate each other, coming to a union more profound than any known in the physical world, but a unity that still preserves differences, even though these are in some senses less important than the unity. The being of God is so open to the other that oneness and multiplicity are just two sides of the same coin. For that reason the coming-to-one of God is creative in the very highest sense of that word.[31]

We have now drawn a thread from chapter two. Since our purpose is not to detail trinitarian doctrine but to locate God's significant union with creatures, we now find ourselves free to sketch the manner in which this union takes place.

III. The Persons of God in Relation to the World

Let us present here a *status questionis* regarding our own thesis so that we can map out trinitarian activity, and because of it, the *locus* of the liturgy. We proceeded on the hunch that God's own relation to the people in worship (liturgy), if intimate enough, held the key to the creation of the liturgy. After establishing the gift of connaturality of people to God, we uncovered two things. First, the history of trinitarian thinking had gradually isolated the reality of the Trinity so that the three persons seem inaccessible and largely irrelevant to human action. This, even though the Church first discovered persons in the Trinity by reflecting on God's action in the world. Second, we began to rethink trinitarian doctrine in order to view God as the most relational being of all. So far from needing protection from earthly—and trinitarian—otherness in order to maintain Godliness, we saw that God is most Godself only when relating to "the other," both the others in the immanent Trinity and, following upon creation, the others of the economy of salvation. Finally, we can saw even the language of economic and immanent Trinities plays false to the reality of God-with-us. One comprehensive arc of Godly oneing would be the best way of describing the mystery of God, any moment of which can be viewed, but only without isolation from the rest.

LaCugna proposes to revise thinking about God and the world. She endorses vigorously Rahner's statement that the economic Trinity is the immanent Trinity. The so-called immanent Trinity does not thereby disappear but is placed in its proper context as the mystery of God, which is beyond creatures and which corresponds to the mystery left in any communicating partner.

> For Rahner, the idea of God as self-communicating does not oppose but includes the belief in God as mystery, for the self-communication itself transcends the creature. Unlike us, God really communicates God's self without either losing or keeping to God's self (GFU 233, n 3).

Put simply, God-within and God-in-the-world are two countenances of one reality, which is the mystery of divine-human communion. This understanding, she says, reflects the biblical and pre-Nicene sense of the "economy" as "one dynamic movement of God (Father) outward, a personal self-sharing by which God is forever bending toward God's 'other'" (GFU 222), and returning.

Such thinking allows LaCugna to present an initial diagram of the Trinity as "a point moving along a parabola":

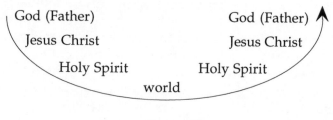

FIGURE 9

This "chiastic" model represents a revision of the trinitarian framework, one which moves directly along the lines of the analogy of the present book. There exists no gap to be closed between the economy of the world and the immanent God.

> *Oikonomia* is not the Trinity *ad extra* but the comprehensive plan of God reaching from creation to consummation, in which God and all creatures are destined to exist together in the mystery of love and communion. Similarly, *theologia* [study of

God as such] is not the Trinity *in se*, but, much more modestly and simply, the mystery of God. As we know from the experience of being redeemed by God through Jesus Christ, the mystery of God is the mystery of God with us (GFU 223–4).

LaCugna then moves to recast trinitarian theology by revising the notion of *person* as substance, which she replaces with person as relationship. She notes that the method of Descartes isolated the self from the world, apart from relationship to anyone or anything else (GFU 251). Indeed Descartes had to work very hard to establish the existence of anything outside the self, and had to rely finally on a truthful God as *deus ex machina* to guarantee knowledge of the outside world.[32] She turns to the philosophy of John Macmurray, to the theology of the contemporary Greek Orthodox writer, John Zizioulas, and most tellingly to liberation theologies, including the feminist critique (see GFU 250–289). She concludes that relationship is a defining characteristic of person, a conclusion that supports the direction of our previous chapters and brings light to trinitarian theology. The diversity of her considerations prohibit summation here.[33]

A. An Abundance of Conception

Other theologians have shared the vanguard of trinitarian renewal, perhaps with a less overtly radical approach than LaCugna's. Where she is intent on the historical "defeat" of trinitarian doctrine and its present emergence, theologians such as Edward Kilmartin and David Coffey rely on traditional doctrine but add important new aspects to it. By these they are able to see the trinitarian persons active in the economy and to find the relationality we have underlined. Kilmartin in particular states as his purpose the founding of liturgical theology on trinitarian doctrine.[34]

> The mystery of the liturgy is the mystery of the history of salvation, fully revealed in the special missions of the Father's one Word and one Spirit. It is, at its depth, the life and work of the Triune God in the economy of salvation. This fundamental Christian belief provides the clue to the proper, comprehensive approach to the theology of the liturgy. As yet, however, few modern Catholic theologians have taken up the challenge of working out a systematic Trinitarian theology of the liturgy (CL I 180).

Because our topic is none other than liturgy, Kilmartin will serve as a guide on our journey toward the unity-at-the-heart-of-liturgy.[35] We will have equal recourse to three other authors especially favored by Kilmartin: Coffey, Jean Corbon, and the trinitarian theologian William Hill. Where Kilmartin summarizes/builds upon them, each of these presents his own rigorously argued case. Their stated purpose is not liturgical theology, as is Kilmartin's, but rather the urging out of real meanings from traditional doctrine for the renewed relevance of trinitarian meaning to daily life. We want a broad view of how God (in the action of the three persons) comes to the world in profound union. If the "mystery of the liturgy is the mystery of the history of salvation, fully revealed in the special missions of the Father's one Word and one Spirit" (CL I 180), then only by seeing these activities in particular will we see the true foundation of liturgy.

1. *Procession versus Bestowal Models.* Four preliminary observations are in order. First, in all of the following, the theologians in question understand the "immanent Trinity" to be one with the "economic Trinity," not isolated in practice or principle. With suitable adjustments they would endorse Rahner's axiom that the economic Trinity is the immanent Trinity, and vice versa. Second, these theologians understand that all our knowledge of God-as-such, if we may so refer to the immanent Trinity, comes from our knowledge of God-with-us. This prohibits beginning with the immanent Trinity and concluding to, say, Christ and the Holy Spirit given to us. Christians in the New Testament began to reason to the three persons in God from what happened in Jesus' life and their own lives.[36] Thus, even though our exposition will begin with a treatment of God within the Trinity, this is only the order of presentation, not of discovery. Third, our explanation will follow the theology of the west (where the Holy Spirit comes forth from the Father *and* the Son) rather than that of the east (where it comes forth from the Father *through* the Son). We do not intend to neglect the latter, but the complicated results of this difference are too many for our summary. Fourth, though we will talk of one person coming forth from another in the Trinity, we must bear in mind the metaphorical nature of such language. It represents an ordering of nature or essence, not one of time.[37]

We have observed—in bits and pieces—the speculation of theologians up to St. Thomas on the immanent Trinity. Their speculations were legitimate and brilliant, even if the practical consequences might have tended toward what LaCugna and Rahner observed. The traditional doctrine is expressed most commonly as "procession." The persons *proceed* outwards from the Father as source. That is to say, it shows us "the other two persons radiating out from the Father, their source, and extending this movement into the world in execution of the Father's plan of salvation" (Coffey 1984, 470). Coffey therefore calls this way of characterizing the Trinity "outgoing or centrifugal." It is the "processional model."

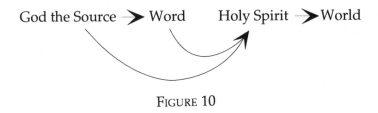

God the Source ⟶ Word   Holy Spirit ⟶ World

FIGURE 10

This understanding presumes the "psychological analogy" of Augustine, which is to say that these "processions" come forth in the way that knowledge and love proceed from the human soul.[38] The Father as Source knows him- (or her-?) self, and therefore utters the Word, which is the fullest possible expression of the Source's being. Mutual love of Source and Word proceeds forth, and we call that love the Holy Spirit. The three persons together create and redeem the world.[39]

This model of thinking adds much to the understanding of God as Trinity. The analogy to human knowing boosts us toward an understanding of God, who is the supreme fulfillment of the "both/and" of consciousness. As analogies from knowledge and love, all three persons co-exist together without compromising the unity of God, any more than knowing and loving overthrow the unity of a human person. This is one of the "yields" of the procession model. Like any model, however, it cannot do full justice to the reality of God-with-us. Both Coffey and Kilmartin remark that the *purpose* of the Holy Spirit's procession is not accounted for, and therefore the Spirit can seem to proceed purposelessly into the void (CL I 131; GGHS 31). Thus the procession model is able to tell us *the fact* that procession takes place, but not the *manner* in which it does. Also it seems unable to account for the order of God's action in the world. The procession model is linear, with action beginning from the Father, proceeding to the Son, and breathing forth the Holy Spirit. Scriptural evidence, however, seems to present the opposite order. The Holy Spirit overshadows Mary, which union produces Jesus (the Word), whose life is a return to the Father (see GGHS 110–113 and CL 160).[40]

A different model might soften these difficulties. Coffey suggests that this second model, which he calls the "bestowal model," was known and treated as far back as Augustine, Richard of St. Victor, and Thomas, though not by that name. Instead of being linear, it is circular, based on "different but complementary aspects of the mystery of Christ, so that [the two models] should be regarded not as exclusive but as complementary" (Coffey 1984, 470).

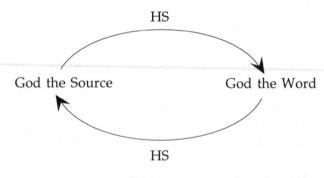

FIGURE 11

God the Source regards and "bestows" love on the Word. The Word bestows the same love upon the Source. That love is the Holy Spirit. The Source's love evokes the Word's love. The action is centripetal or inward moving because instead of representing God's outward action to the world, it shows the Godly love that human beings can be drawn into. Thus, if a person

> is to come into contact with God, the freedom of God in His saving plan is emphasized and the movement which takes place is seen to be ultimately one of assimilation of man[/woman] to God. God reaches out to man[/woman] only to draw him[/her] back into His own life (Coffey 1984, 470).[41]

The "yield" of the bestowal model helps us to account for God's action in the world. The Holy Spirit is bestowed "in two directions," as mutual regard, rather than a linear procession into the world. Thus, if we find Jesus loving the God he called *abba*, we can find this reality echoed in the immanent Trinity. Moreover, if we find the Father sending the Spirit to engender Jesus, we again find this reality not in contradistinction to the (processional model of) the Trinity but in full accord.[42]

I take as my goal in the following pages the exposition of God-with-us, which is not a different God than God-as-such, but rather an inclusion of the world within God by a series of unions possible only to God. The bestowal model makes room for this understanding.

2. *The Birth and Life of Jesus.* The birth of Jesus is God's primary action in the world. The Holy Spirit overshadows Mary, which action creates the human being, Jesus (Luke 1:35). Thus the same Holy Spirit who comes to ordinary human beings serves as the "grace" of Jesus' conception.[43] Another way to put this is to say that "the Father bestows love on the sacred humanity of Jesus." Three things take place simultaneously in this bestowal: the Father's Spirit *creates* Jesus' humanity, *sanctifies* it, and *unites* it to the pre-existent divine Son.

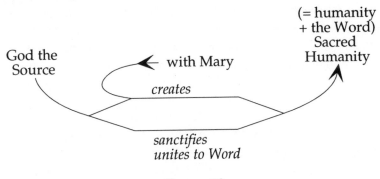

FIGURE 12

Why three actions, or three aspects of one action?[44] Earlier theology did not provide for such things. We can use our own work on Thomistic theory of knowledge (according to Maritain) to clarify. In our chapter on Maritain we said that

> *a lower "grade" of being has to be elevated*
>
> *if it is to come into union with a higher one.*

We recall once more that consciousness had to "raise" the material thing to its own, less-sticky level so that it may become one with that thing's sensed and intellected realities. The same is true of the humanity created by God's oneing with Mary. Considered by itself, without sanctification, this humanity would be of the same order as any other human being. It would be a "lower grade" or intensity of being than the divine. Elevation would boost it to the divine realm so that it could become one with the person of the Son. Sanctification of the humanity provides this elevation.[45] The Holy Spirit sanctifies the sacred humanity and then unites it to the second person of the Trinity. This union is more than a coming together; it results in an identification of the Son and Jesus. Now the humanity of Jesus *is* the Word, the second person of the Trinity, insofar as humanity's structure will allow. Of course Jesus' humanity did not exist *before* it was sanctified and united to the Word. The three are distinctions of essence within the one incarnation, not "before and after" events in time.[46]

So Jesus is born. The bestowal model is unique in that it understands the Holy Spirit (love) as not only being bestowed by the Father upon the Son—and thus on Jesus, as we have just seen—but also by the Son upon the Father. How does this take place in Jesus of Nazareth?

Because Jesus was a material being, his reality unfolds through time. Clearly the Jesus who preached represented a development over Jesus in the crib. And his death on the cross, the consummate act of love and surrender, must be considered an advance in personal character over the man who preached and acted out of everyday love. All human beings *come to be* who they really are, and they do this only through time. We could say of Jesus that

> it was only to the extent that his humanity was developed that
> the divine Sonship was realized in it, for humanity is to be
> conceived not as a static given but rather as spirit in matter,
> which grows in being through its personal history, which
> embraces not only life but also death (GGHS 74).

In a sense the gift of divine Sonship was woven outwards, developed in exactly the way other people develop into what they previously held only in potency within their inner being. It would be true to say that a human life continues to *gestate* after being born, that only a state of relative stability is reached when the baby is born. When his earthly life had been consummated, Jesus could fully take up his oneness with the Word, thereby sending back and bestowing the Spirit on the Father.[47] He did this in partial and ever increasing ways during his life.

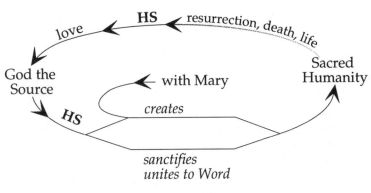

FIGURE 13

The gradually darkening line under the words "life, death, resurrection" indicates this increasing development of Jesus' oneness with the Word. Jesus' life is also an ever increasing *revelation* of the life of the Trinity—which we can now understand because of the circular nature of the bestowal model—a revelation of Jesus' Sonship that is complete only in the resurrection. In a sense there is revealed at that time the "hidden event of the incarnation." In this diagram we can find the inverse ordering of the processions of the Trinity: Holy Spirit, Son, Father. The Holy Spirit draws the sacred humanity into unity of person with the Word, making Jesus in his humanity Son of the eternal Father (GGHS 113. Cf. also Coffey 1986, 230–231).

We have achieved a certain overview of the trinitarian action, then, as correlated to the birth, life, death, and resurrection of Jesus. By it we seem to have accomplished part of what LaCugna wants for the re-emergence of the Trinity as a co-partner with the world. Can we go further? Can we find traces of trinitarian action in the life of other people in the world besides Jesus?

3. The Rest of Humanity.

Pentecost represents a new beginning, for the Spirit is no longer simply the one whom the Father sent with and for his beloved Son; henceforth the Spirit is poured out by the Father *and* his Christ. The river flows henceforth from the throne of God *and* the Lamb. He will show himself from now on as the Spirit of Jesus and as the power that raised Jesus from the dead. Most important of all, from this day forth he is "given" and will be received and recognized as the gift of the risen Lord (Corbon 1988, 46–47).

Pentecost represents the creation of the Church, the constitution of human beings besides Jesus as children of God. According to the processional model, The Father and Christ send the Spirit. Jesus' radical love of his Source turns out to be a similarly radical love for and solidarity with all human persons. We will examine this connection below. Scripture, especially the gospel of John, shows that Jesus will "pray to the Father," who will give a new Counselor to Jesus' followers, the Spirit of truth (John 14:26). This Spirit will declare all Jesus' truths to them (John 16:14). But this can happen, for reasons we have seen, only after Jesus' ordeal.[48]

Coffey and Kilmartin point to the fact that while bestowal of the Spirit *creates* with Mary the sacred humanity of Jesus, the case is different with the rest of us. In our case the Spirit finds already existing persons. We stand already established in our life patterns, our personalities, our attitudes. We seek for something that would fulfill us completely—a godlike answer to our longings. Indeed, we sometimes elect other human beings to fill this role for us—to our disappointment when we find them merely human. We too must be raised to God's level if we are to seek for the actual God instead of something unknown which might answer our quest. The Spirit enters us not as a material being to be known, but as the Spirit of othering, elevating our capacity to seek.

A new factor enters. Instead of the simple bestowal of the Spirit, which was the way God created, sanctified, and united Jesus with the Word, we are given the *offer* of that bestowal. We can respond with either a "yes" or a "no." We saw in Haughton that refusal comes at many levels, all of which have the effect of damming the flow, jaundicing the wondrous exchange that is our real vocation. No wonder Jesus could be called the "great receiver." His very being was not yes and no, but only yes (cf. 2 Cor 1:17).[49] Great patterns of confusion and hardship follow upon our manifold "no," our refusal not only of each other but of the offer of love which is the Holy Spirit. It is important to note that the story could end here for us. Human beings could wander aimlessly, seeking without knowing it that which they have refused.[50]

When we say "yes" we become—not yet children of God—but men and women who *seek* God. Specifically we are now able to seek Jesus, who is God's entrance into the world.

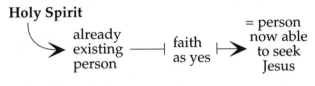

FIGURE 14

Rahner's *Hearers of the Word* establishes this point. Persons are connatural with God only when elevated by a previous oneing with the Holy Spirit, called in that instance, grace. Then they are open to and seeking a union with God that comports itself to their material existence. We are spirit-in-the-world, and so our seeking is for God-in-the-world. The church does not depend utterly upon the "yes" of this or that person—Christ as a human being constitutes humanity's yes to the bestowal, and therefore became the foundation of what we call the church. Those who accept are in a position to join this great, flawed, sometimes calcified body of Christians who stand alongside Jesus in the world.[51]

We saw God's primary and unsurpassed entry into the world through the Spirit, Jesus the Christ. How could it ever be possible actually to find Jesus, who is God in the world? The last two millennia are crammed with schemes, attempts, interpretations, possibilities for doing this: the mystical way, with its journey of ascent; separation from the world, with its ascetical denial; the lure of bypassing God's saving deeds in the world in order to find God within one's self; the supernatural appearances of heavenly creatures that dot the landscape, especially at the turning of the millennia; the cult of the saints as a way to reestablish closeness to the divine when the Christ of the Trinity became otiose.[52]

4. The Trinity and Sacramental Liturgy. Kilmartin, Coffey, and Corbon each concentrate on sacraments as the most intense or especial locale for finding Jesus. I also choose this emphasis. I understand sacraments here in the post-conciliar sense, as an "act of the whole assembly and its total liturgical action," rather than in terms of the older theology, using "the traditional and more restricted focus on matter, form, minister, and recipient alone" (Fink 1991, 7).[53] This interpretation means basing liturgy and church in the "primordial sacrament," Christ.

> As a rule, modern Catholic theology formulates the question of the institution of sacraments by Christ from the background of the Augustinian concept of sacrament as visible form of invisible grace. In this sense Christ himself is the prototype of sacrament. The Church, on the other hand, is sacrament as fruit of salvation: the social situation of the abiding presence of Jesus Christ. As such, the Church is the place where salvation is offered to humanity in a visible way, in the scope of the community of the new people of God. Sacraments are, therefore, to be understood as ways in which the Church actualizes herself as a sacramental reality (Kilmartin 1989, 533).

Christ is the sacrament of God's presence. The church, which is his presence throughout history, is sacrament of Christ, and the individual sacraments establish the church. We will see how this takes place. For now we need only say that, when the church gathers for worship, there Christ is to be found within the sacramental liturgy.[54]

If we proceed in our diagram, the picture would be this:

Holy Spirit

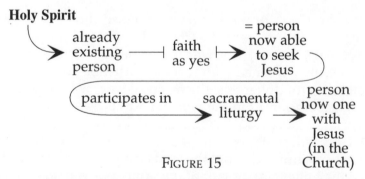

FIGURE 15

This model has the advantage of locating a prime meeting ground for the seeking individual and Jesus in his symbolic representation. The sacrament effects what it signifies. The presence of Jesus in the sacraments of the church effects union with the participants in the liturgy.[55]

A question arises here. Whose work is the liturgy—God's or people's? Variations on the answer would cover the field. The liturgy of the eucharist has been seen as the "Lord's Memorial" in which believers simply call to mind the deeds and teaching of Jesus as a model for life, but without any divine intervention to help.[56] If this viewpoint could be seen at one end of a spectrum, at the other end we would find liturgies entirely caused by God, with human beings as privileged observers.[57]

Jean Corbon structures his book *The Wellspring of Worship* around the idea of the "heavenly liturgy," which is identical to the action of the Trinity in the world.

> The liturgy is not reducible to the content of our celebrations of it. Christ, in the Holy Spirit and together with "the assembly of the first-born," is at every moment celebrating the liturgy before the Father. It is this liturgy that shapes history and gives vitality to the Church in our world; it is constantly at work and is offered to us (Corbon 1988, 78).

This world view seems to comport itself well to the eastern church's manner of celebrating the liturgy. In it, the sacraments are not so much something done by the people but givens, moments of the heavenly liturgy in which we are privileged to take part. Corbon holds it to be a fact of tradition that the "great sacraments are 'covenant signs,' seals upon fidelity, 'moments' of union, which the Lord gives and entrusts to his Bride in his Spirit" (Corbon 1988, 85).

In Corbon's vision, it is the church which presents and guarantees the sacraments, the church looked upon as the acceptance over time and space of the bestowal of grace. The sacraments and therefore the liturgy do not exist baldly as a fact given by God; *they exist as offspring of some kind from Jesus' life in the Spirit.* A view (not Corbon's) that they are simply given by God would seem to race ahead of the facts. Even with this balance, we could place the eastern church's view, at least as expressed by Corbon, toward that end of the spectrum where God's action is primary.

We might fancifully place at the leftmost extreme those theorists who would see liturgical and sacramental action primarily and perhaps only as an externalization by the community gathered together (through time and space).[58] We could find such opinions not only in religious circles, as above, but in sociological theories. Much work has been done on the similarities between types of rituals and symbolism in the history of religions. Christianity's sacramental symbols cannot be called unique in their general shapes.[59] This brings the question of human production of rituals. If human cultures externalize rituals similar to each other, in what way are the sacraments given in any sense by God? Why not say that sacramental liturgies are simply externalizations of human culture, referring to but not deriving from God?

We must listen to this viewpoint as well as the other, since both offer clues as to how liturgy comes to be. For the moment let us take time with the one just mentioned. Even though we cannot do justice to their theory in the space we have, perhaps we could mention a few premises from the sociology of knowledge of Peter Berger and Thomas Luckmann.

In Berger and Luckmann, a culture *externalizes* meanings, constituting thereby a structure in which the meanings become "objectified." That is, they are crystallized and experienced "as existing over and beyond the individuals who 'happen to' embody them at the moment" (Berger and Luckmann 1966, 58). The objectivized institutions then have to be *legitimated*—which is to say, presented in a manner that promotes their acceptance—and passed on to new generations. This is done at a popular level and also on a theoretical basis. The present book could be viewed as a theoretical legitimation of the church's institution of liturgy. Berger and Luckmann say that *symbolic universes* are constructed for the purpose of this legitimating; language is, for them, the most important member of this universe. *Processes of signification* may be developed that refer the meanings to realities other than those of everyday experience (sacraments would seem to do precisely that). These "become modes of participation in a universe that transcends *and* includes the institutional order" (Berger and Luckmann 1966, 96–97). Such referral gives hefty legitimation to the objectified meanings. At the extreme of objectifying is a process called *reification*. Here the meanings are no longer seen as the product of human externalization. The human being, who is

> the producer of a world, is apprehended as its product, and human activity as an epiphenomenon of non-human processes. Human meanings are no longer understood as world-producing but as being, in their turn, products of the "nature of things" (Berger and Luckmann 1966, 89).

Thus the position is reversed. Human beings, who actually give birth to the (sociological) world, are seen as products of that world. The world they produce (and continue to produce without knowing it) is seen as the producer of them.[60] Perhaps on the popular level, trinitarian theorizing had become such a reification, sacrosanct and not subject to its human producers.

Let us try to apply this summarized sociology to an arbitrary example: parenting in the family. The biological fact of the parent-child relationship does not automatically set up any pattern of family life. But neither do patterns have to be dreamed up afresh in each new family. Culture transmits a whole set of expectations, attitudes, roles, rewards to its members who take part in family life. Children take out the garbage, clean up their rooms, feed the dog, do homework. Parents fix meals, establish norms, seem godlike (at first), bring in the money, buy cars, send to college, etc. Arrangements change through the years of children's growth, but in general offspring are supposed to respect, love, and learn from their parents, while the parents are to love and care for the children. To a greater or lesser degree, this kind of pattern is objectified: understood to be "just the way things are." It is legitimated over generations. Teachings from the Bible, for instance, attribute the legitimation "honor thy father and thy mother" in a most dramatic way to a commandment etched on stone by God's own hand. Finally, the pattern can become reified, giving rise to the oft heralded entrapment that family members sometimes feel in a family system that "cannot be changed."

Such theoretical considerations hold great potential for understanding liturgy. At first glance, however, one might see them as freezing the discussions of this chapter. After all, do not all arguments about trinitarian participation in the world constitute a theoretical legitimation of church activities by appealing to other-worldly—and therefore unchallengeable—reality? They do. Would it be right, then, to say that liturgy is a purely human event, able to be described completely by sociology? But here we must be careful to retain our both/and balance. We are choosing a middle point in the fanciful spectrum of the previous pages. Rather than say that sacramental liturgy *either* is the activity of God's Spirit *or* it is the externalization of the community, we must say that it is both of these. God becomes one with nature, and human nature externalizes its (now God-filled) meanings into symbol systems. When the Godly and the human come together in union, people still act as people-in-groups do. Sociology describes this. But God also still acts as God does: the Spirit is able to come together with an other without taking away the identity and characteristics of that other, but also as being truly present in the union. The result is an offspring: a human liturgy in which God's Christ is truly present through the Spirit, but which is also the projection of the people.

People thus serve as the manner in which the Spirit sanctifies otherwise merely material elements in a sacramental action. "Liturgy is the work of the people,"[61] who are however filled with the Spirit. The oneing of Spirit and persons (through time and space) produces the offspring which is sacramental liturgy.

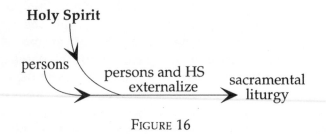

FIGURE 16

This kind of viewpoint not only does not distort the argument we have been pursuing about God-with-us, it harmonizes completely with it. The Spirit is sent by the risen Christ into the deep souls of human beings, who together with other human beings in the church (through time and across space) portray this union in the externalized sacramental liturgy. A momentous oneing takes place and the offspring is the liturgy.[62] This is the first moment of union to be described as regards the liturgy.

There is also what we will call a second moment of union, which we must now describe. Corbon's emphasis (as well as Vatican II's and Berger and Luckmann's) on our humble stance before the liturgy must not be forgotten. The church having externalized (and objectified, legitimated, and perhaps even reified) the liturgical system, the people now partake of it on a regular basis and there find explicit, conscious, material oneness with the risen Lord within the material world. If we return to our previous emphasis on the individual person, we could present this diagram:

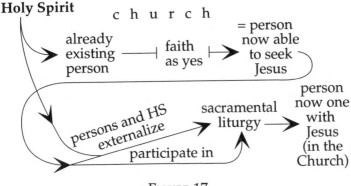

FIGURE 17

The church is established by Christ's life, death, resurrection, and glorification (which is his full realization of his status as Word). Within it persons whose faith says yes to the bestowal of the Holy Spirit on them become one with Christ in the sacraments. Thus, sacraments are the "way in which God's grace is accepted" (Kilmartin 1989, 539).[63] Kilmartin sees sacraments (and the church before them) as a share in the self-offering of Christ, which is the interior of God's self-communication anyway. In the same way, sacraments are an act of worship since they are a participation in the life of the Trinity, in which the heart of worship takes place (Kilmartin 1989, 538). Thus the individual's faith prepares that person to join in a full offering along with Jesus.

> Faith as the act of acceptance of God's self-communication, the realization of the basic attitude of self-offering to God to receive the meaning of one's life from God, is given the opportunity for an offering that embraces the whole person in an especially intensive and extensive way because of the expressiveness of the sacramental celebration (Kilmartin 1989, 539).

Participation in the sacramental liturgy is a new moment, the second one, of significant oneing. The self-offering that is Communion (and communion with Christ throughout the whole liturgy) is a most pregnant union, and

> *its outcome is the birth of Christian,*
> *loving action in the world.*

Any series of liturgies that produces no change in the lives of the participants, that generates no credible action in the world, will

have to be questioned as to its authenticity. A genuine communion with Christ must do what every other substantial union
does: generate a birth that is identical with that union as gestated. The objective Christ/person union is given birth outside
the doors of the Church, as love between spouses and friends,
service of the poor, acts of generosity, and in general the relaxing
of all the boundaries to loving exchange that are so much a part
of human life.

From now on, I will refer to the conception, gestation and
birth of the liturgy itself as "the first moment," and the conception, gestation and birth of Christian action as "the second moment." The first is more preconscious and projective; the second
is more objective and open to consciousness—like the beholding
of a work of art. But, as we will see, both unions originate in
Maritain's pre- or unconscious, and work their way out to the
full light of day.

5. Symbolism and the Spirit of Liturgy. One of the most influential works on the nature of sacrament is Rahner's "The Theology
of the Symbol" (Rahner 1966c, 221–253). There he parlays his
root metaphysics into a theory of being as symbolic, a task too
lengthy and involved for complete explicitation here. We will
begin, however, with certain aspects of it. These will indicate its
accord with our own basic premises, and will enable the continuation of our argument.

Rahner agrees that all being is pluriform—if not specifically
that all creation is co-creation. Even in God's great unity, as we
have seen at length, there is a gestation into plurality: the three
persons. Because of this revelation Rahner holds that being cannot "be" otherwise. It accomplishes its existence by pluralizing.[64]
This is the way any being, material, human, Godly, maintains
itself. It comes into union with itself and so accomplishes its
being. If this were not so, the being would "collapse into lifeless
identity." It pluralizes in order to come into union with itself
through the plural other and thereby become a living union with
itself.[65]

If this is true of all being, then the generated plural member
is symbolic. It discloses the unified whole with which it is one.
My arm is a symbol of my whole self. The Word has always been
held to be the disclosure of the Father-Source. That is why it is
called the "Word." To take another more mundane example
used by Maritain, the hand of the beloved simultaneously *is* the

beloved, and so is a manifestation of him or her. Because the plural is unified with the whole, the hand manifests the whole being, through its partiality and its union with the being. This means that all being is symbolic. It discloses something (else) which it is not, but at the same time is.

In order to think this kind of proposition, we must have recourse to our own premise about the oneing nature of God. The more perfect the being, the more it can "other" without losing itself or the other. God is the consummate example of both/and. Because of the "both," there are three persons. Because of the "and" there is such a unity that we can speak truly of *one God*. By beholding the gestated member of the "both," Christ, I know the "and," the Source. By this reasoning, Christ is the perfect symbol of God the Source. This description resembles closely the classic definition of sacrament: *sacramenta efficiunt quod significant et significant quod efficiunt* (the sacraments do or are what they signify and signify what they do or are). So Christ is the primordial sacrament. And the sacrament of Christ is the Church. By indwelling, the Spirit makes the church the highest symbol of God the Source and God the Word. In knowing the church we observe what is really within it, Christ, through his Spirit.

If human beings were ever to know God, it was necessary for God to utter a Word that contains the whole reality of God. Since humans are enmeshed in material reality as their environment, that Word will be an expression in matter. Thus, Jesus is the fullest symbol of God the Source possible in the material world. We saw that Jesus' full revelation does not take place until he completes his death and resurrection. It is almost as if he had to leave the world just when an encounter with him would finally have told people fully about God. Granted, we have stories about him, and the Holy Spirit has been sent. But finally, having returned to God-his-Source, Jesus now must let himself be present to human beings in another (material) way. That is to say, Christ must come to one with (in the instance of the eucharist) bread and wine so that believers can find him there, in the action of eating and drinking.

How does this oneing with bread and wine happen? Here we return to our own diagram: first, the Spirit comes to oneness with those human beings who say "yes" in faith. These persons, through time and space, *externalize, with the Holy Spirit who is one with them*, the sacramental reality. The subconscious oneing of Spirit and persons allows this externalization to be *a birth* instead of a mere sociological event. Born are sacramental elements with God at their depths. They signify what is within them.[66]

Kilmartin gives a thoroughgoing summation of sacramental theories in chapters thirteen through eighteen of *Christian Liturgy I.* These chapters have already the nature of summary and so resist abridgment here. We can cite, however, his brief overview from chapter fourteen:

> The Spirit, who founded and structures the Church, established the sacraments as constitutive elements of the life of faith. Therefore the sacraments are Spirit-endowed realities of the Church. When the Church actualizes itself in its liturgical celebrations, its sacramental character is most clearly manifested. Here the Church appears as sacrament of the activity of the Spirit and so, in this sense, sacrament of the Spirit. But this activity of the Spirit is an instance of the Spirit working through the participants of the sacramental celebration, in which all of the assembly have their special roles to play (CL I 232).

We see here the elements of our last diagram. We could reach back to elaborate as follows: the Spirit is bestowed upon Jesus in the very act of his creation. The "yes" of Mary and the life of Jesus constitute the irreversible affirmation of this bestowal by humanity, and therefore the existence of the church. From Jesus' life, death, and resurrection emerges the complete revelation of the life of the Trinity-with-us, and the sending of the Spirit upon all humankind. This happens through Jesus' request of the Father. Now the church widens as it comes to include all believers who in their faith say "yes" to the bestowal of the Spirit in their lives. Under the impetus of this Spirit, the church community at large "externalizes" the liturgy's character and meaning, and this is repeated and endorsed at each local liturgy. Individuals are made one with Christ in a way analogous to the unifying of Jesus with the divine Son at conception. The Holy Spirit does both works. Believers are not made *identical* with Christ, as Jesus was with the Word; instead they are *united* to Christ by the mediation of the Holy Spirit. Here we see again a yield of our theory of oneing, in which both parties retain their identity.

> On the one hand, an immediacy must be maintained without this implying the absorption of believers into Christ by over-

drawn identity. On the other hand, the distance between Christ and believers must be affirmed, but not at the cost of denial of immediacy. The correct perspective is given by the introduction of pneumatology. The Holy Spirit, whom Christ possesses in fullness, was sent by him from the Father to form believers into the Church. Hence the same Spirit in Christ and in the communion of believers enables the immediacy of Christ to believers, and yet an immediacy that is mediated (Kilmartin 1989, 535-536).

Once the Spirit is bestowed, its recipient partakes of God's "both/and" nature, and therefore is enabled to "one" with Jesus in the sacraments. Both retain their identities in a union or love or exchange.

When the faithful assembly comes to eucharistic liturgy, then, they use the eyes of the Spirit within them to behold Christ born (in part) of their very own union. When they consume the sacred elements they become not just seekers of the Word but receivers of the Word. They continue to grow toward their destiny as (adopted) children, unified with Christ who is signified. As Coffey puts it, eucharist is the way the community as church is summoned into full existence and celebrated. Eucharist and church show the very nature of God standing revealed, offering God's own trinitarian self to the world (GGHS 175).[67]

Now the circle of love implied by the bestowal model is completed. If the Trinity others itself into the world, it cannot stop there, as the procession model for all its strengths might be thought to imply. In the bestowal model, the imparting of the Spirit upon the Word is completed always by the bestowal of the same Spirit upon the Father by the Son. Human beings are included in that return. By sacramental liturgies believers are made one with Christ in the Holy Spirit. Through their life and their death they realize this oneness completely, even as Jesus realized his oneness with the Word. In all of this they join Jesus in bestowing the Spirit of love back upon God the Source of all.

B. Conclusions and Final Word

I present here a grand diagram of the God-with-us picture, the numbers of which refer to the numbered sections that follow. The explication we are about to begin will serve as a summary of all we have said thus far.

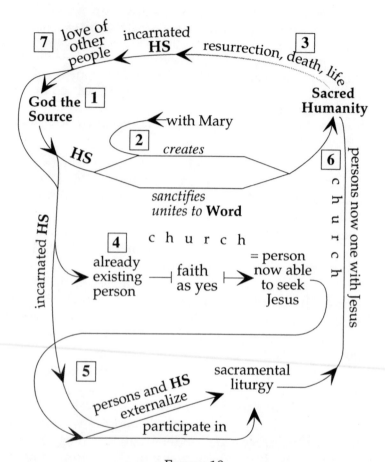

FIGURE 18

(1) We began within the so-called immanent Trinity, making the proviso even so that all our speculations about it are deductions from God's action in the world. We saw that God the Source, the first person of the Trinity, engendered the second person, who is called by the metaphorical or analogical name Word. The procession model told us this *fact*, along with the additional fact that the Source and the Word together "breathe out" the Spirit. The bestowal model told us the *manner* of this procession, that is, that the Source bestows love upon the Word and the Word bestows love upon the Source. This mutual love is called the Holy Spirit.

(2) We went immediately to the mystery of the incarnation (description of creation would have taken us beyond our pur-

poses). For whatever free reason, God decided to enact the "othering" at the heart of Godly being and share with the created world the very life of the Trinity. Since the Word expresses fully the being of God the Source and is the only expression that can be, then the only possible externalization of God into the world has to be the same Word. So the Source sends God's own othering Spirit into the world to accomplish that externalization. In logical order (not temporal), the Spirit ones with Mary and so *creates* the humanity of Jesus, *elevates* or sanctifies that humanity so that it can belong not only to the worldly human sphere but also at the same time to the Godly realm, and finally *unites* unto identity that humanity with the fullest expression of the Source's being, God the Word.

(3) This "sacred humanity," the child Jesus, is born of Mary, grows to an adult, pursues a loving career of preaching the life which is his very nature—we called it the great exchange, characterized by receiving and letting go. This activity comes into mighty conflict with the great philosophy of refusal, Satan's stated mode in Luke. When the antagonism comes to full flower, Jesus characteristically releases everything he is to the powers of evil, because to hang on to anything, even before the face of so great a foe, would reverse the great exchange. The cross follows. One inmost element cannot be taken away because its very nature already consists of letting go and therefore it has no "handle." If we call that activity of exchange by the name love, then love survives. Love as exchange is invisible to the evil of refusal. We can refer to the resurrection, then, as a triumph not just of love, but of the very innermost essence of God. That essence is "exchange" but we could as well call it "othering," or "the highest intensity of being," or simply "Godlove."

This ultimate triumph of God's being within humanity fulfilled Jesus' complete identity with the Word, concluding the circle of bestowed love we inferred in the "immanent" Trinity. It also made Jesus able to join with the Father in sending the same Spirit of love to all the people of the world. The Holy Spirit now has a "christological" character. The Spirit sent out upon all humankind takes the shape of Jesus' own relationship to his Source. It is not a generalized power of God but the highly personal relation between God the Source and the human being Jesus, made possible first by the "othering" nature of God that we remarked, and by the utterly specific birth, life, death, and resurrection of Jesus. The Holy Spirit is now fully incarnate and is marked as the bestowed love of the Father upon Jesus (the Son) and of Jesus upon his Source.[68] As we will see, Jesus' love for the Source is identically a love for all human beings, and through them for all creation.

(4) The now incarnated Spirit is sent upon the human world by the Father and by Jesus. It encounters human beings, each of whom has a history, a culture, biological and psychological determinants, and a will to receive or not. "To those who received him," that is to those who say "yes" to the offer of bestowal, the Spirit is granted, given by the Father in the inner recesses of their souls. They now exist as seekers of the Word, able to find that Word within the world where God-with-us now dwells.

(5) Because they are human beings and not angels, these people act as people do through time and space. They give external form to their meanings, structuring them, objectifying them, teaching them to new generations. The Spirit is with them in this because the Spirit, once bestowed, has become one with their souls, has come into a significant union with them. This union retains the identities of each. People are not "turned into" Jesus or the Spirit but are made intimate co-partners because of their own, personal, internal structure. The Spirit of God has come to one with them, and dwells in their unconscious. Since more than just words about the Word are needed, the externalizing takes form in liturgy and sacrament. If it is people that give meaning to their symbols, and if only the Holy Spirit can give Godly presence, then this marriage produces sacramental liturgies in which not only meaning is given, but a symbol in which God dwells in person, the eucharist.

(6) If these seekers of the Word act to commune with the bread and wine thus constituted, thereby completing their participation in the liturgy, they will be in communion—oneness— with the very Word they quest for. "Seek and you shall find, knock and it shall be opened to you" (Mt 7:7, Lk 11:9). As other Christs, "children of God" in the most profound sense, they join in Christ's life of exchange, sacrifice, self-surrender. They are able to join with Jesus in bestowing the love which is the Holy Spirit upon God the Source. This is the second moment of union in eucharistic liturgy: the engendering of Christian action in the world.

This portrayal relieves one of the problems we alluded to earlier as a defect in the older theology.

> The absolute certainty of a hearing when the prayer is made in the name of Jesus implies that the prayer is integrated into the prayer of the one *mediator who is always heard* (Kilmartin 1989, 537).

In this model it is no longer possible to wonder whether "God has any need of our prayer," the awkward words we noted in one of the Roman prefaces, or whether God is changed by it. The Church, joined to Jesus' prayer, takes humble part in the interior life of the Trinity now widened to include it. Unless the bestowal of love by the Son on the Father is purely medicinal—good for the Son, but not affecting the Father—then prayers and works of the people are certainly received by the Father and find a place in God's own being.[69] Thus the circle is closed. This is the life of the Trinity in the world.

Except for one detail.

(7) What about love of neighbor? Have believers merely been commanded to do this? Jesus died for all people: how is this a love of God the Source? And how are other people connected to his love of God the Source? Why did Van Beeck include the "other moments" of conduct and teaching (to other Christians) within the life of the Church? Why do we fall short of trinitarian life if we merely go to Mass and pray to God? In a word, do we find an intrinsic connection between love of God and love of neighbor? Its placement in our diagram (at #7) would seem to plead for explanation. And so we must attend to the last task of this chapter, the union of love for God and love for others.

We might, of course, rightly suspect from the nature of Godly being that we cannot apply either/or to this problem. Surely the love that is exchange will encompass other people in the returning love of God. Let us see why this might be so, at least for our writers.

Coffey and Kilmartin hold, with Rahner, that love of God and of the neighbor are identical. Kilmartin says that the

> sending of the Spirit by the risen Lord is a kind of prolongation of the answering love of the Son for the Father in the immanent Trinity. It is ordered to enabling a corresponding response of love for the Father from all humanity. At the same time, it is the highest expression of the human love of the risen Lord for the Father, for the explicit love of the neighbor, ordered to the fulfillment of the neighbor's existence, communion with God, is the primary act of human love of God (CL I 189).

These last words, baldly stated, seem to lie at the heart of Christian tradition. Jesus, after all, approves the lawyer's recitation of the law as "you shall love the Lord your God with all your heart, and with all your soul, and with all your strength, and with all your mind; and your neighbor as yourself" (Luke 10:27). But in Matthew Jesus enunciates them as not one but two commandments, numbering them "the first and greatest," and "the other" (Matthew 22:38–39). Is it two realities or one reality? At this crucial juncture Coffey most surprisingly spends just seven lines summarizing Rahner's conclusions on the subject and then moves on.[70]

We must here delve one layer deeper into Rahner if we are to comprehend. We saw above that Rahner (like Maritain, LaCugna, and the present writer) understands the human person as an openness to the other. We understood that, lodged beneath explicit human knowing, is a deep questing, which constitutes a reaching out for what is. At its very center consciousness knows about being and wants explicit objects to enter it and fulfill its seeking for *explicit* knowledge of whatever exists.[71] The Spirit mingles with the preconscious depths of the person. Now the person is acquainted preconsciously with God's own self in its othering: the Spirit. Now he or she can reach out for the real God instead of for some unknown and ideal realization of perfect being.[72]

Mystical knowledge may well put one in touch with the mystery of God, but explicit concepts can only know God as present in the material world. How can the thirst for God in the world be slaked? We have seen sacraments as a privileged place for this union. But Rahner holds that it happens primarily in the most complete and self-realizing act possible for human beings: love of other human beings. This is not a love of neighbor *instead of* God, but love of neighbor as the only way human beings can possibly return to the Father and thereby join in the great circle of love that is the Trinity.[73] Indeed, constitution of the sacraments cannot happen without this act. It is as if—in our terms— a person with the grace of the Holy Spirit partakes of God's ability to go-out-to and to receive-within him/herself the other. Since persons come to their identity only by othering—by, in Coffey's language, bestowing their love on others (centrifugal) and inviting that love to return (centripetal)—then God's Spirit within them can only be incarnated in this activity. Otherwise the presence of God would be trapped inside. To put it more simply, human beings realize themselves only by going out to the other. Their union with Christ in the Spirit can be brought to human fullness only in the same kind of othering that Christ-the-Word carried out: the relation of love for the neighbor. The circle is thus really fulfilled only *within the world, where God the Trinity dwells*. The love of neighbor reveals itself as an act "whose movement is directed towards the God of eternal life" (Rahner 1969, 241).[74]

This consideration, very important in the history of theology, also shows the intrinsic unity of Jesus' message of love for the neighbor, his death for all people, and his love of God. If the love of neighbor is the primary act of love of God, then as a human being Jesus would complete the circle of bestowed love back to the Source only by utter love of other human beings. This also illustrates why what we have called the "second moment of the liturgy" is an engendering union. Its offspring is the love and service of the neighbor, which results from the union with Christ as present in the liturgy. The life of Jesus with which an assembly communes is already a Spirited life of service to other persons.

Our trinitarian path is complete. The life of the Trinity is the stuff of human, Christian life. It encompasses many "significant unions." Our language of oneing and othering has provided the key for understanding the Trinity as wellspring for all Christian acts. We can now consider specifically the yield of our own model of liturgy as conception, gestation, and birth. We can then turn to the question of whether liturgy constitutes an art form, or whether it is only a union.

NOTES

1. Karl Rahner and others consider grace as the self-communication of God, rather than primarily as God causing from outside certain changes in the recipient of grace (Cf. Rahner 1954, 1961b; and 1992, 117–126). And at this point I will define nature as the essential structure of a human being, characterized by openness to the other. This definition will gain precision as the argument proceeds. Also, I would like to note here that the discussion of nature and grace in this book comes from a Roman Catholic viewpoint. This is my own heritage and therefore the place from which I am most likely to speak sensibly. But I hope the conclusions I reach will comport themselves *mutatis mutandis* to any Christian worshipping body.

2. "The stage of immediate preparation has to consist of some experience which dislocates the person, shaking up habitual ways of thinking and acting, creating one of those weak spots at which the demand for breakthrough to the new and prophetically promised life can be experienced" (Haughton 1981, 131).

3. The first temptation would have Jesus show his power by turning stones to bread. In this way the power would return in upon itself, and the spheres "though breached, are kept separate." Nor would Jesus make a spectacular descent from the temple (showing the vast power available to him) or seize political power by "worshipping" Satan (that is by subscribing publicly to Satan's refusal) (Haughton 1981, 118–126).

4. GE II §79, 4, quoting Augustine from *De fide et symbolo*, 7 (*Corpus Scriptorum Ecclesiasticorum Latinorum* 41, p. 11).

5. Van Beeck has an interesting though brief treatment of nature as a present experience of the past, or in other words, a secondary experience of the present. Grace has the characteristic of seeming to come from the future, since the factuality of Jesus Christ strikes the believer as belonging to the future, in that it presents itself as something "I can never take solid possession of, as something I will never quite know my way around in. The Incarnation is not finished; Jesus is still in agony till the world's end; without hope there is no faith now" (van Beeck 1979, 289. Cf. also pp. 286–293). Thus the quest for God in Christ is always unfinished.

6. See Rahner 1969, 111–163. Another way to say this is that grace requires the elevation by grace. "In order to be able to accept God without reducing him, as it were, in this acceptance to our finiteness, this acceptance must be borne by God himself. God's self-communication as offer is also the necessary condition which makes its acceptance possible" (Rahner 1992, 128). Cf. also ibid., 118.

7. Freud, for instance, held that the God representation in an individual is formed by a transmutation of the imago of that person's own father. This would happen at the resolution of the Oedipal conflict. "The psychoanalysis of individual human beings teaches us with quite special insistence that the god of each of them is formed in the likeness of his father, that his personal relation to God depends on his relation to his father in the flesh and oscillates and changes along with that relation, and that at bottom God is nothing other than an exalted father" (Freud, *Totum and Tattoo*, 147; quoted by Rizzuto 1979, 16). Religion is therefore an illusion, an infantile wish for parental protection in the face of life's difficulties. For treatment of this see Rizzuto 1979, chapters 1–3. Cf. also Berger 1969, for a sociological elaboration.

8. In another book, van Beeck attaches names to each stage, names which are the substance of his book *Catholic Identity After Vatican II*

(1985). The teaching stage he calls *Pistic*, from the Greek word *pistikos*, meaning "faithful" or "believer." The "mature" or motivational stage he names *charismatic*, from the Greek word *charismatikos*, meaning gift. This is not to be confused with the current Charismatic renewal movement: van Beeck uses the name to designate those who have deepened their Christian motives and therefore act according to their gifts. Finally, as we might expect at this point, the worshipping church is designated by the name *mystic*. It would seem that these elements in the church can harden what are described in GE II as stages of growth. Thus the dialectical relationship between them is thwarted. Van Beeck does not hesitate to point out the negative results of this calcifying tendency along with the positive points of each. Since a further discussion of this book would lead the present discussion astray, I have placed a somewhat lengthy summary of its theses in Appendix Five. The occurrence of the same motifs in *God Encountered* and *Catholic Identity* illustrates the consistency of van Beeck's thought, especially since the latter is an analysis of the (sometimes warring) elements of the contemporary church.

9. Quoting Ruusbroec *Die geestlike brulocht*, 468–475.

10. Ruusbroec: "And in its created being, it accepts without intermission the impress of its eternal image, just like the untarnished mirror, in which the image constantly remains, and which renews, without intermission, the knowledge of it with new clarity, every time it is looked at anew. This essential unity of our spirit with God does not exist in and of itself, but it abides in God, and it flows forth from God, and it depends on God, and it reverts into God as into its eternal cause, and, accordingly, it does not part from God nor will it ever do so. For this unity is in us in [our] bare nature. And were the creature ever to part from God, it would fall into a pure nothing" (GE II §90, 3, again translating *Die geestlike brulocht*, 468–475).

11. At GFU 8 and 198 (and elsewhere) LaCugna speaks of the "defeat" of trinitarian doctrine, and Part I of that book is an illustration of her thesis. On page 18 n 4 LaCugna attributes the metaphor of defeat to Wendebourg 1982, 194-197.

12. Formal introduction of the name "Father" allows me to comment on my usages throughout the remainder of this book. Along with many theologians of the 1990s, I believe that continued and continuous reference to trinitarian persons as "Father" and "Son" presents a hazard not only to the devotion of many but to understanding of the trinitarian reality. As is clear from the earlier sections of this book, ascription of gender, together with popular attitudes toward it, does connote and denote much besides "general personhood." Woman is privileged to provide the "mothering wing" of the womb to shelter the yet to be born child. This does not make her better or worse than the

male; in fact father and mother each are fertile and in potency. Nevertheless, at the level of gross bodily function, the woman's body is built to be the (centripetal) locus of the fertilizing, and the man's to deposit into that locus (centrifugal). This biological formation was one factor giving rise to the stereotype of males being the progenitors, the cause of the generations to follow, and females just being a means.

The very point we will make regarding procession and bestowal models thus bears on this problem, and we must anticipate that discussion here. The procession model, we will see, is linear and "product oriented." It tends to be a male-based model in other words, and centrifugal. The bestowal model will be seen to be circular, (in part) receptive, and centripetal. Here for the first time we will be able to envisage the "Father" as not only generating and producing, but also as being the locus for *receiving* the "Son's" bestowal of love. This feminine function is not adequately referred to by the name tradition has staunchly used, "Father."

I cannot hope to solve this literally age-old problem in the present pages. I have to be content to utilize "Father" and "Son," even though I think they prejudice the very point I am trying to make about the bestowal model. I have tried to reduce the collective weight of such references by alternate use of the term "God the Source" for the first person, and "the Word" for the second. While these provide variety and lighten the sexual stereotyping, I am aware that they still derive from the processional, production oriented model—the Source as one from whom all else comes forth, and the Word as that which is spoken or generated. Still, women are the human birthing sources and thus mirror the Source. For that reason "God the Source" may begin to be more apt than "Father." I do have hope that renewal in trinitarian theology of the kind I will trace in this chapter will provide rich soil for a renewal of language as regards the Trinity so that we become able as theologians to say with our terms what we really mean.

13. LaCugna points out that the view of Arius must be differentiated from those of his followers. R. C. P. Hanson (1988, 557–636) distinguishes between the early Arians, who subordinated the son in order to explain how the immutable God could have contact with the world; the *homoians,* who declared the incomparability of Father and Son, with the Father greater; the *anhomoians,* who said that Father and Son are unalike in all things; and the *neo-Arians,* who held God the Father to be entirely incomprehensible because of ungenerate essence.

14. LaCugna traces the developing meaning of "economy" (GFU 24–41). In general the phrase "economic trinity" means "the three 'faces' or manifestations of God's activity in the world, correlated with the names, Father, Son, and Spirit" (GFU 211).

15. The emanation of Son and Spirit is not temporal but represents an "essential" ordering. Creation of the world is of course not part of

the inner, immanent Trinity, but takes place in time, subordinate to the Trinity.

16. This explanation causes him difficulty, since a relative name might seem to leave no real identity to the person in question. So Augustine says that the Father, for instance, is an absolute person even without relation to Son or Spirit, in the same way that an earthly father remains a father even if his offspring dies. But when considered not by itself but along with the others, Father is a relative name. This very difficult idea does seem logically contradictory, and it has caused great controversy among scholars. LaCugna quotes the text in question and some of the interpretations (GFU 88-89).

William Hill says "it is true that the fullest implications of Augustine's thought are that God is *one* 'Person,' within whose divine consciousness there is a threefold self-relatedness. He has already grasped that the trinitarian use of the term *personae* conveys relationship, but—proceeding introspectively and using human consciousness as an analogue of divine conscious reality—he understands this as a relationality internal to individual consciousness" (Hill 1982, 61). Hill goes on to clarify and defend Augustine from these implications.

17. "Du Roy maintains that Augustine in his own piety centered less and less on the Father or on the Trinity of persons but addressed his prayer to God without distinction of persons, or to Christ, but not to the Father through the Son in the Spirit" (GFU 109, n 87). Reference is to Du Roy 1966, 462.

18. Quoting Heribert Mühlen (1965, 41).

19. LaCugna traces the effects of such speculation on faith and on the liturgy, showing the gradual conversion of early formulas of prayer in various stages. She says the historical progression of doxological formulas is as follows:

- to God through Christ
- to God through Christ in the Holy Spirit
- to the Father through the Son in the Holy Spirit
- to the Father and the Son together with the Holy Spirit
- to the Father, through Christ and in Christ, in the Holy Spirit
- to the Father and the Son and the Holy Spirit (GFU 127).

It would seem that LaCugna relies too heavily in her chapter four on authors from the 1960s such as Jungmann and J.N.D. Kelly, whose work has been continuously corrected and updated in the intervening three decades. Cf. for example the four volumes of *L'Eglise en Prière* (Martimort 1983–1984), translated as *The Church at Prayer* (1986–1988).

20. Rahner: "The very isolation of the treatise on the trinity proves at once that something is wrong; the thing is impossible! For the trinity is a mystery of *salvation*. Otherwise it would never have been revealed. But then it must be possible to see why it is a mystery of salvation. And

then it must be possible to show in *all* dogmatic treatises that the realities of salvation with which they deal cannot be made comprehensible without recurring to the primordial mystery of Christianity" (Rahner 1966a, 87).

LaCugna believes that #3 is erroneous, since Thomas intended both *De Deo Uno* and *De Deo Trino* as integral and essential components of the larger science of "God-in-himself." Of course this does not deny the *impression* created, which is Rahner's point in the previous paragraph. Moreover, Rahner himself notes the provisional nature of his objection (ibid.). As to the other objections, LaCugna notes that Thomas has been defended on each of them by other theologians (GFU 172, n 11).

21. Or in other words, to begin from a theology "from below" which never loses sight of the fact that all we know about God is the manner(s) in which God comes to live among us. In this sense, incarnation and grace should precede or be concurrent with God as three persons and should precede consideration of the "immanent trinity."

22. Traditional Thomistic doctrine of the analogy of being can also be found in the philosophy of Karl Rahner. Rahner bases his ladder of being on the capacity of all being to be present to itself. "The *degree* of self-presence, of luminosity for oneself, corresponds to the intensity of being, to the *degree* in which being belongs to some existent, to the *degree* in which, notwithstanding its non-being, a being shares in being" (Rahner 1989, 12. Cf. also 10–14 and Rahner 1963, 1969. 31–50). Rahner holds that being and knowing are the same thing for Thomas; both are intrinsic characteristics of being itself (Rahner 1957, 1968, 68–77).

23. William Hill points to Aquinas's "ontologizing" of relationship within the Trinity as heralding this startling insight: "that at the very heart of being as such, of all being, there resides a mysterious *respectus ad alterum*. A certain inner-relationality is revealed in the depths of reality that is not merely incidental. And, what is more, the inner-relationality is not reducible to mere *essential* otherness" (Hill 1982, 73).

24. Quoting Du Roy 1966, 463.

25. Kilmartin: "The fact of the new relational connection between God and creature, in turn, raises the issue of the nature of the receptivity of the unchangeable God to the response of the creatures who have been placed in the new personal relation to God. In other words, if God himself has established new personal relationships with his creatures, whereby they are made capable of personal communion with God, how does their response to God's offer of personal communication with himself affect God himself?" (CL I 136).

26. Such thinking is in no way absent in Aquinas, whose theology in fact provides a foundation for it. William Hill, summarizing Aquinas, says that "God the Father 'prolongates' his utterance of his eternal

Word so as to utter man as his finite, temporal, and non-divine 'word.' Then the Father's loving himself in both his divine Image and his human images is, in effect, a dynamism of reuniting them to himself (without any merging of their identity in his own) in the Holy Spirit" (Hill 1982, 76).

27. LaCugna makes a similar point, basing it on the "relational ontology": the theory that being is first and foremost a relation to others: "Since according to a relational ontology being is found always in being-with-another, it is impossible to say what something is by-itself or in-itself. This is particularly so in the case of God. God's existence is grasped in relationship to us; we do not know God 'in Godself' or 'by Godself.' As soon as we try to prescind from God's existence in relation to us to say something about God's existence in itself, we lose our basis in the economy of revelation. If we try to determine what God is apart from how God exists concretely in the communion of persons, if we isolate God's nature or essence from the divine personhood, then we violate the unity of *theologia* and *oikonomia* as well as the principle that *to-exist-as-person-in-communion is more ultimate than to be*" (GFU 334, last italics mine).

28. Rahner emphasizes that a statement suggesting "necessary plurality" in God does not represent a philosophical deduction about how God must be, but instead a theological statement that *began* with the revelation of God's trinitarian plurality, and therefore is able to postulate plurality in all being. Cf. Rahner 1966c, 226–227. As regards the formal meaning of "person" when applied to the Trinity, cf. GFU 243–250.

29. Likewise *Apollinarianism*, in which flesh is considered corrupt and therefore admitting of no union with God—therefore the second person of the Trinity becomes the soul of Christ. This is unnecessary if the nature of human beings is understood to be a (mitigated) openness to God, whose nature it is to become one with the other insofar as the other is able. Likewise *Docetism*, in which Christ was held to have only an apparent body and only appeared to suffer; and *Macedonianism*, which held the Holy Spirit to be created; and *Monarchianism* in which there was no trinity in God—related to *Adoptionism*, where Jesus was simply a human being, possessed of divine spirit, and adopted by God as son. All of these were methods of avoiding the scandal of a God who can become truly one with the other without losing the Godly identity.

30. It could be justly said that LaCugna's whole book is a working out of this dictum. Rahner questions the alternative by asking "is it correct to affirm that *each* divine person can become man? Our answer is that this pre-supposition is both not proved and false. It is not proved: the most ancient tradition, before St. Augustine, never thought of the possibility and really pre-supposed the contrary in its theological reflexions. The Father is by definition the unoriginated who is

essentially invisible and who shows and reveals himself only by utter-
ing his Word to the world. And the Word, by definition, is both
immanently and in the economy of salvation the revelation of the
Father, so that a revelation of the Father without the Logos and his
incarnation would be the same as a wordless utterance. But the pre-
supposition is also false: one cannot deduce from the mere fact that one
divine person became man that this 'possibility' exists for another"
(Rahner 1966a, 91). Cf. this entire article ("Remarks on the Dogmatic
Treatise *'De Trinitate'*," Rahner 1966a, 77–102) for the working out of
this thesis.

31. "Bonaventure embraced the Dionysian axiom *bonum est
diffusivum sui*. By combining the two characteristics of the Good, productivity and finality, Bonaventure was able 'by a truly profound
metaphysical intuition [to make] the voluntary act and its efficiency
spring simply from the essence of good considered as such'" (GFU 164,
quoting Etienne Gilson 1965, 163).

32. And after Descartes, Locke, Leibnitz, and Kant, for all of whom
the self of the person, apart from the world, provides the starting place
(and seemingly the ending point) for their philosophies. She also criti-
cizes Barth and Rahner for reverting to a substance view of person and
the persons of God (GFU 251).

33. In GFU pages 288–292 LaCugna gives seven points that belong
to her definition of person. (1) *A person is an ineffable, concrete, unique,
and unrepeatable ecstasis of nature.* "Ecstasis" means that to exist as a
person is to be referred to others. The modes of this reference are
"sexuality (and its desire for union), the *'intentionality' of intelligence*
(the desire to know the truth) and *love* (the desire to be united with
another), *hope and anticipation for the future* (seeking permanent con-
summation and fulfillment), and *freedom* (seeking to transcend limita-
tion through conformity to ourselves as creatures ordained for love
and communion with God and with others)" (GFU 289, italics mine).
(2) *The person is the foundation of a nature.* It is "natural" for persons to be
in full communion with each other. (3) *The freedom of the deified human
being consists in being free-for, free-toward others, poised in the balance
between self-possession and other-orientation.* This means a balance between self-love and self-gift. (4) *Persons are catholic, in two respects:*
persons are inclusive of everything that exists, and, each human person expresses the totality of what it means to be human. (5) *The
achievement of personhood requires ascesis,* i.e., putting to death all those
practices that confine us to mere biological existence and lead to death.
(6) *Person is an exponential concept.* Each new relationship and cluster of
relationships make us exist in a new way. (7) *Living as persons in
communion, in right relationship, is the meaning of salvation and the ideal of
Christian faith.*

34. See, for instance, CL I 93-98. Also: "The reduction of the theology of liturgy to the one divine plan of God is the aim of this theology. The one mystery of Christian faith is the Triune God in his self-communication to humanity" (CL I 98).

35. The nature of Kilmartin's first (and thus far only) volume on liturgy, *Christian Liturgy, Vol. I, Theology* presents formidable obstacles to the reader. The text is written in a dense, highly concentrated style. *Christian Liturgy I* reads like a compendium of opinions, perhaps the harvest of a lifetime of work. Moreover, Kilmartin does not always distinguish between his own opinion and that of an author. Kilmartin follows the main direction of David Coffey, for example, but departs from him in unspecified instances. In the case of Jean Corbon, Kilmartin does make an attempt at distinguishing the two. He says that frequently "the exposition of this chapter merely paraphrases what Corbon writes." But there are major differences. Whereas Corbon works with a procession model of the immanent Trinity and only incidentally introduces elements of an ascending christology, Kilmartin's outline of a theology of worship in that context incorporates the bestowal model and an ascending christology, and integrates the notion of the incarnation of the Spirit in Jesus' transcendental love of the Father (CL I 181). In any case, the mixture of summary and new, together with the writing's nearly outline status gives the reader pause as to which theologian is being represented, Kilmartin or those he summarizes. This state of the matter by no means ruins the worth of *Christian Theology I*, but it certainly warns us against the methods of presentation we have used so far with such authors as Langer, Maritain, van Beeck, and LaCugna. In a truer sense than those authors Kilmartin will serve best as a *guide*, instead of mainly a source. Kilmartin does offer his own position, as he says, in the article "Sacraments as Liturgy of the Church" (Kilmartin 1989, 529), and in the synthetic article "Theology of the Sacraments" (Kilmartin 1987). For that reason we will have ample recourse to these articles.

36. Coffey endorses and nuances this dictum which he got from Schoonenberg through Kasper (see Coffey 1986, 248 n 39). First came the biblical understanding of Jesus. "Historically, reflection on this biblical understanding led to the formation of the doctrine of the immanent Trinity in the patristic age, which doctrine acquired precise formulation in the first two ecumenical councils. . . . But coming to the economic Trinity, we see that the process is now, and legitimately in this case, reversed. For the new information about the Trinity is fed back into the biblical understanding to produce the doctrine of the economic Trinity" (Coffey 1986, 248).

37. The models we will follow here are ways of thinking about the Trinity and the world. They have the dignity of being traditional, even

if the bestowal model has been neglected. It is important to maintain the element of mystery about God and God's work, especially by refusing to absolutize models.

38. "Augustine was simply seeking in man's psyche something that might serve to illumine what was believed of God. What he finds is a certain threeness (that of *mens, verbum,* and *amor*) that does not violate an underlying unity. . . . His analogies, consequently, have an extrinsic character: their illuminative power is akin to that of metaphor; what is true of the human psyche suggests in a creative and symbolic way something of what it means to speak of God as triune. Aquinas then moved the analogy into the essence of God. Since God's essence is a pure act of being, to-be, to-know, and to-love all coincide. God's 'othering' is so complete that they are identical, except that they are different relations of the same God" (Hill 1982, 70ff).

39. Here the objection may be brought that at last we have discovered an exception to our principle that two come together to make a third. The Father generates the Word by himself, by knowing himself. Perhaps we could appeal to the ultimate perfection of God's existence. in matters of God, otherness and being one are so closely related that they are, as we have said, two sides of the same coin. Also, as we have remarked, the so-called procession in no way implies *temporal* succession, merely an ordering in essence. The bestowal model will show that relations within the Trinity have also existed from eternity, with the Father receiving as well as giving. Nevertheless, the heart of the ancient doctrine of the Trinity holds that the Father is unoriginate from eternity, whereas the Son receives and further originates, while the Spirit only receives.

Coffey reminds us that in Thomistic epistemology knowledge is ultimately self-knowledge anyway (GGHS 27). In other words, the "thing" has been elevated and received into the conscious sphere. Since this sphere is "within the knower," then, in a manner of speaking, the knowledge union does take place *within* the knower and thus can be called self-knowledge, or knowledge of that which is within oneself already. In Rahner's version of Thomism, identity of a being with itself through self-knowing describes the most important quality of being. Human persons become one with the thing through sense knowledge, become one with the thing as object (and therefore "opposite" to the knower) in intellectual knowing, and knowledge of the self comes about by the final act of "returning" (*conversio*) to sense knowledge and judging that the object is different from the self that is knowing (Rahner 1957, 1968, 67–77). In God, however, the reception of material things into consciousness is unnecessary for self-knowledge. God does not have a consciousness which is potency, waiting to be activated by the object. Therefore "otherness" in this sense does not have to enter into the act of the Father knowing himself. This "otherness" can be present without the "object," implying as it does the relation between subject and object. If we recall Rahner's definition of being as that which is present to itself, then *something* has to be present and placed into unity with the self. Even if this happens at in the very highest possible level, it is still an example of profound union, which is therefore generational.

40. There is disagreement as to whether the Holy Spirit represents a "term" or fixed state of being within the process, as does the Word, or whether it is simply the act of mutual love. Coffey says that the early Aquinas held for the Holy Spirit as the operation of love itself, not a term like the concept is in knowledge. Later, Coffey says, Aquinas changed his mind about human love and therefore the Spirit, holding that love proceeds into an affection which is something like an impression of the thing loved. It follows from this that the Holy Spirit is thus a term rather than the operation of love. "According to the operation of the will, however, there is found in us another procession, viz. of love, according to which the thing loved is in the lover, just as through the conception of the word something said or known is in the knower. Therefore in God in addition to the procession of the word (that of the Son), there is another procession (that of the Holy Spirit), viz. of love" (*Summa Theologica* I, 27, 3). Both Coffey and Kilmartin stand against this latter interpretation because it seems to make the Spirit into "not precisely the bond of union between Father and Son, but a kind of bridge that stands in the way of the 'mediated immediacy' of Son to Father" (CL I 131; see also 128–29, GGHS 11–19, and Coffey 1984, 471). Even though Hill speaks of the affective presence of the beloved in the intentions of the lover, this "does not represent a term analogous to the concept, but an orientation or conative *élan* that orients the lover *through the cognitive symbol* out towards union with the beloved in the latter's own otherness" (Hill 1982, 263; italics mine).

41. I have taken the liberty to insert "man/woman" for the word "man" in this text because Coffey himself adopts this usage in his later writings. Cf., for example, Coffey 1986.

42. One goal of Coffey's theology, as of LaCugna's, is to understand the action of the Trinity as specific to the persons of the Trinity, rather than as proceeding from the divine essence. Coffey says the early Aquinas held that the distinct persons placed the acts of knowing and loving, but the late Aquinas said the processions come from the essence of God, not the persons. For Thomas, creation of the world is done by the essence, not the persons. In this way Trinity of persons is distanced from the world. Coffey argues that it is not necessary for the preservation of God's unity to posit actions proceeding from the essence. Knowing and loving are unified acts of the one God because there is one center of consciousness

performed now by the Father alone, now by the Son alone, now by the Father and Son alone (GGHS 16–28).

43. This sentence represents the purpose of GGHS, describing an action which Coffey calls elsewhere "the incarnation of the Holy Spirit" (cf. Coffey 1984, esp. 476–480).

44. The diagram is intentionally ambiguous as to *which* creates Jesus' humanity: the Father or the Holy Spirit. Coffey says that the "Father bestowed the Holy Spirit on the humanity of Jesus in an act by which at the same time that humanity was created, sanctified and united in person to the divine Son" (GGHS 91; cf. also GGHS 109, and Coffey 1986, 238). Thus the Father creates the humanity (by bestowing the Spirit). Creation could also be called the work of the Holy Spirit (as bestowed by the Father). Coffey espouses the position that "as an operation of God in the world the Incarnation is the work of all three persons" (Coffey 1986, 229). Taken as a whole the incarnation comprises all three of the actions we are now describing: bestowal by the Father, elevation by the Holy Spirit, and identification with the Son.

One of the most significant results of Coffey's labor is not only to overthrow the doctrine of appropriation, but to establish a proper mission in the world for the Holy Spirit. Though the Holy Spirit entered the plan of salvation through being bestowed on the sacred humanity of Jesus, the proper mission of the Spirit arrives only at the end of Jesus' life: being sent as *Christ's love of his brethren* (Coffey 1986, 237–239).

45. Coffey adduces many texts from scripture and the early writers to verify sanctification as one of the "steps" in the conception of Jesus. (See for instance GGHS, chapter seven.) One of the main gains in this schema is to provide a closer solidarity for human beings with Jesus. They are not only human like Jesus, but they arrive at oneness with God in much the same way. The same Spirit, the reality of grace for ordinary human beings, is the source of Jesus' own uniting with the Father (GGHS 118). Coffey means the bestowal model to show that all grace is the gift of the Holy Spirit.

46. "To say that the divinity of Christ *is* his humanity is not to say that the divine person of the Son comes to perfect or adequate expression in the human nature of Christ. It is only to say that he comes to the most perfect expression of which humanity is capable, which is different from, and less than, the expression which he has in his divine nature in the eternal Trinity" (Coffey 1984, 468).

47. Coffey spends time reiterating Rahner's theology of death, which underlies this viewpoint, in GGHS 150–151.

48. "It was only when his humanity was fully realized, through his free obedience to the Father throughout life and particularly in death, that the grace of the incarnation was fully realized in him. And hence

it was only thorough his death that he became, along with the Father, source of the outpoured Spirit" (GGHS 59).

49. (GGHS 65–69). Kilmartin paraphrases this by saying that the difference between Jesus and other persons is that Jesus is the highest possible actualization of a humanity, whereas lesser actualizations result in the union of already constituted human beings with the Holy Spirit (CL I 153-154).

50. Rahner definitely holds that the individual can accept or reject the offer of grace: ". . . that which we call sanctifying grace and the divine life is present *everywhere* where the individual does not close himself to God who creates salvation [,] by a real and culpable denial, and further on the fact that in a real sense, albeit to some extent unconsciously, this grace is brought about and made manifest in the concrete conditions of history and of human life wherever men live and die so long as this life of theirs has not come to imply mortal guilt" (Rahner 1976a, 166). Also Rahner says in 1992, 98 that "there is always present, as the condition of possibility for [every free] act, transcendence towards the absolute term and source of all of our intellectual and spiritual acts, and hence towards God, there can and must be present in every such act an *unthematic 'yes' or 'no'* to this God of original, transcendental experience. Subjectivity and freedom imply and entail that this freedom is not only freedom with respect to the object of categorical experience within the absolute horizon of God, but it is also and in truth, although always in only a mediated way, a freedom which decides about God and with respect to God himself."

He also holds that the person is conscious of this grace, though not with an objective awareness. Cf. Rahner 1976b, 288. If we used Maritain's terms, we might say that the grace is present to the "unconscious" or "preconscious," prior to the knowledge of an "object." But, Rahner says, the experience of opening oneself to the transcendental experience of mystery means that a person finds that "this holy mystery is also a hidden closeness, a forgiving intimacy, his real home, that it is a love which shares itself, something familiar which he can approach and turn to from the estrangement of his own perilous and empty life" (Rahner 1992, 131).

51. Since this offer of bestowal has been made to all humankind, there is no such thing as a human nature which is innocent of the means to accept it. This ability Rahner calls the "supernatural existential." McCool summarizes as follows: "God's decree elevating man to the supernatural order produces an intrinsic ontological effect on man's human nature. For, if that decree is to be a real offer of grace, it must make human nature capable of accepting it. Therefore God's real offer of his grace produces a 'supernatural existential' in the human soul. This 'existential' is a permanent modification of the human spirit

which transforms its natural dynamism into an ontological drive to the God of grace and glory. The supernatural existential is not grace itself but only God's offer of grace which, by ontologically modifying the soul, enables it to freely accept or reject grace. The pain of loss is the effect of the free rejection of grace in the damned soul. In face, the soul is damned precisely because its inbuilt longing, elevated by the supernatural existential, cannot be satisfied without the Beatific Vision of which it is forever deprived" (McCool 1989, 185). See also Rahner 1954, 1961a, esp. 310–317, and 1992, 126–133.

52. This latter perhaps recalls Eliade's description of myths in which the supreme being is replaced by "lesser divinities," closer to humanity and more able to help. See for instance Eliade 1963, 94–98. In primitive cultures, Eliade says, the pattern contains three essential elements: "(1) God created the World and man, then withdrew to the Sky; (2) his withdrawal was sometimes accompanied by a break in communications between Sky and Earth, or in a great increase in the distance between them . . . ; (3) the place of this more or less forgotten *deus otiosus* was taken by various divinities, all of whom are closer to man and help him or persecute him in a more direct and constant way" (*op. cit.*, 98).

53. "Although this way of looking at sacraments may seem obvious to some, it represents a radical shift away from the traditional understanding of sacraments as metaphysical entities which are communicated (in the traditional terminology, 'administered' and 'received') to a recipient from God through the instrumentality of a properly performed (or valid) liturgical ceremony" (Martos 1991, 124). See Rahner 1992, chapter eight for his summary of sacraments in the church.

54. See Fink 1991 for an account of the shift to this newer sacramental thinking. Kilmartin also gives a brief summary in 1989, 527–529. "The language now employed to explore what is common to the church's sacraments is liturgical rather than structural. Emphasis is on their relationship to the mystery of Christ and to the church as a whole, both of which are expressed in each liturgical act. The concept of *sacramenta in genere* has receded somewhat, and, if it were to gain renewed attention again, it would do so only after due consideration of individual sacraments in their uniqueness; it would not be the point of departure" (Fink 1991, 46).

55. Edward Schillebeeckx pioneered the viewpoint that, because sacraments are outward signs revealing a divine, transcendent reality, they provide an encounter with Christ. In the words of Martos, "Schillebeeckx suggests that the closest equivalent to what happens in a sacramental experience is an existential encounter between persons. When two persons deeply encounter each other—in contrast to simply meeting each other—they discover something of the mystery that the other person is. Those who fall in love, for example, see beyond the physical appearance

of the other person to a beauty and a value in that person that others cannot see" (Martos 1991, 111). Cf. Schillebeeckx 1963. For a summary of Schillebeeckx's doctrine, see Martos 1991, 111-113.

56. Thus the early Anabaptists, for example. White says: "The desacralized worldview of many modern Protestants makes sacraments or any other divine intrusions into the world questionable" (White 1989, 60). Eliade says that "the foremost function of myth is to reveal the *exemplary models* for all human rites and all significant human activities—diet or marriage, work or education, art or wisdom" (Eliade 1963, 8, italics mine).

57. Presumably in the middle would be gatherings in which Jesus is present, but mainly on the strength of his dictum "where two or three are gathered in my name, there am I in the midst of them" (Mt 18: 20).

58. In *From Temple to Meeting House* Harold Turner presents the interesting thesis that places of worship have alternated between two poles: the temple, considered as the house of God, and the meeting house, considered as the place where the people of God encounter each other. He sees the synagogue as an early example of the latter (Turner 1979). The two extremes of temple and meeting house fit, of course, at opposite ends of our spectrum. The Roman Catholic Church's renovation of liturgy and churches could be understood as a changeover from what had been in the modern era "God's house" (where worshippers came mainly to adore and kneel in the presence of the living God) to meeting house (where the faithful gather to be the people of God). Revitalization of the greeting of peace, the altar turned toward the congregation, altar as table instead of place of sacrifice, and church as a place to meet and greet, might be manifestations of this attempted change.

59. For non-Christian parallels to each of the seven Roman Catholic sacraments, see Martos 1991, 143–144,179–180, 204–208, 269–271, 318–321, 344–347, 393–396.

60. Cf. Berger and Luckmann 1966, 1–92.

61. Summarized at Fink 1991, 50 as the teaching of the Constitution on the Sacred Liturgy. It is necessary to emphasize here the point we are making, that liturgy is by no means *only* or *first* the work of the people; liturgy is first the benefaction/work of God toward us. Also, this emphasis on the people does not exclude ordained ministers. Kilmartin says that "as the head of the local church the priest is servant of Christ through the Spirit who creates the church's ministries. Hence in his official capacity the priest connotes, for the eyes of faith, the activity of Christ working through the Spirit. In this sense the priest can be said to act *in persona Christi per Spiritum* and, incidentally, be described as participation in the Spirit of the priesthood of Christ. This latter idea guards against the possibility of an overdrawn identification of the priest with Christ" (Kilmartin 1989, 531).

62. The manner by which Christ, through the Holy Spirit, is present in the eucharist remains disputed in theology. The view of externalization presented here is my own, not taken from Kilmartin or Coffey. More work would have to be done to harmonize it (or not) with, Kilmartin's views, for instance, especially as presented in Kilmartin 1989. Here it can be noted that Kilmartin does give attention to the communitarian aspect of sacraments, as in the following: sacraments "are the social expression of the response of faith to the word of revelation: the word of promise of the presence of the risen Lord and the Spirit of God to the community, and in the community for the 'many' called to share in salvation. In brief, the 'sacraments of faith' are a form of the answering self-offering of the Church to God bound up with her prayer of petition and accompanying symbolic actions, made for the salvation of individuals" (Kilmartin 1989, 534). Cooke believes, however, that in CL Kilmartin does not do justice to the community's sacramental role, but moves too soon to the ordained presider as causative symbol of Christ's action (cf. Cooke 1991, 159).

63. Kilmartin says "the Church is the enduring communion of those who participate in Christ's response of faith to the Father, and thereby are united to Christ and share in the fidelity that the Father worked in him. The Church came into existence through the mission of the Holy Spirit, who formed the disciples into the communion. But this forging of the bond of communion was conditioned by their free response to the gift of faith bestowed by the Holy Spirit. Through their free response the faith of the Church became historically accessible to others, and for all time" (Kilmartin 1989, 543).

64. He is careful to say, however, that "the original unity, which also forms the unity which unites the plural, maintains itself while resolving itself and 'dis-closing' itself into a plurality in order to find itself precisely there." He bases this on the Thomistic dictum *non enim plura secundum se uniuntur*: a plurality cannot unify itself by its own means. In other words, significant unity must in essence "precede" any plurality that is unified (Rahner 1966c, 227).

65. We are in a position from chapter two to understand how human beings effect this unity for themselves. In brief summary, knowledge is a pluralizing. It allows the self a union with the other by placing the potency of the knowing faculty into act, in Thomas's language, and by that means comes to itself. As we remarked with Maritain, there is nothing to know about a specific human's consciousness unless it is in act, and to be in act it must contain within itself the other as other.

66. Coffey brings forth an elegant solution to the problem of material elements in the sacraments, particularly the eucharist: he calls it the theology of sanctification. We recall from above that "sanctifica-

tion" is his word for the "elevating" action of the Holy Spirit. The Spirit elevates the humanity of Jesus while creating it, so as to bring it to connaturality with the Godly reality with whom it is to become one. The same goes, *mutatis mutandis*, for the elevation of believers by the Holy Spirit. In the case of material realities, this sanctification consists of adding significance to the elements. Jesus did this at the last supper by pronouncing blessings based in Jewish prayer over them so that the communion effected by eating and drinking bread and wine signifies Jesus' communion with God. The material elements thus have a status in both realms, the sphere of the world and the sphere of God.

But this sanctification goes beyond a simple giving of new meaning. It *issues in unity of being* of the bread and wine with the sacrificed Christ. The giving of new meaning adduces new being. This new meaning is given to elements in all the seven sacraments recognized by the Roman Catholic Church. For instance the bestowal adds new meaning to the wedding ring in marriage. But in sacraments other than the eucharist the new meaning does not result in unity of being between sign and the reality signified. This happens only in eucharist, which is thus the primary sacrament among the seven. This new union of being differentiates Coffey's theology of sanctification from "trans-significa-tion" (GGHS 196–206). The presence of significance means that Coffey recognizes as do we in our diagram the "externalization" of sacraments by the community-at-one-with-the-Spirit.

67. Another word about the sacramental elements: Coffey states what he understands to be binding for faith as regards transubstantia-tion: by the power of God bread and wine are truly changed so as to become Christ in his full saving effectiveness. The result is that Christ becomes present in the eucharist in his total being though under signs rather than in the historical form he had in Palestine. Coffey finds fault with the "transubstantiation" metaphor because in it the elements *cease to be bread and wine* as they become the body and blood of Christ. But nothing in the institutional narratives suggests that the bread and wine cease to exist. Biblical scholarship finds that body and blood are the language of sacrifice, and as such should have a foot in "both worlds," the sacred realm and the mundane realm. In the same way that my desk remains a desk even when it is elevated to the realm of consciousness, so should the bread and wine remain themselves while elevated to the sacred realm (GGHS 189–193). For this reason Coffey chooses his theology of sanctification to explain eucharist instead of the theology of transubstantiation.

68. Cf. Coffey 1984, especially pp. 476–480.

69. "The sacramental celebration, the symbolic action and accom-panying verbal formula, represents objectively the faith of the Church in God's promise of fidelity to his people. God's promise is repre-

sented in word and act as unbreakable—a free promise bound up with the placing of the sacramental celebration in accord with the sense of the Church.

"Concretely, this promise is represented in the liturgy in the form of the prayer of the Church made to the Father through the incarnate Son in the Holy Spirit, with absolute confidence in God's fidelity. In other words, what is represented in the sacramental celebration is the confident response to the promise which the Lord gave to the Church of absolute certainty of a hearing when the community of faith prays in the name of Jesus" (Kilmartin 1989, 537).

70. GGHS 150. This lacuna surely must be regarded a serious flaw in Coffey's otherwise splendid presentation, because it does not allow us to see how Coffey understands Rahner's difficult presentation. The little Coffey does say at least appears to say something Rahner did not. In Coffey 1984, 478, we find this sentence: "We have from the pen of Rahner an essay in which he explains the profound unity which exists between love of God and love of neighbor even in this life." But Rahner's argument does not support the word "even" in this life. Rahner argues that *specifically* in this life, and *essentially* in this life— because human beings are constituted within the material world— they can come to the full love of God mainly (and it seems only) by loving the neighbor. The word "even" seems to imply that somewhere else the principle applies more fully than "in this life." Such an implication is wholly at variance with Rahner's presentation in the article referred to (Rahner 1969). Coffey holds that the Holy Spirit is incarnated in Jesus' specific earthly love and bears the marks of that personality "even" back to the immanent Trinity. This kind of implication is not in the Rahner article and therefore must be explained to the reader of Coffey, on pain of seeming to argue (wrongly) from authority. See also Coffey 1986, 236–238 for the central importance of Rahner's (there unexplained too) article to Coffey's argumentation.

71. This "outreach," or *Vorgriff* in Rahner's German, resembles a horizon before which a person can know, say, the buildings on the skyline. The difference is that in the case of human knowing we can never focus on the horizon and know it explicitly. It remains a preconscious presence.

72. For a most detailed presentation of the above in Thomistic terms cf. *Spirit in the World* (1957, 1968) and in terms of question theory, *Hearers of the Word* (1963, 1969).

73. In Rahner's considerably more technical language, "the transcendentally original *a priori* experience of his original reference to God and thus of God himself (an experience which must in some measure also be objectified in categories) can be made only in an always already achieved going-out into the world which, understood

as the world of man, is primarily the people *with whom* he lives. Precisely because the original reference towards God is of a transcendental kind and hence does not fall into any category but is given in the infinite reference of the spirit of man beyond every mere object of his personal and material surroundings, the *original* experience of God (as distinct from his separating representation in an individual concept) is always given in a 'worldly' experience. This, however, is only present originally and totally in the communication with a 'Thou'" (Rahner 1969, 245–246). Cf. also Rahner 1992, 51–55.

74. Rahner does make room for the mystical "moment" in the church that we saw in van Beeck: "It must be said, of course, that not every act of the love of God is also a formal act of love of neighbor, if and in so far as the love of neighbor means an act in which our neighbor is envisaged and loved as the conscious object in its categorized and conceptual representation. If one relates oneself explicitly by prayer, trust and love to God, then this is in *this* sense an act of love of God and not an act of love of neighbor" (Rahner 1969, 238). Later he says that, even though this kind of "reflected religious act" has a higher dignity, still it remains secondary in comparison to love of neighbor (Rahner 1969, 246). But obviously, all prayer to God includes the neighbor as a background and condition for human existence, and often as specific content.

CHAPTER FIVE

LITURGY AS CREATION, LITURGY AS ART

Two broad questions concern us here, liturgy as creative in itself—distinguished from creative in its historical inception, its particular manner of performance, or in its subsidiary arts—and liturgy as an art form.

Much depends on how one considers the vast interconnections between Trinity and world. If these add up mainly to "meetings" or "causation," then the previous chapter's story will tabulate in a more or less extrinsic manner. Even if grace be considered as Rahner's "self-communication" of God, an undeserved gift, still any gift from a friend could be received gratefully but mainly as something enjoyed in itself and leading to nothing further. This is not Rahner's meaning, of course, but he could be interpreted that way unless understood deeply. Not until one grasps fully the meaning of a "union that engenders" can God's trinitarian action in the world (and within "God-as-God") be comprehended at its fruitful depths.

We begin chapter five, then, by listening again to the trinitarian chronicle with ears sharpened to the creative potential of each point of union. Since liturgy is one privileged moment of this story, we will test it by each of the seven characteristics of co-creation from chapter one. By that time we will have understood that liturgy is itself a creative act. We will be ready to consider next liturgy as art. Can we say that liturgy IS an art form? If not, can we at least draw a fruitful analogy to art and its workings? If either is the case we can move to liturgy as it

229

happens and say in what way our considerations make a difference to it. What does it mean to say that the people participate fully, consciously, actively in it? How do the creative arts cohere to a liturgical form that is not indifferent to them but shares their artistic nature? And how is liturgical music changed when it finds a place in this conception?

I. Liturgy as Creative

All sacramental liturgies result from a "oneing" of God's Spirit with human beings. This union is fruitful. Let us look at both "parents" of this offspring. I have no intention here of referring to or establishing God as male or as only Father and the church as feminine or only mother. These traditional categories of the church through history have had many advantages, but as I have already noted, disadvantages as well. God perforce must have feminine and mothering qualities—as the Bestowal model of the Trinity demonstrates—and the assembly is by no means simply and only feminine or mothering. It does happen that in the present discussion, as in that of art, the analogous roles are identified by locating where the mothering womb is to be found. By this standard and in this case, the assembly is analogous to a mother.[1] Their activity of symbolizing or externalizing gives birth to the rites of their liturgies. We warned ourselves not to interpret this information in an "either/or" fashion. Liturgy is not simply a human, sociological activity, something that could happen even if there were no God, or no God-with-us. Liturgy is *both* the saving action of God *and* the externalizing action of people. In other words, it is the direct result of a union between persons and the Holy Spirit. Human ritual events are permeated with the Spirit of God, both in their meaning and, in the case of the eucharist, in their being. The liturgy is God's, and it is the people's, even as a human child is offspring of both parents. In this we have discovered the reason for Vatican II's affirmation about participation by the people. Instead of being an innovation or an ephemeral trend, "participation" describes the origin of liturgy. In liturgy's second moment there is a oneing of the assembly with Christ-in-the-sacrament, a union that becomes Christian action in the world.

God is analogous to the human father, because the gestation and labor take place physically in the assembly. This does not mean that God is absent from the gestation and birth. God's oneing nature allows the unique presence of the Holy Spirit through the whole process—something a human father cannot have. Only God can provide sacraments in which God is truly and completely present. Liturgy is itself an offer of bestowal because it has God within it. If this were not the case, sacramental liturgy would be only human memories or a sociological event.[2] To apply our thesis to one aspect of the eucharist, the simple material elements of bread and wine have been elevated to the Godly realm and have received oneness with God within the action of the liturgy. Liturgy is human because of its human assembly-mother. It is Godly because of the Spirit-father.

A note about discernment may be in order at this point. It may seem from what we have discovered, and will further determine, that each and every liturgy throughout time has to have been the wholesome outcome of a union between the Holy Spirit and an assembly. Of course this is not so. It would be difficult to find the action of the Spirit, for instance, in Hitler's great pageants. And what about the apostle Paul railing against the divisions in the Corinthian church and the eating and drinking to excess. He tells them that "it is not the Lord's supper that you eat" (1 Cor 11:17-22).[3] Who is to be the judge, then, of whether a liturgy comes from the Spirit of God or from a spirit of darkness?

Of course, the Great Tradition of the church and its teaching tradition will be able to give many guidelines, but these vary from tradition to tradition. Within any Christian liturgy there can be elements that restrict the faith of the people and actually work against the presence of Christ. Human beings remain limited and drawn to sin even within the holiest events. The judge of whether and how much a liturgy comes from union with the Holy Spirit will be exactly the one Paul specifies in the same letter to the Corinthians: the spiritual person. "We have received not the spirit of the world, but the Spirit which is from God, that we might understand the gifts bestowed on us by God," he says (1 Cor 2: 12).[4] Even as the mystic's utterances can be judged only from within the Spiritual reality of the church, so the authentic Spirit of the liturgy can be discerned only by those who are already somewhat proficient in the life and conduct of true Christian life. This is why holiness and prayer are bedrock necessities of every minister of the liturgy.

Now we need to go into practical details. Our purpose is to apply the principles we encountered initially in the first analogy of this book, the one to human reproduction. The point is not to reduce liturgy in some way to the physical events of procreation, but to see the deep human creativity that is active in both. In this way we will confirm how each liturgy is creative in itself, not just in its subsidiary creative arts. Let us verify liturgy as off-spring of the union between God and assembly by asking how the seven characteristics of human co-creating apply.

One important distinction must be noted first. We must in-voke a principle that Maritain insisted on for artistic creativity. Though our analogy might seem to imply a temporal succession of events—*first*, the conception, *then* the gestation, *after that* the birth—the ordering in creation of liturgy is not one of time at all but of an order of nature. This means that each of the steps depends on the one that precedes it in nature, so that if a prior one is absent, the next one cannot take place. But often certain of the seven characteristics can take place at the same time. Con-ception may continue well into the enactment of the liturgical event. Gestation may overlap the performance, so that newness occurs even as the liturgy takes place. Think, for instance, of the homilist who finds that his or her well-prepared text is being met with boredom and disinterest; if able, that presider will discard parts or all of the premeditated homily and initiate a whole different line of thought. In this case, portions of the conception and gestation are simultaneous with the birth of the liturgical event. Priority of nature means merely that gestation depends on conception, and birth depends on gestation—no matter how the temporal sequence may occur.

The advantage of this distinction is that it helps avoid a certain "predetermined" idea of liturgical creativity. If the or-dering were one strictly of time, then everything about the par-ticular liturgy could already be given ahead of time, and merely unfolded (temporally) from what was already essentially formed. This would run contrary to the way every liturgist knows things happen. Seldom does the liturgy simply unfold in an orderly and methodical fashion. It is a living event, an occurrent art, Langer would call it. As in any living organism, the rhythm and intricate relation of event to event happen when they happen, not when some rigorous, detailed plan dictates.

Moreover, the commanding form resists interpretation as a kind of pre-compacted work of art. Langer stresses that it con-tains only the general gestalt from which artistic choices will be made. It is a dynamic form within which the work will develop. We heard her speak of the "relentless strain" on the artist because of the wealth of possibilities given in any commanding form. Since not all can be realized, each choice involves giving up other possibilities. *Possibilities* are found within the commanding form, not realizations. There is no "expressionist" or idealistic tendency in the present theory because without gestation and labor—wrestling with the materials—difficult choices guided by but not dictated by the commanding form, there could be no work of art.

(1) *Connaturality.* We have seen that the connaturality of man and woman for each other needs no "sanctification" or "elevation," but that this is not so with art, or with the relation of God to the world. In these, connaturality must be brought about. The higher entity, longing for union with the lower, frees the lower being from some of its "sticky" either/or status. Connaturality is achieved and union can follow. Liturgy involves this principle of elevation quite necessarily. Human beings do not have the capability to project a liturgy in which God is actively present. They must receive elevation from the Grace of bestowal, in order to be able even to accept the offer. Acceptance allows the preconscious union with the Holy Spirit that conceives the liturgy. The projection of ritual symbols then necessitates the raising of material things—not just to the conscious realm as in knowledge, but to the Godly realm. No human assembly could claim such a power, but an assembly, a church that has God's othering Spirit at its core can. Human beings are the means God utilizes to constitute sacramental liturgies. Two connaturalizing moments, then, are involved in liturgy, as follows:

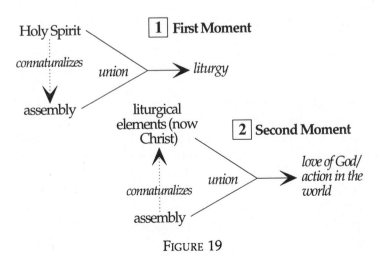

FIGURE 19

In the first moment, persons are raised to connaturality with God by the Holy Spirit and come into union with that Godly being. The communal offspring is liturgy, for the reasons we have seen. In the second moment, material elements are made connatural to Spiritualized human beings by being born from the union of God and people;[5] all the ritual elements—which means the words, actions, gestures and not just, e.g., bread and wine—are infused with the Spirit of Christ. People of the assembly partake of the liturgy, come into communion with Christ present. The offspring of this second and now "explicit" or "objective" union is return of love to God the Source (in Christ), which is love of neighbor and Christian action in the world.[6]

We have said that the party analogous to the mother is always the one which provides the "womb" where gestation takes place. In artistic creation, the father element must be elevated in order to enter artistic, mothering consciousness. It is the opposite in liturgy. God's Spirit gives a fathering seed, yet the mothering agent, human persons, must be elevated. Thus, neither the feminine nor masculine element is *in principle* "inferior" to the other, though of course creatures always remain lesser beings than God.

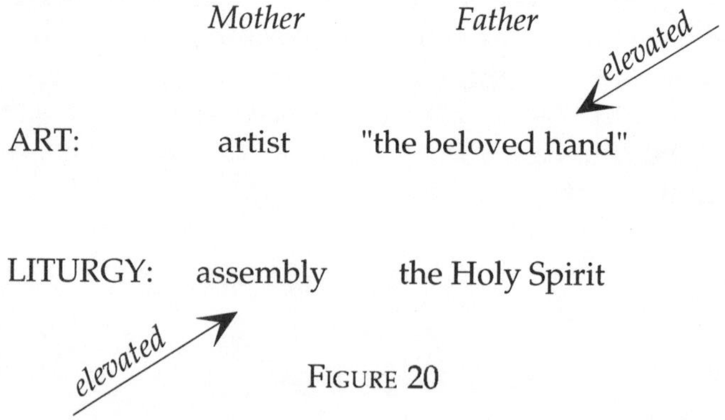

	Mother	*Father*
ART:	artist	"the beloved hand"
LITURGY:	assembly	the Holy Spirit

FIGURE 20

Two further clarifications must be given. First, connaturality does not in any sense mean an ironing out of the differences between God and human beings, making them equal partners. The very fact that "elevation" is needed reveals that God and the human being stand in a most unequal relationship. The point is not to envision a situation similar to the equality of man and woman in the procreative process, but to see how any relationship at all could exist between such dissimilar agents as God and people. The most that can be said of human beings of themselves is that they have an openness that does not exclude the entrance of God's Spirit. This openness is limited because human beings are creatures and have no ability even to reach toward God unless God supplies that ability. As we have noted, God must be the power that enables a human being even to accept the offer of the grace of the Holy Spirit, which even so can be rejected. If the offer is accepted, a person—still radically unequal to God—nevertheless is able then to seek the real God wherever the Godly presence can be found on earth.

If I may be permitted fanciful terms, the person needs only to be admitted into the Godly realm, even as my lowly, high-piled desk was allowed within the conscious realm—without somehow becoming consciousness itself. The person does not become God, but is sanctified or elevated so that, once within the Godly reaches, he or she can have converse with the great God in person.

In the last chapter I speculated that one of the deepest descriptions of God is that God is the one most able to come into union with an other, a profound union that leaves the integrity and identity of that other intact. A union with God compromises neither the union nor the distinction. I noted that the identity of the second person of God with the human being, Jesus, in no way threatens to lessen the infinity of God. For this reason subordination of the second person or of Jesus is unnecessary in order to retain the greatness of God. The same reasoning applies when God comes into union with human beings other than Jesus. A union is possible which neither lessens God nor somehow raises the human being to parity with the divine being. Each retains its own infinity or finitude but comes into penetrating union with the other. It is by God's condescension that the Holy Spirit and assemblies of human persons can do this, can come into a oneness that is the conception of the liturgy.

Secondly, connaturality is not itself union but the condition for union. Prevenient grace allows a person to say yes to the offer of bestowal, but it is not itself the union. The possibility of refusal underlines the reasons for declining to call the elevation itself a engendering union. Human sinfulness remains fully in force along with the capability of accepting the Holy Spirit. After an "unthematic" yes, the union allowed for by bestowed connaturality takes place.

(2) *Fertility.* There are at least four ways to look at fertility in the creation of liturgy. First, grace is everywhere. The offer of grace to every human being surely offers an abundant fertility. Second, the very number of liturgies throughout even one year should alert us to fertility. We would have to examine questions such as the diminished number of eucharistic liturgies possible, say in certain Latin American countries because of the lack of ministers, and in the USA because of lack of vocations to the priesthood. Nevertheless, the general point can be taken. If one were able to add up the number of Masses celebrated throughout the world since the church began, this very large number would attest to fertile abundance.

A third fertility is the "proleptic" nature of liturgy. The people of an assembly are a profusion of Spirited hearts. This does not mean that every assembly member achieves exemplary holiness on each liturgical occasion. At times some or even many will have very little interest or even belief in the events of the celebration. Perhaps a turn of personal life has left them isolated and far from acceptance. Perhaps the new liturgy does not speak to them. Or maybe their embodied faith journey has yet to round an important corner. Still, in varying degrees a number of people, through the eyes of faith, grasp clearly the life of Jesus present in the rites. Liturgy is "proleptic" because it looks forward to the moment when faith will be full, when Christians whose "yes" is now interlaced with "no" will have gradually converted to the simple yes.[7] When any of us wavers, he or she takes support from the rest who do not, at least that day. The abundance of grace and of "projecting" members makes a place for all of us, no matter the state of our unbelief. Of course the church's existence through time and across space magnifies this statement. Moreover, liturgy is founded on Christ's acceptance of grace once and for all. The church was fully founded when Jesus accepted the bestowal of love and lived it out. The "rest of us," to whatever degree, join in Jesus' return to the Source. Here there is much room for the "not yet" of faith life.

We could address fertility finally by drawing away from liturgy as such and turning to what tradition calls the "sacramentals." This word is variously understood, but generally refers to symbolic actions such as use of holy water, rings blessed at a wedding, parents invoking God's favor upon their children, the sign of the cross, blessed ashes, religious vows, etc.

We could refer also to what some call "secular sacraments." Here, for instance, a parent instructs a son or daughter about table manners, or friends recall a special song together. Any breakthrough to love means that the walls of division are breached and allow room for exchange. Especially when this breakthrough is symbolized, a sacramental presence is achieved. The world is fertile with such opportunities.

(3) From such extravagant Spiritual gift comes *onement*. First there is union of individuals with the Holy Spirit, when they (begin to) accept its bestowal. It is difficult to discern exactly when this happens in an individual human life. At baptism? But of course we are talking about a grace prior to the sacraments. At the age of reason? Before? When faith first becomes explicit? On the edge of sleep one cool night when a sub-teenager first comprehends that God is real and somehow present?

Then there is the union of the church-assembled with God's Spirit. Like any large historical organization, the church does not depend on each local assembly to make up its mind about symbols. These are established and held in common through long generations. Like any society, the church depends on *socialization* to pass on the meanings and values of its central symbols. The local assembly does *own* its liturgies because otherwise the symbols would fail to speak. But each assembly appropriates the symbols and meanings of the church. In union with the Holy Spirit it projects their meaning and being. Oneing therefore does take place afresh in each liturgy, at the same time as the church (the habitual union of members with the Spirit through space and time) carries forth the deepest oneing subconsciously from year to year. In short, liturgy can take place through traditional symbols because and only because of the oneing of God's Spirit with the assembly in the many hearts and souls.[8] Obviously, this oneing does not take place in a vacuum. It happens along with the lifelong insertion of the individuals into the life of Christ and the church.

The second moment of onement in liturgy is communion with the presence of Christ throughout the liturgy. Sacramental Communion is more than simply an eating of something or other in fellowship with other Christians. Because Christ is intentionally (really) present in the liturgical sacrament of the eucharist, Communion qualifies as a most important union, a oneing with Christ that is physical and spiritual at the same time. The presence of Christ, of course, is not limited to the elements of bread and wine; it is spread throughout all the liturgical action: readings, eucharistic prayer, music, and so on. Communion with Christ-present is the essence of the liturgy, as we will see in more detail in Part II of this chapter, and Communion represents the symbolic (real) high point of this union. As we have said, this second moment of union takes place between the objective presence of Christ and the participating members, in contrast with the completely pre-conscious union with the Holy Spirit of the first moment.

Of course, this is not to say that the "objective" liturgy enters the participants at a completely conscious and articulate level. Many times an assembly cannot be truly aware of the meaning of their participation or of the presence of Christ. The fullness of any ritual action enters deep into the unconscious of the partaker, something that ritual repetition makes more possible. Only gradually do the full implications make their way into consciousness, in the manner of all gestation, and come to birth as action. Often the meaning of a reading or of Communion may be recognized only later, after the liturgy has ended.

(4) This *union itself becomes the third.* We saw this principle amply evident in physical co-creation, in creation of the work of art, and in, for example, the "spiration" of the Holy Spirit within the Trinity. We said that the union does not cause the third, it *is* the third. If we are to say, with the church, that Christ is really present (in his Spirit) within the sacramental liturgy, then we have to be able to explain how this can be. Without rehearsing our entire argument, we can say again that a doctrine of the Spirit's generative presence within assembled human beings is able to demonstrate how God is truly present in liturgical action and its elements. The onement is already the liturgy in germ. It is a union of God and people, which union itself gestates and becomes the God/human liturgy.

We recall that, for Maritain, the creative idea once conceived must externalize itself into the outer world. The same is true, *mutatis mutandis,* of the church assembled. Human beings *must* express themselves symbolically. God's presence in the warm recesses of their selves cannot simply slumber there, removed from the outer world. The union is pregnant in exactly the same way that creative intuition is. Its purpose is to work its way into the outer world so that men and women can know themselves as one with Christ in his Spirit. Assemblies behold that identity symbolized in sacramental liturgy. They can receive their very identity from the liturgy because it proceeds from their God-oned subjectivity. The liturgical event *is* their real union with the Spirit, gestated and born. Their identity is more than an "understanding of who I am." They have entered a union with the othering One, a pregnant union that will not abide until it has been born.

Once born, the liturgy serves as fathering element for the assembly in what we have called the second moment of union. We said that the assembly partakes of Christ present in the eucharist, and that this union or communion engenders Christian action in the world. Here the principle we have seen in all our analogates so far becomes most clear. Christian action in the world is nothing but the union of an assembly member with Christ. To say it another way, the member has made real again what first came about in baptism, has become "another Christ." Loving action is nothing else than that union, played out in action. In other words, the union itself has become the third: action in the world.

(5) *Gestation* begins in the lives of individual Christians. In whatever way they first broke through to accepting the bestowal of Love upon them, clearly the maintenance of such a "yes" requires their whole life. It gestates there. When babies are born they do not have a sense of "the other." Their boundaries include everything as "me." Only gradually, through trauma and adventure, do infants understand "me" and the "stuff out there" as different from each other. With exquisite finesse human beings learn to break through to the other, while each remains still his or her own self. This is a search for love, and it is elevated into a search for the God of love. As it externalizes itself into the many relationships of their lives, in the commitments of love that they avoid and also seek, it can properly be said to gestate.

As members of an assembly, the individuals-seeking-Jesus work throughout the week toward the regular liturgies that express Jesus' presence. People are inexplicitly aware of these communal events throughout their day or week. If the seasons of the church year are enacted well in a church community, the awareness of the upcoming midnight Mass might become explicit. Immediate anticipation of the events of liturgy resembles the intuitive "pulsions" that are the first stirrings of the creative onement within. Ministers come to awareness of how the Spirit's bestowal is to be born in this season or that, and this gradual awareness represents a gestation of the bestowal union.

Planners and musicians are part of a more defined gestation. They and all other ministers are like internal organs of gestation. They further focus the assembly's growing preparation for a particular liturgy. The planner must articulate designs and strategies for actual implementation. Will there be a wreath for Advent? A procession? Shall we use all the readings? What about movement? Lighting? Pace? This year should we at last get new vestments exclusively for Christmas? The choir director, choir, and instrumentalists work far in advance to prepare music. Here especially, as we will see in the next section, music does not *belong* to the musicians but to the assembly, even in the case of a choral piece to which the congregation simply listens. The creativity of these ministering artists of the liturgy is subsumed under that of the church assembled, and there is no question of a virtuosic show for its own sake. The moment belongs to the minister only insofar as he or she is a member (albeit specialized) of the assembly at large.

It might be objected that the assembly does not in fact gestate a liturgical event, the ministers do. The people's worry centers instead around daily decisions, reactions, crises and resolutions—not around liturgical events. This is true, but here is a new feature of our analogy. The assembly entrusts portions of its job of conceiving to specific members, in the same way that the mother entrusts gestation to her relevant body parts. No part does the job of the other. All parts interact to carry out the primary work which is not theirs alone but the mother's. All of her does the job *through* the relevant parts. Another way to say this is that the ministries are *delegated*. The assembly, within the church, delegates to its ministers the work of developing its own newly conceived life-in-the-Spirit as liturgical action. They leave practical matters to be handled by an "official" portion of the community, the ministers.

Again, this does not mean that the assembly is *not* doing these tasks. Delegation does not mean abdication. The church assembled carries out gestation in a *both/and* rather than an *either/or* fashion. Because the assembly is a corporate entity, it again must act (through space and time) as any human society acts. It must deputize certain of its members to carry out crucial tasks on behalf of it, not instead of it. Benefits accrue to all parties on this account. The assembly retains its authorship of the liturgy, even though all members cannot be expected to carry out all the artistic details. Likewise, the various liturgical artists stand free from the necessity that would fall upon them if they were solo artists: to express their own subjectivity (filled with the other) in their works of art. It is the subjectivity of the assembled church that they carry out, a subjectivity filled with the Jesus-incarnated Spirit of God. What an individual artist did in the arts now takes place in a corporate artist, the assembly, through its ministers—who maintain great vigilance toward the people to assure that the liturgical realization is *theirs*, that it issues from this particular assembly.

This interpretation does not deny to liturgical ministers their own, individual artistic gestation process, in the meaning Maritain described. The question is not whether a liturgical composer acts like a composer, but whose subjectivity is being expressed. A liturgical musician, composer, preacher, or dancer is artist indeed, but all join their subjectivity to that of the whole assembly. Their individual artistic sensibilities act in much the same way as the "secular" painter or composer, but now as specifying the gestation of the whole assembly: conception brinks over into consciousness as inarticulate pulsions, swimming together, bumping and sharing each other's reality. These become more and more discrete, then head toward and through the realm of consciousness. How will this particular piece of music affect the overall flow? What ideas should be preached to bring out the nature of the liturgical event (not: how can I reach them with my preaching this Sunday)? Artists remain artists but conception and gestation are sharings in the larger, mothering assembly.

The highly analogous nature of our comparison has to be born in mind. To say it once more, liturgy does not result from *first*, a conception within the assembly, *second*, a gestation in the manners related above, and *third*, a performance of the liturgy which was already in a sense complete at the moment of conception. This would represent a temporal ordering, exactly like the timing of physical conception, gestation, and birth. But we have said that the ordering in liturgy, as in art, is an ordering of nature, not of time. That is, the gestation depends in principle on the conceptive union, but they may actually take place at the same time. Again, birth cannot take place except on the condition of gestation, but ministers may find at times that part of the gestation takes place only in the actual celebration itself, and that the conception is concurrent and still happening even at the same time as the gestation and birth. The materials of good liturgy can resist control, and ministers of the liturgy have to wrestle with them, even as artists must with the materials of their particular art form.

We have been describing moment one of liturgical creativity, the emergence of the liturgy from the "collective unconscious" of the assembly into the light of objective day. We must also spend a moment on the gestative quality of the second moment of creativity. Here the people, with their unconscious or preconscious thirsting for God in the world, encounter the intentional presence of Christ in the liturgical action. Their union with Christ throughout the liturgy, culminating in physical Communion, presents a most important example of significant, engendering union. The birth resulting from this oneing, Christian action in the world, is the same thing as the return of the Father's love to its source. Gestation takes place as the communion comes to fruition during the week. "Inspired," in the full sense of the word, the members of the assembly mull the significance of Jesus' servant status, his breakthrough into full exchange, his unstinting love of each person. The Holy Spirit within them guides the transition of this communion with Christ into actions of love that are like his, that are the actions of the body of Christ in the world.

(6) *Labor.* Until Christmas or Holy Week is over it is not safe to ask an active liturgist about labor. Yes, a woman forgets the pain of labor when her child is born, but an ample cooling off period is still required. The work of planning and ministering to liturgy's great events absorbs toil in the same way that birth of a child does, in the same way that writing a great work does. Emergence of inner ideas into actual material reality places great demands upon the human psyche and body, and this tells especially on the ministers. The sensations are oddly like a mother's labor. *Push.* I don't feel like it. *Push.* I'm tired. Appropriate habits will help, but the strain is evident. That which was hidden in the collective pre-conscious of people readies itself for birth.[9]

(7) *Birth.* Now the hearing. Now the power. Now the vessel brimmed for pouring. Now the joyful celebration.[10] The assembly's songs, responses, their beholding presence, all are moments in this great coming to be. Believers throng, and maybe the aisles even have extra chairs. A nervous soloist and reader

now must perform. They are helping to birth that which was conceived within the very people of God, through the centuries, through the season, and through the preceding week. Their song or reading *is* the onement of God and people now being born.

The second moment of union arrives. Assembly members partake of the sacramental liturgy they have parented. The liturgy, displaying their union with God's Spirit, their searched for oneness with the resurrected Christ, makes present a specific event of Christ's sacrifice. The people commune with it, partake of their God-oned identity. Their union with Christ-present produces a new offspring: Christian action. It had gestated through time and is born one day when a member joins a church committee or agrees to give out soup. With Christ the assembly members bestow the Spirit of love upon the Father, through love of neighbor. They join in the Spirit-engendered sacrifice; they say yes to receiving all from God, yes to releasing everything in gratitude and surrender.

Every form of Christian sacrament should be considered in this way. Sacraments of initiation give birth to new Christian identity and membership. Marriage engenders committed Christian love between woman and man, and Christian family. Orders becomes official ministry. Reconciliation gives loving ties in place of broken ones. The sacrament of the sick gives birth to patience and acceptance, a wholeness of spirit that can usher in physical healing. Eucharist is called the first of sacraments because it gives the saving action of Jesus for every occasion, not just for this or that specific event, as do the other sacraments. Eucharist provides *par excellence* the new significant union that will gestate within church members and come to birth in the myriad events of daily life. But all the liturgical sacraments flow into action, and specifically in this century into social action. Love of neighbor opens out into love of the poor. The sacraments are meant to engender lives filled with the breakthrough to exchange first accomplished in Christ's life. "By their fruits you shall known them."[11]

It is possible, then, to affirm liturgy as intrinsically creative in both its moments of union. It forms a true analogate to the first of our models, human birth. Now we must turn to our second model, that of art. We understood art by means of human reproduction. Now can art explain liturgy?

II. Liturgy as Art

The first step can be taken simply. Liturgy is not itself an art genre. If it were, it would have to do what music, dance, painting, drama, and poetry all do, in the ways we have discovered. A creative artist would have to one with experienced reality. His or her union with the world would have to become a charged kernel, a zygote, which could otherwise be described as a commanding form. The pulsions within this particle would then have to stir and edge over into the conscious of that mothering artist. They would pass through the conceptual realm, which in this case would mean the articulated material realm of the symbol, and develop into the art object. The birthed work would then stand before beholders, who would find in it the oned subjectivity of an artist written into the forms of the art piece. We placed our objection to this interpretation of liturgy in the introduction to Part Two of this book: liturgy would turn into a personal vehicle, as does a work of art, even in the midst of its universal worth. But liturgy is not the child of a single artisan, as we have seen above in detail. It does not reveal a single person's subjectivity but that of a people. Therefore liturgy does not qualify as an art genre alongside the others.

This "negative insight" in no way compromises the work of the previous chapters. We did not set out to establish a univocal likeness between liturgy and art, or between art and human reproduction. We sought an *analogy* between the three. Here we find bountiful yield. To gather that yield, let us consider liturgy as analogous to an art form, according to the various insights of Maritain and Langer.

A first and perhaps terrifying question emerges. For Langer every work of art has the goal of presenting an illusion. Her greatest contribution was to name a primary illusion for each art genre. Can religious sensibilities rest serene when liturgy is called an *illusion*? Even Langer's friendly critics hesitated to accept the word as applied to art. It sounded too much like another, delusion. This difficulty becomes more severe when we remember the etymology of the word "illusion": it comes from the Latin *in* + *ludere*, meaning to "play against," or to mock. Dictionaries tend to define illusion as a misleading image.[12] But we have worked the question long enough to understand that illusion in art meant, for Langer, "simulation": giving to the beholder something that was not there bodily, but was truly present in another sense, with Maritain's intentional reality. Can this be said of liturgy too?[13]

Maritain's use of the word "intentional" gave us a new way to understand "illusion." Materials of an art work are arranged in such a way that consciousness can find within them what is "virtually" present until then: the forms of inner life. If these forms were present literally, the work of art would be inner life itself, which is impossible. Instead, the *both/and* consciousness of an artist has left its mark on the otherwise *either/or* world of material. The painting is *both* an arrangement of stolid, dried, material paints, *and* an intentional pattern that communicates its intentional meanings to the beholder. Meaning is encapsulated, waiting to be found by the consciousness that frees it. The intentional reality is truly there, but not literally so.

If we are correct in interpreting Langer in this quasi-Maritainian fashion, then no objection can be lodged against liturgy being "illusory," or better, "presence-making." It contains an intelligible structure born from consciousness that is more than the simple material gestures, sounds, smells, and movements of which it consists. In liturgy's narrative character we are beholding not the literal historical actions of Jesus' life but a storied semblance of those actions. Liturgy (if it is good liturgy) is a "making-present" in that it consists of an intentional structure.

"Illusion," in Langer's sense, does not mean that God fails to be "really" present in the liturgy and its elements. Just the opposite. God's presence is achieved precisely by the intentional projection of the human beings who make up the church assembled. God's Word is born into the world of liturgy *because* the Spirit has first come to inhere in the inner life of the individuals who make up the church. Liturgical life is not *like* the Spirit's union with us; it *is* that Spiritual oneing, gestated and given birth in the intentional structure of the liturgy. Externalization of symbolic rites is the only way and the best way that God's Word comes to be present within the ritual. That which is deep in the inner life of the assembly, God's othering Spirit in fertile union with the people, is projected into liturgical rite. This is the "real presence" accomplished by the "illusion" or "semblance," or "making-present."

With that understanding in mind, we now need to establish the "elements," the "basic abstraction," and the "primary illusion" of liturgy. It is already clear that technical "materials," while necessary, can by no means suffice for sacramental liturgy by themselves. According to Roman Catholic tradition, words, actions, and the intention of the presider (to do this according to the mind of the church) are needed to constitute a sacrament— we would say to impart the "intentional" meaning/being or to "make-present."[14] In another context we said that the materials have to be "sanctified," or elevated to the level of Godly othering in order to be sacramental symbols. The "sanctification" *consists of* admitting the materials into the sacred consciousness of the mothering assembly, and through this, birthing of "intentional" meaning into the "materials" of the art-like liturgy.

In Langer's terminology, materials become "elements" when they take on a semblance meaning.[15] What are the elements of liturgy, in her meaning of the word? Without attempting thoroughness or ranking, let us list a few, using the eucharist as our prime example.

- Entrance and exit processions
- Movement within sacred space
- Symbolic gesture
- Word as recited—story, theological and
  ethical reflection
- Word as preached
- Words of praise and of invocation (*epiclesis*)[16]
- Formulaic language
- Repetition
- Specific foodstuff (e.g., bread and wine,
  canonically specified)
- Eating and drinking
- Participation in spoken and sung responses
- Subsidiary arts (music, dance, homiletics, decor)
- Vestments

Clearly, each of the elements already consists of a semblance, the presence of virtual "intentional" meaning. We can see that one of our questions from the introduction to Part Two has been answered. There we objected that the *repetition* found in liturgy would disqualify it as an art form; no other art would be content simply to repeat literally the words and actions of a former work. Here we understand repetition—both within the liturgical event and repetition of the whole form, time after time—to be one of the *elements* of liturgical art. Repetition works to establish the primary semblance that is abstracted.

What is that semblance? Patrick Collins suggests *virtual action* as the answer (Collins 1983, 113), and with qualifications we take that as our answer here. Liturgy's primary element, which everything works to establish, is "sacred action as present." The great deeds of the God-man are called to mind in the specific readings of the day. Hebrew scripture readings tell of God's intervention in history prior to Jesus. The gospel presents one or two incidents from his life, theologically and artistically elaborated, in order to make present Jesus' saving life. The reading from the letters gives theological precision and exhortation to deepen the point. Then enactment of the eucharistic prayer narrates the essential saving action and applies it to the materials about to be received by the assembly. The short narration that used to be called "the consecration" is preceded and followed by words of invocation, praise, and petition. The *epiclesis* asks God's Spirit to make Jesus' resurrected life really present here and now—to make *the action* present. Communion effects oneness with the trans-historical actions.

Processions into and out of the liturgical area symbolize (roughly) entrance into and exit from the space where the semblance is to be carried out, the "sacred space." Of course, the entrance of members in to the place of assembly has a similar symbolic meaning. We have seen at length the "elevation" required—not as the physical raising of the bread and cup, but in our previous meaning of "sanctification"—if persons are to meet God's Spirit and unite through it with Christ. We spoke metaphorically about this as an "entrance into the sacred sphere." "Sacred space" is a *semblance* of this elevation to God's sphere. Of course there are a number of other reasons for processions; one is simply to get the ministers up to the altar from their vesting place. Another is to enact a dramatic beginning and ending. These practicalities are baptized, so to speak, by the semblance they effect, entrance into sacred space. Vestments add to this semblance. All movements within the designated space, whether this be only the sanctuary or includes the whole interior of the church or room, work to establish the primary semblance: sanctified actions within God's sphere. For its part, repetition works to establish the depth of the Spirit's penetration into our lives. Repeated words and actions are like a stairway worn smooth; the daily act of ascending the stairs takes place without thought, even as the bestowal of the Spirit happens prior to thinking. With the comfort of repetition comes an ability to attend interiorly to what one already knows and barely listens to. The memory of Christ's saving deeds runs very deep, and the presence of those actions does not and should not come as news.

Talk of sacred space should be balanced by allusion to the world as sacred. In a sense, Jesus sanctified the secular by offering grace to everyone, everywhere. The birth of Christian action as an offspring of liturgy means that Christ is present throughout the world, not just in a church building.

This realization gave rise, perhaps, to the informal liturgies that Thomas Day decries. If Christian life is a daily thing, if it is within the world, then why should the presider not say "good morning" at the beginning of Mass? This interpretation, however, misses a point brilliantly established by Northrop Frye in *The Anatomy of Criticism*. Frye shows that daily talk can suffice in small groupings, where the participants are of one mind already, but not in "formal" gatherings.

> Ordinary speech is concerned mainly with putting into words what is loosely called the stream of consciousness: the day-dreaming, remembering, worrying, associating, brooding and mooning that continually flows through the mind and which, with Walter Mitty, we often speak of as thought. This ordinary speech is concerned mainly with self-expression. Whether from immaturity, pre-occupation, or the absence of a hearer, it is imperfectly aware of an audience. Full awareness of an audience makes speech rhetorical, and rhetorical means a conventionalized rhythm. The irregular rhythm of ordinary speech may be conventionalized in two ways. One way is to impose a pattern of recurrence on it; the other is to impose the logical and semantic pattern of the sentence (Frye 1963, 20–21).

Daily speech has an inarticulate structure, an abhorrence of the final stop (period), and a tendency to be spoken as it is being thought. It does not need to project "across the footlights." The distancing found in a formal situation requires speech that is formally structured, thought out ahead of time, clearly articulated, and to some degree repetitious (Frye 1963, 13–51). The same goes for liturgical speech and action. Because of its distance from its hearers—be they audience or congregation—it must become conventionalized. The inarticulate "good morning" has to become "the Lord be with you," a phrase formalized and hallowed by time.

There is another reason for conventionalized liturgy, a reason founded on our prior considerations. The goal of a semblance is to establish another kind of *distance*, so that the art will not be taken merely for something literal. Its stylization and repetition removes it from daily events and builds the illusion necessary for symbolic action. In order to birth externally something so intimate and shrouded as pre-conscious union with the Spirit, sacred space and formal language are required, on pain of bypassing the hearers. Liturgy is formalized not out of encrustation or ignorance, but because of its primary semblance: remembered sacred action projected as present.

We recall that a work of art is composed of various semblances ("intentional presences") combined to present one primary illusion. What is the primary illusion in liturgy? Patrick Collins chooses *presence* for this role. But presence serves as a fitting primary illusion for the old Latin Mass, not for the Mass as renewed by Vatican II. In the Latin Mass I did have the feeling I was walking comfortably into the presence of God. The language, perhaps because in my childhood days I did not understand it, gave a sense of mystery. Perhaps Latin helped establish the sacred space. The priest was reciting words and carrying out rubricized movements hallowed by generations—millennia, to be more literal. This specialized formula worked its way toward the great moment, the words of consecration.[17] At that instant I knew that God had become *present* in the bread and the wine. They were now the body and blood of Christ. Priest and people faced the same way, toward the mystery—not toward each other for the sake of "interface." In my childhood we knew that we had not come to church to meet one another or even mainly to eat, but to kneel in the presence of a God who had bent down to our level. Many and perhaps most people bypassed communion. At times our prayer was not precisely liturgical but a kind of devotion carried out in solidarity with others. Here was the one time during our week when we knew for sure that God was there waiting for us. We basked in that presence.[18]

Presence is a precious commodity only when the trinitarian God is distant and other. The "defeat" of the Trinity perhaps contributed to the quite human reaction of humility before God's great epiphany. As we have seen amply above, trinitarian eucharistic liturgy does not really support such an experience. God's othering does not ask us to stand before it but to *partake* of it. The moments of fertile oneing we have traced in this chapter require parties who commingle: humans who are raised to a connaturality in the sacred realm of God in order to allow union. The comfort of the old way—we were favored children in the presence of the Great One—has to give way to the more adult mode of *communion*. [19]

The primary illusion or semblance of Christian liturgy, then, especially eucharistic liturgy since that is what we are concentrating on, is *communion*: oneness with Christ in his sanctified, resurrected life. The liturgy of the word, the liturgy of the eucharist, and the communion rite all have this as their purpose, to establish the presence of Christ's sacred actions in order to lead the assembly to union with Christ (to "more clearly apprehend, more dearly love, and more nearly imitate" the life of Christ made present in them for this liturgical event). Here we arrive at the essence of the argument of this whole book. The ability to become one with an other is the essence of God's being, and of other beings insofar as they are able. Human beings come to liturgy to recognize their Christlife (clearly apprehend), enter into union with it (dearly love), and by so doing give birth to their Christian lives in the world (nearly imitate). Any other reading would fail to do justice to the nature of God, of human beings, and of the liturgy.

Our statement of the primary illusion of liturgy should not be taken in an either/or manner. We do not enter into communion with Christ in the Spirit *to the exclusion of other people*. No horizontal-vertical warfare exists between our attention to other persons and to Christ. We spent time toward the end of the last chapter establishing the point that human love of God the Father (-Mother) is identical to love of other persons. Unless we intend to fence in our love so that it can only reach God, we have to imitate Jesus more nearly in loving the people around us. The important premise that "the original experience of God . . . is only present originally and totally in the communication with a 'Thou'" (Rahner 1969, 246) shows us that the assembly and its interrelationships do not stand accidental to the liturgy. Because of people's love for one another the liturgy can exist as communion with the person who loved people unto death.

Next we can speak of the talents of liturgical artists, those who shape the primary illusion with and for the rest of the assembly. We detailed Maritain's, Langer's, and even Maslow's understanding of talent versus genius. Genius is the power of conception; talent is the capability of bringing that conception to birth. We can account for the genius of liturgical conception, essentially a power of othering, by the presence of the great othering one, God's Spirit. No matter how human partners fail and negate, in the long run conception is sure in the church. Jesus is the foundation of this "yes," and the rest of us yearn toward it.

When we come to talents we have to admit different amounts and kinds within liturgical ministers. Some could easily have been (or are) solo artists on their own. They have chosen to contribute their abilities in service of God's people assembled. Others, we have to say, possess very little of the artist's training and talent that they might focus upon the liturgy. Does this mean that congregations are forced to sit through grade-school-like performances that would never succeed elsewhere? It can often seem so. Here Thomas Day's diatribes regarding music may have a point.

> "Good morning," Mr. Caruso says to us. A few people in the pews mumble a "Good morning" back at him.
>
> "Let us all sing hymn number one hundred," he cheerfully announces.
>
> Then, for the next couple of minutes, Mr. Caruso roars into the microphone at the top of his voice and performs a duet with the organist, while most of the assembled worshipers watch him in stupefied silence. Sometimes the congregation tries to project its singing, sometimes the organ tries to assert its presence but, whatever happens, Mr. Caruso makes sure that his voice, his immensely amplified voice, will be the loudest thing there and will crest *over* the sound made by everyone else (Day 1990, 51).

We could multiply such examples. A guitar group that performs beautiful, folk-like tunes whose intricate charm forbids participation. A pianist-soloist who modifies a familiar melody with artistic decorations and ornamentations—in other words, plays in a way that no congregation could ever mimic. Or a liturgist who selects hymns too complicated, too new, or simply too "other" from the congregation they serve.

We might allege that these musicians are trying to be soloists—they have not yet grasped their place in the birthing event. But two other points need to be made. For one, the prime talent necessary for a liturgical musician is one of *solidarity with the people*. This talent stands prior to the capacity to make exquisite music. Even trained musicians cannot be assumed to have this ability. Churches have to seek out musicians who have developed "the liturgical talent": an ability to discern and foster the assembly in its singing. Congregations are nowhere near as trained or able in music as musicians are. Strict musical training has a single goal in mind for its professional: to take him or her out of the realm of the amateur and into that of the professional. What conservatory or teacher wants to produce amateurs? But ninety-nine percent of the congregation is exactly that: musically amateur. Granted, the Mennonites and some other church groups have been largely able to produce assemblies who sing and sing well, but most of the liturgical churches have not. A wide gulf opens. The more trained the musician, the less able to abide amateurs he or she will be. Should the musicians then be untrained, so they can work with untrained congregations? Or must professional musicians perform music *instead of* the congregation? Our hypothesis provides an answer. Trained musicians take part first in the liturgy's birth. Their job is not just to provide music, even great music. They are the way in which an assembly externalizes its Spirit-filled subjectivity in song and then becomes one with it. Musicians must have "the liturgical talent" because otherwise they will not be able to fill their role in the assembly.

Next we can come back to a question raised in chapter one: how can the church at large ever supply the talents needed for the very large number of liturgies throughout just the USA in a year? To answer, the early historical stage of present liturgical development has to be kept in mind. The Roman Church is still at its very earliest level of developing a liturgical form. The old Latin liturgy did not so acutely need the "liturgical talent" in its ministers because the rite had subsumed much of the gestation into itself. We remarked in chapter one that simply to perform the Latin Mass, whatever else may have been wrong with it, was to include mystique and reverence at its core. So far the new liturgy demands much creative attentiveness and talent on the parts of its ministers, including the presider. Day's endless complaints against the cult of personality have this as their cause: the rites have not yet settled into themselves. As time goes by the artistic production of each (or at least each special) liturgy will rest on decisions long since made and become traditional. Liturgy will not have to be re-invented each time and will not require such a degree of talent. We should not be interpreted as saying, however, that some day good liturgy will not require liturgical talent or the specific liturgical artist at all. It always will, but the need will not be so critical.

It is important to note that this book has not urged an "artistic" style for liturgy. James Empereur has laid out seven current patterns of liturgy in his book *Models of Liturgical Theology* (1987), and none of these qualify as "artistic." Each of his liturgical gestalts centers on a theological theory of liturgy, and the models range from "institutional" to "liberation." The theology of the present book does not adhere exclusively to any one of these theological models; in fact, it adopts tenets held by each. Our contention has been that liturgy is artistic in principle, at least by analogy. Its creative nature must be regarded, no matter in which model, and this regard will give subsidiary arts their place. If liturgy is artistic in principle, it is not necessarily so in style. The important goal is to create liturgy's semblance, not to project artiness.

It is time to leave this section, even though much more could be said. Looking back, we can see the special pertinence of an analogical concept of liturgy as art. Considerations from Maritain and Langer elicit the nature of sacramental liturgy as no other categories can. Because the being of God consists of fruitful union, so does Christian life, so does liturgy. We have caught our analogy at work not only in art but in the Trinity itself, God-with-us, and especially in liturgical worship. Assemblies act as analogous mothers of each liturgical event, with God/Christ's Spirit as fathering component. The dark and stilly womb of assembled Christians conceives and nurtures a complicated, delegated gestation, whose outcome is the birth of the liturgical Christ, ready for union with the same assembly. This is the vision. It is time to listen briefly to some of its implications.

III. Special Questions

Liturgy reveals Langer's organic principle very well. Many people are involved in coinciding activities, delegated by the Church assembled; actions and words flow in and out of each other; numerous art forms insinuate themselves into the overall effect. As does any organism, liturgy's process involves coinciding activities, growth and decay, fragility to hostile forces (what if the lights go out; what if a man with a knife walks up the middle aisle). Most interesting is the presence of *rhythm*, in Langer's sense of the word. The cessation of one dynamic tension prepares the next by its close. The end of an entrance procession calls out for the greeting. Words of welcome prepare for the readings. Readings awaken a hunger for the central event of cross-and-resurrection-as-present-now. The eucharistic prayer delivers this event, rendering sanctified the bread and wine of life. Their presence demands communion. Finally, the natural impulse toward rest after a meal sets up a conclusion and then an exit from the sacred space. This vital rhythm gives the art of liturgy for all its participants, and it is what Don Saliers was talking about when he said that liturgy IS art (Saliers 1990, 33).

Langer highlighted the fact that inner organic life *feels* like something. This feeling enabled artists to bring forth felt, organic structure in the work of art. A new question for liturgists, following the liturgical reform, is how will today's celebration *feel?* In the present state of eucharistic liturgy the presider controls more than just the homily. We remarked in chapter one that his ability makes or breaks the Mass. He is a main controller of its organic rhythm. For this reason, parishioners find nothing unusual in "shopping" for a Sunday liturgy, driving sometimes even far distances to find the right one. The priest serves as a quasi-iconic presence. Liturgy demands from the presider an integral sense of *and display of* the vital rhythms of the liturgical event. This felt quality has to be established rather than merely performed. When people "celebrate" an event, they are glad and rejoice. This is a mood. We said that this standard term in the liturgy points toward feeling.[20]

What shall that feeling be? If Christ's Spirit reconciles and brings together, should not liturgies too reflect and deliver peace? Quasten reports that the early church thought so. Belief in divine unity and the communion of souls (*koinonia*) meant that the church should sing "with one voice." Quasten interprets this phrase to mean unison singing without instrumental accompaniment, a hazardous statement.[21] At least this much is true: in partial reaction to pagan instrumental music excesses, the early church chose music that would express inner devotion, "adoration in Spirit." It was peaceful rather than cathartic. Instruments used in liturgy early on (Quasten 1983, 73) certainly were of mild effect (e.g., cithera and lyre) instead of the highly strident, oboe-like, Phrygian flute or *aulos* by which pagan rites attempted to obtain catharsis, divination, or even divine presence (Quasten 1983, 150). After about 400, church decrees specifically prohibited use of any instrument (Quasten 1983, 54).[22] Certainly the long centuries of chant—at least as scholars interpret it to have been performed—evidence a preference for peace and simplicity as the mood for worship.

If the centuries of Latin Mass possessed serenity at their core, is that the mood contemporary liturgies should convey? One answer could be *solvitur ambulando*, it is solved by walking.[23] We will find out as the decades pass in what way the artistic decisions are absorbed into the rite, and therefore what mood settles in as the predominant one. A bit more can be said, however. We have stated that the dynamic form of a liturgy is identical to that of the assembly's intimate, felt experience of God within. Its dynamic expressions are those of the Christian people. But human life is not so simple as "peace" might seem to imply. Insofar as we have said "yes" to the Spirit, not just as a lark but as a serious, thoroughgoing emendation of our lives, perhaps we will experience some of the heavenly peace. But other conjoined seasons of life come into play. Our yes is interlaced with no, with the compounded refusals of our lives and of our culture. Perhaps we are more intimate with sin than with acceptance. Thus our joy will be mixed with sorrow, our acceptance with resistance; the strength of Christ will contend with our struggle; the vast landscape of God's love will be closed within rigid walls of our lives. Christ embraced the grayness of our shadowy existence with open arms.[24]

Thus a second answer to our question about the mood of liturgy might be this: it varies. If the entire scope of Christlife is to be projected, then the mood will change from season to season. The church year, far from being just a mechanism, gives the church a means to display the many hues of Christ's life in us. Good Friday's darkness holds up the shroud of human refusal. The light of Easter illumines our human face with Christ's dazzling breakthrough to exchange. Christmas shows Godly othering as born into the world, prepared by Advent's waiting. "Ordinary time" perhaps reflects the humdrum reality of lives partially taken up into the mystery of grace. Artistic expression of liturgy should give full scope to Godlife within us.

A question might be raised about the tone of Sunday versus daily eucharist. It has been said that the Roman Church today has too many eucharistic celebrations. Another interpretation might say that we have attempted without realizing it to deliver the same mode of ritual every day of the week. Daily eucharist need not have the same tone and scope as that on Sunday. The

"Lord's Day" deserves a larger framework than regular days, and so music is certainly in order. The homily has to be more polished and perhaps longer than for weekdays. Processions and recessions will give a higher value to the sacred space of the larger community gathered together.[25] On weekdays, in principle and in practice, there is not so much space to be filled, literally and figuratively. Simple, short preaching, scaled down processions, fewer complications are in order. One might ask also whether music really is "normative" for the liturgy as such. This writer is calmed and helped by "dry" weekday liturgies, i.e., ones with no music. Music's machinery seems to complicate something that is, after all, quotidian rather than festive. Recalling Frye, we might say that less formality is called for, and that music's normativity therefore can be held at bay.[26]

Style will also depend on two poles between which liturgy always must swing. On the one hand there is attention to communion with Christ, whose sanctified life has become present. On the other there is communion of the assembly among its members. Each implies the other. No communion with Christ can be innocent of its human realization, love of the neighbor. No interaction among Christian peoples can be founded except in the divine, othering unity that gives it birth. In pre-Vatican II times it was possible to image liturgy as "my" time with the Lord. "I" ("and coincidentally these others") am privileged to stand before the great, mysterious God now present. In these latter times the opposite is sometimes the case: some liturgical gatherings seem more like social meetings in which conviviality is the order of the day. If we over-emphasized the one in former ages, we perhaps now over-accent the latter, at least in some churches in some cities. The style of liturgical enactment will center on whether "*communion with Christ* in union with these others" is emphasized, or else "communion with Christ *in union with these others*" be. Many liturgical changes took their cue from the latter polarity, such as *coram populo*, removal of communion rails, reconstitution of the greeting of peace, etc. Perhaps the first pole needs some stress again, especially in light of the complaint that "all the mystery is gone" from contemporary liturgy.[27]

Let us concentrate now upon the arts in liturgy, a major question. Clearly, every force within the liturgical event belongs there only insofar as it contributes to the primary rhythm. Subsidiary arts in particular must fit or be abolished. Liturgy has elements of drama, narrative poetry, public speaking, dance/ movement, and music, to name a few. We have said that none of these stand alone as artistic conceptions, but are moments within a gestating conception that is wider and better than they are. The *commanding form* has already been conceived and it is being nurtured within the assembly through all the arts and artists involved. An overly dramatic interpretation of the reading, for instance, will call attention to itself and rupture liturgy's primary semblance. An arresting piece of dance, no matter how wonderful in other contexts, could eclipse liturgy's goal. And liturgical musicians know well that a favorite hymn during preparation of the gifts may well be the only thing people remember from that Sunday's Mass.

Thus we must invoke again Langer's "principle of assimilation." Two primary art forms cannot successfully co-exist within a single work of art. For one thing, human beings cannot attend simultaneously to two main events.[28] For another, the organic character of a work of art demands a single commanding form, not two. Text is subordinate to music.[29] Analogously, liturgical music is, or should be, subsumed by the liturgy. The main commanding form is already given in the assembly/Spirit conception. This form is what should occupy the attention of the congregation, not the necessary commanding form of the piece of music itself. When liturgy and music meet, liturgy should win.

Let us look briefly at what one author calls the decline of this ideal. Karl Gustav Fellerer divides his great book, *The History of Catholic Church Music*, into three historical sections. The first, "Music *of* Worship," spans the development of liturgical chant through the Gregorian systematization and into the first tracings of polyphony. The reason this was music *of* the liturgy, in the sense we have been talking about, is that "the musical expression grew with, and out of, the liturgical form. As liturgical song, church music was the music of the liturgy in the fullest meaning of that phrase" (Fellerer 1961, 3).

The second section is called "Music *for* Worship." During the formative years of polyphony, the chant element declined, finally remaining only as a *cantus firmus* or fixed melody, with additional contrapuntal lines added to it.[30] By the thirteenth and fourteenth centuries polyphony had developed such extensive devices that their expressive quality quite outpaced the words, and began to overrun the rites. Numerous objections were raised, attempting "to recall church music to an awareness of basic principles. They even called for a rejection of the newly acquired melodic forms" (Fellerer 1961, 55). Music's purpose had been to heighten the liturgical text and not go its own way autocratically. Now its own way was becoming apparent and irresistible. Fellerer calls this era music *for* the liturgy, because, even though it was based on "extra-ecclesiastical artistic principles" (Fellerer 1961, 3), it still served the liturgy, but at one step removed.

We saw that a reformation of this style was reached by Palestrina in the sixteenth century, but that soon after his death, music had moved light years beyond his stylistic synthesis, with the innovations of the later Monteverdi. For this reason, section three of Fellerer deals with music not *of* or *for* worship, but music *at* worship.

> Thus, around 1600, a fundamental break occurred in church music both in setting and expression. Emotionalism had created not only new forms but new possibilities of expression which, because of their subjective tendency, drew church music away more and more from its liturgical ties. Divine worship came to be regarded as the external scene for the development of musical media (Fellerer 1961, 114).

Baroque ideals created music that ran by its own rules, with sacred texts mainly as pretext. In the eighteenth century a new vocal form for church music came about, based on the symphonic principles then being developed at Mannheim. It was an "art for art's sake" idea of church music, something Fellerer calls a "complete severance of church music from its liturgical foundation" (Fellerer 1961, 158). With Mozart's *C Major Mass*, masses by Schubert and Weber in the classical era, and church music by Beethoven, Berlioz, Liszt, and Bruckner in the romantic, the disjunction was complete. Though profound, great, and deeply religious, these compositions were more at home on the concert stage than at the liturgy. When they came to church, their performance took place on the occasion of liturgy, but without much connection with it. Music's commanding form had won. It could not be held in bounds.

There were movements toward reform, and the history of the "four hymn Mass" leading up to liturgical renewal in this century is well known. Today, the church stands at the beginning of a new, long period of development both in liturgy and in music.

My contention can be stated as follows: if there is to be a chance that liturgical music will remain, through the centuries, music *of* worship, instead of *for* or *at*, creativity has to be given play even as it is restricted. To say it differently, the restrictive principle for music has to be itself creative. If the liturgy be understood from the outset as something creative in principle, of its very nature, as something analogous to the great art forms, then musical imagination can be content to play, free and unbound, but within liturgy's creative parameters. It would share in a creativity larger and more potent than itself. Creative arts would be *enhanced* by being part of a larger creative event, instead of *restricted* by papal decree, conciliar pronouncement, and so on. They would be restrained by their sharing in the wider commanding form of the liturgy. This is really the duty of any artist: to fit the elements into the commanding form. Mozart always checked his otherwise untrammeled imagination to the work at hand; in my premise he would fit it to the liturgical form conceived by the assembly. He would be first a member of the assembly that creates liturgy, and his music would by nature enhance that liturgy. The theories of these pages are one attempt to articulate a vision to let this happen.

What kind of music are we talking about? The ages behind us saw eucharistic liturgy as so great an event that only the very fullest artistic expression would suit it. This resulted in "classical music" for the liturgy, something that comports itself to listening, but not generally as well to participation by assemblies. This problem is made more acute in the twentieth century when contemporary classical music stands not only above the capabilities of ordinary persons, but beyond their taste as well. Like the modern poetry we found Maritain discussing, modern concert music has dispensed with the formal conceptual elements that made it approachable. In poetry these were the reign of concepts, rhymes and verse. In serious music it is melody, harmony, and regular rhythms. We said above that in their wake Maritain's intuitive pulsions may have their chance to control the music outright.

The picture we have been drawing of liturgy as participatory might prohibit such expression, at least for the most part. In general, liturgical music contributes to the primary semblance of liturgy by the clarity of its intent, the discrete moods it portrays, and by its overt connection to the Jesus-expressing rite. Like "classical" poetry, music's melody, harmony, and rhythm will form the ordinary home for intuitive pulsions, at least on most occasions. Creativity will have to find its playground there. Its genius will be to reach within the people and find their music. Of course at times and places "serious" or "classical" music will find a haven too, even "contemporary" strains of it, so long as the intuitive content can speak to the people instead of alienating them. Here above all musical art is not a self-expression by the artist, but the subjectivity of the Spirit-oned people externalized from and for union. If such a vision of liturgy does not prepare fertile ground for musical imagination, nothing does.[31]

We spoke above about different styles of liturgy. What about musical styles? If liturgical music must remain largely music of the people, must it use only "pop" style? Space will not allow development of this question, but a single observation can be made. Nothing is wrong with employing any style whatever, as long as it truly grows out of the primary commanding form of the liturgy. Does it contribute to the purpose we have been at pains to describe? If it does, then a balladic sound can be appropriate; classical strains cannot be ruled out. Nor, interestingly, can "churchy" pieces—which some people hear as dated and obscure—or folk styles. Experimentation with forms also would be in place, since lifeless adherence to the same old formulas will stifle liturgy. The one standard that can exclude aberrations has been stated above: how does a style serve the liturgy (in this place at this time)?

Erik Routley said that hymnody is the folk music of the church:

> When we speak of folk song now we still mean songs which have survived through many generations and whose origins are buried in mystery. But of course there are folk songs whose origins are perfectly discoverable and may be quite recent. As soon as a song becomes the property of people who are not in any sense natural singers (still less professional ones) it is a folk song (Routley 1982, 2).

We would add responsorial psalms, holies and amens to the list and say that in them and in hymns we find the mandate of liturgical music played out. It is not that the people "deserve" to possess their music at worship; they are the very parents of it, the artist of it on the larger plane. Some long for a return to Gregorian Chant, some want good old "mediocre" hymns, to which the congregation is accustomed (Day 1990, 118–121), but these opinions seem like stopgaps. On the objective level, music must attempt mainly to establish the primary semblance. Music stands perhaps in closest intimacy of all the arts to felt awareness. Its *raison d'etre* is to assert subjective time in its passage. Therefore, music plays an irreplaceable role in expressing the seasonal, collective, inner experience of the assembly, oned-with-Christ in the Spirit.[32]

We spoke above about the seasonal, subjective time of the church. How does this apply to music? In Langer we found music's organic forms to be the passage of human tensions of any kind: physical, emotional, intellectual. Its rhythm, in the larger Langerian meaning, consisted of transit from one felt event to the other: from the traffic light on a congested street as I hurry to a concert hall; from a crowded life to the peace of my vacation spot as I forget about all the demands of daily appointments. Christian subjective time can be expected to add a new dimension to music. If we are correct about the enhanced questing granted by bestowal of the othering Spirit upon our depths, then all our experience will be tinged by this new reality. I might think twice before blasting the horn at someone who forced my car from the lane. My relation to significant others may well be transformed into real respect for the other person, a love that echoes all the way back to God the Source. My search for God in the world, Jesus, certainly can have produced significant longing, delight, nostalgia, pain, hope, empathy, yearning. This is the stuff of Christian subjective time and of liturgical music.

It is possible that older "church music" of this century was expressing the stodgy rhythms of a bogged down liturgy. On the other hand, it might have been reflecting the Christian solidity that stands behind the ups and downs of life. The point is to give birth to the dynamic forms of Christian inner "time." Even popular music can be adapted to liturgy. The tune for "Sacred Head Surrounded" was written as a love song.[33] This in no way gives license to incorporate just any folk or pop melody. Church music is in the world but with a different basis, an enhanced subjective time. Its wide rhythm is that of the church's seasons. These echo and emerge from human life's oneing with the Spirit in its own many seasons.

There is also the ecology of the liturgical event itself. Entrance songs should not ordinarily lumber or quieten. The excitement of gathering wants livelier tempos and texts. Responsorial psalm settings for the most part need to be shorter and more meditative—in proportion to the readings, not eclipsing them. Also, Roman Catholics might consider the Lutheran "hymn of the week" for Roman liturgies. There, after the homily, all other action would cease and the singing of an appropriate hymn would serve as the liturgical event. A hymn of the week would fittingly climax the liturgy of the word and help the (rhythmic) transition to the eucharistic prayer. It would express, in other words, the felt experience of passing from one section of Mass to another, and be an expression of Christian subjective time. As yet there is no sung eucharistic prayer that completely satisfies, though many settings have been tried. Music for this prayer must take a low profile, so that the crucially important words can have prominence. And so on through the whole Mass.[34]

The difficult question of beauty has to be approached. As we noted, musicians complain that the aesthetically beautiful music of older Roman rites has been sacrificed on the altar of relevance. Chant is one example, but so are the Renaissance settings by Byrd and Palestrina, and the "masses" of Mozart, Handel, and Schubert. These play well on the concert stage and it seems a shame to deny them to liturgy itself. What about beautiful music by great composers?

We touched upon the (scholastic) meaning of beauty in our chapter on Maritain. Let us use that approach now, for simplicity's sake. For Maritain, beauty is a transcendental because it is an aspect of being itself. Successful works of art rank especially high in beauty, since there is in them the "intentional" presence of creative intelligence. They are born, not made. The key, then, lies in asking what is being born in liturgy. Not a piece of music which is then somehow imposed upon the ritual. The church assembled is birthing an expression of its collective Christian subjectivity—which of course expresses not itself but that which fills it: Christ-life. Therefore beauty has to be sought first within the liturgy itself, and only then in its music. Compositions and performances that are too perfect and beautiful in themselves may be like the dog sharing its owner's bed: finally there is no room for the human. Liturgy's beauty consists of a certain perfection in realizing the Christ event. Beauty will be encountered, in the classical sense, when liturgy is an organic expression. Its music will fulfill this kind of standard of beauty when it enacts organic motions deeply coherent with the main event.

How then does a composer come up with a form for an individual liturgical piece, music that is supposed to be beautiful in this sense? He or she should not write "for the recording" of his or her best-selling liturgical music. The assembly and its liturgy have to be in the composer's heart and mind at the very moment of conception of the musical piece. Great care is required in writing such music. The music must be excellent in itself, and composers have to attend to that task. But, as we have said, they must also turn a keen ear to the local assembly. If composers write in the abstract, far from any assembly, the danger is insurmountable that they will conceive a work that finally *does not fit* into the organic liturgy. What is the level of the congregation's spiritual awareness? What is their ability to "pick up" a new and possibly complicated piece? What kind of music do they like? What kind of accompaniment helps them birth the sacramental liturgy of which they will partake? How much do they like to listen and how much to sing actively? Questions such as these are not answered by survey but by attentive membership in the assembly, without which liturgical music loses its head.

A final observation is that there are liturgical encroachments even at this early date. The practice of having just one reader for all the readings except the gospel is working its way in. At smaller gatherings it is taken for granted that the proclaimer of the first reading will also read the responsorial psalm. We can discern already in this practice a movement toward one person doing the work of all, just as the priest did in the old days. Is it a kind of new clericalism? Another example is the new practice of singing every verse of liturgical music. This custom arises out of insistence by hymn promoters that the hymn writer intended an integrated text which is not complete until all verses have been rendered. Liturgists seem to have widened this perspective to include even the responsorial psalm. From our considerations above, we have to question this practice. Liturgical music is not played in order to display a discrete artistic project by the text writer or composer. If it were, then the commanding form of the hymn would take precedence over that of the liturgy. The only valid reason for singing any or all verses of a liturgical piece is *that they are called for by the course of the liturgy itself.* This question becomes acute in the responsorial psalm, which anyway stands in danger of encroaching upon the readings. Many composers set all the verses of a psalm precisely so that the liturgist may have a choice—not because the composer wishes a recital performance of the entire composition. Even hymns which were written with verses that interlock (and therefore must all be performed) can warp a liturgy. Their verses-*in-toto* will be appropriate when the liturgical action consists only of singing the hymn; in the Roman liturgy such a moment does not presently exist. In churches that do have a hymn-of-the-day, or whose liturgy consists mainly of music and readings, this kind of hymn has a better chance. Music that accompanies liturgical action, on the other hand, must do just that, and not insist on its own priority.

Nevertheless, in spite of this kind of counter-trend, great opportunities exist. Whatever its future trends, no matter how many artistic decisions are absorbed into the character and mood of the rite itself, the liturgy which people create from their oneing with the Spirit of Christ seems alive and well, ready to grow.

Summary

Time has come to rest from this long journey. If the reader will permit, we can now sit like travelers before the fire, recalling favored moments from our trip. Besides, it is necessary to gather dispersed insights into summary form, to collect the mind and focus our vision. Here, then, is a summary of aesthetic liturgy.

We began our considerations with a look at the creative fertility in each and all of God's relationships. God is, after all, the most related of all. Following Rahner, we said that all being, even God's, is pluriform. That is, everything that exists can complete itself only by coming together with that within itself which is not (yet) itself. The Godhead itself possesses plurality. If this were not true, we could not confess three persons in one God.

God-the-Source, then, in a manner of speaking, knows him/her-self, and that knowledge union gives or is the Word. The loving union between Source and Word is what we call the Holy Spirit, as traditional theology has said. Then we turned to the world. We saw that each time God came into union with the created world, that onement became a new being, something which eventually came to birth. The Holy Spirit's "overshadowing" of Mary became Jesus. Jesus' love of his Source, displayed in his marvelous love of human beings, not so much "became" the

Holy Spirit, but *was* that Spirit, now in Christic form, returning to the Source, and sent upon the world through the resurrection.

God offers to bestow this Spirit of love on every human person. Reception of the Spirit qualifies as a most important oneing, a conceiving that gestates and is born as sacramental liturgy. To them that receive it, God gives the privilege of seeking the Word. And so, as all human beings must, the assembled seekers externalize that which already resides within them inchoatively: the Spirited life of Jesus. Thus is born the liturgy. It is the symbolic presence of Jesus, now in a form external to the assembly and waiting for their participation. When Christians encounter Christ in the liturgy, another significant onement takes place, union with the symbolic, real presence of that which was previously only within them. In Christian liturgy, this is Jesus present intentionally within his historic deeds. The seekers have found the Word they sought.

The church is analogously the mothering womb where liturgy, Christ's presence, is nurtured and prepared. This understanding gave us the reason why Vatican II called for full, conscious, and active participation in the liturgy by the assembly. Liturgy "belongs to" the church assembled, in just the way a child belongs to its parent: not by ownership or possession, but by kinship and love. The assembly *does* have a constitutive, originating role in liturgical ritual, something theirs by their very nature, not superadded. Yet we never lost sight of the fact that liturgy is most fully God's—God in intimate and fecund union with the people. God sanctifies and elevates these people so that they can become humble, creaturely, yet "connatural" partners in this great act of birthing.

We saw this "elevation" activity throughout the entire course of our investigation. A man and woman, of course, were already connatural to each other, and therefore needed no further conditioning. But we understood that, for Maritain, the things of experience had to be "enlightened" by intelligence in order to be known. The word enlighten had a double meaning, since the "heaviness" of material things needed to be "lightened" so that they could be *both* themselves *and* something within the conscious field. From there we traced creative emotion, imbued with an intelligence that was not yet differentiated from it. It elevated and then received dear moments of experience. A pregnant union resulted, bringing forth eventually the work of art.

Then we realized that even the humanity of Jesus itself had to be "sanctified" in order to let go of itself and become identical with the second person of the Trinity, the Word of God. This identity, once given, had to "gestate" throughout the life, death, and resurrection of Jesus, in order to reveal fully to the world its Godly nature.

Ordinary human beings, all too aware of their mundane state, could not dream of being somehow connatural to all this, to the eternal God. But God graciously raised them, "connaturalized" them, so that they became in fact ready to receive the Christ they now sought. They look for him within liturgical symbols, and this was the last elevating act we saw. The ordinary things of liturgy, even the familiar bread and wine, became symbolic so that they could carry the presence of Christ.

In terms of our analogy from human procreation, we said that the preconscious union of Spirit and persons was just like a zygote. That is, the union itself *was* the liturgy in germ, waiting to gestate and be delivered. In the manner of any human group, the assembly accomplished gestation by the device of *delegation*, of consigning certain jobs to certain ministers. This was equivalent to differentiation of arms from arm buds, brain from brain stem, and so on, nurtured and carried out by various organs within the mother. It was not as if *either* the assembly as a whole planned and executed liturgy *or* the ministers did it. Liturgy is gestated *both* by the assembly *and* the ministers, since the latter are fully members, and carry out their tasks only by virtue of that membership. Finally, birth provided the place where Jesus could be encountered by those who seek him. At that point a new union took place. The assembly came into communion with Jesus present, became pregnant with him. They went out to give birth throughout their lives to love of neighbor, virtuous life, Christian action, love of the poor, and Christian action through the world. All of this represented a "closing of the circle" of love between Source and Word in the Spirit. Jesus' love returned to the Source from which it came, because of and in the midst of Christians in the world.

We then began to harvest insights from the aesthetic model. We stopped short of calling liturgy an art form alongside music and painting and the rest. We found it more helpful to draw an analogy between art and liturgy. By this means we were able to make good use of the insights of Susanne Langer. First we listed some of the many "elements" used by liturgy, remembering that elements already represented a "making-present" or "intentionality." The entrance procession, not just a walk up the aisle, contained within itself the semblance of entering sacred space. The Word-as-proclaimed made present the actions of God in the world and in Jesus, as reflected upon spiritually and theologically. The word-as-preached heightened, clarified, and applied this presence to the specific circumstances. We spoke about bread and wine in the eucharist, and the symbolic and real presence they contain. Most interestingly, we were able to answer one of the objections we had raised in chapter one, that no art form could be content simply to repeat itself time after time. Repetition, an integral requirement for all liturgy, stood as an element or semblance from which liturgy is dynamically formed. It alleviated the need to listen and be informed anew as if the Spirit of Christ did not already inhere in us.

Then we asked about the key or prime element abstracted and brought forth. In our formulation, it was "sacred action as present." Each of the "elements" of liturgy contributed to this kind of semblance to a greater or lesser degree. It is a semblance because the sacred action—say of the sermon on the mount, or the crucifixion—is not literally present but figuratively so. This gives foundation for the traditional statement that the Mass is the *unbloody* sacrifice of the cross. The cross is "intentionally" present, in Maritain's meaning of that word, not literally.

Finally we asked about the "primary illusion" of liturgy. Langer had held the primary illusion to be the key unifying principle for each art form. It was already clear, from our considerations about relationality, oneing, and significant union, that "presence" could not be the primary illusion of liturgy. Two lovers cannot beget a child by just standing present to each other. Liturgy's entire purpose is to provide *communion*, the oneing of assembled members with Christ in his sanctified, resurrected life now present in the sacramental "elements." Here the people become "other Christs," become pregnant with the Spirit of Christ who has begotten within them the life of Christ in the world. They go from the sacred space of church to bring that life into the now sacred space of the world.

Identification of this primary semblance was the highlight of our considerations. We went from it to reflect on some specifics of liturgy. We saw clearly realized in liturgy the organic principles Langer had noted in art. Actions and words flowing in and out of each other, growth and decay, one moment preparing the other's way by its own demise—this is the *rhythm* of liturgy, the delicate preparation and realization of each segment. In this sense liturgy IS art, or at least stands in high analogy to it.

When we came to reflect on music, we recalled Langer's "commanding form." In it we had already found something like a zygote: a locus of all the potentials that were to be realized through gestation. The commanding form remains as the formal center of the person or work, even after they are "born." But only one commanding form can hold sway in any work of art. When different arts combine, as they do in song, one or the other form has to be in command. This is Langer's principle of assimilation. Liturgy's combination of many arts, including music, raises the danger of competition between them. This was a specific worry for us at the start of this book: which commanding form wins? The answer is, liturgy's. Music, dance, homiletics, gesture, and decoration partake of this overarching form, each contributing its own substance to liturgy's semblance. Thus our theory of aesthetical liturgy overcomes one of the seemingly inevitable problems of liturgy down through the ages: the renegade status of the subsidiary arts. Composers, musicians, choreographers, etc., must be masters first of the liturgy and only then artists of their art form. In this way, great composers can work in liturgy and remain unthwarted and unconstrained. They are to be masters of the liturgical art.

Langer had identified music's primary illusion as that of *passage*, the expression of subjective time. Liturgy, as an analogous occurrent art, also has subjective time as its illusion. It expresses the subjectivity of its artist, the assembly, as filled with the life of Jesus in the Spirit. In this we see Maritain's principle displayed: there is no subjective, inner life unless it is filled with the things of experience. In other words, subjectivity is a marriage of the world and the subject. Christian subjectivity is imbued with Jesus' life both in history and in the world today. This the assemblies gestate over time and deliver as the liturgical event. Christian life has many seasons, as does the liturgy in its seasons of the Church year. The seasonal rhythms of Christian subjective life (filled with the Spirit) find a perfect home in the liturgy.

We also seemed to answer the cry of musicians and music lovers for *beauty*. Beauty must describe first the liturgy, not just music as a thing unto itself. Beauty resides most fully in the birth of the living liturgy, the expression of Christian collective subjectivity. Liturgical music has to be an expression of the same. If music is so exquisite that it severs this connection and becomes lovely in contradiction to the liturgy, it has ruptured the very art it was trying to ply. Music's intrinsic beauty and elegance must be *assimilated* to the primary analogous art form, liturgy.

It followed that liturgical musicians have to possess an "art of the assembly"; they must "know" the assembly and its contours, like a midwife knows the mother. Years of musical practice and training can never make up for a lack of this. We said that the assembly is made up of amateurs in the realm of music. But it is composed of "professional Christians," seekers of the Word of God, who are full partners in the labor of giving birth to liturgical communion with Christ. Music is "of the people" not when it is simplistic or folky or popular, but when it expresses seamlessly the artwork aborning from the very womb of the assembly: presence-for-communion of Christ's life.

We have sought a new theory of liturgy, one based in creativity and explicitly in aesthetics. We have moved toward that goal. From the deeply human and Godly core of liturgy we have located a unity that shelters the arts within its own art.

Afterword

The theologian who discourses about such strong stuff as God-with-us is left feeling small. What is our humble durance that it could deal with the mystery of human art, with God's very self, with the loving and intimate converse God's Trinity has with the world, and with the unique parenting act of liturgy? We have rounded great mountains of aesthetical theory, erected by Jacques Maritain and by Susanne Langer. We found numerous principles in them that we could coax, by the machine of analogy, into sacramental liturgy. If we have done justice to any of this, it is because of the host of profound thinkers and lovers of God whose work we have touched upon so lightly. Most of all we have been privileged to stand before the high mystery of the God whose love empowers us all, artist and worshipper and ordinary folk.

In the end, liturgy is like art, which is like human reproduction. All of them show forth the dynamic of a power that is hidden within being itself. When fertility abounds in parties connatural to each other, when a significant and even momentous oneing follows, this onement itself becomes a new life, enclosed upon itself, yet waiting to unfold, novel and vital simply because it is. Theologians and liturgical artists all serve as midwives to the great event of birth, helpers in something they feel deep within their own selves as well: generous, humble, receptive, laborious creativity. They have opened their arms to the other, who childs them.

NOTES

1. In the first instance it is the human being Jesus.

2. In his otherwise admirable book, *Liturgy Made Simple*, Mark Searle seems to come close to describing the Roman Catholic eucharist as a simple remembering of Jesus. God seems to be present in the world, but not actively present in the sacraments. See, for example, Searle 1981, pp. 43, 56, 63-64.

3. And apparently some of the Corinthian Church were partaking of pagan sacrifices as well as of the cup of the Lord. Paul forbids the worship of demons to all who worship the Lord (1 Cor 10: 14-22).

4. See also I Cor 2: 6-16.

5. Here is an indication of the sacralization of the earth. In the view of sacraments we have been describing, the material world is reborn as a dwelling place for God, by means of human beings. Care for the earth in this sense bears an analogy to parental care for a beloved child. Tenderness and wisdom are required, not brutal manipulation.

6. As regards the Old Testament, Zimmerman suggests that "doing for the downtrodden of Israel, as symbolized by the liturgical phrase 'the sojourner, the fatherless, and the widow,' is not motivated simply by humanitarianism, but also by a sense of what cultic life entails: 'intention and motive are the same, viz. what may be called the *Godward* view; the doing of an act for the sake of God, and not only because it is a kindness to a fellowman'" (Zimmerman 1993, 14; quote is from Oesterly, *The Wisdom of Egypt and the Old Testament in the Light of the Newly Discovered "Teaching of Amen-em-ope,"* London: SPCK, 1927, p. 77). As regards the New Testament, "In part, loving service flowed form the shape of the liturgy itself; as such it is an extension of the liturgy, as Justin attests in his *First Apology*" (Zimmerman 1993, 26).

7. "The offer of personal communion in the grace events of the liturgy of the sacraments is total on the side of God; it is not total on the side of believers. First, they are not able to make a decision which holds once and for all in their condition of historical existence. Second, the capacity for openness to God's personal offer of loving communion

is determined by detachment from self-seeking and self-justification" (Kilmartin 1987, 166).

8. "It can be safely said that there is no universal Church which has a place against and over the local communities and which realizes itself in the activity of the local communities. The Church exists historically and visibly where a community of faithful lives an ordered life according to the Gospel and ecclesiastical tradition. These communities, living in communion with one another, are truly churches and are the basic sacrament from which the sacramental celebrations derive" (Kilmartin 1987, 139).

9. See my article in Foley 1972 for some comments on planning and team meetings.

10. From *Now the Silence* by Jaroslav Vajda, 1987.

11. For an excellent account of practical measures to orient liturgy toward justice, see Empereur-Kiesling 1990.

12. So the American Heritage Dictionary.

13. R. Taylor Scott proposes a "dramatic" character for liturgy, in which aesthetic distance is achieved to maintain the events as "not real," or in our own terms, "illusory." But he says liturgy is also "political," in that its action is "for real," because it is done "directly among persons engaging them in the *realities* of their common situation" (Scott 1980, 104–105). Susan A. Ross says that both the work of art and the sacrament are representative of reality. "The work of art does not claim to be a literal representation of reality but an interpretation of reality which then makes possible a fuller understanding of reality" (Ross 1985, 4).

14. I would add that the intention of all "celebrants" of the liturgy must be present, including those of the other ministers and the whole congregation, in at least a proleptic fashion.

15. This usage has to be distinguished from the technical term "elements" in the church's sacramental language. In that case "elements" are what Langer means by "materials."

16. Corbon in particular makes much of *epiclesis* as a key to every sacrament. He says that "each sacrament is distinguished from the others by its special *epiclesis*. At this point in the celebration the Church is simply a 'handmaid of the Lord.' It asks the Father that the Spirit of Jesus may be poured out on the member of his body that is here being offered. In this context the divinizing energy of the Paraclete is a response of tender love and fidelity, of grace and truth" (Corbon 1988, 110). See also chapter ten, "The Sacramental Epicleses" in Corbon 1988.

17. Even today composers give special prominence in their settings to "the institutional narrative." Perhaps this is precisely because of its narrative form—the only straight narration in the eucharistic prayer. Story always reaches listeners in a more direct and vital manner.

18. Worgul reports that D. R. Brinkman too chooses the "descriptive term" presence to describe the ultimate goal of religious behavior. Brinkman describes the sailor who kisses the photo his girlfriend gave him. The sailor thinks of that photo, fixed above his bunk, as a comforting presence of some kind, a symbolic reality. In his imagination, the sailor recreates the relationship between himself and his girl. This, Worgul says, is like a sacrament (Worgul 1985, 90-91).

19. Zimmerman quotes Mowinckel's definition of cult as "the socially established and regulated holy acts and words in which the encounter and communion of the Deity with the congregation is established, developed, and brought to its ultimate goal" (Zimmerman 1993, 8).

20. Ralph Keifer attributes the prominence of the priest to the newness of the changes. "Perhaps the greatest disservice to the Catholic Church in the introduction of the new Mass Rite was that it threw the role of the celebrant into a new prominence. The chief cause was the novelty of the celebrant speaking aloud in English and facing the congregation; another cause was that other ministries, especially the ministry of music, were ill developed for the new liturgy. Inevitably, the Mass looked as if everybody else was merely gathering around the priest, as it still does in most conventional forms of parish worship. We tend to experience celebration of the Eucharist as 'Father X's' Mass" (Keifer 1980, 98). He also notes that the pre-Vatican II Mass was not a *clerical* rite because "the personalities of the clergy were totally subordinated to the rite, and their ritual gestures served that dramatic central moment of the consecration. The rite was altar-centered, not clergy-centered" (Keifer 1980, 99–100).

I am saying that, even when the novelty of the new liturgy has worn off, the presider still has greater prominence, and his talents as a leader play an important role.

21. Quasten 1983, 67 et passim. It is by no means clear what *miaphone* (with one voice) means. I think "unanimity" or "consonance" would be all that Quasten could support from his evidence. In addition to "with one voice," early writers also speak in ways that could be interpreted as meaning precisely harmony. Athanasius (293–373) hopes that "one and the same voice might rise *in harmony* from" worshippers in Alexandria (cited by Quasten 1983, 69, italics mine). Before him Clement (150–220) says that "we shall choose temperate harmonies . . . [and] leave chromatic harmonies to immoderate revels and to the music of courtesans" (Quasten 1983, 68). Whatever these writers meant, is it right to interpret them as referring exclusively to unison singing? For indication of further research on this topic, see Jeffrey 1984 and McKinnon 1965.

22. A Pseudo Justinianic tract gives a penance of seven weeks to a lector who learns to play the guitar, and excommunicates him if he keeps at it (Quasten 1983, 72)! This kind of church prohibition perhaps demon-

strates that instrumental music was in fact used at the time, since one does not proscribe what does not exist.

23. This saying arose from Zeno's paradoxes. He said that one can never cross a room, since you first cross half the room, then half of the remainder, after that half the new remainder, and so on. Since you can always divide the remainder in half, you can never cross the room. Critics' rejoinder was, *solvitur ambulando*.

24. Though he was not a Christian, Tagore captured something of this reality:

THY sunbeam comes upon this earth of mine with arms outstretched and stands at my door the livelong day to carry back to thy feet clouds made of my tears and sighs and songs.

With fond delight thou wrappest about thy starry breast that mantle of misty cloud, turning it into numberless shapes and folds and colouring it with hues ever changing.

It is so light and so fleeting, tender and tearful and dark, that is why thou lovest it, O thou spotless and serene. And that is why it may cover thy awful white light with its pathetic shadows.

Tagore 1939, 1972, 32

25. J. Hild gives three factors that occasion a celebration in everyday life: (1) there is usually an important or sensational event, which (2) leads to calling an assembly together. (3) This leads to festal action (Martimort 1986-88, Vol I, 239-40). The eucharist is "celebrated" on account of the life/death/resurrection of Christ, an important event, to be sure. Nevertheless the liturgical seasons begin to lose their meaning if all eucharists are treated as full celebrations. The seasons and feast days are invoked, so to speak, because of this or that remarkable event within the life of Christ or the church. These should be "celebrated," and the Masses of the ordinary season should be left as ordinary.

26. For a discussion of daily eucharist, see Baldovin 1991, chapter eight, esp. pp. 108-110. Baldovin holds that daily eucharist cannot appropriately build up the church as the body of Christ, and that therefore it should not be a norm. As regards music at Mass, he holds that "as a true celebration, it [the eucharist] also implies music and singing. This full image of the eucharist is truncated and short-circuited in all but a few daily celebrations" (Baldovin 1991, 108). I am saying here that perhaps daily Mass *should* be "truncated" or restricted. Cf. also Saliers 1981 and Tegels 1985.

27. In certain worship spaces half of the congregation directly faces the other, with the altar to one side and the podium to the other. The assembly is thereby given, at least in glance, to other people, more directly than to the altar and ambo. This increases the sense of pres-

ence within an assembly. Disadvantages include the need to twist in order to see the altar or ambo, and the observable need to avert one's glance to avoid staring into the eyes of friends, casual acquaintances, or total strangers directly in front of one. This practice may slight the need of the assembly to collect itself and be present to the love bestowed (preconsciously) by the Holy Spirit.

28. In counterpoint, composers are taught that only one melodic line can have full integrity. The second contrapuntal line has to be "less interesting" than the first. The third must be considerably less interesting, on pain of dividing and thwarting attention. Bach's use of *stretto* illustrates this. *Stretto* is the imitation of the fugue subject in close succession, with the answer entering before the subject is finished. The *Harvard Dictionary of Music* says that the "resulting dovetailing of the subject and its imitation[s] produces an increased intensity that is particularly suitable for the close of the fugue" (Apel 1975, 809). The intensity results from the listener's attempt to attend to the subject in three or four voices at nearly the same time. One gets a hazy awareness that the theme in all its details is happening everywhere, but it is impossible to follow it in each of its incarnations.

29. This may be the reason that people who stutter when speaking can sing without a stutter. They are not really speaking words at all; they are singing first, and the words come along for the ride.

30. Before long (by the thirteenth century) the increasing polyphonic devices made it only a small step to "discontinue the *cantus firmus* altogether and invent all the voices" (Fellerer 1961, 49).

31. This understanding will lay to rest certain unfounded objections to some contemporary liturgical pieces. The objection is raised that church music texts should never be written in the first person. The pronoun "I," according to this criticism, stands against the "we" of the struggling Christian people. Thomas Day finds it an exercise in ego renewal. He lists and ridicules eight such pieces (Day 1990, 61). The reproach can be accurate in the case of songs that truly promote individualism. But psalms use the first person neither as thinly veiled self-aggrandizement nor as a code word for "us."

> O Lord, you have searched me and known me!
> You know when I sit down and when I rise up;
> you discern my thoughts from afar (Ps 139: 1-2).

The interchange between God and the individual makes a starting place for the assembly's projection of sacramental liturgy. This is not the individual *over against* the assembly, but the individual as someone who is *both* a person *and* a member of the people. "I's" and "me's" are iconic in their individuality. They are a projection of the individual's place in the "great liturgy" of life and of the church. As such they are their own refutation of the critique against them.

A second objection takes offense at song texts that speak with the "voice of God," or, in other words, texts that are settings of God's words instead of our words to God. Day asserts that a congregation which sings the words of God "is really in love with itself" instead of with God (Day 1990, 66). He gives a list of twenty-seven pieces speaking with God's words (Day 1990, 64–65). The protest is voiced also by serious people beyond Day.

Can it be appropriate for an assembly standing before God to sing words not belonging to them but to God? A first reflection might say that the question itself echoes a theology in which God is distant and beyond, not God-in-our-midst. The othering God is *always* God-with-us, expressed in Jesus as fully as human reality can do so. This does not erase the need for humility and reverence, but it does melt an overly firm boundary between us and God. The assembly should never pretend that it is God, but why can it not quote God's words in a liturgy that is first and foremost a semblance and birth of God-with-us? Each piece of musical text has to be judged by that standard.

The objection itself may also mask an overly literal understanding of dialogue. "Let God speak to us in the readings and let us respond with our own voice." Because liturgy is analogous to art, the projection of dialogic factors does not have to be so rigid. Many agents and ministers of the word are called for in the complex organic liturgy; prohibition of congregational quotation of God's word seems to forbid one of the artistic means by which liturgy comes to be: externalization of the spirit/person union within. I would emphasize that the line can be difficult to discern between fitting and unfitting use of this device. Good judgment is called for.

32. Reinstatement of chant is more difficult than it might seem. Routley says that chant was never music of the people, but was always performed by "professional" groups: a *schola* in cathedral versions, monks in the monastery type, monks who of course spent their whole adult lives learning and singing chant many times per day (Routley 1982, 10–13). The version of chant we have received from the Solesmes Abbey's tremendous recovery effort was altered in some markings so as to encourage its singing by congregations at large. But congregations are amateur musicians in principle, as we have noted, and therefore the vast majority of chants stand outside their capability.

33. For a partial list of vernacular hymn texts being set to popular tunes in seventeenth century France, see Delumeau 1977, 191.

34. E. Foley and M. McGann give four categories of ways that music, words, and ritual interact: 1) music alone as a liturgical action; 2) music wedded to ritual action; 3) music united to text, without liturgical action; and 4) music wedded to text, accompanying an action. Foley, McGann 1988, 11-15.

APPENDICES

APPENDIX ONE

FREEDOM AND THE ACCESS TO CREATIVE (POETIC) INTUITION

The access which an artist in the various genres has to the intellective act called poetry will show how free that genre is. Maritain says clearly that the poet has more of such access than does the painter.

> While grasping some aspect of visible corporeal existence as a reality, [the painter] grasps it also as a sign, through which are brought to him [or her], in a kind of indeterminable fluidity, the same secret meanings, correspondences, echoes, and inter-communications which the poet obscurely catches in the universe of Being and the human universe. *Yet the painter catches them still more obscurely, and only in the manner of resonances or overtones* (CI 130, italics mine).

The "intellectual" act that lies behind poetry receives "secret meanings," etc. of the universe, what Maritain calls "the very object of intelligence, that is, the ocean of being, in its absolute universality" (CI 129). But in the painter, this act limits itself to one main aspect of the universe, that of "visible corporeal being" (CI 130); in other words, only one aspect of that which is given in abundance to the interior of the poet. Since an art form can be judged by the width of its opening to "creative intuition" ("poetry"), Maritain must say that painting is a more obscure art form, in the sense that it confines the scope of intuition. It knows through sight, rather than through any and all senses, as does poetry.

279

Another way to look at this is by means of the object pro-duced by the art form. Maritain says that the painter ("artist") has a work to be made. The creativity of the intellect has to be subordinated to the object, to the "making" process. "All the activity of art is specified and formed by the rules intended for the object to be made to exist" (CI 169). The spontaneous creativ-ity which human beings are capable of must be subordinated to an object, rather than issuing forth as free creativity. Poetry, he says, has no object, and therefore the creativity of the spirit is free. Obviously Maritain is using the word poetry here to mean the act of writing poems, and opposing it to the act of painting.

Of course the reader is quite aware that there is also an object involved in poetry even as there is in any art form: "an arrange-ment of words on paper, or of notes on a score, or of colors on a canvas," as Maritain puts it (CI 254-255). This point does not escape him. He says that poetry has no object *in the act of perceiv-ing*, but that since the intuition is precisely *creative*, it must "make or create an object for itself. For no power can proceed to act without an object" (CI 170). It yearns to give expression to its poetic intuition, so it overflows, so to speak, into the production of an object.

This is a difficult distinction to understand, but Maritain's section on music provides some clues. He says that melody is the "pure and direct expression of poetic experience in the com-poser" (CI 253).

> Less bound to the universe of human ideas and human values than [one] who creates with the vocables of the language of men [and women], less bound than the painter or the sculptor to the forms and images of things, less bound than the architect to the conditions for the use of the thing created, it is in the composer that are verified in the most limpid fashion the metaphysical exigencies of poetry (CI 141).

Here it seems that the issue is how directly the utterance is connected with the creative intuition that brings it forth. Even poetry is bound to words and sentences—still objects, though certainly more inward than the oils and canvas. In a sense, words are direct utterances whereas paints are not. And music, especially melody, is a still more immediate assertion of inward intuition.

In any case, "poetry," now in the sense of creative intuition, is at the root of all creative art.

If the fine arts are able to behave in accordance with their name, and to engender in beauty, this is, in the last analysis, because the virtue of art, at its very origin, in the soul, is moved by the grace of poetry (CI 173-174).

The fact remains that by essence poetry, the preconceptual life of the intellect, is the firmament of the virtue of art (CI 238).

APPENDIX TWO

THE LEVELS OF UNION IN MARITAIN'S THEORY OF KNOWLEDGE

The union that is consciousness takes place at various levels. Let us take first the sense level. For Maritain, sense qualities are individual or "particular." They are the aspects our external senses pick up. Coldness, brown color, rough feel, etc. It is not the *idea* of these but the actual physical sensation that we are talking about. Without consciousness these aspects of a thing are inert; their potential to be known is passive. Step one, these are "elevated," or released from the principle of identity.[1] Brown is now brown-color-as-present-in-consciousness. It is no longer just the physical property of the desk thing. Notice, it is still stuck to itself to some degree because it still can only be the color it is, this particular brown, not just any brown, or any color. To this extent it is still close to the material or entitative realm. Even at this "stage," both consciousness and the sense quality of the thing have a certain freedom from the principle of identity.

Step two: the object in its sense qualities is received into oneness with sense consciousness. The senses (as receptive) have now *become* the object.[2] But the object as sensed cannot yet enter the intellectual region. Step three: the Illuminating Intellect raises the sense "image" and thereby (further) frees its intelligibilities from the principle of identity.[3] Why? Because "intelligible" qualities seem to be a step further removed from matter and its principle of identity. When I sense the coldness of my desktop (under the papers) it cannot be anything else but this particular cold feeling. It is "stuck to itself" to that extent. But an intelligibility has more "freedom." What I know about "desk" can apply to any desk I can find. It is not stuck to the specific.[4]

The sensed object has to be elevated in order to have that freedom. While still in the sense realm its "intelligibilities" are passive and supine. Another power is necessary, an active one.

> It is under the pressure of this necessity that Aristotle was obliged to posit the existence of a merely active and perpetually active intellectual energy, . . . the *Illuminating Intellect*, which permeates the images with its pure and purely activating spiritual light and actuates or awakens the potential intelligibility which is contained in them (CI 96, italics mine).[5]

The illuminating intellect (or intellect as illuminating) has seemed to some readers through history as an unnecessary and even downright silly appendage, like a vestigial organ. But it expresses here only the logic of connaturality: two realities can come into union only when they are "unstuck" from themselves to the same degree, and able therefore to unite with each other. Action from the intellect—"illumination"—does this for the object: we might say it connaturalizes it.

Step four: the receptive intellect *receives* the object in its intelligible aspects. Here again we find the curious phrase that speaks right to the heart of our hypothesis: not that the intellect "looks upon" the lighted sense image; not that they communicate or even unite while remaining two parties. The intellect *becomes* the desk in its intellectual qualities. The fertile emptiness of consciousness has been filled by the spiritual contours of the object. Now all of what the object is—at both sensory and spiritual level—is one with the sensing, intellecting subject. Intellect and object are one, senses and the object are one, and so consciousness *has become the object*.[6]

Ordinary knowledge would seem to be complete at this point. It has become the object; what more could be desired? But so far consciousness has missed the most important aspect of all about the thing. The color of a thing, what feel it has, what kind of thing it is, these knowings all belong to a category designating *what* the object is. For Maritain there is something far more important about the desk as it stands burdened in the real, material world. It *exists*. It has entitative existence. Metaphorically speaking, when the thing made its transition into consciousness it acquired *intentional existence,* as opposed to its entitative existence. But if consciousness could not know a thing *in its extramental existence,* for Maritain the most important reality about it, it really does not know the thing at all, only aspects about it. What a thing is and *that it is* are different intelligibilities. Maritain attributes to Thomas Aquinas what he calls a rethinking of the "most characteristic metaphysical thesis of Aristotelianism" to yield the real distinction between essence and existence (EE 45). To know brown color about my desk is not the same as knowing that the desk *exists* in this brown way. None of the knowledge union thus far is enough if it ends without knowing existence.

And so Maritain does not end there. On top of the "simple apprehension" we have seen so far, there is the *judgment.* Through judgment, consciousness says that everything it knows already about the object (knows by becoming it) *is true of the thing in the entitative order.*

> The function proper to judgment thus consists in transposing the mind from the plane of simple essence, of the simple *object* presented to thought, to the plane of the *thing,* of the subject possessing existence. . . (EE 26).

Entitative existence has only to be *affirmed* of the object. It does not need any further action or elevation in order to be known. When such existence is affirmed, therefore, consciousness becomes one with the thing *in its extra-mental existence.*

> In other words, when the intellect judges, it lives intentionally, by an act proper to itself, this same act of existing which the thing exercises or is able to exercise outside the mind. Existence is thus affirmed and intentionally experienced by and in the mind, of intelligibility in act (EE 27).[7]

By means of the judgment I say that the sense aspects and intelligible aspects go together with each other in the object (i.e., within consciousness), but more importantly that they are true of the thing outside my mind. For this reason, judgment is a power by which consciousness can become one with the thing in the *way* it exists and in the *fact* that it exists. Maritain can now give the thing a new name. He called it "object" when it entered consciousness' realm; now, since consciousness knows it even in its extra-mental existence, it can be called "being," or "a being."

The intellect is set up to know *being*, the thing existing as other than the knower. Now knowledge is complete, and the knower has completely become the other, the existing thing.[8]

It can be objected that judgment does not really bridge the gap between knower and the extra-mental thing, that judgment is more equivalent to a "guess" about what is "out there." I do not think Maritain's Thomism is vulnerable to this charge, and to me that is its most interesting aspect. Maritain and the others did not take the knower as their only beginning datum, as Descartes seemed to, making it necessary to work outwards (if possible) from the knower to the then external world. They began instead with a primary datum of consciousness, that the knower is precisely *not* separate from the rest of the world but is in intimate and thoroughgoing union with it. This union is Maritain's beginning datum, instead of being a conclusion from other, prior data. Thus his starting principle does not necessitate a gap between the knower and the existing-being-out-there as such. Only a mechanism is needed, not to *establish* the presence of the thing "out there," but merely to recognize the presence. That mechanism is judgment.

In brief summary, at least two aspects of its reality become one with my knowing: the sense aspects and its less material "intelligible" countenance. The senses enlighten and then become the object's sensed aspects: its particular color, feel, sound (when I strike it) and even taste. A new key is needed for the object's entrance into the intelligible realm. Its intelligible realities are present in the object from the beginning, but needed to be "illuminated" if they are to be known. The active power of the intellect called "illuminating intellect" obliges and gives passage into the new region by (1) noting their intelligibility, and by (2) thereby releasing them further from the either/or hold that materiality kept on them. Once in the new region of consciousness, the newly "intelligible" object is ripe for union with the receptivity of the intellect. This union, together with the sense union, represents the "becoming" of the object by consciousness in regard to *what* it is.

Finally, a strong identity is needed between the object—which is the thing as present within consciousness and oned with it—and the thing existing in the material world. By affirming that the facets of the object at each level, sense and intellectual, *actually exist as such* in the thing out there, consciousness comes at last into intentional union with the thing's trans-objective being. Consciousness becomes the other *as other*. This shows us how, for Maritain, a human being comes to know real things in the world. The person now can be said to know "beings," or "being."

NOTES

1. Only at this point and beyond can it can be called an object (*ob* + *jacere:* to throw against). Maritain says the object is nothing other than some aspect(s) of a thing (which is itself a subject, though of a lower kind) "transferred into the state of immaterial existence of intellection in act" (EE 74).

2. In chapter three we spoke of the organizations of data, what Langer calls "forms." Conscious data might be thought of in that way. In *Creative Intuition* Maritain actually renames the "impressed species" as the "impressed pattern."

3. When this happens the result is called the "impressed species" (from Latin *species:* appearance) because it is a likeness which is "pressed into the knower." When the senses or intellect place the act of knowing, it will become the *"expressed* species." In other words, a process must take place that is similar to the one we saw in sense knowing—the *receptive* power of the intellect requires another *active* power which will elevate the object to its realm.

4. To say it a different way, the quality of desk *is not limited to any one desk*. This intelligibility has been liberated from the principle of identity not only because it can let go and enter into conscious union, but also because it releases itself from this or that object and becomes the intelligibility of any appropriate thing. There its freedom ends, since it is not able to be, say, a sandwich or a hat. Its freedom is limited, but it is more free than the sense aspect. This is the reason that even the intelligibility "desk" has to be elevated in order to have this immateriality. In the entitative world, "desk" is nothing more than mute surfaces and colors (etc.). Entrance into the intentional realm requires that a knower's powers be in attendance.

5. In Latin this is "intellectus agens." Maritain seemed to search for a more expressive translation of these words all through his career. In his first book, *Bergsonian Philosophy and Thomism*, translators render his French as "formative intellect" (BP 157), and in *Degrees of Knowledge* the "acting intellect" (DK 116). In *Creative Intuition* he came forth with the term "illuminating intellect."

6. Because, for Maritain, intellectual aspects are general or "universal" in themselves, it is not necessary for consciousness to restrict them to this or that object. Reasoning, speculative knowledge could be said to be the mind working with such aspects, called concepts, apart from the individual object. As we have seen, the number four does not care what it numbers.

7. Cf. DK 90–101.

8. "True knowledge consists in a spiritual super-existence by which, in a supreme vital act, I become the other as such, and which corresponds to the existence exercised or possessed by that other itself in the particular field of intelligibility which is its peculiar possession" (EE 21).

APPENDIX THREE

QUALITIES OF PEAK-EXPERIENCES AND THEIR SUBJECTS ACCORDING TO A. H. MASLOW

The qualities of a peak experience as Maslow describes them in *Toward a Psychology of Being*[1] are:

1. The object tends to be seen as a whole, as a complete unit detached from relations, from possible usefulness, from expediency, and from purpose (70).
2. The percept is exclusively and fully attended to (70).
3. The world is seen as if it were independent not only of them [the cognizers] but also of human beings in general (72).
4. Repeated cognizing seems to make the perception richer (72).
5. The perceptions are relatively ego-transcending, self forgetful, egoless (74).
6. The peak-experience is felt as a self-validating, self-justifying moment which carries its own intrinsic value with it (74).
7. There is a very characteristic disorientation in time and space (76).
8. The experience is only good and desirable, and is never experienced as evil or undesirable (76).
9. It is more absolute and less relative (80).
10. It is much more passive and receptive than active (81).

11. The emotional reaction in the peak experience has a special flavor of wonder, of awe, of reverence, of humility and surrender before the experience as before something great (82).
12. The whole of the world is seen as a unity, as a single rich live entity (83).
13. People who have peak experiences have simultaneously the ability to abstract without giving up concreteness and the ability to be concrete without giving up abstractness (83-84).
14. At the higher levels of human maturation, many dichotomies, polarities, and conflicts are fused, transcended or resolved (86).
15. These people exhibit complete, loving, uncondemning, compassionate and perhaps amused acceptance of the world and of the person (87).
16. Perception in the peak moment tends strongly to be idiographic and non-classificatory (88).
17. In the experience there is a complete, though momentary, loss of fear, anxiety, inhibition, defense and control, a giving up of renunciation, delay and restraint (89).
18. There seems to be a kind of dynamic parallelism or isomorphism here between the inner and the outer. This is to say that as the essential Being of the world is perceived by the person, so also does he concurrently come closer to his own Being (89).
19. These people deal less in what psychoanalytic study calls "secondary processes" (logic, common sense, good adjustment, enculturation, responsibility, planning, rationalism) and more with "regression in the service of the ego": a kind of "healthy childishness" (90-91).

1. All page numbers refer to Maslow, 1962.

APPENDIX FOUR

LATER LANGER AND THE RESPONSE OF OTHER CRITICS

Later in her writings Langer seems truly to erase any possibility of an epistemology to back up the concrete apprehension I have posited. If to some she seemed to have reductionistic tendencies when dealing with the arts, in her last period of writing such tendencies toward knowledge seem to have won out. As she emerged from her mainly aesthetical writings, she began to worry about the division between subject and object and the division between material and immaterial. In *Philosophical Sketches* she plays with a hypothesis

> which I have found rewarding beyond expectation, . . . that sentience is a phase of vital process itself, a strictly intraorganic phase, i.e., an appearance which is presented only within the organism in which the activity occurs. Each organism, therefore, feels its own actions if they enter this phase, and not any other creature's (PS 9).

Much later, in *Mind,* she says more clearly that feeling is not an entity of any kind, but a phase of the biological process. "Being felt is a phase of the process itself. A phase is a mode of appearance, and not an added factor" (MIND I, 21). She compares feeling to the heat of an iron, which is not a thing but an "agitation, measurable in degrees, not amounts." Then she speculates that

> the wide discrepancy between reason and feeling may be unreal; it is not improbable that intellect is a high form of

feeling—a specialized, intensive feeling about intuitions. There
are corroborations of this idea in the psychological literature
(MIND I, 149).

The epistemological reality that had been implicit throughout her aesthetical period now disappears. The relation between
the self and the world becomes biological.

> By "subjective" I mean whatever is felt as action, and by
> "objective" whatever is felt as impact. . . . The first consequence
> of these definitions is that one does not find a class of objective
> things, with which the scientist is concerned in his laboratory,
> and another class of subjective things which are scientifically
> embarrassing. . . . The properties in question are two possible
> modes of feeling, i.e., of psychical phases of activity (MIND I,
> 31).

This represents what Richard Liddy calls her empiricist bent,
which he finds inadequate to the needs of her aesthetic theory.
Indeed, he notes that in her last phase, Langer's purpose was
"the construction of a biological concept of mind adequate to the
phenomenon itself" (MIND I, 74). A brief look at Liddy's critique of Langer will complete this appendix.

Liddy's *Art and Feeling* (1970) represents a thoroughgoing
critique of such presuppositions from a Lonerganian standpoint.
In his chapter three he argues that Langer has neglected the
human act of understanding in favor of images, which imply
"seeing" as the central paradigm for knowing. Her discussions
of feeling leave the impression "that she is talking about an
object in which she recognizes no element of genuine active
subjectivity or self-presence" (Liddy 1970, 111). One of Lonergan's
assertions is urged against Langer, that "in order for an object to
be present to a knowing subject, the subject must be present to
him-[or her-] self." Liddy believes that Lonergan has assessed
the data about human consciousness far better than Langer, who
in her epistemology seems to have only naive self knowledge.
For Lonergan, human knowing is well explained with three
basic terms: "experience, understanding and judgment, dynamically and functionally related to each other and to the whole
which is concrete human knowing" (Liddy 1970, 137).

Liddy notes that throughout her discussions Langer has in
place a "duality of the 'outer' world of objective impressions and
the 'inner' subjective activity of cognitive formulation" (Liddy

1970, 96). If these are thought of as too distinct and separate, it will be very difficult to bring them together in any meaningful way. We might say that the connaturality of each for the other is too greatly compromised. This is precisely the reason for Langer's interest in the "objective" art work as *revealing* the "private" interior life of feeling. It has to be revealed because it is hidden and unknown in "the other's" realm. Of course, the "concrete apprehension" I think implicit and imperative in Langer's aesthetics has to rest on a different foundation. Instead of what Liddy rightly calls a "confrontational analogue of knowledge and objectivity"—Langer's impact theory of objects as felt—it requires a kind of concrete knowledge that begins from (1) a unity of the knower and known instead of from a duality, (2) a uniting that is not yet differentiated into subject and object.

Lonergan's theory is like the one we saw in Maritain: (1) Lonergan makes reference to Aristotle's dictum that "sense in act is the sensible in act, intellect in act is the intelligible in act" (Lonergan 1959, 290). That is, there is an identity in the conscious realm between whatever object is being known and the faculty that is knowing it. The reality of one is the reality of the other, at least within the conscious field. In Lonergan's theory, knowledge begins by this identity of knower and known within the conscious field, but cannot stop there. The two are then understood as differentiated by means of a pattern of judgments (Lonergan 1959, 290–291). Therefore, instead of assuming from the start that subject and object are separate and separated, this theory assumes as a starting point that they are together. Lonergan calls this "intersubjectivity," and "*Mitwelt*: a world-with-him[/her] of other persons who are there and who he is aware of and living with" (Lonergan 1959, 282).

(2) In ordinary knowing, consciousness then can differentiate itself, extracting general intelligibilities and relating them to one another without reference to their concrete embodiments. Examples of this differentiated consciousness are mathematics, science, and philosophy (Lonergan 1959, 281). Lonergan then makes a statement that founds his reflections on art:

> Differentiated consciousness is, as it were, a stage in the development. It is a withdrawal from the total activity, total actuation, for the sake of a fuller actuation when one returns. And what one returns to is the concrete functioning of the whole. In that concrete functioning there is an organic interre-

lation and interdependence of the parts of the subject to the whole, and of the individual subject to the group. *Art mirrors that organic functioning of sense and feeling;* of intellect, not as abstract formulation, but as concrete insight; of judgment that is not just judgment but moving into decision, free choice, responsible action (Lonergan 1959, 282, italics mine).

This paragraph of course bears the marks of Lonergan's whole discussion of the human knower. The purpose of the present book is not to adopt a particular philosophy, whether of Lonergan, Maritain, or Langer. The Aristotelian starting point of Lonergan's discussion is an illustration that it is possible to read Langer's complex theory with a different underlying theory of knowledge—the union of knower and known—and to find her contribution to the field of aesthetics intact and now more stable.

SUMMARY NOTES FROM FRANS JOZEF VAN BEECK S.J. *CATHOLIC IDENTITY AFTER VATICAN II: THREE TYPES OF FAITH IN THE ONE CHURCH.*[1]

Chapter One

"Vatican II, in taking four centuries of religious and cultural developments seriously in a novel fashion, and in facing up to an unprecedented global challenge, must be understood to *have inaugurated a significant rearrangement of the themes and emphases of the Catholic faith and identity experience*" (4, italics mine).

This in Creed, Conduct, and in Cult.

This change is like continental drift, in which both the continuity and the discontinuity are obvious. But the "rearrangement of the continents on the globe was not a matter of superficial change. Continents drift, but they drift deeply; they do not float" (21).

"We must reckon with the likelihood of a continued process of negotiation to achieve a new balance between identity and openness" (19).

Chapter Two

A. The Pistic (= Traditional or Believers') experience

Pistic from the Greek word *pistikos* meaning "faithful" or "believer" (24).

Characteristics:
   Doctrine = definitions
   Life = precepts and commandments
   Worship = rubrics

Good points: "To believe also means to believe articulately; to behave also means to behave in a responsible and disciplined fashion. To worship also means to act ritually" (27). The pistic experience emphasizes the institutional church, which preexists the individual believer.

Problems:
   1 Feudalistic distinction between leaders and led. Inorganic relationship between clergy and laity. "This development is *theologically* unnecessary and hence not authoritative" (28).
   2 Hardening of boundaries and definitions, with corresponding de-emphasis of dialogue, openness, and synthesis.

The intersection of (a) the normativity of the pistic experience, together with (b) the visual, objectifying approach to knowledge and experience has determined the traditional arrangement of themes and emphases in the Catholic faith-experience (29).

Negative Characteristics of the Pistic Identity Experience:
   1. Inappropriate lay dependency
   2. The suspicion that (Roman) Catholicism is inherently totalitarian and clerical
   3. Structurally impatient and inhospitable
   4. Glorification of the past

B. The Charismatic (= Motivational) Experience

Charismatic taken from the Greek word *charismatikos*, meaning gift (*not* to be confused with the "charismatic movement"!).

Two reversals in the church lead to it:
   1. Realization that "the Church is not the Kingdom of God, but the sacrament of that Kingdom. In other words, the Church *mediates* between God and the world" (34).
   2. "Vatican II did not conceive the Catholic Church as simply identical with the Church of Christ. Rather,

it taught that the Church of Christ 'subsists in' the Catholic Church, thus leaving room for the recognition of ecclesial reality in other Christian bodies" (43).

This leads to an "unprecedented *widening* of perspective and involvement" (34).

Characteristics of the Charismatic identity experience:

In general, "Christians who are in this general category tend to be

1. less dependent on ecclesiastical and clerical assurance and tradition.
2. They are bent on leading lives of active virtue on the strength of a more personalized experience of faith. Hence they tend to manifest
3. a desire to put themselves, along with their gifts, at the service of Church and world" (37).
4. They operate in the *diaspora,* not primarily defined by boundaries. They tend towards *solidarity and communication.*
5. Tend to be *actualists,* motivated by the call of the moment, with strong emphasis on immediate involvement and on the imitation of Christ, of the historical Jesus. An active life of responsibility and involvement.
6. They are *personalists:* conscientious and resistant to general rules. Searching for authenticity, integrity, and personal responsibility.
7. Pluriformity and differentiation of ministries. This is accompanied by confusion and uncertainty, since deeper integration requires experience of deeper conflicts. It creates serious pressures on religious life, priesthood, etc.

Good points:
1. The emergence of ministerial practice and education among lay people and religious women and men.
2. The rise of the many informal "basic communities": prayer groups, Bible study groups, student ministry groups, etc., all organized for the purpose of mutual help and support and upbuilding.

3. Sizable groups that adopt issues of public policy and social and international justice as their special concern (36).

Serious Problems:

1. Risk of diffuseness and compromise. Risk of being measured principally by the yardstick of public relevance.
2. Danger of a serious *loss of tradition*. The appeal to experience may cloak a polemical rejection of whatever used to be intellectually established and authoritative. Charismatic liberalism can therefore be superficial.
3. Dissipation. Variety of agendas, competitive, rejection of what does not appeal.
4. Tendency to adopt a completely moralistic version of the Catholic faith and identity experience (44).
   a) Catholic identity experience, "which must involve *membership in a community, tends to be reduced* to a sense of being part of a broad *movement* called Christianity" (45). What is so compelling about being a Roman Catholic?
   b) May involve a *contempt of the weaker brothers and sisters* in the church.
   c) The "Christian identity-experience ceases to have a compelling center; *the person of Christ tends to lose its decisiveness*. Socrates, the Buddha, Mahatma Gandhi, and so many other great and generous souls have labored and are still laboring for a better world or for a higher humanity without the awkward claim to being the key to the universe" (45).

C. *Common Limitations of the two experiences:*

1. Both are concerned with the past and the present, but not with the future.
2. The Pistic stance is excessively forensic and judgmental vis-a-vis the world, but the charismatic one is wide open to the covert judgmental activities of *permitting and condoning*. Both must find deeper anchorage than judgment.
3. The Pistic experience is structurally impatient and inhospitable. The Charismatic one is "so open that by now everything has dropped out of it" (in the words of Chesterton)

(47). "It takes a true sense of identity to be really patient, to let the pain of another person's estrangement really get to one. It takes a true home to open itself to receive guests, even difficult ones" (47).

Chapter Three:

The goal:

"Vatican II came to deal in a prophetic manner with the fact that the Catholic Church is now for the first time in history actually faced with the challenge of becoming a global Church, of becoming the Church Catholic, not only as a matter or principle, but also in the empirical order" (51). The two themes, 1) demand for a truly universal church and 2) the call for a truly open future are associated in the New Testament with the Resurrection of Jesus Christ.

If the renewal is to be authentically Christian, it "must go back to the original and abiding realization that Christ is alive and present in the Spirit, a realization found everywhere in the New Testament and one that remains the original source of all Christian faith and identity-experience."

Believers of the charismatic type emphasize the ministry of the historical Jesus, and pistics take their cue from the authoritative past—their favorite christological theme tends to be the Incarnation (56).

But:

1. These concerns do not in and of themselves furnish us with a reliable sense of Christian identity and openness. Christian identity is fundamentally a matter of *worship,* and therefore of *mystical* experience.
2. The emphasis on past and present do not give us Christian openness and identity. These come from an appropriate response to Christ's resurrection, which response is *witness,* determined by the demand of the future.
3. Worship and witness, taken together, are mutual safeguards. And, the person of Jesus Christ alive in the Spirit is the source of Christian identity-experience as well as the Christian experience of openness to the world (57).

Worship, Witness, Mysticism:

Worship is the heart of the mystical experience. In liturgy the church "receives and celebrates, enacts and experiences her identity" (61). The pistic concern has marked the liturgy with boundaries, rules, and rubrics; the charismatic has marked it with concern for relevance. But the "roots of the liturgy go to levels deeper than stability or relevance, to where its fundamental dimension, that is to say, its *mystical* depth, is found" (63).

Three elements demand special attention: awe, hope, and the *gift* of identity (an ecstatic sense of identity, born of total abandon and surrender).

Conclusions:

1. The Catholic faith and identity-experience stand to gain decisively from *liturgical spirituality,* as opposed to the "single most dangerous threat to the new liturgy, whether of the authorized or the experimental variety," prayerlessness (67).

2. The widespread current search for prayer, spirituality, and spiritual direction among motivated Catholics over the past ten or fifteen years deserves to be viewed as a most significant development (68).

3. Ecumenism and evangelization are, at heart, a mystical venture (69). "Sensitivity to a Church's holiness is a *sine qua non* for all ecumenical endeavor, including ecumenism at the pistic and charismatic levels" (70).

Patience and hospitality:

"Both the pistic concern with identity by self-preservation and the charismatic concern with identity by compliance have this in common, that they are *impatient and inhospitable*" (75). "Only a deep sense of identity—that is to say, only worship—can enable the Church to desire to be . . . deeply patient and hospitable. This applies not only to the Church's relationships with other Churches and the non-Christian world; it also applies to the community of the Church itself" (76).

1. Van Beeck 1985.

WORKS CITED

Abbott S.J., Walter M., ed. 1966. *The documents of Vatican II.* New York: Guild Press.

Apel, Willi, ed. 1975. *Harvard dictionary of music.* Cambridge MA: The Belknap Press of Harvard University Press.

Aquinas, Thomas. 1846. *Summa totius theologica.* 6 Vols. Neapoli: Ex typographia Virgilii.

Baldovin, John F. 1991. *City, Church and renewal.* Washington DC: The Pastoral Press.

Balthasar, Hans Urs von. 1973–1983. *Theodramatic.* 4 vols. Einsiedeln: Johannes-Verlag.

Beeck, Frans Jozef van, S. J. 1979. *Christ proclaimed: christology as rhetoric.* New Jersey: Paulist Press.

_____. 1985. *Catholic identity after Vatican II: three types of faith in the one Church.* Chicago: Loyola University Press.

_____. 1989. *God encountered: a contemporary Catholic systematic theology.* Vol. 1: Understanding the Christian Faith. San Francisco: Harper and Row, Publishers.

_____. 1992. *God encountered: a contemporary Catholic systematic theology.* Vol. 2. n.p.

Berger, Peter L. 1969. *The sacred canopy: elements of a sociological theory of religion.* Garden City, NY: Anchor Books.

Berger, Peter L., and Thomas Luckmann. 1966. *The social construction of reality: a treatise in the sociology of knowledge.* Garden City, NY: Anchor Books.

Best-Maugard, Adolfo. 1937. *A method for creative design.* New York: A. A. Knopf.

Bishop, Patrick S. J. 1990. Sacramentals. *The new dictionary of sacramental worship*, pp. 1114–1116. Ed. Peter E. Fink, S. J. Collegeville MN: The Liturgical Press.

Bufford, Samuel. 1972. Susanne Langer's two philosophies of art. *The journal of aesthetics and art criticism* 31.1.9-20.

Carrit, E. F. 1955. Review: Feeling and form. *Philosophy* 30.75-76.

Coffey, David M. 1979. *Grace, the gift of the Holy Spirit*. Sydney, Australia: Catholic Institute.

_____. 1984. The incarnation of the Holy Spirit in Christ. *Theological studies*, 45.473-474.

_____. 1986. A proper mission of the Holy Spirit. *Theological studies*, 47.227–250.

Collins, Patrick. 1983. *More than meets the eye*. New York: Paulist Press.

Cooke, Bernard. 1991. Review: Christian liturgy: theology and practice. Vol 1. Systematic theology. *Horizons*, 18.158–159.

Corbon, Jean. 1988. *The wellspring of worship*. Tr. Matthew J. O'Connell. New York: Paulist Press.

Crocker, Richard L. 1966. *A history of musical style*. New York: Dover Publications.

cummings, e.e. 1963. *a selection of poems*. New York: Harcourt, Brace & World, Inc.

Day, Thomas. 1990. *Why Catholics can't sing: the culture of Catholicism and the triumph of bad taste*. New York: Crossroad Publishing Co.

Delumeau, Jean. 1977. *Catholicism between Luther and Voltaire: a new view of the counter-reformation*. Tr. Jeremy Moiser. Philadelphia: Westminster Press.

Doty, William C. 1986. *Mythography: the study of myths and rituals*. University AL: University of Alabama Press.

Du Roy, Olivier. 1966. *L'intelligence de la foi en la trinité selon saint Augustin: genèse de sa théologie trinitaire jusqu'en 391*. Paris: Etude Augustiniennes.

Eco, Umberto. 1988. *The aesthetics of Thomas Aquinas*. tr. Hugh Bredin. Cambridge: Harvard University Press.

Eliade, Mircea. 1963. *Myth and reality*. New York: Harper and Row.

Eliot, T.S. 1920. *The sacred wood*. London: Methuen.

Empereur, James, S.J. 1987. *Models of liturgical theology*. Bramcote: Grove Books Limited.

Empereur, James L., S.J., and Christopher G. Kiesling O.P. 1990. *The liturgy that does justice*. Vol. 33. Theology and Life Series. Collegeville MN: The Liturgical Press.

Evans, Donald D. 1963. *The logic of self-involvement*. New York: Herder and Herder.

Fellerer, Karl Gustav. 1961. *The history of Catholic Church music*. Tr. Francis A. Brunner, C.Ss.R. Baltimore: Helicon Press.

Fergusson, Francis. 1963. Poetic intuition and action in Maritain's "Creative intuition in art and poetry." *Jacques Maritain: the man and his achievement*, pp. 128–138. Ed. Joseph W. Evans. New York: Sheed and Ward.

Fink, Peter E., S. J. 1991. *Praying the sacraments*. Washington DC: The Pastoral Press.

Foley, Edward, and Mary McGann. 1988. *Music and the Eucharistic Prayer*. Washington DC: The Pastoral Press.

Foley, John B. 1972. First, you must plan . . . . *Music in Catholic worship: the NPM commentary*. Washington, DC: National Association of Pastoral Musicians. 37-41.

Foley, John B., S. J. Autumn, 1989. Christ, priest and poet. *The way, supplement #66, "Spirituality and the artist,"* 87-95.

Frye, Northrop. 1963. *The well tempered critic*. Bloomington: Indiana University Press.

Gilson, Etienne. 1965. *The philosophy of St. Bonaventure*. Paterson, NJ: St. Anthony Guild Press.

Hanke, John W. 1973. *Maritain's ontology of the work of art*. The Hague: Martinus Nijhoff.

Hanson, R. P. C. 1988. *The search for the Christian doctrine of God: the Arian controversy 318–381*. Edinburgh: T&T Clark.

Haughton, Rosemary. 1981. *The passionate God*. New York: Paulist Press.

Hausman, Carl R. 1960. Maritain's interpretation of creativity in art. *The journal of aesthetics and art criticism*, Winter. 215-219.

Hill, William J. 1982. *The three-personed God: the trinity as a mystery of salvation*. Washington DC: Catholic University Press.

Hoffman, Lawrence A. 1988. *The art of public prayer: not for clergy only*. Washington: The Pastoral Press.

Hopkins, Gerard Manley, S. J. 1988. *Poems and prose*. London: Penguin Books.

Huijbers, Bernard. 1969. *The performing audience: vernacular liturgy and musical style*. Cincinnati: North American Liturgy Resources.

Jasper, R. C. D., and G. J. Cuming. 1987. *Prayers of the Eucharist: Early and Reformed*. New York: Pueblo Publishing Company.

Jeffery, Peter. 1984. Review: music and worship in pagan and Christian antiquity. *Worship*, 58. 3.261–263.

Jeunhomme, J.M.P. 1985. The symbolic philosophy of Susanne K. Langer. *Neue zeitschrift für systematische theologie und religionsphilosophie* 27.2.159-176.

Keifer, Ralph A. 1980. *To give thanks and praise*. Washington DC: National Association of Pastoral Musicians.

Kilmartin, Edward J., S. J. 1971. Sacramental theology: the Eucharist in recent literature. *Theological studies*, 32. 2.233–277.

_____. 1976. Liturgical theology II. *Worship*, 50. 4.312–315.

_____. 1982. The active role of Christ and the Spirit in the divine liturgy. *Diakonia (NY)*, 17. 2.95–108.

_____. 1984. The active role of Christ and the Holy Spirit in the sanctification of the eucharistic elements. *Theological studies*, 45.225–253.

_____. 1987. Theology of the sacraments: toward a new understanding of the chief rites of the Church of Jesus Christ. *Alternative futures for worship*. Ed. Regis A. Duffy, O. F. M. Collegeville MN: The Liturgical Press.

_____. 1988. *Christian liturgy*. Vol. I. Theology. Kansas City: Sheed & Ward.

_____. 1989. Sacraments as liturgy of the Church. *Theological studies*, 50.527–547.

Kitzinger, Sheila. 1989. *The complete book of pregnancy and childbirth.* New York: Alfred A. Knopf.

LaCugna, Catherine Mowry. 1991. *God for us: the trinity and Christian life.* San Francisco: Harper San Francisco.

Lakoff, George, and Mark Johnson. 1980. *Metaphors we live by.* Chicago and London: The University of Chicago Press.

Lang, Berel. 1962. Langer's arabesque and the collapse of the symbol. *The review of metaphysics* 14.2.349-365.

Langer, Susanne K. 1930. *The practice of philosophy.* New York: Henry Holt and Co.

_____. 1942, 1957. *Philosophy in a new key: a study in the symbolism of reason, rite, and art.* Third ed. Cambridge: Harvard University Press.

_____. 1950. The primary illusions and the great orders of art. *Hudson review* 3.2.219-233.

_____. 1950. The principles of creation in art. *Hudson review* 2.4.515-534.

_____. 1953. *Feeling and form.* New York: Charles Scribner's Sons.

_____. 1957. *Problems of art.* New York: Charles Scribner's Sons.

_____. 1958. *Reflections on art: a source book or writings by artists, critics, and philosophers.* Baltimore: Johns Hopkins Press.

_____. 1962. *Philosophical sketches.* Baltimore: The Johns Hopkins Press.

_____. 1967. *Mind: an essay on human feeling.* Vol. 1 of 3. Baltimore: Johns Hopkins Press.

_____. 1972. *Mind: an essay on human feeling.* Vol. 2 of 3. Baltimore: Johns Hopkins University Press.

_____. 1982. *Mind: an essay on human feeling.* Vol. 3 of 3. Baltimore: Johns Hopkins University Press.

Lear, Jonathan. 1990. *Love and its place in nature.* New York: Farrar, Straus & Giroux.

Liddy, Richard M. 1970. *Art and feeling: an analysis and critique of the philosophy of Susanne K. Langer.* Rome: Tipografia di Patrizio Graziani.

Little, Arthur, S. J. 1930. Jacques Maritain and his aesthetic. *Studies,* 19.467-480.

Lonergan, Bernard J. F. , S. J. 1957. *Insight: a study of human understanding.* New York: Harper & Row.

_____. 1959. *Unpublished notes on art.* 280-315.

_____. *Method in theology.* Toronto: University of Toronto Press, for Lonergan Research Institute of Regis College, Toronto.

Madden, Lawrence J. 1988. *Liturgical renewal: 1963–1988; a study of English speaking parishes in the United States.* Washington DC: Georgetown Center for Liturgy, Spirituality and the Arts. Ptd.

_____, ed. 1992. *The awakening Church: 25 years of liturgical renewal.* Collegeville MN: The Liturgical Press.

Margolis, Joseph. 1955. Review: Feeling and form. *Journal of philosophy* 52.291-296.

Maritain, Jacques, and Raïssa Maritain. 1938, 1955. *The situation of poetry.* Tr. Marshall Suther. New York: Philosophical Library.

Maritain, Jacques. 1914, 1955. *Bergsonian philosophy and Thomism.* Tr. Mabelle L. Andison, J. Jordon Andison. New York: Philosophical Library.

_____. 1924. *Réflexions sur l'intelligence et sa vie propre.* Paris: Nouvelle Librairie Nationale.

_____. 1927, 1935, 1954. *Art and scholasticism and the frontiers of poetry.* Tr. Joseph W. Evans. New York: Scribner.

_____. 1941. *Ransoming the time.* Tr. Harry Lorin Binsse. New York: Charles Scribner's Sons.

_____. 1943. *Art and poetry.* Tr. E. de P. Matthews. New York: Philosophical Library.

_____. 1946, 1952. *The range of reason.* Tr. Mrs. Pierre Brodin. New York: Charles Scribner's Sons.

_____. 1946, 1959. *The degrees of knowledge.* Tr. Gerald B. Phelan. London: Geoffrey Bles Ltd.

_____. 1946. *Raison et raisons.* Paris: Egloff.

_____. 1948, 1960. *Existence and the existent.* Tr. Lewis Galantiere and Gerald B. Phelan Garden City, NY: Doubleday & Company.

_____. 1953. *Creative intuition in art and poetry.* New York: New American Library.

_____. 1962, 1987. *A preface to metaphysics: seven lectures on being.* Salem NH: Ayer Company Publishers, Inc.

Martimort, A. G., ed. 1986–1988. *The Church at prayer.* 4 Vols. Tr. Matthew J. O'Connell. Collegeville MN: The Liturgical Press.

Martos, Joseph. 1991. *Doors to the sacred: a historical introduction to sacraments in the Catholic Church.* Tarrytown NY: Triumph™ Books.

Maslow, Abraham H. 1962. *Toward a psychology of being.* Princeton: D. van Nostrand Co. Inc.

McCartney, Marion, and Antonia van der Meer. 1991. *The midwife's pregnancy and childbirth book: having your baby your way.* New York: Harper Collins Publishers.

McCool, Gerald A., ed. 1989. *A Rahner reader.* New York: Crossroad Publishing Co.

McKinnon, James, ed. 1990. *Antiquity and the middle ages.* Englewood Cliffs NJ: Prentice Hall.

Mitchell, Nathan OSB. 1982. *Cult and controversy: the worship of the Eucharist outside mass.* New York: Pueblo Publishing Company.

Mühlen, Heribert. 1965. Person und appropriation. *Müchener theologische zeitschrift,* 16.

Nagel, Ernest. 1943. Review: Philosophy in a new key. *The journal of philosophy* 40.323-329.

Ouspensky, Leonid. 1978. *Theology of the icon.* Crestwood NY: St. Vladimir's Seminary Press.

Quasten, Johannes. 1983. *Music & worship in pagan & Christian antiquity.* Tr. Boniface Ramsey, O.P. Washington, DC.: National Association of Pastoral Musicians.

Rader, Melvin. 1954. Review: Feeling and form. *Journal of aesthetics and art criticism* 12.3.396-398.

Rahner, Karl, S.J. 1954, 1961a Concerning the relationship between nature and grace. *Theological investigations, I,* pp. 297–317. Baltimore: Helicon Press.

_____. 1954, 1961b. Some implications of the Scholastic concept of uncreated grace. *Theological investigations, I,* pp. 319–346. Baltimore: Helicon Press.

_____. 1957, 1968. *Spirit in the world.* Tr. William Dych, S.J. New York: Herder and Herder.

_____. 1963, 1969. *Hearers of the word.* Tr. Michael Richards. New York: Herder and Herder.

_____. 1966a. Remarks on the dogmatic treatise 'de trinitate.' *Theological investigations IV,* pp. 77–102. Baltimore: Helicon Press.

_____. 1966b. Nature and grace. *Theological investigations IV,* pp. 165–188. Tr. Kevin Smyth. Baltimore: Helicon Press.

_____. 1966c. The theology of the symbol. *Theological investigations IV,* pp. 221-252. Tr. Kevin Smyth. Vol. IV. Baltimore: Helicon Press.

_____. 1967, 1970. *The Trinity.* Tr. Joseph Donceel. New York: Herder and Herder.

_____. 1969. Reflections on the unity of the love of neighbor and the love of God. *Theological investigations VI,* pp. 231–249. Tr. Karl-H and Boniface Kruger. Baltimore: Helicon Press.

_____. 1976a. Considerations on the active role of the person in the sacramental event. *Theological investigations XIV*, pp. 161–184.

_____. 1976b. Observations on the problem of the "anonymous Christian." *Theological investigations XIV*, pp. 280–294.

_____. 1992. *Foundations of Christian faith: an introduction to the idea of Christianity*. Tr. William Dych. New York: Crossroad. Originally published as *Grundkurs des Glaubens: Einfürung in den begriff des Christentums*, 1976.

Ratcliff, E. C. 1950. The Sanctus and the pattern of the early anaphora. *Journal of ecclesiastical history*, 1.29–134.

Rizzuto, Ana-Maria. 1979. *The birth of the living God: a psychoanalytic study*. Chicago: The University of Chicago Press.

Ross, Susan A. 1985. The aesthetic and the sacramental. *Worship*, 59.1.2–17.

Routley, Erik. 1982. *Christian hymns observed: when in our music God is glorified*. Princeton: Prestige Publications.

Rover, Thomas, O.P. 1965. *Imitation and transcendence in the poetics of Maritain*. Washington: The Thomist Press.

Saliers, Don E. 1981. The integrity of sung prayer. *Worship*, 55.290–303.

_____. 1990. Liturgical aesthetics. *The new dictionary of sacramental worship*. Ed. Peter E. Fink, S. J. Collegeville MN: The Liturgical Press.

Schillebeeckx, Edward. 1963. *Christ the sacrament of the encounter with God*. New York: Sheed and Ward.

Scott, R. Taylor. 1980. The liklihood of liturgy: reflections upon prayer book revision and its liturgical implications. *Anglican Theological Review*, 62.2.103–120.

Schulz, Hans-Joachim. 1986. *The Byzantine liturgy: symbolic structure and faith expression*. New York: Pueblo Publishing Co.

Searle, Mark. 1981. *Liturgy made simple*. Collegeville MN: The Liturgical Press.

Simcoe, Mary Ann, ed. 1985. *The liturgy documents: a parish resource*. Chicago: Liturgy Training Publications.

Taft, Robert, S. J. 1984. *Beyond East and West: problems in liturgical understanding*. Washington DC: The Pastoral Press.

Tagore, Rabindranath. 1939, 1972. *Collected poems and plays of Rabindranath Tagore*. London: Macmillian & Co Ldt.

Tegels, Aelred. 1985. Chronicle. *Worship*, 59.154–155.

Turner, Harold W. 1979. *From temple to meeting house: the phenomenology and theology of places of worship*. Vol. 16. Religion and Society. New York: Mouton Publishers.

Vajda, Jaroslav J. 1987. *Now the joyful celebration: hymns, carols, and songs*. St. Louis: Morning Star Music Publishers.

Verny, Thomas, and Pamela Weintraub. 1991. *Nurturing the unborn child*. New York: Dell Publishing.

Weitz, Morris. 1954. Review: Feeling and form. *Review of metaphysics* 7.27.467-481.

Wendebourg, D. 1982. From the Cappadocian Fathers to Gregory Palamas: the defeat of trinitarian theology. *Studia patristica,* 17. 1.194–97.

Wertz, Richard W., and Dorothy C. Wertz. 1989. *Lying-in: a history of childbirth in America.* Expanded ed. New Haven: Yale University Press.

Wheelwright, Philip. 1982. *The burning fountain, a study in the language of symbolism.* Gloucester, Mass: Peter Smith.

White, Eric Walter. 1979. *Stravinsky: the composer and his works.* London and Boston: Faber and Faber.

Worgul, George S. 1985. *From magic to metaphor: a validation of Christian sacraments.* Lanham MD: University Press of America, Inc.

Zimmerman, Joyce Ann, C.PP.S. 1993. *Liturgy as living faith: a liturgical spirituality.* Scranton: University of Scranton Press.

INDEX

A

Ab esse ad posse: 169

Abbreviations: v

Abstract: 28, 36, 97, 111, 115, 116, 125, 129, 263, 290, 294; abstraction, 95-97, 116, 123-124, 135 n7, 136-137 nn7, 8, 245; abstractive, 125; abstractness, 125, 290

Abstracto: 108; "generalizing abstraction," 135-136 n7

Academic: 5-6, 28 n10, 41

Action: as Christian conduct, 148, 154, 170, 199-200, 206, 230, 234, 238-239, 242, 243, 248, 266; as primary semblance abstracted in liturgy, 247-248, 267; in drama, 120, 130; liturgical, 143-147, 161 n16, 194, 195, 198, 201, 230, 231, 238, 240, 242, 247-249, 264, 273 n25, 275 n34; of the Trinity, 182, 183, 186, 188, 189, 191, 195, 204, 219 n42, 220, 224 n62, 224-225 n66, 229; sacramental, 225-226 n69, 230; subjectivity as, 292

Activities in coordination (organic): 100

Adoptionism: 215 n29

Aesthetic: 1-7, 38, 51, 74, 89 n56, 108, 121, 123, 130, 144, 158 n2, 264, 266, 271n13, 292; aesthetics, 3, 2, 7, 43, 59, 78 n8, 93, 129, 269, 293, 294; aesthetical, 1, 4-6, 8, 27, 27 n3, 28 n11, 40, 47, 74, 80 n17, 93, 94, 102, 123, 130, 268, 269, 291, 292; aesthetician, 6, 7, 40, 71, 134, 136; aesthetic liturgy, 4, 264, 266, 268

Agent: 4, 85 n40, 86 n47, 140 n42, 163, 234

Alio esse, in: 74

Amateur: 252, 275 n32

Analogy: between art and liturgy, 244-253, 268; defined, 11-15, 68; of being, 180, 214 n22; of generative union, 17, 34, 35, 37, 39, 51, 59, 60, 63, 94, 127, 130, 134, 157, 184, 229, 231-232, 240, 244, 253, 266

Anamnesis: 151

Anatomy of Criticism: 248

Apollinarianism: 215 n29

Apprehension: 71, 81 n23 89 n56, 93; simple, 82 n29, 285, 291, 293; concrete, 124-125, 127, 139 n38

Appropriation: 176, 181, 220 n44

Aquinas, Thomas: 78 n8, 80 n18, 81 n23, 82-83 n32, 83 n33, 90 n62, 176-177, 179, 186, 188, 189, 213-214 nn20, 23, 214-215 n26, 218 nn38, 39, 219 nn40, 42, 285

Architect: 9, 130, 280

Architecture: 39, 77, 116, 117

Arians: 212 n13

Aristotle: 48, 81 n23, 284, 293, 294

Arius: 174, 212 n13

Art and Feeling: 292

Art and Scholasticism: 88 n51, 133

Art: 1-4, 6-11, 13-15, 17, 19, 21, 24, 26, 33-92, 93-142, 143-147, 158 n2, 170, 200, 209, 223 n56, 229-230, 232-233, 238, 241-246, 249, 253-254, 257-260, 262, 265-269, 271, 275, 279-281, 292-294; art-as-communication, 70-71, 85 n45; art as creative, 9, 33-40; art-form(s), 43, 143-144; art-genres, 121, 126, 130, 244; art-work, 244; artistic skill, 4-5; liturgy as art, 143-144, 243, 244-253, 255; arts in liturgy, 246, 256-259

K

Kant, Immanuel: 40, 216 n32
Kaspar, Walter: 217 n36
Keats, John: 36, 59
Keifer, Ralph: 27 nn6, 8, 272 n20
Kelly, J. N. D.: 213 n19
Kerygma: 153, 162 n17
Kilmartin, Edward: 159 n7, 185-189, 192-194, 199, 202-203, 207, 214 n25, 216 nn34, 35, 217 n35, 219 n40, 221 n49, 222 n54, 223 n61, 224 nn62, 63, 225-226 n70, 270 n7
Kitzinger, Sheila: 23, 30 n25
Knowledge: abstract, 102, 106; active and passive, 49; artistic, chs 2 and 3, 42-43, 58, 128, 279; as biology, 126, 136 n13, 291-292; as union, 47, 51, 57, 82-83 n32, 130, 218-219 n39, 224 n65, 264, 283-288; by connaturality, 44-46, 55, 79-80 n14, 80 n20, 128, 140 nn41, 42, 172, 189; creative, 46, 50, 51-61, 58, 79 n11, 82 n3; creative knowing as leading to art-work, 59, 61, 67-68, 130; emotion as power of knowing, 54-56, 84 n39; mixture of powers, 53-56; felt awareness, 98-100; Freudian unconscious, 43; gestation of, 58-59, 61-69, 86 n47; immanent, 82 n28; in Descartes, 185; in Hegel, 148; in Lonergan, 291-294; mystical, 81 n21, 208; of artistic materials and elements, 61, 99-100, 103, 106, 116, 126; of being, 74, 84 n40, 169, 208, 214 n22; object of creative knowledge, 56-57, 58-59, 84-85 n41; "ordinary" knowledge, 44, 28 n17, 46, 51-60, 71, 74, 79 n13, 82 n28, 83 n37, 95, 128, 129; "poetic, 42-43, 46, 79 n12; powers of, 44, 48, 51-52, 78 n8; reflexive, 42, 43, 46, 57-58, 71-72, 79 n13, 82 n25, 106, 126, 129, 130 n10, 137 n18, 139, 175, 187, 238-239; sociology of, 196-197; sub/pre-conscious, 12, 37, 43-44, 53-56, 221 n50; theory of, 47-50; through symbol, 72-74, 76, 89-90 n57, 107-109, 122-126

Koinonia: 254

L

Labor: artistic, 9, 39, 133; in liturgy, 230, 233, 242, 269; in physical birth, 23-24, 26, 30 n28
LaCugna, Catherine: 28 n13, 174-178, 183-185, 187, 191, 208, 211 n11, 212 nn13, 14, 213 nn16, 19, 213-214 n20, 215 n27, 215-216 n30, 217 n35, 219 n42
Lakoff/Johnson: 28-29 n17
Lang, Berel: 122, 125, 137 nn22, 23, 138 nn 26, 35, 139 n39
Langer, Susanne K.: 37, 38, 40, 57, 65, 71, 80 n17, 83 n37, 89-90 n60, 93-140, 232, 244-245, 250, 253, 254, 257, 266, 268, 291-294
Language-as-mirror: 121
Lear, Jonathan: 28 n10, 29 nn18, 19, 21, 80 n16, 82, n25, 83-84 n38, 85 n42
Lectio divina: 160 n9
Legitimation: 196, 197
Leibnitz, G. W.: 216 n32
Leonardo: 2
Lex orandi lex credendi: 147, 159 n7
Liberation: 150, 185, 253
Liddy, Richard: 135 n1, 292-293
Liszt, Franz: 258
Liturgy: 1-8, 10-11; and symbol, 200-203; and sacraments, 193-200; and the Trinity, 185, 193-200, 217 n34; as creative, 27 n1, 229-243, 231-233; as worship, 147-157, 173; as art form, 143-144, 146, 244-253; as union/communion, 237-238, 238-239, 242-243; as work of God and of people, 195, 197, 198, 223 n61; beauty of, 262-263; birth of, 198, 231, 245; creativity and, 15, 146-147, 240, 243; discernment of Spirit in, 231; elevation and, 233-234; feeling in, 254-256; fertility and, 236-237; liturgy's arts, 145, 256-264; music as assimilated in, 257-259; music in, 27 n6, 158 n45, 256-263; organic nature of, 253-254; sociol-

F   I

by H   ecki

for
dummies®
A Wiley Brand

Football For Dummies®, 6th Edition

Published by: **John Wiley & Sons, Inc.,** 111 River Street, Hoboken, NJ 07030-5774, www.wiley.com

Copyright © 2019 by John Wiley & Sons, Inc., Hoboken, New Jersey

Published simultaneously in Canada

For general information on our other products and services, please contact our Customer Care Department within the U.S. at 877-762-2974, outside the U.S. at 317-572-3993, or fax 317-572-4002. For technical support, please visit https://hub.wiley.com/community/support/dummies.

Wiley publishes in a variety of print and electronic formats and by print-on-demand. Some material included with standard print versions of this book may not be included in e-books or in print-on-demand. If this book refers to media such as a CD or DVD that is not included in the version you purchased, you may download this material at http://booksupport.wiley.com. For more information about Wiley products, visit www.wiley.com.

Library of Congress Control Number: 2019940398

ISBN 978-1-119-55300-7 (pbk); ISBN 978-1-119-55299-4 (ebk); ISBN 978-1-119-55301-4 (ebk)

Manufactured in the United States of America

C10010106_050719

Contents at a Glance

Table of Contents

CHAPTER 20: More Than Ten Top Non-Quarterback Offensive Players

CHAPTER 21: More Than Ten Greatest Quarterbacks of All Time

Introduction

Millions of people across the United States are intrigued by football — all types and levels of it. These people may have friends or family who have made the football season a ritual, from the last weekend in August through the college bowl games in December until Super Bowl Sunday at the start of February. To be a part of that experience, you need to have a working knowledge of the game.

Football For Dummies, 6th Edition, serves to give you that knowledge and help you better facilitate interaction with your friends, family, or whomever you watch football with. For many people, on the surface, football seems to be a complicated game. Twenty-two players are on the field at one time, plus a number of officials. The intricacies of first down, second down, and third down, and everything from how many offensive linemen there are to what the quarterback really does or doesn't do, all need to be explained and simplified. This book will help; that's why I decided to write it.

I think football is far less intimidating when you have a basic working knowledge of the game. After you break through that initial fear of being overwhelmed by football and what you don't understand, everything else about the game falls into place. You begin to see the game clearly, like when you wipe the early morning dew off your windshield — suddenly everything becomes crystal clear.

Today I know a lot more about the game as a whole than I did when I was a player. I played in high school and in college, plus I played for 13 seasons in the National Football League (NFL). But being a television analyst — 2019 will be my 26th season working for FOX Sports — has forced me to learn even more about this game that I love.

As a player, I had a working knowledge of the passing game, of how a secondary works in coverages, and of the offensive and defensive line formations. I also had a working knowledge of general managers, scouts, and head coaches. But working as an analyst, I've been forced to cover the entire game. I no longer view football from a defensive lineman's perspective. Instead, I look at football as a whole. And I'm still learning every day. That never changes. I don't think you'll ever stop learning when it comes to football. It's the same for everyone — the players, the fans, the coaches, and the television experts. So don't feel alone out there.

About This Book

I wrote *Football For Dummies,* 6th Edition, to help you find out what you want to know about football. Therefore, I don't expect you to read every single page in order. Sure, you can read the book from front to back if you want, but if you'd rather skip around and just read about the topics that interest you, that's fine, too.

And I don't make you remember obscure facts from earlier chapters to make sense of later chapters. If you need to know something that I cover in an earlier chapter, I either define it again or refer you to the chapter that contains the information. Also, if you don't know certain football jargon, you can turn to the Appendix, which explains some of the most common terms. What could be simpler?

I also use diagrams — you know, those X and O things — to show you what I'm talking about when I describe lineups, formations, and plays. So you aren't left wondering what all those little symbols mean, here's a key to the diagrams used in this book:

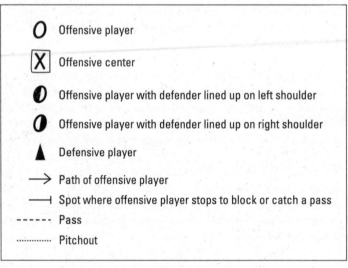

© John Wiley & Sons, Inc.

Foolish Assumptions

Here's what I'm assuming about you: You're interested in football and want to get familiar with the sport, including its history, so you can watch games in person and on television, follow all the action, and enjoy football games to the hilt. You may not know much about football, but I know that you're no dummy either. You may, however, have burning questions like these:

>> Is the ball really made of pigskin, or is that an inside joke?

>> Why do you get six points for a touchdown but only three points for a field goal?

>> Does it really matter how all those guys line up on the field?

>> Does it really mean something when the officials do those funny signals with their arms, or are they just bored out there?

This book answers all these questions and more.

Icons Used in This Book

To help you navigate your way through this book, I place icons in the margins. These little pictures point you to a particular type of information. Here's a list of the icons in this book and what they mean:

HALL OF FAME

A book about football wouldn't be the same without tales of the sport's greats. This icon flags stories about the game's greatest, most recognized players.

HOWIE SAYS

Being a commentator, I can't help but want to throw in my two cents once in a while. When I have my own tale to tell on a subject, I mark it with this icon.

REMEMBER

When you see this icon, you know you're reading a piece of information that's especially important to remember. If you take away nothing else from this book but the paragraphs flagged with this icon, you'll have a solid understanding of football.

TIP

Look for this icon if you want to know all the helpful tidbits of info that can make you a more informed fan.

Beyond the Book

This book provides great information to help you learn about football, but you can find additional resources on Dummies.com. You can download the book's Cheat Sheet at www.dummies.com. Just type "*Football For Dummies* cheat sheet" in the Search box. It's a handy resource to keep on your computer, tablet, or smartphone.

Where to Go from Here

So you're geared up and ready to play, metaphorically speaking. Where you go from here depends on the type of information you're looking for. If you want a primer on football starting at square one, head to Chapter 1. If you want to know about how a particular phase of the game — say, the offensive line or the kicking game — works, head to that specific chapter. And if you want to read about some of the greatest players in football history, head to Part 6. Wherever you start, enjoy the game!

1

Getting Started with Football

IN THIS PART . . .

Get an overview of football's history, the players and personnel involved, and the roots of the world's greatest game.

Look at the field and equipment and the meanings behind the uniforms.

Review the rules of football and understand its ins and outs.

Chapter **1**

America's Greatest Game

When I was 14, a sophomore in high school, I moved out of Boston to live with my uncle. During my first weekend in Milford, Massachusetts, I saw my first high school football game. I had never seen anything like it. Before the game, an antique fire engine led a parade on the track around the football field while the crowd clapped and cheered. The players then thundered across a wooden bridge over a pond and burst through a banner to enter the stadium. I said to myself, "Wow, this game is for me."

I wasn't necessarily drawn to the game itself; I simply loved what came with the sport: *respect.* For me, football was an opportunity to belong to something, giving me confidence for the first time in my life. It was more of a personal thing than it was about playing football. It wasn't so much the football, but what football did for me. Football gave me a sense of self-worth, which I've carried with me throughout my life.

Sure, I experienced down periods when I first started playing, but I never thought about quitting. My first high school coach, Dick Corbin, was great to me and encouraged me to continue playing the game. Believe me, coaches are important. I've always had the support of football coaches, both on *and* off the field.

Football is responsible for everything that I've accomplished in my life. The discipline and hard work that made me a successful athlete have helped me in other areas of my life, allowing me to venture into new careers in movies and television.

Why Football Is the Best

Baseball may be America's pastime, but football is America's passion. Football is the only team sport in America that conjures up visions of Roman gladiators, pitting city versus city, state versus state — sometimes with a Civil War feel, like when the Jets play the Giants in New York or the Dallas Cowboys play the Washington Redskins.

Football is played in all weather conditions — snow, rain, and sleet — with temperatures on the playing field ranging from −30 to 120 degrees Fahrenheit. Whatever the conditions may be, the game goes on. And unlike other major sports, the football playoff system, in the National Football League (NFL) anyway, is a single-elimination tournament. In other words, the NFL has no playoff series; the playoffs are do-or-die, culminating in what has become the single biggest one-day sporting event in America: the Super Bowl.

Or, in simpler terms, anytime you stick 22 men in high-tech plastic helmets on a football field and have them continually run great distances at incredible speeds and slam into each other, people will watch.

Football has wedged itself into the American culture. In fact, in many small towns across the United States, the centerpiece is the Friday night high school football game. The NFL doesn't play on Fridays simply to protect this great part of Americana, in which football often gives schools and even towns a certain identity. For example, hard-core fans know that tiny Massillon, Ohio, is where the late, great Paul Brown of the Cleveland Browns began his coaching career. To this day, Massillon's high school has maintained a tremendous high school football tradition. With so many factions of the student body involved, plus their families, a strong core of fans is built. For many, this enthusiasm for football continues in college.

You may not think it now, but millions of people are familiar with the strategy of the game, and most of them pass it down through their families. A lot of fathers coach their sons, and on rare occasions, their daughters. Although the focus may have changed in today's society, at one time the only team that mattered in high school was the football team. The pace of the game — stoppage after every play with a huddle — is perfect for most fans because it allows them time to guess what the team will try next.

FOOTBALL IS *IT* IN THE UNITED STATES

Since 1985, Harris Interactive (a global marketing research firm) has been conducting polls to determine which sport is the most popular in the United States. Pro football has been ranked number 1 in 30 straight polls. In 2014, 35 percent of Americans polled chose pro football as their favorite sport. Baseball came in second at 14 percent. Guess which sport came in third? That would be college football at 11 percent. Any way you slice it, football is unquestionably the most popular spectator sport in the United States.

TIP

On two particular holidays, sitting down and watching football has become an American tradition:

>> **Thanksgiving Day** is reserved for a turkey dinner with the family, followed by a pro football game. The Detroit Lions started the tradition in 1934, and they continue to play a game every Thanksgiving. There have been at least two pro football games on Thanksgiving Day every year since 1960. Since 2006, fans have enjoyed three NFL games on that holiday.

>> **New Year's Day** has long been the day for college football bowl games, which generally match up some of the nation's finest teams.

Who's Playing Football

Football is suited to all sizes of athletes. Larger athletes generally play on the offensive and defensive lines — what are called the *trenches.* Leaner athletes who are faster and quicker generally play the skill positions, such as quarterback, running back, and receiver. But no matter how big or how talented you are, you must have inner courage to play football. This game requires strength and perseverance. If you don't believe you're tough enough to play, then you probably shouldn't try.

And if you're not up to the full-force-hitting variety of football, you can still enjoy the sport as a player. Touch football is totally different from tackle football. All you need are a ball and maybe six players, three per team. Anyone can play this game, and the players decide the rules and the size of the field at the start of the game. I've seen people playing touch football on the streets of New York City and in parks and front lawns all across America — the beauty of the game is that you can play anywhere.

HOWIE SAYS

Of all the team sports, football is the most violent and dangerous, with hockey a distant second. I played football for respect, and I believe that it builds character. Considering some of the problems in society today, football can give a youngster's life some structure and can also teach discipline. All the players who belong to a football team are in the struggle together, sharing in the joy and the pain of the sport. Every play can be such an adrenaline rush.

How Football Began

Just as many fans get caught up in the hype and hoopla of today's NFL, many others love the game for its sense of tradition. The game itself has endured for more than 150 years.

Games involving kicking a ball into a goal on a lined field have existed for more than 2,000 years. American football evolved from two particular games that were popular in other parts of the world: soccer (as it's known in the United States) and rugby. Both the Romans and the Spartans (remember that movie *Spartacus*? Now those guys were tough!) played some version of soccer. Soccer and rugby came to North America in the 19th century, and historians have noted that the first form of American football emerged on November 6, 1869, when teams from Princeton and Rutgers, two New Jersey universities, competed in a game of what was closer to rugby than football. Rutgers won that game 6–4.

The following sections introduce you to the contributions of two key individuals in the football world: Walter Camp and Harold "Red" Grange.

Camp defines the rules

HALL OF FAME

Walter Camp, a sensational player at Yale University and a driving force behind many football rules, is known as the father of American football. Around 1876, when football was already being played in universities on the East Coast and in Canada, Camp helped write the game's first rules. In 1880, he authored rules that reduced the number of players per team from 15 to 11 (today's total) and replaced the rugby scrum with the center snap to put the ball in play. (In a *scrum*, players from both sides bunch tightly together, butting heads while the ball is thrown between them. The players then try to gain possession of the ball with their feet. Using your hands to gain possession is unique to American football — both rugby and soccer forbid it.)

Camp also championed the rule that a team needed to gain 5 yards in three plays in order to maintain possession. Today, teams must gain 10 yards in four plays. (Head to Chapter 3 for more information about these and other rules.)

Camp devised plays and formations and instituted referees. However, his biggest proposal was tackling, which was introduced in 1888. *Tackling* — the act of hitting players below the waist — made the game more violent. It also popularized an offensive strategy known as the *flying wedge*, where an entire team (ten players) would mass in front of one ball carrier in the form of a wedge. Football was almost banned in 1906 after a dozen and a half deaths (and many more serious injuries in the preceding season), but President Theodore Roosevelt saved the game by convincing college representatives to initiate stricter rules to make the game less brutal and dangerous.

REMEMBER

Football has been cleaned up a great deal over the years and has come a long way from clothesline shots and quarterbacks taking late hits and direct blows to the head. But let's not kid one another: Football is a high-impact collision sport, and with collision comes pain and injury. Even with the rules being adjusted to protect today's quarterbacks, rarely does a Monday morning come without the news that at least one quarterback sustained a concussion. Players are bigger, faster, and stronger. Let me put it this way: You're driving down the road traveling at 35 miles per hour. Would you rather be met head-on by a car of similar size or by a truck? Well, that's the difference between 20 years ago and now. Only thing is, the truck's now going 45 miles per hour rather than 35.

Grange helps spread the popularity of pro ball

Americans started playing football in colleges and on club teams in the 1870s. Football became a source of identity for collegians and a regular Saturday afternoon activity by the turn of the century.

In the first 90 years of football, college football was far more popular than pro football; it was (and still is, at many schools) all about tradition and the many rivalries between colleges. Ninety years ago, having more than 50,000 fans attend a great college game wasn't unusual. During that same period, games in the NFL, which officially began in 1920, were fortunate to draw 5,000 fans.

HALL OF FAME

Two days after the 1925 college season ended, Illinois All-American halfback Harold "Red" Grange (see Figure 1-1) signed a contract to play with the struggling Chicago Bears. On Thanksgiving Day of that year, 36,000 fans — the largest crowd in pro football history at that time — watched Grange and the Bears play the league's top team, the Chicago Cardinals, to a scoreless tie in Cubs Park (now called Wrigley Field, the home of the Chicago Cubs baseball team). The Bears went on to play a barnstorming tour, and in New York's Polo Grounds, more than 73,000 fans watched Grange — nicknamed "the Galloping Ghost" — compete against the New York Giants. Although Grange did attract new fans to the pro game, fewer than 30,000 fans attended championship games in the early 1930s.

HALL OF FAME

FOOTBALL IMMORTALS

With every sport comes a list of immortals — those great players who nurtured the game and made it what it is today. Following are some of the early legends of American football:

- **John W. Heisman:** The annual award given to the nation's best college player — the Heisman Trophy — is named after this Brown University (and later University of Pennsylvania) player. Heisman was also a member of New York's Downtown Athletic Club, where the award was presented every December until the building was damaged in the September 11, 2001, terrorist attacks. Heisman was an early advocate of the forward pass.

- **Fritz Pollard:** Pollard starred for Brown University in 1915 and 1916 and was the first African American player to appear in the Rose Bowl. He's also considered the first African American football player to turn professional, the first to be selected to the college All-American team, and the first African American pro head coach (of the Akron Pros in 1921). In 1954, he became the first African American inducted into the College Football Hall of Fame.

- **Amos Alonzo Stagg:** Stagg was a famous University of Chicago coach who developed the "Statue of Liberty" play, in which a halfback takes the ball from the quarterback who has his hands raised as if to throw a forward pass. (I explain offensive positions in Part 2.) He was also the first coach to put numbers on players' uniforms.

- **Jim Thorpe:** A Native American who won the decathlon and pentathlon in the 1912 Stockholm Olympics, Thorpe was an All-American at Carlisle (Pennsylvania) Indian School and was the first big-time American athlete to play pro football. He was paid the princely sum of $250 to play a game for the Canton Bulldogs in 1915. Today, Canton, Ohio, is the home of the Pro Football Hall of Fame.

- **Pop Warner:** The national tackle youth league (described in Chapter 15) is named after this famous coach, who developed the single-wing formation, which snaps the ball directly to the running back and has four linemen to one side of the center and two to the other side. Warner was the first to use the hidden ball trick, in which an offensive lineman slipped the ball under his jersey. The first "hunchback play" went for a touchdown against Harvard in 1902.

FIGURE 1-1:
Harold "Red"
Grange, known as
"the Galloping
Ghost," played for
the Chicago Bears
in 1925.

Pro football emerged as an equal to college football after its games began being televised nationally in the 1960s, but it took decades for the NFL to supplant college football. And to this day, many colleges have as much fan support as some NFL franchises. Universities such as Nebraska, USC, and Notre Dame can claim more fans than, say, the Atlanta Falcons.

How the Football Season Is Set Up Today

Football as an organized sport has come a long way since the early years. Teams at every level play during a standard season and are governed by various football leagues, such as the NFL and NCAA (National Collegiate Athletic Association).

REMEMBER

The heart of the football season is during the fall months. However, training camps, practices, and preseason games often begin in the summer, and playoffs and bowl games are staged after Christmas and into February. Here's how the season breaks down for each level of play:

>> **High school football teams** usually play between eight and ten games in a season, starting after Labor Day. If teams have successful league seasons,

they advance to regional or state playoff tournaments. Some schools in Texas play as many as 15 games if they advance to the state championship game. Most high school teams play in a regional league, although some travel 50 to 100 miles to play opponents. You can find out more about high school football in Chapter 15.

» **College football teams** play generally a schedule of 12 games, the majority in a specific conference — Pac-12, Big Ten, SEC, ACC, and so on. The top teams in the Division I FBS (Football Bowl Subdivision), which constitute the largest schools that offer the most money for athletic scholarships, advance via invitation to postseason bowl games or a four-team playoff for the national championship. Beginning with the 2014–2015 season, the top four teams play in two semifinal games, with the winners facing each other in the College Football Championship Game. This playoff system replaced the controversial BCS system, which had been in place from 1998 through the 2013–2014 season. Read more about college football in Chapter 16.

» **NFL teams** play 16 regular-season games, preceded by a minimum of 4 preseason games that are played in August. The 32 NFL teams are divided into two conferences, the NFC (National Football Conference) and the AFC (American Football Conference), and the four division leaders and two wild card teams from each conference advance to the playoffs with hopes of reaching the Super Bowl, which is played in early February. Chapter 17 gives you all the details about the NFL.

Football is pretty much a weekend sport, although a few games are played on Monday and Thursday, particularly in the NFL. In general, however, the football season, which begins in earnest right around Labor Day, follows this orderly pattern:

» High school games are usually played on Friday nights.

» College games are played on Saturdays, mostly during the day, although a few are held on Thursday and Friday nights.

» The NFL plays on Sundays for the most part. For television purposes, games are played in the early and late afternoon (Eastern time).

How Television Helped Increase Football's Popularity

Today, most football fans are introduced to the game through television, which brings the game right into everyone's home. The action in a football game translates well to television. The field and all the action that takes place upon it fit just as nicely on a big screen as they do on a smaller model. Because television networks use up to 20 cameras for most games, viewers rarely miss out on plays. And with replay machines, the networks can show critical plays from several different angles, including a viewer-friendly angle for fans watching at home or at the neighborhood tavern.

Television shows like *FOX NFL Sunday* also help to make the game more personal by promoting the personalities under the helmets. Fans, for example, can watch and listen to a Drew Brees interview and feel like they know the New Orleans quarterback as a person.

In addition, with round-the-clock NFL coverage on sports cable networks like ESPN, FOX Sports, and the NFL Network, fans can tune in pretty much 24 hours a day to get the latest news and updates about their favorite players and teams. This kind of coverage keeps football at the forefront of fan awareness all season long.

Why Millions Cheer Each Year for College Football

As much as I prefer the NFL, I have to acknowledge that for many fans, college football is the game to watch. The level of play isn't as high in college, but the collegiate game has more history and pageantry. Marching bands, mascots, pep rallies, and cheerleaders add a fun dimension to college football. Some teams, such as Notre Dame and Michigan, are steeped in folklore and tradition. Notre Dame, for example, has the Four Horsemen, the Seven Mules, and the Gipper.

College football fans can be every bit as passionate as NFL fans, especially when they root for a team that represents the college or university they attend or once attended or when they don't have a professional team to cheer on. Los Angeles, for example, doesn't have an NFL football team — the Rams left for St. Louis in 1995, and the Raiders returned to Oakland that same year — but its football fans make do based on the strength of two local college football teams, the USC Trojans and the UCLA Bruins. USC and UCLA consistently field excellent teams.

What Makes the Super Bowl Number One

Almost every year, the highest-rated show on network television is the Super Bowl, with whatever the number-two show is running a distant second. Of the ten most-watched shows in the history of television, four of them are Super Bowl games. Clearly, the Super Bowl has become an event that all of America, both casual and hard-core fans alike, focuses on. Even if it's the only game they watch all season, people tune into the Super Bowl and attend Super Bowl parties in massive numbers (would you believe these parties are more popular than New Year's Eve parties?).

The Super Bowl has also become an international event. More than 200 countries and territories, including Slovenia and the People's Republic of China, televise the game. In the United States, the typical audience is over 100 million viewers.

REMEMBER

The main reason the Super Bowl is so popular is that pro football is the only major professional team sport with a single-elimination playoff system. The other major sports declare their champions after a team wins four games in a best-of-seven series. The Super Bowl is do-or-die; that's what makes the game so special.

And it isn't just the game itself that attracts viewers. Companies pay advertising firms lots of money to create commercials. In fact, watching the Super Bowl to see the commercials has become a part of what makes Super Bowl Sunday so special. All the commercials are judged and summarized because hundreds of millions of potential customers are watching, making the commercial stakes almost as high as those on the field.

HOWIE SAYS

THE ROAD TO THE SUPER BOWL

I played in my only Super Bowl after my third season in the NFL, and I thought I'd make it back at least two or three more times during my career. Unfortunately, that never happened.

The media attention back in 1984 wasn't nearly as expansive as it is today. In fact, tracing the growth of the media from 1984 to today is like comparing the size of Rhode Island to the size of Montana. I remember taking a cab to Tampa Stadium to play in the Super Bowl. The traffic was so bad that I ended up walking the last three-quarters of a mile to the stadium. Today, the NFL provides police escorts for the players. The fanfare surrounding a team's arrival is as if the president is coming to town.

Chapter 2

Meet Me on the Gridiron

I've spent a lot of time on football fields. Although the dimensions are the same, from high school to the NFL, every field seems different. That's because all across America, the atmosphere inside each stadium, or the architectural character of the stadium itself, tends to be unique to that region. But every field shares some common characteristics.

In this chapter, I explain the basics of a football field and why teams don't always play on my favorite surface — good old green grass. I also talk about the number of players on the field, what they wear, and that odd-shaped ball they play with.

The Big Picture: Stadiums

As you probably know, a *stadium* is the whole structure or area in which football and other games are played: the field, the stands, and so on. Stadiums come in all shapes and sizes. The important thing is that they allow room for the 100-yard-long football field, which is, of course, obligatory. (See the next section for more on the football field.)

NFL and college stadiums come in two main varieties: domed stadiums and outdoor stadiums. Domed stadiums are designed so that the players and the fans don't have to deal with the weather; they always have a roof over their heads, and the teams always play on artificial turf. When you're talking about big-time football, both types of stadiums generally seat between 50,000 and 107,000 screaming fans.

THE BEST STADIUM IN PRO FOOTBALL

There's no better setting in pro football than Lambeau Field in Green Bay, Wisconsin. With its circular seating and lack of an upper deck, Lambeau is a fan-friendly stadium. Every seat offers a good view of the action.

For a potentially cold arena, Lambeau is also a player-friendly stadium. To improve their field in freezing conditions, the Packers installed SportGrass in 1997. This new surface consists of natural grass planted on a recyclable, synthetic surface below field level. This setup creates a stable base that can't be destroyed by the physical wear and tear on the field when coupled with soggy, wet conditions. The old field, by the way, was packed into "Frozen Tundra" boxes and sold to fans to help pay for the new field.

New stadiums, many financed through public support and tax dollars, have become one of the NFL's top priorities. Between 1992 and 2010, a total of 22 new stadiums were built. These stadiums offer luxury boxes, state-of-the-art video systems, and other amenities for fans. Reliant Stadium, home of the Houston Texans, boasts natural grass and a retractable roof, the first of its kind in the NFL. Ford Field, the home of the Detroit Lions, includes a six-story atrium. In 2010, proving once and for all that Texans like all things big, the Dallas Cowboys inaugurated Cowboys Stadium, the largest domed stadium in the world. The stadium includes an 11,520-square-foot video display screen, the — you guessed it — largest high-definition screen in the world.

Getting Down to Business: The Field

There's nothing like a football field. If I could wish something for everyone, it would be for them to stand on the sideline at an NFL game and hear, sense, and feel the impact of the collisions and see the speed of the game up close. The selected areas around the sidelines for photographers and television cameramen are my favorite places to watch the game. The following sections tell you what you see on a football field, whether you're on the field or in the stands.

Field dimensions

The dimensions of a football field haven't changed much through the years. The field has been 100 yards long and 53 yards wide since 1881. In 1912, the two end zones were established at 10 yards deep and have remained so ever since. Consequently, all football games are played on a rectangular field that's 360 feet long and 160 feet wide.

The marks on the field

All over the field, you see a bunch of white lines. Every line has a special meaning, as shown in Figure 2-1:

>> **End lines:** The lines at each end of the field are called the *end lines.*

>> **Sidelines:** The lines along each side of the field are called the *sidelines.*

>> **Goal lines:** The *goal lines* are 10 yards inside and parallel to each end line.

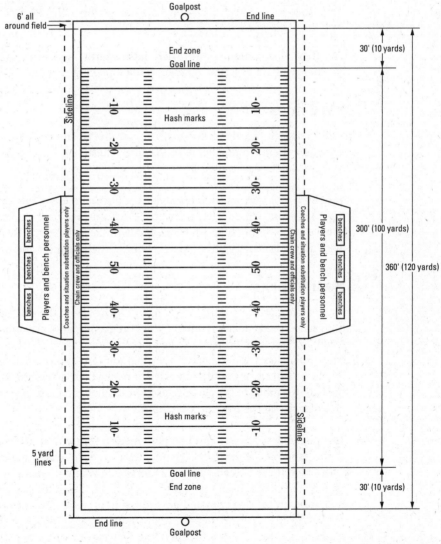

FIGURE 2-1:
The playing field.

>> **Field of play:** The area bounded by the goal lines and sidelines is known as the *field of play.*

>> **50-yard line:** The field is divided in half by the *50-yard line,* which is located in the middle of the field.

>> **End zones:** The two areas bounded by the goal lines, end lines, and sidelines are known as the *end zones.*

To make all these white lines, teams use paint or marking chalk. They're even painting grass fields these days. The end lines and sidelines are 4 inches wide and rimmed by a solid white border that's a minimum of 6 feet wide. All boundary lines, goal lines, and marked yard lines are continuous lines until they intersect with one another.

The field also contains yard lines, hash marks, and lines marking the player benches, which I describe in detail in the following sections.

Yard lines

Yard lines, at intervals of 5 yards, run parallel to the goal lines and are marked across the field from sideline to sideline. These lines stop 8 inches short of the 6-foot solid border in the NFL.

Yard lines give players and fans an idea of how far a team must advance the ball in order to record a *first down.* As Chapter 3 explains in detail, an offensive team must gain 10 yards in order to post a first down. Consequently, the field is numbered every 10 yards, starting from the goal lines. All these lines and numbers are white.

Hash marks

Hash marks mark each yard line 70 feet, 9 inches from the sidelines in the NFL. On high school and college football fields, the hash marks are only 60 feet from the sidelines. Two sets of hash marks (each hash is 1 yard in length) run parallel to each other down the length of the field and are approximately 18½ feet apart. When the ball carrier is either tackled or pushed out of bounds, the officials return the ball in bounds to the closest hash mark. Punted balls that go out of bounds are also marked on the nearest hash mark.

The hash marks are used for ball placement prior to most offensive plays so more of the game can be played in the middle of the field, which makes the game more wide open. If the ball was placed 20 feet from where it went out of bounds rather than on the closest hash mark, offenses would be restricted to one open side of the field for many of their run and pass plays. In other words, they would have to run or pass to the right or the left, and wouldn't have the option to do either. But, when teams run the football and the ball carrier is tackled between the hash marks, the ball is declared dead at that spot and generally is placed where the ball carrier was tackled and stopped.

REMEMBER

An important thing to remember is that an incomplete pass is returned to the spot of the preceding play, not where it actually goes out of bounds or where the quarterback was standing when he threw it.

Out of bounds

A player is *out of bounds* whenever he steps from the field of play and touches (or flies over) the white sidelines or end lines. To remain in bounds for a catch, an NFL player must have both feet (including the toes of his shoes) touching the ground inside the end lines and sidelines and must be in possession of the football; in college and high school football, a player needs to have only one foot inside the end lines and sidelines to be considered in bounds.

Player benches

Six feet outside the border of the field, or 6 feet from the sidelines, is an additional broken white line that defines an area in which only coaches and substitute players may stand. Six feet farther behind this broken white line is where the *bench area* begins (refer to Figure 2-1). The team congregates in the bench area during a game, watching teammates play or resting on the benches. Within this area, team doctors and trainers also examine injured players.

The playing surface

Two types of surfaces are used in football — natural grass and artificial turf. Each has its pros and cons.

>> **Natural grass:** Many natural grass surfaces exist, depending on the region's temperature and the stadium's drainage system. Generally, though, natural grass is similar to your backyard lawn or any baseball outfield: It's green, soft, and beautiful, but it needs to be mowed, watered, and replaced. Many companies have invested a lot of time and effort into perfecting a combination of natural grasses that can withstand the heavy and destructive wear that football presents (after all, cleats can rip up turf).

>> **Artificial turf:** Some artificial surfaces are made from synthetic nylon fibers that resemble very short blades of grass; other artificial surfaces have tightly woven fibers that give the feel of a cushioned carpet. Artificial surfaces are cheaper to maintain than natural grass. Plus, many football stadiums are multipurpose facilities that are used for outdoor concerts, political and religious rallies, and other sports, such as baseball and soccer. When such events are held, some areas of the grass can become trampled and destroyed

by the thousands of fans sitting or walking on it, so having an artificial surface is advantageous.

Then again, in many stadiums, the artificial surface is also harder than natural grass because it's often laid over cement, blacktop, or dirt. And on extremely hot days, artificial surfaces retain the heat, making a day that's 95 degrees Fahrenheit feel like a 100-degree day.

HOWIE SAYS

GRASS BEATS ARTIFICIAL SURFACES

I must admit that artificial surfaces today are a lot better than the ones I played on in the 1980s. There are several brands — I guess there are about 200 such companies — that do provide a decent playing surface, with an acceptable base with varying compounds, including pieces of rubber tires and synthetic grass blades. Where the Seahawks play in Seattle, they have an artificial field that really drains well during a rainstorm.

My problem with artificial surfaces is that there are so many different companies, and consequently, there can be extreme differences in the level of quality. But such artificial surfaces are all over America, somewhere between 12,000 to 13,000 of them, because the manufacturers say they are cheaper to maintain than natural grass. And there is no question that cities, colleges, high schools, and even professional teams may cut corners on the overall cost simply to save money. I find that unacceptable when the biggest concern for parents, coaches, and owners is the safety of the players. So why wouldn't you put them in the best possible position to succeed and also be safe.

I have two sons playing in the NFL now, and both prefer playing on grass. Unquestionably, grass is more forgiving. To understand why, all you need to see is a quarterback's head bouncing off an artificial surface. I realize that in some cities like Pittsburgh, the grass gets worn down because both the Steelers and the University of Pittsburgh use Heinz Field. Later in the season, the Steelers allow state championship high school games to be played there. That's great for the kids but not for the condition of the grass, especially when the weather turns cold.

You can also have a grass field in a domed stadium. The Arizona Cardinals play in a dome, but their field rolls out on a giant tray and sits in the sun for six days. Then it is rolled back in on game days. My Raiders are building a new stadium in Las Vegas and are considering an identical system with a grass field on a giant tray.

If you watch a lot of football, you will notice that many players wear elastic sleeves over their arms to protect them from what I call turf burns when playing on artificial surfaces. I disliked wearing those sleeves because they always seemed to slip and slide when I started sweating. I realize artificial turf is here to stay, but there's no question in my mind that natural grass is the best surface for football on any level from Pop Warner to the NFL.

Most players prefer natural grass to artificial turf. Playing on an artificial surface is much like playing on green-colored wall-to-wall carpeting.

Goalposts and other on-the-field equipment

The *goalpost* serves as the guideline for the kicker, whose goal is to sail the ball high between the goalpost's two vertical bars, an act that's sometimes called *splitting the uprights*. The goalpost rises from the back of the end zone. When a ball carrier reaches the end zone, he has scored a touchdown worth six points. The *goal line* is 8 inches wide (twice as wide as the typical yard line) in the NFL, and 4 inches wide at the high school and college levels. The goalposts were originally located on the goal line, but they were moved inside the goal line, and finally, in 1974, they were moved permanently from the goal line to the end zone's end line (refer to Figure 2-1).

NFL goalposts are a single standard type, known as the *sling-shot* design; on some high school and youth fields, however, you may still find goalposts in the shape of an H. A sling-shot goalpost has one post in the ground and a curved extension that sweeps the crossbar into place, as shown in Figure 2-2. This post is fully padded to protect players when they collide with it in the back of the end zone. The *crossbar* is 10 feet above the ground and 18 feet, 6 inches long in the NFL and college. In high school football, the crossbar is 23 feet, 4 inches long. The *uprights*, the two poles extending up from both ends of the crossbar, rise about 35 feet (30 feet in college and 20 feet in high school) and are 3 to 4 inches in diameter.

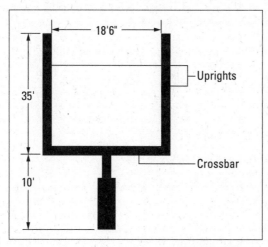

FIGURE 2-2:
The NFL goalpost.

© *John Wiley & Sons, Inc.*

The goalposts generally are painted yellow or white. A 4-x-42-inch ribbon is attached to the top of each goalpost to aid the officials in determining the exact top of the upright when judging whether a kick has passed through the uprights. The ribbons also give kickers an idea of the wind conditions.

Goalposts aren't the only things you see sitting on the field; you also see the chains and down marker along one sideline, marking the spot of the ball and other important information. For more information about the chains and the people who work them, see Chapter 3.

Looking at That Funny-Shaped Ball

The ball is an important component of a football game — you couldn't very well play *football* without the *ball* part. But you can't use just any old ball; strict rules govern the ball's size, weight, and even brand.

In the NFL, the ball must be a Wilson brand, bearing the signature of the commissioner of the league, Roger Goodell. The ball can be inflated to between $12\frac{1}{2}$ and $13\frac{1}{2}$ pounds of air pressure. It's made of an inflated rubber bladder enclosed in a pebble-grained, leather case of natural tan color without grooves or ridges of any kind. The ball is the form of a *prolate spheroid* (basically an oblong shape with pointed ends). You may have heard a football referred to as a *pigskin*. But, don't worry, footballs just *resemble* a toughened pig's skin, and in the game's early days, they were swollen like a chubby little piggy. And today, the NFL "Duke" footballs are actually made from cowhide.

To make it easier to grip and throw, the ball has eight raised white laces in its center. A quarterback can wrap his pinkie, fourth finger, and middle finger between these laces for a perfect grip. The size and weight of the ball must conform to these specifications:

>> **Long axis:** 11 to $11\frac{1}{2}$ inches

>> **Long circumference:** 28 to $28\frac{1}{2}$ inches

>> **Short circumference:** $20\frac{3}{4}$ to $21\frac{1}{4}$ inches

>> **Weight:** 14 to 15 ounces

College and high school balls are the same size as NFL balls, although you may find a white stripe encircling the tip area at both ends of the college and high school ball. The white stripe supposedly helps receivers see the ball better, which may be helpful for night games.

In the NFL, the home club supplies 36 footballs in an open-air stadium or 24 footballs in a domed stadium, and the league supplies another 12 K-balls used only for kicking. (*K-balls* are sealed in a special box to be opened by the officiating crew and held in their custody until two hours before kickoff so they can't be "doctored" by kickers and punters.) Outdoor stadiums require more balls in case of inclement weather, such as rain, sleet, or snow. The referee is the sole judge as to whether all balls comply with league specifications. The referee tests each football with a pressure gauge approximately two hours prior to kickoff.

Meeting the Cast of Characters

Each football team has 11 players per side: 11 on offense and 11 on defense. Teams are allowed to play with fewer than 11 players (why would they want to do that?), but they're penalized for having more than 11 players on the field during play, which is also known as *live action.* In high school, three or more talented players may play both offense and defense. And a few rare athletes may play both offense and defense in major college football and the NFL.

The *nonstarting players* (that is, those who aren't among the 22 or so players who are listed in the starting lineup) are considered reserves, and many of them are specialists. For example, defenses may play multiple schemes employing a *nickel back* (a fifth defensive back) or two *pass rushers* (linebackers or defensive ends who are used strictly on passing downs to rush the quarterback). Also, an extra player is often used as the *long snapper* who snaps (hikes) the ball for punts, field goal attempts, and extra point attempts. Some of the reserves make the team because they're excellent special teams players who are great on punt and kick coverages because they're fearless tacklers in the open field. (See Chapter 12 for the scoop on special teams.)

REMEMBER

The roster sizes in high school and college football tend to be unlimited, especially for home games. The NFL, however, limits active, uniformed players to 45 per team on game day. A typical NFL game-day roster includes three quarterbacks, a punter, a placekicker, a kick return specialist, eight offensive linemen, four running backs, five receivers, two tight ends, seven defensive linemen, seven linebackers, and six defensive backs.

In the NFL, an additional player can be in uniform, but he must be a quarterback and enter the game only after the other quarterbacks have been removed from the game because of injury. When this extra quarterback, or 46th player, enters the game, the other quarterbacks are deemed ineligible and can't return to that game even if they're healthy.

What Football Uniforms Are All About

Youth football (described in Chapter 15) has weight and size limitations, but as boys advance in football from high school to college to the pros, the uniform is the one common denominator. If you can play (and play well), a uniform will always be waiting for you in some team's locker room.

It isn't the uniform that separates one player from the others; it's his talent and heart. But the uniform and its protective pads are a necessary part of the game, something any player would be foolhardy to take the field without. Think of this: Only 60 years ago, many men wore helmets without face masks, meaning they had some pretty rugged noses and required more dental work during football season.

Why the need for all this protection? Well, the NFL is made up of players ranging in weight from 150 to 360 pounds and in height from 5'5" to 6'9". Some of these assorted sizes are able to bench-press 550 pounds and run the 40-yard dash in as fast as 4.2 seconds. Because of the varied weights, sizes, strengths, and speeds of NFL players, the best protection possible is necessary. Smaller players want to be able to play without worrying about being crushed by all those large bodies. (Chapter 17 looks at health risks and the challenge of keeping football players healthy.)

Figure 2-3 shows a typical football uniform, and the following sections talk about the various components of the uniform and the pads that go underneath it.

The jersey

The *jersey* is the uniform's shirt. The jersey is basically each player's identity and marks his allegiance to a specific team. The jersey must be large enough to cover the shoulder pads.

Every NFL team jersey comes with a different numeral to distinguish one player from another. The numerals, which appear on the front and back of the jersey, are 8 inches high and 4 inches wide. Most high school and college teams have the same specifications, and some also place the number on the jersey's sleeve.

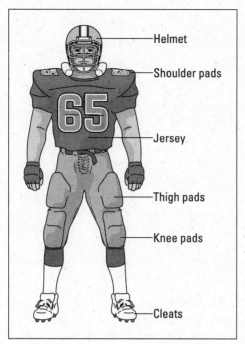

FIGURE 2-3:
The football
uniform.

Helmet

Shoulder pads

Jersey

Thigh pads

Knee pads

Cleats

© John Wiley & Sons, Inc.

TIP

In the NFL, specific positions wear certain numerals. For example:

» Quarterbacks and kickers wear from 1 to 19.

» Running backs and defensive backs wear from 20 to 49.

» Linebackers wear from 50 to 59 or 90 to 99.

» Offensive linemen wear from 50 to 79.

» Defensive linemen wear from 60 to 79 or 90 to 99.

» Receivers wear from 10 to 19 or 80 to 89.

On the back of each NFL jersey is the player's surname in letters that are 2½ inches high. His name appears across the upper back just above the numerals.

Team jersey colors and designs further separate one team from another. And most team colors have been with particular teams since their inception. In Green Bay, for example, the jerseys are green with gold trim. In Oakland, the Raiders always wear black. At Nebraska, the color is bright red; at Texas, it's orange. The different colors add to the spectacle of the game. In the NFL and college, the visiting team usually wears a white jersey. The colors for visiting teams vary on the high school level.

THROWBACK JERSEYS

A *throwback jersey* is a uniform from a team's past. In 1994, to mark the 75th anniversary of the NFL, the league started permitting teams to wear throwback jerseys. Throwback jerseys add a little more color and pageantry to the pro game. They give teams a chance to reconnect with their past. And let's face it, throwback jerseys are a great merchandising tool. Fans who like to wear their favorite team's jersey sometimes shell out a few more dollars to purchase the throwback jersey, too.

NFL teams can decide when they want to wear throwbacks, and some teams actually wear their throwback uniforms in every game. Not that these teams like reliving the past — they wear throwback jerseys because they've always had the same jersey. The Indianapolis Colts, New Orleans Saints, and Cleveland Browns have never redesigned their jerseys. They've worn the same uniforms, more or less, from the beginning.

For specific nationally televised games, the NFL allowed teams to wear what they called *Color Rush* uniforms. For example, the Seattle Seahawks use lime green jerseys and pants, and the Tampa Bay Buccaneers' uniform is all red. The designs are a marketing tool for the league, and many fans like the change in uniform colors.

Helmets and face masks

The helmet and face mask are designed to protect a player's face and head from serious injury. Many players also wear a mouth guard to protect their teeth and prevent themselves from biting their tongues. A few players even wear another protective cap on the outside of the helmet for added protection.

Helmets are equipped with chin straps to keep them snugly in place. To prevent serious concussions, many helmets have air-filled pockets inside them. A player tests his helmet by sticking his head inside it and then shaking it for comfort, also making sure that it's snug. If it's too tight, he simply releases air from the air pockets.

Player safety is an increasingly important issue with concussions and other head injuries becoming a major concern. The NFL and the NFL Players Association, the union that represents all players, have worked together for years on uniform and helmet improvements to better protect players from injury. As part of the NFL's "Play Smart, Play Safe" initiative, the league allocated $60 million toward the development of better protective equipment, including helmets. Because of the increase in concussions, the NFL reached a one-billion-dollar concussion settlement in 2017 with former players and their dependents. Families of all players, from Pop Warner to high school, to college to the NFL, should be aware that many constructive and valuable helmet designs have been made in the last few years.

The NFL has worked with the players and its biomedical experts to assess 34 helmet models made by six companies that were worn in the 2018 season, determining which was best at reducing head impact severity experienced by players on the field. You can see the results at this website: www.playsmartplaysafe.com/resource/helmet-laboratory-testing-performance-results.

The VICIS ZERO1 helmet ranked number one. However, 15 other helmets from Schutt, Xenith and Riddell are listed in the top performing group after laboratory testing. The NFL went so far as to ban 10 helmet models, although four of those designs were permitted to be worn by veteran players like Tom Brady and Drew Brees who were comfortable with the older helmets and didn't want to change. However, rookies were forbidden to wear similar models to what Brady and Brees use.

When you're watching a game, you may notice players wearing helmets of slightly different shapes and designs. Players are allowed to choose the helmet design that works best for them as long as the helmet design is certified by the National Operating Committee on Standards for Athletic Equipment.

All helmets are equipped with face masks. The rounded metal material that composes all face masks can't be more than 5/8-inch in diameter. Most linemen wear a face mask called a *cage,* which has a bar extending down from the middle and top of the helmet to below the nose area. There, this bar joins two or three bars that extend from both sides that completely prevent an opponent's hands from reaching inside the face area and under the chin. However, few quarterbacks and receivers have a face mask with a bar coming between their eyes, because they want to ensure they can see clearly; many also leave the chin exposed. Twenty years ago, some quarterbacks wore a helmet with a single bar across the face. Today, you may see a punter or kicker with a helmet that has a single bar, but players who encounter more contact during games want more protection.

Some helmets also have a sunshade across the eyes to prevent sun glare from interfering with the player's vision. This sunshade also keeps opponents from seeing the player's eyes, which may give the player an advantage because opponents can't see where the player is looking.

Pads

Pads are necessary to absorb the many physical blows a player takes during a game and protect every part of his body. Second only to the helmet, the shoulder pads are probably the number-one protective gear players wear. These pads protect a player's shoulders, plus his sternum region, from injury. Some of these pads also cover the top of the arm and the rotator cuff. Other pads include thigh pads, elbow pads, hip pads, tail pads, and knee pads, although not all players wear them. Some quarterbacks even wear flak jackets to protect their rib cages, which are vulnerable when they lift their arms to throw the ball.

Shoes and cleats

Football cleats come in ½-inch, ⅝-inch, ¾-inch, and 1-inch lengths. Wearing the right cleat is definitely important for traction. If a player doesn't have the proper traction indoors or outside on a muddy surface, he simply can't do his job and perform at the highest level. The shorter cleat, which makes a player less prone to injury, is worn on dry, firm fields because it provides the ideal traction for these fast fields. On a slippery grass field, a player — especially a big lineman across the line of scrimmage — needs to dig deep to gain traction. In that situation, the player switches to a ¾- or 1-inch cleat, depending on how he's maneuvering (stopping and going) during warm-ups. Receivers and running backs often wear shoes with fewer cleats than the larger, more physical players do.

NFL UNIFORM CODES

In a high school game, you may see a player wearing a torn jersey or exposing his midriff area, or you may see five different styles or brands of shoes on 11 different players. None of this occurs in the NFL, where violations of strictly enforced uniform codes can lead to players being fined. Here are some of the NFL rules:

- The NFL shield or logo must be visible on pants, jerseys, and helmets.

- Tear-away jerseys, which would make it more difficult for defensive players to grab and tackle their opponents on the other side of the ball, are prohibited.

- All jerseys must remain tucked into the uniform pants.

- Sleeves can't be torn or cut.

- Stockings must cover the entire leg area from the shoe to the bottom of the pants and meet the pants below the knee. Uniform stockings may not be altered, and they must be white from the top of the shoe to about mid-calf.

- Size and locations of shoe logos must be approved by NFL Properties. Players aren't allowed to wear shoes from companies not approved by the league.

- All tape used on shoes, socks, or pants must be either transparent or a color that matches the team uniform.

- Towels can be only 8 inches long and 6 inches wide and must be tucked into the front waist of the pants. (Quarterbacks and wide receivers often wear towels tucked into their waists to wipe their hands clean of mud and moisture between plays.)

For artificial surfaces, most players wear a shoe that has a sole of dozens of rubber-nubbed, ½-inch cleats. Some linemen prefer a basketball-type shoe, especially on indoor turf where there's no chance of rain and the surface isn't as slick. Because artificial surfaces tend to be sticky, players want to be able to glide over the surface. They don't want to stop on a dime and change directions. Many players believe that instant stop and restart can be hazardous to their knees and ankles.

Most teams are equipped with all sizes and types of shoes in case the weather changes during the course of a game. You often see players changing their shoes on the sidelines. On mushy days, you see them cleaning the cleats on their shoes to maintain the necessary traction. In the NFL, players test the playing surface an hour prior to the game and then go into the locker room and, if necessary, have an equipment manager change their cleats with a power drill, like a pit crew changing tires at a stockcar race.

Chapter **3**

Them's the Rules (And Regulations)

Football is a pretty complicated game. Twenty-two players are on the field at all times, plus a host of officials, not to mention all those people running around on the sidelines. But after you figure out who's supposed to be where, and what they're supposed to do there, following a football game is pretty easy.

This chapter walks you through all the phases of a game, from the coin toss to the opening kickoff to halftime to the time when the fat lady sings. It also explains how the clock works, how you score points, what the officials do, what every penalty means, and much more.

The Ins and Outs of the Game Clock

To keep things in small, easily digestible chunks, every football game is divided into *quarters*. In college and pro football, each quarter lasts 15 minutes; high school teams play 12-minute quarters. After the second quarter comes halftime, which lasts 12 minutes in the NFL, 15 minutes in college, and 15 to 20 minutes in high school. Halftime gives players time to rest and bands and cheerleaders time to perform (it also gives fans time to go get a hot dog). Coaches, players, or alumni are sometimes honored at halftime.

REMEMBER

The game clock, which is operated by a timekeeper in the press box, doesn't run continuously throughout those 15- or 12-minute quarters. (If it did, when would they show the television commercials?) The clock stops for the following reasons:

» Either team calls a timeout. Teams are allowed three timeouts per half.

» A quarter ends. The stoppage in time enables teams to change which goal they will defend (they change sides at the end of the first and third quarters).

» The quarterback throws an incomplete pass.

» The ball carrier goes out of bounds.

» A player from either team is injured during a play.

» An official signals a penalty by throwing a flag. (I tell you all about penalties in the later "Penalties and Other Violations" section.)

» The officials need to measure whether the offense has gained a first down, or they need to take time to *spot* (or place) the ball correctly on the field.

» Either team scores a touchdown, field goal, or safety. (I explain what these achievements are and how much they're worth in the later "Scoring Points" section.)

» The ball changes possession via a kickoff, a punt, a turnover, or a team failing to advance the ball 10 yards in four downs.

» The offense gains a first down (college and high school only).

» Two minutes remain in the half or in overtime (NFL only).

» A coach has challenged a referee's call, and the referees are reviewing the call (college and NFL only).

» A wet ball needs to be replaced with a dry one.

REMEMBER

Unlike college and professional basketball, where a shot clock determines how long the offense can keep possession of the ball, in football the offense can keep the ball as long as it keeps making first downs (which I explain a little later in this chapter). However, the offense has 40 seconds from the end of a given play, or a 25-second interval after official stoppages, to get in proper position after an extremely long gain. If the offense doesn't snap the ball in that allotted time, it's penalized 5 yards and must repeat the down.

OVERTIME AND SUDDEN DEATH

If a game is tied at the end of regulation play, the game goes into overtime. To decide who gets the ball in overtime, team captains meet at the center of the field for a coin toss. The team that wins the toss gets the ball and the first crack at scoring.

The NFL changed its overtime rules in 2012. And they are slightly different for regular season games and playoff games. Scoring a touchdown is the ultimate goal in overtime, but that doesn't always happen, and the 2018 season proved to be anamoly, as there were overtime games in each of the first six weeks of the season. Two of those games still ended in a tie despite a 10-minute overtime period, or essentially a shortened fifth period of play.

When a game is tied at the end of regulation, the referee will immediately toss a coin at the center of the field. The captain of the visiting team will call the toss prior to the coin being flipped. Following a 3-minute break, there is a maximum of one 10-minute period. Each team must possess or have the opportunity to possess the ball unless the team that has the ball first scores a touchdown on its initial possession. The game also ends if the defense scores on the intial possession (via an interception or fumble return for a touchdown or a safety). Each team is entitled to two timeouts, and disqualified players from regulation are not allowed to return.

- In the regular season, if the score is tied at the end of the 10-minute overtime period, the game shall result in a tie. Neither team is allowed to challenge a play via instant replay in the OT period.

- In playoff games, when regulation ends in a tie, the extra period is 15 minutes in length, and the same scoring rules from regular season overtime apply. If the first team to possess the ball scores a touchdown, the game is over. If the score is tied after the 15-minute period, the game will continue with another 15-minute period, and the first team to score in any fashion wins the game.

- Under college rules, each team gets the ball for alternate possessions starting at the 25-yard line. If the team that wins the coin toss scores, its opponent still gets a chance to score and tie the game again. If a college football game goes past two overtimes, teams must try for two-point conversions after touchdowns (instead of kicking for an extra point — a PAT) until one prevails. (See the later section "Extra points and two-point conversions" for additional information on PAT kicks versus going for two.)

With the exception of the last two minutes of the first half and the last five minutes of the second half of an NFL game, the officials restart the game clock after a kickoff return, after a player goes out of bounds on a play, or after a declined penalty.

The Coin Toss and Kickoff

Every football contest starts with a *coin toss*. Selected members of each team (called *captains*) come to the center of the field, where the referee holds a coin. In the NFL, the coin toss is restricted to three captains from each team. In college football, four players may participate. However, only one player from the visiting team calls heads or tails, and that player must do so before the official tosses the coin into the air (hence the name *coin toss*). If that player calls the toss correctly, his team gets to choose one of three privileges:

>> **Which team receives the kickoff:** Generally, teams want to start the game on offense and have the opportunity to score as early as possible, so the team who wins the toss usually opts to receive. They're known as the *receiving team*. The referee, swinging his leg in a kicking motion, then points to the other team's captains as the *kicking team*.

>> **Which goal his team will defend:** Instead of receiving the kickoff, the captain may elect to kick off and choose a goal to defend. Captains sometimes take this option if they believe that weather will be a factor in the outcome of the game. For example, in choosing which goal to defend, the player believes that his team will have the wind at its back for the second quarter and the crucial final quarter of the game.

>> **When to decide:** The team that wins the coin flip can *defer*, giving it the right to choose between kicking and receiving the second-half kickoff.

The team that earns the right to receive the ball gets the ball via a *kickoff*. To perform this kickoff, the kicking team's *placekicker* places the ball in a holder (called a *tee*, which is 1 inch tall in the NFL and 2 inches tall in high school and college) on his team's 35-yard line (NFL and college), or 40-yard line (high school). The kicker then runs toward the ball and kicks it toward the other team. Figure 3-1 shows how teams typically line up for a kickoff in the NFL.

At the far end of the field from the kicker, one or more *returners* from the other team await the kickoff. The returner's goal is to catch the ball and score a touchdown or run the ball as far back toward the opponent's goal line as he can. After the return is complete, the first set of *downs* begins.

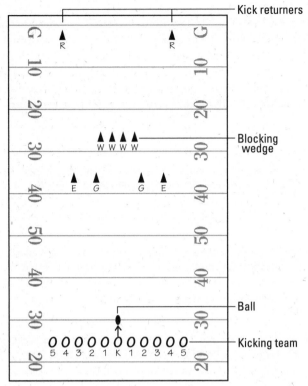

FIGURE 3-1:
Players line up in this formation for a kickoff in the NFL.

Kick returners

Blocking wedge

Ball

Kicking team

© John Wiley & Sons, Inc.

Downs Plus Yardage Equals Excitement

Watching a game in which the offense keeps running plays but never goes anywhere would be really boring. To prevent that, the fathers of football created the *down system*. The offense has four downs (essentially four plays) to go 10 yards. If the offensive team advances the ball at least 10 yards in four tries or fewer, it receives another set of four downs. If the offense fails to advance 10 yards after three tries, it can either punt the ball on the fourth down (a *punt* is a kick to the opponent without the use of a tee) or, if it needs less than a yard to get a first down, try to get the first down by running or passing.

You may hear television commentators use the phrase "three and out." What they mean is that a team failed to advance the ball 10 yards and has to punt the ball. You don't want your team to go three and out very often. But you do want to earn lots of *first downs*, which you get after your team advances the ball 10 yards or more in the allotted four downs. Getting lots of first downs usually translates to more scoring opportunities.

Football has its own lingo to explain the offense's progress toward a first down. A first down situation is also known as a "first and 10," because the offense has 10 yards to go to gain a first down. If your offense ran a play on first down in which you advanced the ball 3 yards, your status would be "second and 7"; you're ready to play the second down, and you now have 7 yards to go to gain a first down. Unless something really bad happens, the numbers stay under 10, so the math is pretty simple.

TIP

As a viewer, you aren't expected to remember what down it is and how many yards the offense needs to advance to gain a first down. Football makes it easy by providing people and signs to help you keep track. On the sideline opposite the press box is a group of three people, known as the *chain gang* or *chain crew*, who hold three 8-foot-high poles. Here's an explanation of that crew:

>> Two people called *rodmen* hold metal rods with Xs at the top connected by a thin metal chain that stretches exactly 10 yards when the two rods are thoroughly extended. One rod marks where the possession begins, and the other extends to where the offensive team must go in order to make another first down.

>> The third person, known as the *boxman,* holds a marker that signifies where the ball is and what down it is. Atop this rod is the number 1, 2, 3, or 4, designating whether it is the first, second, third, or fourth down.

>> In all NFL stadiums, a person also marks where the *drive* began (that is, where the offensive team assumed possession of the ball). Many high school and college fields don't have these markers.

Whenever the officials need to make a critical measurement for a first down, the chain crew comes to the hash marks nearest where the ball is positioned, and the officials use the rods to measure whether the offense has obtained a first down. The home team supplies the chain crew and also the *ball boys*, who are responsible for keeping the balls clean and free of excessive moisture.

Thanks to the miracle of technology, determining where a team has to advance the ball to get a first down is easier than ever — but only if you're watching television. On the television screen during a game, you see an electronic line across the field that marks where a team must go to get a first down.

Scoring Points

Teams can score points in several ways — and scoring more points than the other team is the object of the game. The following sections explain each method of scoring.

Touchdowns

A *touchdown* is worth six points — the ultimate goal. A team scores a touchdown, plus the loudest cheers from fans, when an offensive player carrying the ball, or a defensive player who has obtained the ball from the other team after recovering a fumble or intercepting a pass, advances from anywhere on the field and breaks the plane of his opponent's goal line with the ball. (*Breaking the plane* means that a ball carrier can soar over the goal line in midair and have his efforts count for a touchdown — even if he's hit in midair and lands back on the 1-yard line — as long as the ball crosses the plane.) Figure 3-2 shows New Orleans Saints' running back Pierre Thomas scoring a touchdown in the Super Bowl.

FIGURE 3-2: Pierre Thomas of the New Orleans Saints scores a touchdown against the Indianapolis Colts in Super Bowl XLIV.

Photo credit: © Elsa/Getty Images

A team is also awarded a touchdown when any player who's inbounds catches or recovers a loose ball behind his opponent's goal line. This sort of touchdown can occur on a kickoff, a punt, or a *fumble* (when a player drops the ball).

Extra points and two-point conversions

A try for an *extra point*, also known as a *point after touchdown (PAT)*, is attempted during the scrimmage down that's awarded after a touchdown. The extra point is successful when the kicker kicks the ball between the uprights of the goalpost and above the crossbar, provided that the ball was snapped 2 yards away from the opponent's goal line (or 3 yards away in high school and college). Teams almost always make their extra point attempts — especially beyond the high school level — because the kick is a fairly easy one. (See Chapter 2 for more information about the goalposts.)

When a team is feeling particularly confident — or desperate — it might attempt a *two-point conversion* after scoring a touchdown. (Chapter 8 talks about situations in which a coach might decide to have his team "go for two.") Two-point conversions, which were added to the NFL for the 1994 season, have always been a part of high school and college football. The offense gets the ball on the 2-yard line (the 3-yard line in high school and college) and must advance the ball across the goal line, or break the plane, as if scoring a touchdown. In the NFL, the try (called a *conversion attempt*) is over when the officials rule the ball dead or if a change of possession occurs (meaning the defense intercepts a pass or recovers a fumble). In college, the defensive team can return a fumble or interception to its opponent's end zone and score two points.

Field goals

A *field goal*, often the consolation prize for an offense that tries to score a touchdown but stalls within its opponent's 30-yard line, is worth three points. A team scores a field goal when a kicker boots the ball entirely through the uprights of the goalpost without the ball touching either the ground or any of the offensive players. The kicked ball must travel between the uprights and above the crossbar of the goalpost.

AN EXTRA POINT EXPERIMENT

In the preseason games of the 2014 season, the NFL moved the spot where extra points are kicked from the 2-yard line to the 15-yard line, making the kick 33 yards. (Two-point conversion attempts remained at the 2-yard line.) The reason for this experiment was to see if the game would be impacted at all if extra points were made more difficult. Before the experiment, kickers were making 99.6 percent of extra point attempts from the 2-yard line. Well, due to the increased distance, the success rate has dropped through the years. The success rate for the 2018 regular season was 94.2 percent. So increasing the distance of the extra point attempt definitely made a difference in the game.

The league will likely continue to experiment with rule changes involving extra points and two-point conversions. Many fans of the game think that extra points are too easy and that two-point conversions should be attempted more often. However, league-wide teams only converted 66 of 130 two-points conversions in the 2018 season, a rate of 50.7 percent.

You get the distance of a field goal by adding 10 yards (the distance from the goal line to the end line where the goalposts are placed) to the yard line from which the ball is kicked. Or simply add 17 to the number of yards that the offense would have to advance to cross the goal line (the extra 7 yards represents the typical distance of a snap for a field goal attempt). For example, if the offense is on its opponent's 23-yard line, the offense is attempting a 40-yard field goal.

Safeties

A *safety* occurs when a player on the offensive team is tackled in his own end zone or goes out of bounds in his own end zone. A safety scores two points for the defensive team. After a safety, the team that was scored on must punt the ball to the other team from its own 20-yard line. For the offensive team, a safety is a bad thing. The other team gets not only two points but also the ball in good field position. Normally, teams kick off from the 35-yard line. Having to punt from the 20-yard line allows the other team to advance the ball farther up the field after the punt.

Frankly, a safety is embarrassing to the offense, and offensive players will do just about anything to prevent a safety. Besides being tackled in the end zone, here are other instances when a safety is awarded:

>> A quarterback knows he's about to be tackled in his end zone, and to prevent the other team from scoring a safety, he chucks the ball out of bounds. If a referee thinks the quarterback threw the pass solely to prevent a safety, the referee awards the safety to the defensive team.

>> The offensive team commits a penalty (say, holding a defensive player who's preparing to tackle the ball carrier in the end zone) that would otherwise require it to have the ball marked in its own end zone.

>> A blocked punt goes out of the kicking team's end zone.

>> The receiver of a punt muffs the ball and then, when trying to retrieve the ball, forces or illegally kicks it into the end zone and it goes out of the end zone.

>> A muffed ball is kicked or forced into the end zone and then recovered there by a member of the receiving team.

The Role of the Officials

Officials play many important roles in a football game. In fact, they basically have control of every game. For example:

>> They're responsible for any decision involving the application of a rule, its interpretation, or its enforcement.

>> They keep players from really hurting each other and making other illegal actions.

>> They enforce and record all fouls and monitor the clock and all timeouts that are charged.

All officials carry a whistle and a weighted, bright yellow flag, which they throw to signal that a penalty has been called on a particular play. In the event that an official throws his yellow flag during a play and then sees yet another penalty, he throws his hat.

Officials are part-time workers for NFL, college, and high school football. They're paid for working the game and are given travel expenses. In the NFL and in college football, the work can be financially rewarding. For instance, depending on seniority and experience, these officials may earn between $25,000 and $80,000 a season. High school officials, on the other hand, aren't paid nearly as well; they generally do it for the love of the game.

If you want, you can just call them "the officials," or — if you're in a particularly belligerent mood — you can call them "the idiots who aren't even qualified to officiate a peewee football game." Either way, true diehards know that each of the seven officials (five or six at some levels) has a different title and task. The sections that follow explain who they are and what they do.

Referee

The *referee* has general oversight and control of the game. He's the final authority for the score, the number of a down in case of a disagreement, and all rule interpretations when a debate arises among the other officials. He's the only official who wears a white hat; all the other officials wear black hats.

The referee announces all penalties and confers with the offending team's captain, explaining the penalty. Before the snap of the ball, he positions himself in the offensive backfield, 10 to 12 yards behind the line of scrimmage, and favors the right side if the quarterback is right-handed or the left side if the quarterback is left-handed. The referee also monitors any illegal hits on the quarterback, such as *roughing the passer* (you can read more about this penalty in Chapter 5). He follows the quarterback throughout the game and watches for the legality of blocks made near him.

At the end of any down, the referee can request the head linesman (see the later related section for details on this official's role) and his assistants to bring the yardage chains onto the field to determine whether the ball has reached the necessary line for a new first down. The referee also notifies the head coach when any player is ejected for unnecessary roughness or unsportsmanlike conduct.

Umpire

The *umpire* is responsible for the legality of the players' equipment and for watching all play along the *line of scrimmage,* the division line between the offensive and defensive players. He makes sure that the offensive team has no more than 11 players on the field prior to the snap of the ball. At the start of a play in college football, he positions himself 4 to 5 yards off the line of scrimmage on the defensive side of the ball. In the NFL, he's positioned in the offensive backfield until the final five minutes of each half, when he takes his traditional position on the defensive side.

Because he's responsible for monitoring the legality of all contact between the offensive and defensive linemen, this official calls most of the holding penalties. He also assists the referee on decisions involving possession of the ball in close proximity to the line of scrimmage. He records all timeouts, the winner of the coin toss, and all scores, and he makes sure the offensive linemen don't move downfield illegally on pass plays. Finally, when it's raining, the umpire dries the wet ball prior to the snap.

Head linesman

The *head linesman* sets up on the side of the field designated by the referee. He straddles the line of scrimmage and watches for encroachment, offside, illegal men downfield, and all the other line-of-scrimmage violations (which you can read more about in the later "Penalties and Other Violations" section). He's also responsible for ruling on all out-of-bounds plays to his side of the field.

The chain crew (described earlier in this chapter) is the responsibility of the head linesman. He grabs the chain when measuring for a first down. He's usually the official who runs in after a play is whistled dead and places his foot to show where forward progress was made by the ball carrier at the end of the play. He assists the line judge (who stands opposite the head linesman) with illegal motion calls and any illegal shifts or movement by running backs and receivers to his side. Also, during kicks or passes, he checks for illegal use of hands, and he must know who the eligible receivers are prior to every play.

Line judge

The *line judge* lines up on the opposite side of the field from the head linesman and serves as an overall helper while being responsible for illegal motion and illegal shifts. He has a number of chores. He assists the head linesman with offside and encroachment calls. He helps the umpire with holding calls and watching for illegal use of hands on the end of the line, especially during kicks and pass plays. The line judge assists the referee with calls regarding false starts and forward laterals behind the line of scrimmage. He makes sure that the quarterback hasn't crossed the line of scrimmage prior to throwing a forward pass. And if all that isn't enough, he also supervises substitutions made by the team seated on his side of the field. On punts, he remains on the line of scrimmage to ensure none of the ends move downfield prior to the ball being kicked.

REMEMBER

One of the line judge's most important jobs is supervising the timing of the game. If the game clock becomes inoperative, he assumes the official timing on the field. He advises the referee when time has expired at the end of each quarter. In the NFL, the line judge signals the referee when two minutes remain in a half, stopping the clock for the *two-minute warning*. This stopping of the clock was devised to essentially give the team in possession of the ball another timeout. During halftime, the line judge notifies the home team's head coach when five minutes remain before the start of the second half.

Back judge

The *back judge* has similar duties to the field judge (see the following section) and sets up 20 yards deep on the defensive side, usually to the tight end's side of the field. He makes sure that the defensive team has no more than 11 players on the field and is responsible for all eligible receivers to his side.

REMEMBER

After the receivers have cleared the line of scrimmage, the back judge concentrates on action in the area between the umpire and the field judge: It's vital that he's aware of any passes that are trapped by receivers. He makes decisions involving catching, recovery, or illegal touching of loose balls beyond the line of scrimmage. He rules on the legality of catches or pass interference, whether a receiver is interfered with, and whether a receiver has possession of the ball before going out of bounds.

The back judge calls clipping when it occurs on punt returns. (The upcoming "Recognizing 15-yard penalties" explains clipping and similar penalties.) During field goal and extra point attempts, the back judge and field judge stand under the goalpost and rule whether the kicks are good.

Field judge

The *field judge* lines up 20 yards downfield on the same side as the line judge. In the NFL, he's responsible for the 40/25-second clock. (When a play ends, the team with the ball has 40 seconds in which to begin another play before it's penalized for delay of game. If stoppage occurs due to a change of possession, a timeout, an injury, a measurement, or any unusual delay that interferes with the normal flow of play, a 25-second interval exists between plays.)

The field judge also counts the number of defensive players. He's responsible for forward passes that cross the defensive goal line and any fumbled ball in his area. He also watches for pass interference, monitoring the tight end's pass patterns, calling interference, and making decisions involving catching, recovery, out-of-bounds spots, or illegal touching of a fumbled ball after it crosses the line of scrimmage. He also watches for illegal use of hands by the offensive players, especially the ends and wide receivers, on defensive players to his side of the field.

Side judge

With teams passing the ball more often, the *side judge* was added in 1978 as the seventh official for NFL games. Some high school games are played without a side judge, but, like the NFL, college teams have adopted the use of the seventh judge. The side judge is essentially another back judge who positions himself 20 yards down field from the line of scrimmage and opposite the field judge. He's another set of eyes monitoring the legalities downfield, especially during long pass attempts. On field goal and extra point attempts, he lines up next to the umpire under the goalpost and decides whether the kicks are good.

Familiarizing Yourself with Referee Signals

Because it's awfully hard to yell loud enough for a stadium full of people to hear you, and because someone has to communicate with the timekeepers way up in the press box, the referee uses signals to inform everyone of penalties, play stoppages, touchdowns, and everything else that transpires on the field. Table 3-1 shows you what these signals look like and explains what they mean.

TABLE 3-1

Signaling Scoring Plays, Penalties, and Other Stoppages

Signal	What It Means
	Clock doesn't stop. The referee moves an arm clockwise in a full circle in front of himself to inform the offensive team that it has no timeouts, or that the ball is in play and that the timekeeper should keep the clock moving.
	Delay of game. The referee signals a delay of game by folding his arms in front of his chest. This signal also means that a team called a timeout when it had already used all its allocated timeouts.
	Encroachment. The referee places his hands on his hips to signal that an offside, encroachment, or neutral zone infraction occurred.
	Face mask. The referee gestures with his hand in front of his face and makes a downward pulling motion to signal that a player illegally grabbed the face mask of another player.
	False start/illegal formation. The referee rotates both forearms over and over in front of his body to signify a false start, an illegal formation, or that the kickoff or the kick following a safety is ruled out of bounds.
	First down. The referee points with his right arm at shoulder height toward the defensive team's goal to indicate that the offensive team has gained enough yardage for a first down.
	Fourth down. The referee raises one arm above his head with his hand in a closed fist to show that the offense is facing fourth down.
	Holding. The referee signals a holding penalty by clenching his fist, grabbing the wrist of that hand with his other hand and pulling his arm down in front of his chest.

Signal	What It Means
	Illegal contact. The referee extends his arm and an open hand forward to signal that illegal contact was made.
	Illegal crackback block. The referee strikes with an open right hand around the middle of his right thigh, preceded by a personal foul signal, to signal an illegal crackback block.
	Illegal cut block. From the side, the referee uses both hands to strike the front of his thighs to signal that a player made an illegal cut block. When he uses one hand to strike the front of his thigh, preceded by a personal foul signal, he means that an illegal block below the waist occurred. When he uses both hands to strike the sides of his thighs, preceded by a personal foul signal, he means that an illegal chop block occurred. When he uses one hand to strike the back of his calf, preceded by a personal foul signal, he means that an illegal clipping penalty occurred.
	Illegal forward pass. The referee puts one hand waist-high behind his back to signal an illegal forward pass. The referee then makes the loss of down signal.
	Illegal motion. The referee flattens out his hand and moves his arm to the side to show that the offensive team made an illegal motion at the snap or prior to the snap of the ball.
	Illegal push. The referee uses his hands in a pushing movement with his arms below his waist to show that someone on the offensive team pushed or illegally helped a ball carrier.
	Illegal shift. The referee uses both arms and hands in a horizontal arc in front of his body to signal that the offense used an illegal shift prior to the snap of the ball.
	Illegal substitution. The referee places both hands on top of his head to signal that a team made an illegal substitution or had too many men on the field on the preceding play.
	Illegal use of hands. The referee grabs one wrist and extends the open hand of that arm forward in front of his chest to signal illegal use of the hands, arms, or body.

(continued)

TABLE 3-1 *(continued)*

Signal	What It Means
	Illegally touched ball. The referee uses the fingertips of both hands and touches his shoulders to signal that the ball was illegally touched, kicked, or batted.
	Illegally touched pass. The referee is sideways and uses a diagonal motion of one hand across another to signal an illegal touch of a forward pass or a kicked ball from scrimmage.
	Incomplete pass. The referee shifts his arms in a horizontal fashion in front of his body to signal that the pass is incomplete, a penalty is declined, a play is over, or a field goal or extra point attempt is no good.
	Ineligible player downfield. The referee places his right hand on top of his head or cap to show that an ineligible receiver on a pass play was downfield early or that an ineligible member of the kicking team was downfield too early.
	Intentional grounding. The referee waves both his arms in a diagonal plane across his body to signal intentional grounding of a forward pass. This signal is followed by the loss of down signal.
	Interference. The referee, with open hands vertical to the ground, extends his arms forward from his shoulders to signify pass interference or interference of a fair catch of a punted ball.
	Invalid fair catch. The referee waves one hand above his head to signal an invalid fair catch of a kicked ball.
	Juggled pass. The referee gestures with his open hands in an up-and-down fashion in front of his body to show that the pass was juggled inbounds and caught out of bounds. This signal follows the incomplete pass signal.

Signal	What It Means
	Loss of down. The referee places both hands behind his head to signal a loss of down.
	Player ejected. The referee clenches his fist with the thumb extended, a gesture also used in hitchhiking, to signal that a player has been ejected from the game.
	Personal foul. The referee raises his arms above his head and strikes one wrist with the edge of his other hand to signify a personal foul. If the personal foul signal is followed by the referee swinging one of his legs in a kicking motion, it means roughing the kicker. If the signal is followed by the referee simulating a throwing motion, it means roughing the passer. If the signal is followed by the referee pretending to grab an imaginary face mask, it's a major face mask penalty, which is worth 15 yards.
	Reset 25-second clock. The referee makes an open palm with his right hand and pumps that arm vertically into the air to instruct the timekeeper to reset the 25-second play clock.
	Reset 40-second clock. With the palms of both hands open, the referee pumps both arms vertically into the air to instruct the timekeeper to reset the 40-second play clock.
	Safety. The referee puts his palms together above his head to show that the defensive team scored a safety.
	Stop the clock. The referee raises one arm above his head with an open palm to signify that excessive crowd noise in the stadium has made it necessary for the timekeeper to stop the clock. This signal also means that the ball is dead (the play is over) and that the neutral zone has been established along the line of scrimmage.

(continued)

TABLE 3-1 *(continued)*

Signal	What It Means
	Timeout. The referee signals a timeout by waving his arms and hands above his head. The same signal, followed by the referee placing one hand on top his head, means that it's an official timeout, or a referee-called timeout.
	Touchback. The referee signals a touchback by waving his arms and hands above his head and then swinging one arm out from his side.
	Touchdown. The referee extends his arms straight above his head to signify that a touchdown was scored. He also uses this signal to tell the offensive team that it successfully converted a field goal, extra point, or two-point conversion.
	Tripping. The referee repeats the action of placing the right foot behind the heel of his left foot to signal a tripping penalty.
	Uncatchable pass. The referee holds the palm of his right hand parallel to the ground and moves it back and forth above his head to signal that a forward pass was uncatchable and that no penalty should be called.
	Unsportsmanlike conduct. The referee extends both arms to his sides with his palms down to signal an unsportsmanlike conduct penalty.

Penalties and Other Violations

A *penalty* is an infraction of the rules. Without rules, a football game would devolve into total chaos because the game is so physically demanding and the collisions are so intense. A dirty deed or a simple mistake (like a player moving across the line of scrimmage prior to the ball being snapped) is a penalty. Football has more than 100 kinds of penalties or rule violations. Don't worry, though. The next sections get you acquainted with several of them.

REMEMBER

The specific penalties and their ramifications can get pretty complicated. You may want to read through Parts 2 and 3 to get a handle on the offense and defense first if you're a beginner and really want to understand this stuff. If you have trouble with a particular term, turn to the Appendix. By the way, I describe how these penalties are called and enforced in the NFL. Some of these penalties are slightly different in the college ranks.

Looking at 5-yard penalties

The following common penalties give the offended team an additional 5 yards. Some of these penalties, when noted, are accompanied by an automatic first down.

>> **Defensive holding or illegal use of the hands:** When a defensive player tackles or holds an offensive player other than the ball carrier. Otherwise, the defensive player may use his hands, arms, or body only to protect himself from an opponent trying to block him in an attempt to reach a ball carrier. This penalty also includes an automatic first down.

>> **Delay of game:** When the offense fails to snap the ball within the required 40 or 25 seconds, depending on the clock. The referee can call a delay of game penalty against the defense if it repeatedly charges into the neutral zone prior to the snap; when called on the defense, a delay of game penalty gives the offense an automatic first down. The ref can also call this penalty when a team fails to play when ordered (because, for example, the players are unsure of the play called in the huddle), a runner repeatedly attempts to advance the ball after his forward progress is stopped, or a team takes too much time assembling after a timeout.

>> **Delay of kickoff:** Failure of the kicking team to kick the ball after being ordered to do so by the referee.

>> **Encroachment:** When a player enters the neutral zone and makes contact with an opponent before the ball is snapped.

>> **Excessive crowd noise:** When the quarterback informs the referee that the offense can't hear his signals because of crowd noise. If the referee deems it reasonable to conclude that the quarterback is right, he signals a referee's timeout and asks the defensive captain to use his best influence to quiet the crowd. If the noise persists, the referee uses his wireless microphone to inform the crowd that continued noise will result in either the loss of an existing timeout or, if the defensive team has no timeouts remaining, a 5-yard penalty.

>> **Excessive timeouts:** When a team calls for a timeout after it has already used its three timeouts allotted for the half.

>> **Failure to pause for one second after the shift or huddle:** When any offensive player doesn't pause for at least one second after going into a set position. The offensive team also is penalized when it's operating from a no-huddle offense and immediately snaps the ball without waiting a full second after assuming an offensive set.

>> **Failure to report change of eligibility:** When a player fails to inform an official that he has entered the game and will be aligned at a position he normally doesn't play, like an offensive tackle lined up as a tight end. In the NFL, all players' jersey numbers relate to the offensive positions they play; consequently, the officials and opposing team know when it's illegal for a player wearing number 60 through 79 (offensive linemen generally wear these numbers) to catch a pass.

>> **False start:** When an interior lineman of the offensive team takes or simulates a three-point stance and then moves prior to the snap of the ball. The official must blow his whistle immediately. A false start is also whistled when any offensive player makes a quick, abrupt movement prior to the snap of the ball.

>> **Forward pass is first touched by an eligible receiver who has gone out of bounds and returned:** When an offensive player leaves the field of play (even if he's shoved out), returns inbounds, and is therefore an ineligible receiver.

>> **Forward pass is thrown from behind the line of scrimmage after the ball crosses the line of scrimmage:** When a player catches a pass, runs past the line of scrimmage, and then retreats behind the line of scrimmage and attempts another pass. However, a player is permitted to throw the ball to another player, provided that the ball isn't thrown forward. A ball thrown this way is called a *lateral*.

>> **Forward pass touches or is caught by an ineligible receiver on or behind the line of scrimmage:** When an offensive lineman catches a pass that isn't first tipped by a defensive player.

>> **Grasping the face mask of the ball carrier or quarterback:** When the face mask is grabbed unintentionally and the player immediately lets go of his hold, not twisting the ball carrier's neck at all.

>> **Illegal formation:** When the offense doesn't have seven players on the line of scrimmage. Also, running backs and receivers who aren't on the line of scrimmage must line up at least 1 yard off the line of scrimmage and no closer, or the formation is considered illegal.

>> **Illegal motion:** When an offensive player, such as a quarterback, running back, or receiver, moves forward toward the line of scrimmage moments prior to the snap of the ball. Illegal motion is also called when a running back is on the line of scrimmage and then goes in motion prior to the snap. It's a penalty because the running back wasn't aligned in a backfield position.

» **Illegal return:** When a player returns to the field after he has been ejected. He must leave the bench area and go to the locker room within a reasonable time.

» **Illegal substitution:** When a player enters the field during a play. Players must enter only when the ball is dead. If a substituted player remains on the field at the snap of the ball, his team is slapped with an unsportsmanlike conduct penalty (see the later section "Recognizing 15-yard penalties" for more on this penalty). If the substituted player runs to the opposing team's bench area in order to clear the field prior to the snap of the ball, his team incurs a delay of game penalty.

» **Ineligible member(s) of kicking team going beyond the line of scrimmage before the ball is kicked:** When a player other than the two players aligned at least 1 yard outside the end men go downfield when the ball is snapped to the kicker. All the other players must remain at the line of scrimmage until the ball is kicked.

» **Ineligible player downfield during a pass down:** When any offensive linemen are more than 2 yards beyond the line of scrimmage when a pass is thrown downfield.

» **Invalid fair catch signal:** When the receiver simply extends his arm straight up. To be a valid fair catch signal, the receiver must fully extend his arm and wave it from side to side.

» **Kickoff goes out of bounds between the goal lines and isn't touched:** When the kicking team fails to keep its kick inbounds, the ball belongs to the receivers 30 yards from the spot of the kick or at the out-of-bounds spot unless the ball went out-of-bounds the first time an onside kick was attempted. In this case, the kicking team is penalized 5 yards and the ball must be kicked again.

» **More than 11 players on the field at the snap:** When a team has more than 11 players on the field at any time when the ball is live. The offense receives an automatic first down if the penalty is committed by the defensive team.

» **More than one man in motion at the snap of the ball:** When two offensive players are in motion simultaneously. Having two men in motion at the same time is illegal on all levels of football in the United States. Two players can go in motion prior to the snap of the ball, but before the second player moves, the first player must be set for a full second.

» **Neutral zone infraction:** When a defensive player moves beyond the neutral zone prior to the snap and continues unabated toward the quarterback or kicker even though no contact is made by a blocker. If a defensive player enters the neutral zone prior to the snap and causes an offensive player to react immediately and prior to the snap, the defensive player has committed a neutral zone infraction.

>> **Offside:** When any part of a player's body is beyond the line of scrimmage or free kick line when the ball is put into play.

>> **Player out of bounds at the snap:** When one of the 11 players expected to be on the field runs onto the field of play after the ball is snapped.

>> **Running into the kicker or punter:** When a defensive player makes contact with a kicker or punter. Note that a defender isn't penalized for running into the kicker if the contact is incidental and occurs after he has touched the ball in flight. Nor is it a penalty if the kicker's own motion causes the contact, or if the defender is blocked into the kicker, or if the kicker muffs the ball, retrieves it, and then kicks it.

>> **Shift:** When an offensive player moves from one position on the field to another. After a team huddles, the offensive players must come to a stop and remain stationary for at least one second before going in motion. If an offensive player who didn't huddle is in-motion behind the line of scrimmage at the snap of the ball, it's an illegal shift.

Surveying 10-yard penalties

These penalties cost the offending team 10 yards:

>> **Deliberately batting or punching a loose ball:** When a player bats or punches a loose ball toward an opponent's goal line, or in any direction if the loose ball is in either end zone. An offensive player can't bat forward a ball in a player's possession or a backward pass in flight. (The nearby sidebar titled "The Holy Roller" explains the genesis of this rule.)

>> **Deliberately kicking a loose ball:** When a player kicks a loose ball in the field of play or tries to kick a ball from a player's possession. The ball isn't dead when an illegal kick is recovered, however.

>> **Helping the runner:** When a member of the offensive team pushes or pulls a runner forward when the defense has already stopped his momentum.

>> **Holding, illegal use of the hands, arms, or body by the offense:** When an offensive player uses his hands, arms, or other parts of his body to hold a defensive player from tackling the ball carrier. The penalty is most common when linemen are attempting to protect the quarterback from being *sacked* (tackled behind the line of scrimmage). The defense is also guilty of holding when it tackles or prevents an offensive player, other than the ball carrier, from moving downfield after the ball is snapped. On a punt, field goal attempt, or extra point try, the defense can't grab or pull an offensive blocker in order to clear a path for a teammate to block the kick or punt attempt.

THE HOLY ROLLER

The rule that forbids offensive players from batting the ball forward came about after a controversial play that took place in a 1978 game between the Oakland Raiders and San Diego Chargers. Trailing the Chargers 20–14 with 10 seconds left in the game and desperately needing a touchdown to win, Raider quarterback Ken "The Snake" Stabler deliberately fumbled the ball forward at the Charger 14 yard line. The ball bounced to the 8-yard line, where Raider Pete Banaszak swatted the ball across the goal line. There, Raiders' Hall of Fame tight end Dave Casper fell on the ball for a touchdown.

The controversial play became known as the "Holy Roller." Said Oakland guard Gene Upshaw about the episode, "The play is in our playbook. It's called 'Win at Any Cost.'" Whatever you want to call the play, the NFL made it illegal to advance the ball by kicking or swatting it the following season.

>> **Offensive pass interference:** When a forward pass is thrown and an offensive player physically restricts or impedes a defender in a manner that's visually evident and materially affects the opponent's opportunity to gain position to catch the ball. This penalty usually occurs when a pass is badly underthrown and the intended receiver must come back to the ball and interfere rather than allow the defender to intercept the pass.

>> **Tripping a member of either team:** When a player, usually close to the line of scrimmage, sees someone running past him and sticks out his leg or foot, tripping the player.

Recognizing 15-yard penalties

These are the penalties that make coaches yell at their players because they cost the team 15 yards — the stiffest penalties (other than ejection or pass interference) in football:

>> **A tackler using his helmet to butt, spear, or ram an opponent:** When a player uses the top and forehead of the helmet, plus the face mask, to unnecessarily butt, spear, or ram an opponent. The officials monitor particular situations, such as when a

- Passer is in the act of throwing or has just released a pass

- Receiver is catching or attempting to catch a pass

- Runner is already in the grasp of a tackler

- Kick returner or punt returner is attempting to field a kick in the air

- Player is on the ground at the end of a play

>> **A punter, placekicker, or holder simulates being roughed by a defensive player:** When these players pretend to be hurt or injured or act like a defensive player caused them actual harm when the contact is considered incidental.

>> **Chop block:** When an offensive player blocks a defensive player at the thigh or lower while another offensive player occupies that same defensive player by attempting to block him or even simulating a blocking attempt.

>> **Clipping below the waist:** When a player throws his body across the back of the leg(s) of an opponent or charges, falls, or rolls into the back of an opponent below the waist after approaching him from behind, provided that the opponent isn't a ball carrier or positioned close to the line of scrimmage. However, within 3 yards on either side of the line of scrimmage and within an area extended laterally to the original position of the offensive tackle, offensive linemen can block defensive linemen from behind.

>> **Delay of game at the start of either half:** When the captains for either team fail to show up (or fail to show up in uniform) in the center of the field for the coin toss three minutes prior to the start of the game. A team whose captains fail to show loses the coin toss option and is penalized from the spot of the kickoff. The other team automatically gets the coin-toss choice.

>> **Face mask:** When a tackler twists, turns, or pulls an opponent by the face mask. Because this move is particularly dangerous, the penalty is 15 yards and an automatic first down. If the referee considers his action flagrant, the player may be ejected from the game.

>> **Fair catch interference:** When a player from the kicking team prevents the punt or kick returner from making a path to the ball or touching the ball prior to the ball hitting the ground. This penalty isn't called when a kick fails to cross the line of scrimmage or a player making a fair catch makes no effort to actually catch the ball.

>> **Helmet lowering:** The NFL implemented a new helmet rule in 2018. This foul can be called on both offensive and defensive players. It is a foul if a player lowers his head to initiate and make contact with his helmet against an opponent. Contact does not have to be to an opponent's head or neck area, as lowering the head and initiating contact to an opponent's torso, hips, and lower body is also a foul. Violations of the rule are easier to see and officiate when they occur in open space — as opposed to close line play — but this rule applies anywhere on the field at any time. This penalty was called a couple times in 2018 when a running back lowered his head into an oncoming tackler. In extreme cases, if the player is considered to have delivered the blow when it was clearly avoidable, the officials have the power to eject the player from the game.

>> **Illegal crackback block by the offense:** When an offensive player who lines up more than 2 yards laterally outside an offensive tackle, or a player who's in a backfield position at the snap and then moves to a position more than 2 yards laterally outside the tackle, clips an opponent anywhere. Moreover, the offensive player may not contact an opponent below the waist if the blocker is moving toward the position from which the ball was snapped and the contact occurs within a 5-yard area on either side of the line of scrimmage.

>> **Illegal low block:** When a player on the receiving team during a kickoff, safety kick, punt, field goal attempt, or extra point try blocks an opponent below the waist.

>> **Piling on:** When a ball carrier is helpless or prostrate, defenders jump onto his body with excessive force with the possible intention of causing injury. Piling on also results in an automatic first down.

>> **Roughing the kicker:** When a defensive player makes any contact with the kicker, provided the defensive player hasn't touched the kicked ball before contact. Sometimes this penalty, which also results in an automatic first down, is committed by more than one defensive player as they attempt to block a kick or punt.

>> **Roughing the passer:** When, after the quarterback has released the ball, a defensive player makes direct contact with the quarterback subsequent to the pass rusher's first step after the quarterback releases the ball. The NFL wants to protect its star players, so this penalty is watched closely. Pass rushers are called for this penalty if they fail to avoid contact with the passer and continue to *drive through* or forcibly make contact with the passer. The defensive player is called for roughing if he commits intimidating acts such as picking up the passer and stuffing him into the ground, wrestling with him, or driving him down after he has released the ball. Also, the defender must not use his helmet or face mask to hit the passer. Finally, the defender must not strike the quarterback in the head or neck area or dive at his knees. Roughing the passer results in an automatic first down.

>> **Taking a running start to attempt to block a kick:** When a defender takes a running start from beyond the line of scrimmage in an attempt to block a field goal or extra point and lands on players at the line of scrimmage. This penalty prevents defensive players from hurting unprotected players who are attempting to block for their kicker.

>> **Targeting:** Lowering your head and using the crown of your helmet when tackling a defenseless receiver, running back, or quarterback in the head or neck area. College football has strict rules on this 15-yard penalty. The game officials use replay officials in order to consider intent, and if replay shows the defender struck the offensive player in the head or neck area, it results an automatic ejection of the player who commits the foul. Replay is used to clarify that the player used his helmet, not his shoulder pads, when tackling.

If the foul occurs in the second half, the player must sit out the first half of his next game.

» **Unnecessary roughness:** This penalty has different variations:

- Striking an opponent above the knee with the foot, or striking any part of the leg below the knee with a whipping motion

- Tackling the ball carrier when he's clearly out of bounds

- A member of the receiving team going out of bounds and contacting a player on the kicking team

- Diving or throwing one's body on the ball carrier when he's defenseless on the ground and is making no attempt to get up

- Throwing the ball carrier to the ground after the play is ruled dead (when an official has blown the whistle)

- Hitting a defenseless receiver in one of the following ways: leaving one's feet and launching into the receiver or using any part of the helmet to initiate forceful contact

» **Unsportsmanlike conduct:** When a player commits any act contrary to the generally understood principles of sportsmanship, including the use of abusive, threatening, or insulting language or gestures to opponents, officials, or representatives of the league; the use of baiting or taunting acts or words that engender ill will between teams; and unnecessary contact with any game official.

Identifying specific pass-play penalties

These penalties occur only when the offensive team has attempted a forward pass. Here are three of the most common penalties you see on pass plays:

» **Illegal contact:** When a defensive player makes significant contact with a receiver who's 5 yards beyond the line of scrimmage. Illegal contact is a 5-yard penalty and an automatic first down. This penalty has become much more prevalent in the NFL as the league no longer wants to see receivers impeded as they go out into their pass patterns.

» **Intentional grounding:** When a passer, facing an imminent loss of yardage due to pressure from the defense, throws a forward pass without a realistic chance of completing it. If he throws such a pass in his own end zone, a safety (two points) is awarded to the defense. It is *not* intentional grounding when a passer, while out of the *pocket* (the protected area within the area of two offensive tackles), throws a pass that lands at or beyond the line of scrimmage with an offensive player having a realistic chance of catching the ball. When out of the pocket, the passer is allowed to throw the ball out of bounds.

The penalty is loss of down and 10 yards from the previous line of scrimmage if the passer is in the field of play, or loss of down at the spot of the foul if it occurs more than 10 yards behind the line.

» **Pass interference:** When a defensive player physically restricts or impedes a receiver in a visually evident manner and materially affects the receiver's opportunity to gain position or retain his position to catch the ball. This penalty is an automatic first down, and the ball is placed at the spot of the foul. If interference occurs in the end zone, the offense gets a first down on the 1-yard line. However, when both players are competing for position to make a play on the ball, the defensive player has a right to attempt to intercept the ball.

Disputing a Call: The Instant Replay Challenge System

Under the *instant replay challenge system*, a coach who disagrees with a call can ask the referees to review it with instant replay. (The NFL resurrected this system in 1999 after trying and abandoning it in the late 1980s and early 1990s, and the NCAA has been using it since 2004.) Coaches can challenge up to two calls per game. However, if they challenge a call and the referees decide after reviewing it that the call stands, the team that issued the challenge loses a timeout. In the rare instance of a coach making two successful challenges within a game, he is allowed a third challenge.

To challenge a call, the coach must make the challenge before the ball is snapped and the next play begins. To signal a challenge, the coach throws a red flag onto the field of play. Usually, coaches wait for the replay to be reviewed in the coaches' booth upstairs, or they view the play on the stadium's big screen before issuing a challenge.

In the NFL, in the final two minutes of each half, neither coach may challenge a call. A replay official monitors all plays and signals down to the field to the referee if any play or call needs to be reviewed. In addition, in the NFL, all scoring plays and turnovers (fumbles and interceptions) are automatically reviewed by the replay official and also the NFL's officiating executives in their New York replay room.

New for the 2019 season, coaches will be allowed to challenge pass interference penalties. They also will be able to challenge a non-pass interference call like the one that Saints' fans believe cost them a win in the 2019 NFC Championship game. Supporters of instant replay say that this challenge will make the game fairer. But challenging whether a penalty should have been called or not called will put immense strain on replay officials and the officiating executives in New York to make the correct call.

Go, Offense!

Find out what it takes to be a quarterback, physically and mentally.

Discover how teams throw and run the ball and compare passing patterns.

Examine offensive strategies and get to know the people who play the ground game.

» **Recognizing the qualities that make a good quarterback**

» **Deciphering quarterback language and fundamentals**

» **Figuring out a quarterback's rating**

Chapter **4**

The Quarterback, Football's MVP

Being a former defensive player, I hate to admit that the quarterback is the most important player on a football team. My only consolation is that although quarterbacks command the highest salaries in the NFL, my fellow defensive linemen are number two on the list. That's because their job is to make the quarterback's life miserable. Quarterbacks get all the press during the week, and defensive guys knock the stuffing out of them on weekends.

HOWIE SAYS

I like my quarterback to be the John Wayne of the football team. He should be a courageous leader, one who puts winning and his teammates ahead of his personal glory. Tom Brady, who has won six Super Bowls with the New England Patriots, and John Elway, who won two Super Bowls with the Denver Broncos, quickly come to mind. Both of them played with toughness, although they also had plenty of talent, skill, and flair to somehow escape the worst situations and throw the touchdown pass that won the game. Brady, a true workaholic, also is like a coach on the field, knowing exactly what plays will succeed against a particular defense.

In this chapter, I reveal the fundamental skills necessary for a quarterback. I also discuss stance, vision, and arm strength and solve the puzzle of that mysterious quarterback rating system.

Taking a Look at the Quarterback's Job

With the exception of kicking plays (described in Chapter 12), quarterbacks touch the ball on every offensive play. A quarterback's job is to direct his team toward the end zone and score as many points as possible. The typical team scores on one-third of its offensive possessions, resulting in either a touchdown or a field goal. So you can see that the quarterback is under enormous pressure to generate points every time the offense takes the field.

The quarterback (QB) is the player directly behind the center receiving the ball, as shown in Figure 4-1, where the center is the X. He's the player who announces the plays in the huddle, but he doesn't call them on his own. Coaches on all levels of football (peewee, high school, college, and the NFL) decide what plays the offense will use.

The QB lines up directly behind the center at the beginning of each play. In the NFL, a quarterback receives plays from a coach on the sidelines via an audio device placed in his helmet. In high school and college football, an assistant coach generally signals in the plays from the sidelines after conferring with the head coach or offensive coordinator. In critical situations, a player may bring in the play when being substituted for an offensive player already on the field.

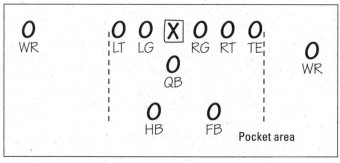

FIGURE 4-1:
The quarterback lines up behind the center.

© John Wiley & Sons, Inc.

When Terry Bradshaw, my partner at FOX, played in the NFL in the 1970s, many coaches allowed their veteran quarterbacks to call their own plays after practicing and studying all week. But eventually the coaches wrested control of the play calling away from the quarterbacks, believing that the responsibility was too much of a mental burden for them. When the game became more specialized (with multiple substitutions on both offense and defense) in the 1980s, coaches decided that they wanted the pressure of making the play calls. They didn't think that a quarterback needed the additional responsibility of facing the media after a game and explaining why he called certain plays in a losing game. Head coaches were also fully aware that they kept their jobs by winning as many games as possible. This is especially true in the NFL, but it also happens on the high school and college level. Basically, coaches prefer to have total control of what happens on the field.

Although NFL coaches don't allow quarterbacks to call their own offensive plays (except in no-huddle situations when little time remains on the clock), a player must be prepared to change the play at the line of scrimmage if it doesn't appear that the play will succeed. Changing the play at the line of scrimmage in this way is called *audibilizing* (see the later "Calling Plays and Audibilizing" section for more on this topic).

After the quarterback is in possession of the ball, he turns and, depending on which play was called, hands the ball to a running back, runs with the ball himself, or moves farther back and sets up to attempt a pass. Depending on the design of the offense, the quarterback takes a three-step, five-step, or seven-step drop before throwing the ball.

The area in which the quarterback operates, most likely with a running back (RB) and the offensive line protecting him from the defense, is called the *pocket.* It's as wide as the positioning of the quarterback's offensive tackles (refer to Figure 4-1). The quarterback is instructed to stay within this so-called protective area; if he ventures out of the pocket, he's likely to suffer a bone-crushing tackle. And the last thing a coach wants is for his quarterback, the leader of his team, to get injured.

The quarterback's main job is to throw the football and encourage his teammates to play well. In college, especially if the team runs a spread formation, the quarterback may run the ball as often as he passes. Most NFL teams don't like their quarterbacks to run, but many of them do to avoid being tackled. Cam Newton of the Carolina Panthers and Russell Wilson of the Seattle Seahawks are very good runners and often make positive plays when leaving the pocket. A basic run play among all quarterbacks is the quarterback sneak. Teams run this play when the offense needs a yard or less for a first down. In a *quarterback sneak,* the quarterback takes a direct snap from the center and either leaps behind his center or guard or dives between his guard and center, hoping to gain a first down.

In passing situations when the team has many yards to go for a first down or touchdown, quarterbacks sometimes take a *shotgun snap.* In this instance, the quarterback stands 5 to 7 yards behind the center and receives the ball through the air from the center, much like a punter does. Starting from the shotgun position, the quarterback doesn't have to drop back. He can survey the defense and target his receivers better. However, defending against a quarterback who lines up in the shotgun position is easier for the defensive players, because they know the play is very likely to be a pass instead of a run.

While the quarterback is setting up a play, he must also be aware of what the defense is attempting to do. Later in this chapter, I explain how quarterbacks "read" a defense.

Determining What a Quarterback Needs to Succeed

When scouts or coaches examine a quarterback's potential to play in the NFL, they run down a checklist of physical, mental, and personality traits that affect a quarterback's success on the field. These qualities are required for success at all levels of football. However, in this chapter, I discuss them in terms that relate to a professional athlete.

Note: Some scouts and coaches break down a quarterback's talent and abilities further, but for this book's purposes, the following are the main criteria necessary to excel. If a quarterback has five of these eight traits, he undoubtedly ranks among the top 15 players at his position.

Arm strength

Unlike baseball, football doesn't use a radar gun to gauge the speed of the ball after the quarterback releases it. But velocity is important when throwing a football because it allows a quarterback to complete a pass before a single defensive player can *recover* (react to the pass) and possibly deflect or intercept the ball. The more arm strength a quarterback has, the better his ability to throw the ball at a high speed.

Many good quarterbacks, with practice, could throw a baseball between 75 and 90 miles per hour, comparable to a Major League Baseball pitcher. Because of its shape, a football is harder to throw than a baseball, but NFL quarterbacks like Matthew Stafford of the Detroit Lions and Carolina's Cam Newton throw the fastest passes at over 45 miles per hour.

Accuracy

Defensive coverage has never been tighter than in today's NFL. When a receiver goes out into a route, most of the time he's open for only a tiny window of space and time. The best quarterbacks can put the ball in the ideal spot for the receiver to not only catch the ball but to catch it in stride to gain more yards down field. Elite quarterbacks make the perfect throw play after play, often releasing the ball before the receiver even turns around in order to catch the ball. Plenty of quarterbacks have strong arms, but the ones who succeed at the highest levels make their living with accurate throws, generally delivering the ball chest high where the receiver can extend his arms to catch the ball with his hands.

Competitiveness

A player's competitiveness is made up of many subjective and intangible qualities. A quarterback should have the desire to be the team's offensive leader and, ideally, overall leader. He should be the hardest working player in practice.

REMEMBER

The quarterback's performance affects the entire offensive team. If he doesn't throw accurately, the receivers will never catch a pass. If he doesn't move quickly, the offensive linemen won't be able to protect him. He also should have the courage to take a hard hit from a defensive player. During games, quarterbacks must cope with constant harassment from the defense. They must stand in the pocket and hold onto the ball until the last split second, knowing that they're going to be tackled the instant they release the ball.

To be a competitive player, a quarterback must have an inner desire to win. The quarterback's competitive fire often inspires his teammates to play harder. Competitiveness is a quality that every coach (and teammate) wants in his quarterback.

Intelligence

The quarterback doesn't have to have the highest IQ on the team, but intelligence does come in handy. Many NFL teams have a 3-inch-thick playbook that includes at least 50 running plays and as many as 200 passing plays. The quarterback has to know them all. He has to know not only what he's supposed to do in every one of those plays but also what the other *skilled players* (running backs, receivers, and tight ends) are required to do. Why? Because he may have to explain a specific play in the huddle or during a timeout. On some teams, the quarterback is also responsible for informing the offensive linemen of their blocking schemes.

HALL OF FAME

Many quarterbacks are what coaches call *football smart:* They know the intricacies of the game, the formations, and the defenses. They play on instinct and play well. Former San Francisco quarterback Steve Young is both football smart and book smart. Young was a lot like former great quarterbacks Otto Graham of the Cleveland Browns and Roger Staubach of the Dallas Cowboys. Being book smart and football smart can be an unbeatable combination on game days.

Mobility

A quarterback's mobility is as important as his intelligence and his arm. He must move quickly to avoid being tackled by defensive players. Therefore, he must move backward (called *retreating*) from the center as quickly as possible in order to set himself up to throw the ball. When a quarterback has excellent mobility, you hear him described as having *quick feet*. This term means that he moves quickly and effortlessly behind the line of scrimmage with the football. A quarterback doesn't have to be speedy to do this. He simply must be able to maneuver quickly and gracefully. In one simple step away from the line of scrimmage, a good quarterback covers 4½ feet to almost 2 yards. While taking these huge steps, the quarterback's upper body shouldn't dip or lean to one side or the other. He must be balanced.

Mobility is also critical when a quarterback doesn't have adequate pass protection and has to move out of the pocket and pass while under pressure and on the run. Coaches call this type of mobility *escapability*. Both Russell Wilson, shown in Figure 4-2, and Carson Wentz of the Eagles are great at escaping defensive pressure. Maybe the best of the old-timers was Fran Tarkenton, who played with the New York Giants and the Minnesota Vikings. Roger Staubach of the Cowboys was nicknamed "Roger the Dodger" because he was tough to trap.

FIGURE 4-2: Quarterback Russell Wilson of the Seattle Seahawks is one of the more mobile quarterbacks in the NFL.

Photo credit: © Norm Hall/Getty Images

Release

If a quarterback doesn't have exceptional arm strength, he'd better have a quick *release*. After the quarterback raises the ball in his hand, usually near his head or slightly above and behind it, he *releases*, or rapidly brings his arm forward and lets the ball loose. Former Miami Dolphins quarterback Dan Marino probably had the game's quickest release. His arm and hand remained a blur when filmed and replayed in slow motion.

Quarterbacks with great releases generally are born with the ability. Average quarterbacks can improve and refine their releases, but their releases will never be great. A quarterback either has this coordinated motion between his arm, elbow, and wrist, or he doesn't. Throwing a football isn't a natural arm movement like slinging your arm to roll a bowling ball.

Size

Players of all different heights and weights have played the quarterback position, but NFL quarterbacks are preferably over 6'1" and 210 pounds. A quarterback who's 6'5" and 225 pounds is considered ideal. A quarterback wants to be tall enough to see over his linemen — whose average height in the NFL is 6'5" to 6'7" — and look down the field, beyond the line of scrimmage, to find his receivers and see where the defensive backs are positioned.

Weight is imperative to injury prevention because of the physical wear and tear that the quarterback position requires. A quarterback can expect a lot of physical contact, especially when attempting to pass. Defenders relentlessly pursue the quarterback to hit him, tackling him for a *sack* (a loss of yards behind the line of scrimmage) before he can throw a pass or making contact after he releases a pass. These hits are sometimes legal and sometimes illegal. If the defensive player takes more than one step when hitting the quarterback after he releases the ball, the hit is considered late and therefore illegal. Regardless, defensive linemen and linebackers are taught to inflict as much punishment as possible on the quarterback. They want to either knock him out of the game or cause him enough pain that he'll be less willing to hold on to the ball while waiting for his receivers to get open. When a quarterback releases a pass prematurely, it's called *bailing out of the play*.

Vision

A quarterback doesn't necessarily need keen peripheral vision, but it doesn't hurt. A quarterback must quickly scan the field when he comes to the line of scrimmage prior to the snap of the ball. He must survey the defense, checking its alignments and in particular the depth of the defensive backs — how far they are off the receivers, off the line of scrimmage, and so on. After the ball is snapped, the quarterback must continue to scan the field as he moves backward. Granted, he may focus on a particular area because the play is designed in a certain direction, but vision is critical if he wants to discover whether a receiver other than his first choice is open on a particular play. Most pass plays have a variety of options, known as *passing progressions.* One pass play may have as many as five players running pass routes, so the quarterback needs to be able to check whether any of them is open so that he has an option if he's unable to throw to his intended (first choice) receiver.

A quarterback needs to have a sense of where to look and how to scan and quickly react. Often, a quarterback has to make a decision in a split second or else the play may fail. Vision doesn't necessarily mean that the quarterback has to jerk his head from side to side. Instead, his *passing reads* (how a quarterback deciphers what the defense is attempting to accomplish against the offense on a particular play) often follow an orderly progression as he looks across the field of play. A quarterback must have an understanding of what the defensive secondary's tendencies are — how they like to defend a particular play or a certain style of receiver. Sometimes, after sneaking a quick glance at his intended target, the quarterback looks in another direction in order to fool the defense. (Many defensive players tend to follow a quarterback's eyes, believing that they'll tell where he intends to throw the pass.)

Quarterbacking Fundamentals

Playing quarterback requires a lot of technical skills. Although a coach can make a player better in many areas of the game, I don't believe that any coach can teach a player how to throw the football. Otherwise, every quarterback would be a great passer. And if such a coach existed, every father would be taking his son to that coach, considering the millions of dollars NFL quarterbacks earn every season. However, there are dozens of quarterback coaches around the country that truly can fine-tune a player's throwing motion. Many quarterbacks, including greats like New England's Tom Brady, work with a former baseball pitcher, Tom House, on their delivery and throwing motion.

REMEMBER

You can teach a quarterback how to deal with pressure, how to make good decisions, and how to make good connections with his receivers and predict where they'll be. But quarterbacks either have the innate talent to throw the football — that natural arm motion and quick release — or they don't. Think of how many good college quarterbacks fail to survive in the NFL. Plus, NFL scouts, coaches, general managers, and so on will tell you that the league has only 10 to 15 really good quarterbacks. If throwing could be taught, all quarterbacks would be great.

Quarterbacks *can* improve and refine their skills in the following areas with a lot of practice and hard work.

Settling into the stance

To play the most important position in football, a quarterback must begin with his stance under center. The quarterback takes his stance behind the center to receive the ball; the center snaps it back to him, as shown in Figure 4-3. The quarterback's stance under center starts with his feet about shoulder width apart. He bends his knees, flexes down, and bends forward at the waist until he's directly behind the center's rear end. The quarterback then places his hands, with the thumbs touching each other and the fingers spread as far apart as possible, under the center's rear end. Because some centers don't bring the ball all the way to the quarterback's hands, the quarterback will lower his hands below the center's rear end in order to receive the ball cleanly. The quarterback needs to avoid pulling out early, a common mistake when the quarterback and the center haven't played together very much.

Quarterback   Center

FIGURE 4-3:
A quarterback usually lines up behind the center, who snaps the ball to him to start the play.

© *John Wiley & Sons, Inc.*

Dropping back

After he masters the stance, a quarterback learns how to *drop back* and set up to pass. Dropping back is what a quarterback does after he receives the ball from the center. Before he passes the ball, he must move away from the line of scrimmage (and the opposing defense) and put himself in a position to be able to throw the football.

You see quarterbacks backing up from center, or *backpedaling,* when the offensive formation is aligned to the left of a right-handed quarterback. Backpedaling is essential in those alignments so that the quarterback can see whether the linebacker on that side is *blitzing* (rushing across the line of scrimmage in an attempt to tackle the quarterback). The quarterback must be alert to a possible blitz; consequently, he can't afford to half-turn his back to that side.

The depth to which a quarterback drops in the pocket generally is determined by how far from the line of scrimmage the receiver is running. If the receiver is running 5 to 6 yards down the field and then turning to catch the ball, for example, the quarterback takes a drop of no more than three steps. The quarterback generally moves farther away from the line of scrimmage as the *pass routes* (the paths receivers take when going out for a pass) of his receivers get longer. For instance, if the receiver is running 10 to 12 yards down the field, the quarterback takes five steps to put himself about 7 yards back from the line of scrimmage.

On a *post route* (a deep pass in which the receiver angles in to the goalpost) or a *streak route* (a deep pass straight downfield), the quarterback takes a seven-step drop. Taking a longer drop when a shorter one is required enables the defense to recover and may lead to an interception or an incompletion.

All these drop-backs are critical to the timing of the receiver's run, move, and turn and the quarterback's delivery and release. In practice, the quarterback works on the depth of his steps according to the pass route.

Handing off

One of the most important things for a quarterback to master is the running game and how it affects his steps from center (head to Chapter 6 for the scoop on the running game). Some running plays call for the quarterback to open his right hip (if he's right-handed) and step straight back. This technique is called the *six o'clock step.* The best way to imagine these steps is to picture a clock. The center is at twelve o'clock, and directly behind the quarterback is six o'clock. Three o'clock is to the quarterback's right, and nine o'clock is to his left.

For example, a right-handed quarterback hands off the ball to a runner heading on a run around the left side of his offensive line (it's called a *sweep*) at the five o'clock mark. When handing the ball to a runner heading on a sweep across the backfield to the right, the quarterback should hand off at the seven o'clock mark.

Getting a grip

Because different quarterbacks have different-sized hands, one passing grip doesn't suit everyone. Some coaches say that a quarterback should hold the ball with his middle finger going across the ball's white laces or trademark. Other coaches believe both the middle and ring finger should grip the laces. Some quarterbacks can still grip the ball solidly while not placing their fingers on the laces.

Many great quarterbacks have huge hands, allowing them to place their index finger on the tip of the ball while wrapping their middle, ring, and small fingers around the middle of the ball. However, the ball slips from many quarterbacks' hands when they attempt to grip the ball this way. So, basically, every quarterback needs to find the grip that works for him.

Reading a Defense

When a quarterback prepares for a game, he wants to be able to look at a specific defensive alignment and instantly know which offense will or won't succeed against it.

Many quarterbacks are taught to read the *free safety,* or the safety positioned deepest in the *secondary,* the part of the field behind the linebackers that the safeties and cornerbacks are responsible for. (See Chapter 10 for more on the secondary and Chapter 11 for the full scoop on defensive schemes and strategies.) If the free safety lines up 5 to 7 yards deeper than the other defensive backs, the safeties are probably playing a zone defense. A quarterback also knows that the defense is playing zone if the cornerbacks are aligned 10 yards off the line of scrimmage. If the cornerbacks are on the line of scrimmage, eyeballing the receivers, they're most likely playing man-to-man. Knowing whether the defense is playing zone or man-to-man is important to the quarterback because he wants to know whether he's attacking a zone defense or man-to-man alignment with his pass play.

Although a defense may employ 20 to 30 different pass coverages in the secondary, four basic coverages exist. Because most defenses begin with four players in the secondary, the coverages are called *cover one, cover two, cover three,* and *cover four.* The following list gives a description of each.

Cover one

In this coverage, shown in Figure 4-4, one deep safety is about 12 to 14 yards deep in the middle of the field, the two cornerbacks (CB) are in *press coverage* (on the line of scrimmage opposite the two receivers), and the strong safety (SS) is about 5 yards deep over the tight end. Cover one is usually man-to-man coverage. Some teams today call this defense *single high free.* A running play works best against this type of coverage.

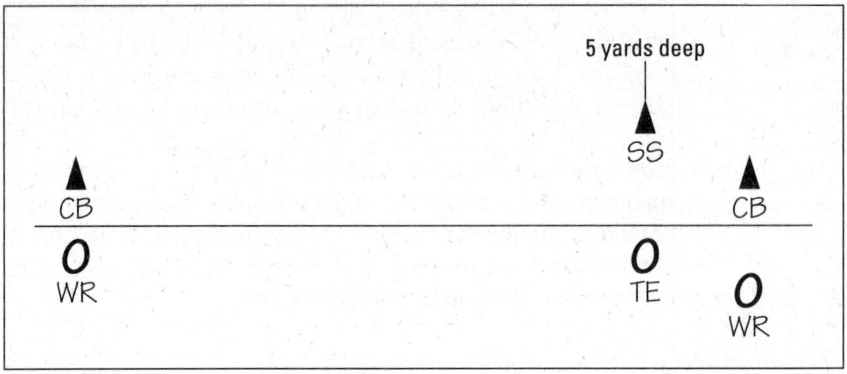

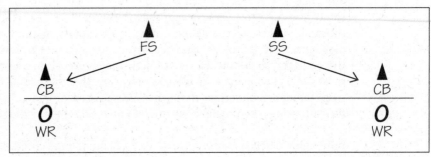

FIGURE 4-4: Cover one puts one safety or secondary player close to the line while the free safety (not pictured) plays deep.

© John Wiley & Sons, Inc.

Cover two

This time, both safeties are deep, 12 to 14 yards off the line of scrimmage, as shown in Figure 4-5. The two cornerbacks remain in press coverage, while the two safeties prepare to help the corners on passing plays and come forward on running plays. A deep comeback pass, a crossing route, or a swing pass works well against this type of coverage.

FIGURE 4-5: Cover two puts both safeties deep.

© John Wiley & Sons, Inc.

Cover three

This coverage, shown in Figure 4-6, has three defensive backs deep. The free safety remains 12 to 14 yards off the line of scrimmage, and the two cornerbacks move 10 to 12 yards off the line of scrimmage. Cover three is obvious zone coverage. The strong safety is 5 yards off the line of scrimmage, over the tight end. This cover is a stout defense versus the run, but it's soft against a good passing team. In this cover, a quarterback can throw *underneath passes* (short passes to beat the linebackers who are positioned underneath the defensive back's coverage). Staying with faster receivers in this area is difficult for some linebackers to do.

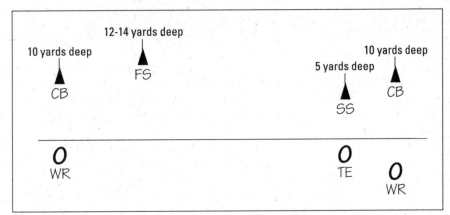

FIGURE 4-6: In cover three, three defensive backs line up deep.

Cover four

In cover four, what you see is what you get, as shown in Figure 4-7. All four defensive backs are off the line of scrimmage, aligned 10 to 12 yards deep. Some teams call this coverage "Four Across" because the defensive backs are aligned all across the field. The cover four is a good pass defense because the secondary players are told to never allow a receiver to get behind them. If offensive teams can block the *front seven* (a combination of defensive linemen and linebackers that amounts to seven players), a running play works against this coverage.

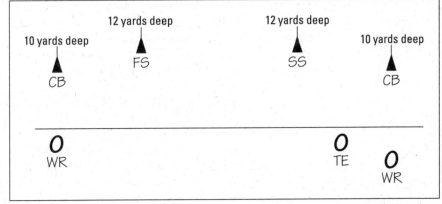

FIGURE 4-7: Cover four aligns all four secondary players off the line of scrimmage.

Calling Plays and Audibilizing

The quarterback relays to his teammates in the huddle what play the coach has called. The *play* is a mental blueprint or diagram for every player on the field. And everything the quarterback says refers specifically to the assignments of his receivers, running backs, offensive linemen, and center.

For example, the quarterback may say "686 Pump F-Stop on two." The first three numbers (686) are the passing routes that the receivers — known as X, Y, and Z — should take. Every team numbers its pass routes and patterns (look for them in Chapter 5), giving receivers an immediate signal of what routes to run. On this play, the X receiver runs a 6 route, the Y receiver an 8 route, and the Z receiver another 6 route. "F-Stop" in this case refers to the fullback's pass route. And "two" refers to the *count* on which the quarterback wants the ball snapped to him. In other words, the center will snap the ball on the second sound.

Most teams snap the ball on the first, second, or third count unless they're purposely attempting to draw the opposition offside by using an extra-long count. For example, if the quarterback has been asking for the ball on the count of two throughout the game, he may ask for the ball on the count of three, hoping that someone on the defense will move prematurely.

After the quarterback reaches the line of scrimmage and puts his hands under the center, he says "Set" (at which point the linemen drop into their stances) and then something like "Green 80, Green 80, Hut-Hut." The center snaps the ball on the second "Hut." "Green 80" means absolutely nothing in this case. However, sometimes the quarterback's remarks at the line of scrimmage prior to the snap count inform his offensive teammates of how the play will be changed. The offensive linemen also know that the play is a pass because of the numbering system mentioned at the beginning of the called play.

Teams give their plays all sorts of odd monikers, such as Quick Ace, Scat, Zoom, and Buzz. Peyton Manning had a favorite one, Omaha, that you may have heard on television. These names refer to specific actions within the play; they're meant for the ears of the running backs and receivers. Each name (and every team has its own terms) means something, depending on the play called.

REMEMBER

Quarterbacks are allowed to *audibilize*, or change the play at the line of scrimmage. A changed play is called an *audible*. Quarterbacks usually audibilize when they discover that the defense has guessed correctly and is properly aligned to stop the play. When he barks his signals, the quarterback simply has to say "Green 85," and the play is altered to the 85 pass play. Usually, the quarterback informs his offensive teammates in the huddle what his audible change may be.

A quarterback may also use an offensive strategy known as *check with me,* in which he instructs his teammates to listen carefully at the line of scrimmage because he may call another play, or his call at the line of scrimmage will be the play. To help his teammates easily understand, the play may simply change colors — from Green to Red, for example.

Acing Quarterback Math

Quarterbacks are judged statistically on all levels of football by their passing accuracy (which is called *completion percentage*), the number of touchdowns they throw, the number of interceptions they throw, and the number of yards they gain by passing. This last statistic — passing yards — can be deceiving. For example, if a quarterback throws the ball 8 yards beyond the line of scrimmage and the receiver runs for another 42 yards after catching the ball, the quarterback is awarded 50 yards for the completion. (You may hear television commentators use the term *yards after the catch* to describe the yards that the receiver gains after catching the ball.) Quarterbacks also receive positive passing yards when they complete a pass behind the line of scrimmage — for example, a screen pass to a running back who goes on to run 15 yards. Those 15 yards are considered passing yards.

TIP

For a better understanding of what the quarterback's numbers mean, take a look at New Orleans quarterback Drew Brees' statistics for the 2017 season. Brees, who already has thrown for over 500 touchdowns and owns the best completition percentage in the NFL, played in all 16 regular-season games. Brees is impressive because he is barely 6-feet tall, proving that height isn't always a requirement to be a great quarterback.

Att	Comp	Pct Comp	Yds	Yds/Att	TD	Int	Rating
536	386	72.0	4,334	8.09	23	8	103.9

Examining Brees' statistics, you see that he attempted 536 passes (Att) and completed 386 of those passes (Comp) for a completion percentage of 72 (Pct Comp). In attempting those 536 passes, his receivers gained 4,334 yards (Yds), which equals an average gain per attempt of 8.09 yards (Yds/Att). Brees' teammates scored 23 touchdowns (TD) via his passing while the defense intercepted (Int) 8 of his passing attempts.

When you see a newspaper article about a football game, the story may state that the quarterback was 22 of 36, passing for 310 yards. Translation: He completed 22 of 36 pass attempts and gained 310 yards on those 22 completions. Not a bad game.

Last but not least you have the NFL quarterback rating formula, also called the passer rating formula. It makes for an unusual math problem. Grab your calculator and follow these steps to figure it out:

1. **Divide completed passes by pass attempts, subtract 0.3, and then divide by 0.2.**

2. **Divide passing yards by pass attempts, subtract 3, and then divide by 4.**

3. **Divide touchdown passes by pass attempts and then divide by 0.05.**

4. **Divide interceptions by pass attempts, subtract that number from 0.095, and divide the remainder by 0.04.**

The sum of each step can't be greater than 2.375 or less than zero. Add the sums of the four steps, multiply that number by 100, and divide by 6. The final number is the quarterback rating, which in Brees' case is 103.9.

REMEMBER

A rating of 100 or above is considered very good; an average rating is in the 80 to 90 range; and anything below 75 is considered a poor quarterback rating.

Chapter **5**

The Passing Game

Although the strategies of offenses change and sometimes favor running over passing, throwing the football is a major part of football's excitement. Some of the most memorable plays in football are those long passes (or throws) that win games in the final seconds or pull a team ahead in the score and turn the game around. Who can resist joining in the collective cheer that erupts when the ball is hurtling through the air and looks as if it's about to drop into a receiver's hands? And when a defensive player catches the ball (known in football jargon as an *interception*), the play can be just as exciting and influential to the outcome of the game.

An offense scores points by moving the ball into the opponent's end zone. This chapter focuses on one half of the offensive attack: the passing game. The other half, the running game, is covered in Chapter 6. In the 1980 NFL season, pass plays exceeded running plays for the first time since 1969, and that trend has continued ever since.

Getting to Know the Passing Game

To many fans, the passing game is the most exciting aspect of football. Seeing the quarterback throwing a long pass and a fleet-footed receiver jumping up to grab it is exciting. Earl "Curly" Lambeau, the founder and player/coach of the Green Bay Packers, made his offenses throw the football in the mid-1930s. But teams eventually moved away from throwing the ball. In the 1960s and 1970s, the running game and zone defenses (where players defended deep and covered every area of the field) choked the life out of the passing game.

Two significant rule changes in 1978 spurred the growth of the passing game in the NFL. First, defenders were permitted to make contact with receivers only within 5 yards of the line of scrimmage. Previously, defenders were allowed to hit, push, or shove ("chuck") a receiver anywhere on the field. (In 2014, NFL officials were instructed to pay close attention to illegal contact by defenders against receivers, further opening up the passing game.) Also, offensive linemen were allowed to use open hands and fully extend their arms to block a pass-rusher. The liberalization of this offensive blocking technique led to better protection for the quarterback and ultimately more time for him to throw the football. But not satisfied, both the NFL and college football added more rules in 2017–2018 to protect the quarterback and also defenseless receivers.

All of these pro-offense rule changes not only created more scoring but led to more creativity by offensive coaches. In today's game, virtually on every level from high school to the pros, there are more spread offenses with maybe as many as five receivers aligned across the formation. The Kansas City Chiefs employed this formation often in 2018 when Patrick Mahomes passed for 50 touchdowns in basically his first full season of NFL play. What propelled Mahomes was the spread formation that he learned at Texas Tech, the well known Air Raid offense of Kliff Kingsbury, now the head coach of the Arizona Cardinals. However, several coaches, including Washington State's Mike Leach, helped invent the Air Raid offense. The late Bill Walsh pioneered the *West Coast offense* when he became the head coach of the San Francisco 49ers in 1979. Walsh instituted the short, but highly successful passing game by using the running-back-as-receiver concept. For the first time, teams were running out of passing formations, and the pass was setting up running plays instead of vice versa.

REMEMBER

To make a pass successful, quarterbacks and receivers (wide receivers, tight ends, and running backs) must work on their timing daily. To do so, the receivers must run exact *pass patterns* with the quarterback throwing the football to predetermined spots on the field. Although passing the football may look like a simple act of the quarterback throwing and a receiver catching the ball (often in full stride), this aspect of the game is very complex. For it to be successful, the offensive linemen must provide the quarterback with adequate protection so that he has time to throw the football (more than 2 seconds), while the receivers make every attempt to catch the ball, even if it's poorly thrown. Sometimes, a receiver must deviate from his planned route and run to any open space to give the quarterback a target. Some NFL quarterbacks, like Tom Brady, can release the ball in around 2.5 seconds.

Recognizing the Role of Receivers

A quarterback wouldn't be much good without receivers to catch the ball. *Wide receivers* and *tight ends* are the principal players who catch passes, although *running backs* also are used extensively in every passing offense. (See Chapter 6 for more on running backs.) During the 2018 season, 29 players in the NFL had over 860 receiving yards, and of those 29, only 5 were not wide receivers. However, one was a running back, Carolina's Christian McCaffrey, who had a franchise-record 107 receptions.

Receivers come in all sizes and shapes. They are tall, short, lean, fast, and quick. To excel as a receiver, a player must have nimble hands (hands that are very good at catching the ball) and the ability to concentrate under defensive duress; he must also be courageous under fire and strong enough to withstand physical punishment. Although receiving is a glamorous job, every team expects its receivers to block defensive backs on running plays as well (head to Chapter 7 to find out more). Every team wants its receivers to be able to knock a defensive cornerback on his back or at least prevent him from making a tackle on a running back.

Tight ends aren't as fast as wide receivers because many of them are also asked to play the role of heavy-duty blockers on many plays. But even the role of a tight end has evolved in the last decade or so as more teams are flanking them away from the formation, occasionally putting them in the backfield, in order to match up their size, speed, and height against a smaller defender. Twenty years ago, teams expected tight ends, who may outweigh a wide receiver by 30–35 pounds, to have the ability to also block a defensive end or linebacker, but today, Rob Gronkowski of the New England Patriots and Kyle Rudolph of the Minnesota Vikings are probably the best at doing both receiving and blocking. Like Hall of Famer Tony Gonzalez (see Chapter 20), today's tight ends can run and definitely catch in traffic, like Zach Ertz of the Philadelphia Eagles and George Kittle of the San Francisco 49ers. Blocking is a sidelight for them, considering Ertz caught 116 passes in 2018, a league record for tight ends, and Kittle set a new tight-end yardage mark of 1,377 yards.

REMEMBER

Basic offenses have five possible receivers: one or two running backs, one or two tight ends, and multiple wide receivers. You might see formations five wide receivers, or one tight end and four wide receivers, or one running back, one tight end, and three wide receivers. The wide receivers are commonly referred to as X and Z receivers. The X receiver, or *split end,* normally aligns to the weak side of the formation, and the Z receiver, or *flanker,* aligns to the strong side of the formation. The tight end is known as the Y receiver. (In simplest terms, the strong side of the formation is the side with the most distance to the sideline.)

The split end received his name because he was the end (the offenses of the 1930s used two ends) who aligned 10 yards away from the base offensive formation.

Hence, he *split* from his teammates. The other end, the tight end, aligned next to an offensive tackle. The *flanker* position was originally a running back, and as offenses developed, he flanked to either side of the formation, but never on the line of scrimmage like the split end and tight end.

In many offenses, on passing downs, the tight end is replaced by another receiver. In Figure 5-1, the Y receiver is the one who replaces the tight end.

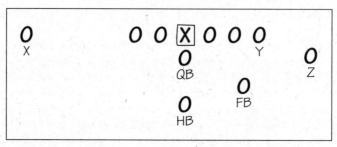

FIGURE 5-1: The Y receiver can replace the tight end on passing downs.

And as an odd-ball example, late in Super Bowl LIII, the New England Patriots successfully employed against the Los Angeles Rams a five-receiver formation that consisted of two running backs, two tight ends, and one wide receiver with an empty backfield.

The following sections offer insight into the nitty-gritty details of the receiver's role in the passing game. Read on to find out everything from the stance that receivers use to the ways they overcome man-to-man coverage.

Achieving the proper stance

Before receivers work on catching the ball, they need to learn the proper stance to create acceleration off the line of scrimmage while also using their upper bodies to defend themselves from contact with defensive backs. Receivers must understand, even at the beginning level, that they must get open before they can catch the ball and that the proper stance enables them to explode from the line of scrimmage. A quarterback won't throw the ball to a receiver who isn't open, and when it comes to being able to complete a pass to an open receiver, every step counts.

In the *stand-up stance,* the receiver's feet remain shoulder width apart and are positioned like they're in the starting blocks — with his left foot near the line of scrimmage and his right foot back 18 inches. With his shoulders square to the ground, he should lean forward just enough so that he can explode off the line when the ball is snapped. The receiver's lean shouldn't be exaggerated, though, or he may tip over.

REMEMBER

A good receiver uses the same stance on every play because he doesn't want to tip off the defense to whether the play is a run or a pass. Bad receivers line up lackadaisically on running plays.

Lining up correctly

One wide receiver, usually the split end, lines up on the line of scrimmage. The other receiver, the flanker, must line up 1 yard behind the line of scrimmage. A combination of seven offensive players must always be on the line of scrimmage prior to the ball being snapped. A smart receiver checks with the nearest official to make sure he's lined up correctly.

The tight end and the split end never line up on the same side. If a receiver is aligned 15 to 18 yards away from the quarterback, he can't hear the quarterback barking signals. Therefore, he must look down the line and move as soon as he sees the ball snapped. Once off the line of scrimmage, a receiver should run toward either shoulder of a defensive back, forcing the defender to turn his shoulders perpendicular to the line of scrimmage to cover him. The receiver hopes to turn the defender in the direction that's opposite of the one in which he intends to go.

Catching the ball

Good receivers catch a football with their hands while their arms are extended away from their bodies. They never catch a football by cradling it in their shoulders or chest, because the ball frequently bounces off.

The best technique a receiver has for using his hands is to place one thumb behind the other while turning his hands so that the fingers of both hands face each other. He spreads his hands as wide as possible while keeping his thumbs together. Then he brings his hands face-high, like he's looking through a tunnel (see Figure 5-2). He wants the ball to come through that tunnel. He wants to see the point of the ball coming down the tunnel, and then he wants to trap it with his palms, thumbs, and fingers. This technique is called *getting your eyes in line with the flight of the ball*. If a ball is thrown below a receiver's waist, he should turn his thumbs out and his little fingers should overlap. A receiver with good fundamentals also keeps his elbows close to his body when catching a football, which adds power to his arms.

FIGURE 5-2:
The right way to catch a football.

© John Wiley & Sons, Inc.

Beating man-to-man coverage

Man-to-man coverage is a style, like in basketball, in which one man guards (or defends) another. The defender stays with a single receiver no matter where he runs. His responsibility is to make sure the receiver doesn't catch a pass. (Head to Chapter 10 for more on man-to-man coverage.)

Defensive players use the in-your-face technique of putting their bodies on the line of scrimmage and trying to knock the receivers off stride and out of their routes (see the later section "Looking at Passing Patterns" for more info on routes). The defensive back's objective is to "hurt" the receiver first and then try to push him out of bounds (it's illegal for a receiver to return to the field and catch a pass) while trying to get the receiver's mind off running a perfect route and making a catch. The entire defensive attitude is to take the receiver out of the game, mentally and physically.

A receiver must approach this in-your-face technique as if he's in an alley fight against someone who wants to take him down. When the center snaps the ball, the receiver must bring his arms and hands up to his face just like a fighter would. The receiver wants to prevent the defensive player from putting his hands into his chest by counterpunching his attempts. The working of the receiver's hands is similar to the "wax on, wax off" style taught in the movie *The Karate Kid.*

After the receiver fights off the defensive back's hands, he must dip his shoulder and take off running. This technique is called *dip and rip* because the receiver dips his shoulder and rips through the defender's attempt to hold or shove him with a strong punch, like a boxer throwing a great uppercut to his opponent's chin. This move was a favorite of Hall-of-Famer Jerry Rice, who's possibly the greatest receiver of all time.

Another method of defeating man-to-man coverage is to use the *swim technique.* With the swim, the receiver's arms and hands are still in the same position as the dip and rip, and the receiver must again get his hands up in a boxing position. But at the snap of the ball, instead of lowering his shoulder and ripping through, the receiver tries to slap the defensive back's hands one way while heading in the opposite direction. When the defensive back reacts, the receiver uses his free arm and takes a freestyle stroke (raises an arm up and forward and then brings it back to the side) over the defensive back while trying to pull the arm back underneath and behind him. This entire action takes a split second. With the swim technique, it's critical that the receiver doesn't allow the defensive back to catch his arm and grab hold under his armpit to prevent him from running downfield.

Note: Bigger, stronger receivers use the dip and rip method, whereas smaller, faster receivers usually use the swim technique.

Defining Important Passing Terms

This section lists the words and descriptions frequently mentioned when discussing the passing game. As a player, my favorite word was *sack:* a defender's dream and a quarterback's nightmare (you can find a definition in the following list). I had 84 sacks in my career, every one a great thrill. I deflected quite a few pass attempts, too. Read on and you'll get my meaning:

» **Deflection:** A *deflection* happens when a defensive player uses his hands or arms to knock down (or deflect) a pass before it reaches the receiver. This act usually occurs near the line of scrimmage when defensive linemen jump, arms raised, into a quarterback's visual passing lane, hoping to deflect the pass. Deflections can lead to an interception or incompletion.

>> **Holding:** *Holding* is the most common penalty called against the offense when it's attempting to pass. The offense receives a 10-yard penalty (and repeat of down) when any offensive player holds a defensive player by grabbing his jersey or locking his arm onto the defensive player's arm while that player is trying to sack the quarterback. This penalty is also known as illegal use of the hands, arms, or any part of the body.

>> **Illegal forward pass:** A quarterback can't cross the line of scrimmage and throw the ball. This penalty often occurs when the quarterback runs forward, attempting to evade defensive players, and forgets where the line of scrimmage is. The offense is penalized 5 yards from the spot of the foul and loses a down.

>> **Intentional grounding:** This penalty occurs when a quarterback standing in the pocket deliberately throws the ball out of bounds or into the ground. It can be interpreted in the following three ways, with the first two drastically penalizing the offense:

- **No. 1:** The quarterback is attempting to pass from his own end zone and, prior to being tackled, intentionally grounds the ball, throwing it out of bounds or into the ground. The defense is awarded a safety, worth two points, and the offense loses possession of the ball and has to kick the ball from its own 20-yard line.

- **No. 2:** The quarterback is trapped behind his own line of scrimmage and intentionally grounds the ball for fear of being tackled for a loss. This penalty is a loss of down, and the ball is placed at the spot of the foul, which in this case is where the quarterback was standing when he grounded the ball. Otherwise, the intentional grounding penalty calls for loss of down and 10 yards. However, a NFL quarterback can intentionally ground the ball when escaping the pocket while also out of the tackle box. Of course, there must be a receiver in the vicinity of where he throws the football.

- **No. 3:** The quarterback steps back from the center and immediately throws the ball into the ground, intentionally grounding it. This is referred to as *spiking the ball.* This play is common when an offense wants to stop the clock without calling a timeout because it either wants to preserve its timeouts or is out of timeouts. For this type of intentional grounding, the penalty is simply a loss of a down.

>> **Interception:** An *interception* is the act of any defensive player catching a pass. Along with a fumble, an interception is the worst thing that can happen to a quarterback and his team. It's called a *turnover* because the defensive team gains possession of the ball and is allowed to run with the ball in an attempt to score. (Deion Sanders was probably the greatest threat on an interception because of his open-field running ability.)

>> **Roughing the passer:** This penalty was devised to protect the quarterback from injury. After the ball leaves the quarterback's hand, any defensive player must attempt to avoid contact with him. Because a defensive player's momentum may cause him to inadvertently run into the quarterback, he's allowed to take one step after he realizes that the ball has been released. But if he hits the quarterback on his second step, knowing that the ball is gone, the *referee* (the official standing near the quarterback) can call *roughing*. It's a 15-yard penalty against the defense and an automatic first down. This penalty is difficult to call unless the defensive player clearly hits the quarterback well after the quarterback releases the ball. After all, it's pretty tough for defensive ends, who are usually over 6 feet and weigh 250 pounds, to come to an abrupt stop from a full sprint.

Roughing the passer penalties can also be called on defenders who

- Strike the quarterback in the head or neck area, regardless of whether the hit was intentional.

- Flagrantly hit the quarterback in the knee area or lower when the defender has an unrestricted path to the quarterback.

- Put their body weight on the quarterbacks while making a sack. I feel that league officials went overboard with this rule. It's asking too much of defensive players to tackle without using their weight in the process.

Keep in mind that these penalties apply only when the quarterback is acting as a passer. If the quarterback tucks the ball and runs, defenders can hit him just like any other ball carrier. However, quarterbacks have the option of giving themselves up while running, which basically means that they slide feet first to avoid being hit. If a defender hits a sliding quarterback, he's assessed a 15-yard unnecessary roughness penalty.

>> **Sack:** A *sack* happens when the quarterback is tackled behind the line of scrimmage by any defensive player. The sack is the most prominent defensive statistic, one the NFL has officially kept since 1982. (All other kinds of tackles are considered unofficial statistics because individual teams are responsible for recording them.) Colleges have been recording sacks for the same length of time.

>> **Trapping:** Receivers are asked to make a lot of difficult catches, but this one is never allowed. *Trapping* is when a receiver uses the ground to help him catch a pass that's thrown on a low trajectory. For an official to not rule a reception a trap, the receiver must make sure either his hands or his arms are between the ball and the ground when he makes a legal catch. Often, this play occurs so quickly, only instant replay can verify whether or not the ball was cleanly caught. The NFL now allows for the ball to touch the ground as long as the receiver has total control of it during the catch.

Looking at Passing Patterns

When watching at home or in the stands, you can look for basic pass patterns used in all levels of football. These pass patterns (also known as *pass routes*) may be a single part of a larger play. In fact, on a single play, two or three receivers may be running an equal number of different pass patterns.

TIP

By knowing passing patterns, you can discover what part of the field or which defensive player(s) the offense wants to attack, or how an offense wants to compete with a specific defense. (Sometimes, a pass pattern is run to defeat a defensive scheme designed to stop a team's running game by moving defenders away from the actual point of attack.) The following list includes the most common patterns receivers run during games:

» **Comeback:** Teams use this pass pattern effectively when the receiver is extremely fast and the defensive player gives him a 5-yard cushion, which means that the defensive player stays that far away from him, fearing his speed. On the comeback, the receiver runs hard downfield, between 12 and 20 yards, and then turns sharply to face the football. The comeback route generally is run along the sideline. To work effectively, the quarterback usually throws the ball before the receiver turns. He throws to a spot where he expects the receiver to stop and turn. This kind of pass is called a *timing pass* because the quarterback throws it before the receiver turns and looks toward the quarterback or before he makes his move backward.

» **Crossing:** The crossing pattern is an effective pass against man-to-man coverage because it's designed for the receiver to beat his defender by running across the field. The receiver can line up on the right side of the line of scrimmage, run straight for 10 yards, and then cut quickly to his left. When the receiver cuts, he attempts to lose the man covering him with either a head or shoulder *fake* (a sudden jerk with his upper body to one side or the other) or a quick stutter-step. This route is designed for two receivers, usually one on either side of the formation. It allows one receiver to interfere with his teammate's defender as the two receivers cross near the middle of the field. The play is designed for the quarterback to pass to the receiver on the run as the receiver crosses in front of his field of vision.

» **Curl:** For this 8- to 12-yard pass beyond the line of scrimmage, the receiver stops and then turns immediately, making a slight curl before facing the quarterback's throw. The receiver usually takes a step or two toward the quarterback and the ball before the pass reaches him. The curl tends to be a high-percentage completion because the receiver wants to shield the defender with his back, and the intention is simply to gain a few yards. Big tight ends tend to like the curl.

>> **Hook:** This common pass play, which is also known as a buttonhook, is designed mostly for a tight end, who releases downfield and then makes a small turn, coming back to face the quarterback and receive the ball. A hook is similar to a curl, except the turn is made more abruptly and the pass is shorter, at 5 to 8 yards. It's a timing pass, so the quarterback usually releases the ball before the tight end starts his turn.

>> **Post:** This is a long pass, maybe as long as 40 to 50 yards, in which the receiver runs straight downfield, and then cuts on a 45-degree angle toward the "post," or goalposts. (Most teams use the hash marks as a guiding system for both the quarterback and the receiver.) A coach calls this play when one safety is deep and the offense believes it can isolate a fast receiver against him. The receiver runs straight downfield, possibly hesitating a split second as if he might cut the route inside or outside, and then cuts toward the post. The hesitation may cause the safety, or whoever is positioned in the deep center of the field, to break stride or slow down. The receiver needs only an extra step on the defender for this play to be successful. The quarterback puts enough loft on the ball to enable the receiver to catch the pass in stride.

>> **Slant:** This pass is designed for an inside receiver (a flanker) who's aligned 5 yards out from the offensive line, possibly from a tight end or the offensive tackle. The receiver runs straight for 3 to 8 yards and then slants his route, angling toward the middle of the field. A slant is effective against both zone and man-to-man coverage because it's designed to find an open space in either defensive scheme (see Chapter 10 for details on both of these types of coverage).

>> **Square-out:** The receiver on this pattern runs 10 yards down the field and then cuts sharply toward the sideline, parallel to the line of scrimmage. The square-out is also a timing play because the quarterback must deliver the pass before the receiver reaches the sideline and steps out of bounds, sometimes before he even cuts. The quarterback must really fire this pass, which is why commentators sometimes refer to it as a *bullet throw*. The route works against both man-to-man and zone coverage. The receiver must roll his shoulder toward the inside before cutting toward the sideline. The quarterback throws the pass, leading the receiver toward the sideline.

>> **Streak (or Fly):** This is a 20- to 40-yard pass, generally to a receiver on the quarterback's throwing side (which is right if he's right-handed or left if he's left-handed). The receiver, who's aligned wide and near the sidelines, runs as fast as he can down the sideline, hoping to lose the defensive man in the process. This pass must be thrown accurately because both players tend to be running as fast as they can, and often the cornerback is as fast as the receiver. This play is designed to loosen up the defense, making it believe the quarterback and the receiver have the ability to throw deep whenever they want to. Moving a defense back or away from the line of scrimmage allows the offense

an opportunity to complete shorter passes and execute run plays. To complete this pass, the quarterback makes sure a safety isn't playing deep to that side of the field. Otherwise, with the ball in the air for a long time, a free safety can angle over and intercept the pass. If the quarterback sees the safety near his streaking receiver, he must throw to another receiver elsewhere on the field.

» **Swing:** This is a simple throw to a running back who runs out of the backfield toward the sideline. The quarterback generally throws the pass when the running back turns and heads upfield. The swing is usually a *touch pass,* meaning the quarterback doesn't necessarily throw it as hard as he does a deep square-out (described earlier in this list). He wants to be able to float it over a linebacker and make it easy for the running back to catch. The area in which the back is running is known as *the flat* because it's 15 yards outside the hash marks and close to where the numbers on the field are placed. The receiver's momentum most likely will take him out of bounds after he catches the ball unless he's able to avoid the first few tacklers he faces.

Figure 5-3 shows the many pass patterns and how they funnel off what's called a *route tree.* The tree is numbered: 4 is a square-out; 5 is a slant; 6 is a curl or a hook; 7 is a post; 8 is a streak or fly; and 9 is a corner route. When calling a pass play, these numbers, which can vary by team, refer to the specific pass pattern (or route) called by the quarterback.

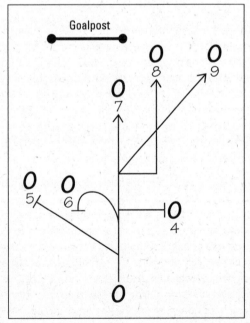

FIGURE 5-3:
A route tree with the pass patterns numbered.

© John Wiley & Sons, Inc.

Getting into the Shotgun Formation

In football terminology, *formation* describes how the players on offense line up before the ball is snapped. As football has evolved, so have the formations. The *shotgun* passing formation was devised by San Francisco 49ers head coach Red Hickey in 1960. Hickey feared the Baltimore Colts' great pass rush, so he had his quarterback, John Brodie, line up 7 yards behind the line of scrimmage (see Figure 5-4). Hickey figured that Brodie would have more time to see his receivers and could release the ball before the defensive rush reached him. The strategy worked, and the 49ers upset the mighty Colts.

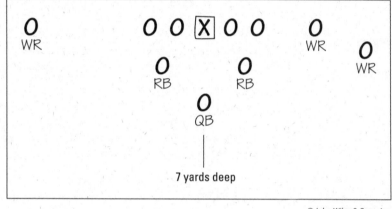

FIGURE 5-4: The shotgun formation puts the quarterback 7 yards behind the line of scrimmage.

© John Wiley & Sons, Inc.

Offenses use the shotgun when they have poor pass blocking or when they're facing excellent pass rushers. Teams also use the shotgun when they want to pass on every down, usually when they're behind. However, many offenses use the shotgun simply because the quarterback and the coach like to use it. Other teams use the shotgun only when they're in obvious passing situations — such as on third down when they need 4 or more yards for a first down, or anytime they need more than 10 yards for a first down.

REMEMBER

Despite its versatility, the shotgun formation has a couple downsides:

>> The center must be able to make an accurate, chest-high, 7-yard snap to the quarterback.

>> You can't fool the defensive players; they know you're probably throwing the ball, and the pass rushers won't hesitate to sprint for your quarterback in hopes of a sack.

PASSING AND CATCHING GREATS

A football team needs all kinds of warriors to make the passing game work. Here are a few snapshots of the performers who are worth remembering. Many of them mixed style with grace, talent, and toughness.

- The San Diego Chargers had a receiver named "Bambi." Lance Alworth hated his nickname, which was given to him by a teammate who thought he had the speed and grace of a deer. Alworth had short hair and brown eyes and ran like the wind — right into the Pro Football Hall of Fame. Alworth was the second player to reach 10,000 receiving yards.

- Joe Willie Namath was one of the first players to wear white football shoes. "Broadway Joe" was a flashy bachelor quarterback for the New York Jets in the 1960s and early 1970s who once wore a fur coat on the sidelines. In the 1967 season, he threw for 4,007 yards in just 14 games. And Namath followed through on his guarantee to beat the heavily favored Baltimore Colts in Super Bowl III.

- Earl "Curly" Lambeau was the first quarterback/coach of the Green Bay Packers. In the 1930s, Coach Lambeau (the Green Bay stadium is named after him) opted for a wide-open passing game when most NFL teams were still slugging each other with the running game. Lambeau made stars of players like receiver Don Hutson (whom I describe in Chapter 20).

- Johnny Unitas is in the Hall of Fame, but he wasn't always a Baltimore Colts star. He played minor league football in 1955 for $3 a game. The Pittsburgh Steelers drafted him but then didn't believe that he was good enough to make their team and released him from their roster. Unitas, famous for his black high-top football shoes, ended up being the first quarterback to pass for 40,000 yards.

Teams need a quick-thinking quarterback who can set his feet quickly in order to use the shotgun formation effectively. In recent years, football coaches on all levels have decided to use the run-pass-option (known as RPO) from the shotgun formation, aligning a running back next to the quarterback. This formation allows the option of also running from the shotgun formation by either the quarterback, or, if he hands off, the running back.

Chapter **6**

Hitting the Ground Running

Running back may be the most physically demanding position in football. A great running back, whose productivity dictates his team's success, is asked to take a tremendous beating on a weekly basis. Every game he faces 11 angry men who have a license to physically punish him. Rarely does one defensive player bring down a great running back. He gets hit from every angle — high and low. Often, one player grabs hold of the running back while a number of defenders take clean shots at him.

HOWIE SAYS

One of the toughest football players I played with was running back Marcus Allen. Despite the continual beating he took, Allen would pick himself off the ground and, without showing any emotion, walk back to the huddle and prepare for the next play. I don't know how many times I saw Marcus look like he'd just gotten his head taken off and then come right back for more on the very next play. He was especially determined at the goal line, scoring a then–NFL-record 123 rushing touchdowns even though everyone in the stadium knew he would be running with the ball.

This chapter goes into detail about what makes a great running back — or a good one, for that matter. Obviously, a running back needs to be able to do more than just run with the football. A running back must also know his assignments, know the opposing defenses, and be aware of all the players on the field. So, in this chapter, I explain the many different running plays and the varied styles and types of people who fit the mold of a running back.

An Overview of the Ground Game

REMEMBER

In football, the *ground game* refers to running the football (as opposed to passing it). Running the ball is the basic premise of football, and it's the easiest way to move the ball. A team runs three times and gains 10 yards, and that's good enough for a first down and another set of four downs. What could be easier? In youth football, every team runs. After all, what 11-year-old can pass like former Miami Dolphins quarterback Dan Marino? Plus, learning the fundamentals of running the ball is much easier than learning how to run pass routes.

Most championship football teams are excellent at running the football. The Denver Broncos won the Super Bowl in 1998 because they had a better running game than the Green Bay Packers. The Broncos could run, and the Packers couldn't stop them and their talented running back, Terrell Davis. In fact, Denver's offensive line was really fired up for that game — they wanted to block and open holes — because they felt that the Packers, the media, and some NFL insiders weren't giving them enough respect.

The New York Giants won their second Super Bowl after the 1990 season, beating a superior Buffalo Bills team, because they could run the ball and keep the clock moving. They also kept the ball away from Buffalo's high-powered offense. This ploy is called *ball control*, which is a common football term. Running the ball is the best way to maintain possession and keep the clock moving when a team is ahead because the clock doesn't stop if a player is tackled in bounds. However, if the quarterback throws an incompletion, the clock stops. Stopping the clock is advantageous to the defense; it gives them a breather and the hope that they may get the ball back. So when a team is running the football successfully, usually it's physically whipping the other team. And that's the object of the game!

The NFL has become somewhat of a pass-happy league, but the running game is still vitally important. In 2018, 16 running backs rushed for more than 900 yards, with Ezekiel Elliott of the Dallas Cowboys leading the way with 1,434 yards. He averaged 4.7 yards per carry. Elliott, like most great running backs, was an above-average receiver, catching 77 passes for 567 yards, giving him 2,001 yards from scrimmage

Meeting the Men Who Play the Ground Game

Understanding what's going on during running plays is much easier when you know who's responsible for the running game. The next time you see an offense set up, look for the two players who line up in the *offensive backfield* (the area of the field behind the quarterback and the line of scrimmage). These players are the *running backs.* The smaller one is the main ball carrier, and the larger one is the guy charged with protecting the ball carrier. Read on to find out what each type of running back does, who tends to play in these positions, and how each player lines up behind the quarterback.

The halfback, a team's principal ball carrier

On most teams, the principal ball carrier is called the *halfback* (also called the *tailback* or the *running back*). When teams — be they high school, college, or NFL teams — find a good running back, they give him the ball. And they give it to him as often as he's willing and able to carry it. Figure 6-1 shows Los Angeles Rams running back Todd Gurley in action.

Most runners would probably tell you that they wouldn't mind carrying the ball even more often than they actually do. Toting the football is a status symbol, after all. The NFL record for rushing attempts in a single season belongs to Larry Johnson, then of the Kansas City Chiefs, who carried the ball 416 times in the 2006 season. That's an astonishing 26 carries per game! With passing dominating NFL offense, rookie running back Saquon Barkley of the New York Giants showed fans that receiving is almost as important as carries in 2018. The former Penn State back displayed his versatility by catching 91 passes to go with his 261 carries to lead the NFL with 2,028 yards from scrimmage.

FIGURE 6-1:
Running back
Todd Gurley of
the Los Angeles
Rams stretches
over the goal line
for a touchdown.

Photo credit: © Jonathan Bachman/Getty Images

The fullback, protector of the halfback

When a team employs two running backs in the offensive backfield, the bigger of the two is usually called the *fullback.* He's there to block and clear the way for the *halfback*, who's the main ball carrier. You may think that the fullback's job is a thankless one, but most fullbacks get a lot of satisfaction from making a great block (generally on a linebacker) and winning the physical battle against players who tend to be bigger than they are. However, most NFL teams these days don't have a fullback, preferring to use a tight end as an extra blocker. Others do use one as primarily a blocker and short-yardage ball carrier.

**HALL OF
FAME**

In the old days, some of the best runners were fullbacks. Marion Motley of the 1949 Cleveland Browns weighed almost 240 pounds and carried defenders down the field. Cookie Gilchrist was a 252-pound fullback with the Buffalo Bills in the mid-1960s; he was one devastating blocker and could run, too. So could 237-pound Larry Csonka, a former Miami Dolphin, who, along with 230-pound John Riggins of the Washington Redskins, was the dominant fullback of the 1970s. Riggins led the Redskins to Super Bowls in the early 1980s and scored 38 touchdowns in two consecutive seasons.

It's interesting to note that because of the way offenses have evolved, especially in college football, the traditional fullback position appears to be going the way of the dinosaur. Some NFL teams have no true fullback on their roster. The spread offense, with its emphasis on passing, doesn't require a fullback. Big, strong, fast players who in previous years might have played fullback are now playing on the other side of the ball, in the linebacker position.

RUNNING BACKS COME IN ALL SIZES AND SHAPES

You may hear football coaches say that a particular player is the prototype performer at a particular position, but no such prototype exists at running back. Running backs come in all sizes and shapes. Little guys like former Detroit Lion Barry Sanders, former Chicago Bear Walter Payton, and former Buffalo Bill Thurman Thomas, who were quick and slippery players, excelled at the highest level. Big brutes like Jim Brown of the Cleveland Browns, Earl Campbell of the Houston Oilers (now the Tennessee Titans), Jim Taylor of the Green Bay Packers, and Riggins also had successful NFL careers.

Running back Emmitt Smith, who scored a then-record 25 touchdowns in 1995 and who holds the NFL record for yards gained, was an example of the tough, physical inside runner who weighed only 210 pounds. Pittsburgh Steelers Hall of Fame tailback Jerome "The Bus" Bettis was 40 pounds heavier than Smith, but I still considered him a halfback rather than a fullback because he was the main runner on his team. And I can't forget former Dallas Cowboy Tony Dorsett, the great Marcus Allen, and former San Francisco 49ers Roger Craig and Tom Rathman — all good backs, but never listed as little guys *or* big brutes.

Next, let me clear up the myth that you have to be extremely fast to be an excellent running back. Marcus Allen had only average speed; in fact, some scouts thought he was too slow. But in his outstanding career, he scored 145 touchdowns and gained 12,243 yards rushing. Allen was elected to the Football Hall of Fame on his first try in 2003. He was football's finest *north/south runner* — which means he didn't mess around dancing "east" or "west" behind the line of scrimmage. When trapped by defensive players, the quickest and best way to gain yards is to go straight ahead; that's the primary trait of a north/south runner.

Little guys slip by opponents in the open field. They're difficult to grab hold of and tackle — it's almost like their shoulder pads are covered with butter. Barry Sanders fell into that group. So did Dorsett and Alvin Kamara, who scored 18 scrimmage touchdowns with the New Orleans Saints in 2018. On the other hand, big brutes like Jim Brown simply run over everyone. Brown never concerned himself with making tacklers miss him. At some point, every coach looks for a big back who can run over everyone in his way.

Regardless of their size or skill level, the common denominator among all these men is that they were physically tough, determined, and talented football players. Any type of runner can be a good running back, as long as he's playing in the right system and gets help from his teammates.

Exploring Running Back Fundamentals

Running backs need more skills than players at other positions. That's because on any given play, a running back may run the ball, catch a pass, or block an opposing player. Occasionally running backs are even called upon to throw a pass or kick the ball. To help you appreciate what running backs do, the sections that follow look at what goes into playing this very important position.

The basic skills

On most football teams, the running back is the best athlete on the team. The demands on him, both physical and mental, are great. Every running back must be able to do the following well:

>> **Line up in the right stance:** The most common stance for a running back is the *two-point stance.* A tailback in the I formation (I tell you all about this in the later "Lining Up: The Formations" section) often uses the two-point stance with his hands on his thighs, his feet shoulder width apart, and his weight on the balls of his feet. His head is up, his legs are slightly bent at the knees, and his feet are parallel to one another, with his toes pointed toward the line of scrimmage. (For more information on running back stances, see the later "The stances" section.)

>> **Receive a handoff:** A runner must receive the football from the quarterback without fumbling. To do this properly, his arms must form a pocket outside his stomach. If the back is right-handed, he bends his left arm at the elbow in a 90-degree angle, keeps his forearm parallel to the ground, and turns up the palm of his left hand. His right arm is up to receive the ball so that when the quarterback places the ball in his stomach area, his right forearm and hand close around it. Figure 6-2 shows how a running back takes a handoff and holds the ball while running. After he has possession of the ball, the back grips the ball at the tip and tucks the other end into his elbow with one side of the ball resting against his body (so his arm is in somewhat of a V-shape).

>> **Run at top speed:** Ideally, a running back is running at near top speed when he grabs a handoff. His head is upright and his shoulders are square to the line of scrimmage. He's also leaning forward slightly to keep his body low, and his legs are driving forward. When making cuts, the back plants and accelerates off the foot that's opposite of the direction he's running (for example, if he wants to go left, he plants on his right foot). When running behind a blocker, he's behind the blocker's outside hip. When the block is made, the back cuts quickly behind the blocker's inside hip when turning upfield. For *cut-back running,* the back fakes a step away from the defender (trying not to shift too much weight) and then turns quickly to the inside of the defender (of course, the defender must move for the cut-back to be successful).

>> **See the field:** When you watch video highlights of a great running back like Barry Sanders of the Detroit Lions, you'd swear he had eyes in the back of his head. How else can you explain his cuts and moves and his escapes from defensive trouble? Like a basketball guard running a fast break, a back needs to have peripheral vision. He needs to be able to see what's coming at him from the corners of the field. Backs with exceptional speed (4.4 seconds in the 40-yard dash) can gain many more yards by seeing where the defensive pursuit is coming from and running away from it. However, backs without great speed can be successful by sensing danger while trying to maintain a straight line to the end zone (these backs are called *north/south runners*). But backs with great speed can outrun many defenders by heading to the corner of the end zone if a defender is 10 yards away to their left or right.

>> **Block for another back:** A team's principal running back is rarely a good blocker. The best blockers among the backs are the fullbacks, who are asked to block players 30 to 100 pounds heavier than they are. A running back needs to stay low and explode into the defender's upper body while using his hands (in closed fists) and forearms to make contact. A lot of backs try to block a linebacker or defensive back low (at his legs), but this technique is rarely successful. Many defensive players are capable of jumping up and then shoving the back down to the ground as they move past him. Coaches want their backs to get a piece of the defender and knock him off his line to the quarterback or ball carrier. Many backs in the NFL are also frequently asked to block as a form of pass protection for the quarterback.

FIGURE 6-2:
One of a running back's main concerns is protecting the ball by receiving the quarterback's handoff properly.

© John Wiley & Sons, Inc.

The job description

A running back has a responsibility, or assignment, on every play. I think running backs have the toughest job on the football field because they have to not only know every play like a quarterback but also make physical contact on virtually every down.

HOWIE SAYS

No matter how fast an athlete is, how big a brute he is, or how slippery or quick he is, he won't be able to play as a running back if he doesn't have a brain and can't think on his feet. I think the main reason many outstanding college runners never make it in professional football is that the pro game simply overloads their brains.

Here's a rundown of a running back's job description:

» **He's an every-minute player.** While he's on the field, he never has a minute to let up, and he never has a chance to take a play off. He can't afford to line up and merely go through the motions. When he doesn't have the ball, he must follow through with his fakes and pretend that he has the ball.

» **On every play, he must know what down it is and how many yards the team needs for a first down.** He must know when to lower his shoulder and go for a first down and when to keep a drive alive by making a move and gaining a little extra yardage, helping his team move into scoring range.

» **He must know the time on the clock in order to know when to go out of bounds and when to turn upfield and gain extra yardage.** Stopping the clock is critical when a team is behind in the score.

» **He must know the defense's various alignments and then adjust his thinking to those alignments on pass plays and running plays.** On a pass play, he must know the protection scheme because he may be asked to throw a block to give the quarterback time to pass.

» **He must know every play and all its variations.** For example, on one running play, he may have to block a linebacker. But on the same play called against a different defensive front, he may be asked to block a defensive end.

On running plays, a running back must know the opposition's defensive schemes so he can predict which defender will be the first guy coming to make the tackle. Although this information may not be important to the runner carrying the ball, it's valuable for the other back who's asked to block on the play.

COLLEGE RUNNING BACKS VERSUS PRO RUNNING BACKS

In college, coaches give a great high school running back a scholarship, and they have him for three or four years. Now, it doesn't look good for your program if you beg a player to come to your school and then end up cutting him or taking away his scholarship because he doesn't live up to your expectations. This is what I mean when I say that he's yours for four years.

The difference for pro running backs is that the NFL is a big business. Running backs can be signed to big contracts, but teams can always cut them and lose nothing but a few days or weeks of coaching time and a few dollars. Today, such dismissals are viewed simply as bad money deals or bad investments. Therefore, when a head coach finds a runner who can run for more than 1,000 yards a season, score whenever he needs to, and carry the team when the quarterback is having an off day, he knows he has a winner.

>> **He must know every pass route called because he may be the first receiving option on a play.** He must know the defense's coverage in order to adjust his route accordingly. For example, if the linebacker goes out, he may have to go in, and vice versa. He must know how deep he has to get on every pass route so that he's timed up with the quarterback's drop. Because the quarterback may throw the ball before the runner turns to catch the ball, he must run the exact distance; if he doesn't, the timing of the play will be messed up.

>> **He must know every hole number in the playbook.** A typical NFL playbook may contain between 50 and 100 running plays. The *holes* (the spaces opened up by blockers), which are numbered, are the only things that tell the running back where he's supposed to run with the ball. The play will either specify the hole number or be designed for a specific hole.

The stances

A running back can use two stances: One is the *up stance*, in which he has his hands resting on his thighs, a few inches above his knees, as shown in Figure 6-3. This stance is also called the *two-point stance*.

FIGURE 6-3:
A running back's up stance (or two-point stance).

The second is the *down stance*, in which he puts his right hand on the ground like a lineman, as shown in Figure 6-4. It's also called the *three-point stance* because one hand and both feet are on the ground.

FIGURE 6-4:
A running back's down stance (or three-point stance).

Runners can use the two-point stance when they're in the *split-back formation*, with one back aligned to the left of the quarterback and one to the right. However, most coaches prefer their runners to use the three-point stance in this alignment because they believe it provides the runner with a faster start than the two-point stance — much like a sprinter bursting from his blocks. Some runners remain in the two-point stance in split backs, which can tip off the defense that they're going to pass-protect for the quarterback or run out for a pass. The running backs can then resort to a three-point stance with the intention of confusing the defense.

In the *I formation,* so named because the center, quarterback, fullback, and half-back line up behind one another to form a letter *I,* the deep back is always in a two-point stance. The fullback in the I formation is in front of the tailback. He can be in either a two-point or a three-point stance because he's blocking on 95 percent of the plays. The two-point stance is better on passing downs because it enables the running back to see the defensive alignment better — meaning he can see whether a linebacker may be blitzing, especially if he must block this defender. The three-point stance is better for blocking because the running back can exert his force upward and into the defender's chest and upper body.

The number one priority

The most important aspect of a running back's game is protecting the football. On the first day of practice, the first thing the coach tells his running backs is this: If you don't protect the football, you won't play. By *protecting the football,* I mean not fumbling the ball and leaving it on the ground where the opposition can recover it and gain possession. How well you protect the football is more a matter of how well you concentrate, not how big you are.

To help them protect the ball (and themselves), running backs have to know *pursuit* and *angles.* I'm talking football language here, not physics. What I mean is that the runner must understand where the defensive players are coming from (the pursuit) and from what direction (the angle) they plan on tackling him. If a runner understands these basic principles, he can figure out the direction the defensive players are coming from and prepare for contact and protecting the football.

Before contact, the running back braces the ball against his body while protecting the outside of the ball with his hand and forearm. Some backs prepare for the collision by wrapping their other arm around the football as well. Also, the back dips his shoulders and head and rolls his shoulders inward away from where he expects the first contact to come from. When facing smaller defenders, the running back may use a *stiff arm* (extending his free hand) to jostle the defender in his face mask or shoulder area. A back uses a stiff arm to push a tackler away from him or to reduce the tackler's ability to go after his legs.

DORSETT GOES THE DISTANCE

A player can return a kick, punt, or interception for 100 yards or more to score a touchdown, but the longest possible run is 99 yards. Former Dallas Cowboys running back Tony Dorsett, a Heisman Trophy award winner from the University of Pittsburgh, covered exactly that distance in 1983.

The amazing part about the play is that Ron Springs, the Cowboys' other running back, was supposed to get the ball; the play was designed for him. But Springs misunderstood quarterback Danny White's call and left the huddle, returning to the sidelines. With Springs gone, Dallas had only ten players on the field. And because quarterbacks don't do much blocking, only 8 Cowboys were available to block 11 Minnesota Vikings (I say only 8 because one of the remaining 9 was Dorsett, who was carrying the ball).

Dallas, coached by the highly specialized and inventive Tom Landry, always did a lot of substituting. But White didn't know that Springs had left the huddle. As White turned away from the line of scrimmage, looking for Springs, he instead came face to face with Dorsett. White did what any panicked quarterback would do: He handed the ball to Dorsett. But the play didn't end up being a flop. Dorsett faked left, stopped, and then headed around the right end. He broke through the first line of defenders and was off to the races.

Dorsett's run still stands as the longest run from the line of scrimmage in NFL history. It was equaled in 2018 by Derrick Henry of the Tennessee Titans. Henry was a Heisman Trophy winner at Alabama, but his production has been shy of Dorsett's and many other NFL running backs.

Lining Up: The Formations

An offensive *formation* is how the offense aligns all 11 of its players prior to using a particular play. A team can run or pass out of many formations, but for this chapter, I selected three backfield formations that focus specifically on running backs. One is the *pro-set,* which is also known as the *split-back* or *split T formation.* Another is the *I formation* — where both runners are aligned together behind one another and behind the quarterback and center. The third formation is the I formation's hybrid, the *offset I formation.* Most teams give these offset formations names like Jack, Queen, Far, Near, and so on.

Split-back formation

In the split-back formation, the runners are aligned behind the two guards about 5 yards behind the line of scrimmage, as shown in Figure 6-5. Teams use this formation because it's difficult for the defense to gauge whether the offense is running or passing. With split backs, the backfield is balanced and not aligned toward one side or the other, making it more difficult for the defense to anticipate what the play will be. This formation may be a better passing formation because the backs can swing out of the backfield to either side as receivers.

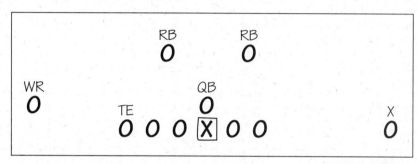

FIGURE 6-5:
In the split-back formation, the two RBs line up behind the two guards.

I formation

In the I formation, the tailback (TB) — the runner who will carry the ball — can place himself as deep as 7 yards from the line of scrimmage, as shown in Figure 6-6. By stepping this far back, the runner believes he'll be in full stride when he nears the line of scrimmage. Consequently, the I formation is ideally suited to a team with a great running back. Also, the depth allows him to have complete vision of his blockers and the defensive players' first reaction to the run. This formation is called the I because the quarterback (QB), fullback (FB), and tailback form an *I*, with the fullback between the quarterback and tailback.

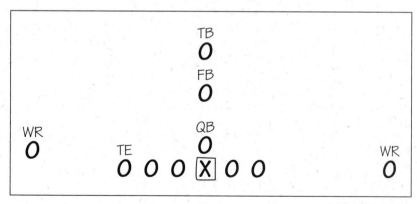

FIGURE 6-6:
In the I formation, the TB lines up 7 yards behind the line of scrimmage with a FB in front of him.

SINGLE WING

The *single wing* was an offensive formation that was popular in the early years of the NFL. Pop Warner developed the formation around 1908. It used four players in the backfield: the quarterback, tailback, wingback, and fullback. In the single wing, the tailback, not the quarterback, was the primary passer and runner. The quarterback was a blocking back like today's fullback.

In this formation, the quarterback was positioned close to the line of scrimmage and in a gap (the spacing) between two offensive linemen. The wingback was aligned behind and outside the strong-side end. The fullback was a few steps from the tailback and also aligned to the strong side. Back then, the offensive line generally was unbalanced — two linemen were to one side of the center and four were to the other side. The strong side was the side where the four offensive linemen were lined up. The ball was snapped to the tailback, not the quarterback, who was about 4 yards behind the center.

Most of the time, offenses ran the ball from the single wing; it was a power football formation. However, with the tailback doing a lot of spinning and faking, the single wing added deception. The tailback often would lateral the ball to another back. Teams would run reverses, counters, and trap plays from the formation while also passing the ball.

Offset I formation

In the offset I formation, the running back (RB) remains deep, 5 to 7 yards from the quarterback. When the running back is this deep, the majority of the time the team plans to run the ball. The fullback (FB), or blocking back, can be as close as 3 yards to the line of scrimmage, as shown in Figure 6–7. The other back wants to be close to his target: the defender he must block. A good fullback needs only 2 yards before making blocking contact. Also, he's deep enough in case the play requires him to go in motion to either side and swing to the outside for a possible reception. The fullback can be set to the strong side or the weak side of the formation.

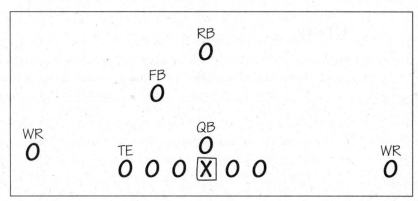

FIGURE 6-7:
The FB is set to the strong side in this version of the offset I formation; the RB remains deep.

Walking through the Basic Running Plays

If you're watching closely, you may notice your local high school football team using some of the same running plays that the NFL pros do. That's because the following basic running plays are used in all levels of football.

Blast or dive

Every team has the blast or dive run in its playbook; it's the simplest of carries. Usually led by a blocking fullback, the running back takes a quick handoff from the quarterback and hits a hole between an offensive guard and a tackle. On some teams, this run ends up between a guard and the center. The offense calls this run when it needs a yard or two for a first down. The runner lowers his head and hopes to *move the pile* (or push through defenders) before the middle linebacker tackles him.

Counter

This play is an intentional misdirection run on the part of the offense. The quarterback fakes a lateral toss to one back who's heading right, running parallel to the line of scrimmage. He's the decoy. The quarterback then turns and hands off to the remaining runner in the backfield, generally a fullback, who runs toward the middle of the line, hoping to find an opening between either guard and the center.

Draw

This is a disguised run, which means it initially looks like a pass play. The offensive linemen draw back like they're going to pass-protect for the quarterback (QB). The quarterback then drops back and, instead of setting up to pass, he turns and hands the ball to the runner, as shown in Figure 6-8. After the running back (RB) receives the ball, he wants to reach his maximum speed quickly to take advantage of the anticipated huge holes at the line of scrimmage. The goal of every draw play is to get the defensive linemen charging at the quarterback, only to be pushed aside by the offensive linemen at the last second. To fool the defense with this run, a team must have an above average passing game.

FIGURE 6-8: How the RB moves in the draw play.

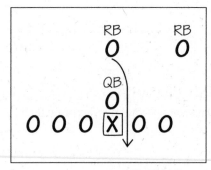

Off-tackle

The off-tackle is the oldest run around — it's a byproduct of the old single wing offense from more than 100 years ago (see the nearby "Single wing" sidebar for more information on this offense). It's a strong-side run, meaning the halfback (HB) heads toward the end of the line where the tight end, the extra blocker, lines up. The runner wants to take advantage of the hole supplied by the tackle, tight end, and his running mate, the fullback (FB). He can take the ball either around the tight end, as shown in Figure 6-9, or outside the tackle. He hopes that the fullback will block the outside linebacker.

Pitch

This run is usually from a two-back formation. The quarterback (QB) takes the snap and fakes a handoff to the first back (HB), who's heading directly toward the line of scrimmage; he then tosses (or pitches) the ball laterally to the other runner (FB), who has begun to move to the outside, as shown in Figure 6-10. The runner can either take the pitch outside or cut back toward the inside. Pitch plays can be designed to go in either direction.

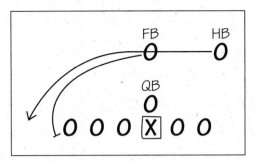

FIGURE 6-9:
The FB clears a path for the HB in the off-tackle run.

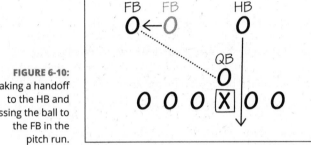

FIGURE 6-10:
Faking a handoff to the HB and tossing the ball to the FB in the pitch run.

Reverse

For this play, the halfback (HB) receives the handoff from the quarterback (QB) and then runs laterally behind the line of scrimmage. (The play can be designed for the back to run in either direction.) The ball carrier meets up with a wide receiver (WR) or flanker running toward him and then hands the ball to that receiver or flanker, as shown in Figure 6-11. The offensive line blocks as if the ball were intended for the halfback so that the defensive players follow him. After the receiver is in motion and has the ball, he runs in the opposite direction, or against the flow of his own blockers. This play really works if the receiver is a fast and tricky runner. It helps if the interior defensive players and linebacker fall for the halfback's initial fake. Also, the weak-side defender, the last line of defense, must leave his position and chase the halfback. Otherwise, this weak-side defender is in perfect position to tackle the receiver.

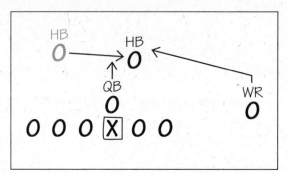

FIGURE 6-11:
For a reverse, the
QB hands off to
the HB, who then
hands the ball to
the WR.

Slant

This run is exactly like it sounds. Instead of running straight toward the line of scrimmage, the runner (HB) slants his angle outside after he receives the ball, as shown in Figure 6-12. A slant is used to take advantage of defenses that over pursue, allowing offensive linemen to be more effective by pushing the defenders to one side.

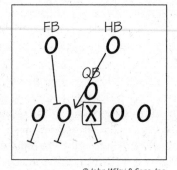

FIGURE 6-12:
The HB runs to
his right after
aligning on the
left side in a slant
play.

Sweep

This run is pretty common in every team's playbook. As shown in Figure 6-13, it begins with two or more offensive linemen (which in the figure are labeled as LG and RG) *pulling,* or leaving their stances and running toward the outside of the line of scrimmage. The ball carrier (HB) takes a handoff from the quarterback (QB) and runs parallel to the line of scrimmage, waiting for his blockers to lead the way around the end. The run is designed to attack the defensive end, outside linebacker, and cornerback on a specific side. Most right-handed teams (that is, teams that have a right-handed quarterback) run the sweep toward the left defensive end. The sweep can begin with the other back faking receipt of a handoff and running in the opposite direction of where the sweep run is headed. Many teams simply have the other back, a fullback (FB), help lead the blocking for the ball carrier.

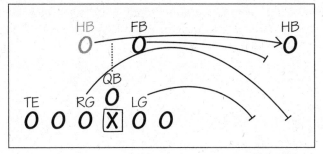

FIGURE 6-13: The sweep calls for the HB to follow the two pulling guards and FB around to the weak side.

Fly sweep

This play has become common in the last decade as teams with versatile receivers use them as runners. As shown in Figure 6-14, the receivers line up in their normal positions, and one of them goes in motion toward the quarterback. After the ball is snapped, the quarterback simply flips the ball to receiver as he passes in front of him. The play is blocked like a typical sweep run. Teams that use this play a lot, like the Los Angeles Rams, can also use the fly sweep design as deception, faking the handoff and then either throwing to the receiver as he runs downfield or to another receiver.

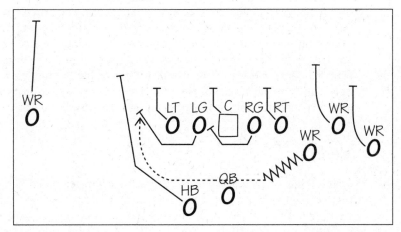

FIGURE 6-14: In a fly sweep, the receiver is the ball carrier.

Stretch

The stretch play, or outside zone run, has become more popular in recent years. The quarterback (QB) takes the snap from under center and sprints into the backfield to meet the ball carrier (HB) as he runs toward the edge of the formation, outside the tight end. As shown in Figure 6-15, the strong side guard and tackle pull to lead the runner as the tight end blocks down to seal off any defenders coming from the inside.

FIGURE 6-15:
The stretch play allows the running back to quickly reach the edge of the formation.

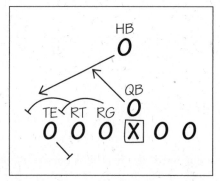

Trap

Teams don't use this run very often because it requires quick and agile offensive linemen, and most teams use big blockers these days. As shown in Figure 6-16, the trap is a sucker run that, like the draw, is intended to take advantage of the defensive players' willingness to attack the offense. The trap works well against an aggressive defensive line and linebackers. On the trap, a guard (LG in the figure) vacates his normal area, allowing the defensive player to cross the line of scrimmage and have a clear lane into the backfield. The guard from the opposite side then moves across the line and blocks the defender. This action by the guard is called *pulling*, hence the term *pulling guard*. The trap play has to be well-timed, and after the ball carrier receives the ball, he must quickly dart through the hole behind the trap block.

Veer

College teams run this play more often than pro teams do because it generally requires a quarterback who's quick-footed and an excellent ball-handler — in other words, a quarterback who can run if he has to. As shown in Figure 6-17, the veer is a quick-hitting run in which the ball can be handed to either running back, whose routes are determined by the slant or charge of the defensive linemen. The term *veer* comes from the back veering away from the defense. In Figure 6-16, the quarterback (QB) hands off to the halfback (HB), who veers to the right behind his blockers.

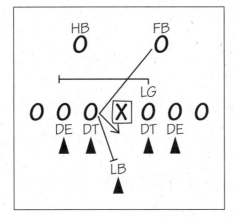

FIGURE 6-16:
As the FB takes a handoff for the trap play, the LG pulls to his right.

© John Wiley & Sons, Inc.

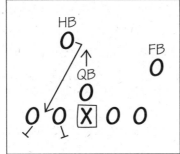

FIGURE 6-17:
In the veer run, the QB hands off to the HB, who veers to the hole on the right.

© John Wiley & Sons, Inc.

Run-pass option

For a quarterback to run this play, he must possess the skills and toughness of a running back. But he also must correctly read the intent of defenders. The beauty of the play, if performed correctly, is the stress it puts on the defense. Not only can the quarterback pull the ball back from the running back and take off running, but he can step back and throw to a receiver running a slant pass. In high school and college, teams with exceptional athletic quarterbacks can have a high-scoring offense because defenses at that level generally don't have enough speedy defenders to stop this play. As you can see in Figure 6-18, the quarterback reads a second-level defender and decides whether to pass the ball or hand it off based on the defenses post-snap movement. If he doesn't like either of those options, the quarterback can elect to run where the blockers planned to block for the running back or make a split-second decision to find his own running lane. If the "read" defenders attacks the line of scrimmage to help against the run, the QB throws to the WR running a slant. The WR should be open with the defender vacating his area of the field. If the "read" defender decides to defend the slant pass, the QB hands the ball off to the RB. Now the offense has as many blockers as the defense has run defenders in the tackle box.

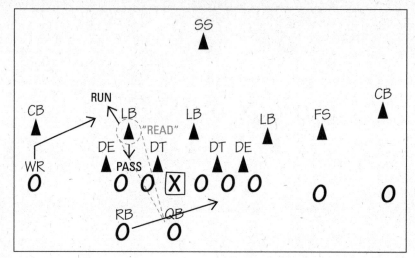

FIGURE 6-18:
In the run-pass
option, the QB
has to option to
hand off, run, or
pass the ball.

© *John Wiley & Sons, Inc.*

Chapter **7**

The Offensive Line at Work in the Trenches

ootball isn't a relationship-driven business. If any positions could be used to illustrate that point, they would be the offensive and defensive lines. The offensive and defensive lines are the sharks and the dolphins, the mongooses and the cobras, of football. In other words, they're natural enemies. Being a defensive lineman, I never encouraged friendships with offensive linemen, but I always respected them. My job was to beat and overpower them in order to help my team win.

HOWIE SAYS

When I was with the Raiders in the 1980s, two opposing offensive linemen stuck out: Anthony Muñoz, a tackle with the Cincinnati Bengals, and Dwight Stephenson, the Miami Dolphins' center. Unlike many offensive linemen, both of these men were very athletic in addition to being rugged and physical. That's the ideal combination for this position. I've seen Muñoz play basketball, and for a 280-pounder, he moved as if he were 100 pounds lighter. Great feet. When the ball was snapped, I wanted to be quicker than the man blocking me. My plan was to beat him off the ball and get by him before he could react.

The job of offensive linemen? To protect the most hunted commodity in the game — the quarterback — and to block for the ball carrier. The line also opens up *holes* in the defense for the running backs (by *blocking*, or impeding the movement of, defenders). Ball carriers try to go through these holes, which are also called *running lanes.* The ability to run effectively in a football game is the end result of the offensive line winning the war at the line of scrimmage. It's man against man, and whoever wants it more usually wins.

The offensive line is also essential to the passing game. Its job is to shield the quarterback, allowing him two or three seconds of freedom in which to throw the ball. The more time the line gives the quarterback to scan the field and find an open receiver, the better chance the quarterback has of a completion or a touchdown pass. Without the offensive line (or *O line*), the offense would never get anywhere.

This group, more than any other, needs to work together like the fingers on a hand. The linemen want their offensive teammates to gain yards — the more the merrier. You'll notice that when a team has a great running back who's gaining a lot of yards, the offensive line is usually mentioned as doing its job.

In this chapter, I explain the positions that make up the offensive line, give some insight into the personalities of offensive linemen, and cover some of the techniques that offensive linemen use to block for the quarterback and running backs.

Looking Down the Line

The offensive line is made up of five players, with the man in the middle called the *center.* Every offensive line position is based on the center. To the right of him is the *right guard,* and outside the right guard is the *right tackle.* To the left of the center is the *left guard,* and outside the left guard is the *left tackle.* Figure 7-1 helps you see the positioning of the offensive line's personnel.

FIGURE 7-1:
The personnel on the offensive line.

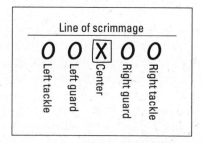

If the quarterback is right-handed, the left tackle is also referred to as the *blind-side tackle*. Why? Well, a right-handed quarterback generally drops back to pass and turns his head to the right while doing so. He can't see behind him, so his left side is his blind side.

The following sections give some generalities about the players at the three main offensive line positions — center, guard, and tackle.

THE MOST SPECIAL OFFENSIVE LINEMAN: THE BLIND-SIDE TACKLE

Most coaches put their best athlete at left tackle if their quarterback is right-handed (and more than 90 percent are). Ideally this player has quick feet and a good sense of balance.

The blind-side tackle doesn't have to be the biggest, baddest player on the team; he can weigh 300 pounds and be quite adequate. But *reach* (arm length) is important, and knowing how to use your arms and hands to block or *jam* (place your hands on the top of your opponent's jersey number) is critical. Getting his hands on the defensive player's numbers, so to speak, guarantees that the lineman is keeping a distance between himself and the defensive player. Gaining this advantage is imperative.

By maintaining proper distance, the offensive lineman isn't as susceptible to the defensive lineman's techniques and moves. If he keeps that distance, he has more time to get his feet into position to block the defender on each move. Also, distance gives the lineman time to adjust laterally and get in front of his man. If the defender is body to body or hip to hip with the offensive lineman, the lineman is beaten because the defensive player can grab him. The closer the defensive player gets to you, the harder it is to recover and get the correct positional leverage on him.

In his 2006 book *The Blind Side: Evolution of a Game* (W.W. Norton & Company), author Michael Lewis described why the blind-side tackle became such an important position and how blind-side tackle Michael Oher rose from poverty with the help of friends and family to become a professional player with a nine-year career and playing in two Super Bowls. *The Blind Side* was made into a movie in 2009 starring Sandra Bullock as the wealthy society lady who adopted Oher. I highly recommend the book and the movie, and not just to football fans. Oher's story is heartwarming and gives a good, although humorous, glimpse into the inner workings of football and college recruiting.

Centers

Like a center in basketball, a football center is in the middle of the action. He's the player who *snaps* (or delivers) the ball to the quarterback. As the snapper, he must know the *signal count* — when the quarterback wants the ball to be snapped, indicated by a series of commands, such as "Down. Set. Hut hut hut!"

REMEMBER

This center-quarterback exchange initiates every offensive play. Before the play begins, the center stands over the ball and then bends down, usually placing both hands around the front tip of the football. He snaps (or *hikes*) the ball between his legs to the quarterback. (Refer to Chapter 4 for an illustration of the snap.)

The exchange of the football is supposed to be a simple action, but occasionally it gets bungled, resulting in a *fumble*. A fumble can be caused by the center not snapping the ball directly into the quarterback's hands (perhaps because he's worried about being hit) or by the quarterback withdrawing his hands before the ball arrives. Because hands are essential to good blocking, centers sometimes worry more about getting their hands into position to block than cleanly snapping the ball to the quarterback. Coaches refer to those poor snaps as *short-arming the ball.* In other words, the center doesn't bring the ball all the way back to the quarterback's hands.

In addition to delivering the ball cleanly to the quarterback, a center must know the blocking responsibilities of every other offensive lineman. The offense never knows beforehand how the defense will set up. And unlike the offense, the defense may move before the ball is snapped, which allows a defense to set up in a vast array of formations. The center is essentially a coach on the field, redirecting his offensive line teammates as necessary based on how the defense aligns itself. On nearly every play, the center points to the defenders and, using terminology that the defense can't decipher, gives his fellow linemen their blocking assignments.

REMEMBER

Centers tend to be quick, smart, and even-keeled. The other linemen look to the center for leadership and stability. In addition to being mentally tough, a center needs to be physically tough so he can absorb hits from defensive players while he's concentrating on cleanly delivering the football to the quarterback.

Guards

Guards, who line up on either side of the center, should be some of the best blockers. In a *block*, an offensive lineman makes contact with a defensive player and uses his hands, arms, and shoulders to move him out of the way. A guard is doing his job if he clears the way, creating a hole for a running back to run through. A guard also must be able to fight off his man — stopping the defender's forward momentum — and prevent him from rushing the quarterback on a pass play.

THE NEUTRAL ZONE

The *neutral zone* is the area between the offensive and defensive lines. It's the length of the ball in width. Only the center is allowed in the neutral zone until he snaps the ball. If a lineman from either team lines up in this zone prior to the snap of the ball, his team incurs a 5-yard penalty.

Tackles

Tackles tend to be the biggest linemen, and in the NFL they're generally the most athletic. (Figure 7-2 shows one of the NFL's best tackles, Lane Johnson of the Philadelphia Eagles.) Tackles should be the stars of the offensive line because their job on the ends of the line is to repel some of the game's best defensive linemen and pass-rushers. They need to have great agility and the strength necessary to seal off the outside when a running play occurs. (*Sealing off the outside* means preventing the defensive players from reaching the corner of the line and tackling the ball carrier.)

FIGURE 7-2: Lane Johnson preparing to block against the Tennessee Titans.

Photo credit: © Frederick Breedon/Getty Images

Sometimes a tackle must shove a defensive player outside when the play is designed to go toward the middle of the field. He has a lot of responsibility on the *edge* (the outside shoulder of the defensive end or linebacker aligned over him) because, if the tackle succeeds in containing the defensive players, the ball carrier has an open field in which to run. I believe in today's NFL game the lines are blurred between right and left tackle because a lot of right tackles are often asked to block some of the sport's best pass rushers. This has happened because the game has evolved with quarterbacks running more and also utilizing the run-pass option plays. Sometimes the tackle must block his man toward the inside, thus allowing the ball carrier to run wide and outside the edge. In some plays, a tackle blocks down on the defensive tackle while the guard pulls to block the defender aligned over the tackle, moving that defender away from the running lane.

REMEMBER

Not all running plays are designed to go inside the tackles. *Off-tackle* runs are usually run to the strong side of the formation, where the tight end, who serves as another blocker, lines up. On off-tackle runs, the tackle must contain his man and push him inside toward the center of the line as the ball carrier runs wide, or outside the tackle. If the tackle can't move his man, he must prevent this defensive end or linebacker from reaching the edge of the line of scrimmage, shielding the ball carrier from the defensive pursuit.

The Lineman Physique: Fat Guys Doing the Job

Fans often look at offensive linemen and say that they're out of shape because they have big, round bodies. But that's the kind of physique most offensive line coaches look for. They don't want sculpted bodies; they want bulky players like guard Quinton Nelson, a 330-pounder with the Indianapolis Colts who starred as a rookie in 2018, and Philadelphia Eagles tackle Jason Peters. These players have great body mass and great natural strength. If you've been carrying 300+ pounds around most of your life, you tend to develop good leg strength and a powerful torso. If you're a big man, though, you must have quick feet and good athletic ability to play on the offensive line — that way you can move the weight and move people out of the way. That's what Peters has.

The perception used to be that you should stick the biggest, least athletic men on the offensive line, but today's offensive linemen have gone a long way toward shattering that notion. Players like Nelson, Peters, Johnson, and left tackle David Bakhtiari of the Green Bay Packers range in size from 310 to 330 pounds, and they're fast, agile, and mean.

Today, offensive linemen fall in two categories:

>> **The big, burly (heavyset) lineman:** During the Cowboys' Super Bowl run from 1992 to 1995, when Emmitt Smith was the best runner in pro football, the Dallas line consisted of this type of lineman. These players imposed

their will on their opponents and pounded them repeatedly — considered a *power offense.* Their style was to beat their opponents into submission. They limited their running plays to maybe five or six; they had those plays and stuck with them.

The power offense is common when a coach believes that his offensive line is bigger and stronger than the opposition's defensive line. The Cleveland Browns had such an offensive line for Jim Brown. The problem defensive players face against such a powerfully built line isn't the first running play, or the second running play, but the ninth play and beyond. As a defensive player, you get tired of 300-pound guys hammering at your head.

>> **The smaller, quicker lineman:** This type of lineman is light and agile, with the ability to run and block on every play (they call that *pulling*). This lineman takes more of a surgical approach, slicing and picking the defense apart. The best example of this type of line play is the classic *West Coast offense.* This scheme involves a lot of *angle blocking,* which means an offensive lineman rarely blocks the defensive player directly in front of him; he does everything in angles.

The San Francisco 49ers used this finesse offense exclusively while winning four championships in the 1980s. The Denver Broncos won Super Bowl XXXII and XXXIII in 1998 and 1999 with what's considered by today's standards to be a small offensive line, with an average size of 290 pounds. The Broncos used a variation of the West Coast offense, which their head coach, Mike Shanahan, incorporated into his offense after serving as the 49ers' offensive coordinator for three seasons.

HOWIE SAYS

I see the difference between these two offensive line styles as the difference between heavyweight boxers George Foreman and Muhammad Ali, with the West Coast style being Ali and the power offense style being Foreman. Every one of Foreman's body punches is magnified by ten — all brute force — whereas Ali works you over like a surgeon, slicing and picking you apart.

REMEMBER

What style a team chooses often depends on its quarterback, the size and ability of its offensive linemen, and the coach's offensive preference. If your quarterback has the ability to escape the rush, the West Coast finesse works fine. If you have an immobile quarterback, you may want Foreman-like blockers who are difficult to get past.

Understanding the Keys to Successful Offensive Line Play

Because the offensive line's job is so important, linemen need to develop certain characteristics, both individually and as a unit. The sections that follow outline some of those critical traits.

The proper stance

Offensive linemen often use a *two-point*, or *up, stance*, especially if the team plans to pass. The best two-point stance for a lineman is to be balanced, meaning that the right foot isn't way back. When the foot is back too far, the lineman has a tendency to turn a little more. A lineman must not turn his body to the outside or to the interior. If he gets caught leaning to the outside, he could give the defensive player the corner (the outside edge). When a lineman gives the defensive player the corner, the defender simply dips his shoulders and then runs forward to that corner. Figure 7-3 shows the proper two-point stance for an offensive lineman.

FIGURE 7-3: An offensive lineman's two-point stance ensures that he remains balanced.

© John Wiley & Sons, Inc.

On normal downs in which the offense may opt to run or pass the football, many teams put their linemen in a three-point stance, which means right hand on the ground and right foot back, as shown in Figure 7-4. A player must get comfortable in this stance and also maintain his balance so that he doesn't telegraph what he intends to do. The hand on the ground shouldn't be too far forward as to cause a dip in the shoulders; those should be square. From that stance, you can pull to the right, pull to the left, set up and hold your ground, or drive straight ahead.

FIGURE 7-4: On normal downs, offensive linemen assume a three-point stance.

But in a definite passing situation, such as third-and-long, being in a two-point stance is perfectly fine. Moving and maintaining positional leverage is easier and quicker from a two-point stance (see the "Leverage" section later in this chapter for more information). You can also run a draw or trap play from that position.

By the same token, if it's first-and-10, an offensive tackle may be able to remain in the up position. Say the play is a run designed away from the tackle. From a two-point, up position, he can pull to the inside and help block for the ball carrier. *Note:* Linemen want to change stances occasionally to prevent defensive players from zeroing in on exactly what the offense is doing; this changing is known as *giving the defensive player different looks.*

A solid base

An excellent offensive lineman is able to maintain proper balance. The key to proper balance is having a solid base. A lineman's feet should be set a little wider than the width of his shoulders; that way, the torso is set like a perfect upside-down *T*. If the lineman can maintain this stance, in most cases he won't be knocked off his feet.

If offensive linemen can maintain a good base, they can utilize their feet and whatever quickness they have. The same principle applies in boxing and basketball. A boxer always maintains that good base while keeping any lean to a minimum. He doesn't want to overextend his body to one side, thus becoming more susceptible to being knocked off his feet. A basketball player on defense wants to be able to move right and left while maintaining a good center of gravity.

Leverage

Maintaining positional leverage is important for an offensive lineman. He needs to anticipate where the defensive player is going and then get himself between that player and the quarterback, whom he's trying to protect. The point between the blocker and the quarterback, where the offensive lineman wants to meet the defender he plans to block, is called the *intersection point*. The offensive lineman needs to reach that point as quickly as possible. The slower the lineman assumes that position, the easier it is for his opponent to get him turned. That's really what the defensive player is trying to do — turn the offensive lineman. After the offensive lineman is turned, the defensive player can shorten his distance to the corner. And after he accomplishes that, the defender can make an inside move because he has the offensive lineman pointed in the wrong direction.

Toughness

An important ingredient in offensive line play is toughness. Generally, toughness is an attitude a player develops over time. He must have a lot of self-pride and tell himself that no one will beat him. Being tough is a big part of every sport, and it's a sign of a true competitor.

So much of toughness is mental. Many times, a football game is like a 15-round prizefight. At some point, one of those boxers slows down. I don't want to say that he quits, but working hard simply becomes less important to him. That phenomenon happens on a football field, too, and that's where mental toughness comes in. Toughness is essential when run-blocking because it's basically about being tougher than your opponent and wearing him down. Linemen win the fight when they rob their opponents of mental toughness.

HALL OF FAME

STANDING TOGETHER: THE OFFENSIVE LINE

Offensive linemen tend to hang in a group: They practice together and go out together.

For example, in 2017, the Philadelphia Eagles had a typical group. Philadelphia's offensive linemen would spend every Tuesday at a downtown steak house where the bill would be around $2,000. They generally rotated the check, although center Jason Kelce got stuck with it more than once. Other teams, like the Denver Broncos in 1997, instituted a kangaroo court — no defense attorneys allowed — in which they fined each other for being quoted in newspapers or talking on radio shows. The plan was for them to be anonymous; they were against publicity. Prior to the Super Bowl, when the NFL ordered the Bronco linemen to talk — 2,000 reporters were asking questions every day — they bit their tongues when they heard how the more-talented Green Bay Packers defensive line was going to overpower them. On game day, they opened huge holes for running back Terrell Davis, who scored three touchdowns and rushed for 157 yards in Denver's 31-24 victory.

There is probably not a closer group generally on a team than the offensive line. And one thing they usually count on are presents for a job well done. Quarterbacks and running backs are known to give outrageous presents to their primary blockers. Jacksonville's Leonard Fournette gave each of his linemen Rolex watches after his successful 2017 season. The Los Angeles Rams offensive line in 2018 received Polaris Rangers from NFC champion quarterback Jared Goff and running back Todd Gurley, who led the NFL with 21 touchdowns that season. The New York Jets offensive linemen didn't like their Christmas presents — $300 gift cards for steaks and personalized grilling equipment — from Sam Darnold, so they pulled a prank on the rookie quarterback in 2018. They removed the front wheels from his SUV in the players-only parking lot. Darnold eventually found his wheels, but he got the message that when you sign for a guaranteed deal worth $30 millon, the gift to your linemen should suit your salary.

Repetition

Another key to an effective and cohesive offensive line lies in its practice repetition. On any level, many of the best running teams are those that run three or four basic plays. They keep repeating them, doing them over and over until they're so proficient that no opponent can stop them. In NFL training camps, offensive lines constantly work together, everyone going through the hard times, the long, hot muggy days — everyone working when he's tired. At some point, you have to rely on the guy next to you. Working together over and over in the heat of the day can develop real cohesiveness.

Uncovering a Lineman's Worst Offense: Penalties

When the ref blows the whistle because an offensive lineman committed a transgression, he blows the whistle because the lineman did one of the following:

- **Clipping:** When an offensive lineman blocks an opponent from behind, hitting him in the back of the legs or in the back. The infraction costs the offense 15 yards. However, clipping above the knee is legal within 3 yards of the line of scrimmage.

- **Chop blocking:** This dirty play (which draws a 15-yard penalty) is when a lineman dives at an opponent's knees anywhere outside a designated area 3 yards beyond the line of scrimmage. The same block is considered legal when it occurs within 3 yards of the line of scrimmage. Go figure. The worst chop block is when linemen double-team a defender; one restrains the player around the shoulders while another hits him below the waist.

- **Encroachment:** Encroachment happens when a player enters the neutral zone before the ball is snapped and makes contact with the opposition. This is a 5-yard penalty. The offense repeats the down.

- **False start:** A false start is when an offensive lineman who's in a stance or set position moves prior to the snap of the ball. This is a 5-yard penalty with a replay of the down.

- **Helping the runner:** After the ball carrier crosses the line of scrimmage, an offensive lineman can't push or pull him forward, helping him gain extra yardage. Helping the runner is a 10-yard penalty with a replay of the down.

- **Holding:** When an offensive lineman grabs and holds onto a defensive player, it's called *holding,* and it's one of the worst things an offensive lineman can get caught doing. An offensive lineman is whistled for holding when he grabs an arm or a jersey, or even tackles a player who has managed to get around him. Linemen are allowed to use their hands, but they can't use them to clamp onto an opposing player and limit his movement. If a lineman is caught holding a defensive player in the NFL, the penalty is 10 yards from the line of scrimmage.

Now, some people will tell you that offensive linemen hold on every play, but mainly those accusations are coming from defensive guys like me. Generally, if the offensive lineman's hands are inside the opponent's shoulder and his chest area (where the jersey number is), he can grab and hold all he wants as long as he keeps the defender in front of him. But if a defender goes to the ground really fast for no apparent reason, it's obvious that he's being held, even if the offensive lineman's hands are inside.

>> **Ineligible receiver downfield:** A quarterback would never throw the ball to his blockers, but the blockers can be penalized for running downfield if they aren't trying to block defensive players. Linemen who are no longer blocking or have lost their man can't run past the line of scrimmage when the quarterback is attempting to pass. Ineligible receiver downfield is a 5-yard penalty with a repeat of the down.

>> **Offside:** This happens when an offensive player lines up over the designated line of scrimmage, trying to gain an edge on blocking or simply forgetting where he should be. Generally, the lineman either places his hand over the line of scrimmage or tilts his upper body over the line of scrimmage. Offside is a 5-yard penalty with a repeat of the down.

Getting Acquainted with Blocking Terms

You hear a lot of terms thrown around when it comes to blocking. Knowing one type of block from another really isn't that important unless you're trying to impress a diehard fan or you happen to play on the offensive line. If you're interested, here's the lowdown on some of the most common blocking terms:

>> **Cut-off block:** Generally used on running plays, which are designed to allow a defensive player to come free, or untouched, across the line of scrimmage. After that happens, an offensive lineman deliberately gets in the way of this on-rushing defender. This block is sometimes called an *angle block* because the offensive lineman hits the defensive player from the side, or from an angle.

>> **Chop block:** The legal variety is used within 3 yards of the line of scrimmage to slow the opposition's pass rush. A lineman blocks down low with his shoulders and arms, attempting to take the defender's legs from underneath him and stop his momentum. If this play occurs 3 yards or more beyond the line of scrimmage, the blocker is penalized 15 yards. Defensive players wish this type of block would be outlawed permanently on all parts of the playing field.

>> **Drive block:** This one-on-one block is used most often when a defensive lineman lines up directly over an offensive lineman. The blocker usually explodes out of a three-point stance and drives his hips forward, delivering the block from a wide base while keeping his head up and his shoulders square.

>> **Double-team:** Two linemen ganging up on one defensive player is known as double-teaming. It's more common on pass plays when the center and a guard work together to stop the penetration of a talented inside pass-rusher.

However, the double-team also works well on running plays, especially at the point of attack or at the place where the play is designed to go. The double-team blockers attack one defender, clearing out the one player who might stop the play from working.

» **Man-on-man blocking:** This is the straight-ahead style of blocking, with a defender playing directly over you and you driving straight into him. Most defenses use four linemen, so man-on-man blocking is common on pass plays, with each offensive lineman choosing the opponent opposite him, and the center helping out to either side.

» **Reach block:** A reach block is when an offensive lineman reaches for the next defender, meaning he doesn't block the opponent directly in front of him but moves for an opponent to either side. The reach block is common on run plays when the play calls for a guard to reach out and block an inside linebacker.

» **Slide block:** This is when the entire offensive line slides down the line of scrimmage — a coordinated effort by the line to go either right or left. It's a good technique when the quarterback prefers to roll or sprint right, running outside the tackle while attempting to throw the football. In that case, the line may slide to the right to give the quarterback extra protection to that side. With a talented cutback runner, this scheme may give the illusion of a run to the right, as the line slides that way while the ball carrier takes an initial step to the right and then cuts back to his left, hoping to gain an edge.

» **Trap block:** In a trap block, the offensive line deliberately allows a defensive player to cross the line of scrimmage untouched and then blocks him with a guard or tackle from the opposite side or where he's not expecting it. The intent is to create a running lane in the area that the defender vacated. The trap block is really a mind game. The offense wants the defender to believe it has forgotten about him or simply missed blocking him. After the defender surges upfield, across the line of scrimmage by a yard or two, an offensive lineman blocks him from the side.

Depending on the play's design, this block can come from a guard or a tackle. Teams run this play to either side, and it's important for the center to protect the back side of this lane, negating any pursuit by the defense. The trap block is also called an *influence block* because you want to draw the defender upfield and then go out and trap him. Good passing teams tend to be good trapping teams because defenders usually charge hard upfield, hoping to reach the quarterback.

» **Zone block:** In this block, each lineman protects a specific area or zone. Even if the defensive player leaves this area, the blocker must stay in his zone because the play or ball may be coming in that direction and the quarterback wants that area uncluttered. Blocking in a zone is generally designed to key on a specific defensive player who's disrupting the offensive game plan.

Chapter **8**

Offensive Plays and Strategies

hen I played defense, I knew that the offensive coaches were trying to get into my head and into the minds of my defensive buddies. When calling a specific play, the offensive coaches wanted to not only beat us but also make us look foolish. This chapter unmasks some of the tricky tactics those offensive geniuses come up with when they're burning the midnight oil studying defensive tendencies.

When football teams decide which play or formation to use, they base the decision on the personnel matchups they want. Coaches study the opposition and examine hours of video hoping to find the weak links in the opposing defense. No defensive team has 11 great players. So, the offense's design is to move away from the opposition's strengths and attack the weaknesses.

REMEMBER

Here's another thing you should know about offensive strategy: No perfect play exists for every occasion. In strategy sessions prior to a game, a play may look like it will result in a long gain, but in reality it may not succeed for various reasons. It may fail because someone on the offensive team doesn't execute or because a defensive player simply anticipates correctly and makes a great play. Things happen!

In this chapter, I explain the basic offensive approaches to the game and walk you through some particular plays and overall schemes. Then I discuss which offensive plays or formations work well against particular defenses and in specific situations. When does a quarterback sneak work? When is play-action passing ideal? What goal-line run plays really work? What does a team do on third-and-long? This chapter has answers for all these questions and a whole lot more.

Offense Begins with Players

The first thing you should know about offense is that *players* win games — schemes, formations, and trick plays don't. If a player doesn't execute, none of the decisions that the coaches made will work. And I'm not talking merely from the point of view of an ex-player; coaches, owners, and scouts all know that this is true.

The opposite scenario applies, too: A play designed to gain the offense only a couple of yards can turn into a score unexpectedly if a defensive player misses a tackle or turns the wrong way or if an offensive player makes a spectacular move. Having been a defensive player, I know that we sometimes had players placed in the right situations to defend a play perfectly, but the play still succeeded because of an offensive player's outstanding effort.

And look at the size of today's offensive players — who can stop them? So many runners and receivers weigh 200 pounds or more, and they all can run 40 yards in 4.5 seconds or faster. (The 40-yard dash is a common test that teams use to measure players' talents.) Aaron Rodgers, quarterback of the Green Bay Packers, weighs 225 pounds and is 6 feet 2 inches tall. Quarterback Ben Roethlisberger of the Pittsburgh Steelers is 6 feet 5 inches tall and weighs 240 pounds.

And it isn't just the quarterbacks. Runners and receivers are growing in size. Some teams have 325-pound offensive linemen who can run 40 yards in 5 seconds flat, and some are as agile as men half their size. They're as big as the defensive linemen, therefore giving the skilled players on offense an opportunity to succeed. Every great ball carrier will tell you that he can't gain his 1,000 yards a season without a very good offensive line.

HELPING OFFENSES BY ENFORCING AN IMPORTANT RULE

What has aided offensive production in the last dozen or so NFL seasons is the enforcement of the *5-yard bump rule,* which forbids defensive backs from pushing or shoving receivers 5 or more yards beyond the line of scrimmage in hopes of pushing them off their pass routes. The 5-yard bump rule was originally instituted in 1978, but through the years, officials started allowing defensive backs to again use their hands and arms in this manner. This liberal interpretation of the rule hurt the passing game because it prevented offenses from executing their carefully designed plays.

But because the rule is being enforced properly in the NFL today, offenses are taking charge. Referees are calling many more illegal contact and defensive holding penalties, resulting in defenders not playing as aggressively as they once did. Offenses are doing a much better job of spreading out the defenses, knowing that they can throw to their outside receivers. Forcing defenses to defend a larger area of the field has not only improved the passing game, but also created more opportunities for running backs. With defenders spread out across the line of scrimmage, a runner now has a chance at a longer run if he breaks through the first line of defense.

Specialized Pass Offenses

Few passes travel more than 10 or 12 yards. I'm sure you've heard about *the bomb* — a reference to a long pass — but those 40- to 45-yard or longer pass plays are pretty rare, thanks to the modern pass offenses that are run in the NFL and college football. As a fan, you should be aware of two types of pass offenses, which I describe in the sections that follow.

West Coast offense

Currently, Aaron Rodgers and a handful of other NFL quarterbacks operate a short, ball-control passing game called the *West Coast offense.* It got this name because it was developed by coach Bill Walsh, who directed the San Francisco 49ers to three Super Bowls. The West Coast offense's popularity spread throughout the NFL in the 1990s and 2000s while today's young head coaches like the Los Angeles Rams Sean McVay and San Francisco's Kyle Shanahan have injected their own ideas into Walsh's design, hoping to find more explosive plays. Many college teams use variations of this offense, depending on the talent of their receivers.

The West Coast offense uses all the offense's personnel in the passing game, as opposed to an I-formation team that's structured to run the ball and rarely throws to the running backs. (I tell you all about the I formation in Chapter 6.) Rather than running long routes downfield, the wide receivers run quick slants or square-out patterns toward the sidelines, hoping to receive the ball quickly and gain extra yards after the catch. The receivers run a lot of *crossing routes,* meaning they run from left to right or right to left in front of the quarterback, maybe 10 yards away. Crossing routes are effective because they disrupt many defensive secondary coverages. To this day, the crossing route is one of football's favorite plays.

If a running back is good at catching the ball, he becomes a prime receiver in the West Coast offense. This offense also uses a tight end on deeper routes than most other offenses. Because the offense has so many potential pass catchers (two receivers and two running backs or three receivers and one running back) on a typical pass play, the tight end can often find open areas after he crosses the line of scrimmage. The defensive players in the secondary tend to focus their attention on the wide receivers. The West Coast offense incorporates the tight end into most pass plays, so that player must be an above-average receiver.

REMEMBER

The premise of the West Coast offense is to maintain possession of the ball. Although it has quick-strike scoring possibilities, it's designed to keep offensive drives alive by passing rather than running the ball. One of the basic theories of this offense is as follows: If the defense is suspecting a run, pass the ball to the running back instead.

Shotgun offense

For obvious passing downs, some teams use the *shotgun offense.* In the shotgun, the quarterback (QB) lines up 5 to 7 yards behind the center and receives a long snap, as shown in Figure 8-1. The pass plays used in this offense are identical to those used when the quarterback is under center; offenses use the shotgun simply to allow the quarterback more time to visualize the defense, particularly the secondary's alignment. On an obvious passing down, nothing can be gained by keeping the quarterback under center. Why have him spend time dropping back to pass when he can receive a long snap and be ready to throw?

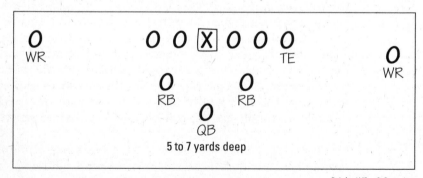

FIGURE 8-1:
The QB is positioned 5 to 7 yards behind the center in the shotgun offense.

To run this offense, you want a quarterback who's quick with his decisions and also able to run with the football if the defense's actions make it possible for him to gain yardage by carrying the ball himself.

RED GUN (OR RUN-AND-SHOOT) OFFENSE

The *red gun offense,* or *run-and-shoot offense,* uses four receivers and one running back. The Houston Oilers and the Atlanta Falcons used this offense in the early 1990s, but both teams have since abandoned it for a more conventional approach because it places too much emphasis on passing. (The Houston Oilers have since moved out of Texas, and now they're called the Tennessee Titans with a home in Nashville.)

The red gun is a great offense for fans to watch because it uses so many pass plays. Also, only five offensive linemen are blocking on every play, which creates more opportunities for the defense to place more pass-rushers to one side (called *overloading*); the offensive linemen can't possibly block every one of these pass-rushers. These types of gambles may lead to a sack or a big play — feast or famine. When a red gun offense gives the ball to a running back, he has a chance to make a big play because the defense is concentrating on pressuring the four wide receivers. Depending on how deep the receivers run their patterns, the running back may have a lot of open area on the field in which to run.

No NFL team has won with the red gun, but the University of Florida won two national championships with it. Both Baker Mayfield and Patrick Mahomes played in a very similar offense in college, where any combination of five receivers was the norm on every play. Defenses need to practice and prepare for running offenses, too, and with a limited amount of practice time on a typical weekday, the red gun offense never gives the defense that opportunity. Instead, the defensive players become accustomed to defending the pass. Defenses have to be good at stopping the run, too, in order to win. Also, the red gun doesn't employ a tight end — another thing the defense needs to know how to defend.

I always had problems with the red gun offense as a player because it was an unconventional system. It was difficult to key on the lone running back and anticipate what the play was going to be. This running back usually was in the same alignment, so, to me, some passes looked like run plays, and run plays ended up being pass plays. Offenses often ran *draw plays* (running plays) from an unusual perspective. For example, the team would run a draw as the quarterback was faking like he was going to run around the end (called a *bootleg*), but actually he had already given the ball to the running back; the quarterback was simply pretending to have the ball while running wide. I know this offense frustrated our defensive coaches. They never seemed sure of which defense worked best against it, especially for us defensive linemen.

The best shotgun quarterback I ever saw was John Elway of the Denver Broncos. Jim Kelly of the Buffalo Bills truly excelled in the shotgun, too. Elway and Kelly seemed more comfortable and confident in this formation than other quarterbacks. But so many of today's young quarterbacks like Baker Mayfield with the Cleveland Browns and Patrick Mahomes, the MVP quarterback of the Kansas City Chiefs, love to operate out of the shotgun because they played exclusively in that style while in college. It made their transition to the NFL game so much easier.

From a defensive lineman's viewpoint, the shotgun is okay because you don't have to concentrate on defending the run; you know that the offense is going to pass. In other formations, a defender has to be prepared for both possibilities: run or pass. He has to think before reacting. When facing the shotgun, a defensive lineman has only one mission: to get to the quarterback as fast as he can.

Some Newfangled Offenses

One of the great pleasures of following the game of football is seeing it evolve over time. Coaches are always trying innovative new schemes on offense and defense to catch their opponents off guard. Consequently, the game keeps changing. If you watch a football game from years past (you can watch these games on DVD, on ESPN Classic, and at www.nflnetwork.com/nflnetwork), the first thing you notice is how different the game is now, especially on offense. The previous century saw offenses use and abandon these formations: the flying wedge, the single wing, the wing T, the Notre Dame Box, and the wishbone. Recent years have seen four new offensive formations: the wildcat, the spread, the run-pass option, and the pistol. I describe them in the next sections.

The wildcat

The *wildcat* formation is unique in football because, when an offense runs the wildcat, the quarterback isn't on the field. His place is taken by a running back or sometimes a wide receiver, who takes the snap shotgun-style from 5 to 7 yards behind the center. The running back or receiver then runs the ball (or sometimes hands it to another running back).

The wildcat offers a couple advantages to the offense. Without a quarterback on the field, the offense has an extra blocker to help the runner advance the ball. And because the halfback takes the snap from center, the offense wastes no time handing off the ball. The runner can make his move as soon as the ball is snapped. Moreover, by starting from 5 to 7 yards behind the offensive line, the runner has a good field of vision. He can better see where the defenders are and where his offensive line has busted a hole in the defense for him to run through.

In the 2008 season, the Miami Dolphins ran the wildcat with talented running backs Ricky Williams and Ronnie Brown, and they won 11 games. But for the most part the wildcat is used sparingly in the NFL and in college. If a team runs the wildcat, it frequently does so only when it needs 2 to 3 yards to get a first down. The wildcat is a one-dimensional offensive formation. Most of the advantages of running the wildcat are cancelled out by the fact that the defense can focus on the run — it doesn't have to defend against a player who is good at passing the ball — when it sees its opponent lining up in the wildcat.

The spread

The *spread* gets its name because, in this formation, the offense spreads out across the width of the field, causing the defensive players to spread out accordingly. The quarterback takes the snap shotgun-style, after which he can run the ball, pass it, or hand it off, often to a runner who's going in motion across the backfield. The idea behind the spread is to open up the field and create more offensive opportunities — more seams for runners to attack and more space in which receivers can get open.

The spread is used far more often in high school and college football than in the pro game for a very important reason: In the spread, the quarterback runs as well as passes the ball, and in the NFL, where players are faster and bigger, and where the quarterback is a very valuable commodity, teams don't want to risk an injury to the quarterback by allowing him to run the ball. But many NFL teams have adopted this formation, coupling it with the run-pass option, because they don't mind their quarterbacks running, as Russell Wilson does so effectively with the Seattle Seahawks.

Still, with all its option and misdirection plays, the spread formation makes for very exciting football, and many college teams have found success with the spread. The 2011 Bowl Championship Series (BCS) championship game (see Chapter 16 for information about the BCS) featured two teams that ran the spread offense: the Oregon Ducks and the Auburn Tigers. However, in the 2019 national championship game, both winner Clemson and Alabama ran a conventional I-formation offense with a slew of shotgun formations.

The pistol

The pistol, like the wildcat and the spread formation, is run from a shotgun snap. The quarterback lines up 4 yards behind center, and a running back lines up 3 yards behind the quarterback. The pistol combines the advantages of the shotgun formation and the I formation. Lining up 4 yards behind center gives the quarterback a better view of the defense and allows him the opportunity to throw quick passes without having to drop back before passing the ball. The running back, meanwhile, also gets a good look at the defense, because he's even farther behind the line of scrimmage than the quarterback. Like the spread, the pistol requires a quarterback who can run as well as pass. Running quarterbacks, however, take a lot more hits than pocket quarterbacks, and injuries are often a factor over the course of a season. This offense is run a lot in high school, but when Colin Kaepernick played in the NFL he led the San Francisco 49ers to a Super Bowl in the 2012 season.

Beating a Defense

One of the primary factors that helps a coach decide what offense to run and what plays to call is how the defense sets up. Various defenses call for different strategies to beat them. The following sections describe some defenses and the offensive plays or formations that may work against those defensive schemes. For more information about any of these defenses, flip to Chapter 11.

Battling a 3-4 front

When facing a 3-4 *front* (three down linemen and four linebackers), the offense's best strategy is to run *weak side,* or away from the tight end (which is always the strong side of any offensive formation). One possible running play is called the *weak-side lead.* With this play, the defensive end (DE) usually attempts to control and push the offensive tackle (LT) inside toward the center of the line, leaving the linebacker behind him (OLB) to defend a lot of open area. The offense is in the I formation, and the fullback (FB) runs to the weak side and blocks the linebacker, shoving him inside. The left offensive tackle allows the defensive end to push him a little, letting the defender believe that he's controlling the play. However, the offensive lineman then grabs the defender, containing him, and moves him out of the way to the right. The ball carrier should have a clear running lane after he hits the line of scrimmage. Figure 8-2 diagrams this play.

Running against a 4-3 front

An offense can attack a 4-3 *front* (four down linemen, three linebackers) in many different ways, but one common strategy is to attack what coaches call the *bubble side* (the defensive side where the two linebackers are positioned). Remember, the 4-3 defense employs both over and under slants that the four-man defensive line uses. *Overs* and *unders* are basically the alignments of defensive linemen to one particular side of the offensive center (see Chapter 11 for further details). When the defensive front lines up in an under look, the offense attacks the bubble.

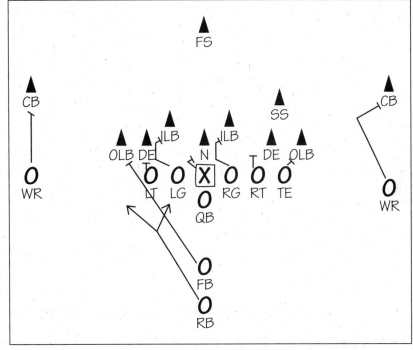

© John Wiley & Sons, Inc.

FIGURE 8-2:
Running the ball to the weak side is a good offensive strategy against a 3-4 defense.

The offensive play shown in Figure 8-3 is called a *delay draw* to the strong side (the tight end side) of the offensive formation. When the defense is positioned like this, three defensive linemen line up over the center, left guard, and left tackle. These offensive linemen are also called the weak-side guard and tackle. This defensive alignment leaves only one lineman and two smaller linebackers (DE, ILB, and OLB) to defend the strong side of the offense's I formation (turn to Chapter 6 for the scoop on this formation).

On the delay draw, the right guard (RG) blocks down on the defensive nose tackle (N), and the fullback (FB) runs into the hole and blocks the front-side linebacker (ILB). The right tackle (RT) blocks the defensive end (DE), keeping him out of the middle, and the tight end (TE) blocks and contains the outside linebacker (OLB). This approach is known as *running at the defense's weakest point.* When the ball carrier reaches the line of scrimmage, he should find open space between the offense's right guard and right tackle.

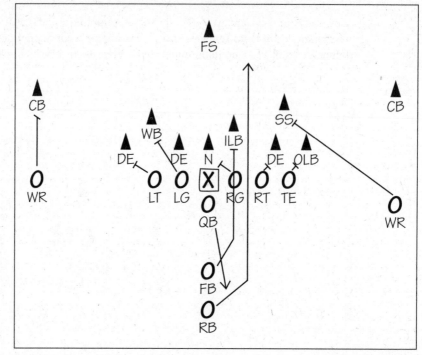

FIGURE 8-3:
The delay draw takes advantage of the fact that only one lineman and two linebackers are on the strong side.

Defeating the four-across defense

In the *four-across defense*, the defense plays all four secondary players deep, about 12 yards off the line of scrimmage. To beat this defense, the offense wants to have two wide receivers (WR) run comeback routes, have the tight end (TE) run a 16-yard in route, and have the two backs (RB) swing out to the right and left. The running back to the quarterback's left side should run more of a looping pattern. The quarterback (QB) throws the ball to the wide receiver on the left, as shown in Figure 8-4.

TIP

The quarterback throws to his left because the ball is placed on the left hash mark, which is the short side of the field. Throwing a 15-yard comeback pass to his left is much easier than throwing a 15-yard comeback to the right, or the wide side of the field. The pass to the wide side would have to travel much farther, almost 42 yards, as opposed to just 15 yards. From the left hash mark to the numbers on the right side of the field, the distance is more than 19 yards. And the comeback to the right is always thrown beyond those numbers (10, 20, 30, 40), going down the length of the field.

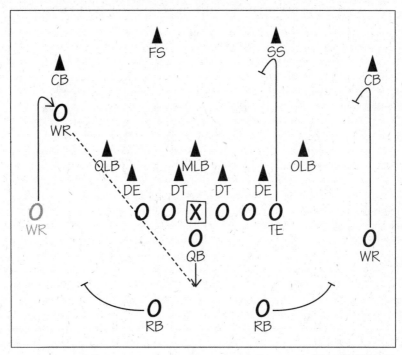

© John Wiley & Sons, Inc.

FIGURE 8-4: This play is good for beating the four-across defense.

If the defense senses that the quarterback is going to throw to the wide receiver on the left side and then decides to drop a linebacker into underneath coverage, hoping to intercept, the quarterback can't throw that pass. By *underneath*, I mean that the linebacker is dropping back to defend the pass, but safeties are still positioned beyond him. Hence, the linebacker is underneath the safeties. Instead, the quarterback throws to the running back on the same side. The quarterback simply *keys* (watches) the linebacker. If the linebacker drops into coverage, the quarterback throws to the running back because he won't be covered. If the linebacker takes the running back, the quarterback throws to the receiver.

Beating press coverage

Press coverage is when the defensive team has its two cornerbacks on the line of scrimmage, covering the outside receivers man-to-man. One tactic against this defense is to throw to the tight end (TE), who runs to the middle of the field, as shown in Figure 8-5.

Another option is to throw to the running back (RB), who's swinging out to the left. The wide receivers (WR), who are being pressed, run in the opposite direction, away from the area in which either the tight end or the running back is headed, as shown in Figure 8-6.

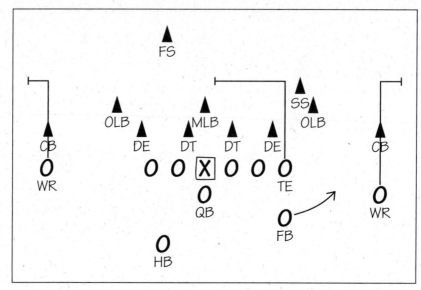

FIGURE 8-5:
One option for beating press coverage is to throw to the tight end in midfield.

© John Wiley & Sons, Inc.

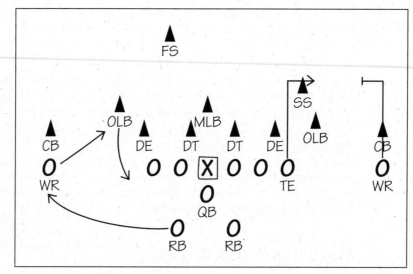

FIGURE 8-6:
Throwing to the running back, who swings out to the left, is another way to beat press coverage.

© John Wiley & Sons, Inc.

Passing against a zone coverage

When I say "passing against a zone coverage," I'm talking about a defensive secondary that's playing zone — meaning the cornerbacks are playing off the line of scrimmage. They aren't in press coverage or man-to-man coverage. The best pass against a zone coverage is the curl, and the best time to use it is on first-and-10.

A receiver (WR) runs 10 to 12 yards and simply *curls*, or hooks back, toward the quarterback (QB), as shown in Figure 8-7. He usually curls to his left and attempts to run his route deep enough to gain a first down. The coverage should be *soft* enough (meaning the defensive back, CB, is playing 5 to 7 yards off the receiver) on these routes that the receiver's size shouldn't matter. However, against a man-to-man scheme, a smaller receiver may be ineffective when running patterns against a taller, stronger defensive back.

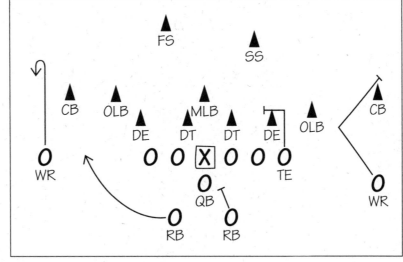

FIGURE 8-7: The receiver runs 10 to 12 yards out and then curls back toward the quarterback when facing zone coverage.

© *John Wiley & Sons, Inc.*

Attacking a zone blitz

Pittsburgh Steelers defensive coordinator Dick LeBeau invented the *zone blitz* in the late 1980s, giving his team the nickname "Blitzburgh" (see Chapter 11 for details on the zone blitz). Sustaining a running offense is difficult against teams that run a zone blitz. Some offenses have had success running against zone blitz defenses, but I don't think you can beat them consistently by running the ball.

When facing a defense that blitzes a lot off the corner (linebackers or safeties coming from either wide side of the line of scrimmage against your offensive tackles), the offense should align with two tight ends in order to help pass-protect. To beat a zone blitz with a passing attack, the offense must find its opponent's weakest defender in the passing game (be that cornerback, safety, or linebacker).

The quarterback must throw to the side opposite where the defense is *overloaded* (has more players). For example, if the defense positions four players to the quarterback's left, as shown in Figure 8-8, the quarterback should throw to his right. But the offense must still block the side from which the defense is attacking.

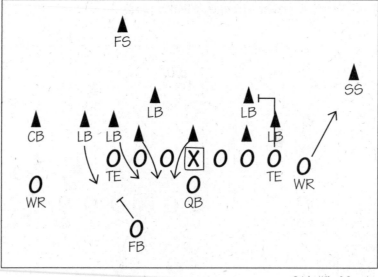

FIGURE 8-8:
With the defense overloaded to the QB's left, the QB attempts to avoid the zone blitz from that side by throwing a short pass to the WR on his right.

© *John Wiley & Sons, Inc.*

Throwing the post versus blitzing teams

Most defenses protect against quarterbacks attempting to throw the *post route*, which is when a receiver fakes to the outside and then runs straight down the field toward the goalpost. The quarterback lines up the throw by focusing on the hash marks. When he releases the ball, he tries to *lead the receiver,* or throw the ball slightly in front of him, so that the pass drops to the receiver over his shoulder. That way, if a defensive player is chasing the receiver, the defender shouldn't be able to intercept the pass or deflect it away.

The deep post doesn't really work well against zone blitz defenses. Why? Because these teams rarely leave the post open. They defend it pretty well.

However, other teams that blitz from a basic 4-3 defense may use a safety to blitz the quarterback. When a team uses a safety to blitz, usually the defense is vulnerable in the center of the field, where both safeties should be. Still, very few teams leave the deep post wide open because it can give the offense a quick six points.

Wearing out a defense with the no-huddle offense

In need of a score late in a game, every team runs a *no-huddle offense* in an attempt to move down the field quickly. (See "Running the two-minute drill" later in this chapter for more info on late-game tactics.) In essence, by quickly running plays without pausing to huddle, the offense prevents the defense from substituting players and changing its scheme. The quick pace of play can tire out a defense, leaving it vulnerable to a score.

A handful of teams with elite quarterbacks — the New England Patriots with Tom Brady, the New Orleans Saints with Drew Brees, and the Green Bay Packers with Aaron Rodgers — have the knowledge and ability to run their two-minute, or no-huddle, offense throughout the game if they so choose.

Gaining Better Field Position

Of course, scoring is always an offense's ultimate goal, but to score, you have to move down the field toward your opponent's end zone. In the next sections, I describe the various strategies for gaining yards and, consequently, a better field position.

Throwing a field position pass

When offenses face third down and more than 6 yards, which is known as *third-and-long,* the safest play is for the quarterback to throw to a running back who's underneath the coverage of the defensive secondary. Why? Because in such situations, the defensive secondary, which is aligned well off the line of scrimmage, is always instructed to allow the receiver to catch the ball and then come up and tackle him, preventing a first down.

Early in the game, when your offense is down by ten or fewer points, you want to run a safe play on third-and-long, knowing that you'll probably end up punting the ball. In other words, your offense is raising its white flag and giving up. That's why this pass to the running back is called a *field position pass.* Maybe the back will get lucky, break a bunch of tackles, and gain a first down, but basically you're playing for field position. The odds of beating a good defensive team under third-and-long conditions are pretty slim.

Opting for possession passes

Most of the time, a *possession pass* is a short throw, between 8 and 10 yards, to either a running back or a tight end. The intent isn't necessarily to gain a first down but to maintain possession of the ball while gaining yardage. Often, teams call possession passes several times in a short period to help the quarterback complete some easy passes and build his confidence.

If the quarterback wants to throw a possession pass to a wide receiver and the defensive secondary is playing off the line of scrimmage, his best option is to throw a 5-yard hitch. A *5-yard hitch* is when the receiver runs up the field 5 yards, stops, and then turns back so that he's facing the quarterback. When the receiver turns, the ball should almost be in his hands. Coaches call these throws when the quarterback has thrown some incompletions, giving him a chance to calm down and complete a few easy passes.

Another high-percentage pass is the bubble screen pass (see Figure 8-9) in which three potential receivers align to one side of the formation, allowing the quarterback to throw to one of them while the other two receivers block on the play against whatever defenders are aligned to that side. Often the play can pick up big yardage if the blocking receivers do their job effectively. Also, with such a formation, overloaded to one side, teams have been known to run or even throw in the oppostive direction, kind of a misdirection play.

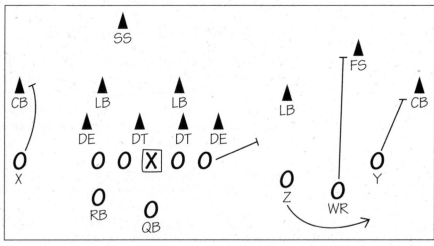

FIGURE 8-9: In a basic bubble screen pass, two receivers (WR & Y) to the right block downfield after receiver Z catches the pass.

© John Wiley & Sons, Inc.

Moving downfield with play-action passes

In a *play-action pass,* the quarterback fakes a handoff to a running back and then drops back 4 more yards and throws the football. The fake to the running back usually causes the linebackers and defensive backs to hesitate and stop coming forward after they realize that it isn't a running play. They stop because they know they must retreat and defend their pass responsibility areas.

If neither team has scored and the offense is on its own 20-yard line, that's a perfect time to throw the football. Some conservative offensive teams run play-action only in short-yardage situations (for example, second down and 3 yards to go). But play-action works whenever the defense places its strong safety near the line of scrimmage, wanting to stuff the run. Because the defensive pass coverage is likely to be soft, the offense has a good opportunity to throw the ball. And the defense shouldn't be blitzing, which in turn gives the quarterback plenty of time to throw.

Offensive Strategies for Sticky Situations

One of the biggest challenges of being a coach — or a quarterback, for that matter — is to lead your team out of the sticky situations that arise. This section explains some of the strategies that offenses use to gain the necessary yardage for a first down, move downfield with little time left on the clock, and more.

Deciding whether to gamble on fourth-and-1

The game is tied, and on fourth-and-1 you have a decision to make: Should your team kick a field goal or go for the first down and maintain possession, hoping to end your offensive possession with a touchdown?

For most coaches, the decision depends on the time of the game and the team they're playing. If a team is on the road against a solid opponent, one that has beaten the team consistently in the past, most coaches elect to kick a field goal. In the NFL, some teams are especially difficult to beat at home. For example, the six-time champion New England Patriots won 21 consecutive home games (including playoff games) in the 2002 through 2005 seasons. The thought process is that any lead, even a small one, is better than risking none at all against such a team when you're on the road. So at Gillette Stadium, where the Patriots play, you kick the field goal and take your three points.

HOWIE SAYS

A coach's strategy may change drastically when his team is playing the same opponent in its own stadium. If I'm playing in my stadium and I'm leading 17–7 in the fourth quarter, I may go for it on fourth-and-1 — especially if we're inside the other team's 20-yard line. I may let my team take a shot, especially if the offense hasn't been very effective. If my team doesn't make the first down, the other team has to go more than 80 yards to score, and it has to score twice to beat me. You'd rather be in the other team's territory when you gamble. Never gamble in your own territory — it could cost your team three points or a touchdown.

However, when my oldest son, Chris, won a Super Bowl with the Philadelphia Eagles in 2017, his coach Doug Peterson somehow perfected a strategy of being successful on 17 of 26 fourth-down gambles in the regular season. The Eagles also converted a critical fourth-down play in their own territory that helped them beat the Patriots in the championship game.

The toughest area in which to make a decision is between your opponent's 35- and 40-yard lines — a distance that may be too far for your field goal kicker but too close to punt. If your punter kicks the ball into the end zone, for example, your opponent begins possession on the 20-yard line, giving you a mere 15-yard gain in field position. When you're making the decision whether to kick or punt in this 35- to 40-yard line area, you may as well toss a coin.

Making a first down on a fourth-down gamble

It's fourth down and 1 yard to go for a first down, and your offense just crossed midfield. You want to gamble, believing that your offense can gain enough yards for a first down. The best play to call in this situation is a run off the tackle and the tight end on the left side of the formation, as shown in Figure 8-10.

Your offense has three tight ends in the game: the standard short-yardage personnel. These players always practice running a few specific plays during the week. Your offense knows that the defense plans to plug up the middle; they don't want an interior running play to beat them. They'll defend that area. To fool the defense and maximize the offense's chance to succeed, the offensive alignment puts two tight ends to the right, hoping the defense will react to the formation and slant its personnel to that side because it believes that the play is centered there. With the defense slanted to prevent a run to the right, the offense runs to the left.

Running a quarterback sneak

The *quarterback sneak* is one of the oldest plays in the book. But it isn't that simple to execute, and it doesn't always succeed. The play is designed for the quarterback to run behind one of his guards, using the guard as his principal blocker. Teams run the quarterback sneak when they need less than a full yard, sometimes only a few inches, for a first down.

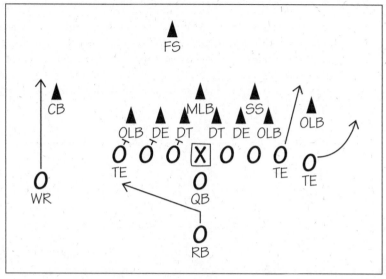

FIGURE 8-10:
Run to the left in a short-yardage situation when the defense believes that the play is centered to the right.

To be successful with the sneak, the quarterback delays for a moment and determines the angle the defensive linemen are coming from. Then he dives headfirst, pushing his shoulders into the crack behind whichever guard (the right or left side) is called in the huddle.

The quarterback wants to run at the weakest defensive tackle. If the Fletcher Cox of the Philadelphia Eagles is aligned over your right guard, you want to sneak over your left guard. You make the sneak work by having your center and guard double-team the defensive tackle (or whoever's playing in this gap opposite the two offensive linemen). These two blockers must move the defensive tackle or the defender in that gap. Many quarterbacks, but especially Drew Brees of the New Orleans Saints, are adept at simply extending their arm and the ball over the line of scrimmage to get the necessary first down. The lone worry about such a play is having a defender knock the ball free, considering the quarterback is holding it with only one hand.

Running the two-minute drill

Your team has two minutes left in the game to drive 70 yards for a score. You must score a touchdown (and successfully kick the extra point) to tie the game. As an offensive coach, you're hoping the defense decides to play a *prevent defense*, which means they use seven players in pass coverage while rushing only four linemen or linebackers at the quarterback. When a defense plays a prevent defense, you may want to run the ball because the running back has plenty of room to run after he crosses the line of scrimmage.

The best pass play to use in this situation is the *triple stretch,* which is also known as the *vertical stretch.* In this play, one receiver runs a deep pattern through the secondary, another receiver runs a route in the middle, and another simply runs underneath, as shown in Figure 8-11. The underneath route may be only 5 yards across the line of scrimmage and *underneath* the linebackers' position in pass coverage.

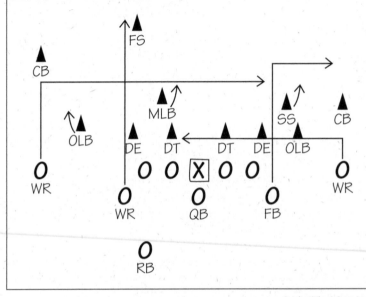

FIGURE 8-11:
The triple
(or vertical)
stretch pass
play is great for
a two-minute
offense.

© *John Wiley & Sons, Inc.*

The intermediate receiver runs a route behind the linebackers and in front of the secondary coverage players. Teams don't necessarily want to throw deep, knowing that the defense is focused on preventing a huge gain, but that receiver must *stretch the defense,* or force the defense to retreat farther from the line of scrimmage. You use the deep receiver as a decoy.

The quarterback's intention is to find the intermediate receiver (WR who comes in from the left). If the intermediate receiver can run behind the linebackers and catch the ball, he'll probably have a 15-yard gain, but he'll have to make sure that he runs out of bounds to stop the clock and conserve time. If the short receiver catches the ball, the linebackers are probably playing deep to prevent the intermediate receiver from catching the ball. In this situation, you dump it to the running back. He catches it and has a chance to run, but he must make sure he gets out of bounds, too. If the defense blitzes, you may be able to complete the deep route for a long touchdown pass. The quarterback normally reads progression from deep to intermediate and underneath, knowing that the defense is set up for the middle route.

Scoring Offenses

After you get the ball downfield and get out of all those sticky situations, your offense is ready to score. In the following sections, you can find plays for various scoring situations.

Making the best run play on the goal line

Actually I can't tell you the *best* run play on the goal line because there's no best play. But I can tell you that teams that have the most success running on the goal line have a great back like Hall of Famers Jim Brown or Marcus Allen in their backfield. Teams are always searching for a great running back, someone who can fight through three defenders, for example, and still reach the end zone.

REMEMBER

The best running back in the NFL isn't necessarily the one that coaches choose when their teams are near the goal line. The "dodger and dancer" type of runner who can break out in the open field isn't as valuable near the goal line as the "pound it in there" guy. Down on the 1-yard line, you need a powerful runner — a tough, physical player — who can bowl over people. Because he's going to be hit, he needs to be able to bounce off one or two tacklers. Well, okay. The best play at the goal line is always something straight ahead.

Scoring inside the opponent's 10-yard line

One pass in today's NFL offenses is perfectly suited to the part of the field inside the 10-yard line: the *quick out.* As shown in Figure 8-12, the outside receiver (WR on the left) runs straight for 5 to 7 yards and then breaks quickly to the outside. Offenses use this pass play a lot because many defenses play the old college zone defense of putting their four defensive backs deep and back, which is called the *four-across alignment* (see the earlier "Defeating the four-across defense" section for more). The play is generally effective if the quarterback is accurate enough to place the ball on the receiver's back shoulder. The back-shoulder pass is pretty common in football because it can prevent the defensive back from tipping the ball away from the receiver, and if he tries too hard, he can make contact before the pass arrives and end up being flagged for interference.

If you have a big, physical receiver, the quick out is the ideal pass. The receiver and the quarterback have to be in unison and time it right. If the quarterback completes the pass, the receiver has a chance to break a tackle and run in for a touchdown. The opportunity to score is there because in the four-across alignment, the defensive back doesn't have help on that side; he must make the tackle by himself. If he doesn't, the receiver can score an easy six points. Of course, the quick out is also a dangerous pass to throw. If the cornerback reads the play quickly and the quarterback fails to throw hard and accurately, the ball is likely to be intercepted by the defensive player and returned for a touchdown.

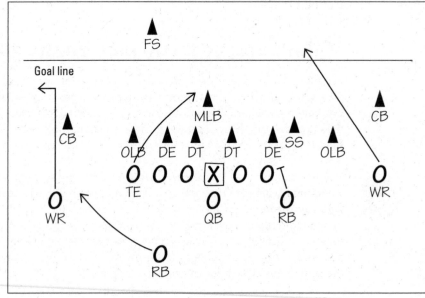

FIGURE 8-12: The quick out to the WR on the left is the perfect pass to throw from inside an opponent's 10-yard line.

Going for two-point conversions

After scoring a touchdown, a team has two options: kick the ball through the uprights for one point or try for a *two-point conversion*. The team earns two points if it successfully reaches the end zone on either a pass or a run after a touchdown.

For a two-point conversion in the NFL, the ball is placed on the 2-yard line, the same spot as for a kick. (College and high school teams must score from the 3-yard line.) You'd think that the two points would be automatic, but over the years, two-point conversions have been successful just 47 percent of the time, whereas kickers convert extra-point attempts at a rate of around 94 percent.

Coaches have a universal chart that tells them when to kick and when to attempt a two-point conversion (the chart was supposedly devised by UCLA coach Tommy Prothro in 1970 with the help of his offensive coordinator, Dick Vermeil). Coaches like the chart because they dislike being second-guessed by players and the media for making the wrong choice — a decision that may result in a defeat. Here's what the chart says:

» If you're behind by 2, 5, 9, 12, or 16 points, attempt a two-point conversion.

» If you're ahead by 1, 4, 5, 12, 15, or 19 points, attempt a two-point conversion.

» If you're behind by 1, 4, or 11 points, you have to make the dreaded judgment call — it can go either way.

TIP

Teams elect to go for two points when they need to close the point differential with their opponent. For example, if a team is behind by five, kicking the extra point would close the gap to four. That means the team could kick a field goal (worth three points) and still lose the game. But a two-point conversion would reduce the deficit to three, and a field goal would tie the game. When behind by nine points, a two-point conversion reduces the deficit to seven, meaning that a touchdown and an extra point could tie the game.

The two-point conversion, with the right multiples of field goals and touchdowns, can close a deficit or widen it, depending on the situation. It's a gamble. But when a team is trailing, it may be the quickest way to rally and possibly force overtime. Most coaches prefer to tie in regulation and take their chances with an overtime period. However, some coaches, especially if their teams have grabbed the momentum or seem unstoppable on offense, may elect to try two points at the end of the game and go for the win rather than the tie. The previous play is more common in high school and college football than in the NFL, where coaches tend to be conservative because of playoff implications — and because a loss might mean unemployment.

Most teams use zone pass plays in two-point conversion situations because defenses aren't playing man-to-man coverages as much anymore. So the following play was designed to succeed against a zone defense. Remember that the offense simply has to gain 2 yards (or 3 in high school and college) to reach the end zone, which doesn't sound complicated.

To attempt a two-point conversion, the offense lines up three receivers to one side. One receiver runs the flat; another receiver runs up about 6 or 7 yards and runs a curl; and the third receiver runs to the back of the end zone, turns, and waits. Figure 8-13 shows three receivers (TE and WR) to one side — the right side. This group of receivers can be a tight end and two wide receivers — it doesn't matter as long as the receivers are bunched together in a close group. One receiver runs straight ahead and about 2 yards deep into the end zone. Another receiver is the inside guy. He runs straight up the field. He heads first to the back of the end zone and turns to run a deep square-out. The other receiver just releases into the flat area, outside the numbers on the field. If the quarterback looks into the secondary and believes that he's facing a zone defense, he wants the receiver running the 6-yard curl to come open.

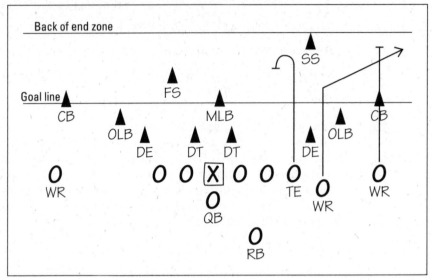

FIGURE 8-13:
A common
two-point
conversion
against a zone
coverage, with
three receivers
(TE and WR) to
one side.

© *John Wiley & Sons, Inc.*

If the defense is playing a man-to-man coverage, the quarterback wants the receiver in the flat to come open immediately. If the defense reads the play perfectly, the quarterback is in trouble because he must find a secondary target while under a heavy pass-rush. Still, this pass is almost impossible to defend because the offense is prepared for every defensive concept.

If the coverage is man-to-man, the offense opens with a *double pick*, which is illegal if the officials see it clearly. By a *pick*, I mean that an offensive receiver intentionally blocks the path of a defensive player who's trying to stay with the receiver he's responsible for covering. Both the tight end and one receiver on the right side attempt to pick the defensive player covering the receiver (refer to Figure 8-13) running toward the flat area. If the receiver who's benefiting from the illegal pick doesn't come open, the first receiver attempting a pick runs 2 yards into the end zone and curls, facing the quarterback. After trying to pick a defender and if he believes he's wide open, the tight end settles, stops to the right of the formation, and waves his arm so the quarterback can see him.

Disguising a Successful Play

During the course of a game, a team often finds that one pass play works particularly well against a certain defense and matchup. To keep using the play in that game and to continue to confuse the defense, the offense often runs the pass play out of different formations while maintaining similar pass routes.

As an example, here's what an offense originally does: It lines up with three receivers (WR), a tight end (TE), and a running back (RB), as shown in Figure 8-14. One receiver is to the left, and the running back is also behind the line to the left, behind the left tackle. The tight end is aligned to the right, and two other receivers are outside of him. The receiver on the left runs down the field 18 yards and runs a square-in (for more on this passing route, see Chapter 5). The tight end runs a crossing route, about 7 or 8 yards from the line of scrimmage. The running back swings out of the backfield to the left.

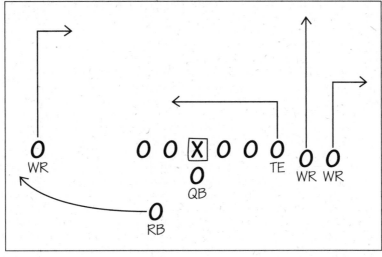

FIGURE 8-14: An example of a successful offensive play.

© John Wiley & Sons, Inc.

The receiver located in the slot to the right simply runs right down the middle of the field. He's the deep decoy receiver who's going to pull all the defensive players out of the middle. The quarterback wants to hit the receiver who lined up on the left side. If he isn't open, he tries the middle with the tight end; lastly, he dumps the ball to the running back.

To modify this successful play, the same receiver on the left runs the same 18-yard square-in, as shown in Figure 8-15. The running back on the left releases to that side, but this time he runs across the line of scrimmage 7 or 8 yards and curls back toward the quarterback. The back is now assuming the role of the tight end in the original formation. This time, the tight end runs down the middle of the field. The receiver in the slot now runs right between the two hashes and hooks. So it's pretty much the same play. The offense's target remains the receiver to the left. And all those other receivers are simply decoys.

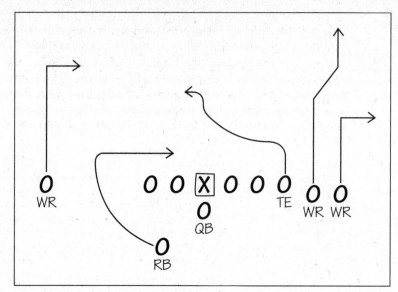

FIGURE 8-15:
An offense can modify a successful play by varying passing routes.

© John Wiley & Sons, Inc.

The Big D

IN THIS PART . . .

Take a look at the defensive line and understand sacks and tackles.

Look at how the secondary — the last line of defense — operates.

Brush up on defensive tactics and how to handle difficult situations on the field.

Chapter **9**

These Guys Are Huge: The Defensive Line

The game of football has changed a lot since I entered the NFL in 1981. Today's defensive linemen are bigger, and maybe faster, than those who played more than 30 years ago. Of course, they've had to keep pace with their main opposition, the offensive linemen. When I played in the NFL, you could count the number of 300-pound offensive linemen on one hand. Now, you need more than two hands to count a single team's 300-pounders!

Defensive linemen have to battle these huge offensive linemen. Then they have to deal with running backs and quarterbacks, whose main function in life is to make the defensive line look silly. Few linemen can run and move, stop and go, like running back Saquon Barkley of the New York Giants and quarterback Russell Wilson of the Seattle Seahawks. These guys are two of the best offensive players in the NFL, and they're also superb all-around athletes. Linemen, who generally weigh 100 pounds more than Barkley or Wilson, have a difficult time catching and tackling players like them. The few who can are the great linemen. However, many linemen have the ability to put themselves in position to stop a great offensive player. The key is: Can they make the tackle?

In this chapter, I address the responsibilities of every defensive lineman and talk about all the linebacker positions, explaining how those two segments of the defense interact.

Those Big Guys Called Linemen

Defensive linemen are big players who position themselves on the line of scrimmage, across from the offensive linemen, prior to the snap of the ball. Their job is to stop the run, or in the case of a pass play, sack the quarterback, as shown in Figure 9-1.

FIGURE 9-1: JJ Watt of the Houston Texans celebrates after sacking Eli Manning of the New York Giants.

Photo credit: © Tim Warner/Getty Images

The play of the defensive linemen (as a group) can decide the outcome of many games. If they can stop the run without much help from the linebackers and defensive backs, they allow those seven defensive players to concentrate on pass defense (and their coverage responsibilities). Ditto if they can sustain a constant pass-rush on the quarterback without help from a blitzing defensive back or linebacker.

For the defense to do its job effectively, linemen and linebackers (the players who back up the defensive linemen) must work together. This collaboration is called *scheming* — devising plans and strategies to unmask and foil the offense and its plays. To succeed as a group, a defense needs linemen who are selfless — willing to go into the trenches and play the run while taking on two offensive linemen. These players must do so without worrying about not getting enough pass-rush and sack opportunities.

The following sections take an in-depth look at the defensive line, which is also known as the *D line.*

A close look at the D line

Defensive linemen usually start in a *three-point stance* (one hand and two feet on the ground). In rare situations, they align themselves in a *four-point stance* (both hands and both feet on the ground) to stop short-yardage runs. The latter stance is better because the lineman wants to gain leverage and get both of his shoulders under the offensive lineman and drive him up and backward. He needs to do anything he can to stop the offensive lineman's forward charge.

REMEMBER

Defensive linemen are typically a rare combination of size, speed, and athleticism, and, in terms of weight, they're the largest players on the defense. A defensive lineman's primary job is to stop the run at the line of scrimmage and to *rush* (chase down) the quarterback when a pass play develops.

Defensive linemen seldom receive enough credit for a job well done. In fact, at times, a defensive lineman can play a great game but go unnoticed by the fans and the media, who focus more on offensive players, like quarterbacks and wide receivers, and defensive playmakers, such as defensive backs and linebackers. Defensive linemen *are* noticed in some situations, though, like when they

» Record a *sack* (tackle a quarterback for a loss while he's attempting to pass)

» Make a tackle for a loss or for no gain

Often, defensive linemen *contain* an opponent (neutralize him, forcing a stalemate) or deal with a *double-team block* (two offensive linemen against one defensive lineman) in order to free up one of their teammates to make a tackle or sack. The defensive lineman position can be a thankless one because few players succeed against double-team blocks. The only place where one guy beats two on a regular basis is in the movies.

The types of defensive linemen

The term *defensive lineman* doesn't refer to a specific position, as you might think. A player who plays any of the following positions is considered a defensive lineman:

» **Nose tackle:** The defensive lineman who lines up directly across from the center, "nose to nose," as shown in Figure 9-2. Like in baseball, you build the strength of your team up the middle, and without a good nose tackle, your defense can't function. This player needs to be prepared for a long day because his job is all grunt work, with little or no chance of making sacks or tackles for minus yardage.

The nose tackle knows he'll be double-blocked much of the game. He's responsible for gaps on each side of the center (known as the *A gaps*). Prior to the snap, the nose tackle looks at the ball. When the center snaps the ball, the nose tackle attacks the center with his hands. Because the nose tackle is watching the ball, the center can sucker him into moving early by suddenly flinching his arms and simulating a snap.

» **Defensive tackles:** The two players who line up inside the defensive ends and usually opposite the offensive guards. The defensive tackles' responsibilities vary according to the defensive call or scheme; they can be responsible for the *A gaps* (the space between the center and guards) or the *B gaps* (the space between the guards and tackles), as shown in Figure 9-3.

Defensive tackles do a great deal of *stunting,* or executing specific maneuvers that disrupt offensive blocking schemes. They also adjust their alignments to the inside or outside shoulders of the offensive guards based on where they anticipate the play is headed. Often, they shift to a particular position across from the offensive linemen when the game unfolds and they discover a particular weakness to an offensive lineman's left or right side.

» **Defensive ends:** The two defensive linemen who line up opposite the offensive tackles or on those players' outside shoulders. Where the defensive ends line up varies according to the defensive call or scheme. For example, in a *4-3 defense,* the defensive ends align wide because they have two defensive tackles to the inside of them (refer to Figure 9-3). In a *3-4 defense,* the defensive ends align tighter, or closer to the center of the line, because they have only a nose tackle between them, as shown in Figure 9-4. To find out more about 3-4 or 4-3 defenses, turn to Chapter 11.

The defensive ends are responsible for chasing the quarterback out of the pocket and trying to sack him. These players are usually smaller than nose tackles and defensive tackles in weight (that is, if you consider 270 pounds small), and they're generally the fastest of the defensive linemen. The left defensive end is usually a little stronger against the run, a better tackler, and maybe not as quick to rush the quarterback. He's generally tougher for an offensive lineman to move off the line of scrimmage. The right defensive end (who's usually on the blind side of the quarterback) is the better pass-rusher. On a few teams, these ends flip sides when facing a left-handed quarterback, making the left defensive end the better pass-rusher.

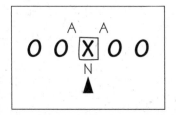

FIGURE 9-2:
The nose tackle (N) lines up opposite the center.

© John Wiley & Sons, Inc.

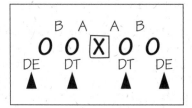

FIGURE 9-3:
The defensive tackles (DT) line up inside the defensive ends (DE).

© John Wiley & Sons, Inc.

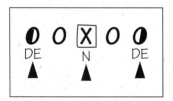

FIGURE 9-4:
The defensive ends (DE) in a 3-4 defense.

© John Wiley & Sons, Inc.

What makes a good defensive lineman

Great defensive linemen, like JJ Watt of the Houston Texans and Aaron Donald of the Los Angeles Rams are very rare players. Watt and Donald have combined to win Defensive Player of the Year five times in a seven-year period. Their combination of size, speed, strength, and durability isn't found in many players. A good defensive lineman has the majority of these qualities:

>> **Size:** A defensive lineman needs to be 260 pounds or bigger.

>> **Durability:** Defensive linemen must be able to withstand the punishment of being hit or blocked on every play. Because they play 16 or more games a season, with about 70 plays per game, defensive linemen are hit or blocked about 1,000 times a season.

>> **Quickness:** Speed is relative, but quickness is vital. A lineman's first two steps after the ball is snapped should be like those of a sprinter breaking from the starting blocks. Quickness enables a defensive lineman to react and get in the

proper position before being blocked. I call this "quickness in a phone booth." A defensive lineman may not be fast over 40 yards, but in that phone booth (5 yards in any direction), he's a cat!

>> **Arm and hand strength:** Linemen win most of their battles when they ward off and shed blockers. Brute strength helps, but the true skill comes from a player's hands and arms. Keeping separation between yourself and those big offensive linemen is the key not only to survival but also to success. Using your hands and arms to maintain separation cuts down on neck injuries and enables you to throw an offensive lineman out of your way to make a tackle.

>> **Vision:** Defensive linemen need to be able to see above and around the offensive linemen. They also need to use their heads as tools to ward off offensive linemen attempting to block them. A defensive lineman initially uses his head to absorb the impact and stop the momentum of his opponent. Then, using his hands, he forces separation. But before the ball is snapped and before impact, the opponents' backfield formation usually tells him what direction the upcoming play is going in. Anticipating the direction of the play may lessen the impact that his head takes after the ball is snapped.

>> **Instincts:** Defensive linemen need to know the situation, down, and distance to a first down or a score. And they must be able to know and read the stances of all the offensive linemen they may be playing against. In an effort to move those big bodies where they need to go a little more quickly, offensive linemen often cheat in their stances more than any position in all of football. By doing so, they telegraph their intentions. Defensive linemen must assess these signs prior to the snap in order to give themselves an edge.

For example, if an offensive lineman is leaning forward in his stance, the play is probably going to be a run. The offensive lineman's weight is forward so that he can quickly shove his weight advantage into his opponent and clear the way for the ball carrier. If the offensive lineman is leaning backward in his stance (weight on his heels, buttocks lower to the ground, head up a bit more), the play is usually going to be a pass; or he may be preparing to *pull* (run to either side rather than straight forward).

D-line lingo

Every football team has its own vocabulary for referring to different positions. For example, some teams give male names to all the defenders who line up to the offense's *tight end side* — they call these defenders Sam, Bart, Otto, and so on. The defenders who align on the *open end side* (away from the tight end) are occasionally — but not always — given female names like Liz, Terri, and Wanda.

Here are some of the most common terms that teams use to refer to defensive linemen and their alignments:

>> **Under tackle:** A defensive tackle who lines up outside the offensive guard to the split end side, as shown in Figure 9-5. The entire defensive line aligns under (or inside) the tight end to the split end side. Some of the NFL's best players are positioned as the under tackle. They possess strength and exceptional quickness off the ball, but they aren't powerful players.

>> **Open end:** A defensive end who lines up to the split end or open end side of the formation — away from the tight end side, as shown in Figure 9-6. (If the offensive formation has two tight ends, there's no open side and therefore no open end.) Coaches generally put their best pass-rusher at the open end position for two reasons: He has the athletic ability to match up with the offensive tackle, and if he's positioned wide enough, a running back may be forced to attempt to block him, which would be a mismatch. Houston Texans end/linebacker Jadeveon Clowney, who had 9 sacks in 2018, typifies the all-around open end.

>> **Elephant end:** The elephant end lines up on the tight end side of the offense, as shown in Figure 9-7, and then attempts to disrupt the tight end's *release* (his desire to escape the line of scrimmage and run down the field) on each play. This position was made famous by the San Francisco 49ers and was suited to the specific skills of Charles Haley, the only defensive player to have earned five Super Bowl rings. Haley was ideal for the position because he was a great pass-rusher as well as strong, like an elephant, which enabled him to hold his position against the run. This position gives the defense an advantage because the tight end generally has trouble blocking this talented defensive end.

>> **Pass-rushing end:** A player on the defense who has superior skills at combating offensive linemen and pressuring the quarterback. These ends can line up on either side of the defensive line. A pass-rushing end, like Chandler Jones of the Arizona Cardinals, has the job of getting the best possible pass-rush, although he reacts to the run if a pass play doesn't develop. If the quarterback is in a *shotgun formation* (see Chapter 5), the pass-rushing end must focus on where he expects the quarterback to be when he attempts to throw his pass.

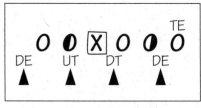

FIGURE 9-5: The under tackle (UT) lines up outside an offensive guard.

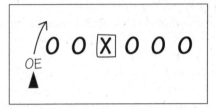

FIGURE 9-6:
The open end (OE) goes head-to-head with an offensive tackle or a running back.

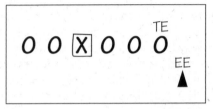

FIGURE 9-7:
The elephant end (EE) is the tight end's greatest foe.

The keys to a defensive lineman

A *key* is what a defensive player looks at prior to the snap of the ball. For example, if it's first-and-5, odds are that the offense will attempt to run the ball. The defensive lineman must *key* (watch) the offensive lineman and be prepared to react to his movements.

Here's a quick rundown of a defensive lineman's thought process prior to any play:

>> **Alignment:** The defensive lineman has to make sure he's aligned correctly.

>> **Stance:** The stance he's using should be to his advantage.

>> **Assignment:** Does he know exactly what to do?

>> **Key:** The lineman considers what/whom he should be looking at.

>> **Get off:** He has to be quick off the football.

>> **Attack:** The lineman thinks about attacking and controlling the offensive lineman with his hands, and then escaping by using his arms and shoulder to push by him.

>> **Execute:** The lineman wants to execute his stunt to a specific area or gap and then react to where the ball is.

>> **Pursue:** He always follows the football.

>> **Tackle:** Finally, he can make the tackle.

And you thought tackling was the only chore of a defensive lineman! Now you know that they have many responsibilities (some of them thankless tasks), and they really have to be thinking to put themselves in a position to make a tackle.

Linebackers: The Leaders of the Defense

By the design of the defense, linebackers are the leaders of that 11-man squad. They're the defensive quarterbacks and coaches on the field, beginning every play by giving the defensive call. Like quarterbacks, one designated linebacker has a speaker in his helmet so that the defensive coordinator can relay the defensive strategy before every play. They set the standard for every defense by being able to get to the ball before anyone else. They're usually emotional leaders who excel in leading by example. If they play hard, their winning attitude carries over to the rest of the defense.

Although a linebacker's main intention is to tackle the offensive player with the ball, the term *linebacker* has become one of the most complicated terms in football. Linebackers have become football hybrids due to their wide variety of responsibilities and enormous talent.

Football is in an age of specialization, and linebackers are used a great deal because they're superior athletes who can learn a variety of skills and techniques. Some of them are suited to combat specific pass or run plays that the coaches believe the opposing offense plans to use. For that reason, coaches make defensive adjustments mainly by putting their linebackers in unusual alignments, making it difficult for the opposing quarterback and offensive players to keep track of the linebackers. Sometimes in a game, three linebackers leave the field and are replaced by two defensive backs and one linebacker who excels in pass defense. The roles are constantly changing as defenses attempt to cope with the varied abilities of a team's offense.

Because linebackers play so many different roles, they come in all sizes, from 215 pounds to 270 pounds. Some are extremely fast and capable of sticking with a running back. Others are very stout and strong and are known for clogging the middle of a team's offensive plans. Still others are tall and quick and extremely good pass-rushers. Regardless of skill or size differences, all linebackers have a few key characteristics in common: They have good instincts, are smart on their feet, can react immediately when the offense snaps the ball, and dominate each individual opponent they face.

The following sections offer insight into just what it is linebackers do, how they get those jobs done, and what kinds of linebackers you may see.

What linebackers do

The job description of all linebackers is pretty lengthy: They must defend the run and also pressure the quarterback. (Vacating their assigned areas to go after the quarterback is called *blitzing*.) They must execute stunts and defend against the pass in a zone or in what are paradoxically known as *short-deep areas* on their side of the line of scrimmage. Also, the middle linebacker generally makes the defensive calls (he informs his teammates of what coverages and alignments they should be in) when the offense breaks its huddle.

Linebackers also are often responsible on pass defense to watch and stay with the tight end and/or running backs. In other pass defense coverages, a linebacker may be responsible for staying with a speedy wide receiver in what's known as *man-to-man coverage* (more on this in Chapter 10).

To fully understand linebacker play, you need to be aware that every linebacker wants to coordinate his responsibilities with those of the defensive line. A linebacker is responsible for at least one of the *gaps* — the lettered open spaces or areas between the offensive linemen — in addition to being asked to ultimately make the tackle.

Every team wants its linebackers to be the leading tacklers on the team. It doesn't want its players in the *secondary,* the last line of the defense (see Chapter 10), to end up as the top tacklers, because that means the other team's running backs have consistently broken through the line.

TIP

To keep your sanity when watching a game, just try to remember which players are the linebackers and that the bulk of their job is to do what Bobby Wagner of the Seattle Seahawks (shown in Figure 9-8) does: make tackles from sideline to sideline and constantly pursue the ball carrier.

How linebackers operate

Linebackers must take full advantage of what they can see, feel, and do. Every drill they do in practice, which carries over to the game, is based on these things:

>> **Eyes:** Linebackers must train their eyes to see as much as possible. They must always focus on their target prior to the snap of the ball and then mentally visualize what may occur after the snap.

>> **Feet:** Everything linebackers do involves their ability to move their feet. Making initial reads of what the offense is going to do, attempting to block offensive linemen and defeat them, and tackling the ball carrier are all directly related to proper foot movement.

» **Hands:** A linebacker's hands are his most valuable weapons. They also protect him by enabling him to ward off blockers and control the offensive linemen. A linebacker uses his hands to make tackles, recover fumbles, and knock down and intercept passes.

The types linebackers

The following definitions can help you dissect the complex world of the linebacker:

» **True linebacker:** Linebackers who line up in the conventional linebacker position — behind the defensive linemen — are true linebackers. They align themselves according to the defensive call. Their *depth* (or distance) from the line of scrimmage varies, but it's usually 4 yards.

» **Sam linebacker:** A linebacker who lines up directly across from the tight end (the strong side of the formation) and keys the tight end's movements, as shown in Figure 9-9. His responsibility is to disrupt the tight end's release off the line of scrimmage when he's attempting to run out for a pass. The linebacker must then react accordingly. Depending on the defensive call, he either rushes the passer or moves away from the line of scrimmage and settles (called a *pass drop*) into a specified area to defend potential passes thrown his way. The ideal Sam linebacker is tall, preferably 6 feet 4 inches or taller, which enables him to see over the tight end. (Tight ends also tend to be tall.)

When he played with the New York Giants in the 1980s, Carl Banks was a perfect fit for the Sam linebacker position. He had long arms and viselike hands, giving him the ability to control the tight end or *shed* him (push him away) if he needed to run to a specific side. The Sam linebacker needs to immobilize the tight end as well as have the athletic ability to pursue any ball carrier.

>> **Will linebacker:** The macho term for a *weak-side linebacker* (see Figure 9-10), the Will linebacker has the most varied assignments of any linebacker: He rushes the passer or drops into coverage, depending on the defensive call. He tends to be smaller, nimbler, and faster than most other linebackers.

>> **Mike linebacker:** This is the glory position of the linebacker corps. Every defensive player — from boys playing pickup games on the sandlot to men playing in the NFL — wants to play this position. The Mike linebacker is also known as the *middle linebacker* in 4-3 defenses (which I explain in Chapter 11). He lines up in the middle, generally directly opposite the offense's center and off him 3 to 4 yards, as shown in Figure 9-11. His job is to make tackles and control the defense with his calls and directions. He keys the running backs and the quarterback because he's in the middle of the defense and wants to go where the ball goes.

FIGURE 9-9:
The Sam linebacker disrupts the tight end during the play.

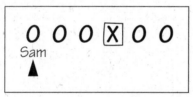

© John Wiley & Sons, Inc.

FIGURE 9-10:
The Will linebacker (W) covers the weak side.

© John Wiley & Sons, Inc.

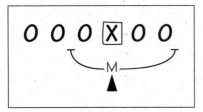

FIGURE 9-11:
The Mike
linebacker (M)
lines up across
and back from
the center.

© John Wiley & Sons, Inc.

Defensive Alignments

To better understand the inner workings of defensive football, you need to know how a defense lines up. Most defenses line up according to where the tight end on offense lines up. A defensive player, generally a linebacker, yells "left" or "right," and the remaining players react and align themselves. Alignments are critical to a defense's success. If the defense isn't in the proper alignment, the players put themselves at a great disadvantage prior to the snap of the ball.

REMEMBER

Here are some helpful explanations of terms used to describe defensive players and their alignments:

» **On or over a player:** The defensive player is directly across from the offensive player and no more than a yard apart — virtually helmet to helmet.

» **Inside a player:** The defensive player lines up with his right shoulder across from the offensive player's right shoulder. The defensive player's right shoulder can be directly across from the offensive player's helmet.

» **Wide of a player:** The defensive player is facing forward, and his entire upper body is outside the nearest shoulder of an offensive player. When the center snaps the ball, the defensive player wants a clear path forward so he can use his quickness to beat the offensive blocker off the line of scrimmage.

» **Over defense:** In this defensive alignment, four members of the defensive team shift position in order to put themselves directly opposite each player aligned on the strong side (tight end side) of the offensive formation.

» **Under defense:** This is exactly the opposite of the over shift. This time, three defensive players line up directly across from the center, guard, and tackle on the weak side (non–tight end side) of the offensive formation, leaving only a defensive end opposite the offensive tackle on the strong side of the formation.

The *open end side,* or weak side, is opposite the tight end, where the split end lines up on offense. Most defenses design their schemes either to the tight end or to the open end side of the field. When linebackers and defensive linemen line up, they do so as a group. For example, they align *over* to the tight end or maybe *under* to the open end.

Sacks, Tackles, and Other Defensive Gems

Defensive players work all game hoping to collect a tangible reward: a sack. Former Los Angeles Rams defensive end Deacon Jones coined the term *sack* in the 1960s when referring to tackling the quarterback for a loss behind the line of scrimmage. (The name comes from hunting: When hunters go into the field planning to shoot a quail or pheasant, they place their trophies in a gunnysack.) Unfortunately for Jones, who had as many as 30 sacks in some of his 14 seasons, the NFL didn't begin to officially record this defensive statistic until the 1982 season. Consequently, Jones doesn't appear on the all-time sack leader list, which is headed by Buffalo Hall of Famer Bruce Smith with 200.

When two defensive players tackle the quarterback behind the line of scrimmage, they must share the sack. Each player is credited with half a sack; that's how valuable the statistic has become. In fact, many NFL players have performance clauses in their contracts regarding the number of sacks they collect, and they receive bonuses for achieving a certain number of sacks.

Unfortunately, in the quest to rack up sacks, defensive players can get penalized for roughing the passer if they're not careful. The NFL has placed special emphasis on protecting quarterbacks from late hits and unnecessary roughness. Defensive players can no longer strike the quarterback in the head or neck area, even with an incidental, glancing blow. Nor can they tackle quarterbacks at the knee or lower. They must also avoid driving the quarterback into the ground when tackling. The bottom line is you can't hit 'em high, you can't hit 'em low, and you can't hit 'em hard. That makes a pass rusher's job pretty tough.

HALL OF FAME

Alan Page, Hall of Famer and defensive end of the Minnesota Vikings in the 1970s, was so quick that opposing quarterbacks often rushed their throws in anticipation of being tackled. Some quarterbacks would rather risk throwing an incompletion — or an interception — than be sacked. Page's coach, Bud Grant, called this action a *hurry.* The term remains popular in football, and pressuring the quarterback remains the number-one motive of defensive linemen on pass plays.

The term *tackling* has been around for more than 100 years. A player is credited with a *tackle* when he single-handedly brings down an offensive player who has possession of the ball. Tackles, like sacks, can be shared. A shared tackle is called an *assist*. Many teams award an assist whenever a defensive player effectively joins in on a tackle. For example, some offensive players have the strength to drag the first player who tries to tackle them. When that occurs, the second defensive player who joins the play, helping to bring down the ball carrier, is credited with an assist.

You may have heard the term *stringing out a play*. Defenders are coached to force the ball carrier toward the sideline after they cut off the ball carrier's upfield momentum. Consequently, the sideline may be the best "tackler" in the game.

A LINEMAN WHO PREFERRED KEYBOARDS TO QBs

HALL OF FAME

Mike Reid was raised in Altoona, Pennsylvania — about the craziest high school football town in the country. Reid became an all-state defensive lineman and a punishing fullback. Before football, his mother made him take piano lessons. So when Penn State offered him a football scholarship, he accepted and majored in classical music.

Reid was a demon on the football field. In 1969, he won the Outland Trophy, emblematic of the best lineman in college football. The next April, he was the first-round draft choice of the Cincinnati Bengals. He enjoyed football, but music remained his passion. He taped his fingers before every game, hoping to prevent them from being broken so that he could play the piano on Monday afternoons. After playing five pro seasons and twice being named to all-pro teams, Reid quit the Bengals in 1975 to join a little-known rock band. Five years later, he moved to Nashville, Tennessee, and began writing country western songs.

Reid has since written such hits as "There You Are" for Willie Nelson and "I Can't Make You Love Me" for Bonnie Raitt. He has won three Grammys and even wrote an opera about football, titled *Different Fields*.

Chapter **10**

The Secondary: Last Line of Defense

The *secondary* is the name given to the group of players who make up the defensive backfield. The basic *defensive backfield* consists of four position players: a right cornerback, a left cornerback, a strong safety, and a free safety. The secondary is the final line of defense, right after the defensive line and the linebackers (head to Chapter 9 for details on these defenders). The players who make up the secondary are known collectively as *defensive backs*, or *DBs*. Basically, their job is to tackle runners who get past the defensive line and the linebackers and to defend — and hopefully break up — pass plays.

Depending on the defensive scheme the coaching staff employs, the secondary can consist of anywhere from three to seven defensive backs on the field at the same time. (In rare instances, I've even seen eight defensive backs on the field at once.) However, most conventional defensive alignments use four defensive backs: two cornerbacks and two safeties. If all of this sounds confusing, never fear — this chapter is here to help you understand how and why a secondary acts in a particular way.

TIP

Be aware that a majority of big offensive plays (gains of 25 yards or more) and touchdowns come from the offense's ability to execute the passing game. Therefore, on the defensive side of the ball, a great deal of attention on television is devoted to the secondary. Often, a defensive back is in proper position or has good coverage technique, but the offensive receiver still catches the pass. Other times, the secondary player is out of position, failing to execute his assignment, or is physically beaten by a better athlete. If you know the difference and what to look for, you'll be regarded as an expert.

Presenting the Performers

All the players who make up the secondary are called defensive backs, but that category is further divided into the following positions: cornerbacks, safeties, and nickel and dime backs. In a nutshell, these players are responsible for preventing the opponent's receivers from catching the ball. If they fail, they must then make the tackle, preventing a possible touchdown. The different players work in slightly different ways, as you find out in the following sections.

Cornerbacks

The *cornerback* is typically the fastest of the defensive backs. For example, Deion Sanders, who played on Super Bowl championship teams in the 1990s with the San Francisco 49ers and the Dallas Cowboys, had Olympic-caliber speed and the explosive burst necessary for this position. The *burst* is when a secondary player *breaks* (or reacts) to the ball and the receiver, hoping to disrupt the play.

The ideal NFL cornerback can run the 40-yard dash in 4.4 seconds, weighs between 180 and 190 pounds, and is at least 6 feet tall. However, the average NFL cornerback is about 5 feet 10 inches tall. Although speed and agility remain the necessary commodities, height is becoming a factor in order to defend the ever-increasing height of today's wide receivers. How many times have you seen a great little cornerback like Antoine Winfield, who's 5 feet 9 inches, put himself in perfect position simply to be out-jumped for the ball by a much taller receiver with longer arms?

The ultimate thrill for a cornerback is the direct challenge he faces on virtually every play, but this is especially true on passing downs. A defensive lineman can win 70 percent of his battle against an offensive lineman and leave the field feeling relieved. However, the same odds don't necessarily apply to a cornerback. He can't afford to lose many challenges because he's exposed one-on-one with a receiver. If his man catches the ball, everyone in the stadium or watching on television can see. And if he's beaten three out of ten times for gains over 25 yards, he may be in the unemployment line or find himself demoted come Monday. Cornerback is a job that accepts no excuses for poor performance. The next sections describe the cornerback's role in two specific types of coverage.

Cornerbacks in man-to-man coverage

Most defensive schemes employ two cornerbacks (CB) in man-to-man coverage (which I explain further in the later "Man-to-man coverage" section) against the offense's wide receivers (WR), as shown in Figure 10-1. The cornerbacks align on the far left and right sides of the line of scrimmage, at least 10 to 12 yards from their nearest teammate (usually a linebacker or defensive end) and opposite the offense's wide receivers. The distance varies depending on where the offensive receivers align themselves. Cornerbacks must align in front of them.

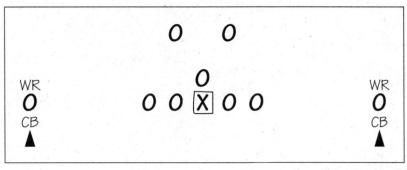

FIGURE 10-1: The two CBs generally line up on the far left and right sides of the line of scrimmage.

© John Wiley & Sons, Inc.

Most teams attempt to place their best cornerbacks against the opposition's best receivers. Coaches generally know who these players are and design their defenses accordingly. Often, they simply need to flop cornerbacks from one side to the other. Some offensive formations place a team's two best receivers on the same side of the field, requiring the defense to place both of its cornerbacks accordingly, as in Figure 10-2.

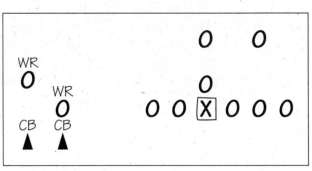

FIGURE 10-2: Placing two top WRs on the same side of the field forces the defense to place both CBs on that side.

© John Wiley & Sons, Inc.

Cornerbacks in zone coverage

Cornerbacks are also used in zone coverage (which I fill you in on in the later "Zone coverage" section). If a team's cornerbacks are smaller and slower than its opponent's receivers, that team usually plays more zone coverages, fearing that fast receivers will expose its secondary's athletic weaknesses. However, if you have two talented cornerbacks, like the Cincinnati Bengals had in the 2010 season with Leon Hall and Johnathan Joseph, your team can play more man-to-man coverage.

HOWIE SAYS

AN OUTSTANDING CORNERBACK PAIR

To win in the NFL today, a team needs to have a good pair of cornerbacks. When I played for the Raiders, we had an excellent pair: Mike Haynes, who was inducted into the Pro Football Hall of Fame in 1997, and Lester Hayes, who may still be inducted. When you have two great players like Haynes and Hayes — guys who can cover the best receivers one-on-one without surrendering any long gains — your front seven defensive players (some combination of linemen and linebackers) are all the more effective.

Cornerbacks are a special breed of athlete. They must be both physically gifted and mentally strong. Haynes was an effortless player, with a fluid stride and graceful movements. And *graceful* isn't a term that's generally associated with football players. Sometimes an opposing coach — the type who likes to take a hit on 17 when playing blackjack — would decide to test him and throw the ball his way, but rarely with any success. More often than not, when you throw toward a great cornerback, your play doesn't succeed. And in the worst-case scenario, the corner intercepts the ball and returns it for a touchdown. Haynes never talked much on or off the field, but he was deadly as a player.

Hayes was just the opposite. He enjoyed talking to newspaper and television reporters and seemed to have an opinion on most subjects. He loved talking on the field, too. He also believed in putting tacky goo on his hands and uniform. We called it "stickum." Stickum was so sticky that it was like having a Velcro glove or playing with a Velcro ball. Hayes covered himself with the stuff. When a pass would come his way, it generally would stick to his body, and then he would grab hold of it. In 1980, Hayes had 13 interceptions, the second-best total in NFL history. Soon after, the NFL outlawed stickum, claiming that it gave players an unfair advantage.

Safeties

Most defenses employ two safeties — a strong safety and a free safety. Safeties often are called the defense's quarterbacks, or the quarterbacks of the secondary. They must see and recognize the offense's formations and instruct their teammates to make whatever coverage adjustments are necessary. These instructions are different from what the middle linebacker (whom I describe in Chapter 9) tells his teammates.

For example, the middle linebacker focuses more on his fellow linebackers and the alignment of the defensive linemen. Also, he's generally too far away from the defensive backs to yell to them. The safeties must coordinate their pass coverages after finding out what assistance the linebackers may offer in specific situations. They often have to use hand signals to convey their instructions in a noisy stadium.

Strong safety

Of the two types of safeties, the *strong safety* is generally bigger, stronger, and slower.

Coaches often refer to (and judge) their safeties as small linebackers. These players should be above-average tacklers and should have the ability to backpedal and quickly retreat in order to cover a specified area to defend the pass (which is called *dropping into pass coverage*). The strong safety normally aligns to the tight end side of the offensive formation (also known as the *strong side,* hence the name *strong safety*), and 99 percent of the time, his pass coverage responsibility is either the tight end or a running back who leaves the backfield.

TIP

Good strong safeties like former Steeler Troy Polamalu are superior against the run offense. Many strong safeties are merely adequate in pass coverage and below average when playing man-to-man pass defense. When you hear a television analyst inform viewers that the strong safety "did a great job of run support," he means that the strong safety read his key (the tight end) and quickly determined that the play was a run rather than a pass. (Chapter 8 has more information on keys.)

The sole reason strong safeties are more involved with the run defense is because they line up closer to the line of scrimmage. Coaches believe that strong safeties can defend the run while also having the necessary speed and size to defend the tight end when he runs out on a pass pattern.

Free safety

The *free safety* (FS) is generally more athletic and less physical than the strong safety. He usually positions himself 12 to 15 yards deep and off the line of scrimmage, as shown in Figure 10-3. He serves the defense like a center fielder does a baseball team: He should have the speed to prevent the inside-the-park home run, which in football terms is the long touchdown pass. He also must have the speed and quickness to get a jump on any long pass that's thrown in the gaps on the field. Derwin James of the Los Angeles Chargers is an excellent free safety.

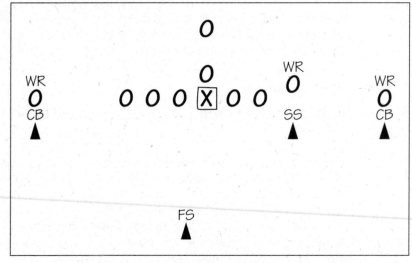

FIGURE 10-3: The FS lines up deep and off the line of scrimmage, hoping to prevent the long pass.

© *John Wiley & Sons, Inc.*

HALL OF FAME

I would be remiss if I didn't talk about Ronnie Lott, a Hall of Fame safety. What made Lott so special was that he could play either safety position. And he was so fast that he began his career as a cornerback. Never has a more intuitive player played in the secondary than Lott, who always seemed to know where the pass was headed.

Being the final line of the defense against the long pass, the free safety must be capable of making instant and astute judgments. Some people say that an excellent free safety can read the quarterback's eyes, meaning he knows where the quarterback is looking to throw the football. The free safety is the only defensive back who's coached to watch the quarterback as his key. The quarterback directs him to where the ball is going.

A free safety must also be able to cover a wide receiver in man-to-man coverage, because many offenses today employ three wide receivers more than half the time. (The first two are covered by the cornerbacks.)

Nickel and dime backs

Some experts try to equate learning the nickel and dime defensive schemes with learning to speak Japanese. Not so! All it's about is making change. When defensive coaches believe that the offense plans to throw the football, they replace bigger and slower linebackers with defensive backs. By substituting defensive backs for linebackers, defensive coaches ensure that faster players — who are more capable of running with receivers and making an interception — are on the field.

The fifth defensive back to enter the game is called the *nickel back,* and the sixth defensive back to enter is termed the *dime back.* The *nickel* term is easy to explain — five players equal five cents. The dime back position received its name because, in essence, two nickel backs are on the field at once. And, as you well know, two nickels equal a dime. However, each team has its own vernacular for the nickel and dime back positions. For example, the Raiders used to refer to their nickel back as the *pirate.* Regardless of the name, these players are generally the second-string cornerbacks. In other words, no team has a designated nickel back or dime back job.

The one downside of using a defensive scheme that includes nickel and dime backs is that you weaken your defense against the running game. For instance, many modern offenses opt to run the ball in what appear to be obvious passing situations because they believe that their powerful running backs have a size and strength advantage over the smaller defensive backs after the ball carrier breaks the line of scrimmage. Although defensive backs should be good tacklers, the prerequisite for the position is being able to defend pass receivers and tackle players who are more your size.

Substituting nickel and dime backs is part of a constant chess game played by opposing coaching staffs. Defensive coaches believe they've prepared for the occasional run and that these extra defensive backs give the defense more blitzing and coverage flexibility.

Figure 10-4 shows a common nickel/dime alignment that has a good success rate against the pass, especially when offenses are stuck in third-and-20 situations. This alignment enables teams to use many different defensive looks, which help to confuse the quarterback. But this scheme is poor against the run, so the defense has to remain alert to the possibility that the offense will fake a pass and run the ball instead.

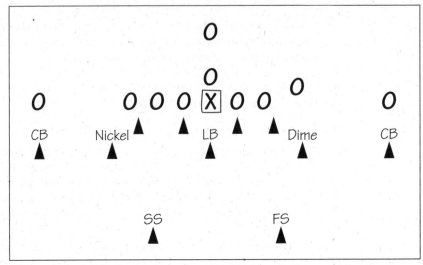

FIGURE 10-4:
A common nickel/
dime alignment
that works well
against the pass.

Studying Secondary Tricks and Techniques

Being a defensive back is pretty scary. Often, the entire weight of the game is on your shoulders. One misstep in pass coverage or one missed tackle can lead to a touchdown. Also, a defensive back may be the only player between the ball carrier and the end zone. So this means that the defensive back has to be a good, smart tackler rather than an aggressive one.

When defensive backs line up, they rarely know whether the play will be a pass or a run. In a split second after the ball is snapped, they must determine the offense's intentions and, if it's a pass play, turn and run with one of the fastest players (the wide receiver) on the field. In the following sections, I introduce you to some of the tricks of their trade.

Doing a bump and run

The meaning of the term *bump and run* has been altered through the years. Thirty years ago, a cornerback could bump a receiver and then bump him again. Many cornerbacks held on for dear life, fearful the receiver would escape and catch a touchdown pass. Mel Blount, a Hall of Fame cornerback with the champion Pittsburgh Steelers of the 1970s, may have had the strongest hands of any defensive back. When he grabbed a receiver, even with one hand, the man could go nowhere; Blount would ride him out of the play. By *ride* I mean Blount (or any strong defensive back) could push the receiver away from his intended pass route. Most defensive backs tend to ride their receivers, if they can, toward the sidelines.

Blount perfected his hands-on technique so well that in 1978, the NFL's Competition Committee (coaches, owners, and general managers who are appointed to study and make rule changes) rewrote the chuck rule, or what's known as the *bump* in bump and run. Consequently, defensive backs are still allowed to hit receivers within 5 yards of the line of scrimmage, but beyond that, hitting a receiver is a penalty. The penalty for this illegal use of the hands gives the offense an automatic first down and 5 free yards (turn to Chapter 3 for the full scoop on penalties).

TIP

Today, you may see defensive backs with their hands on receivers beyond 5 yards. Sometimes the officials catch them, and sometimes they don't. The intent remains the same: Defensive backs want to get in the faces of the receivers and chuck them or jam them (using both hands) as they come off the line of scrimmage. The idea is to disrupt the timing of the pass play by hitting the receiver in the chest with both hands, thereby forcing the receiver to take a bad step. Often, the defensive back pushes the receiver in order to redirect him. A defensive back generally knows which way a receiver wants to go. By bumping him to one side, the defensive back may force the receiver to alter his pass route.

Staying with a receiver

After bumping or attempting to jam a receiver, a defensive back must be able to turn and run with the receiver. Sometimes, the defensive back (especially a cornerback) ends up chasing the receiver. When he needs to turn, the defensive back should make half-turns, rotating his upper body to the same side as the receiver. When the receiver turns to face the ball in the air, the defensive player should turn his body to the side of the receiver to which his arms are extended.

A defensive back must practice his footwork so he can take long strides when backpedaling away from the line of scrimmage while covering a receiver. When he turns, he should be able to take a long crossover step with his feet while keeping his upper body erect. This technique is difficult because the defensive back often has to move backward as quickly as the receiver runs forward. When he turns to meet the receiver and the pass, the defensive back should be running as fast as he can to maintain close contact with the receiver.

Stemming around

The term *stemming around* sounds foolish, and, in all honesty, defensive backs may look foolish while they're stemming around. Well, at least they're not standing around. Anyway, *stemming* describes the action of the defensive backs when they move around after appearing to be settled in their alignments prior to the offense's snap of the ball. By stemming, they attempt to fool the quarterback and force him into making a bad decision about where to throw the football. This tactic is becoming quite popular in defensive football (all players can do it, but it's most noticeable in defensive backs and linebackers) because it creates an uncertainty in the quarterback's mind, thus disrupting his decision making.

The most successful stemming ploy by the secondary is to give the quarterback the impression that they're playing man-to-man coverage when they're really playing zone coverage. This ploy usually results in a *poor read* (an inaccurate interpretation of the defense) by the quarterback. A poor read can lead to a deflected pass, an incomplete pass, or an interception — the secondary's ultimate goal.

Making a Mark: A Good Day in the Life of a Defensive Back

Quarterbacks and receivers tend to pick on defensive backs. Former Miami Dolphins quarterback Dan Marino passed them silly, and receivers like Mike Evans of the Tampa Bay Buccaneers and Julio Jones of the Atlanta Falcons simply push them aside with their size and strength. The only way a defensive back can retaliate is to make a play.

REMEMBER

This list shows some of the positive plays a defensive back can use to make his mark. The first three plays are reflected on the statistical sheet after the game; the rest just go into the receiver's or quarterback's memory bank. Of course, all tackles are recorded, but the ones I list here have a unique style of their own.

>> **Interception:** The ultimate prize is an *interception,* which is when a defensive back picks off a pass intended for a receiver. An even bigger thrill is returning the catch for a defensive touchdown, which is called a *pick-six* (*pick* because the pass was picked off, and *six* because returning the catch for a touchdown scores six points).

>> **Pass defensed:** *Pass defensed* is a statistic that a defensive back achieves every time he deflects a pass or knocks the ball out of a receiver's hands. You can also say that the defensive back *broke up a pass.* A pass defensed means an incompletion for the quarterback.

>> **Forced fumble:** A *forced fumble* is when a defensive back forces the ball away from a receiver after he gains possession of the ball. Defensive backs have been known to use both hands to pull the ball away from the receiver's grasp. This play is also known as *stripping the ball.* Any defensive player can force a fumble, and forced fumbles can happen on running plays, too.

>> **Knockout tackle:** The *knockout tackle* is the ultimate tackle because it puts a wide receiver down for the count. Every safety in the league wants a knockout tackle; it's a sign of intimidation. Defensive backs believe in protecting their (coverage) space and protecting it well. Cornerbacks want these hits, too, but many of them are satisfied with bringing an offensive player down any way they can.

>> **Groundhog hit:** A *groundhog hit* is a perfectly timed tackle on a receiver who's leaping for the ball. Instead of aiming for the body, the defensive back goes for the feet, flipping the receiver headfirst into the ground.

The Problem of Pass Interference and Illegal Contact

When a receiver is running in a pass pattern and is more than 5 yards away from the line of scrimmage, a defensive player can't push, shove, hold, or otherwise impede the progress of the receiver. If he does any of those things before the quarterback throws the ball, he's called for either *defensive holding* or *illegal contact*. Both penalties result in 5 yards and an automatic first down for the offense.

When a pass is in the air, if a defensive player pushes, shoves, holds, or otherwise physically prevents an offensive receiver from moving his body or his arms in an attempt to catch the pass, he's called for *pass interference.* Except for being ejected from a game, pass interference is the worst penalty in professional football for any member of the defensive team. Why? Because the number of yards that the defense is penalized is determined by where the penalty (or foul) is committed. So when the officials call pass interference against a defensive player on a pass attempt that travels 50 yards beyond the line of scrimmage, the penalty is 50 yards. The offensive team is given the ball and a first down at that spot on the field. If a defensive player is *flagged* (penalized) in the end zone, the offensive team is given the ball on the 1-yard line with a first down. (The offense is never awarded a touchdown on a pass interference penalty.)

This penalty is a judgment call, and you often see players from both sides arguing for or against a pass interference penalty. Officials don't usually call pass interference when a defensive player, who also has a right to try to catch any ball, drives his body toward a pass, gets his hand or fingers on the ball, and then instantaneously makes physical contact with the receiver. The critical point is that the defensive player touched the ball a split second *before* colliding with the receiver.

On these plays, the defensive back appears to be coming over the receiver's shoulder to knock down the pass. Often, you can't tell whether the official made the right call on these types of plays until you see them in a slow-motion replay on television. These plays (called *bang-bang plays*) occur very quickly on the field.

In recent years, the NFL has asked officials to pay special attention to defensive coverage of receivers. The result has been a tremendous increase in the number of holding, illegal contact, and pass interference penalties on the defense. Defensive players feel like they can't even breathe heavily on receivers without getting flagged. Any sort of incidental bumping or pushing now warrants a flag.

Defensive backs (safeties and cornerbacks) now can't afford to cover receivers tightly, so they have to give the receivers a bit of a cushion. This softer style has allowed offenses throughout the league to rack up huge passing numbers. Receivers are catching more passes and offenses are gaining more yards. If you like this style of football, the game is more exciting. But if you prefer low-scoring defensive struggles, you're not a happy fan.

Examining the Two Types of Coverage (And Their Variations)

Football teams employ two types of pass coverage: man-to-man coverage and zone coverage. Both coverages have many variations and combinations, but the core of every coverage begins with either the man-to-man concept or a zone concept. I get you familiar with the core coverages first, and then I show you some of the variations.

Man-to-man coverage

Simply stated, *man-to-man coverage* is when any defensive back, or maybe even a linebacker, is assigned to cover a specific offensive player, such as a running back, tight end, or wide receiver. The defender must *cover* (stay with) this player all over the field until the play ends. His responsibility is to make sure the receiver doesn't catch a pass. The most important rule of man-to-man coverage (which is also known as *man coverage*) is that the defensive back must keep his eyes on the player that he's guarding or is responsible for watching. He's allowed to take occasional peeks toward the quarterback, but he should never take his eyes off his man.

Here are the three main types of man–to–man coverage:

>> **Man free:** In this coverage, all defensive backs play man-to-man coverage except the free safety, who lines up or drops into an area and becomes a safety valve to prevent a long touchdown completion. This style of coverage is used when the defense *blitzes,* or rushes four or five players at the quarterback. So, man free is man-to-man coverage with one roaming free safety. Linebackers also cover running backs or even tight ends man-to-man.

>> **Straight man:** The free safety doesn't serve as a safety valve in this alignment — or, as coaches say, no safety help is available. Each defender must know that he (alone) is responsible for the receiver he's covering. The phrase "the player was stuck on an island" refers to a cornerback being isolated with an offensive receiver and having no chance of being rescued by another defensive back. This style of man-to-man coverage is generally used when the defense is blitzing or rushing a linebacker toward the backfield, hoping to sack the quarterback. Defenses use it depending on the strength and ability of their own personnel and the receiving talent of the offense they're facing. So, straight man is pure man-to-man coverage with no roaming free safety.

>> **Combo man:** This category contains any number of combinations of man-to-man coverage. For example, when a team wants to double-team a great wide receiver (with two defensive backs), it runs a combo man defense. A great receiver is someone like Jerry Rice, who owns virtually every pass-receiving record in the history of pro football. The object of such a defense is to force the quarterback to throw the football to a less-talented receiver than someone like Rice (namely, anybody but him!).

In Figure 10-5, the cornerback (CB) is responsible for the star receiver's outside move, while the safety (S) is prepared in case the star receiver decides to run his route inside, or toward the middle of the field. A team's pass defense may be vulnerable on the side of the field opposite where it's double-teaming a receiver. Also, the pass defense may be vulnerable to a short pass on the same side of the field and underneath the double-team.

FIGURE 10-5:
Combo man coverage can prevent a talented receiver from making a big play.

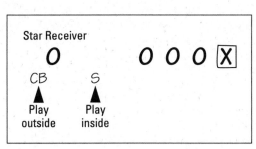

© *John Wiley & Sons, Inc.*

What's fun about man-to-man coverages, especially for players, are the endless personnel matchup possibilities that they provide. Also, against an excellent throwing quarterback like Andrew Luck of the Indianapolis Colts or the New Orleans Saints' Drew Brees, these combinations create something of a chess match between the quarterback and the defensive secondary.

Zone coverage

In *zone coverage*, the defensive backs and linebackers drop into areas on the field and protect those *zones* against any receivers who enter them. The biggest difference between zone coverage and man-to-man coverage is that in the latter coverage, a defender is concerned only about the player he's covering. In virtually all zone coverages, two defensive backs play deep (12 to 15 yards off the line of scrimmage) and align near the hash marks.

In a zone coverage, each defensive back is aware of the receivers in his area, but his major concentration is on the quarterback and reacting to the quarterback's arm motion and the ball in flight. Coaches employ zone coverage against teams that love to run the football because it allows them to better position themselves to defend the run. Other teams use zone coverage when the talent level of their secondary personnel is average and inferior to that of the offensive personnel they're facing.

For defensive backs, zone coverage is about sensing what the offense is attempting to accomplish against the defense. Also, in zone coverage, each defensive player reacts when the ball is in the air, whereas in man-to-man coverage, he simply plays the receiver.

TIP

The simplest way to recognize a zone defense is to observe how many defenders line up deep in the secondary. If two or more defensive players are aligned deep (12 to 15 yards off the line of scrimmage), the defense is in a zone.

Eight men in the box

I'm sure you've heard television commentators mention the term *eight men in the box*. They aren't talking about a sandbox, and they aren't discussing a new pass coverage. Instead, they're talking about a setup that enables a team to defend the run more effectively when it has a strong secondary.

The *box* is the imaginary area near the line of scrimmage where the defensive linemen and linebackers line up prior to the offense putting the ball into play. Usually, a team puts seven defenders, known as the *front seven,* in that box. But a team can put an eighth man — the strong safety (SS) — in the box, as shown in Figure 10-6, if it has two outstanding cornerbacks (CB) who can cover wide receivers (WR) man to man.

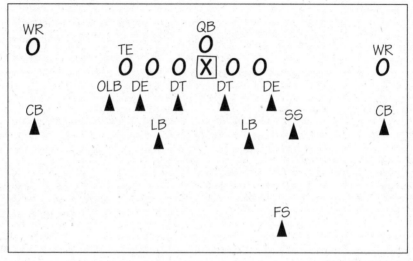

FIGURE 10-6: The defense puts an eighth man, the SS, in the box to improve its odds against six run blockers.

© *John Wiley & Sons, Inc.*

So how does a talented pair of cornerbacks drastically improve a team's defense against the run? By allowing the defense to play an extra (eighth) man in the box, where the defense has to deal with the runner. By placing eight defenders against six blockers — five offensive linemen and a tight end — the odds are pretty good that the running back will have trouble finding open territory. And when a team has talented cornerbacks who can defend the pass effectively, the defensive linemen and linebackers perform with the utmost confidence. They know that they can attack without worrying about their pass coverage responsibilities.

The Nickel 40 defense

By definition, the *Nickel 40 defense* is strictly a pass defense that can employ either a linebacker or another defensive back as the sixth player in pass coverage. It's a substituted defense (one that generally isn't used on every down) by skill and ability level. A defensive team wants to put its four best pass-rushers on the line of scrimmage, with one linebacker and six defensive backs.

THE PRESSURE OF BEING A CORNERBACK

A matchup between a great cornerback and a great receiver is as eagerly awaited as an Old West gunslinger's final duel. On January 7, 1990, the Los Angeles Rams and New York Giants were in overtime of a playoff game. With the ball on their own 30-yard line, the Giants had their defensive backs on the line of scrimmage (called *pressing*), hoping to prevent the Rams from moving into ideal field goal range.

Rams receiver Willie "Flipper" Anderson was lined up on the right side, and Giants cornerback Mark Collins had him one-on-one. If Anderson were to run past Collins, no safety would be available to help. Rams quarterback Jim Everett recognized the coverage and elected to try for the home-run play (a *bomb pass*) rather than a running play.

When the ball was snapped, Collins missed his bump or jam on Anderson. The game was now on the line. Everett floated a *rainbow* (a high-arching pass) down the right sideline toward Anderson, who had a 1-yard advantage on Collins. Near the goal line, Collins jumped, praying that he could deflect the pass. His fingertips missed the spiraling ball by 6 inches. Anderson caught the ball, the officials raised the touchdown signal, and the Rams won the playoff game. Anderson actually ran through the end zone, through the Giants Stadium tunnel, and into the locker room, the ball firmly in his grasp.

Afterward, Collins stood in his locker room aware of his failure, but his confidence wasn't shattered. "That's the life of a cornerback," Collins said. "You make ten good plays and one bad one, and all anyone wants to talk about is the bad. If you're going to play cornerback in this league, you've got to accept that this is your life."

The sixth, or dime back (DB), position can end up being a defensive back as well as a linebacker at times. In this alignment, the linebacker aligns in the middle about 5 yards away from the line of scrimmage (see Figure 10-7). He should be one of the team's fastest linebackers as well as a good tackler. Most teams use four defensive backs near the line of scrimmage with two safeties playing well off the ball, toward the middle of the field near the hash marks.

REMEMBER

The object of the Nickel 40 is to pressure the quarterback, hoping to either sack or harass him. Teams use their four best pass-rushers on the field in this alignment, and these four players will most likely be opposed by only five offensive linemen. Defenses use a Nickel 40 defense only when the offense uses three or more receivers in its alignment.

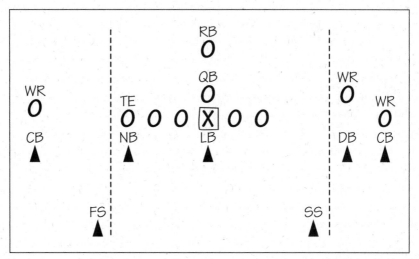

FIGURE 10-7:
In the Nickel 40, the defense puts a sixth player (DB) in pass coverage.

From this defensive look, the pass-rushers may stem or *stunt* (move about on the line of scrimmage), trying to apply pressure by using their best linemen against the offense's weakest blockers. Defenses also have been known to blitz the quarterback with one of the defensive backs or a linebacker in order to overwhelm the offensive blocking scheme. The defensive pass coverage in the secondary can be a mixture of man-to-man and zone alignments.

The Nickel 40 is a good defense against an offense that's fond of *play-action passes* (when the quarterback fakes a handoff to a running back, keeps the ball, and then attempts a pass; see Chapter 8 for more on these) or against an offense that likes to substitute a lot of receivers into the game. I'm talking about offenses that use formations that employ four wide receivers rather than the customary two wide receivers. The Nickel 40 defense, with faster personnel, can compensate and deal with an offense that prefers to always have a player in motion prior to the snap of the ball. It's also adept against other unusual formations.

Chapter **11**

Defensive Tactics and Strategies

Coaches will tell you that defenses win championships, and I'm not being prejudiced when I say that I agree with that statement. When I was in the right defense, in the proper alignment, that was when I had the best chance to succeed. When you're in the right defense, it comes down to you beating the man in front of you. As an athlete, that's all you can ask for.

The defense's battle plans are exactly what this chapter is about. Every team enters a game with a basic strategy. This chapter explains the common strategies — the defense's alignment and look — and how the defense can be "offensive" by dictating the style of play in a game. In this chapter, I cover all the basic defenses and help you figure out which defensive package works best against which offense.

Choosing a Base Defense

NFL coaches love to copy one another, primarily when a coach is successful with a particular offense or defense. For example, a lot of winning teams in the 1970s began to use the 3-4 defense (which uses three down linemen and four linebackers) as their base, or primary, defense. The 3-4 was the defense of choice in the 1980s; only Dallas, Chicago, and Washington preferred a 4-3 scheme (four down linemen and three linebackers). By the time the 1990s came to a close, the 4–3 defense was back in vogue, thanks mostly to the success that Jimmy Johnson had with the Dallas Cowboys in the 1990s. In the 2014 season, a slight majority of NFL teams used some form of the 4–3 as their base defense.

REMEMBER

Basically, what you need to understand is that the goals of any type of defense are to

>> Stop the opposition and get the ball back for the offense.

>> Seize possession of the ball via a turnover. A *turnover* occurs when the defense recovers a fumble or secures an interception.

To compete with sophisticated offenses, defenses have had to keep pace. In fact, some rules have changed simply to negate suffocating defenses. These rule changes have caused defensive coaches to return to the chalkboards and film rooms to devise more dastardly plans — and nowadays, they even use computers to uncover offensive tendencies.

HOW I PREPARED TO TAKE ON AN OPPONENT'S OFFENSE

HOWIE SAYS

When I played for the Raiders in the 1980s, I brought computer printouts to the locker room to glance over on game days. Those computer sheets showed every formation the opposition planned to use against us (or so we thought).

When I went on the road, I carried my own VCR and brought tapes that Johnny Otten, the Raiders' film guy, put together for me. I had him put every run play the team used on one tape, called a *run cut-up*, and every pass play on another, called a *pass cut-up*. These cut-ups showed every play that the opposition ran from a two-back formation, from the I-formation, and from the one-back formation. (I fill you in on these formations in Chapter 6.) Today's players study all of their necessary video on tablets.

We watched hours of film during the week, but on Saturday nights I watched a couple more hours on my own and broke down every formation. By studying and reviewing all the formations, I was prepared. For example, when the opposition's offense came to the line of scrimmage in a split-back formation, my mind immediately computed to "full left, 18 Bob Tray O," a run play.

I know that jargon means nothing to you, but it tipped off my mind. I knew which play was coming, which is more than half the battle as a player. The other half is stopping the play.

Most defenses are named by their *fronts,* or the number of defensive linemen and linebackers who align in front of the defensive backs. The most common front is the *front seven:* four defensive linemen and three linebackers, or three defensive linemen and four linebackers. It's assumed in football parlance that a front seven also includes four defensive backs: 7 + 4 = 11 players on the field.

HOWIE SAYS

I want you to fully understand the history, the reason, and the success/failure rates for each defensive scheme. Knowing why a team uses a specific strategy is important. Choosing a defense is like a game of checkers: A coach wants his team to stay a few offensive moves ahead of its opponent, anticipating the opponent's next move or play. The defense wants to prevent the offense from jumping over its defenders and reaching the end zone (or as they say in checkers, "King me!"). And, like checkers, you may sacrifice a piece in one area of the board (or field) to prevent the opponent from reaching your end of the board. The ultimate goal with any defense is to prevent a touchdown, so sometimes surrendering a field goal is a moral victory.

Examining the Different Defenses

The next time you watch a football game, try this little experiment: Right before the offense snaps the ball, glance at the defense and note where the defensive players are on the field. Then very quickly ask yourself, "What defensive scheme is that?" If you do this for a whole game, you'll start to understand — and appreciate — the different defensive strategies. You'll see why the defense lines up differently, for example, when it's making a goal-line stand or when it's defending against a long pass. You'll begin to see precisely what the defense is trying to do to stop the offense from gaining yards and scoring.

To help you recognize different defensive strategies, the following sections describe a handful of common lineups that defenses use to keep the offense in check.

4-3 front

The majority of NFL teams use the 4-3 *defense,* which consists of two defensive tackles (DT), two defensive ends (DE), two outside linebackers (LB), a middle linebacker (MLB), two cornerbacks (CB), and two safeties (S), as shown in Figure 11-1. The 4-3 was devised in 1950 by New York Giants coach Steve Owen, who needed a fourth defensive back to stop the Cleveland Browns from completing long passes. Owen, whose cornerback was future Dallas Cowboys head coach Tom Landry, called the 4-3 his *umbrella defense* because the secondary opened in a dome shape as the linebackers retreated into pass coverage. In the first game in which the Giants used it, the defense clicked, and the Giants beat Cleveland 6–0, shutting out the Paul Brown-coached team for the first time in its history.

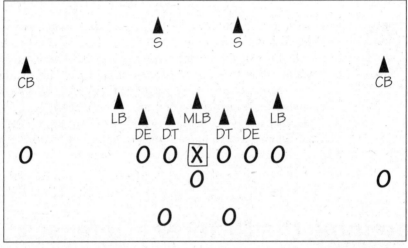

FIGURE 11-1: The 4-3 defense consists of four linemen (DE and DT), three linebackers (LB and MLB), and four defensive backs (CB and S).

© John Wiley & Sons, Inc.

HALL OF FAME

Although it was initially devised to stop the pass, the 4-3 defense should be able to stop both the pass and the run. The 4-3 was first widely used in the late 1950s, when Sam Huff became the Giants' middle linebacker and the Detroit Lions, who also liked the scheme, made Joe Schmidt their middle linebacker. Both of these Hall of Fame players were instinctive and played run defense well because they were strong and exceptional at lateral pursuit of the ball carriers. But they also played the pass well. They could move away from the line of scrimmage (in other words, *drop into coverage*) and effectively defend a team's short-passing game.

On paper, this defense is well-balanced. As with all defenses, having talented personnel is important. The 4-3 defense needs ends who are strong pass-rushers and physically tough against the run. The ideal middle linebacker is someone like former Chicago Bear Dick Butkus (see Chapter 19), who could single-handedly make defensive stops and possessed the all-around savvy to put his teammates in favorable positions. The defensive tackles should be strong against the run and agile enough to sustain pass-rush pressure on the quarterback.

In the 4-3, the stronger and more physical of the two outside linebackers lines up over the tight end, leaving the other, quicker outside linebacker to be more of a pass-rusher. With the exception of all-star teams, it's almost impossible for a team to have superior players at every position. However, teams tend to use a 4-3 when they have four pretty good defensive linemen and a good middle linebacker. If three of those five players have all-star potential, this scheme should be successful.

Later in this chapter, I tell you about variations of the 4-3, including the Dallas 4-3, the over/under, and the Chicago Bears' 46 defense of the mid-1980s. Some teams also use four-man lines but use more defensive backs rather than linebackers behind their four-man fronts.

3-4 front

Bud Wilkinson created the 3-4 *defense* at the University of Oklahoma in the late 1940s, but the 1972 Miami Dolphins, who went undefeated that year, were the first NFL team to begin using it in earnest. And the Dolphins did so out of necessity; they had only two healthy defensive linemen. Chuck Fairbanks, another Oklahoma coach, used the 3-4 as an every-down defense with the New England Patriots in 1974; also in 1974, Houston Oilers coach O. A. "Bum" Phillips did the same.

Unlike the 4-3 defense, the 3-4 defense uses only three defensive linemen, with the one in the middle called the *nose tackle* (N), as shown in Figure 11-2. The prototype nose tackle was the Oilers' 265-pound Curley Culp, who combined strength with exceptional quickness; he was an NCAA wrestling champion. The 3-4 also employs four linebackers (LB), with the other two defensive linemen (DE) usually consisting of one superior pass-rusher and a rugged run-defender. In some 3-4 defenses, all three down linemen are *two-gappers*, meaning they plug the gap between two offensive linemen and aim to neutralize those two blockers, allowing the linebackers to go unblocked and make the majority of the tackles.

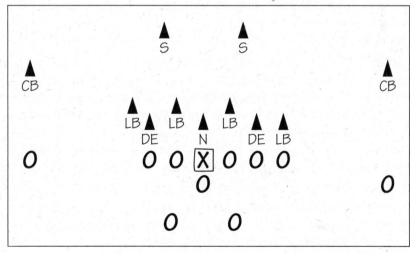

FIGURE 11-2: The 3-4 defense lines up with three linemen (DE and N) and four linebackers (LB).

© *John Wiley & Sons, Inc.*

NFL teams in the 1970s adopted the 3-4 because they lacked quality defensive linemen and had more players who were suited to play outside linebacker. This is also true today in high school and college, where teams may lack quality defensive linemen but have no shortage of athletes who are capable of playing linebacker. The outside linebacker position fits an NFL player who's at least 6 feet 3 inches, 240 pounds (the bigger and taller, the better). This player should have the ability to play the run and rush the passer like a defensive end.

The 3-4 can be a flexible defense. In some instances, the defense may decide to drop seven or eight players into pass coverage. Conversely, the interchangeable personnel of a 3-4 could end up sending three to five players to rush the quarterback. In the 1970s, Miami actually called its 3-4 defense "the 53" after linebacker Bob Matheson's jersey number. Matheson moved around, but he was primarily a pass-rushing linebacker.

The 3-4 defense is ideally suited to defending multiple offensive formations, meaning a defensive coordinator can match his personnel with that of the offense. Also, the physically dominant nose tackle can prove to be a nightmare for the offensive center. The nose tackle can neutralize the center's pass-blocking attempts by constantly shoving his strong head and shoulders to the ground or moving the center sideways, thus negating his effectiveness as a blocker.

The 3-4 defense also spawned the term *two-gap style.* With this technique, the defensive linemen and inside linebackers actually block the offensive linemen to either side, opening a lane for the untouched outside linebacker to make the play. The 3-4 defense focuses on the outside linebackers; in fact, they're the stars of this defense.

HALL OF FAME

The greatest defensive player I ever saw, Lawrence Taylor of the New York Giants, was essentially an outside linebacker in a 3-4 scheme. Although Taylor was great at sacking the quarterback in this scheme, the 3-4 defense generally is better at stopping the run than rushing the passer. And Taylor was exceptional at both aspects of the game — he could rush but also stand his ground and contain the run. Plus, he had the speed to pursue a running back moving away from him and still make the tackle.

The NFL in recent years has seen an increase in the number of teams using the 3-4 defense. The New England Patriots and Pittsburgh Steelers, who between them won five Super Bowls in the first decade of the 2000s, used the 3-4. But for the most part, NFL teams have shied away from the 3-4 defense because, to be successful, they need tall, 250-pound outside linebackers who also have speed. That kind of player is hard to come by.

3-4 eagle

Fritz Shurmur started using the *3-4 eagle defense* with the Los Angeles Rams in the late 1980s. Shurmur's defense used another linebacker in the role of the nose tackle, as shown in Figure 11-3. Instead of having a 300-pound player over the center, Shurmur inserted a 240-pound linebacker, a player who was susceptible to the run because most offensive centers outweighed him by 60 pounds. To succeed against the run, this linebacker needed to use his quickness and guile to shoot offensive line gaps. However, this linebacker was a solid tackler and was also good at dropping into pass coverage. The remaining personnel were identical to a typical 3-4 scheme, so it was sometimes referred to as a 2-5 eagle because of the five linebackers.

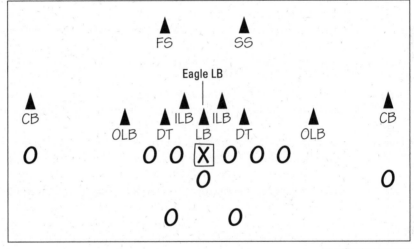

FIGURE 11-3:
The 3-4 eagle defense uses a linebacker (LB) in place of the nose tackle.

© *John Wiley & Sons, Inc.*

Shurmur devised this defense to confront (and ideally confuse) San Francisco 49ers quarterback Joe Montana, who had an exceptional ability to read a defense correctly and complete a pass to the open man. Having a lighter and faster linebacker drop into passing lanes was a totally foreign concept to any quarterback, who was used to that player remaining along the line of scrimmage rather than roaming in the defensive backfield like a defensive back.

The 3-4 eagle evolved from Buddy Ryan's 46 defense (described in detail later in this chapter), which is all about applying pass-rush pressure at the end of the offensive line. The eagle places a premium on above-average linebackers who can sack the quarterback by rushing around the last blocker at the end of the offensive line.

Most pass-rushers in this scheme prefer to line up away from the outside shoulder of the man responsible for blocking them. Outside linebacker Kevin Greene, who collected 46 quarterback sacks in three seasons (1988–1990), was the star (and benefactor) on Shurmur's Rams teams. Greene used his speed and exceptional strength for a 248-pounder to later lead the NFL in sacks twice (in 1994 and 1996). His 160 career sacks are the most ever by a linebacker.

The eagle is more successful with above-average cornerbacks who can play man-to-man defense, or man coverage. Man coverage complements the deep zone drops of two of the five linebackers. To me, it makes more sense to drop a 240-pound linebacker into pass coverage than to use a 310-pound nose tackle, which is what some zone blitz defenses do. That's one of the big differences between these two defenses. This defense can be very effective against a team running the West Coast offense (see Chapter 8), especially one that has a versatile running back who can damage a defense with his receiving as well as his running ability. Linebackers are better suited to catching and tackling this kind of ball carrier, while also being capable of defending the tight end, who's always an important performer in the West Coast offense.

REMEMBER

Despite the lack of a big body over the center, the eagle 3-4 defense isn't susceptible to the run because it employs two very physical inside linebackers and can bring a strong safety close to the line of scrimmage to serve as another tackler (or linebacker). This maneuver allows the eagle to put eight defensive players in the *box*, which is the area near the line of scrimmage where the defense is most effective at stopping the run. Some teams, however (particularly those with a good, versatile running back), have tremendous success running the football against this defense. Why? Because the offense is able to neutralize the light linebacker playing nose tackle and run the ball from formations from which it had always thrown the football. Such tactics confuse the defensive personnel, who are unable to predict what the offense intends to do.

Dallas 4-3

I want to make a distinction here: When Jimmy Johnson coached the Dallas Cowboys in Super Bowls XXVII and XXVIII, Dallas's defense had an abundance of talented players among the front seven but didn't have particularly speedy or skillful cornerbacks. The *Dallas 4-3 defense* used four down linemen and three linebackers but gambled more than Johnson would have allowed and occasionally used more of a nickel scheme, inserting another defensive back in place of a linebacker, as shown in Figure 11-4. This defense is predicated more on a team's personnel than on a particular alignment.

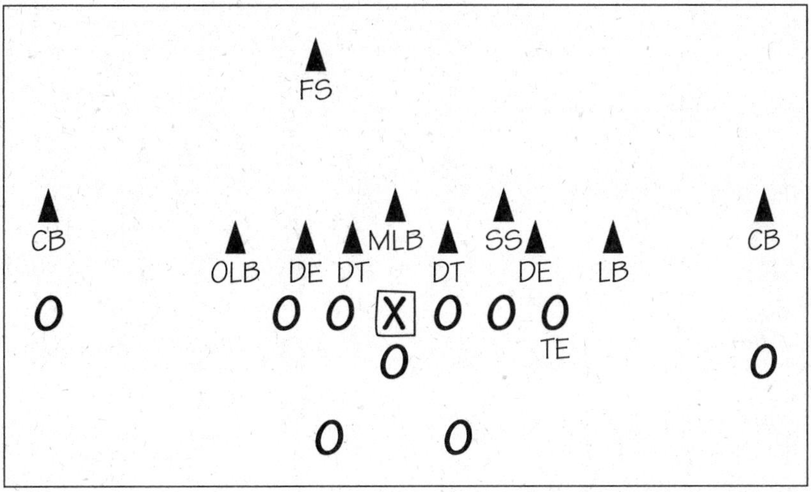

© John Wiley & Sons, Inc.

FIGURE 11-4: The Dallas 4-3 defense uses four linemen (DE and DT) but may use an extra defensive back in place of one of the three linebackers (OLB, MLB, and LB).

But what Dallas was able to accomplish, and what has been copied, was the scheme *cover four* or *four across* in the secondary. Because Dallas's front seven was so talented and could apply extreme pressure on the quarterback, the secondary was able to play deeper and prevent the deep pass. Of course, this scheme puts extra pressure on the two cornerbacks, who are expected to be able to take the opposition's two best receivers man-to-man and shut them down without any help.

In the Dallas 4-3 defense, the safeties also can creep up toward the line of scrimmage to provide support against running plays. Basically, this defense allows the safeties to cheat and overplay one aspect of the offense when they anticipate the play correctly. With the rest of the defense attempting to funnel almost every running play toward these physical safeties, the back goes down if the safeties make good reads. In modern football, in which teams may have physically gifted tight ends, the Dallas 4-3 defense puts the safety in a better position to defend the *seam pass*, the throw right down the hash marks to the tight end or to a receiver running straight upfield.

Flex

Coach Tom Landry invented the *flex defense* for the Dallas Cowboys teams of the 1970s and 1980s. It's a 4-3 alignment, too, but it *flexes* (moves back) two defensive linemen (DT and DE) off the line of scrimmage by 2 or 3 yards, as shown in Figure 11-5. These two offset linemen read the blocking combinations of the offense and attempt to make the tackle (or the sack) while their teammates try to break down the offense's blocking patterns.

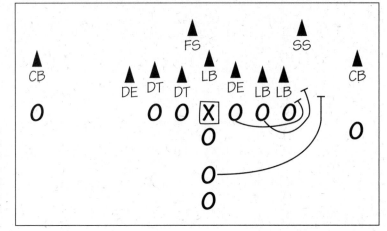

FIGURE 11-5:
The flex defense puts two defensive linemen (DT and DE) 2 or 3 yards off the line of scrimmage.

© John Wiley & Sons, Inc.

The flex defense works only if you have talented defensive tackles. These flexed defensive linemen must have exceptional speed and the ability to react. By being a couple of yards off the line of scrimmage, they should be able to see how an offensive play is developing. But to be able to stop a play from their positions, they also must have the speed to recover the 2 yards while moving forward. Being off the line of scrimmage makes it more difficult for offensive linemen to block them. The blockers have to run a couple of yards to strike them, but meanwhile the defensive linemen are also moving, quite possibly in a different direction.

HALL OF FAME

Bob Lilly (whom I tell you more about in Chapter 19) was one of the greatest defensive tackles of all time; Randy White (nicknamed *The Manster* because he was half man and half monster) was very close to him in ability. The keys to both players' success were their exceptional quickness and strength. White was a converted linebacker playing defensive tackle; you don't find many players capable of making that change. Shifting White's defensive position was a bold move by Landry more than 30 years ago, but this defensive scheme wouldn't work well today. The basic premise of the flex — to have defensive linemen reading — hinders the pass-rush. A player can't be reading and waiting for something to come his way. Instead, he has to react and attack if he wants to tackle the quarterback. The flex seemed like a great defense against the run until Eric Dickerson of the Los Angeles Rams ran for 248 yards against it in a playoff game at the end of the 1985 season.

Zone blitz

Zone blitz sounds like a contradiction in terms: Teams that like to play zone pass coverage generally don't blitz. Zones are safe; blitzes are all-out gambles. Dick LeBeau, a player and coach for 45 years in the NFL, is usually credited with inventing this defense in the late 1980s to take advantage of his huge safety, David Fulcher.

The Pittsburgh Steelers and the Carolina Panthers were the proponents of the exotic zone blitz in the mid-1990s (Figure 11-6 shows a zone blitz). From a base 3-4 alignment, they would overload one side of the offense by placing as many as three of the four linebackers to that side. They might stick a cornerback there, too, or put a safety there in place of a linebacker. The object was to confuse the quarterback and the offensive linemen, forcing them to wonder: How many people (four, five, or six) are really coming at the quarterback?

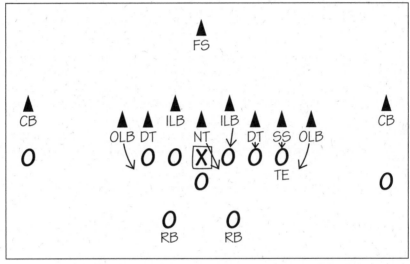

FIGURE 11-6:
The defense lined up in a zone blitz.

© John Wiley & Sons, Inc.

The down linemen in this scheme usually engage the center and guards. Their intent is to occupy these players and give them the impression that they may be rushing the quarterback. Often, the defensive linemen merely hold their ground while waiting for the run, or they stop, peel back off the line of scrimmage (by 5 yards or so), and then attempt to cover that area (this move is referred to as *short zone coverage*) against a possible pass play. The object of a zone blitz is to create one or two free lanes to the quarterback for the linebackers or defensive backs who do the blitzing.

REMEMBER

The zone blitz is an ideal defense against an inexperienced or gun-shy quarterback. The defense wants to get the quarterback thinking. Before any quarterback drops back to pass, he scans the secondary to try to figure out what kind of defense it's playing. This is called *reading the secondary.* When a quarterback looks at a zone secondary, he doesn't usually equate it with blitzing. But in this defense, the quarterback checks out the defensive front, too. He wants to have an idea where the blitz or the most pass-rush pressure will come from. A good quarterback believes that he can move away from the pressure from the suspected overloaded side and gain enough time to complete his pass.

The combinations and varieties of zone blitzes are endless. However, offenses have discovered that a short pass play to the *flat* (outside the hash marks) may be effective against this defense. Most zone blitzing teams give offenses considerable open areas to one side or the other underneath their final line of pass defense. Often, blitzing teams send a player who normally would be in pass coverage toward the quarterback. When a defense blitzes like that, it always keeps two people deep because it doesn't want to surrender a long touchdown.

46

The team most often associated with the *46 defense* is the Chicago Bears of the 1980s. The 46 didn't receive its name from its alignment, but rather because Bears free safety Doug Plank wore jersey number 46 and often lined up as a linebacker. Buddy Ryan, the Bears' defensive coordinator, altered Chicago's original personnel in the 46 defense — five defensive linemen, one linebacker, and five defensive backs — to four defensive linemen, four linebackers, and three defensive backs, as shown in Figure 11-7. The fourth so-called linebacker, the "46," is generally considered a cross between a linebacker and a strong safety.

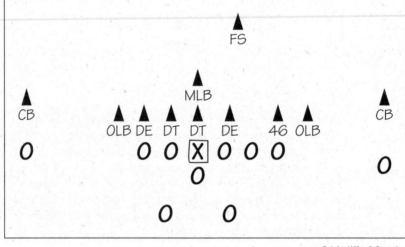

FIGURE 11-7: The Bears' 46 defense used four down linemen (DE, DT), four linebackers (OLB, MLB, 46), and three defensive backs (CB, FS).

© John Wiley & Sons, Inc.

HALL OF FAME

In the 46, three defensive linemen line up across from the offense's center and two guards, making it impossible for those offensive players to double-team the defender opposite the center. In Chicago, this defensive player was Dan Hampton. When Ryan became head coach of the Philadelphia Eagles, the player over the center was Reggie White. Hall-of-Famers Hampton and White were the strongest linemen on their teams; they were also excellent pass-rushers. Their exceptional ability made it possible for them to collapse the offense's pocket, thus ruining the quarterback's protection. They were good enough to beat two blockers in their prime, paving the way for teammates to have a clean shot at the quarterback as White and Hampton occupied his protectors.

The Bears had sensational success with the 46 defense. In 1984, they recorded 72 quarterback sacks, and the following year, they allowed only ten points in three playoff games en route to their Super Bowl XX championship. In one six-game stretch, the defense scored 27 points and allowed 27 points. When the Bears won the Super Bowl, the defensive players carried Buddy Ryan off on their shoulders, while the offensive players took care of head coach Mike Ditka.

In the 46, no defender lines up over the two offensive tackles. Instead, defenders are placed off both of the offensive tackles' outside shoulders. From there, their intentions are straightforward: rush and sack the quarterback.

The biggest downsides to the 46 defense are the pass-coverage limitations. Your cornerbacks are stuck in man-to-man coverage 90 percent of the time, with only one safety to help. You can drop an inside linebacker or two into zone coverage; however, when you line up with basically only three defensive backs on the field, often a linebacker gets stuck one-on-one with the tight end. If the tight end can run, this matchup may be a mismatch for the defense. Also, the 46 defense can struggle against a three-wide-receiver offense because of the man-coverage situations. But, the philosophy of this defense is to attack the quarterback before he can pick apart the secondary.

The 46 is a good defense against offenses with two-back sets. Why? Because such an offense doesn't spread the 46; instead, it condenses it. And that's perfect, because the 46 is an aggressive defense designed to attack. The two-back offense affords the 46 defense the opportunity to send its pass rushers off the corner. When they come off the corner, the edge of the offensive line, no one is there to impede their path into the backfield, where they can cause the most damage.

REMEMBER

The 46 defense can have a soft spot if the offense believes it can run wide against it, particularly in the direction of one of the offensive tackles. If the offense can block the two outside defenders, pushing them outside, the runner can cut inside the offensive tackle and run through that lane. And when the cornerbacks drop deep, the back may be able to gain a lot of yards. In college football, offenses beat the 46 defense by having the quarterback run an *option play*. In the option, the quarterback starts running around the end. He can either turn upfield or lateral the ball to a running back. (Note that pro coaches don't usually allow their quarterbacks to run an option play.)

Over/under 4-3

The over/under 4-3 is basically a scheme with four down linemen and three linebackers — what I call a Sam linebacker on the tight end and then two inside linebackers. The object of this defense is to shift more defensive linemen to the offense's suspected point of attack, which is called the *over*, or to shift the linemen to the weak side of the offensive formation, which is called the *under*. The down linemen are the stars of this show.

In the *under* 4-3, shown in Figure 11-8, one defensive lineman is on an offensive tackle, another is on the guard and center, and another is on the *open side* offensive tackle (the side opposite the tight end). In the *over* 4-3, three of the four defensive linemen shift toward the strong side of the offensive formation (the tight end side), as shown in Figure 11-9. A defender is always directly opposite the tight end in both of these defenses.

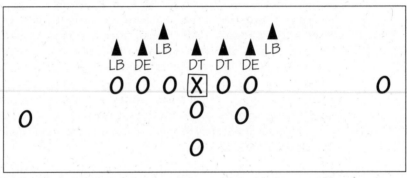

FIGURE 11-8:
The under 4-3 aligns on the weak side of the defense.

© John Wiley & Sons, Inc.

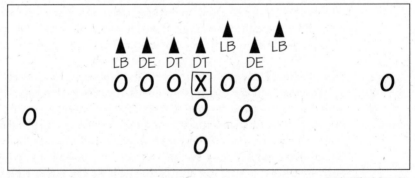

FIGURE 11-9:
The over 4-3 shifts the down linemen toward the offense's strong side.

© John Wiley & Sons, Inc.

The over-and-under scheme gives the defense flexibility in the way it uses its players in the secondary. Tony Dungy, former coach of the Tampa Bay Buccaneers and Indianapolis Colts, used to bring his strong safety close to the line of scrimmage, and suddenly he had an eight-man front. For a change-up look, defenses can drop safeties to their traditional spots 12 yards off the line of scrimmage and roll the two cornerbacks up to or within 3 yards of the line of scrimmage, making the defense look like a nine-man front.

For this defense to succeed, a team needs talented people up front — players capable of dominating the line of scrimmage. This scheme works only if the down linemen are special players like Dungy had with Warren Sapp in Tampa Bay. This defense can survive with average linebackers, decent safeties, and good cornerbacks, but it must have hard-charging linemen who are physically capable of beating offensive linemen.

The over/under 4-3 was a perfect defense for Dungy. Unlike Dungy, some teams and their coaches are very impatient; they want to attack and be aggressive, maybe pushing the panic button and blitzing the opposition before the time is right. But a coach like Dungy was able to sit back. He wasn't emotional. He folded his arms and let the offense keep the ball for seven or eight plays, believing that sooner or later the offense would panic and make a mistake. This defense can force an offense into making mistakes, too. Believe me when I say that some NFL offenses have trouble running eight plays without screwing something up.

Cover two (and Tampa two)

The cover two defense was devised to stop the *West Coast offense,* which relies on short passing routes and running backs coming out of the backfield to catch passes (for more about the West Coast offense, see Chapter 8). When running backs as well as tight ends and receivers all catch passes, how can the defense cover so many receivers?

The answer is the *cover two,* a 4-3 zone defense. Rather than cover receivers man to man, the defensive side of the field is divided into zones, with each zone the responsibility of a safety, cornerback, or linebacker. The deep part of the field (the area starting about 15 yards from the line of scrimmage) is divided into two large zones, each of which is the responsibility of a safety. (The cover two gets its name from these two large zones.) The safeties guard against receivers running downfield to catch long passes. Meanwhile, the area between the line of scrimmage and the deep part of the field is divided into five small zones, each of which is the responsibility of a cornerback or linebacker. The idea is to stop the short pass, or if a receiver succeeds in catching a short pass, to keep him from gaining more than a few yards. If a receiver breaks a tackle and gets downfield, one of the two safeties for which the defense is named is supposed to stop the receiver from breaking off a long gain. The cover two defense requires talented linemen who can pressure the quarterback into throwing the ball before receivers can break into the open areas between zones.

The cover two, designed to stop short passes, is susceptible to a strong running attack. What's more, the area in the middle of the field beyond 10 or 15 yards from the line of scrimmage is vulnerable because it falls between the two major zones. A speedy receiver who slips into this area and catches a pass can torch a team playing the cover two defense.

To protect the middle of the field, the Tampa two, a variation on the cover two, was invented. In the *Tampa two*, the middle linebacker drops back into the defensive secondary to protect against the pass, as shown in Figure 11-10. The Tampa two gets its name from the Tampa Bay Buccaneers, who used this defense starting in the mid-1990s under defensive coordinator Monte Kiffin. Running the Tampa two defense requires a stellar middle linebacker, somebody like Derrick Brooks, who played for the Buccaneers. Brooks had the speed to drop back and cover receivers as well as the strength and stamina to guard against runs up the middle. Most middle linebackers aren't blessed with that combination of speed and strength.

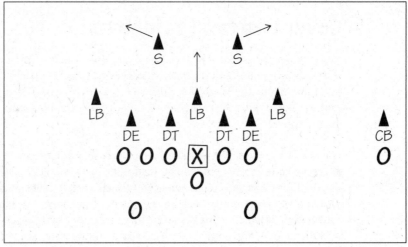

FIGURE 11-10: In the Tampa two, a variation of the cover two, the middle linebacker (LB) drops back into pass coverage.

Tackling Tricky Situations

Defenses are under constant pressure in every game: one mistake (a missed tackle in the open field or a blown assignment, for example) and the opponent has points on the board. The sections that follow tackle a couple of the tricky situations that defenses face and give advice for handling them.

Stopping a superstar

When playing against a superstar, whether he's a running back or a quarterback, the defense must decide what facet of the offense it wants to focus on. In other words, the defense says, "I'm stopping Todd Gurley and forcing the quarterback to throw the ball to beat me." Defenses can't do both — stop the run and the pass — against great offensive teams.

A team with a great safety, such as Harrison Smith of the Minnesota Vikings, can move its safety closer to the line of scrimmage without sacrificing his ability to cover receivers. The safety becomes another linebacker, the eighth man in the box. In other words, you have four defensive linemen and three linebackers, and you bring an extra run defender out of the secondary. If your safety reacts poorly, the defense can be susceptible to being beaten consistently by the pass. The consolation, though, is that the running back isn't going to run for 150 yards.

REMEMBER

Defenders must at least attempt to tackle a great back like Jones-Drew. They should never stand around and wait for a good shot; they should fly at him. If they miss, they miss, but they're definitely not going to bring him down if they don't at least give it a shot.

Stopping the two-point conversion

The two-point play can make or break a game — and ultimately a season. (Check out Chapter 8 for more details on the two-point conversion.) On a two-point conversion attempt, teams try to spread the defense and then run some kind of *pick pass pattern.* Here's how that pattern starts: The offense aligns two receivers on one side of the formation. The outside receiver runs toward the middle of the field, while the inside receiver runs, stops, and then heads in the direction of the outside receiver. When the two receivers cross, that's called a *pick play* because the inside receiver tries to rub the man guarding him against the defender who's covering his teammate. The desired result is an open receiver in the *flat,* the area beyond the defensive linemen but in front of the secondary.

In an effort to prevent the pick play, defenses trying to prevent two-point conversions are playing more and more zone coverage in the secondary. After all, they just can't stop all the combinations of different pass routes, especially when offenses use a three-wide-receiver set. And the pick play is particularly successful against man-to-man coverage. So in trying to prevent a two-point play, the defense anticipates that most teams won't run. Most offenses line up in a one-back formation with three receivers to one side.

REMEMBER

The key to defending against a two-point conversion attempt is not to blitz. Instead, the defense should use a four-man line and play a zone defense behind it. You can play as many as six or seven defensive backs across because the defense doesn't have to worry about the depth of the field. (After all, the end zone is only 10 yards deep.)

Stuffing short yardage

The first thing you have to realize in *short-yardage situations* (third down and 1 yard or fourth down and 1 yard or less) is that you can't stop everything. So you have to prepare your defensive front people — the defensive line and the linebackers — to stop one or two particular plays. Usually, you have eight defenders on the line, a combination of linemen and linebackers, and defensive players over both tight ends. The key play that you have to be able to stop is the offense's isolation play.

An *isolation play* is what happens on a blast play, when a fullback runs inside to block a defensive player standing by himself before the quarterback hands off the ball to the running back behind him. The running play is called the *blast play,* but it works because the fullback isolates a specific defensive player. On this type of play, the defensive linemen must establish positive gap control.

Here's what I mean: In addition to lining up across from an offensive lineman and defeating his block, each defensive lineman must get his body into a gap, either by *stunting* (when the defensive linemen jump to one side or the other, confusing the offensive linemen) or by lining up on the shoulder of an offensive lineman and securing the gap. Next, someone on defense must get some penetration across the line of scrimmage in order to have any chance of disrupting the play. (Offensive linemen have trouble blocking quicker players who are charging straight ahead into a gap.)

4

Meet the Rest of the Team

Chapter **12**

Special Teams, Masters of the Kicking Game

As you probably know, every football game begins with a kickoff. More than 94 percent of the time, a team kicks an extra point after scoring a touchdown. And every time a team scores, the team must kick off again. These are just a few examples of what's known as the *kicking game.* The proper name for the group of players who take care of these tasks is *special teams.*

Overall, this group of players is remarkable. A lot of effort, skill, and courage are involved in manning these positions. But no longer can you play ten years in the NFL, be a tremendous special teams performer, and play in virtual anonymity. Steve Tasker was a great special teams' performer on the Buffalo Bills' teams that lost four consecutive Super Bowls in the 1990s. Today, the perennial contender New England Patriots have one of the league's best special teams' player in Matthew Slater. Slater, the son of Hall of Fame tackle Jackie Slater, is a 7-time Pro Bowler, and Tasker was the MVP of the 1993 Pro Bowl, the all-star game featuring the NFL's very best players. Kickers and some return men garner attention, but for the majority of the other players — the guys who cover kicks and punts and block for kickers — the job is often pretty thankless in the eyes of the public and the media (and even within the team). Special teams players generally are noticed only for doing a poor job — when a punt or field goal attempt is blocked or when the opposition returns a kickoff for a touchdown. After you read this chapter, however, you should have a much greater appreciation for these fine athletes and the important tasks they do.

Who's Who on Special Teams

The players who put their foot to the ball are the *placekickers, punters,* and *field goal kickers.* They're all also known as *specialists.* On some teams, the punter handles kickoff duties, and the placekicker is responsible for field goal and extra point attempts. Other teams have players for all three positions. But there's a lot more to the kicking game than these two or three players.

When a punter attempts a punt, for example, 21 other players are on the field. The ten remaining men on the punting team have two tough responsibilities: to protect the punter's kick from being blocked and then to run down the field and cover the punt. They face ten players who are trying to slow them down, as well as the player who's catching the punt (the *punt returner*). The returner is generally one of the fastest runners on a team and a specialist in his own right. The punting team wants to prevent the return man from gaining a single yard, whereas the punt returner obviously wants to go the distance and score a touchdown. At the very least, he wants to place his team's offense in good field position, shortening the distance that the offense must travel to score.

Specialists have their own coach, known as a *special teams coach,* who serves in a capacity similar to that of an offensive or defensive coordinator in that he coaches a large group of players and not merely a specific position (flip to Chapter 13 for full insight into the coaching lineup). Some teams also have a kicking coach who coaches basically two players, the punter and the kicker.

Special teams are *so* specialized that a single group of players can't cover every situation. Four special teams units exist:

>> The group of players that handles punts, kickoffs, and punt returns

>> The unit that handles field goal and extra point attempts

>> The group that takes care of kickoff returns

>> The unit that attempts to block field-goal and extra-point attempts

Generally, great special teams players are unusual. Travis Jervey, who played for the Atlanta Falcons, Green Bay Packers, and San Francisco 49ers, and was selected for the Pro Bowl, had a pet lion. Special teams players are often the wild and crazy guys on a team, too. When coverage men stop a returner in his tracks, for example, they're usually as excited as offensive players scoring touchdowns.

MY OWN SPECIAL TEAMS EXPERIENCES

I was a special teams player during my first two years in the NFL. Being a small-college player from Villanova, playing on special teams gave me the opportunity to work my way up through the ranks on the Raiders. The NFL is kind of like the Army in that you have to prove you belong.

I was on most of the special teams units. I covered punts and kickoffs, plus I was part of the unit that tried to block field goal and extra point attempts. Matt Millen and I were the two bulldozers on the kick-blocking team. We used to get down in a *four-point stance* (both hands and feet on the ground) and line up on either side of the center, who snaps the ball. Ted Hendricks, who was over 6 feet 7 inches tall and had the longest arms I'd ever seen, would stand right behind us. Millen and I would basically function as a snowplow and clear a path for Hendricks. Ted was in charge; he'd tell us where to line up and what to do, and I remember him blocking a number of kicks.

When I became an All-Pro player in my third year in the NFL, my defensive line coach wouldn't allow me to play on special teams anymore because he didn't want me getting hurt. That's pretty much the philosophy in the NFL today. For example, quarterbacks used to be the holders for field goals and extra points, but it's pretty rare to see any of them holding these days. They don't want to hurt those pretty fingers!

What's So Special about Special Teams

A key thing to know about special teams is that these 11-man units are typically on the field for about 20 percent of the plays in a football game. But coaches often say that special teams play amounts to one-third of a football game — by that, they mean its total impact on the game.

Take scoring, for example — how games were won and lost in the 2018 NFL regular season:

>> **Offenses** scored 1,286 touchdowns and 66 two-point conversions for a total of 7,848 points. Remember, teams earn six points for a touchdown and two points for a two-point conversion.

>> **Special teams** accounted for 802 field goals made and 1,164 extra points for a total of 3,570 points just from kicking. Plus teams scored 7 touchdowns on punt returns and 5 touchdowns on kickoff returns for an additional 72 points.

>> **Defenses** scored 73 touchdowns on interception returns and fumble recoveries, which totals 438 points.

FIELD POSITION TERMINOLOGY

The main line of demarcation on a football field is the 50-yard line. The area on both sides of the 50 is known as *midfield territory*. A lot of football terms are defense-oriented. Consequently, when a commentator says, "The Chicago Bears are starting from their own 18," it means that the ball is on the 18-yard line and that the opposition, should it recover the ball, is only 18 yards away from scoring a touchdown. The Bears may be on offense, but they should be mindful of the precarious offensive position they're in. They want to move the ball away from their goal line, and probably in a conservative fashion (say, by running the ball rather than throwing risky passes that could be intercepted).

So while the offense does most of the scoring, as you would expect, special teams contribute a pretty big chunk of the total points. Another important function of the special teams unit is to maintain good field position and to keep the opposition in bad field position. The main objective of the kickoff, for example, is to pin the opponent as far away from its end zone, and thus a score, as possible. Kickoff coverage teams strive, though, to put the opponent 75 yards or more away from scoring.

Placekicking

Placekicking, which is one half of the special teams' duties, involves kickoffs, field goal attempts, and extra point attempts (an extra point is also known as a *point after touchdown*, or PAT). Unlike punting, which I describe later in this chapter, a kicker boots the ball from a particular spot on the field. You can read about the three types of kicks and the rules and objectives behind them in the next sections.

Kicking off

For fans, the opening kickoff used to an exhilarating start to any game. They see the two-sided thrill of one team attempting to block the other, helping its returner run through, over, and past 11 fast-charging players of the kicking team. (Well, make that 10 players. The kicker usually stands around the 50-yard line after kicking the ball, hoping he doesn't have to make a tackle.) And the kicking team wants to make a statement by stopping the returner inside his own 25-yard line. This is the object on every level of football, from peewee to college to the NFL.

But to improve safety for those on the field, kickers now kick off from the 35-yard line, and most can reach deep into the end zone for a touchback, thus negating most returns. A kickoff is ruled dead in the end zone for a touchback if it lands in the end zone and is not touched by a returner. Touchbacks are now placed on the 25-yard line.

The following sections help you understand what happens during a kickoff, from the decision made at the coin toss to the rules regulating kickoffs in the NFL.

Deciding whether to kick or to receive

At the coin toss, when captains from both teams meet the referee in the center of the field, the captain who correctly calls the flip of the referee's coin decides whether his team is to receive or to defend a particular goal. For example, if the captain says he wants to defend a certain end zone, the opponent automatically receives the ball. If the winning captain wants the ball, the opponent chooses which end of the field his team will kick from (and the goal it will defend). Except in bizarre weather conditions — when it's snowing, raining, or extremely windy — most teams elect to receive the kickoff because they want the ball for their offense.

On some occasions, a team may allow its opponent to receive after winning the coin toss, meaning it *defers* its right to kick off because the head coach probably believes that his defensive unit is stronger than the opposition's offense and wants to pin the offense deep in its own territory, force a turnover, or make it punt after three downs. Adverse weather conditions are also a factor because they may jeopardize the players' ability to field the kick cleanly, and some kickers have difficulty achieving adequate distances against a strong wind. In these conditions, a team may opt to receive the ball at the end of the field where the weather has less of an effect.

Setting up for the kickoff

For kickoffs, NFL and college kickers are allowed to use a 1-inch tee to support the ball. High school kickers may use a 2-inch tee. The kicker can angle the ball in any way that he prefers while using the tee, but most kickers prefer to have the ball sit in the tee at a 75-degree angle rather than have it perpendicular to the ground. During some games, strong winds prevent the ball from remaining in the tee. In those instances, a teammate holds the ball steady for the kicker by placing his index finger on top of the ball and applying the necessary downward pressure to keep it steady.

REMEMBER

The kickoff team generally lines up five players on either side of the kicker. These ten players line up in a straight line about 8 yards from where the ball is placed on the kicking tee. If the kicker is a soccer-style kicker (I describe this type of kicker in the later related sidebar), he lines up 7 yards back and off to one side (to the left if he's a right-footed kicker, or vice versa). As the kicker strides forward to kick the ball, the ten players move forward in unison, hoping to be in full stride when the kicker makes contact with the ball.

In both the NFL and college football, teams kick off from the 35-yard line. But that wasn't always the rule. In the NFL from 1994 to 2010, the kick off was moved back five yards to the 30-yard line. In college, kickoffs came from the 30 from 2007 to 2011.

So why was the kickoff moved up to the 35? The rules committees in both the NFL and college want to improve player safety. When the kickoff comes from the 35 yard line, most kickers place the ball deep in the opposite end zone. These deep kicks mean that the receiving team is less likely to attempt a return and instead accept a touchback. A *touchback* occurs when a receiving player possesses the ball in the end zone and takes a knee (known as downing the ball) or when the kicked ball is allowed to bounce past the end line. Touchbacks automatically give the offense the ball on its own 25-yard line.

When a kickoff isn't deep in the end zone, the receiving team is more likely to attempt a return. If the ball carrier has great blocking and can avoid a few tackles, he might return the ball past the 20-yard line, and that makes for exciting football. Unfortunately, kickoffs feature 22 players running full speed at each other, resulting in dangerous collisions. To reduce injuries, the NFL and the NCAA (National Collegiate Athletic Association) now require kickoff from the 35-yard line.

The move to the 35-yard line has definitely increased the number of touchbacks in the NFL. From 1994 to 2010, the touchback percentage from all kickoffs was around 11 percent. From 2011 to 2013, touchbacks increased to 45 percent. In 2018, the touchback percentage jumped to 59.3.

Kicking the ball

When the referee blows his whistle, the kicker approaches the ball. His objective is to hit the ball squarely in the lower quarter in order to get the proper loft and distance. As soon as the kicker's foot makes contact with the ball, his ten teammates are allowed to cross the line of scrimmage and run downfield to *cover* the kick — basically, to tackle the player who catches the ball and attempts to return it back toward the kicking team. The ideal kickoff travels about 70 yards and hangs in the air for over 4.5 seconds. Maximizing *hang time* (the length of time the football is in the air) is important because it enables players on the kicking team to run down the field and cover the kick, thus tackling the return man closer to his own end zone.

Again, the kicking team's objective in a kickoff is to place the ball as close to its opponent's end zone as possible. After all, it's better for your opponent to have to travel 99 yards to score a touchdown than it is for that team to have to move the ball only, say, 60 yards. Plus, if you can keep the ball close to your opponent's end zone, your defense has a better chance of scoring a touchdown if it recovers a fumble or intercepts an errant pass. And by pinning the opposition deep in its own territory and possibly forcing a punt, a team can expect to put its offense in better field position when it receives a punt.

To keep the kick returner from making many return yards, kickers may attempt to kick the ball to a specific side of the field (known as *directional kicking*) to force the return man to field the kick. The basis of this strategy is the belief that your kick coverage team is stronger than your opponent's kick return unit and that the return man isn't very effective. In this situation, the returner is often restricted, and the defense can pin him against the sidelines and force him out of bounds.

Many teams now opt to force the receivers into a touchback by either kicking the ball to deep into the end zone or out of the end zone completely. This tactic minimizes the risk of a long return. The offense then takes the ball at the 25-yard line.

The kickoff formation shown in Figure 12-1 typifies directional kicking. Instead of simply kicking the ball straight down the middle of the field, the kicker angles the ball to the left side. This style is ideal against a team that lines up with only one kick returner. The directional kick forces the returner to move laterally and take his eyes off the ball. The kicking team's purpose is to focus its coverage to one side of the field, where it hopes to have more tacklers than the return team has blockers.

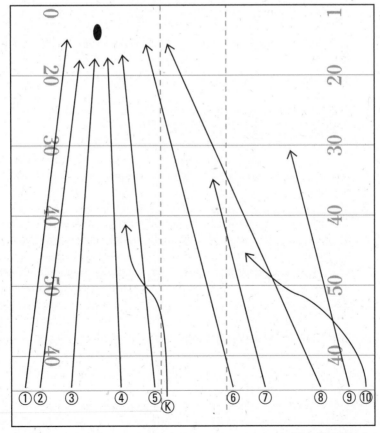

FIGURE 12-1:
Kicking the ball to a specific side of the field forces the returner to field it and allows the kicking team to focus its coverage on that side of the field.

Following the rules of the kickoff

Like virtually everything else in football, kickoffs are strictly governed by a set of rules:

>> The receiving team must line up a minimum of 10 yards from where the ball is kicked.

>> Members of the kicking team can recover the ball after the kick travels 10 yards or the ball touches an opponent. If the kicked ball goes out of bounds before traveling 10 yards, the kicking team is penalized 5 yards and must kick again. If a member of the kicking team touches the ball before it travels 10 yards, the kicking team must kick again and is again penalized 5 yards.

>> A member of the kicking team can recover the ball in the end zone and be awarded a touchdown.

>> Members of the kicking team must give the receiving team's returner the opportunity for a *fair catch*. If he signals for a fair catch, the players can't touch him and can't come within 3 feet of him until he touches the ball.

>> The receiving team gets the ball on its own 40-yard line (25 yards from the spot where the ball was kicked) if the kickoff goes out of bounds before reaching the end zone. If it bounces out before the 40-yard line, the receiving team receives the ball where it went out of bounds.

Returning the kickoff

The ultimate purpose of a kickoff return is to score or advance the ball as close to midfield (or beyond it) as possible. A team's ability to start out on offense in better-than-average field position greatly increases its chances for success.

Kickoff returners don't usually figure greatly in a team's success, but during the 1996 season, Desmond Howard was a major reason that the Green Bay Packers were Super Bowl champions. Howard returned only one kickoff for a touchdown that season, but his long returns always supplied tremendous positive momentum swings for his team. When he didn't go all the way, Howard was adept at giving his team excellent field position. Anytime he advanced the ball to his own 30-yard line or beyond, he put his offensive teammates in better field position and, obviously, closer to the opponent's end zone and a score.

THE WACKIEST KICKOFF EVER

HALL OF FAME

Alumni and fans of the Stanford/University of California at Berkeley rivalry know it simply as "The Play." It's also the only known touchdown scored while running through the opposition's band — as in *marching band.*

Stanford and UC Berkeley have faced each other in more than 110 games, and The Play occurred in the 85th meeting, on November 20, 1982. Stanford was ahead 20–19 with four seconds remaining, and most of the 75,662 fans were heading for the exits in Cal's Memorial Stadium when Stanford's Mark Harmon kicked off from his own 25-yard line because his team had been assessed a 15-yard penalty for excessive celebration following its go-ahead field goal. Given the field position and in an attempt to prevent a runback, Harmon made a *percentage kick* — a low-bouncing squibber. Such kicks are usually difficult to field and, because the ball isn't kicked a great distance, allow the coverage team a shorter distance in which to tackle the opposition. At the time of the kick, the Stanford band, a legendary group known for its zany attire and performances, poured onto the south end of the field (Cal's end zone), believing the game was over.

What happened next goes into football history under the "pretty unbelievable" category. Cal's Kevin Moen caught the bouncing ball on his own 46-yard line and ran forward 10 yards, where he was surrounded by Stanford tacklers. But before he was downed, Moen lateralled to Richard Rodgers. (A *lateral* is a legal play in which the ball is passed or tossed backward; it's illegal to pass forward on any type of running play.) Rodgers kept the ball briefly before tossing it back to running back Dwight Garner, who carried the ball to the Stanford 48-yard line. Garner was being tackled when he flipped the ball back to Rodgers, who started running forward again and, before he was tackled, lateralled to Mariet Ford, who sidestepped two tacklers and rushed to the Stanford 25-yard line.

As Ford was being tackled and falling to the ground, he tossed the ball up in the air, and backward, to Moen, the player who had originally fielded Harmon's kickoff. By this time, Moen and the players who remained were running through the Stanford band. Moen sidestepped some band members and then smashed through the Stanford trombone player to score the winning touchdown.

Final score: Cal 25, Stanford 20.

Great kickoff returners possess the innate ability to sense where the tackling pursuit is coming from, and they can move quickly away from it. A great returner follows his initial blocks and, after that, relies on his open-field running ability or simply runs as fast as he can through the first opening. Both Gayle Sayers of the

Chicago Bears and Terry Metcalf of the former St. Louis Cardinals were excellent at changing directions, stopping and going, and giving tacklers a small target by twisting their bodies sideways.

Teams want their kick returners to be able to run a 4.3-second 40-yard dash, but they also want them to have enough body control to be able to use that speed properly. Being the fastest man doesn't always work because there's rarely a free lane in which to run. Usually, somebody is in position to tackle the kickoff returner. Great returners cause a few of these potential tacklers to miss them in the open field.

The sections that follow offer insight into what happens when the ball lands in the returner's hands, both from the offensive and defensive perspective, and present the kickoff return rules to know.

Understanding the kickoff return rules

The following rules govern the kickoff return:

>> No member of the receiving team can cross the 45-yard line until the ball is kicked.

>> Blockers can't block opponents below the waist or in the back.

>> If the momentum of the kick takes the receiver into the end zone, he doesn't have to run the ball out. Instead, he can down the ball in the end zone for a *touchback,* in which case his team takes it at the 25-yard line.

>> If the receiver catches the ball in the field of play and retreats into the end zone, he must bring the ball out of the end zone. If he's tackled in the end zone, the kicking team records a safety and scores two points.

Before 2009, good return teams set up a *blocking wedge* with three or more huge players aligned together to clear a path for the ball carrier behind them. But in 2009, in the interest of player safety, the NFL prohibited teams from using more than two players to form a wedge on kickoff returns. Then in 2018, the NFL outlawed the two-man blocking wedge, further negativing the possibility of an exciting return. In 2020, WWE founder Vince McMahon will resurrect the XFL professional league. Players on their kickoffs will be separated by only five yards, and the kicking team players won't be allowed to run until a player on the receiving team catches the ball. This is one way to negate injuries, and that's what the NFL did by negating wedge blocking. In the past, defenders on the kicking team would get a 50-yard head of steam and crash into the wedge. Players who did this were known as *wedge busters,* and they were celebrated for their toughness and courage. Unfortunately, wedge busters were constantly risking injury to themselves and the blockers they collided into. The NFL decided that using wedges and busting wedges were just too dangerous.

The NFL made another significant rule change prior to the 2018 season that virtually ruined the onsides kickoff. When teams are trailing late in the fourth quarter, they used to have a fair chance of recovering an onsides kick. But the rule change forbid teams from overloading one side of the coverage team with 7 to 8 players. They can only have five players on both sides of the kickers, so in 2018 teams only recovered 4 of 52 onside attempts, a woeful 7.7 percent. In 2017, prior to this drastic rule chance, teams recovered 12 of 56 attempts, or 21.4 percent.

Covering the kickoff return

Coverage men (the guys whose job it is to tackle the kick returner) must be aggressive, fast, and reckless in their pursuit. They must avoid the blocks of the return team. Special teams coaches believe that a solid tackle on the opening kickoff can set the tone for a game, especially if the return man is stopped inside his own 20-yard line. But the job of the kickoff coverage man isn't an easy one. Players get knocked down once, twice, and sometimes three times during their pursuit of the kickoff returner. Not for nothing is the coverage team sometimes called the "suicide squad."

Kicking field goals and PATs

Most special teams scoring involves the placekicker or field goal kicker. During the 2009 NFL season, the 32 pro teams attempted 930 field goals and converted 756 of them, which is an 81 percent success rate. For the last 35 years, field goal kicking has played a pivotal, often decisive, role in the outcomes of NFL games. Kickers can become instant heroes by converting a last-second field goal to win a game. After an NFL offense has driven to within 30 yards of scoring a touchdown, the coaches know the team is definitely within easy field goal range. In the 2018 NFL season, field goal kickers converted 484 of 498 attempts inside 39 yards for an impressive 97 percent conversion rate. NFL kickers are definitely improving as four of them were perfect inside 50 yards, and many others missed only one of 10 or 11 attempts between 40 and 49 yards. There are currently nine kickers in the NFL with a career conversion percentage on all field goals of 85 percent or above, led by Baltimore's Justin Tucker, whose career average is 90.11 percent. So you can see why head coaches are willing to at least attempt to score three points, knowing that a missed field goal gives the defensive team the ball at the spot of the kick.

Reliable kickers can often claim a job for a decade or more because their ability to convert in the clutch is so essential. For example, Adam Vinatieri, currently with the Indianapolis Colts, has played 23 seasons in the NFL. He holds the record for most career field goals when, in 2018, he surpassed Morten Andersen's career high of 565. Andersen is only the second placekicker in the Pro Football Hall of Fame, and Vinatieri is certain to be the third after he retires.

HIDDEN YARDAGE

Jimmy Johnson, who coached the Dallas Cowboys and the Miami Dolphins, called positive return yards *hidden yardage.* For example, Johnson equated a 50-yard advantage in punt/kick return yards to five first downs. In some games, it may be extremely difficult for an offense to produce a lot of first downs, so return yardage is key.

Johnson reported that his teams won games while making only 12 first downs because they played great both defensively and on special teams. He believed that the team with the best field position throughout the game, attained by excellent punt and kick coverage, generally wins. Also, he believed that if you have a great punt and kick returner, opponents may elect to kick the ball out of bounds, thus giving your offense fine field position.

The following sections explain the roles of the folks involved in field goal and extra point attempts, what makes a kick count, and the rules regarding both types of kicks.

Who does what

On field goal and extra point (PAT, which stands for *point after touchdown*) attempts, the kicker has a holder and a snapper. He also has a wall of nine blockers in front of him, including the snapper, who's sometimes the offensive center. On many teams, the player who snaps the ball for punts also snaps for these kicks. The snap takes approximately 1.3 seconds to reach the holder, who kneels on his right knee about 7 yards behind the line of scrimmage. He catches the ball with his right hand and places the ball directly on the playing surface. (Placekicking tees are allowed in high school football but not in college and the NFL.) The holder then uses his left index finger to hold the ball in place.

The kicker's leg action, the striking motion, takes about 1.5 milliseconds, and the ball is usually airborne about 2 seconds after being snapped.

It's good!

For an extra point or a field goal try to be ruled good, the kicked ball must clear the crossbar (by going over it) and pass between (or directly above one of) the uprights of the goalpost (see Chapter 2 for the specs of the goalpost). Two officials, one on each side of the goalpost, stand by to visually judge whether points have been scored on the kick.

Most college and NFL teams expect to convert every extra point, considering that the ball is snapped from the 2- or 3-yard line. A field goal is a different matter, though, due to the distance involved.

The rules

A few rules pertain strictly to the kicking game. Most of them decide what happens when a kick is blocked or touched by the defensive team. Because three points are so valuable, special teams place a great emphasis on making a strong effort to block these kicks. The team kicking the ball works just as diligently to protect its kicker, making sure he has a chance to score.

The byproduct of these attempts often leads to the defensive team *running into* or *roughing the kicker*. This infraction occurs when a player hits the kicker's body or leg while he's in the act of kicking. A penalty is also enforced when a player knocks down the kicker immediately after he makes the kick. The rules are fairly strict because the kicker can't defend himself while he's concentrating on striking the ball. (Check out Chapter 3 for more on these and other penalties.)

REMEMBER

Some of the other rules regarding field goals and extra points:

>> Either team can advance a blocked field goal recovered behind the line of scrimmage.

>> A blocked field goal that crosses the line of scrimmage may be advanced only by the defense. If the ball is muffed or fumbled, however, it's a free ball and either team can recover it.

>> On a blocked PAT in an NFL game, the ball is immediately dead. Neither team is allowed to advance it. In college football, the defense can pick up the ball and return it to the kicking team's end zone for a two-point score (if they're lucky).

>> The guards may lock legs with the snapper only. The right guard places his left foot inside the snapper's right foot after both players assume a stance so that their legs cross, or lock. The left guard places his right foot on the opposite side of the center. By locking legs, the guards help stabilize the snapper from an all-out rush on his head and shoulders while he leans down over the ball. All other players on the line of scrimmage must have their feet outside the feet of the players next to them.

>> The holder or kicker may not be roughed or run into during or after a kick. The penalty for running into the kicker is 5 yards; the penalty for roughing the kicker is 15 yards and an automatic first down.

DROP-KICKING: THE LOST ART

Before the ball was made thinner and distinctly more oblong to assist passers, the plumped version was easily drop-kicked. Yes, players would simply drop the ball and kick it after it touched the ground. The action was perfectly timed.

The current rules still allow drop-kicking, but the ball's tapered design stops most players from trying it. The last successful drop kick in the NFL occurred on January 1, 2006, when Doug Flutie of the New England Patriots drop-kicked an extra point in the final game of his career. Prior to Flutie's drop-kick, no one in the NFL had succeeded in making a drop-kick since the 1941 championship game, when the Chicago Bears' Ray "Scooter" McLean successfully drop-kicked a PAT.

In a 2010 Thanksgiving Day game, Dallas Cowboys' punter Mat McBriar fumbled the snap from the center, and after the ball bounced a couple times on the grass, kicked the ball in what might be described as a drop kick. The referees, however, ruled that McBriar's kick wasn't a drop kick at all, but a fumble followed by an illegal kick. Nice try, Mat!

However, roughing the holder or kicker is legal if the kick is blocked, the ball touches the ground during the snap, or the holder fumbles the ball before it's kicked.

>> On a missed field goal, the ball returns to the line of scrimmage if it rolls dead in the field of play, is touched by the receiving team, goes into the end zone, or hits the goalpost. The defensive team assumes possession at that time.

Blocking field goals and PATs

Blocking either a PAT or a field goal attempt can change the momentum of a game and eventually decide its outcome. To block kicks, players must be dedicated, athletic, and willing to physically sacrifice themselves for the good of the team, as the players in Figure 12-2 are doing. To have a successful block, each man must do his job.

TIP

Blocked kicks may appear easy, but, as shown in Figure 12-3, a play such as the *middle field goal block* requires talented defensive linemen who can win the battle up front. These defensive linemen position themselves near the center snapping the ball because the quickest way to any field goal or extra point attempt is up the middle. With the ball 7 yards off the line of scrimmage, teams place their best pass-rushers in the middle, believing that one of them can penetrate the blocking line a couple of yards and then raise his arms, hoping to tip the booted ball with his hands. If the kicker doesn't get the proper trajectory, the kick can be blocked.

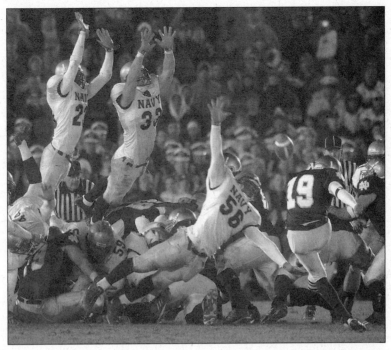

FIGURE 12-2:
Navy defenders try to block a field goal attempt by Notre Dame's D.J. Fitzpatrick in 2003.

Photo credit: © U.S. Navy/Getty Images

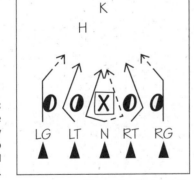

FIGURE 12-3:
The defensive linemen try to penetrate up the middle and block the kick.

© John Wiley & Sons, Inc.

In Figure 12-3, the three interior defensive linemen (LT, N, and RT) are over the two guards and the snapper. RT must align on the inside shoulder of the guard opposite him. N lines up directly across from the center. LT aligns on the inside shoulder of the guard opposite him. These linemen want to be able to gain an edge, an angle, on those blockers. Their attempts to block the kick won't work if the two tackles align squarely on top of the guards. They must pick a particular shoulder of the guard and attack to that side.

SOCCER-STYLE KICKING

One of the biggest developments in kicking came in the late 1950s, when soccer-style kickers began surfacing at U.S. colleges. Before the soccer style came into vogue, the straight-on method was the only way to kick a football. This American style of kicking is totally different from the soccer style. Straight-on kickers approached the ball from straight on, using their toes to strike the ball and lift it off the ground. A soccer-style kicker, on the other hand, approaches the ball from an angle, and the instep of the kicker's foot makes contact with the ball.

In 2010, not one NFL kicker used the straight-on method. For starters, the soccer style creates quicker lift off the ground. But basically, this method has simply stuck and become the pervasive kicking style. Mark Moseley, who retired from the Cleveland Browns in 1986, was the last straight-on kicker.

Both LG and RG (left and right guard) drive through the tackles' outside shoulders. Their objective is to apply enough individual pressure so as not to allow the tackle to slide down the line and help his buddies inside. Both players should attempt to block the kick if they break free. If not, they *contain* the opponent's linemen in case of a fake field goal attempt. Containing means to hold their ground and simply jostle with the players who are blocking them — all while keeping their eyes on the kicker and holder.

REMEMBER

The only chance the middle block has of succeeding is if the pass-rush moves that the three interior defensive linemen make on the offensive linemen work. It's critical that all three players are isolated on one blocker. The defenders can decide to double-team a blocker, hoping one of them breaks free and penetrates the line.

On other kick-block plays, teams attempt to break through from the outside, using two men on one blocker and hoping the single blocker makes the wrong choice and allows the inside rusher to get free.

Punting

Punting occurs when a team's offense is struggling, which means the offense is failing to generate positive yardage and is stuck on fourth down. Teams punt on fourth down when they're in their own territory or are barely across midfield. By punting, the team relinquishes possession of the ball.

One of the most difficult aspects of football to understand initially is why teams punt the ball. A team has four downs to gain 10 yards, and after accomplishing that, it receives a new set of downs. Why not gamble on fourth down to gain the necessary yardage to maintain possession of the football? Field position is the answer. Unless it's beyond the opponent's 40-yard line, a team would rather punt the ball on fourth down, hoping to keep the opponent as far from its end zone as possible (which, of course, stops the other team from scoring).

Teams punt routinely at the beginning of the game, especially when there's no score or the score is close. They rely on their defenses in such situations, believing that the benefits of field position outweigh any offensive risk-taking. Punting in these situations isn't a conservative tactic, but a smart one.

Punting is a critical part of football because some coaches believe it can change the course of a game. And no facet of the game alters field position more than punting. In the NFL, each punt is worth an average of 45 yards per exchange. However, some punters are capable of punting even farther than that, thus pinning opponents deep in their own end of the field and far, far away from a score.

The sections that follow get you acquainted with the punting process, the members of the punting team, the rules regarding punting, and more.

Setting up and kicking the ball

The punter stands about 15 yards behind the line of scrimmage and catches the ball after the snapper hikes it. The center's snap of the ball must reach the punter within 0.8 seconds. Every extra tenth of a second increases the risk that the punt may be blocked.

After receiving the ball, the punter takes two steps, drops the ball toward his kicking foot, and makes contact. This act requires a lot of practice and coordination because the velocity of the punter's leg prior to striking the ball, as well as the impact of his foot on the ball, is critical. The punter needs to strike the ball in the center to achieve maximum distance. When the punter strikes the ball off the side of his foot, the ball flies sideways (such a mistake is called a *shank*).

A punt, from the snap of the ball to the action of the punter, requires no more than 2 seconds. Most teams want the punter to catch, drop, and punt the ball in under 1.3 seconds.

Today's punters must be adept at kicking in all weather conditions and must strive for a hang time of 4.5 seconds. Many have hang time beyond 5 seconds. They must also boot the ball at least 45 yards away from the line of scrimmage. By the way, most punters also serve in a dual role as holder for the field goal kicker.

Meeting the key performers on the punt team

The punter isn't the only important player during a punt play — although it may seem like it sometimes, especially on a bad punt. Following are some of the other key performers:

>> **Center or long snapper:** This player must be accurate with his snap and deliver the ball to where the punter wants it. On most teams, he makes the blocking calls for the interior linemen, making sure no one breaks through to block the punt. The long snapper is such a specialist that many have had careers lasting as long as ten seasons in the NFL.

>> **Wings or gunners:** The *wings* are the players on both ends of the line of scrimmage, and they're generally 1-yard deep behind the outside leg of the end or tackle. These players must block the outside rushers, but they worry more about any player breaking free inside of them.

>> **Ends:** One *end* stands on each side of the line of scrimmage, and they're isolated outside the wings at least 10 to 12 yards. On some teams, these players are called *gunners*. Their job is to run downfield and tackle the punt returner. Often, two players block each end at the line of scrimmage in hopes of giving the punt returner more time to advance the ball.

>> **Personal protector:** The *personal protector* is the last line of protection for the punter. This player usually lines up 5 yards behind the line of scrimmage. If five or more defensive players line up to one side of the snapper, the personal protector shifts his attention to that side and makes sure no one breaks through to block the punt.

Most coaches prefer that a fullback or safety play this position because they want someone who's mobile enough to quickly move into a blocking position. Regardless, the personal protector must be a player who can react quickly to impending trouble and make adjustment calls for the ends and wings.

Figure 12-4 shows a basic punt formation involving these players against what coaches call *man coverage*. X is the center (or snapper); he stands over the ball. PP is the punter's personal protector, and P is the punter. The wings are labeled with Ws, and the Es (ends) are on the line of scrimmage about 10 to 12 yards away from the wings.

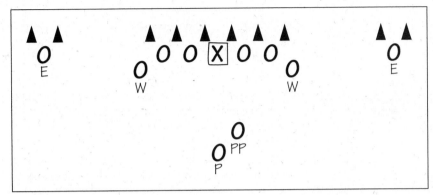

FIGURE 12-4:
A basic punt
formation.

Reviewing punt rules

As with everything else in football, punting has rules. Consider the following:

>> In the pros, only the players lined up on the ends are permitted to cross the line of scrimmage after the ball is snapped to the punter and before the ball is punted. In college and high school, all players on the punting team may cross the line of scrimmage after the snap.

   After the ball is punted, everyone on the punting team is allowed to cross the line of scrimmage with the intent of tackling the player fielding the punt (who's also known as the *punt returner*).

>> Players aren't allowed to block below the waist on punt returns. Such an illegal block is a 15-yard penalty and is marked off from where the team returning the punt gained possession of the ball.

>> If a punt doesn't cross the line of scrimmage, either team may pick up the ball and run toward its own end zone.

>> A *touchback* occurs when a punt touches the end zone before the ball touches a player on either team, or when the punt returner catches the ball in the end zone and drops to one knee. The ball is then spotted on the receiving team's 20-yard line.

>> Either team can *down* a punt after it hits the ground or after one of its players touches the ball past the line of scrimmage. To down the ball, a player must be in possession of the ball, stop his forward movement, and drop to one knee. Such action leads to an official blowing his whistle, signaling the end of action.

>> A partially blocked punt that crosses the line of scrimmage is treated like a typical punt.

TIP

Several times during a game, you see the punt returner stand and simply catch the ball. He doesn't run. In this case, he's probably calling for a *fair catch.* To signal for a fair catch, the player who's preparing to receive the punt must clearly extend his arm over his head and then wave it from side to side to let the officials and the defensive players know that he doesn't plan to run with the ball after catching it. After signaling for a fair catch, the punt returner can't advance the ball. If the defenders tackle him after he signals a fair catch, the kicking team incurs a 15-yard penalty.

However, the player signaling for a fair catch isn't obligated to catch the ball. His only worry is not to touch the ball because if he does so without catching it, the loose ball is treated like a fumble, and the other team can recover it. After he touches it or loses control and the ball hits the ground, either team is allowed to recover the ball.

If the returner *muffs a kick,* or fails to gain possession, the punting team may not advance the ball if they recover it. If the returner gains possession and then fumbles, however, the punting team may advance the ball.

Punting out of trouble

A punter must remain calm and cool when punting out of trouble — that is, anywhere deep in his own territory. Any poor punt — a shank or a flat-out miss — can result in the opponent scoring an easy touchdown, especially if the other team gets the ball 40 yards away from its end zone. Poor punts inevitably mean an automatic three points via a field goal. A dropped snap can mean a defensive score; ditto for a blocked punt — and you'll see little sympathy when that punter returns to the sideline. In 2013, NFL teams averaged 4.9 punts per game, so coaches and players fully expect punts to happen without a hitch.

HOWIE
SAYS

When I played with the Raiders in Super Bowl XVIII, our punter, Ray Guy, won the game for us. You may be thinking, "What role can a punter have when you beat the Washington Redskins 38–9?" Well, after a bad snap early in the game, Guy jumped as high as he could and grabbed the ball one-handed. When he landed, he boomed his punt way downfield. We were deep in our own territory, and if the ball had gone over Guy's head, the Redskins might have recovered it in our end zone for a touchdown. Who knows?

THE QUICK KICK

One of the most underutilized trick plays in football is the quick kick. The *quick kick* is when the offensive team surprises the defense by punting the ball on third or even second down, usually from the shotgun formation (described in Chapter 5), although sometimes the ball is pitched to a halfback who does the punting. Teams try the quick kick when they're deep in their own territory and want to get the heck out of there. A quick kick is a risky play because the kicker is closer to the line of scrimmage, which increases the chances of his kick being blocked, and most quarterbacks and halfbacks aren't capable of punting the ball well. Still, if the play works, the ball can travel many yards because no defender is lined up deep in the defensive backfield to catch the punted ball.

Guy was a fabulous athlete. He was a first-round draft choice (who ever heard of a punter being taken in the first round?) and a tremendous secondary performer at Southern Mississippi. All I remember about him was that he was like Cool Hand Luke, the role Paul Newman played in the 1967 movie of the same name. No matter the situation, even if he was punting from our own end zone, Guy never got frazzled. In all my years in the NFL, he was head and shoulders above every punter I saw. He was such an exceptional athlete that he served as the quarterback on the scout team in practices, but all he ever did for us in games was punt. Guy led the NFL in punting during three seasons and retired after 14 years with a 42.4-yard average. Guy was voted into the Hall of Fame in 2014 after waiting more than 30 years for induction.

Examining the dangerous art of punt returning

Punt returning isn't always as exciting as returning a kickoff because the distance between the team punting and the punt returner isn't as great. A punt returner needs either a line-drive punt or a long punt (45 yards or more from the line of scrimmage) with less than 4 seconds of hang time — or spectacular blocking by his teammates — to achieve significant positive return yards.

REMEMBER

To produce positive return yards, the receiving team must concentrate on effectively blocking the outside pursuit men and the center — the players who have the most direct access to the punt returner. The rest of the unit must peel back and attempt to set up a wall or some interference for the returner. Whenever the return unit can hold up four or five players from the punting team, the returner has a chance.

A returner needs to be a fearless competitor and must be willing to catch a punt at or near full speed and continue his run forward. If the defense isn't blocked, the collisions between a returner and a tackler can be extremely violent, leading to injuries and concussions.

A returner's other necessary qualities are superior hands and tremendous concentration. Because of the closeness of the coverage and the bodies flying around, the returner usually catches the ball in traffic. Several players are generally within a yard of him, so the sounds of players blocking and running tend to surround him. He must close out these sounds in order to catch the ball and maintain his composure. To catch the ball and then run with it, under such conditions, takes guts. A returner's final fear is losing the ball via a fumble, thus putting his opponent in favorable field position.

Punt returns typically average around 8 or 9 yards. Great punt returners, like Tyreek Hill and Dwayne Harris, have the ability to make big gains and even score touchdowns. Hill's 4.2 speed allows him to escape most defenders.

A SPECIAL TEAMS PLAYER WHO'S TRULY SPECIAL

In 1986, the NFL and its players began awarding Pro Bowl invitations to each conference's best special teams player. Mainly, the award winner is the player who's best at covering punts and kickoffs — the one who's a fearless open-field tackler. Steve Tasker of the Buffalo Bills was even named the MVP of the 1993 Pro Bowl for forcing a fumble and blocking a field goal attempt, thereby preserving a three-point victory for his AFC teammates.

their styles

» **Exploring the functions of owners and general managers**

» **Scouting opponents and college prospects**

» **Finding out how trainers take care of players**

Chapter **13**

Coaches, General Managers, and Other Important Folks

epending on the football franchise, a coach, a general manager, or even an owner has the ability to put the team in the best possible position to win. Each person's primary function is to help the team win, assisting the players in any way possible.

HOWIE SAYS

I'm proud to say that I became an All-Pro player because of the late Earl Leggett, who coached the defensive linemen for the Raiders. I had quickness and strength, the skills that I needed to play in the National Football League, but Leggett was the one who taught me how to harness my ability. He showed me how to anticipate an offense's intentions and use my talents on every single play. He was my mentor.

Probably hundreds of coaches, maybe not as gifted as Leggett, have the same impact on players throughout high school, college, and pro football. If a player is willing to commit to a coach's system, a good coach can develop him into a very good player. Michael Strahan, who sits next to me on *Fox NFL Sunday*, was also coached by Leggett, and Strahan became one of the most complete defensive ends in football. Strahan is a Hall of Famer and also holds the single-season sack record of 22½.

In this chapter, I explain how coaches, from the head coach to the strength coach, work together toward one goal: winning. And for NFL coaches to win, they need a personnel department that has the ability to find players and then sign them. Similarly, a college coach needs the support of the school's administration to be able to recruit good players. I guess I'm saying that there's more to playing football and winning than simply the players — coaches, general managers, scouts, and all the rest play important roles on winning teams.

A Team's Fearless Leaders: The Coaches

Every army has a general and a group of lieutenants; similarly, every football team has a head coach and a coaching staff. The coaches are the leaders of the team; they're the men who put the players in the position to win games. They decide what offenses and defenses the team will use, and good coaches devise these schemes to get the most out of their players' talent. In the NFL, the coach is highly visible because the television cameras show him on the sidelines throughout every game.

Some coaches are stars, like the New Orleans Saints' Sean Payton. He has a perfect personality for coaching football because he's charismatic and emotional. Other coaches prefer a low-key, business-like approach, which can be equally successful. Bill Belichick of the New England Patriots and Mike Tomlin of the Pittsburgh Steelers have had great success holding their cards close to the chest.

I'm using NFL coaches as examples because covering them is part of my job, and I know these men personally. I can relate to their powerful impact on a football team. However, thousands of high school and college coaches have the same impact on their teams. Why? Because coaches are special. They devote countless hours to preparing practice schedules and game strategies, working with players in practice and in film sessions, and dealing with them one-on-one when necessary. In high school and college, a coach can be stern and fair like a father. And many coaches have earned players' respect because of their success and longevity — they're revered for being great for the game of football. Alabama's Nick Saban and Clemson's Dabo Swinney are college football's very best at winning and also developing super players for the NFL.

REMEMBER

A good coach is a special man, one who's supremely confident in his ability to build, prepare, and focus a team on winning a championship. Because the season is long and the games are few in comparison to other sports, a football coach must cope with the mood swings of his players during the week and know when and how to be assertive and when to be relaxed. He sets the tone for his team.

The sections that follow give you a better idea of the coaching staff members and their roles, as well as various coaching styles and philosophies and the day-to-day tasks of coaches.

Who does what on the coaching staff

Almost every football team has more than one coach. Some teams have two coaches monitoring special teams: One coach handles the punter and placekicker, and the other coach handles coverages and kick protection. Including strength and conditioning coaches, the typical NFL team averages 20 assistant coaches. (A college team generally has 9 full-time assistants and 2 graduate assistants, not including strength coaches.) Here's a common NFL coaching staff:

>> **Head coach:** The head coach is the main man who gets most of the credit for winning — and most of the blame for losing. Most head coaches are more than 40 years old, have 20 or more seasons of playing and coaching experience, and are experts on one side of the ball or the other. Their styles of coaching vary. Some head coaches demand control over what alignments and plays the team uses on defense and offense. Others delegate one aspect of the game plan, preferring to focus on their particular expertise, whether it's defense or offense. Depending on the franchise's power structure and ownership, the head coach may have a lot of flexibility and control over personnel, or he may have a rather limited role.

>> **Offensive coordinator:** The offensive coordinator is the coach in charge of the offensive players. He usually calls the plays and works directly with the quarterbacks. He's responsible for developing the offensive game plan (the plays he believes will be successful against the upcoming opponent) and works with the head coach on how practice is organized, especially if some of the plays are unusual or somewhat unfamiliar to the offensive personnel. Some coordinators do all the work and are almost as valuable as the head coach. On some NFL teams, the owner is as involved in the hiring of the offensive coordinator as in the hiring of the head coach.

>> **Defensive coordinator:** The defensive coordinator is the coach in charge of the defensive players. He usually decides what defensive schemes to run. Like the offensive coordinator, the defensive coordinator meets with half the team on a typical practice day and prepares them for the upcoming opponent. I've

always thought that a good defensive coordinator is one who can adapt his system to his players' talents rather than the other way around. But sometimes teams want to find players that fit their particular system. The best defensive coordinators are the ones who are really flexible and simply strive to put their players in the best possible situation to succeed.

» **Special teams coach:** The special teams coach supervises the kickers, punters, kick return team, field goal protection team, punt return team, and so on. Generally, he's coaching the younger players on a team, and he must find a way to motivate them to do their jobs. Many of the special teams' stars are backups and reserves — they're players who aren't yet talented enough to be offensive or defensive starters. On some units, the special teams coach may have starters mixed in with rookies, and so he must find a way to get these players to complement one another. He must study the strengths and weaknesses of how teams return kicks and cover kicks. Also, he studies film to discover whether a team is particularly weak in kick protection so he can prepare his team to attempt a block in a specific game.

» **Quarterback coach:** A quarterback coach is an assistant coach who monitors the physical and mental aspects of a quarterback's game. He works on the quarterback's footwork, pass-drop technique, and throwing motion. He makes sure a quarterback doesn't fall into bad mental or physical habits. In training camp, if the starting quarterback is an experienced veteran, the quarterback coach may devote extra hours to the backup and third-string quarterback, hoping to develop them for the future and prepare them to play in an emergency. On some teams, the quarterback coach serves as a sounding board between the quarterback and the head coach. On NFL teams, the head coach and the quarterback are usually under the greatest scrutiny.

» **Offensive line coach:** An offensive line coach works with the offensive linemen and generally has a solid understanding of the team's running game. He and the offensive coordinator spend time discussing what running plays may work, depending on what the offensive line coach views as his unit's strengths and weaknesses against the upcoming opponent. He is also a key component in developing the offense's pass protection schemes. A good offensive line coach can mold five blockers, all with different or varied levels of skill, into a solid, efficient unit. On some teams, the line coach is more valuable than the offensive coordinator.

» **Defensive line coach:** A defensive line coach is the guy who works exclusively with the defensive linemen. He works on individual technique (run stopping, gap control, pass rushing, and so on) and whatever stunts the defensive coordinator wants from these players.

- » **Linebacker coach:** A linebacker coach works with linebackers and, depending on the team's style of defense, ranks a step below the defensive coordinator. Defenses that exclusively use four linebackers need a coach who can teach all the variations necessary for this scheme to work. This coach must work on tackling, pass-rushing off the corner, and particular pass coverage drops.

- » **Secondary coach:** A secondary coach is the coach who works with the defensive backs. He must have a total understanding of pass offenses. He works on all aspects of pass coverage, from footwork and deep zone drops to how to prepare players for the particular receivers they'll face.

- » **Strength coach:** A strength coach specializes in weight training and conditioning. He makes sure the players are strong and in shape throughout the season, and he often coordinates off-season training programs. A strength coach also works with team doctors to prepare and monitor rehabilitation exercises following player surgeries.

A team may also have coaches for specific positions, such as a receiver or running backs coach, depending on how many coaches the team can afford to keep on staff. On smaller staffs, the head coach may also serve as the offensive coordinator, or the special teams coach may also be the strength coach. On some large NFL staffs, the head coach, not the offensive coordinator, calls the offensive plays.

The different coaching styles and philosophies

Without question, a coach can have a dramatic impact on a football team. Some coaches want to control the emotional pulse of their teams; others attempt to use their influence by establishing good rapport with selected team leaders. A coach needs to stand apart as an authority figure, especially if he coaches younger players. He makes the rules, and the players must follow his orders. Still, a coach can't be as demanding as an army sergeant because he wants his players to feel comfortable talking to him about any serious off-the-field problems they may be facing. A pro coach may even allow himself to become friendly with his players and treat them like the adults they are.

No one set standard for being a head coach exists, nor is there a particular philosophy that a coach should adhere to. Good head coaches learn from the men for whom they've worked, absorbing the good qualities and tossing out the bad ones that don't work with their personality. A coach needs to be himself and be true to how he would want to be treated. Players can spot a phony as soon as he walks into the team meeting room. The next sections run through the different types of coaching styles and philosophies.

The yell-your-head-off coach

Players don't like coaches who yell and scream all the time. But I've known some coaches who can communicate only by screaming. They aren't screaming because they're angry; they just know screaming is the only way their instructions are going to sink into their players' heads. (Granted, players can barely think on the practice field when their bodies are tired and aching from a long day.) The screamers are generally defensive coaches; offensive coaches tend to be calmer and more cerebral.

Many of these screamers are good coaches. When Mike Zimmer screamed at any of his Minnesota Vikings, everyone at practice knew he meant business. Zimmer wasn't a screamer by nature, but he, like many other coaches, yelled when a player or unit constantly repeated the same mistake. After all, a coach can be patient for only so long.

TIP

You can spot the yell-your-head-off coach anywhere. Here are some examples of that coaching style:

>> Whenever these coaches believe their teams have been penalized unfairly, you can bet they're yelling at the referee or some official along the sidelines.

>> Whenever a player misses an assignment and causes a critical play to fail, you may see these coaches actually grab the player and tell him, inches away from his face, how and why he screwed up.

>> These coaches often grab a player's face mask and rattle his cage before telling him how poorly he's playing or practicing.

>> These coaches throw things. Coaches who scream a lot love to toss their hats, clipboards, or whatever they're holding to get everyone's attention.

The kinder, gentler coach

Another kind of coach takes the kinder, gentler approach. These coaches rarely yell, and they believe that teaching good character to players can be as important as teaching physical skills. Tom Landry, revered coach of the Dallas Cowboys from 1960 through 1988, was known for his calm, stoic demeanor.

The smash-mouth football coach

Smash-mouth coaches love nothing more than to see a tremendous block by an offensive lineman and then watch their running back gain 10 yards while running over the opposition. Most of these coaches began as defensive coaches, and they believe in dominating the line of scrimmage and want their defense to decide the outcome of a game. On offense, they'd rather win by running the football. Bill Cowher (who won a Super Bowl with the Pittsburgh Steelers and now works as an analyst for CBS Sports) and Hall of Famer Bill Parcells (who won two Super Bowls with the New York Giants) are examples of the smash-mouth coach. They prepared their teams to be the stronger, dominant team in a matchup, and that's why they were successful.

TIP

So that you're sure to recognize this type of coach during a game, take a look at these examples of the smash-mouth coaching style:

>> When the game is close and the offense needs to convert a play on fourth and 1, these coaches are likely to gamble, believing that their offensive line and running back can pick up the first down.

>> These coaches are more apt to continue to run a successful play until the opposition stops it.

>> These coaches' football teams usually focus on both the offensive and the defensive linemen. Their teams may not always win the game, but they plan on winning the war along the line of scrimmage.

>> These coaches rarely waiver from their beliefs in how to approach a game or a particular opponent. They're very strong-minded coaches.

The offensive-genius coach

You see a lot of offensive-genius coaches in the NFL. Mike Shanahan, who directed the Denver Broncos to their 1998 and 1999 Super Bowl wins, typifies this type of coach. An offensive-genius is a coach who seems to have an unlimited ability to develop new plays; defensive coaches know that these coaches will try more than one new play or variation of an old play every week. Offensive-genius coaches aren't always viewed as tough guys because they're so cerebral. Nevertheless, although their minds may be working overtime on the sidelines, they don't tolerate a lack of discipline or shoddy play on the football field.

This kind of coach is constantly looking for an edge on the field. One example of Shanahan's genius took place in the 1997 season when the Broncos had to beat the Kansas City Chiefs to reach the Super Bowl. The Chiefs had a great pass-rusher in Derrick Thomas, and they preferred to line up Thomas on the weak side, away from the tight end. The Chiefs had a strong linebacker, Wayne Simmons, who demolished most tight ends. Prior to the snap, Shanahan would move his tight end off the line of scrimmage and motion him over until he was in front of Derrick Thomas. Then he'd call a running play directly at Thomas. That simple formation adjustment prior to the snap gave Shanahan's offense the matchups that he wanted on a running play. In such a short period of time, Thomas and Simmons couldn't switch sides before the ball was snapped. Denver had success running at Thomas while negating the Chiefs' greatest asset: Thomas's pass-rushing ability.

Here are some typical actions of the offensive-genius coach:

TIP

>> These coaches generally wear headsets on the sidelines to communicate with their assistants upstairs in the press box, and they always have a *playsheet* (the game plan of offensive plays) in their hands. They're more involved with the offensive team than the defensive team during a game.

>> These coaches tend to be more thoughtful and under control during sideline sessions with their players. They don't rattle easily.

>> When they talk during practice, these coaches explain the whole play and show how a small aspect can lead to a gigantic reward. For example, each player's alignment dictates a defensive alignment response. Anticipating the defense's alignment to a certain formation or pass route can lead to an opening to spring a big play.

>> At the training facility, these coaches work alone most of the time. They have a daily staff meeting, but they like to think and tinker with the offense for hours on their own.

What coaches do when they're not yelling on the sidelines

Coaching a football team is a full-time job. While players rest during the offseason, coaches are busy planning for the season ahead. Following is a quick look at what coaches do during the season and in the offseason.

During the season

Coaches at all levels prepare playbooks that every player receives — and many of these playbooks include more than 200 plays for the offense alone. They meet with the general manager and other college and pro scouts regarding personnel — whom to trade for, whom to acquire, and whom to release.

With the head coach leading the way, the coaches meet during the players' day off. During this meeting, they prepare the game plan for the next week and review hours of film of their own players and the opposition, looking for tendencies, strengths, and weaknesses. During training camp, the coaching staff dissects what it wants to accomplish during the season in all phases of the game: offense, defense, and special teams. At the same time, the coaches test to see how the players are adapting to specific plays and strategies. From there, they refine their plan, tinkering with minute details in order to guarantee success.

In the NFL, every play is analyzed and dissected until the coaching staff knows exactly how it wants to instruct the players on the practice field. A coach can break down a single play on videotape to show a player taking the wrong first step, backing up too much, angling his shoulders improperly, or failing to read the other team's intentions.

College and high school coaches meet regularly with their school's athletic director and administrators regarding financial budgets and player eligibility status. They oversee travel schedules and are involved in picking hotels and meals for road trips. College and high school coaches usually work all day on Sunday, examining film of the weekend's game and preparing for the next week. They have staff meetings in preparation for meeting the players on Monday. And, of course, they devote a lot of time to motivating their players. NCAA rules, though, have limited college practice time to 20 hours per week, which has been a drag on player development.

Coaches also deal with the media. In the NFL, coaches may have press briefings with newspaper, radio, and television reporters every day except Tuesday and Saturday. However, on Saturday, they must meet with network television producers and commentators to discuss their opinions of what may occur in Sunday's or Monday's game. College and high school coaches may also deal with local reporters, although on a smaller scale.

During the off-season

Although high school and college football teams are restricted to a certain number of off-season practice days, NFL coaching staffs work virtually year-round making free-agency decisions, scouting potential draft choices, monitoring selective *mini-camps* (three or four days of on-field practice), and attending countless organizational meetings. Most NFL coaches take their vacations in late June and early July, right before the opening of training camp.

An NFL head coach spends his days in the off-season preparing practice schedules for training camp and the regular season. The college coach devotes much of his off-season to *recruiting* high school players and hosting clinics for high school coaches. Recruiting means visiting a potential player in his hometown — which necessitates a lot of traveling — and meeting with his parents, guardians, and high school coaches.

GETTING AXED: THE PRESSURE OF BEING A FOOTBALL COACH

Coaches work long hours because they're usually under enormous pressure to win. If they don't win, even on the high school level, they get fired. As soon as an NFL season ends, several coaches are usually given the ax. Some teams seem to change coaches every year.

When a head coach is fired, usually his coaching staff of 15 to 20 assistants is also out of work. Or, sometimes, a head coach saves his job but is forced by management to fire some or all of his assistants. This situation doesn't happen a lot, but it does occur enough to make assistant coaches realize that coaching is more about business than it is about loyalty. Besides being fired, coaching staffs are constantly turning over as assistants move on to different teams and receive promotions. Changing teams creates a lot of upheaval for a coach's family, especially if he's married with children. Coaches who begin their careers dreaming of the NFL usually bounce around to several colleges, sometimes as many as eight different jobs, before landing a pro position. And I know good NFL assistant coaches who've worked for five different teams during their careers.

The Team's Public Face: The Owners

People buy teams for many different reasons, but most owners simply want to be public figures. The NFL is structured financially so that every club receives an equal share of television revenue and splits the ticket revenue — it's more or less a socialist system. The concept is that the weakest franchise can gross as much revenue as the strongest franchise. However, a team's revenue from local radio broadcasts, luxury boxes, parking, concessions, and private seat licenses (fans pay a fee for the right to own a season ticket) isn't totally shared with the other teams. But the revenue from NFL paraphernalia (income selling NFL logo clothing, hats, and so on) and the Super Bowl is shared. Therefore, you don't have to own a Super Bowl team to do well financially.

After the head coach and the star players on the team, the owner may be the next most visible person. Most football fans know, for example, that Jerry Jones owns the Dallas Cowboys. At one time Jones had his own television show and radio show in Dallas and also wrote a newspaper column. He's very visible in marketing his football team and is very active in network television negotiations. However, many franchise owners are rarely interviewed, choosing to remain behind the scenes, preferring that their coach and general manager speak for the franchise.

The NFL requires one person to own at least 30 percent of a particular franchise and prefers that this person has no financial interest in any other professional sports leagues. Some franchises, such as the Cincinnati Bengals and the Chicago Bears, have been owned for decades by members of one family. The New York Giants have two owners, each with a 50 percent stake in the franchise.

HOWIE SAYS

I don't think any owner in pro football knew more about the game than Al Davis of the Raiders, who passed away in 2011. In pure Xs and Os, the strategy of a game, Davis was like a coach. He actually started in football as a coach and was an excellent one. And in terms of making the financial commitment, Davis always brought in great players. He made every possible effort to improve his team. You can't say that about every NFL owner.

In its August 2018 annual listing of NFL franchise values, *Forbes* magazine placed the value of $2.57 billion on the average franchise with the Dallas Cowboys valued at $5 billion and they haven't won a Super Bowl since the 1995 season. Four franchises — the New England Patriots, the Los Angeles Rams, the New York Giants, and the Washington Redskins — are valued above $3 billion. You must be extremely wealthy to own an NFL franchise. Although the financial return is generous, many business people would tell you that better ways exist to invest that amount of money. Many NFL owners are actually sports fans, people who love the game as much as their pursuit of financial success. Many of them contribute their time, energy, and financial resources to their respective communities, believing that football is part of their region's social fabric.

An Owner's Eyes and Ears: General Managers

On many NFL teams, general managers are the eyes and ears of the owner, and they oversee the day-to-day operation of the team. They must be cold and calculating people because they have to make a lot of difficult personnel decisions. They make the player trades and free agent acquisitions, decide salary levels, and ultimately determine which players to select in the NFL draft. General managers must be excellent judges of every player's ability because they're responsible for doing what's best for the organization. They must have a feel for what the team needs and be able to work in conjunction with the head coach and his needs.

The best possible scenario is to have a solid general manager and a great head coach, who can put their egos aside and work together. But this situation is very rare these days because head coaches usually want total control over personnel, like Bill Belichick has in New England.

REMEMBER

General managers oversee a large front-office staff. Some teams have business, marketing, and public relations personnel. People reporting to the general manager include the following: *capologists* (who monitor a team's salary scale within the salary cap; more on the salary cap in Chapter 17), business managers, contract negotiators (also known as a club vice president), human resources directors, and public relations directors.

The People Responsible for Finding Talent: Scouts

Two basic kinds of scouts exist in the NFL: pro scouts and college scouts.

A team can have a great week practicing, but if the players don't know what to expect from their opponents, they may find themselves behind by 14 points or more in a hurry. *Pro scouts,* people who attend NFL games and study a team's opponents, exist so teams can anticipate what each opponent will do. These scouts attend the games of upcoming opponents and take copious notes, tracking every offensive and defensive tactic, keeping an eye on key players, noting who gets injured, and so on. Then they bring this information back to the coaches, who may devise parts of their game plans around the scouts' input.

A *college scout* examines a pro prospect's every move. He times the player in the 40-yard dash, studies his ability and decisions on every play, and monitors him off the field. NFL teams want to know whether a prospect has ever been arrested and, if so, for what crime. They're concerned about illegal drug use and also about how the player performs in the classroom. They want to know about his attitude, his personality, and his approach to football and to life in general. Every NFL team has a chance to examine and interview prospects at the NFL Combine that is held annually in Indianapolis and also televised by ESPN and the NFL Network. A good college scout watches the prospect in practice and games and also watches film of all his games. The scout then interviews the prospect and members of the college coaching staff. He may even interview opposing coaches to find out their views of the player, and athletic trainers to check on a player's past injuries or training room habits. When scouting the top 100 college players, teams often have two or more scouts examine a prospect.

Keeping Players Strong and Healthy: Trainers and Team Doctors

A team isn't very good if its players don't stay healthy or recover quickly if they get injured. Trainers and team doctors step in to help alleviate these concerns. Most teams have their own orthopedic surgeon and general practitioner. Unless these doctors have total autonomy, they're often put in really difficult positions because their job is to take care of the player, but their employer, who's the owner of the team, wants the player on the field all the time.

A trainer's job is to monitor every injury and then work with the doctor on the rehabilitation process. In some instances, players seek outside medical opinions, especially if the injury is considered serious or the team doctor prescribes surgery. The league monitors injuries and has several medical groups that assist on serious injuries, particularly injuries involving the head and neck.

A trainer also works with the strength trainer to make sure injured players aren't overextending themselves in the weight room or exercising too much. Most pro and college teams have at least two full-time trainers, and some have part-time assistants for training camps. Trainers are responsible for dispensing and monitoring all medicine prescribed by the doctors and all dietary supplements that players are taking. A trainer also inspects team meals to make sure they contain the proper proteins and carbohydrates.

REMEMBER

The best trainer is trusted by both the players and the coaching staff. The worst thing a trainer can do is inform the head coach that a certain player isn't hurting as badly as he claims to be. If the trainer feels that way, he must confront the player as well. Players need to believe that the trainer is concerned about their welfare, regardless of how that concern (possibly in the form of keeping a player off the field) may affect the team's win-loss record.

5

Football for Everyone

IN THIS PART . . .

Follow youth, high school, and college football.

Understand how the NFL has become so successful.

Find out how to play fantasy football.

Chapter **14**

Armchair Quarterbacks and Other Fabulous Fans

ootball is a great sport because you don't have to play it to enjoy it. (In fact, after you watch a few of the hits football players take, you may decide you'd *rather* watch.) This chapter gives you tips for making the most of the viewing (or listening) experience, however you're following the game — on television, from the stands, through your browser or mobile device, or through the radio. I also tell you about all the ways you can keep up with your favorite teams when no games are being played — through newspapers, magazines, and the Internet. Finally, I let you know how to visit the College and Pro Football Halls of Fame.

Deciphering the Announcers' Slang

One of the most difficult and intimidating parts about following a football game is that the announcers sometimes seem to be speaking a foreign language known only to true football enthusiasts. But if you remember a few key terms, you'll be way ahead of the game. Here are some terms you may hear, along with their definitions (the Appendix defines a whole bunch of football terms as well):

» **Corner blitz:** A blitzing linebacker or defensive back rushes the quarterback from the outside edge of the offensive alignment or the *corner* of the offensive line.

- » **Dime back:** When the defense has six players in the secondary, the sixth player is called a *dime back* because he's the second nickel back (two nickels equal a dime).

- » **Forklift:** A defensive lineman lifts an offensive lineman off the ground, moving him aside as he rushes the quarterback.

- » **Franchise player:** Commentators routinely refer to the most important player on a team as the *franchise*. In Indianapolis, for example, quarterback Andrew Luck is the franchise player; the Colts can't win without him.

- » **Looking off a defensive back:** Commentators say this when a quarterback eyeballs a defensive back, giving the defensive player the impression that he's throwing the ball toward his area. In actuality, the quarterback intends to throw in a different direction. He fools the defensive back by *looking him off.*

- » **Muscling his way through:** When a commentator says this, he means a player managed to gain a physical advantage over an opponent.

- » **Nickel package:** The defensive team is using five defensive backs in the secondary to defend the pass. Generally, the nickel back lines up opposite the slot receiver.

- » **Running to daylight:** The running back has found the soft spot in the defense and is running freely down the field toward the end zone.

- » **Shooting a gap:** A defensive player somehow runs untouched through a space that should have been blocked by an offensive player. The gap is often between two offensive players or to the outside shoulder of one player.

- » **Stretch the field:** An offense is employing three to five wide receivers in a formation that's spread out along the line of scrimmage. A defense has to stretch its alignment of players in order to cover all of the receivers.

- » **Zeroing in on a receiver:** The quarterback is focused on throwing to one specific receiver. The quarterback watches the receiver while he's running his route and then releases the ball when he's open.

Following a Game on Television or Radio

If you can't be there in person, the next best thing is to watch the game on television or listen to it on the radio. Hey, don't knock the radio. Radio announcers add pizzazz to the game. They have to paint a picture of the game in words, so most of them have developed a colorful vocabulary and a delivery that makes a game more exciting. I know more than a few fans who get the video portion of the game through their television set and the audio portion from their favorite radio announcer. In the upcoming sections, I share the fine points of following a game on television and the radio. (By the way, I realize you can now watch games online, but the stream is essentially the same as what's broadcast on television.)

Watching a game on television

In a way, television is the best way to watch a football game; you can see up close what's happening on the field, and you can watch replays of the big plays if you missed them the first time around. My innovative bosses at FOX Sports devised the scoreboard clock, which appears in the upper corner of your television screen and gives you a stadium feel. It gives you the score, the down and distance, and how much time is remaining in a particular quarter.

Excellent football analysts add humor and insight to the game. They're also good with a device known as a *telestrator,* which allows them to circle players on the screen or demonstrate how a certain play was successful by diagramming it on the screen.

HOWIE SAYS

I like to watch a game from the inside out; first I look at the quarterback and then I check out the action away from the ball. Because the networks use so many cameras, you can follow the entire game and not miss a play. What's great about television are the replays — you can watch a replay of a critical play from two or three different angles. These different views are often necessary to determine whether a player was in possession of the ball, especially on really close plays involving receptions and fumbles. Also, the different angles help fans interpret whether the officials called the correct penalty, especially on penalties like pass interference (I fill you in on penalties, including pass interference, in Chapter 3).

TIP

Here are some tips to help you become a more savvy and informed viewer when you're watching a game on television:

>> **Start at the line of scrimmage.** Look wide to see how many receivers you spot and where they're located. Scan to see how many players are lined up on the defensive line and in the defensive backfield. Where and how the players line up gives you an indication of what the play may be.

>> **Keep an eye on the game's progress.** In the upper corner of the television screen, check out what the down is, how far the offense needs to go for the first down, how much time is left on the clock, and what the score is. The score and the time left on the clock often dictate whether a team will run or pass.

>> **Check the quarterback.** If he's positioned 5 yards behind the center, he's in the shotgun formation, meaning there's a 90 percent chance he'll pass the ball. The other 10 percent of the time, the quarterback drops back and then hands off the ball to a running back or runs on his own.

>> **Look for movement among the linebackers and defensive backs.** If defenders appear to be creeping toward the line of scrimmage, they're probably going to either blitz the quarterback or fill all the running lanes to neutralize a run play.

>> **Look at the defensive fronts, paying particular attention to the defensive tackles.** If only three linemen are lined up close to the line of scrimmage, the defense expects the offense to pass the ball. If the defense has four down linemen on the field and the linebackers are within a couple yards of the line of scrimmage, the defense expects the offense to try to run.

>> **Count the number of defensive backs.** If more than four defensive backs are in the game, the defense is geared toward preventing a pass completion.

HOWIE SAYS

TALK RADIO: GETTING THE INSIDE SCOOP

I enjoy being a guest on most sports talk shows. To me, talk radio is another way to get information about pro football. These shows discuss the inside scoop and address all the serious issues.

Sports talk radio has altered the landscape of sports journalism. Players and coaches listen to these shows. One season, Philadelphia's WIP radio station was so critical of the Philadelphia Eagles that the team declined to issue game credentials to some of the station's commentators. I know that coaches on the team quit listening to the morning shows because they would get too upset to go to work. This shows you the power of talk radio and how it can irritate people.

However, I recommend listening to the pro football reports in most NFL cities. If the talk radio show includes a lot of conversations about your team and regular player interviews, the program is probably worth listening to. Some talk radio hosts can be more insightful than some reporters; they do their homework on the team.

Other talk radio hosts allow callers to dominate their programs. This kind of interaction with the audience might make for great radio, but you rarely get much insight from local fans, whose commentary, let's face it, generally breaks down into these categories: calling for the quarterback to be benched after a loss, calling for the coach to be fired after a loss, complaining about the refs, or declaring their team an unbeatable playoff contender after any regular-season victory.

Listening to a game on the radio

Every NFL team and most major college teams have a local radio station that owns the rights to the teams' broadcasts. And because of the popularity of sports talk radio, many fans want to tune in to their favorite broadcasters.

Perhaps the best thing about listening to the radio is that you get the home-team announcers' insights into what strategy your team plans to use. These announcers know the players and can immediately tell you which player has the ball and who made the tackle. They also have access to the injury reports, so you can receive player updates throughout the broadcast. You also hear important statistics — such as how many total yards and first downs each team has collected — faster than most scoreboards can provide them.

HOWIE SAYS

The first time I saw a fan listening to a radio in a ballpark was during a Los Angeles Dodgers game. Although the fans were watching the action in person, they wanted to hear Vin Scully, the radio announcer, describe it. Just like these baseball fans, many football fans also enjoy listening to the radio when attending a game.

Attending a Game

To the die-hard football fan, nothing beats watching a football game live. You get caught up in the excitement of cheering for your team. You sometimes get the feeling that the outcome of the game is in your hands — and in a way it *is* in your hands because cheering loudly can disrupt the other team's offense and make it difficult for the other team to hear its quarterback barking plays. Most of all, attending a game is just plain fun. The following sections look into some of the nuances of watching a game in person.

Picking the best seats

TIP

The really good seats in every stadium are near the 50-yard line, 25 rows up, where you can scan the entire field. But those great seats usually belong to long-time season ticket holders. If you aren't a longtime season ticket holder or lucky enough to have an official sideline credential, the end zone can be a good place to watch a game. The best seat in the house, from my perspective, is in the end zone about 20 rows up. Of course, you need good binoculars. I like to see plays developing and watch the line play on both sides of the ball, and the end zone offers the best vantage point to see this action.

Sitting in the end zone, you can focus on a matchup of two linemen, like a defensive end battling an offensive tackle, and watch how they attack each other. Whoever wins this battle is going to win the war (the game). These individual battles can teach you a lot about football, even when the play or ball is going in the opposite direction. For a team to win, its players need to win these individual battles.

HOWIE SAYS

I love to watch a game from the sidelines. It's too bad more fans don't have that same opportunity at least once in their lives. Standing on the sidelines, you see firsthand the speed of the players and the ferocity of their hits. The contact occurs — and the overall game is played — at such a high speed. The players move like bullet trains plowing through a cornfield.

Wherever you sit, make sure you buy a program or check your local newspaper or team website for team depth charts and numbered rosters — these rosters are the only way to identify the many players on the field. A *depth chart* lists the starting lineups for both teams by their positions on offense and defense. It also lists the punter, placekicker, snapper for punts and kicks, and kickoff and punt return specialists. The reserves are listed alongside the starters on the depth chart, so when a player is injured, you can figure out who will replace him.

Knowing what to focus on

The beauty of watching a game in person is that you can see the entire play develop. As soon as the center snaps the ball, all 22 players on the field are moving. Television can't possibly capture that singular moment and every player, too. At the stadium, you can also watch what happens to a quarterback after the ball is released. On television, the camera follows the ball, but in person, you can see whether the quarterback is hit after he releases the ball. Occasionally, the quarterback and a pass-rusher exchange words (or even swings).

The special teams play, especially kickoffs and long punts, is exciting to watch in person because you can follow the flight of the ball and the coverage players running full speed toward the kick returner. Because kickoff and punt plays cover so much of the field, often 50 to 70 yards, television can't capture all the action.

TIP

During commercial timeouts, scan the sidelines with your binoculars. You can spot coaches talking strategy with players, and sometimes you can capture an animated conversation or debate. The more games you attend, the better able you'll be to follow the action and observe the sidelines. The pace is fast during plays, but there's enough down time between plays to check out what's happening on the sidelines and to figure out, by how teams are substituting, which play may be called next.

Enjoying the halftime show

Except for the elaborate halftime shows at the Super Bowl every year, halftime shows aren't televised anymore. To see a halftime show, you must attend a game in person.

College game halftime shows usually feature high-spirited bands, drill teams, and cheerleading squads doing their best to rally the fans. I remember when you used to see *card stunts* at college football games. To perform one, thousands of fans would hold up different-colored cards coordinated to display, for the entire stadium, a team name, mascot picture, or some other message for the faithful.

Some colleges are famous for their halftime performances. The Stanford band, for example, often puts on a comic show. At a show during Stanford's annual game against arch-rival California, the band dressed one member in a California band uniform and had him march around looking extremely confused during the Stanford performance.

Keeping Up with Your Favorite Teams

The fun of football doesn't end when the last seconds of the fourth quarter tick away. Diehard fans love to analyze the statistics of today's games and find out all about the upcoming ones. You can get this type of information from a wide variety of sources; I list some of my favorites in the next sections.

The NFL Network and the NFL Redzone Channel

The NFL Network offers non-stop, continuous coverage of professional football. It's available on most cable and satellite providers in the United States. In addition to game highlights, in-depth analysis, and news coverage of teams and players, the NFL Network broadcasts half of the Thursday night games each season and also shows replays of the most interesting games from the previous weekend. They also have a lot of talk-radio type shows like *Good Morning Football,* which airs for two hours every weekday morning.

The NFL Redzone Channel broadcasts on Sundays during the regular season. Its goal is to provide instant coverage and highlights of every game taking place. If you're watching the Redzone Channel, you'll see every touchdown from every game. It's a great way to follow all the games every Sunday during the season.

Internet sports sites

You can find more football-related information on the Internet than you could read in a whole season — everything from who's being traded and who's injured to who's predicted to go to the playoffs and more. The following websites are great sources of up-to-the-minute football info:

>> **ESPN** (espn.go.com): This online version of ESPN offers in-depth information about the NFL and college football. At espn3.com, you can watch webcasts of college football games (if your Internet connection is good enough).

>> **Pro Football Talk** (www.profootballtalknbcsports.com): This may be the most informative NFL site for daily news on every team and also excellent background information for the most-compelling issues league wide.

>> **NFL.com** (www.nfl.com): This is the official site of the NFL. In addition to scores, statistics, and news, it gives in-depth team coverage, including audio and video clips. The individual team pages offer links to your favorite teams' official websites.

>> **Sports Illustrated** (www.si.com): This website includes comprehensive coverage of the NFL and college football.

>> **Sporting News** (www.sportingnews.com): This site, which is the online version of the magazine, provides an abundance of information about NFL and college football. You can customize this site so that it displays your favorite sports and teams.

>> **Yahoo Sports** (sports.yahoo.com): This sports site is one of the most visited on the Internet. In addition to football scores, news, and stats, it offers commentary from multiple columnists.

>> **CBS Sports** (www.cbssports.com): This site covers the NFL and college football. It's an excellent source for information, such as team updates, schedules, injury reports, and statistics.

>> **The Athletic:** This a very good subscription site that has reports on every NFL team and most of the major college football teams. It features a lot of familiar sports journalists who formerly worked for newspapers.

Fantasy football sites

Many of the major sports websites listed in the preceding section (CBS, ESPN, NFL, Yahoo) offer free fantasy football leagues that you and your friends can join. They are all full-featured and provide up-to-date stats and scoring.

If you need advice on fantasy strategy, you're a simple web search away. Countless sites offer tips, stats, and picks for fantasy enthusiasts. If you're into fantasy football, you're probably visiting multiple sites per week looking for any tidbit of information that might give you an advantage over your opponent.

I offer some information on fantasy football in Chapter 18.

Twitter

It seems like everyone is tweeting these days, even if very few people have anything meaningful to say. Sports figures are no exception. Many football players in both the NFL and college tweet regularly. Sometimes they offer interesting observations; other times they accidentally send inappropriate pictures of themselves to thousands of fans. And a few players use their Twitter accounts to connect with fans and their community. Choose wisely when deciding whom to follow.

Sports columnists as well as radio and television personalities also use Twitter to communicate with fans. Many *live tweet* a game, meaning that they use their Twitter account to provide a running commentary during a live football game. Some of these tweeting marathons can be hilarious, and that's one of the reasons why so many people watch games with one eye on their phone, tablet, or laptop. In addition to following scores and fantasy stats, they're also reading Twitter and sending out tweets of their own. For some, this instant interactivity is a lot of fun. But it's also nice to occasionally put down all the gadgets and just watch the game. (I hope that doesn't make me sound too old.)

Mobile apps

Smartphones and tablets give football fans multiple tools for following their teams. NFL Mobile is a great app for checking scores and viewing highlights as the games are going on. You can also watch NFL games (after paying a subscription fee) using the NFL Sunday Ticket app. NFL Game Rewind, which also requires a paid subscription, gives you the ability to watch full replays of every NFL game.

Visiting the Football Halls of Fame

Visiting one of the football halls of fame — there's one for college, one for exclusively black colleges, and one for professional football — is a terrific way to find out more about how football became what it is today. They are filled with memorabilia from players and teams from the turn of the 19th century to the present. The many exhibits include uniforms and pictures of Hall of Famers in action and screening rooms in which you can enjoy films of legendary players and teams. Here are the websites for the halls of fame:

» **College Football Hall of Fame:** www.cfbhall.com

» **Black College Football Hall of Fame:** www.blackcollegefootballhof.org

» **Pro Football Hall of Fame:** www.profootballhof.com

Chapter **15**

Youth Leagues and High School Football

On the youth level, football isn't like baseball or basketball. My experience with those sports is that not playing well is okay because you're not putting yourself in danger. With football, on the other hand, you can really get hurt if you're not physically and mentally equipped to handle the game — especially if you're a young kid.

But football can teach you a lot about life; it's a character-building sport. Young players can discover the rewards of hard work, dedication, teamwork, and discipline. Football, like a lot of sports, is a great way to bring families together.

In this chapter, I discuss the benefits of youth football, from Pop Warner and flag football to high school football. I offer my own thoughts on coaching, the father-son relationship, and the things that young players need to focus on to be successful with the game and with life. I also look at making the transition from high school to college football.

Determining When to Start Playing

If your young son has the desire to play the game, let him play; just don't push him to play. Football either is or isn't the right sport for him, and everyone will know quickly whether he made a good choice.

I didn't start playing football until I was 15; my oldest son, Chris, played football for the first time when he was 12, and 2018 was his 11th season in the NFL as a defensive end. Because he was bigger than most boys his age, he couldn't play with his friends and other 12-year-olds; he had to play on the junior varsity football team with boys who were 15 and 16. Because of age differences, he got physically whipped. But I tried to help and support him.

REMEMBER

If you want your son to play at a young age, you must be committed to supporting and consoling him during the tough times. Young players — particularly those who have talent but haven't had a lot of success — need encouragement. However, fathers who care *too much* and try to live vicariously through their children often ruin the football experience for their children. Find a good balance.

Pop Warner Football and other local junior tackle programs have teams for 7-year-olds. I think starting football at age 7 is a little too young because kids that age are too small and may get hurt. But if your child is mature for his age he may have fun. With young kids, though, every parent should monitor practices and make sure the coach knows what he's doing and that he encourages the players to have fun.

Signing Up Your Kids for Youth Football

Depending on where you live in the United States, your child has multiple options for playing youth football. The following sections explain what these options are.

REMEMBER

When you sign up your child for youth football, you need a copy of his birth certificate and a current report card. (Most leagues won't enroll students who are failing in school.) Also, examine your health insurance and make sure that your child is covered for all types of injury.

TIP

If you can't find sign-up information, check with your town or city's recreation department. Most know how to locate league officials and know where teams are practicing.

Pop Warner and similar programs

The nation's largest youth football organization is Pop Warner Little Scholars, Inc., which is the legal name for Pop Warner Football. Pop Warner has leagues in 42 states and several countries. More than 300,000 boys and girls (the girls take part in cheer and dance teams) participate in those programs.

Pop Warner has stringent safety rules, including an age-weight schematic. This system ensures maximum safety because players are evenly matched in size and physical maturity. Pop Warner also has a no-cut rule, which means players don't have to try out. "First come, first on" is how Pop Warner operates. Pop Warner has different age-group divisions for players ages 5 to 16. Players move up to different divisions until they reach the Bantam division in which the 16-year-olds play. In many parts of the country, school districts no longer have junior high/middle school football programs, and youth leagues fill that void.

To find a Pop Warner program in your area, check your local phone book; email the organization at football@popwarner.com; write to Pop Warner Little Scholars at 586 Middletown Blvd., Suite C-100, Langhorne, PA 19047; call 215-752-2691; or visit www.popwarner.com.

There are also many flag football leagues in larger cities. Many parents may prefer these leagues because there isn't any physical contact in the game, and their sons (or daughters) can learn the intricacies of football and develop their skills for potentially trying the contact game when they get older.

Punt, Pass & Kick

Every year, thousands of boys and girls ages 6 to 15 participate in the NFL Punt, Pass & Kick competition. Since this competition began in the early 1960s, numerous participants — including quarterbacks Dan Marino, Drew Bledsoe, Brett Favre, Troy Aikman, and Randall Cunningham — have gone on to play in the NFL.

Kids compete by age group in this competition, which is offered on the local level in every NFL city. The competition is then regionalized, and those winners compete at the end of the NFL season in a prearranged NFL city. Every young athlete is judged on how far he or she throws a pass, punts a football, and kicks a football off a tee. Points are awarded by distance and accuracy, and most winners have won one if not two of the three categories. For more information, visit www.nflppk.com.

COACHING A YOUTH FOOTBALL TEAM

To coach any youth team, you must be able to give your time freely and want to do it for the kids. You must be committed to making the game fun; to helping develop a player's physical, mental, and social skills; and to winning the game. There's nothing wrong with trying to win, as long as you encourage the team to play the game fairly and teach your players good sportsmanship. Nothing can be gained from whipping an opponent 40–0 in a league of 10-year-olds. Think of how those kids on the losing team would feel!

You must make sure that *every* child has an enjoyable and successful experience. You need a lot of patience because you have to play every child, and sometimes you have to play a child in a position he isn't very good at. Your job is to make sure each player can cope with his limitations and be placed in a position where he can succeed. Try to get to know your players individually — every kid is different.

To be a coach, you must know the rules of the game and understand the tactics of the game. If you don't, you may want to buy some coaching books and attend coaching clinics, which are held in every state. Check with local high school coaches about available clinics. And consider reading *Coaching Football For Dummies* by the National Alliance for Youth Sports with Greg Bach (Wiley).

Your practices need to be well-organized, and you need to start the season with a set of rules that applies to every member of the team. One rule should be that if a player misses a certain number of practices, he has to sit out a certain number of minutes during the game, even if he's a star player. Rules about players being on time for practices and remembering their equipment teach players how to be responsible. In the end, football is about building character. Remember, too, that children view most adults' actions from a right-or-wrong perspective. They can tell when a coach is playing favorites; that's why your rules need to be uniform.

What Sets High School Football Apart

Some high school principals believe that football is the most important extracurricular activity on campus. Football generally starts off the school year in September, and a winning football team can create a positive attitude on campus. The spirit and enthusiasm that a football program generates can form a building block for a positive school environment.

At most high schools, the number of students who participate in the sport (including student managers and cheerleaders) can amount to 10 percent or more of the student body. For these youngsters, the football experience can create a special bond that lasts forever. Because of its physical and mental demands, football is a sport that can make men out of boys. Of course, it's essential that the young men have the proper role models and authority figures in the head coach and his assistants.

All across America, high school football teams are part of small towns' identities. The team can serve as a rallying point for the community, mainly because of family ties to the players. In small towns, most people know everyone else; consequently, a lot of people take pride in a successful high school team. Local businesses usually purchase advertising in the football program or donate services that help the program succeed financially.

Every state has its own high school federation or association that governs football and other sports. These federations oversee all-state awards, name district all-stars, and compile records of achievement. The following sections provide even more insight into the high school game, including the scoop on rule differences and how to use players who play both offense and defense.

Rule differences

Table 15-1 shows how the rules governing high school football differ from NFL rules.

TABLE 15-1 **Comparing High School Rules to NFL Rules**

High School Rule	NFL Rule
Any ball carrier who touches the ground with any part of his body except his hands or feet is ruled down; the ball is dead at that spot.	A ball carrier is considered down when he's touched by an opponent while on the ground. For example, if an NFL runner slips and inadvertently touches the ground, he can get up and keep moving forward.
The defense can't advance a fumble. The ball is ruled dead where the defensive player recovers it.	The offense and defense can return fumbles.
A player is considered inbounds on a pass reception if he catches the ball with one foot down inside the sideline.	A player must catch the ball with both feet down inside the sideline to be considered inbounds.
The goalposts are 23 feet, 4 inches wide, and they rise to 20 feet.	The goalpost width is 18 feet, 6 inches, and it rises to 35 feet.
The hash marks are 53 feet, 4 inches from each sideline. Because the hash marks are close to each sideline, high school offenses can attempt more running plays to the wide side of the field.	Hash marks are 70 feet, 9 inches from each sideline.
Games are 48 minutes long.	Games are 60 minutes long.

Style of play

With a few exceptions, most high school offenses generally run the ball more often than they throw it. But the top high school programs in California, Texas, and Florida play a wide-open style of offense like the pros. For the smaller high school programs, developing a good running game is easier than finding a quarterback who's capable of accurately throwing 25-yard passes and finding receivers who are fast enough to get off the line of scrimmage to catch the ball. Limited practice time (most states allow only 14 days of practice prior to the first game) is another reason high school teams opt for a run-oriented offense; they can develop this type of offense more quickly.

Offense seems to be the priority in high school football. Coaches gamble more often on fourth down, believing that they can easily gain a yard or two to get the first down and keep the ball. Some of the top programs rarely punt the ball and always go for it on fourth down. Unlike pro quarterbacks, most high school quarterbacks are good runners. You see more old-style offenses in high school, too: You see a *full-house backfield* (three running backs lined up straight across behind the quarterback) and double-wing formations as coaches attempt to use more blockers in the backfield to better the chances of a successful play. For the most part, high school teams concentrate more on offensive preparation than on defensive preparation unless they're facing an opponent that operates a formation that's totally unfamiliar to them.

REMEMBER

High school teams don't kick as often as pro teams because finding an accurate high school field goal kicker can be difficult. Some high school teams can't find a player who can even convert an extra point, which is basically a 20-yard kick. Plus, they don't have the time to concentrate on special teams play because of the time constraints on high school athletes.

Player lineups

The players on a high school roster may not compare in size to those on an NFL team, but high school players are definitely getting bigger. Today, a high school offensive line averaging 260 pounds isn't uncommon, whereas 25 years ago that average may have been 220 pounds. In the last few years, more illegal use of steroids has been reported among boys 18 and under than among college and professional football players. Unlike college and the NFL, no mandatory testing system for steroids is in effect at the high school level. (Some schools do test for marijuana and other drugs, though.)

You will find more two-way players at the high school level because most high school teams don't have enough quality players. A *two-way player* is one who plays both an offensive position and a defensive position. Here are some examples of the different combinations of positions: Receivers may also play defensive back, quarterbacks may lead the offense and spark the defense at safety, and blocking backs are also linebackers.

When a school is forced to use a lot of two-way players, you may see sloppy play in the fourth quarter when the young players tire and begin to lose their concentration, which may lead to injury. Although two-way players don't always run out of steam at the end of a game, an opponent that doesn't need to use two-way players may have an advantage.

Making the Most of the High School Game

The first thing parents and young men should realize about high school football is that players experience many ups and downs. You win a game against your rival and nothing feels better. Next week, you lose and you feel down. But you have to bounce back. Football teaches you to be humble about success because when games go badly, you have to work hard to battle back.

Losing a football game isn't unlike some experiences that you go through in other aspects of life. You have to learn to deal not only with success but also with failure. I think that football is a great teacher of those lessons — more so than any other sport. Unlike high school baseball and basketball teams that play multiple games every week, in football you play only one game, which heightens each game's importance. You focus all week on one game, and if you lose, the pain may linger for days before you get an opportunity to redeem yourself in the next one.

The next sections give some tips to help players, coaches, and parents keep the game in the proper perspective and enjoy football to the fullest.

Players

If you're interested in playing high school football, go to the school's main office and ask where and how to sign up. The employees in the main office can send you in the direction of the athletic director or head football coach.

As a player, you need to adhere to the team rules and most likely get involved in a weight-lifting program. Most schools have programs that are monitored by a coach or teacher. In most parts of the United States, football players have a few weeks in the spring in which they work out without equipment. To make the team, you must take advantage of these training opportunities. Coaches like to see athletes working year-round and attending every practice. If your coach recommends that you attend a football camp, ask your parents for permission and find a way to earn the money to pay your way.

Ultimately, you play football (or any sport, for that matter) to have fun. It should be a worthwhile experience, not drudgery. But if you possess special athletic ability and your goal is an athletic scholarship, remain focused and work as hard as you can. Good things come from hard work.

Coaches

Coaching is a demanding career. High schools are having more and more trouble finding quality coaches because coaching is a time-consuming, low-paying profession. High school head coaches are usually also teachers, and teachers aren't paid well. Still, regardless of the financial rewards (or lack thereof), a high school football coach's chief reward is the personal satisfaction of working with young people and watching them grow. And that satisfaction is so meaningful to many high school coaches that they would gladly work for minimum wage rather than give up coaching.

If you coach high school football, make a point of recruiting other teachers. Get them on your side so that they understand what your values are and how hard your athletes are working. Every week, invite one or two teachers to the pregame meal and ask them to ride the bus to away games. Doing so will make them feel like a part of your program. You must educate them about the game and about what's happening with your team. If they know how much time the kids and coaches spend practicing and working at football, and if they're aware of the discipline you're teaching, they may view your program more favorably. Remember, you're a teacher, too, not just some jock.

The other benefit of building a good relationship with other teachers is that you need to know when players are failing classes. You need to do grade checks every four to six weeks. Some schools don't allow students to play sports if they're flunking one or more classes. Developing a good relationship with the other faculty members helps everybody.

Parents

I think most fathers expect their sons to go out for football because they played the sport in high school. Often, football is a family tradition. The grandfather played, the father played, and the uncles and cousins played, so a boy grows up wanting to emulate his relatives, particularly his father. Kids quickly learn how tough playing football is. Going to football practice is like going to boot camp. It's much different from practicing baseball, where you play catch and run around and have fun, or basketball, where you're mostly playing the sport all the time. With football, you spend a great deal of practice time working on conditioning, as well as hitting — and 2 to 3 hours of practice a day is hardly fun.

TIP

When your child asks you why he should bust his butt for 3 hours a day and have people hit him and yell at him when he can stay home and play video games, that's the time you can have some real influence. Preach the benefits of teamwork and of not quitting something you start. Remind your child how much pride he'll feel in being successful at such a difficult sport.

Here are some other recommendations for parents:

>> A football player has to make a lot of sacrifices, so try to give your son some slack with chores; he has made a huge commitment to the team.

>> Encourage your son to have a good work ethic and to study hard and maintain good grades.

>> If your son has the talent to earn an athletic scholarship, consider sending him to summer football camps during his high school career. Many colleges and universities offer these types of camps. There are also speciality coaches which charge a fee for quarterback training or working to improve a player's speed and conditioning.

JUDGING HIGH SCHOOL PLAYERS' TALENT

The average college football coach would give his right arm to know which high school players will become college football stars. How can you tell whether a high school football player will achieve on the college level? College football recruiters can study tapes of players. They can measure a player's speed (in the 40-yard dash, which is the benchmark for measuring speed in football) and strength (in the bench press and other weight-lifting tests), but being a college star requires an extra something that's hard to quantify. This extra something usually goes by the name "heart" or "desire," and no test has yet been devised for measuring those intangibles.

Still, a cottage industry for judging high school football players has grown up in the past 10 years. Websites such as Rivals (www.rivals.com), Scout (recruiting.scout.com), PrepStar (www.prepstar.com), and ESPN College Football Recruiting (espn.go.com/college-football/recruiting) rate high school players; each year these services rank colleges to determine which have the best recruiting classes. Looking at these services' rankings from past years is fascinating. You can see just how difficult it is to tell which players will succeed in the college game. Some players who are highly ranked never make it in college football; often a player with a low ranking turns into a bright blazing star. For example, the Rams' Clay Matthews was runner-up for the 2010 Defensive Player of the Year award when he played for the Packers, but he started his college career at USC as a walk-on. A *walk-on* is someone who tries out for a college football team without first receiving a football scholarship.

Thinking Ahead to a College Football Career

High school players have many opportunities to play college football and receive financial assistance. In fact, if you include the smaller division schools, I think that more colleges and universities are giving scholarships to play football today than 40 years ago. Just as many schools are recruiting high school players, and the entire recruitment process has really advanced.

Forty years ago, the University of Southern California (USC) could give as many football scholarships as it wanted. Now, all Division FBS schools are restricted to 85 scholarships. Although not as many players have the opportunity to earn football scholarships at big-time schools like USC and Notre Dame as in the past, other colleges are picking up the slack. Colleges like Boise State and Montana go to small suburbs in California to find good players. Long story short? Good athletes don't get overlooked anymore because colleges are on a mission to find them.

TIP

If you're a parent and you believe your son has the ability to play college football, meet with the high school's guidance counselor during your son's freshman year and find out what course work is required by colleges that your son may be interested in. Doing so is a must to ensure that he's eligible to play at the college level when he graduates from high school.

If you're a student, remember that you go to school to receive an education. Of the thousands of young men who play college football, fewer than 240 are drafted by the NFL each year. Because college players have only a 1 percent chance of having a professional football career, education should be the number-one priority.

If you're a parent or coach, prepare young athletes for the realities of college by stressing the importance of academics and keeping track of athletes' academic records. To find out about the eligibility requirements for your son, check with your high school guidance counselor or the NCAA Initial-Eligibility Clearinghouse (www.eligibilitycenter.org). And start your research in his junior year if you believe that he has the ability to play college football.

Chapter **16**

College Football — Where It All Started

E ven though the National Football League is made up of pros, don't let that fool you: The NFL's rules, traditions, and growth were nurtured by college football. In fact, the sport itself began on the collegiate level. The first college football game was played in 1869 between Princeton and Rutgers, and it took professional football almost a century to match America's love affair with college football.

Although the NFL and college football attract many of the same fans today, some of the rules, as well as the levels of competition, are different. In this chapter, I clue you in to the different divisions of college football, shine a little light on the sometimes mysterious inner workings of the College Football Playoff, and reveal the powerful impact of college coaches, among other things.

Why People Love College Football

Fans are passionate about college football because of its local and regional flavor, and also because it's built on more than a century of tradition. A college football fan doesn't have to be an alumnus of a particular college to become a serious fan, either. For example, if you're raised in Ohio and your mother or father is passionate about football, you'll probably have heard about Woody Hayes (a legendary coach) and root for Ohio State.

In every pocket of America, fans are loyal to their state universities, both big and small, and when two state schools collide, a rivalry emerges and fans go wild. Ohio State's major rival is the University of Michigan. In Alabama, nothing is bigger than the matchup between the University of Alabama and Auburn, the state's other major college football team. And in Florida, life stops for three-plus hours when Florida State and the University of Florida play. The same is true when USC and UCLA meet in Los Angeles.

Another primary appeal of college football is its young, amateur players. Even in major college football, you see smaller-sized athletes (the ones who aren't big enough, strong enough, or fast enough to play in the NFL) performing at a high level. And the style of the college game generally isn't as structured as the NFL game. College teams are more open about their approach to the game; coaches will try anything new if they think it will work. They use offenses and defenses that NFL teams would never consider, such as the *wishbone*, which features three running backs and emphasizes the run by using a ball-handling running quarterback. Because not every college team is stacked with great players at every position, superior coaching decides a lot of outcomes with offensive and defensive game plans that exploit specific weaknesses.

Plus, the college game offers pageantry — the tailgate parties, the marching bands, and the Friday night pep rallies. In many cases, a college campus mushrooms to more than twice its normal population on a Saturday afternoon as thousands of adult fans join students at the game. Major college sights and sounds include

>> **The Notre Dame Victory March ("Cheer, cheer for old Notre Dame . . ."):** This school song is one of the most famous songs in the United States, right up there with the national anthem, "God Bless America," and "White Christmas."

>> **The Stanford and Yale bands:** These bands are known for their zaniness, wacky attire, and willingness to attempt any outlandish halftime show imaginable.

>> **The Trojan Horse:** The symbol of Southern California (USC) football is the Trojan Horse — a white horse with a man dressed like a Trojan warrior riding him. The horse's name is Traveler.

>> **Dotting the *i* in Ohio State:** The Buckeye band ends every home pregame performance by spelling out *Ohio* on the field, with the sousaphone player completing the spelling by running to dot the *i*.

RULE DIFFERENCES BETWEEN COLLEGE AND NFL FOOTBALL

If you watch a lot of NFL games, you should know that pro and college rules differ in three important areas:

- In college football, the hash marks are 10 feet 9 inches closer to the sidelines than in the pros.

- In college football, a receiver is ruled inbounds when he has possession of the ball and has one foot inbounds. In the NFL, the receiver must have both feet inbounds.

- In the NFL, any offensive player in possession of the ball — whether a running back, a quarterback, or a kick returner — can fall down, get back on his feet, and continue running if he isn't touched by a defensive player. A college player is considered down whenever one knee touches the ground, whether or not another player has touched him. Consequently, you'd better not slip in college football.

>> **Mascots:** Mascots are huge in college football. Some of the best include the Falcons at the Air Force Academy, which fly at halftime; the real-life Buffalo at Colorado; the ugly-faced bulldog at Georgia; and the little Irish leprechaun at Notre Dame.

>> **Atmosphere:** Atmosphere is what a college football game is all about. Here are some fan favorites: Any night game at LSU; the Florida–Georgia game, usually played in Jacksonville; Ohio State versus Michigan before 110,000 in Ann Arbor; Florida–Florida State and Notre Dame–USC anywhere; and any home game at Tennessee.

>> **Battle of the bands:** The Grambling–Southern University game offers the finest strutting, dancing, and rhythm halftime show in college football.

Big, Medium, and Small

The *National Collegiate Athletic Association* (NCAA), the governing body of college athletics, reports that 778 member colleges fielded football teams during the 2018 season. These colleges are divided into divisions based on enrollment, financial commitment, and the competitive level of the conference to which they belong. The NCAA doesn't want big-time powers like Alabama and Clemson playing small schools like Union College and Wabash. It wants a level playing field to make for more competitive games.

Consequently, as shown in Table 16-1, the colleges are divided into four divisions: Division I FBS (Football Bowl Subdivision), Division I FCS (Football Championship Subdivision), Division II, and Division III. Within each division, teams are members of conferences. A *conference* is similar to a league in professional sports (see "Examining College Conferences" later in this chapter for more on conferences).

TABLE 16-1

Division Breakdown for the 2018 Football Season

Division	Number of Schools	Number of Conferences
I FBS	130	10
I FCS	125	14
II	169	15
III	250	29

Hundreds of junior colleges (two-year programs) also have football teams, as do *National Association of Intercollegiate Athletics* (NAIA) schools, a group of smaller four-year colleges not associated with the NCAA. Unable to qualify academically to receive a four-year scholarship to a four-year college, many athletes attend junior colleges and hope to land a scholarship to a four-year school. Many of the NAIA teams are based in Kansas, North and South Dakota, Pennsylvania, Ohio, Nebraska, and Oregon.

The following sections introduce you to some of the big-time and small-time schools to know.

Big-time schools

Although 130 colleges and universities played Division 1 FBS in 2018, less than half of them had a realistic chance of finishing in the top ten or qualifying for the National Championship playoff system.

HOW THE NCAA GOT ITS START

Although it oversees every sport and both men's and women's teams, the NCAA got its start as a governing body for college football. In 1905, representatives of 13 colleges got together to establish playing rules, and in 1906, 49 schools joined the original 13 to form the precursor of the NCAA: the *Intercollegiate Athletic Association of the United States,* or IAAUS. The IAAUS became the NCAA in 1910.

Traditionally, Alabama, Clemson, Ohio State, LSU, Notre Dame, Michigan, Oklahoma, Penn State, Georgia, Texas, Texas A&M, Washington, Wisconsin, and USC have the best college programs. The state of Florida has four quality programs: University of Florida, Florida State, the University of Miami, and Central Florida. About 60 percent of the players in the NFL in 2018 came from three conferences: the SEC, the Big 10, and the ACC. Table 16-2 highlights the schools boasting the greatest number of college-players-turned-pro.

TABLE 16-2

Where NFL Players Came From, 2018

College	Number of Players
Alabama	44
LSU	40
Florida	38
Miami (Fla)	36
Ohio State	36
Florida State	33
USC	32
Clemson	29
Auburn	28
Georgia	28
Stanford	27
UCLA	27
Tennessee	27
Michigan	26
Notre Dame	26
Iowa	25
Texas	24
Penn State	24
Texas A&M	24
Oklahoma	23

(continued)

TABLE 16-2 *(continued)*

College	Number of Players
Wisconsin	22
California	22
Washington	22
Ole Miss	22
South Carolina	22

HALL OF FAME

Notre Dame, a Roman Catholic university located in South Bend, Indiana, has historically been the most recognized college football power. It began its rise in the 1920s and has maintained a lofty hold on the college scene ever since. Notre Dame's support is nationwide — it recruits high school players from virtually every state — and all of its games are televised nationally. (The term *subway alumni* is used to describe the many fans who support Notre Dame football. These fans act very much like they attended or even graduated from the school.)

The reputations of big-time schools help with recruiting because many of the best high school players want to play for a school where they have a chance to compete for a national championship, possibly prepare for the NFL, and also receive a good education. Every one of the schools mentioned earlier in this section adheres to those criteria.

Small college powers

Although small schools may not achieve national prominence, they certainly play tough football. Some of the winningest teams and coaches aren't at giants like Florida and Nebraska but rather smaller colleges, such as the following:

>> **Mount Union College:** Just 18 miles east of the Pro Football Hall of Fame is the small Ohio town of Alliance, home of Division III powerhouse Mount Union College, the winningest college football program since 1990. In 2012, Mount Union won its 11th Division III Football National Championship in the previous 19 years by defeating the University of St. Thomas (Minnesota) in the Stagg Bowl.

>> **Grambling State University:** From 1941 through 1998 Grambling was led by the great Eddie Robinson, who became the second winningest coach in NCAA Division I history with 408 wins. Among predominantly black colleges, Grambling has been the best producer of NFL players, sending more than 100 to the pros. Robinson, who coached 55 seasons at Grambling, was inducted into the College Football Hall of Fame in 1998. He died in 2007.

HALL OF FAME

Two of the greatest players of all time, Walter Payton and Jerry Rice, were small-college players. Payton starred at Jackson State in Mississippi, and Rice, another first-round draft choice, played at Mississippi Valley State in Itta Bena, Mississippi. Bigger doesn't always mean better!

Examining College Conferences

College football teams play most of their games against schools in their own conferences. Some conferences, such as the Ivy League, formed because their members have a shared focus on academic excellence and don't award athletic scholarships. Brown, Columbia, Cornell, Dartmouth, Harvard, Penn, Princeton, and Yale are in the Ivy League conference (these schools — particularly Harvard, Princeton, Columbia, and Yale — helped spawn football in America). However, most conferences are formed with the goal of bringing together teams on the same competitive level in the same geographical area.

REMEMBER

The best-known Division I FBS conferences are the Big Ten, Pac-12, SEC (Southeastern Conference), ACC (Atlantic Coast Conference), Big 12, and the American Athletic Conference. These conferences supply more than 60 percent of the players on NFL rosters.

Here's the lowdown on these well-known college football conferences:

>> **Big Ten:** This conference, which actually has 14 members, is located mostly in the Midwest. Its members are Illinois, Indiana, Iowa, Maryland, Michigan, Michigan State, Minnesota, Nebraska, Northwestern, Ohio State, Penn State, Purdue, Rutgers, and Wisconsin.

>> **Pac-12 (formerly the Pac-10):** The Pac-12 is located in the western United States. In 2011, Colorado and Utah joined Arizona, Arizona State, Oregon, Oregon State, Stanford, UCLA, University of California at Berkeley, USC, Washington, and Washington State in this conference.

>> **SEC:** The members of the SEC are situated mostly in the southeastern portion of the country. Its members are Alabama, Arkansas, Auburn, Florida, Georgia, Kentucky, LSU, Missouri, Mississippi (also known as Ole Miss), Mississippi State, South Carolina, Tennessee, Texas A&M, and Vanderbilt.

>> **ACC:** The ACC schools are mostly in the Carolinas and along the East Coast. They include Boston College, Clemson, Duke, Florida State, Georgia Tech, Louisville, Miami, North Carolina, North Carolina State, Pittsburgh, Syracuse, Virginia, Virginia Tech, and Wake Forest.

>> **Big 12:** The Big 12 is actually composed of ten teams. The current members are Baylor, Iowa State, Kansas, Kansas State, Oklahoma, Oklahoma State, Texas, Texas Christian University (TCU), Texas Tech, and West Virginia.

>> **American Athletic Conference:** This conference formed during a period of NCAA conference realignments from 2010 to 2013. Many of its members were part of the former Big East conference. It includes these football programs: Central Florida, Cincinnati, Connecticut, East Carolina, Houston, Memphis, South Florida, Southern Methodist, Temple, Tulane, and Tulsa.

The other Division I FBS conferences are Conference USA, Mid-American Conference, Mountain West Conference, and Sun Belt Conference.

THE EVER-SHIFTING DIVISION I FBS CONFERENCES

The year 2011 saw a drastic realignment of teams in Division I FBS conferences. Nebraska left the Big 12 Conference to join the Big Ten. Not to be outdone by its rival the Big Ten, the Pac-10 Conference successfully courted two new members, Utah (formerly in the Mountain West Conference) and Colorado (formerly in the Big 12), which necessitated a name change for the conference; it became the Pac-12 Conference. Then in 2013, the Big Ten added Rutgers and Maryland, for a total of 14 teams. Sounds like a name change is long overdue for that conference.

The Mountain West Conference, smarting from the loss of Utah, signed up three new members in Boise State, Nevada (Reno), and Fresno State — all formerly of the Western Athletic Conference. Not long after, however, the Mountain West Conference received some bad news: Long-time member Brigham Young (BYU) had decided to go solo. The BYU Cougars left the Mountain West Conference to become an independent football team.

Why this game of musical chairs? Why are so many teams jumping to different conferences?

One reason is because the teams are seeking a competitive advantage in the College Football Playoff (CFP), the playoff system used in Division I FBS football that began in 2014. Teams move to different conferences or go independent with the hope of positioning themselves for a shot at one of the four playoff spots. The thinking is that being a top team in one of the major football conferences increases a team's chances of being one of the four playoff teams.

Not all football teams belong to a conference. Navy, Brigham Young, and Notre Dame head the group of football independents. These schools don't have any trouble scheduling games because of their excellent football heritage. Plus, Notre Dame has its own network television contract.

REMEMBER

Although it isn't a national championship, winning a conference championship is a major accomplishment and assists in postseason honors and invitations to bowl games (in Division I FBS) or playoff games (in the other divisions).

The College Football Playoff

From 1998 to 2013, Division I FBS college football used the Bowl Championship Series (BCS) to determine a national champion. The BCS relied on polls and computer rankings to select two teams to play in a single BCS National Championship Game. The BCS was controversial since its inception with many fans arguing that the championship game rarely paired the two best teams in college football. So for 2014, a new system, the College Football Playoff (CFP) was devised.

The CFP is a four-team playoff. Two semifinal games are played first, followed a little over a week later (always on a Monday night) by a championship game pitting the two semifinal winners against each other.

The selection process

A committee of 13 football experts selects the final four teams for the semifinal games. The committee members include athletic directors from the major football conferences along with former athletic directors, coaches, players, and administrators, and even a retired sports reporter.

The four final teams are major conference champions, but as you may know, there are more than four major conferences. So the selection committee has to weigh factors such as overall record, strength of schedule, and head-to-head results. Polls and computer rankings are not used in the selection process. Ultimately, some major conference champions are left out of the playoffs. Those teams play in other bowls instead.

The selection committee seeds the four final teams from 1 to 4, with teams 1 and 4 playing in one semifinal and teams 2 and 3 playing in the other.

The semifinals

The two semifinal games are hosted on a rotating basis by five bowl games: Rose Bowl, Sugar Bowl, Orange Bowl, Cotton Bowl, and Peach Bowl. The games are played on New Year's Day along with other major bowl games featuring teams that didn't make the CFP. For the 2018 season, Alabama and Oklahoma played in the Orange Bowl, with Alabama coming out on top. In the other semifinal game, Clemson and Notre Dame played in the Cotton Bowl, with Clemson easily advancing to the final game.

The national championship game

The championship game is played on the first Monday a week after the semifinal games. Cities around the United States bid to host the game, which is held at a different location every year. For the 2018 season, the game was played at Levi Stadium in San Jose, California, home of the San Francisco 49ers. Clemson won its second National Championship Trophy, beating Alabama for both wins.

COLLEGE FOOTBALL FIRSTS

Here are some firsts in college football:

- White lines are placed on the field at 5-yard intervals in 1882. As a result of the pattern, the playing field is called a *gridiron*.

- A game is played on the West Coast between the University of California at Berkeley and Stanford in 1892.

- *Collier's* magazine publishes the first All-American team in 1898. *Collier's* remains the official selection holder of teams through 1924.

- The length of the football field is reduced from 110 yards to today's standard of 100 yards in 1912.

- The University of Wisconsin erects an electronic scoreboard in 1926, and first uses it in a game against Iowa.

- Although a Fordham practice was shown in the preceding year, the game between Maryland and the University of Pennsylvania on October 5, 1940, is television's first game. Saturday afternoon telecasts emerge nationwide in the 1951 season.

The Heisman and Other Trophies

The Heisman Trophy is awarded annually to America's most outstanding college football player. The trophy is named in honor of John W. Heisman, a legendary football coach. The first Heisman was given to halfback Jay Berwanger of the University of Chicago in 1935. Over the years, the award has traditionally gone to running backs and quarterbacks and some wide receivers. Two exceptions were Larry Kelley of Yale in 1936 and Leon Hart of Notre Dame in 1949, who were both *two-way players* (meaning they played both offense and defense). The third exception is Charles Woodson, a cornerback from Michigan who in 1997 became the first full-time defensive player to ever win the Heisman. (Woodson also returned kicks and occasionally played wide receiver on offense.)

HOWIE SAYS

REMEMBERING MY COLLEGE DAYS

I went to Villanova on a football scholarship, and we never played on television. Our home stadium's capacity was around 7,000. We took buses to a lot of our games and stayed three to a room at motor lodges with two beds a lot of the time. We didn't have the fancy training facilities, film rooms, or big weight-lifting rooms that a Nebraska, Penn State, or a Florida team has. I was just happy to have hot water for my shower.

But we played some big games at Villanova. We played Boston College twice, and Clemson was in the top ten when we faced them. The Boston College game was a big game for me because I was from Boston and was supposed to play for them. I always had some animosity for that game because the day after I had originally signed with Boston College the head coach told me I was going to play offensive guard. I didn't want to play that position. That's how I ended up at Villanova, playing defense.

When we played Clemson, they had something like seven first-round draft choices on their roster, and they beat us 30–0 with their third team. Clemson had the Bostic brothers (Jeff and Joe) playing center and guard, and they simply wore me out. They didn't beat me with athletic ability; they just knew a whole lot more about playing than I did. But I got my revenge in the Super Bowl, playing against Jeff, who was with the Washington Redskins. And our previous matchup definitely was on my mind.

College football has become much bigger since I played — more television, more money, and more exposure. Villanova, though, hasn't changed much. It's still a small college program.

More than 900 people (former winners and 870 college football broadcasters and sportswriters) vote every year for the Heisman winner, which is announced in mid-December. To vie for the award, some college sports information departments wage what's tantamount to a political campaign, producing tons of brochures, handbooks, and campaign literature on their star player. The campaign for the next year's Heisman winner actually begins during spring practice prior to the start of the football season.

Besides the Heisman, college football has other prestigious awards, including the

>> **Outland Trophy:** This trophy has been awarded since 1946 to the nation's top interior lineman. Some notable recipients include Alex Karras, Orlando Pace, and Ron Yary.

>> **Maxwell Award:** Two years younger than the Heisman, the Maxwell Award, which began in 1937, also goes to the top college player of the year. Often, the Maxwell and the Heisman don't agree.

>> **Lombardi Award:** This award is given to the nation's top lineman. Recipients include Cornelius Bennett, Orlando Pace (a two-time winner), and Terrell Suggs.

>> **Davey O'Brien Award:** This award is given to the best quarterback. Steve Young, Peyton Manning, Vince Young, and Tim Tebow have all received the Davey O'Brien Award.

All-American and Other All-Star Teams

The Associated Press All-America team is the most prestigious All-America team, followed by the Walter Camp All-America team. The American Football Coaches' All-America Team, which is selected by the coaches for all NCAA divisions and the NAIA (National Association of Intercollegiate Athletics), is also considered a highly accurate gauge of the best college talent.

These teams are *all-star teams* that honor the best players at their respective positions on a national scale. The Associated Press lists first-, second-, and third-team All-Americans. The selections are subjective. Often, coaches and football writers vote for players they know personally. Voters have their favorites and also their prejudices. Consequently, some deserving players may be ignored or fail to receive the recognition they deserve. In many ways, it's a popularity contest.

Because many of these all-star teams include players who are flunking classes and who have no intention of ever graduating, Academic All-America teams have emerged to recognize student-athletes who've had great careers and been successful in the classroom.

Some all-star teams actually compete in all-star games. Exceptional college football players can look forward to playing in these games when their college careers come to an end:

>> **East-West Shrine Game:** Pits players from the eastern United States against players from the West. The game is held in Orlando, Florida, with proceeds going to benefit the Shriners Hospitals for Children.

>> **Senior Bowl:** Held in Mobile, Alabama, with players divided into North and South teams. The game is considered a venue for players to showcase their talents to NFL scouts and coaches.

MY INVITE TO THE BLUE-GRAY ALL-STAR GAME

HOWIE SAYS

When I was at Villanova, I was fortunate to receive an invitation to a college all-star game called the Blue-Gray Football Classic held in Montgomery, Alabama (the game has since been discontinued). I think another player canceled out, and I got in, sort of as a novelty. I don't think that I projected very high in the NFL draft, maybe a tenth-round pick, until I played in this all-star game.

The week of practice and the game itself helped me a lot. It gave me the opportunity to compete with the top college prospects in America, something I couldn't do every weekend at a smaller school like Villanova. Every NFL team had scouts at this game; very few scouts came to my Villanova games. I ended up playing well against a guy from Texas A&M who was considered to be a high draft choice, a first- or second-round pick. Jimmy Johnson, whom I ended up working with at FOX, coached me in the game. During the game, I blocked a punt and scored a touchdown, and my team won.

I had the opportunity to run for a lot of pro scouts at that game. I was running 4.7s and 4.8s and doing all their little eraser drills where you run 10 yards, pick up an eraser, drop it in a basket, and do it again. Run 20 yards, and pick it up. . . . I was really good at those drills. My vertical jump was good. I had all the intangibles, but I wasn't a good football player. So someone had to take a chance, and the Raiders did, drafting me in the second round. All-star games give a lot of unknown players like me a chance to prove that they belong at the next level.

» **Checking out the NFL's schedule**

» **Assembling a winning team**

» **Exploring the business side of professional football**

» **Surveying the other professional leagues out there**

Chapter **17**

Taking a Look at the NFL (And Other Professional Leagues)

The National Football League (NFL) is the pinnacle of football — it's the ultimate high and the purest acceptance of anyone's ability as a football player or coach.

HOWIE SAYS

When I was a young player in the NFL, I thought I would always enjoy team success. I thought my team, the Los Angeles (now Oakland) Raiders, would go to the Super Bowl every year because we had so much talent. But so many intangibles are involved in reaching that game — things you can't control, such as injuries, complacency, and the loss of talent to free agency. Looking back on my playing career, I now understand and appreciate how lucky I was to play in and win one Super Bowl.

Although regular-season games begin in September and end in December or January (followed by a month of playoffs), the NFL is active year-round. During the off-season, players usually continue working out to remain in condition. The league also experiences coaching changes, players switching teams via free agency, the drafting of college players, and various organized training sessions called *mini-camps,* which last three to four days. Teams report to training camps in late July or early August, where players practice twice a day in preparation for the long season ahead. Preseason games, generally four per team, are played in August, prior to the start of the regular season.

In this chapter, I explain how the NFL started, how it works, how teams reach the playoffs, and how the money filters down to the players. I also demystify the salary cap, player movements, practice schedules, and life in general in the greatest league on earth.

The Birth of Pro Football

In its early days, and I'm talking about the early 20th century, professional football was disorganized because it lacked a league-wide constitution and guidelines. Player movement was rampant, with teams routinely bidding on players. The contracts for star players generally ranged from $50 to $250 a game, which was a considerable amount of money for that time. Many college players assumed aliases so they could earn some of that money by playing on Sunday afternoons with pro teams.

The Ohio League had the strongest professional teams, featuring such legends as the Canton Bulldogs and Olympian Jim Thorpe, until 1920 when a group of seven Ohio League owners/players created the first national professional football league. This organization, known as the American Professional Football Association (APFA), consisted of 14 teams. After the 1921 season, the APFA officially changed its name to the National Football League, or NFL.

In the first few years of the NFL, the championship wasn't decided on the field. Instead, it was awarded based on a vote at league meetings. The league didn't have a playoff system to decide its champion until 1933, and it wasn't until 1936 that every team in the league played the same number of games. In 1933, the NFL divided into a two-division alignment, with the winners of each division meeting for the league championship at the end of the regular season.

In the first 13 years of the NFL, the league lacked franchise stability; numerous teams folded because of a lack of money or fan interest. Nineteen teams lasted only one year, and another 11 managed just two seasons. Only two of today's teams, the Chicago Bears (originally the Decatur Staleys) and the Chicago Cardinals (whose franchise today resides in Phoenix, Arizona) started with the league in 1920. The Green Bay Packers are the third oldest team, joining the league in 1921.

THE AFL JOINS THE NFL

The American Football League (AFL) started in 1960 with eight teams. The pursuit of the same players by both the AFL and the NFL led to escalating salaries, which was great for the players but not for the financial welfare of pro football team owners. The NFL wasn't used to this kind of competition over talent. When the AFL, strengthened by its own network television contract, considered signing away many of the NFL's top quarterbacks, it forced the more established NFL to make peace. A merger of the two leagues was the solution, so the AFL and NFL agreed to merge in 1966 under the umbrella of the NFL. The two leagues held a common draft in 1967 and began interleague play in the 1970 season. The first four Super Bowls were actually between the champions of the NFL and the AFL.

The NFL Conferences

Today, the NFL is divided into two conferences: the *American Football Conference* (AFC) and the *National Football Conference* (NFC). Each conference consists of 16 teams and is divided into four divisions — East, West, North, and South — of four teams each. These division titles generally correspond to geographic parts of the country. There has been recent movement among the California teams with both the Rams and the Chargers returning to their roots in Los Angeles and preparing to share a new $3 billion stadium for the 2020 season. My Raiders, too, are leaving Oakland for a new stadium in Las Vegas for the 2020 season. Here's the division breakdown:

>> **The American Football Conference:** Along with six other teams, this conference includes ten franchises (in bold) that were once part of the old AFL.

- East Division: **Buffalo Bills, Miami Dolphins, New England Patriots, New York Jets**

- West Division: **Denver Broncos, Kansas City Chiefs, Oakland Raiders, Los Angeles Chargers**

- North Division: Baltimore Ravens, **Cincinnati Bengals,** Cleveland Browns, Pittsburgh Steelers

- South Division: Houston Texans, Indianapolis Colts, Jacksonville Jaguars, **Tennessee Titans**

>> **The National Football Conference:** Along with 13 others, this conference includes three franchises (in bold) that once formed the original NFL.

- East Division: Dallas Cowboys, New York Giants, Philadelphia Eagles, Washington Redskins
- West Division: **Arizona Cardinals,** Los Angeles Rams, San Francisco 49ers, Seattle Seahawks
- North Division: **Chicago Bears,** Detroit Lions, **Green Bay Packers,** Minnesota Vikings
- South Division: Atlanta Falcons, Carolina Panthers, New Orleans Saints, Tampa Bay Buccaneers

The Pro Football Schedule

The NFL schedule begins with what's called the *regular season*. In regular-season games, teams compete for the best win-loss records, and the teams with the best records advance to the playoffs. The playoffs, meanwhile, decide who goes on to the Super Bowl. The following sections look at the ins and outs of the NFL football schedule.

The regular-season games

As laid out in the annual *NFL Record and Fact Book,* the NFL follows a formula for devising each team's regular-season schedule. Each team plays 16 games in 17 weeks (the week a team doesn't play is called its *bye week*). In the formula, every team's schedule is as follows:

>> Six games, three at home and three away, against the three other teams in the division.

>> Four games against teams from a single division of the other conference; these divisions rotate on a four-year cycle.

>> Four games against teams from a single division of the franchise's own conference; these divisions rotate on a three-year cycle.

>> Two games against teams within the franchise's own conference, based on the team's finish in the preceding season. (For example, a team that finished second one year plays the two second-place teams in the three divisions of its conference that it is *not* scheduled to play the next year.)

The playoffs

The NFL schedules all those regular-season games — 256 in a typical season — to separate the good teams from the bad. On every level of sports, people want to declare a champion. In the NFL, a total of 12 teams qualify for what amounts to the road to the Super Bowl.

Six teams from each conference qualify for the playoffs, with the four division winners qualifying automatically. These winners are joined by two teams called *wildcard teams,* who qualify based on the win-loss records of the remaining teams in each conference that didn't finish first in their respective divisions. The two division winners with the highest winning percentages host second-round games, skipping the first round of competition. This is known as a first-round bye. The third and fourth division winners host the wildcard teams in the first round.

The winners of the two wildcard games advance to the second round of contests, called Divisional Playoff games. The lowest-rated wildcard winner (the first-round winner with the worst record) plays the division winner with the best record, and the other wildcard winner plays the division winner with the second-best record. Both division winners enjoy *home field advantage,* meaning they host the games.

For the Conference Championship games (the third round), any surviving division champion automatically hosts the game. If two division winners survive, the team with the better winning percentage hosts the championship game. If the two surviving teams have identical records, home field is based first on how the two teams performed in head-to-head competition during the season, and then on who had the best winning percentage in conference games. The winner of each Conference Championship game goes on to the Super Bowl.

The Super Bowl

The Super Bowl is the NFL championship game. It pits the winner of the AFC against the champion of the NFC. The game was born out of the merger agreement between the former American Football League (AFL) and the National Football League (NFL) in 1966 (see the nearby related sidebar).

In the first two years of the pro football championship, the game was billed as the AFL-NFL World Championship Game. But not until the third championship meeting between the two leagues in 1969 did the name "Super Bowl" stick for good. Kansas City Chiefs owner Lamar Hunt coined the name after a toy with super bouncing abilities. That toy was called the Super Ball. He derived the name because the game itself was considered to be "super" (and any fan would agree with that!). The term "bowl" came from the college game, where bowl games remain common post-season rituals (I fill you in on these in Chapter 16).

The Super Bowl is such a huge television and fan attraction that cities routinely bid for the game, offering to defray many of the league's expenses for hotels and travel. In fact, the Super Bowl is so large that cities are selected to host three to four years in advance. This extra time gives the cities the necessary time to prepare.

In the two weeks between the two conference championship games and the Super Bowl, plenty of hype and hoopla about the game arises. The two teams usually arrive in the host city on the Sunday prior to the game, along with more than 2,500 members of the media. The event has a national flavor to it. Week-long events, such as the NFL Experience (an interactive theme park that features more than 50 attractions, including games like Quarterback Challenge, the Extra-Point Kick, and the Super Bowl Card Show) are planned for youngsters and older fans alike. Parties are held at hotels and venues throughout the host city.

With ticket prices ranging from $800 to $2,000, and most fans paying five times that amount thanks to ticket scalping, the Super Bowl has become more of a corporate event than a bastion for hard-core football fans. The average resale price for the 2019 game was over $5,200. You almost have to be somebody important or know somebody important to attend.

Building a Team: It's More than Drawing Straws

As you can imagine, building an NFL team is no easy task. Most teams focus first on acquiring a solid quarterback and then making sure they have highly skilled players at the running back and wide receiver positions. The offensive line is generally built to suit the specific offensive strategy of the team. For example, if the team likes to pass, it pays a premium for linemen who are better pass-protectors than run-blockers. Having linemen equally suited to both styles is best, but sometimes that's a luxury when you're selecting your roster for today's game. Injuries are a factor when most teams have only eight linemen on their 53-player rosters. Teams then place players on a game-day inactive list because teams can only dress 45 players.

In terms of the defense, teams need at least five star performers among the players on the defensive line, the linebacker corps, and secondary. Ideally, these players rank among the top ten players at their respective positions. Most NFL teams have a core of seven to ten potential-superstar players, an average of 6 to 12 rookies, and a group of *veterans* (players with at least one year of pro experience) to round out the roster. Many teams have at least 20 players with five or more years of NFL experience.

All teams acquire players through the draft, and their plan is to develop the players that they draft over a couple seasons. They also acquire players by making trades with other teams and getting players through free agency and also by signing players who were bypassed in the NFL draft. The next sections explore how coaches and general managers build what they hope will be a winning team.

Drafting players out of school

The annual NFL draft of college players occurs in late April or early May. The three-day event begins on a Thursday in prime time with the first round. Rounds 2 and 3 are on Friday evening with Rounds 4–7 on Saturday. The draft, which is televised by ESPN, the NFL Network, and also by one of the national networks, was traditionally held at Radio City Music Hall in New York City, but today the draft takes place at different cities that will change from year to year. Some of the top college players are in attendance. If a college player wants to play in the NFL, he usually enters via the draft. In a typical year, more than 2,500 college athletes become eligible for the draft, but only about 260 players are selected.

If a high draft choice doesn't become a starter by his third season, he's generally considered a bust. The team then attempts to replace him with a veteran or another rookie and starts the process anew.

Who picks when

The draft consists of seven rounds, and each team is allotted one pick in each round. The team with the worst record in the preceding season selects first. The team with the second worst record selects second, and so on, with the Super Bowl champion picking last in the first round and the Super Bowl loser picking next to last. Teams are allowed 10 minutes to make their selections in the first round, 7 minutes to make their picks in the second round, and 5 minutes in rounds thereafter.

How picks are made

At the NFL Scouting Combine in Indianapolis, Indiana, in February, medical doctors and trainers examine prospective players who are hoping to be drafted. These players also submit to weight-lifting and running drills and perform position-specific drills, such as a throwing drill for quarterbacks and a running pattern drill for wide receivers. Players are also tested for illegal drug use and are given intelligence tests, one of which is called the Wonderlic test and has been used for over 50 years. They're measured and weighed and interviewed by countless coaches, scouts, and club officials. This information-gathering process is so thorough that a casual observer might think the teams are conducting research for some sort of science project.

On draft day, every team has a representative at the draft venue, but the teams' coaching, scouting, and executive staffs remain at the training facilities or team headquarters in their respective cities. Teams usually have one huge room called the *War Room* where staff members meet to discuss potential players and formulate their final decisions prior to announcing selections. Depending on the team, the general manager may consult with the owner, the head coach, the director of college scouting, and other club personnel before making a selection.

Usually, the team is in contact with the player on the telephone prior to making the choice in order to inform him of its decision or to ask any last-minute questions regarding health or personal issues. The NFL security department does background checks on all prospective draft candidates and reports its findings to the member clubs when asked. Most teams also have their own security personnel to do further complete investigations.

REMEMBER

A player who isn't selected has the option of signing a free-agent contract with any team that wants him. These players are the lowest-paid players on the rosters, and most are released during training camp. Teams sign many of these players simply to provide bodies for the veterans to practice against during training camp. Of course, some undrafted, free-agent rookies make the team because they have more ability than drafted players. This scenario just shows everyone that scouts, general managers, coaches, and other player-personnel department members can make mistakes when evaluating all the draft-eligible players.

Trading to get who you want

Many trades involve the simple exchange of draft choices as teams want to move either up or down from their assigned selecting spots. The most amazing example of trading for a draft pick occurred prior to the 1999 draft, when Coach Mike Ditka of the New Orleans Saints traded away every pick after his first one, as well as the first- and third-round picks for the following year, to the Washington Redskins to obtain Heisman Trophy winner Ricky Williams, whom he selected fifth overall. The San Diego Chargers, a team in desperate need of a quarterback in 1998, traded two veteran players (running back Eric Metcalf and linebacker Patrick Sapp) and three draft choices (their first-round picks in 1998 and 1999 and a 1998 second-round draft choice) simply to move into the Arizona Cardinals' position in the 1998 draft. This was a blockbuster trade, considering that the Chargers surrendered a lot for the rights to draft Washington State quarterback Ryan Leaf, a huge bust.

Going the free agent route

If a team doesn't want to wait for the draft or can't make a trade, it usually opts to find what it considers a star player by signing a *free agent*, a player who sells himself to the highest-bidding team. Considering the NFL's salary-cap restrictions, a team must be careful in how it pursues free agents because it may not be able to afford a particular player — that player's salary may jeopardize the team's salary scale with its current players (for more information on the salary cap, see the later "The salary cap levels the playing field" section). Players often become upset when a new player earns more than they do, especially if they're considered team leaders or stars.

The free-agent period begins in March. Most of the top players agree to new contract terms in the first six weeks of the negotiating session, which ends in mid-July (usually prior to the start of training camp). A top free agent usually decides on a few teams he'd like to play for, and then he visits each club's facility to meet the coaches and general manager. His agent then begins negotiations with the clubs that are interested. A free agent usually makes his decision based on money, but occasionally his choice is affected by the offensive or defensive system the team uses, how he fits in with the other players, his city preference for his family, or whether he likes the coach. Some players accept less money to play with a team they think has the potential to make the playoffs.

Status Is Everything: Determining Player Designations

While listening to commentary or reading about the NFL, you hear many terms that relate directly to a player's status, such as *franchise player* or *restricted free agent*. Hard-core fans frequently toss around these terms. Many of the terms were agreed on by the NFL owners and the *NFL Players Association* (the union that represents the interests of the players) as part of their collective bargaining agreement (more on that later in the chapter).

TIP

The following list explains some frequently heard words used to describe players (and the people who broker contract deals for them), as well as some terminology that relates to a player's experience or active status:

» **Accrued season:** An *accrued season* is a season when a player spends six or more regular-season games on a club's active/inactive list, injured reserve list, or "physically unable to perform" list.

» **Agent:** An *agent* is a person who represents a player during contract negotiations. Many agents are attorneys, and some are friends and relatives of the players they represent. Agents are banned from most college campuses.

>> **First-year player:** A *first-year player* is either a player who has spent the preceding season on an NFL practice squad or a player who was injured and has never played in the NFL before.

>> **Franchise player:** A team can designate only one of its players as a *franchise player*. This player may not apply to become a free agent and seek a higher salary from another team. In exchange for giving up this right, the franchise player is paid a minimum of the average of the top five salaries at his position or 120 percent of his previous salary, whichever is greater.

>> **Injured reserve:** A team can place an injured player who's deemed a physical risk in the *injured reserve* category. Usually, these players require surgeries for their injuries. A player in this category can't return to the active roster (and play again) during that season.

>> **Practice squad:** Each team can place eight players on the *practice squad*. These players, who are eligible only to practice, are paid $5,200 at minimum per week and are considered free agents. Teams routinely sign players from other teams' practice squads in order to complete their weekly 45-man active rosters when they lose players due to injury or release them due to poor performance.

>> **Pro-Bowler:** A *Pro-Bowler* is a player who's selected by a vote of the fans, players, and coaching staffs to represent his conference in an all-star game that takes place the week before the Super Bowl. Any player chosen to play in the Pro Bowl is considered among the league's elite.

>> **Restricted free agent:** A player who has completed three accrued seasons and now has an expired contract is considered a *restricted free agent*. Under the terms of the collective bargaining agreement, the club basically controls what he will be paid. Most teams attempt to sign this player to a long-term contract if he's deemed a valuable starter. This move prevents the player from being an unrestricted free agent in his fourth season.

>> **Rookie:** A *rookie* is a player who's on an NFL roster for the first time. A player who has played in another league, such as the Canadian Football League or the Arena Football League, is still considered a rookie by the NFL.

>> **Transition player:** A team can designate no more than two *transition players* in the same season (as long it doesn't also have a designated franchise player). This player's club must pay him the average of the prior season's top ten salaries of players at the same position or 120 percent of the player's previous year's salary, whichever is greater. A transition player can seek a contract from another team, but his current team has seven days to match the offer and thus retain his services.

>> **Unrestricted free agent:** An *unrestricted free agent* is a player who has completed four or more accrued seasons and now has an expired contract. Such a player is free to negotiate and sign a new contract with any team.

>> **Veteran:** A *veteran* has played at least one season in the NFL.

>> **Waiver system:** The *waiver system* is a procedure by which a player's contract or NFL rights are made available by his current team to other teams in the league. Teams may waive a player if they no longer need him. During the procedure, the 31 other teams either file a claim to obtain the player or waive the opportunity to do so, thus the term *waiver*.

The Business of Professional Football

Besides being the greatest league in the greatest game on earth, the NFL is also a big business. How big? The 32 teams in the NFL raked in about $14 billion in 2018 despite some TV ratings' decline. The players, of course, want a piece of the action. After all, they're the ones the fans come to see.

Through collective bargaining agreements that players have had with team owners, the players have received a specific percentage of the gross revenue earned by NFL teams. The collective bargaining agreement also stipulates a maximum amount that teams may spend to compensate players, the so-called salary cap. Keep reading to find out about player salaries, the salary cap, and the NFL's collective bargaining agreement. The current CBA expires at the end of the 2020 season.

Show me the money: Player salaries

Salaries in the NFL have risen dramatically since the late 1980s. In 1988, the average salary of an NFL player was $250,000. It jumped to almost $800,000 in 1997, to $1.5 million in 2005, and to $1.9 million in 2014. These increases came about because of the financial impact of the league's television contract, which in the years 2006 to 2011 amounted to $3.1 billion per year (at more than 70 percent, television income is the largest portion of a team's revenue). And in 2014 alone, the major networks and DirecTV paid the NFL 5.5 billion dollars for broadcasting rights. As of 2012, the teams were required under the collective bargaining agreement to share 55 percent of national media revenue, 45 percent of NFL Ventures revenue (merchandising and licensing), and 40 percent of local club revenue with the players.

HOWIE SAYS

My only knock on the wage system is the inequity inside the locker room; a definite caste system exists. According to the way the free agency system has worked since 1993, 20 percent of players tend to receive 60 percent of a team's payroll, leaving 80 percent of the players with the remaining 40 percent share. To simplify this equation, say a team's total payroll is about $100 million for 50 players.

In that scenario, the breakdown would be 10 players earning $6 million each and the other 40 players earning $1 million each. That breakdown of salaries creates a huge disparity, which is unfortunate considering football is such a team game. And a great, highly paid quarterback is nothing without a good offensive line and solid receivers.

The salary cap levels the playing field

To understand how an NFL team decides which players to draft, sign in free agency, or outright release, you must understand the salary cap. As determined by the collective bargaining agreement, the *salary cap* is a limit on the amount of money each team can spend for its players' salaries. When it was introduced in 1994, the salary cap was $34.6 million; by the 2014 season, it had risen to $133 million. The salary cap for the 2019 season will be $188.2 million, a 40-percent increase from the 2014 salary cap. The cap is based on players receiving a certain percentage of the defined gross revenues of the NFL teams, which include revenue from network television contracts, ticket sales, and product sales.

The salary cap was designed to put all the NFL teams on equal footing when competing for free agents and signing their number-one draft choices. Teams that don't charge exorbitant ticket prices or whose stadium leases don't provide extra income from luxury suites, parking, and concessions receive funds from the richer teams to supplement their gross revenues in order to make the cap as equitable as possible.

There is also a rookie salary cap, which has greatly restricted the total amount paid to the first overall draft choice with a downward salary scale on first-round draft choices. So the first overall pick makes a lot more than the last player drafted (32nd overall) in the first round. This system allows for more money to be spent on proven veteran players and prevents teams from gambling too much money on rookies. For example, before the rookie salary cap was in place, Sam Bradford was the first overall pick in the 2010 draft and signed a six-year, $78 million contract with $50 million in guarantees. Bradford earned a lot of money but never took any of his teams to the playoffs, and as of the 2018, he has a losing record. Baker Mayfield, also a Heisman Trophy-winning quarterback like Bradford from Oklahoma, was the first overall draft pick in 2018. But his five-year deal was worth just $32 million. The rookie cap has allowed for more veteran players to receive contracts in the $3 million to $5 million range.

REMEMBER

Every team is allowed a maximum of 53 active players under its salary cap. If a player is injured and unable to play the rest of the season, his salary still counts toward the cap. So, teams do a lot of juggling during the season as players come and go — clubs rework contracts in order to fit an entire roster under the cap. Some teams may have as many as 15 players on injured-reserve lists, meaning those players must also be paid while adding new players under the cap. Each team usually has one executive, called a *capologist,* crunching the salary numbers of the players and making sure everyone fits under the salary cap.

NFL teams actually spend more money on their players than the salary cap allows. Teams are also required to fund pension and health benefits. And some teams spend millions in signing bonuses in order to lure top-notch free agents. Teams have been known to give as much as $35 million in one season in signing bonuses alone. These benefits and bonuses are spread out over a period of years, which lessens the impact on the salary cap and makes these perks possible.

Salaries are on the rise

HOWIE SAYS

When free-agency began in 1993, the wage system didn't improve immediately. There was still inequity inside the locker room; a definite caste system was still in place. But as the salary cap has increased over the years, more players are earning good money with the average salary around $3 million annually. Granted, there are too many players who average only three or four years in the league before being replaced due to injury or poor play. But most teams have five to ten high-salaried stars, generally starting with the quarterback and their best wide receiver or running back. On defense, great pass rushers like the Rams' Aaron Donald can earn as much or more than a starting quarterback. Cornerback Stephon Gilmore, who had an important interception when the New England Patriots won Super Bowl LIII, has an average salary of $13 million. Offensive linemen have been rewarded, too, because protecting the quarterback has become a high priority.

Collective bargaining agreements

A *collective bargaining agreement* is an agreement between employers and employees. Since 1993, team owners and the NFL Players Association have negotiated or agreed to extend their collective bargaining agreement five times. The agreement includes pension benefits and health coverage for retired players. It also dictates what percentage of the league's gross revenue goes to the players and the salary cap amount.

The current collective bargaining agreement runs from 2011 through the 2020 season and the 2021 NFL draft. Players now receive 55 percent of national media revenue, 45 percent of NFL Ventures revenue, and 40 percent of local club revenue.

Big business and the television connection

The best way to explain the popularity of the NFL is to study its network television contract. In 2011, the league signed a nine-year, $28 billion national television contract with CBS, NBC, and Fox. The total obligation of these three networks is about $3.1 billion annually. In addition, the NFL has a separate eight-year broad-casting agreement with ESPN that pays $1.9 billion annually. Now you can understand why Super Bowl commercials are priced at over $5 million per 30 seconds. And that price will only increase in the future.

For NFL owners, these are pretty good times. Annual income from television networks (about $255 million per team) just about covers player salaries and their overall benefits. And owners benefit from the revenue earned from ticket sales, luxury suites, local radio broadcast rights, concessions, and *NFL Properties LLC* (the NFL's marketing arm for hats, T-shirts, company logos, sponsorships, and so on). Individual club revenue adds another $40 million to many teams' bank accounts.

HOW TELEVISION TRANSFORMED THE NFL

No professional sports league is more impressive or more powerful than the NFL. It's a multibillion-dollar empire. In fact, the NFL virtually transformed pro sports into a big business, marketing its on-field product through the magic of television. Walking down the street anywhere in the United States, you're likely to see a fan wearing a ball cap or jersey featuring his or her favorite player or team.

The NFL and television have grown and expanded together over the last 45 years. Television allows cities and states to close ranks; it brings Miami to tiny Green Bay, Wisconsin, and Nashville to New York City. The immediacy of television is picture-perfect for a national league full of nationalized teams. For example, no matter where in the United States you live, you can follow the exploits of your favorite team on television. In the early 1990s, southern California was the site of one of the biggest fan clubs for the Cleveland Browns.

Television is a powerful medium that's perfectly suited to NFL football and its many lengthy timeouts and delays. The timeouts and commercials enable fans to discuss strategy with other fans. In fact, most fans watching at home can actually have a better view of what's going on in a game. But in the last decade, stadiums like the new Mercedes-Benz Stadium in Atlanta where Super Bowl LIII was held in 2019, has a 360-degree halo video screen near the roof, covering over 82,500 square feet, that gives spectators tremendous views of all in-game replays. AT&T Stadium, where the Dallas Cowboys play, has a huge video screen that's 218 feet long and 95 feet high, and many fans actually watch the game off that screen instead of looking onto the field because the picture is so spectacular. Many NFL stadiums have drastically improved their video boards in attempts to make the in-stadium experience a good one. But sitting at home can be more comfortable, and television brings every replay to the screen. What's more, the NFL offers packages where you can see every game (including streaming ones on several internet sites), not just the ones provided by network TV.

HOWIE SAYS

FRANCHISE MOVEMENT

After the NFL lost an antitrust lawsuit in federal court, and thus lost the ability to prevent the Oakland Raiders from moving to Los Angeles in 1982, six franchises have left their home cities in search of better stadium deals.

I started with the Raiders in Oakland, and then played most of my career in Los Angeles. In 1995, unsatisfied with the stadium situation in Los Angeles, the Raiders returned to Oakland. That same season, the Rams vacated Orange County, California, for St. Louis, Missouri, which left the Los Angeles area without a pro football team. In the 1980s, the Colts left Baltimore, Maryland, for Indianapolis, Indiana, and the Cardinals left St. Louis for Phoenix, Arizona. The Rams returned to Los Angeles for 2016 season and the Chargers bolted San Diego for Los Angeles as well in 2017.

The biggest jolt to the NFL landscape occurred in 1996, when the Cleveland Browns left Ohio for Baltimore and changed their name to the Baltimore Ravens. A new Cleveland Browns franchise resumed play in 1999. The Houston Oilers became the Tennessee Oilers in 1997, settling in Nashville but playing their games in Memphis. In 1998, the renamed Tennessee Titans began playing home games at the newly built Coliseum in Nashville.

In case you're wondering, *luxury suites* are the glass-enclosed private boxes within a stadium that seat as many as 22 fans and include private bars, restrooms, couches, and television sets. Some stadiums feature large VIP restaurants and bar lounges for high-roller fans. Some fans have to pay seat licensing fees simply to earn the right to purchase season tickets. These fees are similar to a surtax on each seat and cost fans, on average, between $500 and $2,500 per seat.

When the Carolina Panthers and the Jacksonville Jaguars joined the NFL, beginning play in 1995, the teams had to pay an entry fee of more than $200 million to the NFL. The small-city Panthers were sold last season for over $2.2 billion. The Cleveland expansion team, which began playing in 1999, paid more than double that amount.

Making the Players' Health a Priority

In a sport revered for its hard-hitting play and fast action, making sure that football players are healthy has always been a challenge. As I explain in Chapter 1, the early days of football could be very brutal, and the game was almost banned in 1906 after nearly 20 deaths occurred on the football field. In the years since then, equipment innovations and new rules have been introduced to safeguard the players' health, but football remains a dangerous game.

In 2009, a study commissioned by the NFL determined that retired players were experiencing high rates of Alzheimer's disease, dementia, and memory-related diseases. The study concluded that ex-players had these diseases as a result of untreated concussions they experienced in their playing days. In the wake of the study, the league outlawed deliberate helmet-to-helmet hits, which are considered the chief cause of concussions on the football field. The league also instituted a policy whereby a player who shows symptoms of a concussion can't return to play and must stay off the field until the symptoms disappear.

The current collective bargaining agreement with players (signed in 2011) includes enhanced medical and injury protection benefits. And the NFL has committed to spending close to $1 billion on health insurance and pensions for retired NFL players.

OTHER PRO LEAGUES

The NFL isn't the only professional football league. Diehard football fans can watch football games in the summer months, football's traditional offseason, and watch games in countries other than the United States. Here's a rundown of the NFL's sister leagues:

- **Arena Football:** Arena football is a fast-paced, offense-oriented, indoor sport played with only eight players per team on the field at a time. Six of those eight players must play both offense and defense. The field is 85 feet wide and 66 yards long. Kurt Warner, the MVP of Super Bowl XXXIV, began his professional career with an Arena Football team (the Iowa Barnstormers, to be exact). To find out more about Arena football, visit www.arenafootball.com.

- **Canadian Football League:** CFL play begins in June and ends in late November with the Grey Cup, its version of the Super Bowl. The field is 110 yards by 65 yards, bigger than the 100 yards by 53 yards of a U. S. football field, which gives offenses more room to maneuver and score points. Several former NFL stars, notably Warren Moon and Doug Flutie, got their start in the CFL. You can find out more about the CFL by visiting the league website at www.cfl.ca.

- **Alliance of American Football:** This eight-team professional league started play in February 2019 and failed to complete its inaugural season because of financial issues.

- **XFL:** Vince McMahon, the founder of World Wrestling Federation, which is known now as WWE, plans to resurrect this spring-time league in 2020. The league existed for one season back in 2001 on NBC. The new eight-city league will have franchises in seven NFL cities and also St. Louis. The New York, Tampa Bay, and Seattle teams will play in their respective NFL stadiums. The league has many former NFL executives and coaches in front-office positions, plus former NCAA executive Oliver Luck as its commissioner. Both ABC (with ESPN) and FOX Sports have agreed to televise their games, which will be on Saturdays and Sundays, after the NFL season. Eligibility requirements won't be as restrictive as the NFL, meaning that college freshmen may opt to play in the XFL rather than pursue a college scholarship.

Chapter **18**

Playing Fantasy Football

Have you ever watched a football game and said to yourself, "If I were an NFL team owner, I'd do things differently, and my team would make it to the Super Bowl"? Well, you can live your dream of becoming an NFL team owner by participating in a fantasy football league. These leagues give you the opportunity to put together a dream team of NFL players and pit your team against other fantasy football teams. And at the end of the season, you may even win prize money — and more importantly, bragging rights!

Fantasy football leagues are everywhere, and many types of leagues exist. I know a lot of fans are obsessed with these leagues because people ask me for advice all the time. Some of them would rather have me advise them on whom to trade for than ask for my autograph. For example, during the 1997 season when San Francisco 49ers receiver Jerry Rice suffered an injury that forced him to miss much of the season, fans were asking how they could replace him. But there's no way to replace a player like Rice, the NFL's all-time leading scorer and receiver.

In this chapter, I focus on the rules and method of play of the most popular type of fantasy football league: the head-to-head league. I also point out resources for you to use to investigate other types of leagues.

How Fantasy Football Leagues Work

In a head-to-head fantasy football league, you and your fellow owners draft teams of NFL players and compete against each other's teams each week. Your fantasy team roster includes individual offensive players (quarterbacks, running backs, wide receivers, tight ends, and kickers) and may include defensive or special teams units, depending on the particular setup of the league.

Throughout the season, you track the performance of the players on your team and tally the points, yardage, and other statistics they accrue. You earn points based on those real-life statistics. For instance, if your team's defense or special teams unit scores a touchdown or records a safety, you get points. Table 18-1 lists the common scoring categories and the number of points awarded in most standard leagues.

TABLE 18-1   **Typical Fantasy Football Scoring Categories**

Category	Points Awarded
Touchdown	6 points
Field goal	3 points
Safety	2 points
Two-point conversion	2 points
Interception	2 points
Passing yards	1 point per 25 yards
Rushing yards	1 point per 10 yards
Receiving yards	1 point per 10 yards

REMEMBER

If your team outscores your opponent's team for the week, you get a win. At the end of the season, you compare your win-loss record against those of the other teams to determine who makes the *playoffs* — the head-to-head competition of the top teams in the league, leading up to the Fantasy Super Bowl. The last team standing in the playoffs is the champion.

The Basics of How to Play

Entire volumes have been written on playing fantasy football. I'll skip over most of the intricate details found in other books and instead try to give you the basics you need to get started. Refer to a good fantasy football reference, such as Martin

Signore's *Fantasy Football For Dummies* (Wiley), to get detailed coverage of the nuances of fantasy football.

Starting a league

Starting a fantasy football league is easy. Here's how:

TIP

1. **Recruit enough friends, co-workers, or neighbors to have 8, 10, or 12 teams (each person fields one team).**

   Definitely go with an even number of teams. Scheduling is too difficult with an odd number of teams.

2. **Name your league and have each owner name his or her team.**

   Each owner must submit a team name. (Get creative!)

3. **Select a date for your annual player draft.**

   This date is when you choose the players for your team. The weekend before the start of the NFL regular season usually works best.

4. **Agree on an entry fee.**

   This dollar amount can be as high or low as you like. Pool the entry fees to form the *pot,* the cash paid out as prize money to the lucky winners. (Note that you can skip this step if you and your fellow team owners don't want to play for money.)

That's it! Grab your clipboard and start scouting players as you begin the count-down to the draft.

Choosing a fantasy football site

Your first order of business after forming your league is to appoint an almighty commissioner. The commish arbitrates any and all disputes that crop up (and trust me, controversy rears its ugly head in most leagues).

After a commissioner is in place, find an online fantasy league site to join. (References like *Fantasy Football For Dummies* can help you in this regard.) The sites offer articles, message boards, injury reports, and stats. These head-to-head online fantasy football leagues are the most popular:

» **CBS Sports Fantasy Football:** www.cbssports.com/fantasyfootball

» **ESPN:** http://games.espn.go.com/frontpage/football

>> **Fleaflicker:** `www.fleaflicker.com/nfl`

>> **Fox Sports Fantasy Football:** `www.foxsports.com/fantasy/football/commissioner`

>> **NFL.com Fantasy:** `www.fantasy.nfl.com`

>> **Yahoo:** `http://football.fantasysports.yahoo.com`

>> **RT Sports:** `www.rtsports.com`

Drafting a team

The goal for each owner is to draft a team of 15 to 18 players. (Determine the roster limit for each team beforehand; see the next section for the breakdown of roster spots.) You generally draft offensive players from different teams along with the defense and special teams units from a single NFL team.

REMEMBER

The number of players to draft at each position is up to you, but here's a safe combination for a 16-member team:

>> Two quarterbacks

>> Four running backs

>> Four wide receivers

>> Two tight ends

>> Two kickers

>> Two defense/special teams (punt and kickoff return) units

During the most common kind of draft, the *snake draft,* each owner selects one player at a time. Generally, the commissioner draws numbers out of a hat to determine the draft order. The owners make their picks in order for the first round. Then they reverse this order for the second round. For example, in an eight-team league, Owners 1 through 8 make the first eight selections in order. Then Owner 8 gets the 9th pick, Owner 7 gets the 10th pick, and so on down to Owner 1, who makes the 16th and 17th picks, and so on until all owners fill their rosters.

TIP

Before the draft, designate two people to record all the player selections. Accurate records can help resolve conflicts that may arise later.

Filling out your roster

Each week, you enter a starting lineup — in a standard league, that lineup is made up of a quarterback, two running backs, two wide receivers, a tight end, a kicker, and a defense/special teams (punt and kickoff return) unit.

The remaining players are *reserves.* These players' statistics don't count while the players sit on your reserve squad; instead, reserves serve as backups for your starting lineup. Here's why reserves are important:

>> **They replace poor-performing starters.** If your quarterback, for example, plays poorly, you can replace him in your starting lineup the following week with your backup quarterback.

>> **They replace injured starters.** If your star running back breaks his leg (gulp!), you simply start your backup running back the following week.

>> **They replace players on bye weeks.** Each NFL team has one *bye week* (a week when they don't play). Because of bye weeks, you need to insert backup players for your starters whose teams aren't playing that week.

Managing your team after the draft

Fantasy football requires active weekly participation. You can't just kick back after the draft and expect your team to be successful. For starters, each week you must submit your starting lineup. At a minimum, you should

>> **Monitor the schedule.** Don't start a player whose team isn't playing that weekend.

>> **Check out the injury updates.** You obviously don't want to start an injured player.

TIP

Consider the following options to try to improve your team over the course of the season:

>> **Free agent acquisitions:** Closely monitor the pool of undrafted players; you may be able to acquire a great player no one else drafted.

>> **Trades:** As a general rule, you must trade equal numbers of players. For example, if you trade two players, you must get two players in return to keep your team whole.

Note: The rules for free agent acquisitions and trading vary widely. Consult *Fantasy Football For Dummies* or fantasy football websites to find out more about other leagues' policies regarding free agents.

Figuring your point total and winning

As long as you know how many points go with which actions (see the earlier "How Fantasy Football Leagues Work" section), scoring fantasy football just comes down to basic math. Table 18-2 shows you an abbreviated scoring example. Using this example, you pit your 69 points against your weekly opponent's total. If you outscore that opponent, you get a win; if he or she outscores you, you lose; if you score the same total, you get a tie. Simple, huh? As the season progresses, you can gauge how well (or how poorly) your team is doing by comparing your win-loss record with the other teams' records.

TABLE 18-2   **A Scoring Example**

Player	Scoring Play	Points Awarded
Aaron Rogers, QB	1 touchdown pass, 278 passing yards, 24 rushing yards	6 + 11 (1 point per 25 yards passing) + 2 (1 point per 10 yards of rushing) = 19
Ezekiel Elliott, RB	2 touchdown runs, 149 yards rushing	12 + 14 = 26
Rob Gronkowski, TE	1 touchdown reception, 99 receiving yards	6 + 9 (1 point per 10 yards receiving) = 15
Sebastian Janikowski, K	1 field goal	3
Chicago Bears, defense/special teams	1 kickoff return touchdown	6
		69 (total)

At the end of the regular fantasy season, the teams with the best records make the playoffs. These high-powered playoff teams vie for the pinnacle of fantasy football — the Fantasy Super Bowl!

Of course, financial incentive exists for fielding a strong team (but feel free to eliminate entry fees and play for pride only). Here's one easy way to distribute prize money (dollar amounts will vary based on the number of teams in your league and the entry fee amount):

1. **Award a small amount ($1 or $2) for each win during the regular season.**

2. **Give 20 percent of the pot to the Super Bowl loser.**

3. **Give the remainder of the pot to the Super Bowl champ.**

Tips for fantasy football success

Everyone who plays fantasy football will give you a different set of tips, but here are a few that should serve you well in any league:

>> **Check out the prior year's stats.** Make sure you know who the best players are at each position. Pay special attention to touchdowns scored because that's the name of the game in fantasy football.

>> **In the early rounds of the draft, take the best player available regardless of position.** For example, if most of the top-notch quarterbacks are taken by the time it's your turn to pick, snag the best available player, such as a running back or wide receiver. Remember, however, that you must fill in all the necessary positions to field a legal team.

>> **Don't draft a kicker in the early rounds.** The NFL has plenty of decent kickers, so use your early draft picks to acquire players at other positions.

>> **Consider a player's opponent for the week when selecting your starting lineup.** If one of your running backs is going up against the best run defense in the league, you may want to start another running back.

Finding Information to Help Your Team

Prior to the draft and throughout the season, you need to stay informed about your players. You can stay up-to-date by searching the Internet.

Fantasy football websites abound. The following some sites offer player profiles, team stats, injury reports, lots of good insider information, and links to even more fantasy sites:

>> ESPN Fantasy Football (http://games.espn.go.com/frontpage/football)

>> FOX Sports (www.foxsports.com/fantasy/football/commissioner)

>> NFL.com (www.nfl.com/fantasyfootball)

>> Sporting News (www.sportingnews.com/nfl)

>> Sports Fanatics Player Drafts (www.sportsdrafts.com)

>> Sports Illustrated (www.si.com/fantasy)

>> USA Today (http://fantasy.usatoday.com/category/football)

6

The Part of Tens

Chapter **19**

The Ten (Or So) Greatest Defensive Players of All Time

When creating a top ten list, you're bound to exclude a number of players who could easily make someone else's top ten — it's a subjective, personal thing. Everyone has a top ten list of all-time defensive players, so here's mine (with a couple extra players for good measure). Some of these selections are predictable; others may raise an eyebrow or two.

Doug Atkins

Doug Atkins, a 6-foot-8-inch, 275-pounder from Humboldt, Tennessee, started his athletic career as a basketball player at the University of Tennessee, where he also ran track. One year, he finished second in the Southeastern Conference high jump competition. When the football coach heard of his feats, he asked him to try football and put him at defensive end. Atkins was a natural — he started hurdling offensive linemen like he did high jump bars. He became an All-American at Tennessee and is considered one of the toughest men to ever play football.

Atkins played for 17 years in the NFL, from 1953 to 1969, a total of 205 games, mostly for the Chicago Bears and the New Orleans Saints. He played in eight Pro Bowls. Atkins was a terror on the field, refusing to quit. To keep him from destroying their quarterbacks, most teams used two men to block him.

Atkins was every bit as funny as he was mean. One of the best anecdotes about Atkins is how he literally (and liberally) interpreted the words of the Bears' tough-guy head coach George Halas. During practice one day, Halas was unhappy with Atkins's practice habits and ordered him to take a lap around the field while wearing his helmet. Atkins took his lap with his helmet on — but that's all he wore. His teammates cracked up, and so did Halas.

Dick Butkus

Dick Butkus is arguably the most intimidating player to ever play defense. In fact, I think players were flat-out frightened of him. He was probably the first defensive player who really caught fans' attention. Kids growing up in the late 1960s wanted to hit and tackle like Butkus, the 6-foot-3-inch, 245-pound middle linebacker for the Chicago Bears.

Butkus was so good that he was All-Pro seven times. He had the speed and agility to make tackles from sideline to sideline and cover the best tight ends on pass plays. The NFL didn't officially begin recording quarterback sacks until 1982, but the Bears say Butkus had 18 in 1967, a huge number for a middle linebacker. He averaged 12.6 tackles per game — today's pro players think that 10 tackles is a great game. The growling man dominated games, finishing his career with 22 pass interceptions and 27 fumble recoveries.

Besides being a ferocious and violent player, Butkus was an intelligent linebacker. He studied game film and knew what the opposition liked to do on offense. At the snap of the ball, Butkus seemed to fly to wherever the play was headed. He had super instincts, which is something every player needs to be successful on defense. He played every game as though it were his last, and had he not suffered a serious knee injury in 1970, his career may have lasted a lot longer.

Kenny Easley

Okay, Ronnie Lott was the best safety, bar none. But Kenny Easley, who starred in college at UCLA (University of California, Los Angeles), across town from USC (University of Southern California) and Lott, wasn't too far behind. He was the first player in Pac-10 Conference history to be selected All-Conference all four years, and he was an All-American three times. Easley was a three-sport star at Oscar Smith High School in Chesapeake, Virginia, and was offered college basketball scholarships by ACC (Atlantic Coast Conference) and Big Ten colleges.

Easley played only seven years in the NFL, but he managed 32 interceptions during his career. He was named AFC Defensive Rookie of the Year in 1981 after the Seattle Seahawks drafted him in the first round. In 1984, Easley was voted NFL Defensive Player of the Year when he collected ten interceptions, returning two for touchdowns. He was the defensive heart of his team and a huge reason why the Seahawks finished 12-4 that season.

HOWIE SAYS

Easley was 6 feet 3 inches tall and 206 pounds, and he hit people like a freight train. He was a wild man on the field, playing with a total disregard for his body. His career was cut short by a serious kidney ailment and, believe me, our receivers had mixed feelings. They hated to see Easley retire in the prime of his career, but they sure didn't miss his heavy-handed greeting card when they crossed the middle of the field. As a defensive player, I didn't mind watching him while I rested on the sidelines.

Joe Greene

Most people, especially in Pittsburgh, remember Joe Greene as "Mean Joe Greene." He was the heart and soul of the great Pittsburgh Steelers defensive teams of the 1970s. Pittsburgh's defensive line was so immovable and suffocating that it earned the nickname "The Steel Curtain." In fact, during a stretch of nine games in 1976, Pittsburgh's defense allowed only 28 points while going 9-0.

However, Pittsburgh fans weren't convinced that Greene — a 6-foot-4-inch, 275-pound defensive tackle from unknown North Texas State — deserved to be the club's first-round draft choice in 1969. The team had suffered through five consecutive losing seasons and hadn't appeared in a playoff game since 1947. A quarterback or running back made more sense to fans. Going with his own instincts, Chuck Noll, the first-year Pittsburgh coach, ignored some of the scouting reports and built his team, one of the NFL's best ever, around Greene.

The imposing Greene made an immediate impact in the league and was named Defensive Rookie of the Year. He was named All-Pro five times in the 1970s, played in ten Pro Bowls, and was NFL Defensive Player of the Year in 1972 and 1974. In 1972, with the Steelers needing to beat Houston to clinch their first-ever division title, Greene had an amazing game — five sacks, a blocked field goal, and a fumble recovery — in a 9-3 Pittsburgh win. During Pittsburgh's first Super Bowl–winning season, Greene used a new stance, lining up almost sideways between the guard and center. He was able to neutralize those two linemen or shoot a gap from this stance because he had such an unusual combination of speed, quickness, and sheer power. I can't think of a player who was able to duplicate Greene's production from that stance.

Jack Ham and Ted Hendricks

I couldn't separate Jack Ham and Ted Hendricks; they were two of the best outside linebackers I ever saw play. Both had tremendous range and a rare instinct for the game. They saw offensive plays developing before the ball was snapped: They could interpret any running back's stance. And when an offensive player went in motion, it instantly triggered something in their brains.

Ham — a consensus All-American at Penn State, the school known as Linebacker U — was the first and only linebacker of the 1970s to be named to eight consecutive Pro Bowls. Ham started every game as a rookie and was a Pittsburgh regular until he retired after the 1982 season. He was a big-play performer, much like Hendricks, and was adept at shutting down the short passing game; there were few running backs he couldn't defend.

Besides being extremely quick, Ham was an intelligent player and usually knew his opponents' formations as well as they did. He finished his career with 21 fumble recoveries and 32 interceptions.

Hendricks fell a little short of Ham — 16 fumble recoveries and 26 interceptions — but he was a master when the opposition was pinned near its own goal line. He retired with a record-tying four safeties. Like Ham, Hendricks was a starter on four Super Bowl–champion teams. He won three Super Bowls with the Raiders and his first with the Baltimore Colts in Super Bowl V.

Hendricks and Ham opposed each other in the great Steeler-Raider rivalry of the 1970s. Off the field, the iconoclastic Hendricks was the opposite of Ham. Hendricks was a chain smoker and a Good-Time Charlie. Because he was 6 feet 7 inches tall and gangly looking, Hendricks was nicknamed "The Mad Stork" coming out of the University of Miami, where he was a three-time All-American. He played in 215 regular-season games and was selected to eight Pro Bowls.

Mike Haynes

Mike Haynes was probably the best bump-and-run cover cornerback in the history of the game; he could stick with any receiver. His coverage seemed so effortless because of his superior athletic ability and speed. Haynes was unusually tall

(6 feet 2 inches) for the cornerback position, yet he was so graceful. I like to call him a "black hole player" — any player he covered seemed to go into a black hole, disappearing from the field.

Haynes finished his 14-year career in 1989 with 46 interceptions, which ranks low on the all-time list. But in Haynes's case, statistics don't tell the whole story. He was so good that opposing quarterbacks quit throwing in his direction — which is the highest compliment for a cornerback. In 1976, the New England Patriots drafted Haynes in the first round, and he finished his first season with eight interceptions, a 13.5-yard punt return average, and AFC Rookie of the Year honors.

HOWIE SAYS

Haynes joined me with the Raiders after seven seasons in New England. With the Raiders, Haynes and Lester Hayes formed one of the finest cornerback tandems in the history of the game. During those years, teams threw toward Hayes because they feared Haynes. And Hayes was a great cornerback in his own right; in 1980, he had 13 interceptions, just one shy of the NFL single-season record. You can't play pass defense without solid cornerbacks, and Haynes simply put on a clinic every game, teaching other cornerbacks how the game should be played.

Ken Houston

How great of a strong safety was Ken Houston? So good that Washington Redskins coach George Allen traded five veteran players to the Houston Oilers for him in 1973. Houston was a defensive back who tackled like a linebacker. For 12 consecutive seasons, between 1968 and 1979, Houston was selected to either the AFL All-Star game or the AFC-NFC Pro Bowl. Without question, Houston was the dominant player at his position in that era.

Houston (6 feet 3 inches, 198 pounds) was a long strider with exceptional quickness and strength. He would sit back from his viewpoint as a safety and attack the line of scrimmage. He had tremendous instincts and owned that proverbial "nose for the ball." With the Oilers, he returned nine interceptions for touchdowns, an NFL record at the time. During his career, he intercepted 49 passes and returned them for 898 yards. He also recovered 21 fumbles.

HALL OF FAME

One of the most memorable instances of Houston's signature style of tackling occurred in one of the Redskins' great rivalry games against the Dallas Cowboys in 1973. With seconds remaining, Cowboys running back Walt Garrison caught a short pass and started heading toward the end zone. Houston met him at the 1-yard line, lifted Garrison off his feet (a hit called a *decleater*), and planted him in his tracks. The game ended, and Houston's tackle preserved Washington's victory. Throughout his career, the super-strong Houston repeated this style of bone-chilling tackle.

Sam Huff and Ray Nitschke

Dick Butkus stands alone as the game's best middle linebacker, but Sam Huff and Ray Nitschke stand right behind him in terms of how they tackled running backs from the middle linebacker position. During a 13-year pro career, Huff was a well-known player because his reign of terror emanated from New York City. He appeared on the cover of *Time* magazine when he was 24 and was even the subject of a television special, "The Violent World of Sam Huff." He played in six NFL championship games with the New York Giants before finishing his career with the Washington Redskins.

Both Huff and Nitschke had a nose for the football and were difficult to block from their 4-3 formations. And both seemed to love the violent aspects of the game; losing their helmets after a rousing tackle was a trademark. Both were instinctively tough players who enjoyed football's collisions and brutality.

They were smart players, too. Huff had 30 interceptions; Nitschke had 25. And when Nitschke's team, the Green Bay Packers, beat Huff's Giants for the 1962 NFL championship, Nitschke was named the game's Most Valuable Player. He was a soft-hearted man who was loved by many thousands of Packers fans. He kept a home in Green Bay, Wisconsin, until his death in 1998.

Deacon Jones and Merlin Olsen

Listing one of these great Los Angeles Rams defensive linemen without including the other is impossible. David (Deacon) Jones and Merlin Olsen were a dynamic duo for the Rams for ten seasons (1962 to 1971) until Jones was traded to the San Diego Chargers. Olsen joined the Rams as a first-round draft choice in 1962 after an All-American career at Utah State and was a mainstay on the team's defensive line for 15 seasons. Jones entered the NFL as an obscure 14th-round draft choice who had played at South Carolina State and Mississippi Vocational. But regardless of their backgrounds, these two players worked together to wreak havoc on opposing teams. Because of Jones and Olsen, who lined up side by side on the left, the Rams' defensive line (nicknamed "The Fearsome Foursome") was one of the most feared and successful units in the history of pro football.

Olsen, who was 6 feet 5 inches tall and 270 pounds, was named to the Pro Bowl team a record 14 consecutive times. He was very agile for a big man, and he clogged the middle of the line, enabling speed rushers like Jones to cause trouble from the outside. Jones, 6 feet 5 inches tall and 272 pounds, used his speed, strength, and quickness to beat offensive tackles who attempted to block him. While he played, Jones coined the term *sack*, which is used today to define the tackling of a quarterback behind the line of scrimmage. Jones claims that he's the all-time sack leader. And arguing with him is difficult because the NFL didn't begin to include this defensive statistic officially until 1982 — two seasons after Jones was inducted into the Pro Football Hall of Fame. In 1967 and 1968, Jones was chosen as the NFL's best defensive player.

The Rams teams of his era were defense-oriented, and Olsen was their leader. Olsen was team MVP six consecutive seasons and in 1974 was named NFL Player of the Year by the Maxwell Club, an athletic club based in Philadelphia, Pennsylvania, that conducts an annual poll of the national media. In addition to acting on TV dramas such as *Little House on the Prairie,* Olsen was a football analyst on network television for many years after he retired from football.

Jack Lambert

The beauty of Jack Lambert's career is that he came from a small, non-football power (Kent State) and was rather small by NFL standards, only to rise and become a Hall of Famer. At 6 feet 4 inches and 220 pounds, Lambert was Defensive Rookie of the Year with the Pittsburgh Steelers in 1974 after being a second-round draft choice. He was Pittsburgh's defensive captain for eight years, and many people believe that his presence at middle linebacker solidified the Steelers as a great defensive team. (Lambert is one of three Pittsburgh players I mention in this chapter.)

Lambert had an 11-year career with the Steelers and starred in their four Super Bowl victories. He was known for his toothless glare and confident demeanor. He was both an intimidator and a tormentor. Unlike the prototypical middle linebacker — the big, huge run-stuffers — Lambert could drop 20 yards deep into pass coverage because he was so fast. He had exceptional range while still possessing the toughness to make rock-solid tackles. No one messed with Jack Lambert, including his teammates.

Lambert was All-Pro seven times and was twice named Defensive Player of the Year. He finished his career with 28 interceptions.

Dick "Night Train" Lane

Dick Lane's story is an improbable one. He played one season of junior college football and a few years on a military team at Fort Ord, California. In 1952, he was working at an aircraft factory in California, carrying oil-soaked sheet metal, when he showed up at the Los Angeles Rams offices looking for work. Coach Joe Stydahar was impressed by his workout and signed him. Lane went on to intercept 14 passes in his 12-game rookie season, a league record that still stands.

Most secondary coverage in those days was man to man, and Lane was fast enough to stick with any receiver. Plus, he fully understood the passing game because he had been a receiver on his military team. (Lane shifted to cornerback because the Rams already had Tom Fears and Elroy "Crazy Legs" Hirsch, two future Hall of Fame receivers.) Lane also got his nickname via Fears, who was partial to Buddy Morrow music. "Night Train" was one of Morrow's favorite songs, and a teammate put the tag on Lane one night while he sat in Fears' room listening to Morrow's music.

Amazingly, the Rams kept Lane for only two seasons, trading him to the Chicago Cardinals, who later dealt him to the Detroit Lions. His best seasons were with the Lions, where he played the final six seasons of his 14-year career. Lane never won a championship, but he finished with 68 interceptions, which is fourth all-time behind Paul Krause of the Minnesota Vikings, Emlen Tunnell of the New York Giants, and Rod Woodson of the Pittsburgh Steelers, Baltimore Ravens, and a couple of other teams.

Bob Lilly

Bob Lilly was the first-round draft choice of the Dallas Cowboys in 1961 after being a consensus All-American at Texas Christian in nearby Fort Worth (in fact, Lilly was the *first ever* draft choice of the expansion Dallas Cowboys). He had such a legendary 14-year career that he earned the nickname "Mr. Cowboy." At 6 foot 5 inches tall and 260 pounds, Lilly was built like some of today's pass-rushing defensive ends. And he played outside for two seasons before coach Tom Landry moved him to tackle, where his catlike speed and punishing style forced most opponents to double-team him. Ernie Stautner, his old line coach, remembers some teams putting three blockers in his way.

Lilly was selected to 11 Pro Bowls in his 14 NFL seasons and was so durable that he played in 196 consecutive games. In the early part of Lilly's career, the Cowboys kept winning regular-season games and making title game appearances but couldn't win the championship game. Dallas played in six NFL/NFC championship games in an eight-year period. When the team finally won a title, Super Bowl VI, Lilly sacked Miami quarterback Bob Griese for a record 29-yard loss.

Usually, defensive tackles fall down when they recover fumbles, but Lilly could run. He returned three fumbles for touchdowns and scored again on a 17-yard interception return.

Gino Marchetti

Big Gino Marchetti was to defensive ends what the Cleveland Browns' Jim Brown was to running backs; he was light-years ahead of his time. Marchetti played the run and the pass equally well — he did it all. And he did it with his hands. During his era (the 1950s), most defensive linemen used their forearms and shoulders a lot, but not Marchetti. He kept consistent separation with his hands, meaning he shed blockers instead of battering his way through them by lowering his shoulder or knocking them over with his forearm.

HOWIE SAYS

When I first came into the NFL, I studied four or five players, looking for technique and style. I looked at some of Marchetti's old NFL films, and I tried to play the run like he did. His technique and style would have fit in the 1980s or 1990s — he had all the right pass-rush moves, using his hands so well. Marchetti, who was 6 foot 4 inches tall and 245 pounds, used his long frame to hound opposing quarterbacks. If the NFL had monitored quarterback sacks when he played, he probably would have ranked ahead of great pass-rushers like Reggie White and Bruce Smith.

Marchetti was also a tough guy. In the great 1958 NFL championship game between Marchetti's Baltimore Colts and the New York Giants, Marchetti made a key tackle on Frank Gifford, stopping him short of a first down with two minutes left and forcing the Giants to punt. Marchetti broke his leg making that tackle. (The Colts rallied to win the game in overtime after Marchetti was carried to the locker room.) The injury forced Marchetti to miss the Pro Bowl game. Had he not missed this game, he could have claimed after he retired that he had made ten consecutive visits to that all-star game during his career — a benchmark for many Hall of Fame players.

Ed Reed

The Baltimore Ravens' Ed Reed redefined the position of safety with his size, speed, range, hands, instincts, and intelligence. He was the equivalent of having baseball great Willie Mays in center field at the free safety position. With Reed playing, the field shrunk because he had unnatural anticipation and knowledge of the passing game. When watching Reed play, his talent simply jumped off the

TV screen. His unique ability to know where the quarterback would go with the football made him the best safety I've ever seen.

Reed was selected to nine total Pro Bowls, was a five-time First Team All-Pro, three-time Second Team All-Pro, and was the 2004 NFL Defensive Player of the Year Award winner. He holds the NFL record for the two longest interception returns (106 yards in 2004 and 107 yards in 2008). He also holds the all-time NFL records for interception return yards (with 1,590) and postseason interceptions (9, tied with three other players). His 64 regular-season interceptions ranked him 6th on the NFL's all-time leader list at the time of his retirement.

Edward Earl Reed was born in St. Rose, St. Charles Parish, Louisiana. Reed was a multi-sport athlete excelling in track and field. He was a member of the state champion 4×100 meters relay squad. He set a high school record throw of 56.94 meters in the javelin throw. He played at the Univeristy of Miami, Florida, and was an All-American there on the school's 2001 National Championship team, finishing with 21 career interceptions.

The Ravens selected Reed in the first round (24th overall) of the 2002 NFL Draft. In the 2004–05 season, Reed started all 16 games and recorded 76 combined tackles (62 solo), eight pass deflections, a career-high nine interceptions, three forced fumbles, and two sacks. Reed was named the NFL Defensive Player of the Year by the Associated Press.

In 2013, Reed left the Ravens and played a few games with the Houston Texans and the New York Jets. With Baltimore, he scored 13 touchdowns, recorded three blocked punts, one punt return, two fumble returns, and seven interception returns. He was the first player in NFL history to return an interception, a punt, a blocked punt and a fumble recovery for a touchdown. He has the most multi-interception NFL games with 12.

Deion Sanders

You hear football analysts talk about "pure cover cornerbacks," and there was none better than Deion Sanders. In his best NFL seasons, Sanders could lock onto a wide receiver and deny him the football. He was so good, with 4.2-speed and quickness, that he often didn't even go into the defensive huddle. I mean Deion could be in a closet for six months, open the door, drop himself on any receiver in football, and he would lock him down. No one else could do that! Opposing quarterbacks decided to not even throw in his direction. Basically, Sanders could take away one entire side of the field with his coverage ability.

But there was more to Sanders, who was nicknamed "Prime Time," than just football and playing cornerback. Sanders was one of the best multi-sport athletes ever and one of the most gifted athletes of all-time. Deion played nine seasons of Major League Baseball and 14-seasons in the NFL. During his NFL career, Sanders was a nine-time All-Pro and a first ballot Hall of Famer. Sanders is the only man to play in both a Super Bowl and a World Series, to hit an MLB home run and score an NFL touchdown in the same week, and to have both a reception and an interception in the Super Bowl. He is one of two players to score six different ways on the football field.

In high school in Florida, Sanders was All-State in football, basketball, and baseball. At Florida State, he played baseball and football and also ran on the track team. He was an All-American twice and once returned an interception 100 yards for a touchdown while leading the nation in punt returning.

Sanders had a solid run in the MLB after getting drafted by the New York Yankees, but because of football, he played only nine seasons as a part-time player, finishing with a career .263 batting average, 39 home runs, 168 RBI and 186 stolen bases.

Sanders was the fifth pick overall in the 1989 NFL Draft by the Atlanta Falcons, where he played until 1993. During his time in Atlanta, he intercepted 24 passes, three of which he returned for touchdowns. Over his five years with the Falcons, Sanders scored ten touchdowns (three defensive, three kick returns, two punt returns, and two receptions).

With free agency coming to the NFL, Sanders signed in 1994 with the San Francisco 49ers, eventually helping them win Super Bowl XXIX. Sanders arguably had his best season with the 49ers, recording six interceptions and returning them for an NFL-best and a then–NFL record 303 yards and three touchdowns. Besides being All-Pro, Sanders was named the 1994 NFL Defensive Player of the Year.

The next season, Sanders left the 49ers for the Dallas Cowboys, receiving a $12.9 million signing bonus and becoming the highest-paid defensive player in the league. Sanders helped the Cowboys win their third Super Bowl in four years. He retired with 53 interceptions and 22 touchdowns. He was a member of the 1990s All-Decade team as a cornerback *and* as a punt returner.

Lawrence Taylor

Let's talk about a player who revolutionized the game, dominating and performing like none before him. The New York Giants' Lawrence Taylor was simply the best front-seven player (down linemen and linebackers) I've seen. Taylor was ahead of his time; he was a glimpse into the future that you may see today with young defensive players like Houston's JJ Watt, the Rams' Aaron Donald, and the Bears' Khalil Mack who have rare, unique skill sets.

Not only was Taylor, known at LT, one of the best players to ever play in the NFL, he was probably the best defensive player in league history. Taylor had the size, speed, and skill to do whatever he needed, but he also played with anger. Coaches in his division actually changed their offenses in order to find a way to negate his abilities. When teams decided to run away from him, he had the speed to catch the running back. Yes, the game was simpler when Taylor played in the sense that pro teams still believed that they could win Super Bowls with an exceptional running game and a great defense.

That was the makeup of the Giants under head coach Bill Parcells. Taylor was a feared and intimidating presence on the Giants' two Super Bowl winners, teams that humbled two great offenses and quarterbacks of that era in Denver's John Elway and Buffalo's Jim Kelly, both Hall of Famers. LT finished his career with 132.5 sacks, and that number would be higher, but in his rookie season, the NFL didn't record sacks as a statistic. He's a 10-time All-Pro, 10-time Pro Bowler, 3-time NFL Defensive Player of the Year, and only the second defensive player in history to be named NFL MVP in 1986 when he posted 20.5 sacks.

Taylor was born in Williamsburg, Virginia, and he concentrated on baseball and being a catcher. He didn't play organized football until the 11th grade and was not heavily recruited, going to North Carolina. Taylor switched to linebacker in his final college season and had 16 sacks. He was recognized as a consensus first-team All-American and the ACC Player of the Year in 1980. How valuable did NFL teams view Taylor? Well, the Giants drafted him as the second overall pick after the Saints picked Heisman winner George Rogers. In a poll of NFL general managers taken before the draft, 26 of the league's 28 GMs said they would have selected Taylor with the first pick. He recorded 9.5 sacks in 1981, and his rookie season is considered one of the best in NFL history. One of the more memorable plays of his career occurred in 1985. In a game against the Washington Redskins, Taylor's sack of Redskins quarterback Joe Theismann inadvertently resulted in a compound fracture of Theismann's right leg, ending his career. Replays showed Taylor frantically screaming for medical personnel to come help.

Although Taylor was suspended for four games in 1988, when he returned, he dominated. In his final 12 games of that season, Taylor led the Giants in sacks again, with 15.5. In a crucial late-season game with playoff implications against the New Orleans Saints, Taylor played through a torn pectoral muscle to record seven tackles, three sacks, and two forced fumbles. Parcells said that performance was "the greatest game I ever saw."

Taylor retired in 1993, and since then, I've heard comparisons about various players with comments like "This guy is the next LT." Well, I'm still waiting for that guy to come along.

JJ Watt

Told by his first college coach that he was being moved to offensive tackle, Justin James Watt — known as JJ Watt — left his scholarship behind and returned home to Wisconsin, deciding to walk-on with the Badgers. It was the smartest decision Watt ever made. In his senior season at Wisconsin, he had seven sacks, 21 tackles for loss, and three forced fumbles. He was named team MVP, which led the Houston Texans to draft him in the first round.

Watt, who plays taller than 6-foot-5, received the AP NFL Defensive Player of the Year Award three times in his first five seasons. He and Lawrence Taylor of the New York Giants are the only two players to ever win such a prestigious award three times. Watt's performance in that span was as dominant as any I've seen. He has the ability to rush from either edge, right or left, and also as an interior rusher on either guard, and be totally disruptive. In 2014, Watt became the first player in NFL history to record two 20+ sack seasons in a career. He holds the Texans' franchise records for both sacks and forced fumbles. Watt is a total disrupter along the line of scrimmage. Because of his versatility, opposing offensive coaches have to game-plan for him and try to neutralize him with double-team blocks. With his wingspan, he tips passes at the line of scrimmage and can be impossible to block by a single player.

A four-year stretch, from 2012 to 2015, saw Watt produce one of the best statistically dominant stretches by a defensive end in NFL history. During that span, Watt amassed 69 quarterback sacks, 119 tackles for a loss, 190 quarterback hits, 41 passes defensed, 15 forced fumbles, and 10 fumble recoveries. However, a broken leg and a severe back injury sidelined Watt for most of the 2016 and 2017 seasons. Still, Watt had a major impact on Houston when he started an Internet site to raise money for victims of Hurricane Harvey. He hoped to raise $200,000, but fans across America donated more than $37 million, earning Watt the Walter Payton Man of the Year award in 2018.

What might have been even more impressive is the comeback he made in 2018 following those two devastating injuries. He finished the season with 16 sacks, second in the league behind Aaron Donald, and was named a First Team All Pro for the fifth time in his career. Watt is part of a talented football family. He has two brothers playing in the NFL. T.J. Watt is a great pass rusher with the Pittsburgh Steelers, and Marcus is a fullback with the Los Angeles Chargers.

Reggie White

White's combination of strength and speed was something the NFL had never seen at defensive end when he arrived in 1985 after playing a full season in the USFL. Reggie's intimidation was simple: Blockers knew what was coming, but they couldn't stop him. White employed a hump move, and if the offensive tackle overset, or leaned in the wrong direction to combat his power, the next thing you saw was an offensive lineman literally going airborne.

At the time of his retirement, White was the NFL's all-time sacks leader with 198. He was later surpassed by Bruce Smith, who had 200. But counting his time in the USFL, White has 221.5 sacks in professional football. He recovered 19 fumbles, which he returned for 137 yards and three touchdowns. His nine consecutive seasons (1985–1993) with at least ten sacks remain an NFL record. He was named an All-Pro for 13 of his 15 seasons, including eight as a first-team selection.

White was born in Chattanooga, Tennessee, and immediately became the No. 1 recruit for the University of Tennessee. His 15 sacks in 1983 remain a school record. White was a consensus All-American, SEC Player of the Year, and a Lombardi Award finalist. Hence, it was natural for White to sign with the rival USFL and play for the Memphis Showboats for two seasons, starting in 36 games and collecting 23.5 sacks.

After the USFL collapsed in 1985, White took a salary cut and went to the Philadelphia Eagles. He missed the first few games, but by season's end he had 13 sacks and was named NFC Defensive Rookie of the Year.

He played with the Eagles for eight seasons and posted 124 sacks in 121 games, becoming the Eagles' all-time sack leader. He also set the Eagles' regular-season record with 21 sacks in a single season (1987, a season shortened to 12 games). White also became the only player ever to accumulate 20 or more sacks in just 12 games. He set an NFL regular-season record during 1987 by averaging the most sacks per game, with 1.75. He was named NFL Defensive Player of the Year twice in his career: in 1987 with the Eagles and again in 1998 with the Green Bay Packers. White and Deion Sanders both benefitted when the NFL allowed free agency. But White's impact on free agency changed the way business in our league was done, and brought one of the NFL's truly historic franchises in the Green Bay Packers back from obscurity.

White joined the Packers in 1993 and played there for six seasons. White notched up another 68.5 sacks to become, at the time, the Packers' all-time leader in that category. He helped the Packers win a Super Bowl with a game-ending sack in Super Bowl XXXI. White was a super human being, a preacher when not playing, and he died tragically in 2004 from sleep apnea.

Chapter **20**

More Than Ten Top Non-Quarterback Offensive Players

With a few exceptions, this chapter's main criterion was choosing talented offensive players who were also great champions. And because the NFL has become such a passing league, I decided to list the greatest quarterbacks separately (in Chapter 21).

One player who could have made this list but didn't is Bo Jackson, the most gifted physical specimen I ever played with. Bo won the Heisman Trophy at Auburn University as a running back. In the pros, he was a two-sport star, playing football with the Los Angeles Raiders and baseball with the Kansas City Royals, Chicago White Sox, and California Angels. A severe hip injury suffered in a football game ended his career prematurely. What a shame — he had the most incredible, natural, raw physical talent I've ever seen. I left Bo off this list only because his career was cut too short.

Choosing players for all-time teams is extremely difficult. I ended up with 13 players in this chapter. I just couldn't help myself.

Larry Allen

How good was Larry Allen? Well, he's one of the few players — maybe the strongest offensive guards in history — to be chosen as a member of the NFL's All-Decade Team for the 1990s and the 2000s. A tremendous weight lifter, Allen recorded an official bench of 705 pounds and also squatted 905 pounds. Once Allen got his hands on a defensive linemen, he could move him wherever he wanted to because he had unparalleled strength. Allen is the most dominant guard I've ever seen. In his 14 seasons in the NFL, he was named to the Pro Bowl 11 times, including his last as a 49er in 2006. He was also named All-Pro seven times, six times at guard (1995–1997, 1999–2001) and once at tackle (1998). With his Pro Bowl selection at tackle in 1998, he became just the third player in league history to be selected to the Pro Bowl at more than one offensive line position. It was Allen's blocking with the Dallas Cowboys that helped open the holes for Emmitt Smith, the NFL's all-time leading rusher with 18,355 yards.

I have yet to see a player who possesses Allen's combination of size, the quickness to pull, his otherworldly strength, and the ability to finish blocks.

Allen's background helped toughen his resolve. He was born and raised in Compton, California. At the age of 10, he was stabbed 12 times while protecting his brother. Because he played at four different high schools, he didn't qualify for a Division 1 college scholarship and played in junior college and finally at Division II Sonoma State in California. He was the first player ever drafted out of Sonoma after allowing only one sack in a two-year career. The Cowboys, based on the advice of offensive line coach Hudson Houck, drafted him with the 46th pick in the second round. Nine offensive linemen went ahead of him, but that didn't deter Allen from a Hall of Fame career.

On March 21, 2006, the Cowboys released Allen after spending his first 12 seasons with the organization from 1994 to 2005. Allen proved his worth to his new team, the San Francisco 49ers, by blocking for running back Frank Gore's franchise record 1,695 rushing yards that season and earning another Pro Bowl trip.

Jim Brown

Jim Brown was light-years ahead of his time. He also played in an age (1957 to 1965) when the running game was a big part of the offense. Still, with every team geared to stop him, none of their efforts seemed to work. Brown was 6 feet 2 inches tall and weighed 232 pounds — 10 to 20 pounds heavier than most running backs today and huge for a player in his day. In nine pro seasons, Brown led the NFL in rushing eight times and totaled 12,312 yards, 106 rushing touchdowns, and 756 points. He was Rookie of the Year in 1957 and MVP three times, in 1957, 1958, and 1965.

What's even more amazing about Jim Brown is the fact that he retired from football at age 30. He decided to become an actor and retired during the shooting of probably his most memorable movie, *The Dirty Dozen*. Had he continued to play, Brown might still hold every rushing record, may have gained 20,000 yards, and may have scored 150 touchdowns. To this day, every great runner — from Barry Sanders to Emmitt Smith to Adrian Peterson — is judged by his standards.

Brown, a splendid all-around athlete, dominated his era with a rare combination of power, speed, and size. For such a huge man, his waist was only 32 inches around. He was durable, and his head coach, Paul Brown of the Cleveland Browns, never shied away from using him. At Syracuse University, he lettered in basketball and was an All-American in lacrosse as well as football. He competed in track for one year and finished fifth in the national decathlon championship.

When fans rank their top five players of all-time, Brown should be on everyone's list. Two statistics set him apart: He never missed a game in nine seasons, and his 5.22 yards-per-carry average remains number one.

Earl Campbell

Earl Campbell ran like an out-of-control bulldozer, but he had Ferrari speed after he broke into the open. Campbell was 5 feet 11 inches tall, weighed 233 pounds, and people said that his thighs were as big as tree trunks. If he couldn't run *around* you, he simply ran *over* you. A Texas native, he was given the gentle label "The Tyler Rose," although he simply wreaked havoc on defenses. He won the Heisman Trophy at the University of Texas in 1977 and was an instant superstar when he joined the Houston Oilers the following season.

In his first pro season, Campbell won the rushing title, was named Rookie of the Year, and was the NFL's Most Valuable Player. The highlight of his rookie season was a Monday night game against the Miami Dolphins in the Astrodome. Campbell rushed for 199 yards and four touchdowns to lead the Oilers (a franchise that has since moved to Tennessee and changed its name to the Titans) to a 35–30 victory.

Campbell was a repeat winner of the MVP award in 1979, but his best season was in 1980, when he rushed for 1,934 yards — at the time the second-best single-season mark ever, behind only O.J. Simpson. Campbell made my list because although he was a punishing runner, he missed only 6 games out of 121 due to injuries.

Tony Gonzalez

In the last decade or so, NFL and college teams went looking for the next Tony Gonzalez, a big-body athlete (6-foot-4, 240 pounds) who had the receiving skills and the innate quickness of a player much smaller. Gonzalez, a first-ballot Hall of Famer in 2019 and the game's most complete tight end, was a football freak athletically because of his basketball skills and his 34-inch vertical jump. While at Cal Berkley, Gonzalez was an All-American tight end, and he also helped the basketball Bears advance to the Sweet 16, scoring a season-high 23 points in a second-round NCAA tournament win over Villanova.

Gonzalez was great because he could block like a fullback and also make the tough, acrobatic catch. After scoring a touchdown with the Kansas City Chiefs, he would always dunk the football over the crossbar of the goalposts. Because of Gonzalez, NFL scouts went looking for basketball power forwards to play tight end. The Chargers' Antonio Gates, a basketball player at Kent State, possessed the toughness and had the size and speed to play pro football. In today's NFL, the tight end position has blossomed — Travis Kelce of the Kansas City Chiefs and George Kittle of the San Francisco 49ers are two such stars — and I credit Gonzalez for showing coaches how a big, shifty, and tough guy can play as a receiver. Gonzalez literally changed the game.

Gonzalez never made it to a Super Bowl, but he excelled in the NFL even though his team's passing offense didn't always revolve around him. Tony spent his final four years with the Atlanta Falcons, and he finished his career with the most receiving yards (15,127) for a tight end and also the most receptions (1,325). His 14 Pro Bowls are the most ever by a tight end. In fact, he is one of only five NFL players in history (Tom Brady and Peyton Manning are two others) to be named to 14 Pro Bowls.

John Hannah

John Hannah was big, mean, athletic, and a steamroller — all perfect ingredients for one of the game's finest all-around offensive linemen. When he came into the NFL in 1973, a first-round draft choice of the New England Patriots from the University of Alabama, Hannah was the first guard of such size (6 feet 3 inches, 265 pounds) who could also run well; he was a devastating pulling guard.

Some people had doubts about Hannah's ability to adjust to the pro game because he was strictly a zone, straight-ahead blocker while playing at Alabama. At the time, Alabama ran a wishbone offense, which featured option running by the quarterback, who also pitched wide to running backs. A lineman didn't have to leave his stance and run wide to block or concentrate on pass-blocking techniques in the wishbone offense. But Hannah had football in his genes (Herb, his father, played pro football with the New York Giants), and he was an adaptable athlete, having won varsity letters in wrestling and track, as well as football, at Alabama.

During his career, the Patriots were a few players and a little luck away from being a championship team. Hannah played in only one Super Bowl (and lost), but he was named All-Pro for ten consecutive seasons (1976 to 1985) and Offensive Lineman of the Year by the Players Association four times. In 13 seasons, he missed only 5 of 188 games due to injury.

Don Hutson

Everyone knows that Jerry Rice of the San Francisco 49ers was the best receiver ever, but old-timers will tell you that Green Bay Packer Don Hutson was the best. From 1935 to 1945, Hutson's receptions and receiving totals were almost three times greater than his nearest competitor. Teams didn't throw a lot in those days, but the Packers did because they had "The Alabama Antelope," one of the fastest and most graceful men in football. In 1942, Hutson caught 74 passes, more than all receivers on the Detroit Lions combined; his 1,211 receiving yards were more than two NFL teams; and his 17 touchdown catches were more than six NFL teams. Hutson was the consummate deep-ball threat, leading the NFL in touchdown receptions in 9 of his 11 seasons. In his second game as a pro, he caught an 83-yard touchdown from quarterback Arnie Herber. Teams never double- and triple-teamed players until Hutson showed up on the scene.

In college at the University of Alabama, Hutson was an all-around jock. In fact, one day, he was playing outfield in a baseball game and left to compete in a track meet. He ran a 9.7-second 100-yard dash, winning the event, before hustling back to his baseball game.

Hutson, a charter inductee into the Pro Football Hall of Fame, was a two-way performer, playing at left end and in the secondary on defense. In his final four seasons, Hutson intercepted 23 passes. His record of 99 touchdown receptions stood for 44 seasons. And he was great until the bitter end, leading the NFL with 47 receptions in his final season.

Before he died, Hutson was asked about modern athletes and whether he could play with them. "How many catches would you have today?" the young reporter asked. "Oh, probably about 50," Hutson replied. "Fifty? That's not as many as you had in your prime," the reporter retorted. "Well," Hutson said, smiling, "I am 74, you know."

Jonathan Ogden

Let me be the first to say that Ozzie Newsome deserves to go into the Pro Football Hall of Fame twice. He was a Hall of Fame tight end with the Cleveland Browns, but he was also a Hall of Fame general manager. His first draft choice for the relocated Cleveland franchise, known today as the Baltimore Ravens, was UCLA All-American Jonathan Ogden. And with his awesome wingspan at 6-foot-9 and 355 pounds, Ogden was football's prototypical left tackle.

Ogden was a total athlete. At UCLA, he also was a shot putter, helping the Bruins to win the 1996 NCAA men's Division 1 Indoor Track and Field championships with a personal best of 19.42 in the shot put. Ogden, who started all four years in football at UCLA, was the first of many great draft selections by Newsome, who also drafted great defensive players like Ray Lewis and Ed Reed.

The NFL had never seen a player Ogden's size who was so athletic. He was a glimpse into the future when he arrived, the equivalent of a lunar eclipse at left tackle for over a decade. Everything Ogden did on the football field was picture perfect. His quick feet always had him in the ideal position to devour and negate opposing defensive linemen.

When watching Ogden, his every move and tactic was effortless. Ogden never seemed to be sweating, never in fear of allowing a sack. Before entering the Hall of Fame in 2013, Ogden was an 11-time Pro Bowler, only missing his rookie season. Nine seasons he was All-Pro, a literal giant on the football field. Michael Strahan, one of my sidekicks on *Fox NFL Sunday* and himself a Hall of Famer, once said of Ogden, "You see him, you think to yourself this guy is not mean enough. But Jonathan would rip your limbs off, and he'd smile . . . and wave your arm in front of you."

In 2001, Ogden won a Super Bowl with the Baltimore Ravens when they defeated the New York Giants 34–7 in Super Bowl XXXV.

Jim Parker

Jim Parker was the first offensive lineman elected to the Pro Football Hall of Fame. A first-round draft choice from Ohio State, Parker played both ways — offensive and defensive tackle — but Baltimore Colts coach Weeb Ewbank changed all that by starting him at only offensive tackle in 1957. The plan was pretty simple: Parker, all 6 feet 3 inches and 273 pounds of him, was supposed to protect quarterback Johnny Unitas, one of the greatest passers of all time. Unitas attempted

47 passes in his very first game and wasn't sacked once. Parker was magnificent at his job.

Parker was the first huge man — who possessed the quickness of a man 60 pounds lighter — to emerge as an outstanding blocker. Until men like Parker arrived, defensive players generally dominated pro football's line of scrimmage; most athletic big men preferred playing defense to offense.

Parker's gifts were immeasurable. He was a Pro Bowl player at tackle for four years when Ewbank was forced to shift him to left guard because of injuries to other players. Parker fit perfectly in that role and was named All-Pro at guard for four consecutive seasons. A knee injury ended Parker's career in 1967.

Walter Payton

Mike Ditka, the great Chicago tight end and coach, called Walter Payton the most complete football player he had ever seen. Payton's nickname was "Sweetness," but maybe it should have been "Toughness." He missed only one game in 13 seasons with the Chicago Bears, and that was due to a coaching decision made by Jack Pardee in Payton's rookie season (1975).

Excluding his rookie year and his final season, when he no longer was the hub of Chicago's offense, Payton touched the ball an average of 24 times a game for 119 yards, combining rushing and receiving gains. Payton is the NFL's second-leading all-time rusher with 16,726 yards (Emmitt Smith is first).

Players marveled about Payton because he did whatever he needed to do to win, and he stood out because he spent more than half his career on non-playoff teams. In fact, in Payton's first eight seasons, Chicago was a dismal 61–70. His passion for the game ran deep. He enjoyed blocking and would run a dummy pass route like he was the intended receiver. Heck, he even passed for eight touchdowns. In 10 of 13 seasons, Payton rushed for at least 1,200 yards. He needed arthroscopic surgery on both knees after the 1983 season, in which he gained 1,421 yards on those two gimpy knees. Tragically, he died in 1999 at age 45.

Jerry Rice

If you listen to sports shows on television, you probably have heard the slang reference of GOAT, Greatest of All Time. In recent years, that moniker has been used when referring to Patriots quarterback Tom Brady. But in football reality, there is only one GOAT, and that's wide receiver Jerry Rice. Well, he's at worst the greatest offensive player of all time.

Even though Rice was not heavily recruited out of high school, his world renown work ethic led him to achieve many collegiate records. He starred at Division II Mississippi Valley State University before becoming a first round pick in the 1985 NFL Draft. In a league where speed and quickness are an essential attribute, Rice ran a 4.7 40-yard dash. Tyreek Hill of the Kansas City Chiefs runs a 4.2 40, so you know that Rice wasn't the fastest. But he was football fast. What I mean by that is that there were no wasted motions: Rice was always in the right place on the field; he took all the right angles; and he always caught the football.

Rice was one of eight children, and he always praised his father, a bricklayer, for instilling in him a hard-work ethic. His superior hand-eye coordination came from catching bricks from his father, sometimes hauling them in from the rooftops. Rice played in the NFL for 20 seasons, 16 of those when the San Francisco 49ers were winning three Super Bowls. He also appeared in a losing Super Bowl with my Raiders after the 2002 season.

Rice was All-Pro in 12 seasons, and he still holds 14 NFL records, a remarkable achievement considering how the league has become such a pass-happy sport since he left the game in 2005. Rice set the standard, and what's staggering to me is that when he starred, teams threw the ball nowhere as often as they do today. Rice holds numerous NFL receiving records. His 1,549 career receptions are 307 receptions ahead of the second-place record held by Tony Gonzalez. His 22,895 career receiving yards are 6,961 yards ahead of the second-place spot held by his former 49ers teammate Terrell Owens. His 197 career touchdown receptions are 41 scores more than the second place record of 156 touchdown receptions by Randy Moss, and his 208 total touchdowns (197 receiving, 10 rushing, and one fumble recovery) are 33 scores ahead of Emmitt Smith's second place total of 175. He also threw a touchdown pass against the Atlanta Falcons in a 1995 regular-season game. His 1,256 career points scored make him the highest-scoring non-kicker in NFL history. During a career spanning two decades, Rice averaged 75.6 receiving yards per game.

Barry Sanders

I only played against the Detroit Lions' Barry Sanders once, back in a 1990 Monday night game, and I believe he may be the greatest running back of all time. He was the best back I ever faced. In a league of extraordinary athletes, Barry made them look average throughout his career. His short-space quickness, coupled with a low center of gravity and uncanny vision, made him a nightmare to tackle. I knew it was fruitless to chase him, so it made sense to simply wait because eventually he might circle around and come running toward me.

We beat his Lions that night, 38–31, because my Raiders had three Heisman Trophy winners and they all scored. Sanders won the 1988 Heisman after probably the greatest individual season in college football history, rushing for 2,850 yards and 42 touchdowns in 12 games for Oklahoma State. My 1990 teammates — Tim Brown and Marcus Allen — won the Heisman and are also in the Pro Football Hall of Fame, just like Sanders. The one Raider missing from the HOF that night is Bo Jackson, arguably the greatest athlete I ever saw. Bo could do it all, but a hip injury forced his retirement from major league baseball and football prematurely.

Sanders unexpectedly retired before the 1999 season. Through ten seasons in Detroit, he averaged over 1,500 rushing yards per season and just under 100 rushing yards per game. In 1997, he became the third player to rush for over 2,000 yards in a season and was named the NFL's Most Valuable Player. He was NFL Rookie of the Year when he entered the league in 1989. Sanders made the Pro Bowl in all ten of his NFL seasons and led the NFL in rushing four different years.

Yes, Sanders retired healthy and relatively young from the game he loved so much, and he did so knowing that he was at the time 2,000 yards short of an attainable all-time mark. He was frustrated that he could never take the Lions deep into the playoffs. He did it his way, he played with class, and I have nothing but respect for him. For those of you who never saw Sanders play, check out some of his highlights on YouTube. His moves were unbelievable.

Gale Sayers

Gale Sayers of the Chicago Bears was a speedster with shake-and-bake moves — a dazzler in football pads. The only sad thing about Sayers is that two knee injuries shortened his career. Still, in basically a five-season career, he accomplished enough to gain entry into the Pro Football Hall of Fame on the first ballot. Sayers enjoyed nothing more than returning punts and kicks. In his first preseason game, he raced 93 yards with a kickoff and 77 yards on a punt return, and he also threw a 25-yard touchdown pass with his left (non-dominant) hand.

In 1965, Bears coach George Halas, who coached more than 40 seasons, remarked after Sayers scored six touchdowns on a muddy Wrigley Field against the San Francisco 49ers that it was the greatest performance he'd ever seen. Sayers gained 336 yards that day, and some people say that he covered more than 130 yards while scoring on an 85-yard punt return in which he zigzagged all over the field.

In basically 12 full games that season, Sayers scored 22 touchdowns and averaged 31.4 yards on kick returns and 14.9 yards per punt return. His 2,272 combined yards by a rookie still ranks second in NFL history. Sayers had only two 1,000-yard rushing seasons, but he did average 5 yards per carry and scored a touchdown one out of every 23.7 times he touched the ball.

Art Shell

Art Shell arrived with the Oakland Raiders as a third-round draft choice from tiny Maryland State–Eastern Shore in 1968, a year after Gene Upshaw. However, the two players eventually united to form the best guard/tackle combination in the history of the NFL. Shell, who was 6 feet 5 inches tall and weighed 265 pounds, became the starting left tackle in 1970 and was named to eight Pro Bowls in the 1970s. He became the Jim Parker of his era. Shell and Upshaw worked as one, dominating their side of the offensive formation on run sweeps.

However, Shell also evolved into a picture-perfect pass-blocker. In Super Bowl XI, Shell virtually buried talented Minnesota defensive end Jim Marshall to help lead the Raiders to victory. Shell was a mammoth man with a dancer's feet. He could *slide-protect* (he had quick feet, which allowed him to shift his body easily in any direction when protecting his quarterback in passing situations), and he could also hammer defensive linemen with his brutish strength. Shell developed his agility while earning All-State honors in basketball at Bonds-Wilson High in North Charleston, South Carolina.

Shell later became one of the first African Americans to become an NFL head coach in the modern era. He owns a 56–52 record in his two stints as coach of the Raiders. He opened the door for other African American coaches like Tony Dungy, Marvin Lewis, and Lovie Smith.

Gene Upshaw

Before his untimely death in 2008, many fans knew Gene Upshaw as the executive director of the NFL Players Association, a title that translates into the leader of the players union. As leader of the union, he fought on the players' behalf for better free agency terms, more money, and stronger benefits. The former Oakland Raider seemed destined for such a role because he entered the league in 1967, when its popularity was mushrooming, and left in 1981, knowing that pro football had sur-passed baseball as America's pastime. Also, he was a Raiders captain for eight seasons, which is the same number of years this left guard was named to All-AFC or All-Pro teams.

Upshaw was the first of the really tall (6 feet 5 inches) guards, and he was drafted in the first round to block a specific Oakland opponent: Hall of Fame tackle Buck Buchanan of the arch-rival Kansas City Chiefs. Upshaw had never played guard, but he won the starting job as a rookie and kept it for 15 seasons. Upshaw is the only player to start on championship teams in the old American Football League and in the NFL. The Raiders won the American Football League title in 1967 and then Super Bowls XI and XV, with Upshaw leading the way. Upshaw was a fierce competitor who was equally adept at run-blocking and pass-blocking. All told, he played in 307 preseason, regular-season, and postseason games with the Raiders, 24 of them playoff games.

Chapter **21**

More Than Ten Greatest Quarterbacks of All Time

NFL quarterbacks hold the most highly regarded position in all of sports. When they're good, they're stars in the eyes of the media and the world. When they're great, their exploits become the stuff of legend. Most kids today would rather aspire to be a great NFL quarterback than the president of the United States.

The players in this chapter are listed in alphabetical order. I made no attempt to rank these ten great quarterbacks.

Terry Bradshaw

I had to pick Terry Bradshaw or working at FOX Sports would be unbearable; he's like the older brother I never wanted. But kidding aside, Terry was really something in big games. The bigger the game, the better he played. He and Joe Montana of the San Francisco 49ers are the only quarterbacks to have led their teams to four Super Bowl championships. Bradshaw was voted the Super Bowl MVP twice with the Pittsburgh Steelers. And he was the league MVP in 1978, his best statistical season.

Bradshaw is a great example of a player who refused to quit when his career didn't flourish immediately. Although he was the first player taken in the 1970 college draft, the Steelers didn't immediately turn over the offense and the team to him. But Bradshaw overcame his struggles and his benchings to become one of the all-time greats.

When the Steelers were ready to win, Bradshaw led them to an unprecedented four Super Bowl wins in a six-year period (1974 to 1979). In Pittsburgh's first title run, his touchdown pass to Lynn Swann in the fourth quarter beat the Oakland Raiders in the AFC championship game, and in the Super Bowl that followed, his fourth quarter touchdown pass to Larry Brown clinched the victory over the Minnesota Vikings.

When the NFL liberalized its pass-blocking rules and prevented defensive backs from touching receivers after they ran 5 yards, Bradshaw's throwing talents really blossomed. He had a great arm, and during the 1979 season, the Steelers rode it to the team's fourth championship. In his two championship MVP performances, Bradshaw threw for 627 yards and six touchdowns. Believe me, I know all his stats; I've heard about them enough. If he tells me about the "Immaculate Reception" that robbed my Raiders of a fourth championship one more time, I'll flip!

Tom Brady

Nobody thought Tom Brady would amount to much more than a backup quarterback in the NFL. After a moderately successful stint at the University of Michigan, Brady was selected by the New England Patriots as the 199th pick all the way down in the 6th round of the NFL draft in the year 2000. The draft snub has served as a motivating factor in Brady's career. At the start of his rookie season with the Patriots, he was their fourth-string quarterback. By the end of the season, he was their backup behind Drew Bledsoe.

A serious injury to Bledsoe early in the 2001 season meant that Brady would fill in as the Patriots' starter, and the rest, as they say, is history. Brady led the team to a first place finish in the AFC East and a berth in the playoffs. The Patriots eventually won the Super Bowl in dramatic fashion over the heavily favored St. Louis Rams, one of the biggest upsets in Super Bowl history. At that point, Brady was a star, and his career as one of the NFL's premier quarterbacks has continued for two decades. His quick delivery, pinpoint accuracy, and uncanny ability to read and manipulate defenses have made him incredibly difficult to beat. He plans to play a 20th NFL season in 2019, and he is the only player to become league MVP at the age of 40.

As of the 2018 season, Brady has had 10 consecutive seasons of 10 or more victories in a 16-game season. He will go down as the winningest quarterback with 207 regular-season wins plus another 30 playoff victories. He, along with Coach Bill Belichick, has led the Patriots to nine Super Bowls, winning six of them, surpassing both Montana and Bradshaw. He has thrown for over 70,500 yards and 517 touchdowns, marks that rank just behind Peyton Manning and Drew Brees. In his old age, Brady has become a health nut, training differently than most players in order to keep playing at a high level into his 40s. Brady is certainly one of the all-time greats, and he's bound for the Hall of Fame at the end of his career.

Drew Brees

Given the greatness of current New Orleans quarterback Drew Brees, it's hard to believe that no one wanted him at significant periods of his football life. Size was always an issue — he is barely 6 feet tall — and a torn knee ligament in high school limited his scholarship offers, and that's how Brees ended up at Purdue, where he was a Heisman Trophy finalist and led the Boilermakers to their last Big Ten title in 2000.

Many NFL personnel were concerned about Brees' size, but the Chargers selected him at the top of the second round. While with them, a torn labrum of his throwing shoulder put his professional future in doubt. Doctors for the Miami Dolphins wouldn't give him medical clearance, and thus he signed as a free agent with Coach Sean Payton and the New Orleans Saints. It's been a masterful football marriage as Brees has virtually rewritten every NFL passing record just like he did at Purdue under Coach Joe Tiller.

Brees has set many NFL passing records, but he's best known as being the most accurate passer in NFL history. In 2018, he completed 74.44 percent of his pass attempts, breaking his own completion percentage record.

In 2006, the city of New Orleans needed a new hero after Hurricane Katrina destroyed so much of the city and took so many lives. Brees ended up being that hero, and he has devoted a great portion of his off-the-field life to numerous Louisiana charities.

In 2009, Brees brought home the Super Bowl XLIV trophy, beating the Peyton Manning-led Colts 31–17. Brees is currently the NFL's all-time leading passer with over 74,000 yards and he has seven consecutive seasons (2010–2016) with at least 4,500 yards passing. He and Coach Payton may go down as the smartest quarterback-coach offensive combo ever.

John Elway

The son of a college football coach, John Elway was known as a great athlete as early as his high school days. In college at Stanford University, he excelled at both football and baseball, and a professional career in either sport was an option for him. In the 1981 baseball draft, the Yankees picked him six spots ahead of the late Hall of Famer Tony Gwynn, probably the greatest hitter in San Diego Padres' history.

Elway played his entire NFL career with the Denver Broncos (though he was initially drafted in 1983 by the Baltimore Colts, who subsequently traded him to Denver). His reputation as a great quarterback who could perform at clutch time was cemented in the 1986 playoffs. Down seven in the AFC championship game against the Cleveland Browns, Elway orchestrated a masterful 98-yard, game-tying drive late in the fourth quarter. His Broncos went on to win the game in overtime and go the Super Bowl, only to lose to the New York Giants.

Elway brought the Broncos to the Super Bowl again in the 1987 and 1989 seasons, but in both games, the Broncos suffered blowout defeats. After eight years of continued greatness, Elway led the Broncos to their first Super Bowl victory after the 1997 season. The Broncos won the Super Bowl the following season as well, after which Elway retired. The two championships at the end of his great career erased the sting of three earlier Super Bowl losses and secured his Pro Football Hall of Fame enshrinement in 2004. Elway remains involved in pro football to this day, working in the Broncos' front office for eight seasons, mostly as the team's general manager.

Otto Graham

Any debate over Otto Graham's selection should cease when you consider that he's the only professional quarterback to lead his team, the Cleveland Browns, to ten consecutive championship games. The Browns won seven of those games, and Graham's teams won more than 83 percent of their games during his career. What's also astounding about Graham is that he played tailback, not quarterback, at Northwestern University. And many people in his hometown of Waukegan, Illinois, believed that his best sport was basketball.

Browns coach Paul Brown chose Graham in 1946 for his poise, leadership, and ball-handling skills and believed that he would be a great T-formation quarterback, even though Graham had never played the position. (In the *T-formation*, the quarterback moved behind the center to take a direct snap, and three players — mostly running backs — were aligned behind him, three across.)

In the late 1940s, Graham, who finished his NFL career with a 55.7 completion percentage, excelled at throwing the deep sideline and crossing routes that are prevalent in pro football today. Brown also used receivers in the backfield and put these players in motion, knowing that Graham was smart enough to deal with an evolving offensive strategy. The only knock on Graham and his Browns was that they played in the All-America Football Conference for four years, a league considered inferior to the NFL.

But after Graham and the Browns joined the NFL, their successes continued. In the Browns' 30–28 victory over the Los Angeles Rams in the 1950 championship game, Graham passed for four touchdowns. In the 1954 title game against Detroit, Graham passed for three touchdowns and also ran for three touchdowns. In his final season, Graham led the Browns to another title, again beating the Rams. In this game, he passed for two touchdowns and ran for two more.

Peyton Manning

The son of NFL quarterback Archie Manning, Peyton Manning was destined for greatness. He led the University of Tennessee to the SEC championship during his senior season, and he was runner-up to win the Heisman Trophy, the most prestigious award in all of college football. He was drafted number one overall in the 1998 NFL draft by the Indianapolis Colts, and he immediately became their starting quarterback.

Even though the Colts had a record of 3–13 during his rookie season, Manning showed that he was a top NFL quarterback, setting several records for passing by a rookie. As Manning's career progressed with the Colts, the team became one of the best in the NFL. From 1998 to 2010, the Colts with Manning as quarterback won eight division champions and two AFC championships. Manning and the Colts appeared in two Super Bowls, winning one in 2007.

Manning's career took an abrupt turn in 2011. After a neck injury and multiple surgeries, he was unable to play for the Colts for the entire 2011 season. Despite being the premier player of a successful franchise for over a decade, he and the Colts decided to part ways. Manning signed with the Denver Broncos in 2012 and led them to an AFC championship and a Super Bowl appearance in 2014. A year later, he won his second Super Bowl, beating then MVP Cam Newton and the Carolina Panthers in Super Bowl 50.

Although Manning is the only five-time winner of the NFL's prestigious MVP award, he was on the losing end of more championships than he won. Manning's consistent play throughout his entire career puts him at or near the top of the list of all-time great quarterbacks.

Dan Marino

Dan Marino was the last quarterback selected in the first round of the great 1983 draft class that included John Elway, Jim Kelly, and Tony Eason. According to his Miami Dolphins coach, Don Shula, this perceived slight of being passed over in the draft helped motivate Marino to prove all the other teams wrong.

Marino became the Dolphins' starting quarterback midway through his rookie season. He became known for his strong arm and quick release. Though he wasn't mobile, he was rarely sacked because he was able to get rid of the ball so quickly. You don't know how many times I was so close to sacking him when I played, only to look up and see the ball leaving his hands. One of the game's most beautiful throwers.

In just his second season, Marino set records for most yards and touchdowns thrown as he propelled the Dolphins to the Super Bowl, only to lose to the San Francisco 49ers. Marino would never return to the Super Bowl, but his 17-year career with the Dolphins was notable for his consistent excellence.

Joe Montana

With the game on the line or a championship to be won, Joe Montana is the quarterback I want running my team. When I played against Joe Montana, I was always impressed with his ability to remain calm and focused (after all, many manic things happen on the field during a close game). His composure was merely one characteristic that set him apart. He was also a tremendously accurate passer — his all-time passing accuracy was 63.2 percent, and he once completed 22 consecutive passes.

Montana is one of those great quarterbacks who was raised in and played high school ball in a relatively small corner of western Pennsylvania. Joe Namath, Dan Marino, Jim Kelly, and Montana all come from that part of the state (and all are Hall of Famers). Although he appeared thin in build, Montana was a tough quarterback. After major back surgery in 1986, he returned to perform some of his greatest feats. His most productive seasons were in 1987 and 1989, the latter of which culminated in a 92-yard scoring drive to win Super Bowl XXIII in the final seconds.

Montana was named the Super Bowl MVP a record three times, and in his last two playoff runs to Super Bowl titles, Montana passed for 19 touchdowns with just one interception. The beauty of Montana is that he won at every level — high school, college at Notre Dame, and the NFL — despite some coaches and NFL scouts doubting his abilities. San Francisco Coach Bill Walsh designed an exquisite pass-control offense, and Montana directed it with the passing precision of a surgeon. If he wasn't the best quarterback of all time, he surely was the most instinctive player ever to play this position.

Fran Tarkenton

Mobile quarterbacks are common in the NFL now, but the first great one was Fran Tarkenton, who played for the Minnesota Vikings and New York Giants. Drafted by the Vikings in 1961, Tarkenton play was characterized by his ability to evade pass rushers and extend plays, gaining yardage by both running and throwing.

Tarkenton earned the nickname "Scrambin' Fran" playing for the Vikings from 1961 to 1967 and again from 1972 to 1978 after a stint with the Giants. In the 1970s, he and the Vikings appeared in three Super Bowls but lost all three. When Tarkenton retired, he held the records for most throwing yards, most rushing yards, most completions, and most touchdowns by a quarterback. Almost 40 years later, his numbers in each of those categories are still in the top ten all time.

Johnny Unitas

Johnny Unitas wasn't the first great quarterback in the NFL, but he was arguably the first star. That's not to say he wasn't an amazing quarterback, because he was, but his play made him a popular figure in the media, paving the way for future stars of the NFL.

Unitas' career in the NFL began inauspiciously. He was drafted by the Pittsburgh Steelers in the ninth round in 1955, but he was never given a chance to play. He left pro football and worked construction, playing semi-professional football on weekends. In 1956, the Baltimore Colts gave Unitas a chance. He began as a backup but became a starter due to an injury to George Shaw. His first few games were shaky, but he came into his own by the end of the season. In 1957, Unitas led the NFL in passing yards and helped the Colts to their first-ever winning season. For more than five decades, Unitas held the NFL record of throwing a touchdown pass in 47 consecutive games. Drew Brees set a new mark of 54 games in October 2012.

Unitas and the Colts won NFL championships in 1958 and 1959. The attention his performances garnered in the championship games brought the NFL to a new era of popularity, especially the 1958 overtime win over the New York Giants in Yankee Stadium. That game was the first of many title games shown live on television. Throughout the 1960s, the Colts with Unitas at the helm were consistently one of the top teams in the NFL. Unitas and the Colts lost the Super Bowl after the 1968 season but rebounded to win the Super Bowl after the 1970 season. Unitas played with an injured arm during the later years of his career, which hampered his production. Nonetheless, he was inducted to the Hall of Fame in 1979.

Steve Young

Steve Young excelled as quarterback for Brigham Young University. He was an accurate passer and an elusive runner, but his professional career stumbled out of the gate. Young first signed with the now defunct USFL (United States Football League) after leaving college in 1984. In 1985, he joined the NFL's Tampa Bay Buccaneers, who won a total of four games in their two seasons with Young on their roster. In 1987, Young was traded to the San Francisco 49ers, which already had a great quarterback playing for them, Joe Montana, discussed earlier in this chapter. For a few years, Young was a backup while Montana flourished.

But injuries to Montana allowed Young opportunities to play, and he took advantage. After strong performances by Young in the early 1990s, the 49ers eventually decided to trade Joe Montana, and Young became their starter. Young showed great athletic prowess, throwing the ball with precision in the 49ers' West Coast offense, and he often stymied defenses with his evasiveness in the pocket and ability to run the ball. Young led the 49ers to a Super Bowl victory after the 1994 season. He holds the record for the highest career quarterback rating (96.8) and has the second most career yards rushing by a quarterback.

Chapter **22**

More Than Ten Greatest Coaches in the History of the Game

I don't like choosing sides or picking favorites, so know that I went with my gut (and it isn't that considerable, either) when picking the best football coaches of all time for this chapter. I'm not a big history buff, so I didn't consider all the old-timers like Pop Warner and Curly Lambeau. And I skipped over some terrific former college coaches like Ohio State's Woody Hayes, Nebraska's Tom Osborne, Paul "Bear" Bryant (who actually walked on water in Alabama, I hear).

I spoke with many coaching friends to narrow my list to the following men. Most of them were innovators, and all of them were winners. Everyone speaks of playing hard, win or lose. But I know that a football coach is special when he molds 30 to 53 men into a championship team. All these men are champions. And many of these great coaches are connected to one another. For example, Don Shula and also Pittsburgh Steelers coach Chuck Noll both worked under Paul Brown, and I know they both credit Brown for how well-organized and prepared they were on game days.

Bill Belichick

There has been no greater coach in the modern era of pro football than this former defensive coordinator of the New York Giants under Bill Parcells. Belichick's first job as a head coach was with the Cleveland Browns, but a rift with then owner Art Modell led to his departure after the owner decided to move his franchise to Baltimore. His 11–5 record in 1994 remains Cleveland's best record in more than two decades. My buddy Terry Bradshaw at FOX says that the Lombardi Trophy, emblematic of a Super Bowl champion, could be called the Belichick Trophy because his New England Patriots have played in nine Super Bowls in an 18-year period, winning six championships. In those 18 seasons, his teams missed the playoffs only twice. Only Lombardi, who was 9–1 in playoff games, has a better postseason percentage (minimum 10 games) than Belichick. Belichick, who has total control of the Patriots' personnel, has won 31 of 42 playoff games with the Patriots. His career winning percentage of .685 is tops (292–134) among coaches with at least 190 wins.

Belichick learned the hard way, going to work for $25 week in 1975 watching film for Colts head coach Ted Marchibroda. But undoubtedly his best mentor was his late father, Steve, who coached and scouted for the U.S. Naval Academy for more than three decades. Steve was with his son during much of the 2004 season that ended in a Super Bowl 39 victory.

Belichick has been in control of everything related to football in New England, meaning that he controls the 53-man roster and also makes all decisions relating to trades and the salary cap. Although a defensive coach in the beginning, he also was Tom Brady's quarterback coach early in his career. He is a unique head coach in that he is very capable of coaching every aspect of football, from special teams to offense. His defensive game plan against the high-scoring Los Angeles Rams in Super Bowl LIII, limiting them to only three points, is simply another example of how great and complete he is as a tactician.

When my son, Chris, played for Belichick in New England, he spoke in appreciative terms of how Belichick conducted himself in front of the room and in front of all the players. Belichick made sure that every player was prepared for every conceivable situation that may arise in a game. Having been around the game as long as I have, it is mind-boggling that one man has the answers for everything. For me, Belichick is sitting atop Mt. Everest, and it's not even close. Every other coach is sitting somewhere down at base camp.

I realize there are a few who point to Belichick's involvement in Spygate, when a Patriots video assistant was caught taping the New York Jets' defensive signals from the sidelines, and denigrate his accomplishments. The sideline taping was against NFL rules, and he was turned in by Jets coach Eric Mangini, who had once been assistant under Belichick. The league came down hard on Belichick, fining him a record $500,000 and taking away a first-round draft selection from the team. In the 100-year history of the NFL, the sanctions in 2007 were the harshest ever until Saints Coach Sean Payton was suspended for an entire season (2012) for covering up a scheme in which bounties were paid to his players for deliberately knocking opponents out of the game.

But during all this criticism of Belichick and how he operates a team, he led the Patriots to a perfect 16-0 regular season in 2007 only to lose to the New York Giants in Super Bowl XLII, thus finishing 18-1. Despite all the sideline drama, Belichick was voted Coach of the Year by the Associated Press.

Paul Brown

I loved playing pro football, but I don't know if I could have sat still in a Paul Brown classroom. This man turned football into a science class back in the late 1940s. He graded every player's performance from game film and sent plays in from the bench. Players were turned off by his classroom approach. However, his revolutionary approach to practice sessions and his demands that players take notes and carry playbooks became commonplace and have remained so for decades, from high school ball to the NFL.

In 1956, Brown wired his quarterback's helmet in order to transmit instructions. Nearly 60 years later, the NFL allows every team to do so (although those transmitters don't always work).

The Cleveland Browns are the only team named after a head coach — which proves just how talented Paul Brown was. The Cincinnati Bengals' Paul Brown Stadium is named after Brown as well. After winning a national championship at Ohio State and coaching Washington High School in Massillon, Ohio, to six consecutive state championships, Brown was paid the princely sum of $20,000 to coach and build a professional team, called the Cleveland Browns, in 1945. The Browns won four consecutive championships, but the team's success (52–4–3 record) doomed the All-America Football Conference. But when the mighty NFL absorbed the Browns, the team didn't play like second-rate performers. In their first game in the new league, the Browns defeated the NFL champion Philadelphia Eagles. They won three more championships over the next six seasons.

In the last decade, the Browns have fallen on tough times, losing more than they have won, including a 0–16 record in 2017.

Brown eventually left Cleveland, retiring with a 115–49–5 NFL record. He returned to football in 1968 as the owner and coach of the Cincinnati Bengals, an expansion team. After only three years, the Bengals made the playoffs. Brown died in 1991, and his family continues to have a controlling interest in Cincinnati's NFL franchise.

Joe Gibbs

HOWIE SAYS

Although my Raiders beat his Washington Redskins in Super Bowl XVIII, we also lost to Joe Gibbs's team a couple of times during my career. I never thought that its personnel matched up with ours, but Gibbs always had his team ready to play and exploit our weaknesses. From top to bottom, the Redskins were as well coached as any group I ever faced. His teams always played hard; they were physical as well as daring, and they played together as a team.

Players say that Gibbs was strict but fair. The biggest testament to his abilities is that he won three Super Bowls — and that he won with three different quarterbacks. He didn't need many stars or dominant players to win. He knew how to build on his players' strengths and minimize their weaknesses. Not only was he great with quarterbacks, but he won with big backs (such as John Riggins) and small receivers. His teams were able to play power football (running the ball) one week, and then the next week, he'd open it up and beat you throwing the ball. One of his power football tactics was the three-tight-end offense. Not only did this offense help his team's running game, but it also negated the strength of New York Giants linebacker Lawrence Taylor, the best defender in the history of the NFL.

Gibbs, who won 17 of 24 playoff games, was a tireless worker. I heard he slept in his office two or three nights a week and often worked 20-hour days. I know a lot of people see Joe as a serious guy, but he can also be pretty funny. Current Redskins owner Daniel Snyder coaxed Gibbs out of retirement in 2004, but his second stint in Washington wasn't as successful. He made the playoffs twice in four seasons. Gibbs returned to what he loved, stock car racing, and his very successful NASCAR racing team.

George Halas

George Halas is my first real old-timer. But I probably wouldn't be writing this book or even have my job at FOX if it weren't for George Halas, the father of pro football. When you think of Chicago, the city of broad shoulders, you immediately think of bigger-than-life men like Mayor Richard J. Daley, Al Capone, and "Papa Bear" Halas. I can't think of another large American city that has a bigger connection with a football team than Chicago, and it's all due to George Halas.

Legend has it that Halas was cheap with a buck and was a strict disciplinarian, but he was also a showman. In 1920, in the Hupmobile showroom of a Canton, Ohio, car dealer, Halas represented one of the NFL's original teams, the Decatur (Illinois) Staleys. (Imagine playing for a team called the Staleys!) A year later, Coach Halas wised up and moved the team to Chicago. The next year, he changed the team's name to the Bears.

Halas realized the pro game wouldn't survive without stars, so he signed Illinois All-American Red Grange in 1925. At that time, Grange was the most exciting player in college football. The Bears went on a barnstorming tour and played in packed stadiums, showing thousands of fans how great the pro game was. Halas pioneered radio broadcasts of games, and he was also the first to use a public address system to describe to fans what was happening on the field: how many yards were gained, who made the tackle, and what the down and distance were.

Halas was associated with the Bears from the team's inception until his death in 1983. He stepped away from coaching three times, and each time a rejuvenated Halas returned to lead Chicago to an NFL championship. He believed in hiring the best assistant coaches, and he didn't mind sharing the credit. Clark Shaughnessy drastically altered the Bears' offense in 1940, and the result was a 73–0 victory over Washington in the NFL title game. The lopsided victory provided national attention for the publicity-starved professional game. Until Don Shula broke his record, Halas was the number one coach with 324 pro football victories.

Jimmy Johnson

Jimmy Johnson, like Bill Walsh (whom I tell you about later in this chapter), is a super builder and talent evaluator who also happens to be a great football coach. Nothing ever slips by this man. In his first stint as head coach in the NFL, he totally rebuilt the Dallas Cowboys when that great franchise was on the decline back in 1989. He won two Super Bowls with young, drafted talent (free agency didn't exist in the NFL when he started). Later his replacement, Barry Switzer, won another Super Bowl with players like Troy Aikman, Emmitt Smith, and Michael Irvin — players Jimmy Johnson drafted.

When he left Dallas, the Cowboys were the most talented team in the NFL. Their second-team players could have been starters on other teams — and eventually that's what happened. When free agency began in 1993, Dallas wasn't able to keep all its players, especially the talented reserves.

Jimmy struggled in his second NFL coaching gig with the Miami Dolphins because the NFL system had changed. He inherited someone else's team, and it came furnished, but because of salary cap restrictions and players' possessive contracts (see Chapter 17 for more details about the pro football draft), Johnson could replace only one or two players at a time. Building a franchise through the college draft takes a lot longer these days. Plus, Jimmy believes that you win with defense (so do I) and by running the football, but Miami's best chance to win was with its quarterback, Hall of Famer Dan Marino.

Vince Lombardi

When pro football first started to become popular on television in the 1960s, Vince Lombardi was in the process of transforming tiny Green Bay, Wisconsin, into the biggest franchise in the NFL. The Packers were as popular as baseball's Yankees; they were a national team and they still are to this day. Lombardi was the game's most recognized coach. Like a story fresh off a movie lot, the Packers appealed to many blue-collar fans because they're owned by the Wisconsin fans and not by some giant corporation.

Lombardi wasn't an innovator; he honed and borrowed from other coaches' methods. He learned the passing game from Sid Gillman while the two were assistant coaches at the U.S. Military Academy. He was a lineman in college, so he knew the blocking techniques as a player. While coaching at Army, the great coach Earl "Red" Blaik showed him what organization and execution mean to a team.

Lombardi was a man of basics, and the Green Bay power sweep was one of his productions. On the power sweep, the two offensive guards would run around the end to block, with a fullback leading the way for the halfback carrying the ball. The fans, the opposition, and everyone knew that the play was coming, but the Packers ran it with such precision that few teams were able to stop it consistently.

Over a seven-year period, the Packers won five championships, including the first two Super Bowls. The only championship game Lombardi lost was his first, 17–13 to the Philadelphia Eagles in 1960.

So much about being a football coach is teaching, and Lombardi was one of the best. "They call it coaching, but it is teaching," Lombardi said of his craft. "You don't just tell them it is so. You show them the reasons why it is so, and then you repeat and repeat it until they are convinced, until they know." Lombardi, like

George Halas, is one of the game's legendary heroes, and the Super Bowl trophy honors his accomplishments. After trying his hand at management with the Packers, Lombardi returned to coaching with the Washington Redskins in 1969. He led them to their first winning season in 14 years only to die of cancer the following year at age 57. This great man went too soon.

John Madden

For nearly 30 years, John Madden was a TV football analyst, but before he became a television star and commercial pitchman, he was one of the game's best coaches. His enthusiasm and love of the game were obvious from the very beginning. A knee injury derailed his professional football career. However, he hung around the Philadelphia Eagles for most of the year anyway, learning as much as possible from Eagles quarterback Norm Van Brocklin, a future Hall of Famer.

Madden likes to come across as a lighthearted statesman for the game of football — he loves to garrulously describe the play of the oversized linemen and never seems to take the game too seriously — but he's always been a clever, intuitive leader. Smart like a fox. When you have an opportunity to sit and talk to John, it's like having an audience with the Dalai Lama; you sit, listen, and learn.

Like a lot of famous coaches, Madden began his coaching career at the very bottom, with a small junior college team in rural California. In a few years, Madden moved up to San Diego State, studying under Don Coryell, a great passing coach. "John never let his players give up, even if it was in practice," Coryell remembers. "Our practices got heated because John didn't even like to lose a scrimmage." Eventually, Oakland Raiders owner Al Davis hired Madden as an assistant and two years later elevated him to head coach when he was only 32 in 1969. When the Rams hired Sean McVay at age 30 in 2017, Madden lost the distinction of being the game's youngest head coach.

If you ever watch NFL films on cable television, you may catch a glimpse of Madden during the Raiders' great glory run of the 1970s. A big man, Madden was an emotional coach. He was constantly on the officials, bemoaning calls, waving his arms, and exhorting his players to work harder. Madden coached for only ten years, but he won 100 games faster than any other NFL coach at that time and led the Raiders over Minnesota to win Super Bowl XI. He walked away from the game on top, after the 1978 season, at the age of 42. Many coaches don't even earn their first head-coaching position until they're older than that!

Madden never had a strong urge to return to coaching. He became an icon in sports television, remaining in the game by working as a television analyst. And *Madden NFL*, the popular video game series officially sanctioned by the NFL, has carried his name since 1990.

Bill Parcells

Bill Parcells was a throwback coach in many ways. By that, I mean he could have coached in any era. His greatest strength was his talent to relate to his players and figure out the best approach to use their skills and turn them into a winning team. He knew how to push a player's buttons, strike a nerve, and force him to dig deep for something extra — for whatever it takes to win. Parcells was a defensive coach, so his focus was on that side of the ball, supported by an offense that preferred to run first and pass second. If I were physically able, I'd love to turn back the clock and play for this man. He was a coach who appreciated toughness and personal sacrifice for the good of the team.

Parcells coached the New York Giants to Super Bowl victories in 1987 and 1991. He retired after the second Super Bowl, but returned in 1993 to coach the New England Patriots to the Super Bowl. The Patriots were 2–14 in 1992, but in Parcells' first season, the Patriots won five games, and then an amazing 10 in 1994, which is when he won his third Coach of the Year honor. The 1996 team went 13–6, losing to the Green Bay Packers in Super Bowl XXXII.

A New Jersey guy, Parcells abruptly returned to New York City the next season to coach the New York Jets. And in typical Parcells fashion, he made an immediate impact. The Jets, who'd had eight straight non-winning seasons, finished 9–7 in his first season; the year before, they'd won just 1 of 16 games. Parcells is an expert at turning perennial losers into perennial winners. His first such accomplishment was with the New York Giants. After one bad season, Parcells enjoyed a remarkable run with the Giants, winning 10, 11, 17, 6, 10, 12, and 16 games (including playoffs) between 1984 and 1990 with teams led by linebacker Lawrence Taylor and quarterback Phil Simms. Parcells was named Coach of the Year in 1986 and 1989.

Parcells surprised the football world by taking the Patriots to Super Bowl XXXII, knowing that their only chance to win rested with quarterback Drew Bledsoe. Parcells, who would have preferred to control the clock with a running game, proved to everyone that he could win with an offense that went against his basic beliefs and background. However, his finest coaching job was in the Giants' second Super Bowl run. His team was forced to play the end of the 1990 season without Simms, and they neutralized two great offensive teams, the San Francisco 49ers and the Buffalo Bills, with a stifling defense and a ball-control rushing attack. They beat the 49ers by two points and defeated the Bills 20–19 in Super Bowl XXV.

In 2003, Parcells headed south to coach the Dallas Cowboys, where he was modestly successful with a 34–30 record, making the playoffs twice in four years before he retired at the end of the 2006 season. Parcells is the ninth-winningest coach in the NFL, with an overall record of 183–138–1 (a .570 winning percentage). He returned to the NFL to become the Executive Vice President of Football Operations for the Miami Dolphins from 2008 to 2010. He was inducted into the Football Hall of Fame in 2013.

Knute Rockne

I'm sure many non-football fans have heard of the University of Notre Dame in South Bend, Indiana. Notre Dame is synonymous with college football. And Knute (pronounced *Newt*) Rockne was college football's greatest coach. And what a great name! The sound perfectly suits the image of football: You have to be rock hard and tough to play this game.

"The Rock," as Rockne was affectionately called, guided Notre Dame to six national championships and had a 0.881 winning percentage — the all-time best winning percentage, college or pro. He won 105 games and lost only 12, with 5 ties. In *Knute Rockne — All American*, a great old movie, actor Pat O'Brien immortalizes Rockne's famous "Win one for the Gipper" speech. (Former President Ronald Reagan, who was a Hollywood star before going into politics, plays the ill-fated George Gipp.)

Rockne was a master of the fiery pep talk, a type of speech that even Little League coaches give now and then. When his team was playing badly, he would sarcastically refer to his macho players as girls, which is the last thing tough guys want to hear. But after the game was over and his verbal berating finished, Rockne loved his young players like a father. The players knew Rockne's rough words weren't personal — even though he scared them at times by saying he might die if they didn't win.

Rockne was an inspirational speaker and traveled the country sharing his thoughts and opinions of life and football. He sold football across the land and made many Americans stand up and take notice of the sport.

Rockne was also influential on the field. In 1913, playing end for Notre Dame, he teamed with quarterback Gus Dorais to develop the use of the forward pass in a game against West Point. He was also the first to use *shock troops*, or second-team performers, to wear down the opposition's first string. He believed in playing the best teams every week, which is how Notre Dame became a national team.

Don Shula

I don't know if Don Shula is the best coach who ever walked a sideline, but he certainly is the most successful. After the 1995 season, Shula retired after 33 years of coaching in the NFL with more wins (347, including the postseason) than any-body. He also possesses the league's only perfect season: 17–0 in 1972, a season the Miami Dolphins capped off by winning Super Bowl VII. He was the first head coach to cost his owner a first-round draft choice, the price Miami had to pay Baltimore for hiring him away from that team in 1970. The beauty of Shula, NFL executive George Young said, is that "he was best at playing the cards he was dealt." Shula built his offensive and defensive systems around his players, not the other way around, which is more common in the coaching fraternity.

"We take a lot of pride in that," Shula said of his adaptability. "My philosophy was to get the most out of the talent you have, then design your system to best take advantage of that talent. I'd rather not tell a player, 'Hey, this is my system' and demand they either do it this way, or I'll find someone else."

Shula had tremendous success with three different styles of offenses: He played power football with Larry Csonka in the early 1970s, a more balanced scheme with the Colts back in the 1960s, and at the end of his career he pretty much turned the offense over to Dan Marino's big arm and allowed him to throw as much as he wanted. Players win championships, and Shula was fortunate to have quarter-backs such as Johnny Unitas, Earl Morrall, Bob Griese, and Marino, all Hall of Famers, guiding his teams.

Shula has always been respected by his peers and upper management. He was always at the forefront of advocating better rules, and he supported the instant replay system for rectifying an improperly made call on the field.

Bill Walsh

They don't call Bill Walsh "The Genius" for nothing. He built the San Francisco 49ers out of the ashes (they were a 2–14 team when he took over) and trans-formed them into the dominant franchise of the 1980s. To this day, his imprint on the game remains visible. For example, Walsh created the West Coast offense, and now many NFL teams use a version of it (see Chapter 8 for more on this offense).

In Walsh's third season, the 49ers won their first of his three Super Bowls. His first offensive team had an incredible lack of talent, but he designed a system that truly worked for them. The 49ers, unlike the Raiders, worked on throwing short, possession-type passes. To them, a 5-yard gain was a 5-yard gain, whether it was a pass or a run play. Walsh didn't care; he simply wanted to maintain possession and keep the ball moving.

In the process of devising this offensive system, Walsh developed one of the game's best quarterbacks, Joe Montana. Now, Montana didn't have the greatest arm, nor was he the biggest guy. But he was one of the toughest and definitely one of the greatest quarterbacks under pressure. In fact, Montana may be the best decision maker pro football has ever seen. Walsh deserves a lot of credit for Montana and for designing a passing offense that was an extension of the running game.

Although Walsh was a huge factor in developing quarterbacks like Dan Fouts, Montana, and Steve Young, he's also a great judge of talent at other positions. His drafts built the 49ers into champions, and I know he had to watch only five plays by Charles Haley in college to know that Haley would be a great pass-rusher in the NFL. Jerry Rice, the best receiver who has ever played, was another Walsh selection.

Even though many players benefited from his offensive system, Walsh was often quick to release or trade veteran players that he thought were expendable or were running out of time. This policy caused some animosity in the locker room, but Walsh believed teams needed a constant infusion of young talent. He always seemed to be ahead of the curve, allowing an experienced veteran to depart while grooming a faster, quicker rookie for the role. Walsh was criticized for being cold and calculating, but I know he had a soft spot for many of his players and simply was dealing with the extremely high expectations of pro football owners.

Walsh is another coach connected to Paul Brown's tree. He coached under Brown in Cincinnati, but when he wasn't named Brown's successor, Walsh moved on, thus becoming available to the 49ers.

Appendix

Football Speak

audible: When the quarterback changes the play at the line of scrimmage by calling out prescribed signals to his teammates.

backfield: The group of offensive players — the running backs and quarterback — who line up behind the line of scrimmage.

blitz: A defensive strategy in which a linebacker or defensive back vacates his customary position or responsibility in order to pressure the quarterback. The object of a blitz is to tackle the quarterback behind the line of scrimmage (also known as a sack) or force the quarterback to hurry his pass, thus disrupting the offensive play. (Prior to World War II, this defensive strategy was called a red-dog, but the name was changed to blitz after the German Army's blitzkrieg tactics.)

bomb: A long pass play in which the quarterback throws the ball to a receiver more than 35 yards past the line of scrimmage.

bump and run: A technique used by defensive backs to slow down receivers. The defender bumps the receiver at the start of the play and attempts to keep his hands on him, as rules permit within 5 yards of the line of scrimmage, before running downfield with him.

carry: The act of running with the ball. In statistical charts, a runner's rushing attempts are listed as carries.

center: The offensive player who hikes (or snaps) the ball to the quarterback at the start of each play. The term comes from the fact that this player is flanked on either side by a guard and a tackle; he's the middleman (or center) in a contingent of five offensive linemen or blockers. He handles the ball on every play and also snaps the ball to the punter and holder.

clipping: When a player throws his body across the back of the legs of an opponent or charges, falls, or rolls into the back of an opponent below the waist after approaching him from behind. It's a 15-yard penalty.

coffin corner: The area between the opponent's end zone and 5-yard line. Punters try to kick the ball into the coffin corner so that the offense takes over the ball deep in its own territory.

completion: A forward pass that's successfully caught by an eligible receiver.

cornerback: A defensive player who lines up on one of the wide sides of the field, usually opposite an offensive receiver. Called a cornerback because he's isolated on the "corner" edge of the defensive alignment.

count: The numbers or words that a quarterback shouts loudly while waiting for the ball to be snapped. The quarterback usually informs his teammates in the huddle that the ball will be snapped on a certain count.

counter: A running play designed to go against, or counter to, the expected direction of the defense's pursuit.

defensive back: A member of the defensive secondary. Defensive backs form the line of defense whose job is to prevent receivers from making catches and then gaining lots of yards after the catch. Safeties, cornerbacks, and nickel backs are defensive backs.

defensive end: A defensive player who lines up at an end of the defensive line. His job is to contain any run plays to his side and prevent the quarterback from getting past him. On passing plays, he rushes the quarterback.

defensive line: The defensive players who play opposite the offensive linemen. The defensive line is made up of ends, tackles, nose tackles, and under tackles. Defensive linemen disrupt the offense's blocking assignments and are responsible for clogging certain gaps along the line of scrimmage when they aren't in a position to make the tackle themselves.

defensive tackle: A defensive player who lines up on the interior of the defensive line. His job is to stop the run at the line, or to shoot through the offensive line and make a tackle in the backfield. If he can't make a play, he needs to prevent the opponent's center and guards from running out and blocking the linebackers.

dime formation: When the defense uses six defensive backs rather than the usual four. The dime formation is used in obvious passing situations.

double foul: A situation in which each team commits a foul during the same down.

down: A period of action that starts when the ball is put into play and ends when the ball is ruled dead (meaning the play is over). The offense gets four downs to advance the ball 10 yards. If it fails to do so, it must surrender the ball to the opponent, usually by punting on the fourth down.

down lineman: A defensive lineman.

draft: The selection of mostly collegiate players for entrance into the National Football League (NFL). The draft occurs in late April. The NFL team with the preceding season's worst record selects first, and the Super Bowl champion selects last. Each team is awarded one selection during each of the seven rounds.

draw: A disguised run that initially looks like a pass play. The offensive linemen retreat like they're going to pass-protect for the quarterback. The quarterback drops back and, instead of setting up to pass, he turns and hands the ball to a running back.

drive: The series of plays during which the offense has the football. A drive ends when the team punts or scores and the other team gets possession of the football.

encroachment: A penalty that occurs when a defensive player crosses the line of scrimmage and makes contact with an opponent before the ball is snapped. Encroachment is subject to a 5-yard penalty.

end zone: A 10-yard-long area at both ends of the field — the promised land for a football player. A player in possession of the football scores a touchdown when he crosses the plane of the goal line and enters the end zone. If you're tackled in your own end zone while in possession of the football, the defensive team gets a safety.

extra point: A kick, worth one point, typically attempted after every touchdown (it's also known as the point after touchdown, or PAT). The ball is placed on the 2-yard line in the NFL, or the 3-yard line in college and high school, and generally is kicked from the 10-yard line. It must sail between the uprights and above the crossbar of the goalpost to be considered good. See *two-point conversion.*

face mask: The protective bars on the football helmet that cover a player's face. Also the name of the penalty for grabbing these bars when tackling a player. Grabbing the face mask is subject to a 15-yard penalty.

fair catch: When the player returning a punt waves his extended arm from side to side over his head. After signaling for a fair catch, a player can't run with the ball, and those attempting to tackle him can't touch him.

field goal: A kick, worth three points, that the offense can attempt from anywhere on the field (but most kickers attempt it within 40 yards of the goalpost). The kick must sail above the crossbar and between the uprights of the goalpost to be considered good.

first down: A team begins every possession of the ball with a first down. The offense must gain 10 yards or more (in four downs) to be awarded another first down. Teams want to earn lots of first downs because doing so means they're moving the ball toward the opponent's end zone. See *down.*

flanker: A player who catches passes, also known in more general terms as a wide receiver. In an offensive formation, he usually lines up outside the tight end, off the line of scrimmage.

flat: The area of the field between the hash marks and the sideline and in close proximity to the line of scrimmage. A pass, usually to a running back, in this area is described as a flat pass.

formation: A predetermined setup (or alignment) employed by the offense or defense.

foul: Any violation of a playing rule.

franchise player: A player who's designated by his team and must be paid the average salary of the top five players at his position. Football reporters also use this term to describe a superstar player who's invaluable to his team.

free agency: An open signing period, usually beginning in late February, during which an NFL team can sign any unrestricted player who doesn't have a contract.

free safety: The defensive player who lines up deepest in the secondary. He defends the deep middle of the field and seldom has man-to-man responsibilities. A coach wants this player free to read the quarterback and take the proper angle to break up or intercept any forward pass thrown over the middle or deep to the sidelines.

fullback: A player who lines up in the offensive backfield and generally is responsible for blocking for the running back and pass-blocking to protect the quarterback. Fullbacks also serve as short-yardage runners.

fumble: When any offensive player loses possession of the football during a play. The ball can simply drop from his hands or be knocked free by the force of a tackle. Either the offense or the defense can recover the fumble.

gap: The open space (also called a split) between players aligned along the line of scrimmage. For example, there's a wide gap between the offensive guard and tackle.

goalpost: The poles constructed in a U-shape at the rear of each end zone through which teams score field goals and extra points.

guard: A member of the offensive line. There are two guards on every play, and they line up on either side of the offensive center. The guards protect the quarterback from an inside rusher; they block defenders immediately across from them and also swing out, or "pull," and run toward either end to block any defender when the ball carrier runs wide.

hail Mary: When the quarterback, usually in desperation at the end of a game, throws a long pass without targeting a receiver with the hope that a receiver will catch the ball and score a touchdown.

halfback: An offensive player who lines up in the backfield and generally is responsible for carrying the ball on run plays. Also known as a running back or tailback.

handoff: The act of giving the ball to another player. Handoffs usually occur between the quarterback and a running back.

hang time: The seconds during which a punted ball remains in the air. If the punt travels 50 yards and is in the air for more than 4 seconds, that's very good hang time.

hash marks: The two rows of lines near the center of the field that signify 1 yard on the field. Before every play, the ball is marked between or on the hash marks, depending on where the ball carrier was tackled on the preceding play.

holder: The player who catches the snap from the center and places it down for the placekicker to kick. A holder is used on field goal and extra point attempts.

hole number: The number the offensive coaching staff gives to each gap or space between the five offensive linemen and the tight end. The players, particularly the running backs, then know which hole they should attempt to run through.

huddle: When the 11 players on the field come together to discuss strategy between plays. On offense, the quarterback relays the plays in the huddle. On defense, the captain relays the coach's instructions for the proper alignment and how to defend the expected play.

hurry-up offense: An offensive strategy that's designed to gain as much yardage as possible and then stop the clock. It's generally used in the final 2 minutes of a half when time is running out on the offense. The offense breaks the huddle more quickly and runs to line up in the proper formation, hoping to get off as many plays as possible. (Sometimes teams don't huddle at all.) Offenses tend to pass in the hurry-up, and receivers are instructed to try to get out of bounds, thus stopping the clock.

I formation: An offensive formation that looks like an I because the two running backs line up directly behind the quarterback.

incompletion: A forward pass that falls to the ground because no receiver can catch it, or a pass that a receiver drops or catches out of bounds. After an incompletion, the clock stops, and the ball is returned to the line of scrimmage.

interception: A pass that's caught by a defensive player, and thus stolen from the offense.

key: Either a specific player or a shift in a particular offensive formation that serves as a clue to a defensive player. From studying a team's tendencies, the defensive player immediately knows which play the opponent will attempt to run and to what direction.

kickoff: A free kick that puts the ball into play at the start of first and third quarters, and after every touchdown, field goal, and safety.

lateral: A backward or sideways pass thrown from one offensive player to another. A lateral isn't considered a forward pass, so players can lateral to one another beyond the line of scrimmage.

line of scrimmage: The imaginary boundary between the two teams prior to the snap of the ball. The offense's and defense's scrimmage lines are defined by the tip of the ball closest to them and stretch from sideline to sideline. The defensive team usually lines up less than a yard away from where the ball is placed.

linebacker: A defensive player who lines up behind or beside the defensive linemen and generally is regarded as one of the team's best tacklers. Depending on the formation, most teams employ either three or four linebackers on every play. In a three-linebacker defense, the linebackers are called the strong-side, middle, and weak-side linebacker.

long snap: When the quarterback or punter takes the snap while standing 6 to 15 feet behind the center. A long snap is used in punts, the shotgun formation, and the wildcat formation.

man-to-man coverage: Pass coverage in which every potential offensive receiver is assigned to a particular defender. Each defensive player must stick to his receiver like glue and make sure he doesn't catch a pass thrown in his direction.

motion: When an offensive receiver or running back begins to move laterally behind the line of scrimmage — after his teammates have assumed a ready stance and are considered set — he is in motion. This motion can't be forward, and only one player is allowed to move at a time.

neutral zone: The area between the two lines of scrimmage, stretching from sideline to sideline. The width of this area is defined by the length of the football. Other than the center, no player can be in the neutral zone prior to the snap; otherwise, the official calls an encroachment or violation of the neutral zone (offside) penalty.

nickel back: An extra defensive back used in some defensive formations.

no-huddle offense: When the offense for several plays in succession lines up and snaps the ball without first going into a huddle. The no-huddle offense is used when time is expiring in the first half of the game and the team with the ball doesn't want to use precious time in huddles. Sometimes offenses run a no-huddle offense to confuse the defense or catch it off guard.

nose tackle: The defensive player (also called a nose guard) who lines up directly across from the center, or "nose to nose" with him. His job is to defend the middle of the offense against a running play.

offensive line: The human wall of five men who block for and protect the quarterback and ball carriers. Every line has a center (who snaps the ball), two guards, and two tackles. Teams that run a lot may employ a blocking tight end, too, who's also considered part of the offensive line.

offensive pass interference: A penalty in which, in the judgment of the official, the intended receiver significantly hinders a defensive player's opportunity to intercept a forward pass.

officials: The men in the striped shirts who officiate the game and call the penalties. Their decisions are final, except when overturned by videotape review.

offside: A penalty caused when any part of a player's body is beyond his line of scrimmage or the free kick line when the ball is snapped.

off-tackle: A strong-side run, meaning the running back heads toward the end of the line where the tight end (the extra blocker) lines up. The runner wants to take advantage of the hole supplied by the tackle (the tight end) and his running mate (the fullback). He can take the ball either outside the tackle or around the tight end. He hopes that the fullback will block the outside linebacker, giving him room to run.

onside kick: When the kicking team attempts to get the ball back during a kickoff by kicking the ball so that it travels a relatively short distance (but more than 10 yards) and is recovered by the kicking team.

option: When a quarterback has the choice — the option — to either pass or run. The option is more common in high school and college football, where quarterbacks may be excellent runners.

overtime: Extra playing time tacked on to the end of the game to decide a game that's tied at the end of regulation play.

pass interference: A judgment call made by an official who sees a defensive player make contact with the intended receiver before the ball arrives, thus restricting his opportunity to catch the forward pass. The penalty awards the offensive team the ball at the spot of the foul with an automatic first down. (In college, pass interference is a 15-yard penalty and an automatic first down.) See *offensive pass interference*.

PAT: See *extra point*.

personal foul: An illegal, flagrant foul considered risky to the health of another player.

pick-six: When a defender intercepts, or picks off, a pass and runs it back for a touchdown, thereby scoring six points. See *interception*.

pigskin: A slang term for the football, which is actually made of leather, not pigskin.

pitch: The act of the quarterback tossing the ball to a running back who's moving laterally away from him.

placekicker: The player who kicks the ball on kickoffs, extra point attempts, and field goal attempts. Unlike a punter, a placekicker kicks the ball either off a tee or while it's being held by a teammate.

play-action pass: A pass play that begins with the quarterback faking a handoff to a running back while he's dropping back to pass. The quarterback hopes the defense falls for the fake and doesn't rush him.

pocket: The area where the quarterback stands when he drops back to throw the ball. This area extends from a point 2 yards outside of either offensive tackle and includes the tight end if he drops off the line of scrimmage to pass-protect. The pocket extends longitudinally behind the line back to the offensive team's own end line.

point after touchdown (PAT): See *extra point*.

possession: When a player maintains control of the ball while clearly touching both feet, or any other part of his body other than his hand(s), to the ground inbounds. A team is also considered in possession of the ball whenever it has the ball on offense. A team's possession ends when it scores, turns over the ball, punts the ball, or when a half of the game ends.

post: A forward pass that the quarterback throws down the center of the field as the intended receiver attempts to line up with the goalpost.

punt: A kick made when a player (the punter) drops the ball and kicks it while it falls toward his foot. A team usually punts on a fourth down. The farther the ball flies from the line of scrimmage, the better.

punter: The lone player who stands 10 to 12 yards behind the line of scrimmage, catches the long snap from the center, and then kicks the ball after dropping it toward his foot.

quarterback: The offensive player who usually receives the ball from the center at the start of each play. He informs his teammates in the huddle of the play that will be run and then, after the center snaps the ball to him, either hands the ball to a running back or throws to a receiver.

receiver: See *wide receiver*.

red zone: The unofficial area from inside the 20-yard line to the opponent's goal line. Holding an opponent to a field goal in this area is considered a victory by the defense.

redshirt: A college player who postpones a year of eligibility due to injury or academic trouble or in order to gain another year of physical maturity. For example, a redshirt freshman is a player who's in his second year of school but is playing his first season of football. Players have four years of eligibility and five years in which to use them, so they can be redshirted only once.

return: To catch the ball after a punt, kickoff, or interception (or pick it up after a fumble) and run it back toward your own end zone.

reverse: A play in which the running back receives a handoff from the quarterback then runs laterally behind the line of scrimmage before handing off to a receiver or flanker running toward him.

roll out: When the quarterback runs left or right away from the pocket before throwing the ball.

route: The prescribed direction and exact distance, coupled with specific physical movements, that a receiver follows when he runs from the line of scrimmage for a forward pass. Every receiver has a route that he must run on a particular play.

running back: An offensive player who runs with the football. Running backs are also referred to as tailbacks, halfbacks, and fullbacks, depending on their exact responsibilities and alignment.

rushing: To advance the ball by running, not passing. A running back is sometimes called a rusher.

sack: To tackle the quarterback behind the line of scrimmage, resulting in a loss of down and yardage.

safety: A two-point score by the defense that occurs when one of the defensive players tackles an opponent in possession of the ball in the offensive player's end zone. See also *free safety* and *strong safety*.

salary cap: In the NFL, the maximum amount of money a team can spend on player salaries in a given year under a formula that includes base salaries, prorated portions of signing bonuses, and likely-to-be-earned incentives. The salary cap figure is a league-wide number that every team must adhere to.

scheme: A slang term used to describe offensive and defensive formations and the overall strategy for using such formations.

scramble: When the quarterback, to gain time for receivers to get open, moves behind the line of scrimmage, dodging the defense.

screen pass: A forward pass in which at least two offensive linemen run wide to a specific side of the field and then turn and block upfield for a running back who takes a short pass from the quarterback.

secondary: The defensive players who line up behind the linebackers and wide on the corners of the field opposite the receivers and defend the pass. These defensive players, who are called defensive backs, are separated into safeties, cornerbacks, and, occasionally, nickel backs.

shotgun: A passing formation in which the quarterback stands 5 to 7 yards behind the center before the snap. This setup enables the quarterback to scan the defense while standing back from the line of scrimmage.

sidelines: The sides of the field along its long part, where players, coaches, trainers, and the media stand. These areas aren't part of the actual playing field; they're considered out of bounds.

slant: A run play in which the runner slants his angle forward after receiving the ball instead of running straight toward the line of scrimmage. Or a pass route on which an outside or "wide" receiver "slants" toward the center of the field.

snap: The action in which the ball is handed or hiked by the center to the quarterback, to the holder on a kick attempt, or to the punter.

special teams: The 22 players who are on the field during kickoffs, field goals, extra points, and punts. These units have special players who return punts and kicks, in addition to players who are experts at covering kicks and punts.

spiral: The tight spin on the ball in flight after the quarterback releases it. The term "tight spiral" is often used to describe a solidly thrown football.

split end: A player who catches passes. This player is also known in more general terms as a wide receiver. In an offensive formation, the split end usually lines up on the line of scrimmage to the opposite side of the formation from the tight end.

spread: A type of offense designed to spread the defense on the field. The spread offense features play-action runs, option plays, and roll-out passing. In a spread offense, the quarterback runs as often or nearly as often as he passes.

stance: The position that any player assumes prior to the snap of the ball and after he's aligned.

strong safety: A defensive player who generally lines up in the secondary, but often aligns close to the line of scrimmage. In most defenses, this player lines up over the tight end and is responsible for both playing the pass and supporting the run.

strong side: The side of the offensive formation where the tight end aligns. With a right-handed quarterback, the strong side is usually to his right side.

stunt: A maneuver by two defensive linemen in which they alter their course to the quarterback, hoping to confuse the offensive linemen and maximize their strengths. In most stunts, one defensive lineman sacrifices himself in hopes of his teammate either going unblocked or gaining a physical advantage in his pursuit.

substitution: The act of a player (called a substitute) running onto the playing field, replacing another player.

sweep: A fairly common run in every team's playbook. It begins with two or more offensive linemen leaving their stances and running toward the outside of the line of scrimmage. The ball carrier takes a handoff from the quarterback and runs parallel to the line of scrimmage, waiting for his blockers to lead the way around the end.

tackle: To use your hands and arms or body to bring down an offensive player who has the ball. Tackle also refers to a position on both the defensive and offensive lines. Offensive tackles are outside blockers on the line of scrimmage; on defense, the tackles are in the inside position, generally opposite the offensive guards.

tailback: An offensive player whose primary role is to carry the ball. Also known as a running back or halfback.

takeaway: How a defense describes any possession in which it forces a fumble and recovers the ball or registers an interception. Any turnover that the defense collects is called a takeaway.

tight end: An offensive player who serves as a big receiver and also a blocker. Unlike a wide receiver, this player generally lines up beside the offensive tackle either to the right or to the left of the quarterback. See *strong side*.

touchback: A situation in which the ball is ruled dead behind a team's own goal line, provided the impetus came from an opponent and provided it isn't a touchdown or a missed field goal. After a touchback, the ball is spotted on the offense's 20-yard line.

touchdown: A situation in which any part of the ball, while legally in the possession of a player who is inbounds, goes on or beyond the plane of the opponent's goal line. A touchdown is worth six points.

turnover: A loss of the ball via a fumble or an interception.

two-minute warning: The signal that 2 minutes remain in the half.

two-point conversion: After a touchdown, scoring two points with a pass or run into the end zone rather than kicking through the goalpost to score one point in an extra-point try.

veer: A quick-hitting run in which the ball is handed to either running back, whose routes are determined by the slant or charge of the defensive linemen.

weak side: The side of the offense opposite the side on which the tight end lines up.

wide receiver: An offensive player who uses speed and quickness to elude defenders and catch the football, but who isn't primarily a blocker. Wide receivers are also known as pass catchers. Also called a wideout.

wildcat formation: An offensive formation in which the quarterback doesn't play and the ball is snapped directly to a running back. The formation allows for an extra blocker on the field and permits offenses to strike quickly without taking time to hand off the ball.

zone coverage: Coverage in which the secondary and linebackers drop away from the line of scrimmage into specific areas when defending a pass play. Zone means that the players are defending areas, not specific offensive players.

Index

lateral pass, 52, 219, 359

leading receiver, 142

LeBeau, Dick, 200

left guards, 116

left tackles, 116

Leggett, Earl, 233–234

leverage, positional, 124

Lilly, Bob, 200, 316–317

line judges, 44

line of demarcation, 214

line of scrimmage, 43, 83, 359

linebacker coaches, 237

linebackers

  defined, 359

  job description of, 166

  overview, 165

  players, 167–169

  traits of, 166–167

lining up, 83

listening to game on radio, 253

live action, 25

Lombardi, Vince, 348–349

Lombardi Award, 280

Long, Howie, 213

long snap, 25, 359

looking off defensive back, 250

loss of down signal, 49

Lott, Ronnie, 178, 310

M

Madden, John, 349

man free coverage, 185

Mangini, Eric, 344–345

Manning, Archie, 339

Manning, Peyton, 326, 339

man-on-man blocking, 128

man-to-man coverage

  beating, 84–85

  combo man, 185

  cornerbacks in, 175

  defined, 184–186, 359

  linebacker use of, 166

  man free, 185

  punting, 228–229

  straight man, 185

Marchetti, Gino, 317

Marino, Dan, 261, 340

marks, field, 19–21

masks, face, 28–29

Massillon, Ohio, 8

Matthews, Clay, 267

Maxwell Award, 280

McBriar, Mat, 224

McLean, Ray "Scooter", 224

Metcalf, Terry, 220

middle field goal block, 224–225

middle linebackers, 168

midfield territory, 214

Mike linebackers, 168

Millen, Matt, 213

mini-camps, training, 241

mobile apps, 257

mobility, of quarterbacks, 68

Moen, Kevin, 219

Montana, Joe, 335, 340–341

Moseley, Mark, 226

Moss, Randy, 330

motion, legal, 359

mouth guards, 28

move the pile, 107

muffs a kick, 230

muscling his way through, 250

N

Namath, Joe Willie, 92, 340

national championship game, 278

National Collegiate Athletic Association (NCAA), 13

National Football Conference (NFC), 14, 286

National Football League. *See* NFL

National Operating Committee on Standards for Athletic Equipment, 29

national tackle youth league, 12

NCAA (National Collegiate Athletic Association), 13

neutral zone, 119, 359

New Year's Day game, 9

NFC (National Football Conference), 14, 286

NFL (National Football League)

  birth of, 284

  building teams, 288–291

  conferences, 285–286

About the Authors

Howie Long is a former Oakland/Los Angeles Raider defensive end with eight Pro Bowl appearances, a Super Bowl XVIII victory over the Washington Redskins, a member of the 1980s All-Decade team, and the George S. Halas Defensive Player of the Year in 1985, awarded by the Newspaper Enterprise Association. His size (6'5" and 275 pounds), combined with his speed, strength, intensity, durability, and explosive quickness, set him apart. He retired from the NFL after the 1993 season and was inducted into the Pro Football Hall of Fame in 2000.

Long is currently a commentator on the Emmy Award–winning *FOX NFL Sunday* program, which is the most-watched NFL pregame show in the United States. *FOX NFL Sunday* concluded the 2018 season as the top-rated pregame show for 25 consecutive seasons. His previous television broadcasting credits include ESPN's *Up Close,* on which he had a regular segment discussing current sports issues, HBO's *Inside the NFL,* the weekly *NFL Diary,* NBC's *NFL Live* as a guest studio analyst, and *Costas Coast to Coast.* He also wrote the opening chapter to Bo Jackson's book, *Bo Knows Bo* (Jove).

Long is no stranger to the limelight, as he's been involved in many commercials and campaigns for Nike, Chevrolet, Hanes, Sketchers, Coca-Cola, and Pizza Hut. He also made his big-screen debut in the action-adventure film *Broken Arrow* with John Travolta and Christian Slater and was featured in the 1998 film *Firestorm.*

At Villanova University, Long was a four-year letterman in football as a defensive lineman. He was All-East and honorable mention All-American as a senior, and was tabbed the Most Valuable Player in the 1980 Blue-Gray Game. He was also a champion boxer as an undergraduate, and his $1 million donation in 2015 helped build the Howie Long Strength Training Center at the university.

Howie may be the best football father of all time. He was able to coach his three sons for eight years through high school, and two of them, Chris and Kyle, became first-round NFL draft picks and Pro Bowl players. Chris recently won the 2019 NFL Man of the Year award for his years of charity work. Chris was also a player on two Super Bowl teams, the 2016 Patriots and the 2017 Eagles. His third son, Howie Jr., currently works for the Raiders as they transition from Oakland to Las Vegas.

John Czarnecki has reported on the NFL since 1979. He has consulted for *FOX NFL Sunday* since the program began in 1994, and he previously consulted for *The NFL Today.* He has received four Sports Emmys as an executive producer. A former newspaperman with such dailies as the defunct *Los Angeles Herald Examiner, The National,* and *The Dallas Morning News.* Czarnecki is currently one of 48 selectors to the Pro Football Hall of Fame. He is also a member of the prestigious Seniors Committee.

Dedication

To my wife, Diane, who has been a rock through my 38 years of being part of professional football, and 11 years of watching our sons play. Needless to say, she's been to every stadium over the years, old and new, and logged countless miles supporting us.

To my coach, Earl Leggett, who taught me everything I knew as a player and the foundation of how I see the game. He is the kind of man I strive to be.

Authors' Acknowledgments

From Howie Long:

First, I'd like to thank my wife, Diane, and my three sons for their support. I'd also like to thank my former coach at the Los Angeles Raiders, the late Earl Leggett, who taught me not only how to be a great football player but also how to be a man. And I can't forget my coauthor, John Czarnecki, for all his hard work and dedication to this project. Thanks also to my friends around the NFL, Terry Robiskie, Hudson Houck, and Artie Gigantino, who contributed to this book. Finally, I'd like to thank all the people at John Wiley & Sons who participated in this project.

From John Czarnecki:

Thanks go to my proofreading wife, Vicki. To my mom, who knew that I would do a book one day. To Ben, my computer expert, and Kathy, my transcriber. To the coaches, Earl Leggett, Terry Robiskie, Hudson Houck, and Ernie Zampese. Also to my late friend and football mentor, Fritz Shurmur. To Barry Meier, my neighborly coaching expert. To Artie Gigantino, a special teams/television expert. To Garrett Giemont, a very special strength trainer. To two helpful workers, Conrad Company and Bryan Broaddhus. To Green Bay legend Ron Wolf, for all his insightful football knowledge these past many years, and to my good friend, Peter King, for all his advice.

Publisher's Acknowledgments

Executive Editor: Lindsay Sandman Lefevere

Project Editor: Tim Gallan

Production Editor: Siddique Shaik

Cover Image: © CatLane/Getty Images
Howie Long Headshot: © Fox Sports

PERSONAL ENRICHMENT

Staying Sharp dummies
9781119187790
USA $26.00
CAN $31.99
UK £19.99

Facebook dummies
9781119179030
USA $21.99
CAN $25.99
UK £16.99

Guitar dummies
9781119293354
USA $24.99
CAN $29.99
UK £17.99

Investing dummies
9781119293347
USA $22.99
CAN $27.99
UK £16.99

Beekeeping dummies
9781119310068
USA $22.99
CAN $27.99
UK £16.99

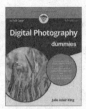
Digital Photography dummies
9781119235606
USA $24.99
CAN $29.99
UK £17.99

Meditation dummies
9781119251163
USA $24.99
CAN $29.99
UK £17.99

Pregnancy ALL-IN-ONE dummies
9781119235491
USA $26.99
CAN $31.99
UK £19.99

Samsung Galaxy S7 dummies
9781119279952
USA $24.99
CAN $29.99
UK £17.99

iPhone dummies
9781119283133
USA $24.99
CAN $29.99
UK £17.99

Crocheting dummies
9781119287117
USA $24.99
CAN $29.99
UK £16.99

Nutrition dummies
9781119130246
USA $22.99
CAN $27.99
UK £16.99

PROFESSIONAL DEVELOPMENT

Windows 10 dummies
9781119311041
USA $24.99
CAN $29.99
UK £17.99

AutoCAD dummies
9781119255796
USA $39.99
CAN $47.99
UK £27.99

Excel 2016 dummies
9781119293439
USA $26.99
CAN $31.99
UK £19.99

QuickBooks 2017 dummies
9781119281467
USA $26.99
CAN $31.99
UK £19.99

macOS Sierra dummies
9781119280651
USA $29.99
CAN $35.99
UK £21.99

LinkedIn dummies
9781119251132
USA $24.99
CAN $29.99
UK £17.99

Windows 10 ALL-IN-ONE dummies
9781119310563
USA $34.00
CAN $41.99
UK £24.99

SharePoint 2016 dummies
9781119181705
USA $29.99
CAN $35.99
UK £21.99

Fundamental Analysis dummies
9781119263593
USA $26.99
CAN $31.99
UK £19.99

Networking dummies
9781119257769
USA $29.99
CAN $35.99
UK £21.99

Office 2016 dummies
9781119293477
USA $26.99
CAN $31.99
UK £19.99

Office 365 dummies
9781119265313
USA $24.99
CAN $29.99
UK £17.99

Salesforce.com dummies
9781119239314
USA $29.99
CAN $35.99
UK £21.99

Coding dummies
9781119293323
USA $29.99
CAN $35.99
UK £21.99